Downcast Eyes

THE
DENIGRATION
OF VISION IN
TWENTIETH-CENTURY
FRENCH THOUGHT

Downcast Eyes

THE DENIGRATION OF VISION IN TWENTIETH-CENTURY FRENCH THOUGHT

Martin Jay

UNIVERSITY OF CALIFORNIA PRESS

BERKELEY   LOS ANGELES   LONDON

University of California Press
Berkeley and Los Angeles, California

University of California Press, Ltd.
London, England

First Paperback Printing 1994

Library of Congress Cataloging-in-Publication Data

Jay, Martin, 1944–
    Downcast eyes : the denigration of vision in twentieth-century
    French thought / Martin Jay.
        p.   cm.
    Includes bibliographical references and index.
    ISBN 978-0-520-08885-6 (pbk. : alk. paper)
    1. Vision.   2. Cognition and culture.   3. Philosophy, French—20th
century.   4. France—Civilization—20th century.   5. France—intellectual
life—20th century.   I. Title.
    B2424.P45J39   1993
    194—dc20   93-347
                                                          CIP

Printed in the United States of America

10   09   08   07   06
14   13   12   11   10   9   8

The paper used in this publication meets the minimum requirements of
ANSI/NISO Z39.48-1992 (R 1997) (*Permanence of Paper*). ∞

For Beth

Contents

Acknowledgments

Registering the many acts of generosity that made this book possible is both a pleasant and melancholy activity. Its pleasure follows from the fond recollection of the people and institutions who were so supportive of the project from the beginning. It is difficult to imagine a warmer or more constructive response to a scholarly enterprise than was forthcoming in this instance. Because the scope of the book is so wide, I have had to rely on the expert knowledge of many people in a multitude of disciplines, all of whom were remarkably willing to share with me the fruits of their own research and learning. The melancholy flows no less inexorably from the fact that several of their number are no longer alive and able to know how deeply I benefited from and appreciated their help.

I would not have been in a position to solicit such aid without the support of the more anonymous benefactors who made the institutional decisions that allowed this project to prosper. Let me thank them first. I was given financial sustenance by the Rockefeller Foundation, the American Council of Learned Societies, the University of California Center for Germanic and European Studies, and the University of California Committee on Research. Clare Hall, Cambridge University kindly provided me a visiting membership while I was engaged in writing the manuscript. And three institutions allowed me to teach courses on its theme: the Collège international de philosophie of Paris in 1985, the School of

Criticism and Theory at Dartmouth College in 1986, and Tulane University, where I was Mellon Professor in the summer of 1990. There can be no better preparation for writing a book of this kind than testing its ideas out in seminars comprising both faculty and advanced graduate student participants, who taught me far more than I taught them. Only they will know how much this book is a collaborative effort. Special thanks are due to Bernard Pulman, Geoffrey Hartman, and Geoffrey Galt Harpham for their respective invitations to conduct those seminars.

During the year I spent in Paris, I also was greatly abetted by the kindnesses of many French scholars, whose names will often be found in the pages that follow. Let me acknowledge them with genuine gratitude: Christine Buci-Glucksmann, Cornelius Castoriadis, the late Michel de Certeau, Daniel Defert, Luce Giard, Jean-Joseph Goux, Luce Irigaray, Sarah Kofman, Claude Lefort, Michel Löwy, Jean-François Lyotard, Gerard Raulet, Jacob Rogozinski, and Philippe Soulez. I have also deeply benefited from conversations with Jacques Derrida, Philippe Lacoue-Labarthe, Jean-Luc Nancy, and the late Michel Foucault during their visits to America.

I also owe an enormous debt to the following friends and colleagues, who in a variety of ways left their mark on this book: Svetlana Alpers, Mitchell Ash, Ann Banfield, Susanna Barrows, William Bouwsma, Teresa Brennan, Carolyn Burke, Drucilla Cornell, Carolyn Dean, John Forrester, Hal Foster, Michael Fried, Amos Funkenstein, Claude Gandelman, Alexander Gelly, John Glenn, Joseph Graham, Richard Gringeri, Sabine Gross, Robert Harvey, Joan Hart, Frederike Hassauer, Eloise Knapp Hay, Denis Hollier, Michael Ann Holly, Axel Honneth, Karen Jacobs, Michael Janover, Dalia Judovitz, Anton Kaes, Kent Kraft, Rosalind Krauss, Dominick LaCapra, Thomas Laqueur, David Michael Levin, the late Eugene Lunn, Jane Malmo, Greil Marcus, Irving Massey, Jann Matlock, Françoise Meltzer, Stephen Melville, Juliet Mitchell, John Durham Peters, Mark Poster, Christopher Prendergast, Anson Rabinbach, Paul Rabinow, John Rajchman, Bill Readings, Eric Rentschler, Irit Rogoff, Michael Rosen, Michael Roth, Michael Schudsen, Joel Snyder, Kristine Stiles, Sidra Stich, Marx Wartofsky, John Welchman, J. M.

Winter, Richard Wolin, Eli Zaretsky, and Jack Zipes. Skilled research assistance was supplied by Berkeley graduate students Alice Bullard, Lawrence Frohman, Nicolleta Gullace, Gerd Horten, and Darrin Zook. It has also been my great good fortune to be able to lecture on aspects of this project to audiences from many different disciplines in Australia, Belgium, Canada, Denmark, France, Germany, Great Britain, Holland, Hungary, India, and Yugoslavia, as well as throughout the United States. I want those who invited me and those who responded with questions I am still struggling to answer to know how much I value their hospitality. I would also like to thank the editors of the journals and volumes in which earlier versions of several chapters or parts of chapters appeared: chapter 4 in the *Visual Anthropology Review*, 7, 1 (Spring, 1991); chapter 5 in *Modernity and the Hegemony of Vision*, ed. David Michael Levin (Berkeley, 1993), chapter 7 in *Foucault: A Critical Reader*, ed. David Couzens Hoy (London, 1986), *ICA Documents* (London, 1986), and chapter 10 in *Thesis Eleven*, 31 (1992).

James Clark and Edward Dimendberg of the University of California Press have supported the book with great vigor and generosity. The readings they provided by Rosalind Krauss and Allan Megill were invaluable. So too were the ones solicited by Harvard University Press from Walter Adamson and Paul Robinson; Aida Donald's efforts on behalf of the manuscript were in this sense not in vain, and I want to express my appreciation for her enthusiasm and understanding. I have also benefited from the computer assistance of Gail Phillips, the copyediting of Lisa Chisholm, and the indexing of Rita Chin.

As always, I am privileged to be able to acknowledge the relentless scrutiny of a pair of very special readers: my wife, Catherine Gallagher and the late Leo Lowenthal. Leo's death at the age of ninety-two earlier this year ended a remarkable friendship, the like of which I will never enjoy again. Two more eagle-eyed critics are hard to imagine. Finally, no acknowledgment section would be complete without mentioning my daughters, Shana Gallagher and Rebecca Jay, who know how to roll their eyes when their father, like George Bush, bemoans yet again his problems with "the vision thing."

Introduction

Even a rapid glance at the language we commonly use will demonstrate the ubiquity of visual metaphors. If we actively focus our attention on them, vigilantly keeping an eye out for those deeply embedded as well as those on the surface, we can gain an illuminating insight into the complex mirroring of perception and language. Depending, of course, on one's outlook or point of view, the prevalence of such metaphors will be accounted an obstacle or an aid to our knowledge of reality. It is, however, no idle speculation or figment of imagination to claim that if blinded to their importance, we will damage our ability to inspect the world outside and introspect the world within. And our prospects for escaping their thrall, if indeed that is even a foreseeable goal, will be greatly dimmed. In lieu of an exhaustive survey of such metaphors, whose scope is far too broad to allow an easy synopsis, this opening paragraph should suggest how ineluctable the modality of the visual actually is, at least in our linguistic practice. I hope by now that you, *optique lecteur,* can see what I mean.[1]

---

1. There are some twenty-one visual metaphors in this paragraph, many of them embedded in words that no longer seem directly dependent on them. Thus, for example, *vigilant* is derived from the Latin *vigilare,* to watch, which in its French form *veiller* is the root of *surveillance. Demonstrate* comes from the Latin *monstrare,* to show. *Inspect, prospect, introspect* (and other words like *aspect* or *circumspect*) all derive from the Latin *specere,* to look at or observe. *Speculate* has the same root. *Scope* comes from the Latin *scopium,* a translation of a Greek word for to look at or examine. *Synopsis* is from the Greek word for general view. These are latent or dead metaphors,

1

Other Western languages also contain a wealth of examples to buttress the point. No German, for instance, can miss the *Augen* in *Augenblick* or the *Schau* in *Anschauung*, nor can a Frenchman fail to hear the *voir* in both *savoir* and *pouvoir*.[2] And if this is so with ordinary language, it is no less the case with the specialized languages intellectuals have designed to lift us out of the commonsensical understanding of the world around us. As Ian Hacking and Richard Rorty have recently emphasized, even Western philosophy at its most putatively disinterested and neutral can be shown to be deeply dependent on occluded visual metaphors.[3]

In addition to the ocular permeation of language, there exists a wealth of what might be called visually imbued cultural and social practices, which may vary from culture to culture and epoch to epoch. Sometimes these can be construed in grandiose terms, such as a massive shift from an oral culture to a "chirographic" one based on writing and then a typographic one in which the visual bias of the intermediate stage is even more firmly entrenched.[4] On a more modest level, anthropologists and sociolo-

---

but they still express the sedimented importance of the visual in the English language. For a discussion of dormant visual metaphors, see Colin Murray Turbayne, *The Myth of Metaphor* (Columbia, S.C., 1971).

2. The French etymologies for these words are, to be sure, different—*voir* coming from the Latin *videre*, *savoir* from *sapere*, and *pouvoir* from *potere*. But sometimes imagined etymologies reveal as much as real ones. For a consideration of this theme, see Derek Attridge, "Language as History/History as Language: Saussure and the Romance of Etymology," in *Post-structuralism and the Question of History*, ed. Derek Attridge, Geoff Bennington, and Robert Young (Cambridge, 1987). That the connections were made is shown by the film theorist Thierry Kuntzel's essay "Savoir, pouvoir, voir," *Ça Cinéma*, 7–8 (May, 1975).

3. Ian Hacking, *Why Does Language Matter to Philosophy?* (Cambridge, 1975); Richard Rorty, *Philosophy and the Mirror of Nature* (Princeton, 1979). For a discussion of the link between knowledge and sight in all Indo-European tongues, see Stephen A. Tyler, "The Vision Quest in the West, or What the Mind's Eye Sees," *Journal of Anthropological Research*, 40, 1 (Spring, 1984), pp. 23–39. He shows that at least one other language family, Dravidian, lacks this linkage.

4. For arguments of this kind, see Walter J. Ong, *The Presence of the Word* (New Haven, 1967); Jack Goody, *The Domestication of the Savage Mind* (Cambridge, 1977); and Donald M. Lowe, *History of Bourgeois Perception* (Chicago, 1982).

gists have examined such visually fraught phenomena as the widespread belief in the evil eye, which has given rise to a no less popular series of countervailing apotropaic remedies.[5] Somewhere in between, historians of technology have pondered the implications of our expanded capacity to see through such devices as the telescope, microscope, camera, or cinema. What has been called the expansion of our "exosomatic organs"[6] has meant above all extending the range of our vision, compensating for its imperfections, or finding substitutes for its limited powers. These expansions have themselves been linked in complicated ways to the practices of surveillance and spectacle, which they often abet.

Because of the remarkable range and variability of visual practices, many commentators have been tempted, in ways that we will examine shortly, to claim certain cultures or ages have been "ocularcentric,"[7] or "dominated" by vision. For them, what may seem a function of our physiology or evolution is best understood in historical terms, with the obvious conclusion often drawn that we can reverse the effects of that domination. Anthropological evidence of radical variations in the intersensory mix of different cultures has been adduced to encourage such an outcome.[8]

But as in so many other similar debates, the threshold between what is "natural" and what is "cultural" is by no means easy to fix with any cer-

5. For recent studies of the evil eye, see Clarence Maloney, ed., *The Evil Eye* (New York, 1976); Lawrence Di Stasi, *Mal Occhio: The Underside of Vision* (San Francisco, 1981); and Tobin Siebers, *The Mirror of Medusa* (Berkeley, 1983). For an account of apotropaic responses to it, see Albert M. Potts, *The World's Eye* (Lexington, Ky., 1982).

6. Robert E. Innis, "Technics and the Bias of Perception," *Philosophy and Social Criticism*, 10, 1 (Summer, 1984), p. 67. Although visual "prostheses" appear to be the most significant extension of human sense organs, such inventions as the telephone, loudspeaker, stethoscope, and sonar demonstrate that hearing has also been exosomatically enhanced. The other senses have perhaps not been as fortunate.

7. As is the case with many neologisms, "ocularcentric" or "ocularcentrism" is sometimes spelled differently in the literature. Often it is rendered "oculocentric," or less frequently "ocularocentric." In previous publications I have followed the first of these usages and will remain with it here.

8. See, for example, the essays in David Howes, ed., *The Varieties of Sensory Experience: A Sourcebook in the Anthropology of the Senses* (Toronto, 1991).

tainty. For example, the psychologists Michael Argyle and Mark Cook have recently concluded that "the use of the gaze in human social behavior does not vary much between cultures: it is a cultural universal."[9] But the implications of the work of another psychologist, James Gibson, suggests otherwise. Gibson contrasts two basic visual practices, which produce what he calls "the visual world" and the "visual field."[10] In the former, sight is ecologically intertwined with the other senses to generate the experience of "depth shapes," whereas in the latter, sight is detached by fixating the eyes to produce "projected shapes" instead. A plate, for example, will be experienced as round in the visual world, but as an ellipse in the visual field, where the rules of perspectival representation prevail. The implication of Gibson's argument is that vision is normally crossed with the other senses, but it can be artificially separated out. Thus, cultures might be differentiated according to how radically they distinguish between the visual field and the visual world.

But whether we identify the latter with "natural" vision is not self-evident. In a series of essays, the philosopher Marx Wartofsky has argued for a radically culturalist reading of all visual experience, including Gibson's two dominant modes.[11] Alternately talking about "visual postures," "visual scenarios," "styles of seeing," or "cultural optics," he concludes that

9. Michael Argyle and Mark Cook, *Gaze and Mutual Gaze* (Cambridge, 1976), p. 169. It should be noted that they use the term "gaze" in a general sense to mean any kind of visual interaction. Unlike some of the authors cited later, they do not contrast it with the less fixating glance.

10. James J. Gibson, *The Perception of the Visual World* (Boston, 1950); *Senses Considered as Perceptual Systems* (Boston, 1966); *The Ecological Approach to Visual Perception* (Boston, 1979). For a recent defense of Gibson, see John Hell, *Perception and Cognition* (Berkeley, 1983).

11. Marx W. Wartofsky, "Pictures, Representations and the Understanding," in *Logic and Art: Essays in Honor of Nelson Goodman,* ed. R. Rudner and I. Scheffler (Indianapolis, 1972); "Perception, Representation and the Forms of Action: Towards an Historical Epistemology," in his *Models: Representation and the Scientific Understanding* (Boston, 1979); "Picturing and Representing," in *Perception and Pictorial Representation,* ed. Calvin F. Nodine and Dennis F. Fisher (New York, 1979); "Visual Scenarios: The Role of Representation in Visual Perception," in *The Perception of Pictures,* ed. M. Hagen, vol. 2 (New York, 1980); "Cameras Can't See: Representa-

"human vision is itself an artifact, produced by other artifacts, namely pictures."[12] *All* perception, he contends, is the result of historical changes in representation. Wartofsky thus presents an intentionalist account of visuality, which verges on making it a product of collective human will.

Judging from the current state of scientific research on sight, which helps in conceptualizing the "natural" capacities and limitations of the eye, Wartofsky's hostility to any physiological explanation of human visual experience may, however, be excessive.[13] Certain fairly fundamental characteristics seem to exist, which no amount of cultural mediation can radically alter. As a diurnal animal standing on its hind legs, the early human being developed its sensorium in such a way as to give sight an ability to differentiate and assimilate most external stimuli in a way superior to the other four senses.[14] Smell, which is so important for animals on

tion, Photography and Human Vision," *Afterimage*, 7, 9 (1980), pp. 8–9; "Sight, Symbol and Society: Toward a History of Visual Perception," *Philosophic Exchange*, 3 (1981), pp. 23–38; "The Paradox of Painting: Pictorial Representation and the Dimensionality of Visual Space," *Social Research*, 51, 4 (Winter, 1984), pp. 863–883. For a similar plea for a culturalist position, see Robert D. Romanyshyn, "The Despotic Eye: An Illustration of Metabletic Phenomenology and Its Implications," in *The Changing Reality of Modern Man*, ed. I. Dreyer Kruger (Cape Town, 1984); and *Technology as Symptom and Dream* (London, 1989).

12. Wartofsky, "Picturing and Representing," p. 314.

13. For helpful recent summaries of the status of scientific knowledge about vision, see M. H. Pirenne, *Vision and the Eye* (London, 1967); Robert Rivlin and Karen Gravelle, *Deciphering the Senses: The Expanding World of Human Perception* (New York, 1984); Anthony Smith, *The Body* (London, 1985); John P. Frisby, *Seeing: Illusion, Brain, and Mind* (Oxford, 1980); Steven Pinker, ed., *Visual Cognition* (Cambridge, Mass., 1985); Walter J. Freeman, "The Physiology of Perception," *Scientific American* 264, 2 (February, 1991). Cognitive faculty psychology influenced by Noam Chomsky has also attempted to establish a modular concept of the mind in which visual perception transcends cultural variations. See, for example, Jerry A. Fodor, *The Modularity of Mind: An Essay on Faculty Psychology* (Cambridge, Mass., 1983).

14. The anthropologist Edward T. Hall has conjectured that even before hominids stood on their hind legs, vision was important: "Originally a ground-dwelling animal, man's ancestor was forced by interspecies competition and changes in the environment to desert the ground and take to the trees. Arboreal life calls for keen vision and decreases dependence on smell, which is crucial for terrestrial organisms. Thus

all fours, was reduced in importance, a fateful transformation that Freud was to conjecture was the very foundation of human civilization.[15] Vision was the last of the human senses to develop fully, its very complexity always proving a difficult case for incremental theories of evolution. It also remains the last of the senses to develop in the fetus, only in fact gaining its true importance for the survival of the neonate some time after birth.[16] The infant, it is sometimes argued, experiences a synesthetic confusion of the senses without vision fully differentiated from the rest. Smell and touch are apparently more functionally vital than sight at this very early stage of development.

With the maturation of the child, however, the superior capacity of the eyes to process certain kinds of data from without is soon established. Having some eighteen times more nerve endings than the cochlear nerve of the ear, its nearest competitor, the optic nerve with its 800,000 fibers is able to transfer an astonishing amount of information to the brain, and at a rate of assimilation far greater than that of any other sense organ. In each eye, over 120 million rods take in information on some five hundred levels of lightness and darkness, while more than seven million cones allow us to distinguish among more than one million combinations of color. The eye is also able to accomplish its tasks at a far greater remove than any other sense, hearing and smell being only a distant second and third.[17]

Despite the frequent characterization of vision as atemporal and static, the eye can only do its job by being in almost constant motion. Either it

man's sense of smell ceased to develop and his powers of sight were greatly enhanced." See Hall, *The Hidden Dimension* (Garden City, N.Y., 1982), p. 39.

15. Sigmund Freud, *Civilization and Its Discontents*, trans. James Strachey (New York, 1961), pp. 46–47.

16. Rivlin and Gravelle, p. 79. It might be noted that they posit a much wider sensorium than the generally accepted five senses. Based on experiments with a variety of animals, science has noted some seventeen different ways in which organisms can respond to the environment. Some of these may have a residual role in human behavior, which possibly accounts for the existence of so-called extrasensory perception. Still, they acknowledge that humans tend to rely on sight more than any other sense.

rapidly jumps from one briefly fixated point to another through what are known as saccadic movements (named after the French for jerk, *saccade*, by Émile Javal, who discovered them in 1878)[18] or it follows a moving object across a visual field. Its so-called vestibulo-ocular reflex makes it turn in the opposite direction of a rapid head movement to retain a continuity of image and its "vergence system" constantly fuses short and long-range focus into one coherent visual experience.[19] Even during sleep, as scientists only learned in the 1960s, rapid eye movement is the norm. Although it is, of course, possible to fix the gaze, we cannot really freeze the movement of the eye for very long without incurring intolerable strain.

Although the optical mechanism of vision has been well understood since the time of Kepler,[20] who established the laws of refraction governing the transmission of light rays through the cornea, viscous humors, and lenses of the eyeball onto the retinal wall at its rear, the precise manner of its translation into meaningful images in the mind remains somewhat clouded. The image received is reversed and inverted, but the physiological cum psychological processes which "read" it correctly are still incompletely known. The binocular or stereoscopic integration of data from the two eyes into one image with apparent three-dimensional depth is also

17. According to Hall, "Up to twenty feet the ear is very efficient. At about one hundred feet, one-way vocal communication is possible, at a somewhat slower rate than at conversational distances, while a two-way conversation is very considerably altered. Beyond this distance, the auditory cues with which man works begin to break down rapidly. The unaided eye, on the other hand, sweeps up an extraordinary amount of information within a hundred-yard radius and is still quite efficient for human interaction at a mile" (*The Hidden Dimension*, p. 43).

18. Émile Javal, *Annales d'oculistique* (Paris, 1878).

19. For a discussion of these systems, see Argyle and Cook, pp. 16–17. See also Claude Gandelman, "The 'Scanning' of Pictures," *Communication and Cognition*, 19, 1 (1986), pp. 3–24.

20. For an excellent history of optics up through Kepler, see David C. Lindberg, *Theories of Vision from Al-Kindi to Kepler* (Chicago, 1976). See also the various histories of Vasco Ronchi, most notably *Optics: The Science of Vision*, trans. Edward Rosen (New York, 1957), and *The Nature of Light: An Historical Survey*, trans. V. Barocas (London, 1975).

not yet fully understood. Indeed, with all the advances science has made in explaining human vision, its complexities are such that many questions remain unanswered. Significantly, attempts to duplicate it through computer simulation have met so far with only very modest success.[21]

If the eye's powers are appreciated by science, so too are its limitations. Human vision can see light waves that are only a fraction of the total spectrum—in fact, less than 1 percent with such phenomena as ultraviolet light, visible to other species, excluded.[22] In addition, the human eye has a blind spot where the optic nerve connects with the retina. Normally ignored because the vision of the other eye compensates for it, the blind spot's existence nonetheless suggests a metaphoric "hole" in vision, which, as we will have ample occasion to witness, critics of ocularcentrism gleefully exploit. Human vision is also limited by its capacity to focus on objects only a certain distance from the eye, a distance that normally increases with age. Thus the eye's superiority at sensing objects from afar is balanced by its inferiority at seeing those very close. Finally, we are often fooled by visual experience that turns out to be illusory, an inclination generated perhaps by our overwhelming, habitual belief in its apparent reliability. Here the compensating sense is usually touch, as we seek confirmation through direct physical contact.

One final aspect of the contemporary natural scientific understanding of vision merits comment. Unlike the other senses of smell, touch, or taste, there seems to be a close, if complicated, relationship between sight and language, both of which come into their own at approximately the same moment of maturation. As Robert Rivlin and Karen Gravelle note, "The ability to visualize something internally is closely linked with the ability to describe it verbally. Verbal and written descriptions create highly specific mental images. . . . The link between vision, visual memory, and verbalization can be quite startling."[23] There is therefore something re-

21. See William J. Broad, "Computer Quest to Match Human Vision Stymied," *International Herald Tribune* (October 4, 1984), p. 7.
22. Rivlin and Gravelle, p. 53.

vealing in the ambiguities surrounding the word "image," which can signify graphic, optical, perceptual, mental, or verbal phenomena.[24]

The implications of this final point are very significant for the problem noted earlier: the permeability of the boundary between the "natural" and the "cultural" component in what we call vision. Although perception is intimately tied up with language as a generic phenomenon, different peoples of course speak different tongues. As a result, the universality of visual experience cannot be automatically assumed, if that experience is in part mediated linguistically. Natural science, therefore, itself suggests the possibility of cultural variables, at least to some degree. It implies, in other words, the inevitable entanglement of vision and what has been called "visuality"—the distinct historical manifestations of visual experience in all its possible modes.[25] Observation, to put it another way, means observing the tacit cultural rules of different scopic regimes.

The cultural variability of ocular experience will be even more evident if we consider it, as it were, from a different perspective. The eye, it has long been recognized, is more than the passive receptor of light and color. It is also the most expressive of the sense organs, with the only competitor being touch. Although the ancient theory of light rays emanating from the eye, the theory called extramission, has long since been discredited,[26]

23. Ibid., pp. 88–89. For a discussion of the complex interaction between vocal-auditory and gestural-visual channels of communication, see Argyle and Cook, p. 124.

24. For an account of its various meanings, see W. J. T. Mitchell, "What Is an Image?" in *Iconology: Image, Text, Ideology* (Chicago, 1986). For a more restrictive notion of the term which attacks its literary use, see P. N. Furbank, *Reflections on the Word 'Image'* (London, 1970).

25. For a discussion of the difference, see Hal Foster, ed., *Vision and Visuality* (Seattle, 1988), especially the editor's preface.

26. Perhaps the belief in rays coming from the eye was due to the phenomenon of light shining off the eyeball through reflection, which is especially evident in certain animals. Descartes, as late as *La Dioptrique*, credited the cat with extramission for this reason. In 1704, however, an experiment showed that if a cat is immersed in water, the lack of corneal refraction prevents the eye from shining. See Smith, *The Body*, p. 380.

it expressed a symbolic truth. For the eye—broadly understood as including the complex of muscles, flesh, and even hair around the eyeball—can clearly project, signal, and emit emotions with remarkable power. Common phrases such as "a piercing or penetrating gaze," "melting eyes," "a come-hither look," or "casting a cold eye" all capture this ability with striking vividness. Aided by its capacity to overflow with the tears necessary to bathe it with constant moisture, a capacity triggered by a multitude of different stimuli, some physical, some emotional (the latter found only in humans), the eye is not only, as the familiar clichés would have it, a "window on the world," but also a "mirror of the soul."[27] Even the dilation of the pupil can unintentionally betray an inner state, subtly conveying interest or aversion to the beholder.

There is, moreover, a learned ability to use the eyes to express something deliberately, a skill more sharply honed than in the case of the other senses. Ranging from the casual glance to the fixed glare, the eye can obey the conscious will of the viewer in a way denied the other more passive senses, once again the only competitor being touch with its ability to strangle as well as caress. The phenomenon of the evil eye, mentioned above, is only one manifestation of this potential for sending powerful messages. As a result, vision is often called "the censor of the senses . . . an arbiter of behavior, an inhibitor or stimulus thereto,"[28] unlike the more accepting touch. Significantly, of all the animals, only man and the primates have the ability to use the gaze to send affiliative as well as threatening signals. Here scientists have conjectured that this ability may be a residue of our visually charged infant feeding position with the maternal look of love the key to later behavior.[29]

27. For a discussion of the importance of crying as an ocular experience, see David Michael Levin, *The Opening of Vision: Nihilism and the Postmodern Situation* (New York, 1988), chap. 2.

28. Ashley Montagu, *Touching: The Significance of the Human Skin*, 3d ed. (New York, 1986), p. 269.

29. Argyle and Cook, p. 26. They suggest that because Japanese mothers tend to carry their infants on their back, their culture is less dependent on the mutual gaze. As for the contention that only humans and primates send affiliative signals, which is

Messages are only such, of course, if they are received, and one of the most extraordinary aspects of vision, most broadly conceived, is the experience of being the object of the look. Here the range of possibilities is exceptionally wide, extending from the paranoid's fantasy of being under constant hostile surveillance to the exhibitionist's narcissistic thrill at being the cynosure of all eyes. There can also be few human interactions as subtle as the dialectic of the mutual gaze, ranging from the contest for domination to the lovers' complementary adoration. Even *not* being the object of the look conveys a powerful message under certain circumstances, as any underling who has become an "invisible man" will quickly attest.

Terms such as paranoia, narcissism, and exhibitionism suggest how powerfully visual experience, both directed and received, can be tied to our psychological processes. In ways we will explore later, vision has been frequently linked by psychologists to the "normal" emotions of desire, curiosity, hostility, and fear. The remarkable ability of images originally construed as mimetic representations or aesthetic ornaments to be transformed into totemic objects of worship in their own right also bespeaks vision's power to evoke hypnotic fascination.[30] And scopophilic and scopophobic inclinations have also been widely acknowledged as fundamental aspects of the human psyche.[31]

With all of these dimensions to the phenomenon we call vision—and others can doubtless be added—it is no surprise that our ordinary language, indeed our culture as a whole, is deeply marked by its importance. An excellent example of its power can be discerned in no less central a human phenomenon than religion.[32] From the primitive importance of

---

also theirs, it might be thought that dogs do the same, at least in their interaction with humans. But do they send each other such messages too?

30. The word *fascination*, it might be noted, has itself an origin in the Latin for casting a spell, usually by visual means.

31. For a recent account of their implications, see David W. Allen, *The Fear of Looking: On Scopophilic-Exhibitional Conflicts* (Charlottesville, Va., 1974).

32. For a recent overview, see David Chidester, *Word and Light: Seeing, Hearing, and Religious Discourse* (Champaign, Ill., 1992). Another obvious area is literature,

the sacred fire[33] to the frequency of sun-worship in more developed religions—such as the Chaldean and Egyptian—and the sophisticated metaphysics of light in the most advanced theologies,[34] the ocular presence in a wide variety of religious practices has been striking. Some faiths, like Manichaean Gnosticism, have fashioned themselves "religions of light"; others, like the often polytheistic Greek religion, assigned a special role to sun gods like Apollo. Unearthly, astral light surrounding the godhead, the divine illumination sought by the mystic, the omniscience of a god always watching his flock, the symbolic primacy of the candle's flame—all of these have found their way into countless religious systems. So too has the remarkable power attributed to mirrors, which so-called scryers or *specularii* have claimed a special gift to read for signs of the divine. At times the insubstantiality of the mirror's image has been taken as a token of the purity of the dematerialized soul. At others, the "spotless mirror" has been analogized to the immaculate nature of the Virgin Mary.[35]

No less symptomatic of the power of the optical in religion is the tendency of the visionary tradition to posit a higher sight of the seer, who is able to discern a truth denied to normal vision. Here the so-called third eye of the soul is invoked to compensate for the imperfections of the two physical eyes. Often physical blindness is given sacred significance, even if at times as a punishment for transgressions against the gods.[36] What

---

where visual imagery abounds. There is an inexhaustible commentary on "the eye in the text."

33. The classic study of its importance is by Numa-Denys Fustel de Coulanges, *The Ancient City: A Study of Religion, Laws and Institutions of Greece and Rome*, trans. Willard Small (Boston, 1873).

34. For a survey of religions of light, see Gustav Mensching, "Die Lichtsymbolik in der Religionsgeschichte," *Studium Generale*, 10 (1957), pp. 422–432.

35. For accounts of the religious importance of mirrors, see Benjamin Goldberg, *The Mirror and Man* (Charlottesville, Va., 1985); and Herbert Grabes, *The Mutable Glass: Mirror-Imagery in Titles and Texts of the Middle Ages and the English Renaissance*, trans. Gordon Collier (Cambridge, 1982).

36. For a discussion of the religious implications of blindness, see William R. Paulsen, *Enlightenment, Romanticism, and the Blind in France* (Princeton, 1987), Introduction.

Thomas Carlyle once called "spiritual optics"[37] has, of course, continued to have a powerful secular effect well after its original religious sources lost much of their legitimacy.

But as might be expected of so deeply affecting a phenomenon, the ocular presence in religion has also aroused a hostile reaction. Its privileged role has been challenged, especially when the gap between spiritual and mundane optics has been perceived as unbridgeable. In fact, suspicion of the illusory potential of images has often led to full-fledged iconophobia.[38] Monotheistic religions, beginning with Judaism, have been deeply wary of the threat of pagan idolatry. The fictional character of artificial images, which can only be false simulators of the "truth," has occasioned distrust among more puritanical critics of representation. St. Paul's celebrated warning against the *speculum obscurum*, the glass (or mirror) through which we see only darkly, vividly expressed this caution about terrestrial sight. Religious distrust was also aroused by the capacity of vision to inspire what Augustine condemned as *concupiscentia ocularum*, ocular desire, which diverts our minds from more spiritual concerns.[39] These and like suspicions have at times come to dominate religious movements and dictate long-standing religious taboos. Moses's struggle with Aaron over the Golden Calf, the Islamic rejection of figural representation, the iconoclastic controversy of the eighth-century Byzantine church, the Cistercian monasticism of St. Bernard, the English Lollards, and finally the Protestant Reformation all express the antiocular subcurrent of religious thought. In fact, this hostility remains alive today in the work of such theologians as Jacques Ellul, whose *Humiliation of the Word*, written in 1981, reads like a summa of every imaginable religious complaint against the domination of sight.[40]

37. Thomas Carlyle, "Spiritual Optics," in *Thomas Carlyle, 1795–1835*, ed. James Anthony Froude, 2 vols. (New York, 1882), 2: 7–12.

38. For a survey of its various manifestations, see Kenneth Clark, "Iconophobia," in *Moments of Vision and Other Essays* (New York, 1981). See also Moshe Barasch, *Icon: Studies in the History of an Idea* (New York, 1992).

39. Saint Augustine, *Confessions*, chap. 35.

40. Jacques Ellul, *The Humiliation of the Word*, trans. Joyce Main Hanks (Grand Rapids, Mich., 1985).

⊙

Ellul's animus against vision cannot, however, be understood solely in the context of the time-honored tradition of religious iconophobia, for it draws as well on a much wider antivisual discourse that extends beyond the boundaries of religious thought. That discourse, I hope to demonstrate, is a pervasive but generally ignored phenomenon of twentieth-century Western thought. Although by no means confined to one locale, it is most prevalent and multifarious in a country where it may seem, for reasons we will examine shortly, highly improbable. That country is France. It will be the main purpose of this study to demonstrate and explore what at first glance may seem a surprising proposition: a great deal of recent French thought in a wide variety of fields is in one way or another imbued with a profound suspicion of vision and its hegemonic role in the modern era.[41]

To establish this argument, I will begin with a general consideration of the history of Western attitudes toward sight in its various guises. After focusing more precisely on the honored place of the visual in French culture since the time of Louis XIV and Descartes, I will turn to the indications of its crisis in the late nineteenth century by examining changes in the visual arts, literature, and philosophy, most notably the work of Henri Bergson. I will then explore more explicit manifestations of hostility to visual primacy in the work of artists and critics like Georges Bataille and André Breton, philosophers like Jean-Paul Sartre, Maurice Merleau-Ponty, and Emmanuel Levinas, social theorists like Michel Foucault, Louis Althusser, and Guy Debord, psychoanalysts like Jacques Lacan and Luce Irigaray, cultural critics like Roland Barthes and Christian Metz, and poststructuralist theorists like Jacques Derrida and Jean-François

41. Other examples of a similar attitude will no doubt occur to readers familiar with different national traditions: for example, American pragmatism with its distrust of spectatorial epistemology or German hermeneutics with its general privileging of the ear over the eye. It would also be possible to pursue the theme in the work of individual thinkers outside of the orbit of French thought, such as Wittgenstein with his subtle ruminations on the distinction between "seeing" and "seeing-as."

Lyotard. In so doing, I hope to clarify the implications of the denigration of vision for the current debate over modernity and postmodernity.

⊙

Before beginning so ambitious an undertaking, a few words of methodological explanation are in order. The focus of this study is on a discourse rather than on a visual culture in its entirety. It would, in fact, be very hazardous to characterize French culture as a whole as hostile to the visual. Paris, "the City of Lights," remains for many the most dazzling and brilliant urban setting ever devised by our species. The fascination of the French with such visually dominated phenomena as fashion, cinema, or public ceremonial remains unabated. And as anyone who has spent the month of August on the Côte d'Azur can easily testify, they are scarcely less fascinated than ancient solar cultists in "worshiping the sun."[42] Indeed, even their intellectuals tend to be obsessed with visual phenomena, as the remarkable preoccupation of so many of them with painting, photography, film, and architecture demonstrates.

And yet, for many that obsession has turned in a negative direction, as an essentially ocularphobic discourse has seeped into the pores of French intellectual life. By choosing to call the complex of antivisual attitudes a discourse, I am fully aware that I am invoking one of the most loosely used terms of our time. It has been employed in a host of different contexts, from the communicative rationalism of a Jürgen Habermas to the archaeology of knowledge of a Foucault; from the computerized Althusserianism of a Michel Pêcheux to the sociolinguistics of a Malcolm Coulthard; from the textual analysis of a Zelig Harris to the ethnomethodology of a Harvey Sacks.[43]

42. See John Weightman, "The Solar Revolution: Reflections on a Theme in French Literature," *Encounter*, 35, 6 (December, 1970), pp. 9–18, for an account of sun worship and its literary manifestations, which he dates from André Gide.

43. Jürgen Habermas, "Wahrheitstheorien," in *Wirklichkeit und Reflexion: Walther Schulz zum 60. Geburtstag* (Pfullingen, 1973), pp. 211–265; Michel Foucault, *The Archaeology of Knowledge*, trans. A. M. Sheridan (London, 1972), in which the term

Despite these contrary and shifting usages, discourse remains the best term to denote the level on which the object of this inquiry is located, that being a corpus of more or less loosely interwoven arguments, metaphors, assertions, and prejudices that cohere more associatively than logically in any strict sense of the term. Discourse in this usage is explicitly derived from the Latin *discurrere*, which means a running around in all directions. The antiocularcentric discourse that I hope to examine is precisely that: an often unsystematic, sometimes internally contradictory texture of statements, associations, and metaphors that never fully cohere in a rigorous way. No single figure expresses all of its dimensions and none would be likely to accept them all, even if they were explicitly posed as positive arguments. Nor has there been anything like a conscious conspiracy determining its dissemination.[44] But as a powerful if at times subliminal context, the discourse we will explore has helped shape the attitudes of a wide variety of French intellectuals who share little else in terms of their disciplines, politics, or theoretical self-consciousness. At times, it provides them with a vocabulary to discuss other issues, such as subjectivity, the Enlightenment, and humanism. At others, it seems to determine the way they approach those same issues, as a powerful metaphoric often does, lending arguments an emotional tone and critical energy that would otherwise be inexplicable.

"Discourse analysis," as James Clifford has noted, "is always in a sense, unfair to authors. It is interested not in what *they* have to say or feel as subjects, but is concerned merely with statements as related to other statements in a field."[45] Discourse as I am using it thus cuts across the bound-

---

"discursive formation" is used; Michel Pêcheux, *Analyse automatique du discours* (Paris, 1969); *Language, Semantics and Ideology* (New York, 1982); Malcolm Coulthard, *An Introduction to Discourse Analysis* (Harlow, Essex, England, 1977); Zelig S. Harris, "Discourse Analysis," *Language*, 28 (1952), pp. 1–30; Harvey Sacks, Emanuel A. Schegloff, and Gail Jefferson, "A Simplest Systematics for the Organization of Turn-Taking for Conversations," *Language*, 50 (1974), pp. 696–735.

44. This disclaimer is necessary to set straight the confusion concerning my intentions evident in John Rajchman's otherwise very interesting essay, "Foucault's Art of Seeing," *October*, 44 (Spring, 1988), p. 90.

aries of what Freud would have called the conscious, preconscious, and unconscious. It includes Pêcheux's "forgetting no. 1," which the subject cannot fully remember, and his "forgetting no. 2," which a certain amount of effort can restore to consciousness.[46] That only perhaps an outsider can bring it more fully to the surface is the justificatory assumption of this study, which aims not only to reveal the extent of this hidden discursive continent, but also to probe its implications in a critical way.

In holding on to such a hope, it will be quickly realized that the author is betraying his sympathy for one of the targets of the discourse in certain of its bleaker moods. That is, I remain unrepentantly beholden to the ideal of illumination that suggests an Enlightenment faith in clarifying indistinct ideas. To make matters worse, I will employ a method that unapologetically embraces one of the antiocularcentric discourse's other major targets, a synoptic survey of an intellectual field at some remove from it. Here I invite the same reproach made in some of the responses to an earlier work that dealt with the Western Marxist concept of totality: that I am tacitly arrogating to myself the very totalizing vantage point called into serious question by the crisis of holistic thinking my narrative has reconstructed.[47]

A fateful, if unanticipated, continuity between the two books is in fact demonstrated by the opening metaphor of the first, which called for "mapping the uncertain terrain" of Western Marxism, a figure of speech that immediately evokes the visual distance of a stranger not at home in the landscape he or she must survey from afar.[48] But as any honest geographer will readily admit, mapmaking cannot escape the bias—both in the literal sense of a slanted perspective and in the metaphorical one of a

---

45. James Clifford, *The Predicament of Culture: Twentieth-Century Ethnography, Literature, and Art* (Cambridge, Mass., 1988), p. 270.

46. Pêcheux, *Language, Semantics and Ideology*, p. 126.

47. Martin Jay, *Marxism and Totality: The Adventures of a Concept from Lukács to Habermas* (Berkeley, 1984); the reproach was made in a thoughtful review essay by Ferenc Fehér in *Theory and Society*, 14, 6 (November, 1985), p. 875.

48. Jay, *Marxism and Totality*, p. 1. For a critique of mapping metaphors, see Pierre Bourdieu, *Outline of a Theory of Practice*, trans. R. Nice (Cambridge, 1977), p. 2.

cultural prejudice—of the mapmaker. There is no "view from nowhere" for even the most scrupulously "detached" observer.

To these charges let me plead guilty, but with extenuating circumstances. First, as I've tried to argue elsewhere, the traditional intellectual historian's tool of synoptic content analysis, when complicated by a healthy distrust of reductive paraphrase, is indispensable in making sense of the past.[49] For it expresses a certain cautious optimism about the potential for a communicative interaction between the historian and his subject matter—the fusion, as Hans-Georg Gadamer would optimistically put it, of their horizons. Horizon is of course itself a visual metaphor, if a less totalizing one than synopsis. It suggests that finite vantage point from which the historian "sees" the past, an insight hermeneutically minded historians since the days of J. C. Chladenius in the early eighteenth century have known well.[50] Even when partial horizons are fused, no absolute God's-eye view above the fray is possible. But perhaps some advantage is nonetheless gained from the attempt to "achieve a perspective," as we say, on the material, and then to compare it with those of the participants involved, as the materials they have left behind allow us to reconstruct them.

In this particular case, I have been fortunate to be able to discuss this argument with several of the figures it purports to explain, thus experiencing a more active fusion—or at least interaction—of horizons than is given to most historians. In a striking number of cases, they were fully conversant with the implications of their own work on visual themes, but

49. Martin Jay, "Two Cheers for Paraphrase: The Confessions of a Synoptic Intellectual Historian," *Stanford Literature Review*, 3, 1 (Spring, 1986), pp. 47–60; reprinted in *Fin-de-siècle Socialism and Other Essays* (New York, 1988).

50. For a discussion of Chladenius's use of "point of view" in history, see Michael Ermarth, "Hermeneutics and History: The Fork in Hermes' Path Through the 18th Century," in *Aufklärung und Geschichte: Studien zur deutschen Geschichtswissenschaft im 18. Jahrhundert*, ed. Hans Erich Bödicker et al. (Göttingen, 1987), pp. 217f. See also the important essay by Reinhart Koselleck, "Perspective and Temporality: A Contribution to the Historiographical Exposure of the Historical World," in his *Futures Past: On the Semantics of Historical Time*, trans. Keith Tribe (Cambridge, 1985).

were unaware of the larger dimensions of the discourse in which it was embedded. Although my attempts to convince them of its extent did not always fully succeed, a kind of fusion seems to have begun. For my own part, I can verify that my horizon has been transformed by this opportunity in ways that I hope have increased the subtlety and plausibility of the book's argument.

Another warrant for the retention of a synoptic approach comes from the methodological reflections of the French intellectual who has himself written among the most trenchant studies of visual themes, Jean Starobinski. In the preface to his collection of essays, *L'oeil vivant*, he comments on the value and the dangers of what he calls "le regard surplombant" (the look from above):

> Despite our desire to lose ourselves in the living depths of a work, we are constrained to distance ourselves from it in order to speak of it. Why then not deliberately establish a distance that will reveal to us, in a panoramic perspective, the *surroundings* with which the work is organically linked? We would try to discern certain significant correspondences that haven't been perceived by the writer, to interpret his mobile unconscious, to read the complex relations that unite a destiny and a work to their historical and social milieu.[51]

After then acknowledging the threats inherent in a one-sided *regard surplombant*, most notably the disappearance of the work itself into its context, Starobinski concludes with a call for a judicious balance, which this study also hopes to maintain:

> The complete critique is perhaps not one that aims at totality (as does *le regard surplombant*) nor that which aims at intimacy (as does identifying intuition); it is the look that knows how to demand, in their turn, distance and intimacy, knowing in advance

51. Jean Starobinski, *L'oeil vivant: Essais* (Paris, 1961), p. 26.

that the truth lies not in one or the other attempt, but in the movement that passes indefatigably from one to the other. One must
refuse neither the vertigo of distance nor that of proximity; one must
desire that double excess where the look is always near to losing
all its powers.[52]

It is, let me end these introductory remarks by emphasizing, such a
willingness to risk this loss that ultimately empowers the intellectual historian to enter the discursive field itself in a critical way. How successful
the present effort will be in this regard remains, of course, very much to
be seen.

52. Ibid.

CHAPTER ONE

The Noblest of the Senses: Vision from Plato to Descartes

Except among heretics, all
Western metaphysics has been
peephole metaphysics. . . . As
through the crenels of a parapet,
the subject gazes upon a black sky
in which the star of the idea, or of
Being, is said to rise.

THEODOR W. ADORNO[1]

The eyes are the organic prototype
of philosophy. Their enigma is that
they not only can see but are also
able to see themselves seeing.
This gives them a prominence
among the body's cognitive
organs. A good part of
philosophical thinking is actually
only eye reflex, eye dialectic,
seeing-oneself-see.

PETER SLOTERDIJK[2]

All the management of our lives
depends on the senses, and since
that of sight is the most comprehensive and the noblest of these,
there is no doubt that the inventions which serve to augment its
power are among the most useful
that there can be.

RENÉ DESCARTES[3]

"Clearly outlined, brightly and uniformly illuminated, men and things
stand out in a realm where everything is visible; and not less clear—
wholly expressed, orderly even in their ardor—are the feelings and
thoughts of the persons involved."[4] So Erich Auerbach described the
world of Homeric Greece in the celebrated opening chapter, "Odysseus'
Scar," of his classic study of literary realism, *Mimesis*. In the dominant
reading of Greek culture that has so influenced the West, this assumption
of the Hellenic affinity for the visible has enjoyed widespread popularity.
Hans Blumenberg, for example, expresses a typical judgment when he

1. Theodor W. Adorno, *Negative Dialectics*, trans. E. B. Ashton (New York, 1973),
pp. 139–140.

2. Peter Sloterdijk, *Critique of Cynical Reason*, trans. Michael Eldred (Minneapolis,
1987), p. 145.

3. René Descartes, *Discourse on Method, Optics, Geometry, and Meteorology*, trans. Paul
J. Olscamp (Indianapolis, 1965), p. 65.

4. Erich Auerbach, *Mimesis: The Representation of Reality in Western Literature*, trans.
Willard R. Trask (Princeton, 1953), p. 2.

writes, "The light in which the landscape and things that surrounded the life of the Greeks stood gave to everything a clarity and (in terms of optics alone) unquestionable presence that left room for doubt regarding the accessibility of nature to man only late and only as a result of thought's experience with itself."[5] Although there have been dissenting voices— William Ivins's was the most persistent[6]—it is generally agreed that classical Greece privileged sight over the other senses, a judgment lent special

5. Hans Blumenberg, *The Legitimacy of the Modern World*, trans. Robert M. Wallace (Cambridge, Mass., 1983), p. 243.

6. William M. Ivins, Jr., *Art and Geometry: A Study in Space Intuitions* (Cambridge, Mass., 1946), which says the Greeks were more tactile than visual. Ivins's argument is based on the claim that vision is inherently relational, relativist, and continuous, moving as it does through a process of gradual transitions from focused attention to peripheral inattention. Touch, in contrast, is based on the immediate, discontinuous, unrelational contact with the discrete objects it can grasp in the here and now. It lacks, so Ivins contends, the capacity to deal with duration or becoming and fails to get a full "picture" of the whole. Greek art, he then argues, was itself cold, static, and lacking in any sense of history or development. Greek geometry was also based on touch, as shown by its metrical bias, which derived from what could be measured by hand. As such, it lacked a true sense of perspective with a converging vanishing point at infinity, believing instead with Euclid that parallel lines never converge. Ivins attempts to clinch his argument that the Greeks were more tactile than visual by noting Plato's hostility to sight and speculating that this negative attitude toward the mimetic arts was due to their failure to deal satisfactorily with becoming and growth.

Although Ivins's point about tactile versus visual qualities in geometry is suggestive, his general argument is unconvincing. First, vision is just as likely to lead to a frozen and static appropriation of the world as touch; in fact, we will see that many commentators damn it precisely for that reason. Second, touch can certainly give the experience of continuity over time through an exploration of a surface. Although, to be sure, it is far less capable than vision of giving a sense of the whole with which it comes into contact, such a synoptic view is more likely to lead to a synchronic denial of becoming than touch's probing movement. Nor is touch as foreign to relational, interactional experience as Ivins assumes. What, after all, is the meaning of the lovers' caress? His characterization of Plato's hostility to sight depends on a very restricted notion of vision. In fact, whatever hostility Plato did harbor against sensual vision was directed at precisely what Ivins claims vision cannot do, but Plato thought it could: register becoming. For Plato, becoming was the realm of illusion.

weight by the contrast often posited with its more verbally oriented Hebraic competitor.[7]

There is, in fact, ample warrant for this generalization in Greek art, religion, and philosophy. Even linguistic evidence has been adduced to show that the scattered verbs employed during the Homeric period to designate aspects of visual practice coalesced into only a few during the classical era, suggesting an essentializing of vision itself.[8] The Greek gods were visibly manifest to humankind, which was encouraged to depict them in plastic form. They were also conceived as avid spectators of human actions, as well as willing to provide the occasional spectacle themselves. The perfection of idealized visible form in the Greeks' art accorded well with their love of theatrical performance. The word *theater*, as has often been remarked, shares the same root as the word *theory, theoria*, which meant to look at attentively, to behold.[9] So too does theorem, which has allowed some commentators to emphasize the privileging of vision in Greek mathematics, with its geometric emphasis.[10] The importance of optics in Greek science has also been adduced to illustrate its partiality for sight. Even the Greek idealization of the nude body, in con-

---

For all of these reasons, Ivins's argument about the Greek attitude toward vision has not become the dominant view, although it is not without influence. See, for example, William Kuhns, *The Post-Industrial Prophets: Interpretations of Technology* (New York, 1971), p. 130; and Walter J. Ong, *The Presence of the World: Some Prolegomena for Cultural and Religious History* (New Haven, 1967), p. 4.

7. See Thorlieff Boman, *Hebrew Thought Compared with Greek* (Philadelphia, 1954); and Susan A. Handelman, *The Slayers of Moses: The Emergence of Rabbinic Interpretation in Modern Literary Theory* (Albany, N.Y., 1982).

8. Bruno Snell, *The Discovery of the Mind: The Greek Origins of European Thought*, trans. T. G. Rosenmeyer (Oxford, 1953), p. 4.

9. For a history of the word, see David Michael Levin, *The Opening of Vision: Nihilism and the Postmodern Situation* (New York, 1987), pp. 99f.

10. Abel Rey, *La science dans l'antiquité*, 5 vols. (Paris, 1930–1948), esp. vol. 2, pp. 445f, and vol. 3, pp. 17, 389. It can, however, be argued that the importance of proofs in Greek geometry involved a shift from the purely visual to propositional language instead.

trast with the Hebrew stress on clothing, has seemed consonant with a bias for visual clarity and transparency.[11]

But nowhere has the visual seemed so dominant as in that remarkable Greek invention called philosophy. Here the contemplation of the visible heavens, praised by Anaxagoras as the means to human fulfillment,[12] was extended to become the philosophical wonder at all that was on view. Truth, it was assumed, could be as "naked" as the undraped body. "Knowledge (*eidenai*) is the state of having seen," Bruno Snell notes of Greek epistemology, "and the *Nous* is the mind in its capacity as an absorber of images."[13]

In a seminal essay entitled "The Nobility of Sight," Hans Jonas has outlined the implications of this visual bias both for Greek thought and for the subsequent history of Western philosophy.[14] Because of their favoring vision, a number of its apparent inclinations influenced Greek thinking. Sight, he contends, is preeminently the sense of simultaneity, capable of surveying a wide visual field at one moment. Intrinsically less temporal than other senses such as hearing or touch, it thus tends to elevate static Being over dynamic Becoming, fixed essences over ephemeral appearances. Greek philosophy from Parmenides through Plato accordingly emphasized an unchanging and eternal presence. "The very contrast between eternity and temporality," Jonas claims, "rests upon an idealization of 'present' experienced visually as the holder of stable contents as against the fleeting succession of nonvisual sensation."[15] Zeno's paradox, which so perplexed Greek thought, shows how beholden it was to a

11. Mario Perniola, "Between Clothing and Nudity," in *Fragments for a History of the Human Body*, part 2, ed. Michel Feher with Ramona Naddaff and Nadia Tazi (New York, 1989), p. 238.

12. For a discussion of the Greek contemplation of the skies, see Hans Blumenberg, *The Genesis of the Copernican World*, trans. Robert M. Wallace (Cambridge, 1987).

13. Snell, p. 198.

14. Hans Jonas, "The Nobility of Sight: A Study in the Phenomenology of the Senses," in *The Phenomenon of Life: Toward a Philosophical Biology* (Chicago, 1982).

15. Ibid., p. 145.

detemporalized notion of reality (a central target, as we will see, of the French antiocularcentric discourse that began with Bergson's critique of Zeno). Greek science, which was crowned by optics, was also incapable of dealing successfully with motion, in particular with the problem of acceleration.[16] Its understanding of vision was itself basically reduced to the geometry of light rays in Euclidean terms.

Medusa

Jonas's second contention is that the externality of sight allows the observer to avoid direct engagement with the object of his gaze. Thus, the very distinction between subject and object and the belief in the neutral apprehension of the latter by the former, a distinction so crucial for much later thought, was abetted by the ocularcentrism of Greek thought. "The gain," Jonas writes, "is the concept of objectivity, of the thing as it is in itself as distinct from the thing as it affects me, and from this distinction arises the whole idea of *theoria* and theoretical truth."[17] Perhaps lost by this "dynamic neutralization," as Jonas calls it, is a clear sense of causality, because the constitutive link between subject and object is suppressed or forgotten.

Finally, the advantage given sight in the apprehension of great distances, Jonas claims, had several consequences. The Greek idea of infinity was encouraged by contemplating the vast reach of our ocular range.[18] So too the pull of the eye into a distant landscape seemed to grant the viewer the all-important "prospective" capacity for foreknowledge, which was the premise of instrumental and adaptive behavior. Because the Greeks often depicted their seers as blind (Tiresias, for example) and had their oracles deliver verbal rather than pictorial predictions, it would be problematic to contend that they always "saw" the future. But if seeing the open landscape in front of one provided a spatial experience of appre-

16. For a discussion of later attempts to set it right, see Amos Funkenstein, *Theology and the Scientific Imagination from the Middle Ages to the Seventeenth Century* (Princeton, 1986), pp. 165f.

17. Jonas, p. 147.

18. In contrast, Ivins in *Art and Geometry* claims that because of their tactile bias, the Greeks never "made use in proof of the idea of infinity" (p. 50).

hending what was likely to come next, foresight could be and was translated into temporal terms as well.

To these arguments, other commentators like Eric Havelock and Rudolf Arnheim have added that visual primacy helps account for the Greek penchant for abstraction, its awareness of the dialectic of permanence and change, and even the general supplanting of Mythos by Logos in classical thought.[19] Once the battle against Sophism, which defended rhetoric and the ear, was won, Greek philosophy could elevate a visually defined notion of disinterested, monologic, epistemic truth over mere opinion or *doxa*. Although the Sophist alternative was never entirely forgotten—indeed it lingers in the very form of Plato's dialogues—its reputation remained low until figures like Lorenzo Valla and Giambattista Vico revived it many centuries later.

The importance of sight is evident throughout Plato's writings. In the *Timaeus*, for example, he distinguished between the creation of the sense of sight, which he grouped with the creation of human intelligence and the soul, and that of the other senses, which he placed with man's material being.[20] For Plato, truth was embodied in the *Eidos* or Idea, which was like a visible form blanched of its color.[21] The human eye, he contended, is able to perceive light because it shares a like quality with the source of light, the sun. Here a similar analogy holds between the intellect, which he called "the eye of the mind," and the highest form, the Good. Although at times he was uncertain of our ability to look directly at the sun (or the Good),[22] in *The Republic*, Plato claimed that the just man can indeed face it squarely and "is able to see what is, not by reflections in water or by fantasms of it in some alien abode, but in and by itself in its own place."[23]

19. Eric Havelock, *A Preface to Plato* (Oxford, 1963); Rudolf Arnheim, *Visual Thinking* (Berkeley, 1969).

20. Plato, *Timaeus*, 61d–68e.

21. For a discussion of Plato's elevation of form over color, see Havelock, p. 274.

22. Plato, *Phaedo*, 99e.

23. Plato, *The Republic*, 516b.

Plato and sight

A closer examination of Plato's celebration of sight will, however, correct too one-dimensional an assessment of Greek ocularcentrism. For in his philosophy, "vision" seems to have meant only that of the inner eye of the mind; in fact, Plato often expressed severe reservations about the reliability of the two eyes of normal perception. We see *through* the eyes, he insisted, not *with* them. The celebrated myth of the cave, in which the fire is substituted for the sun as the source of a light too blinding to be faced directly, suggests his suspicions of the illusions of sense perception. Ultimately, the prisoners in the cave do escape and find their way into the world, where after an initial dazzlement they can face the sun. But their normal sense perception in the cave is of the fleeting and imperfect shadows cast on its wall. Whatever the implications of this founding myth of Western culture—and we will later encounter criticisms of it by antivisual French feminists like Luce Irigaray—it is clear that it demonstrates Plato's uncertainty about the value of actual sense perception, including vision.

From this distrust followed Plato's notorious hostility to the mimetic arts—most notably painting, which he banned from his utopian state in *The Republic*.[24] Theater was equally suspect for its fictitious simulation of true action.[25] Of all the arts, only music with its mathematical rather than imitative relationship to the higher realm of forms (a relationship grounded for Plato in Pythagoras's discovery of the numerical nature of musical intervals) was not dangerously deceptive. Thus, the Plato who tells us in the *Timaeus* that vision is humanity's greatest gift[26] also warns us against the illusions of our imperfect eyes. True philosophers, he insists, are not mere "sight-seers," advice taken very much to heart by later thinkers like Democritus, who was said to have blinded himself in order to "see" with his intellect.

Although one can certainly find a more positive attitude toward the

24. For a general discussion of Plato's hostility to mimetic art, see Iris Murdoch, *The Fire and the Sun: Why Plato Banished the Artists* (Oxford, 1977).

25. For an account of Plato's criticism of the theater, see Jonas Barish, *The Anti-Theatrical Prejudice* (Berkeley, 1981).

26. Plato, *Timaeus*, 47b.

actual eyes in Greek philosophy, most notably in Aristotle's defense of induction and the power of sight to discriminate among more pieces of information than any other sense,[27] it is thus apparent that Greek culture was not as univocally inclined toward celebrating vision as may appear at first glance. Indeed, a certain anxiety about vision's malevolent power is expressed in many of the central Greek myths, most notably those of Narcissus, Orpheus, and Medusa.[28] And the all-seeing Argus, nicknamed Panoptes, is ultimately undone by Pan, whose enchanting music lulls him to sleep.[29] The very appearance of the Gods in anthropomorphic images was, in fact, called into question by one critic, the sixth-century B.C. philosopher Xenophanes. The frequent existence of apotropaic amulets and other devices to disarm the evil eye (which the Greeks called the *baskanos opthalmos*) also suggests how widespread the fear of being seen existed here as elsewhere.[30]

And yet, having thus demonstrated that the Greek celebration of sight was more equivocal than is sometimes claimed, it must still be acknowledged that Hellenic thought did on the whole privilege the visual over any other sense. Even in its negative guises, its power was evident. Indeed, it might be argued that the very ambiguities that we've noted in Plato's thought were instrumental in elevating the status of the visual in Western

27. Aristotle's considerations of vision appear most notably in *De Anima* and the *Metaphysics*. For an account, see John I. Beare, *Greek Theories of Elementary Cognition from Alcmaeon to Aristotle* (Oxford, 1906). For a history of the reception of his famous dictum that "nothing is in the intellect which was not first in the senses," see P. Cranfield, "On the Origins of the Phrase *Nihil est in intellectu quod non prius fuerit in sensu*," *Journal of the History of Medicine*, 25 (1970).

28. For a suggestive interpretation of their significance, see Hartmut Böhme, "Sinne une Blick. Variationen zur mythopoetischen Geschichte des Subjekts," in *Konkursbuch*, vol. 13 (Tübingen, 1984).

29. For a suggestive analysis of the implications of this struggle, see Michel Serres, "Panoptic Theory," in *The Limits of Theory*, ed. Thomas M. Kavanagh (Stanford, Calif., 1989).

30. For a discussion of Greek apotropaic reactions to the evil eye, see Albert M. Potts, *The World's Eye* (Lexington, Ky., 1982), chap. 4.

culture. For if vision could be construed as either the allegedly pure sight of perfect and immobile forms with "the eye of the mind" or as the impure but immediately experienced sight of the actual two eyes, when one of these alternatives was under attack, the other could be raised in its place. In either case, something called vision could still be accounted the noblest of the senses. As we will note in the case of Cartesian philosophy, it was precisely this creative ambiguity that lay at the origins of modern ocularcentrism.

It was an ambiguity that also had a correlate in the way light itself was conceptualized for a long time in Western thought. Light could be understood according to the model of geometric rays that Greek optics had privileged, those straight lines studied by catoptrics (the science of reflection) or dioptrics (the science of refraction). Here perfect linear form was seen as the essence of illumination, and it existed whether perceived by the human eye or not. Light in this sense became known as *lumen*.[31] An alternative version of light, known as *lux*, emphasized instead the actual experience of human sight. Here color, shadow, and movement was accounted as important as form and outline, if not more so. In the history of painting, as well as optics, these two models of light vied for prominence.

This dual concept of light nicely complemented the dual concept of vision, even if they weren't perfectly congruent. What might be called the alternating traditions of *speculation* with the eye of the mind and *observation* with the two eyes of the body provided fertile ground for the varieties of ocularcentrism that have so deeply penetrated Western culture. In fact, if we divide them further, we can discern still other opportunities for privileging the visual. Speculation can be construed as the rational perception of clear and distinct forms with the unclouded eye of the mind or as the irrational and ecstatic dazzlement by the blinding light of God, the "vision" of the seer. Here a metaphysics of light could turn into a full-

31. For an account of the *lux/lumen* distinction, see Vasco Ronchi, *Optics: The Science of Vision*, trans. Edward Rosen (New York, 1957), chap. 1.

fledged mysticism of light.[32] Observation could be understood as the unmediated assimilation of stimuli from without, the collapse of perception into pure sensation. Or it could be construed as a more complicated interaction of sensations and the shaping or judging capacity of the mind, which provided the Gestalt-like structures that made observation more than a purely passive phenomenon. And within these broad categories, many differentiated variants could proliferate. In all of them, however, something called sight was accorded a fundamental place in our knowledge of the world.

If the Greek ambiguities about speculation and observation and the two types of light created opportunities for ocularcentrism to take root, so too did the complicated relationship between the eye and its object implicit in the idea of *theoria*. As already noted, commentators like Jonas have emphasized the distancing function of sight in creating the subject/object dualism so typical of Greek and later Western metaphysics. A closer examination of what the Greeks meant by theory suggests a second possible inference that might be drawn. If Plato argued that the eye and the sun are composed of like substances, and the Greeks believed that the eye transmitted as well as received light rays (the theory of extramission), then there was a certain participatory dimension in the visual process, a potential intertwining of viewer and viewed.[33]

32. See Hans Blumenberg, "Licht als Metapher der Wahrheit," *Studium Generale*, 10 (1953), p. 434, where he denies the existence of a light mysticism in Plato, calling it instead a light metaphysics.

33. According to Böhme (p. 29), this communion-oriented notion of vision was especially evident in pre-Socratic thought. Support for this interpretation comes from F. M. Cornford, *From Religion to Philosophy: A Study in the Origins of Western Speculation* (New York, 1957). He notes that the Orphic version of *theoria* involved emotional involvement, whereas its Pythagorean replacement did not (pp. 198f.). In another sense as well, *theoria* seems to have suggested more than the isolated gaze of a subject at an object. According to Wlad Godzich, the word designates a plural collective of public figures, who as a group provided certain knowledge for the *polis*. As such, *theoria* was the opposite of the individual perception known as *aesthesis*. See Godzich, "Foreword: The Tiger on the Paper Mat," in Paul de Man, *The Resistance to Theory* (Minneapolis, 1985), p. xiv.

Mindful of this possibility, Hans-Georg Gadamer has in fact contended that *theoria* was not as completely disengaged and spectatorial as was more modern scientific epistemology. Instead, it contained a moment of "sacral communion" beyond mere disinterested contemplation. "Theoria," he argues, "is a true sharing, not something active, but something passive (pathos), namely being totally involved in and carried away by what one sees. It is from this point that people have tried recently to explain the religious background of the Greek idea of reason."[34] Residues of such reciprocity in the notion of theory may well in fact have persisted until the late Middle Ages, when belief in extramission was finally laid to rest.

From this beginning—which led in a different direction from the more spectatorial tradition stressed by Jonas—arose an especially important strain in the tradition of speculation, which was to be a particular target of the antivisual discourse in twentieth-century France. That strain we might call the argument for specular sameness. The Latin *speculatio*—along with *contemplatio*, the translation of *theoria*—contained within it the same root as *speculum* and *specular*, which designate mirroring.[35] Rather than implying the distance between subject and object, the specular tradition in this sense tended to collapse them. As Rodolphe Gasché has argued in *The Tain of the Mirror*, the reflection of the speculum was potentially an absolute one.[36] That is, speculation could mean the pure knowledge of self-reflection, a mirror reflecting only itself with

34. Hans-Georg Gadamer, *Truth and Method* (New York, 1975), p. 111.

35. It was Cicero who seems to have derived *speculatio* from *specularis*, which may have been a mistake. See Rodolphe Gasché, *The Tain of the Mirror: Derrida and the Philosophy of Reflection* (Cambridge, Mass., 1986), p. 43. If wrong, it was nonetheless a very suggestive etymology.

36. Gasché, p. 54, where he contends that "unlike reflection, which, as a function of understanding, perpetuates division and absolutely fixed opposition, absolute reflection, or speculation, deliberately pursues a totalizing goal." Interestingly, Nietzsche claimed that mirrors defeat the ideal of specular sameness. In aphorism 243 of *Daybreak*, he wrote, "When we try to examine the mirror in itself we discover in the end nothing but things upon it. If we want to grasp the things we finally get hold of

no remainder. Later in medieval Christianity, the materiality of the human mirror, or the mirror of creation, as it was known, could be subordinated to the divine mirror in which only perfect truth was reflected. Dante in the *Paradiso* was able to describe his journey as a transition from the *speculum inferius* of man (the glass through which we see only darkly) to the *speculum superius* of heavenly illumination.[37] And in the great speculative philosophies of the modern era, most notably nineteenth-century German Idealism, speculation as self-reflection was given a secular expression. As Gasché notes, this process was designed to reveal the same amidst all apparent diversity.

> Speculative thought is grounded in this reflecting mirroring of what is positively in opposition. It coincides with the reciprocal mirroring and unification of the conflicting poles. The mirroring that constitutes speculative thought articulates the diverse, and the contradictions that exist between its elements, in such a way as to exhibit the totality of which this diversity is a part. Speculation, then, is the movement that constitutes the most complete unity, the ultimate foundation of all possible diversity, opposition, and contradiction.[38]

In short, the faith in the nobility of sight bequeathed to Western culture by the Greeks had many, often contrary implications. It could mean the spectatorial distancing of subject and object or the self-reflective mirroring of the same in a higher unity without material remainder (the mirror's tain in Gasché's metaphor). It could mean the absolute purity of geometric and linear form apparent to the eye of the mind or it could mean the uncertain play of shadow and color evident to the actual senses.

---

nothing but the mirror.—This, in the most general terms, is the history of knowledge." *Daybreak: Thoughts on the Prejudices of Morality*, trans. R. J. Hollingdale (Cambridge, 1982), p. 141. I am indebted to Allan Megill for drawing my attention to this passage.

37. For a discussion of mirrors in Dante, see James L. Miller, "The Mirrors of Dante's Paradiso," *University of Toronto Quarterly*, 46 (1977).

38. Gasché, p. 44.

language = doxa
vision = truth and knowledge } *Greek world*

It could mean the search for divine illumination or the Promethean wresting of fire from the gods for human usage. And it could mean the contest for power between the Medusan gaze and its apotropaic antidote (a contrast with gender implications occluded until recent feminist critiques made them explicit).[39]

One final point needs emphasizing before we leave the classical world. The Greek privileging of vision meant more than relegating the other senses to subordinate positions; it could also lead to the denigration of language in several respects. Outside of the often maligned tradition of Sophism, language was deemed inferior to sight as the royal road to the truth. It was the realm, as we have noted, of mere *doxa* (opinion) instead. Rhetoric was thus banished from genuine philosophy. Even when the Greeks discussed verbal phenomena like metaphors, they tended to reduce them to transparent figures, likenesses that were mimetic resemblances, not the interplay of sameness and difference. "To produce a good metaphor," Aristotle claimed in his *Poetics*, "is to see a likeness."[40]

Not surprisingly, when recent French commentators on metaphor examined their Greek predecessors, they condemned precisely this Hellenic inclination toward pure specularity.[41] Other contributors to antiocularcentric discourse made similar accusations against the specular implications of Greek tragedy, claiming that it recuperated indigestible horror in a theatrical economy of the same.[42] Greek metaphysics and Greek poetics, they charged, were at one in their ocularcentric bias. If the Jews could begin their most heartfelt prayer, "Hear, O Israel," the Greek philosophers were in effect urging, "See, O Hellas."

---

39. On the links between femininity, vision, and Greek epistemology, see Genevieve Lloyd, *The Man of Reason: "Male" and "Female" in Western Philosophy* (Minneapolis, 1984), pp. 2f.

40. Aristotle, *Poetics*, 1459a, 7–8.

41. Jacques Derrida, "White Mythology: Metaphor in the Text," in *Margins of Philosophy*, trans. Alan Bass (Chicago, 1982); and Paul Ricoeur, *The Rule of Metaphor* (Toronto, 1978). For a helpful summary of their arguments, see Handelman, pp. 15f.

42. Philippe Lacoue-Labarthe, *La césure de spéculatif* (Paris, 1978). He contends that the key link between tragedy and speculative thought is mimesis (p. 195).

Western culture has often seemed like a struggle to respond to one or the other of these two injunctions, even if, as we have argued, the opposition can be too starkly drawn. One of the major battlefields of that contest was medieval Christianity. This is certainly not the place to rehearse in detail the history of the Christian attitude toward vision or the complex intertwining of Hellenic and Hebraic impulses in that history. But it will be necessary to spend some time with it, if only to caution against a widely influential but oversimplified version that has had special importance in France. Its perpetrators are Lucien Febvre and Robert Mandrou, two of the most distinguished historians of the late medieval, early modern period, both of them luminaries of the celebrated *Annales* school.

In his much-admired study of *The Problem of Unbelief in the Sixteenth Century*, Febvre argues,

> The sixteenth century did not see first: it heard and smelled, it sniffed the air and caught sounds. It was only later, as the seventeenth century was approaching, that it seriously and actively became engaged in geometry, focusing attention on the world of forms with Kepler (1571–1630) and Desargues of Lyon (1593–1662). It was then that *vision* was unleashed in the world of science as it was in the world of physical sensations, and the world of beauty as well.[43]

In his *Introduction to Modern France, 1500–1640*, Mandrou makes a similar assertion: "The hierarchy [of the senses] was not the same [as in the twentieth century] because the eye, which rules today, found itself in third place, behind hearing and touch, and far after them. The eye that

---

43. Lucien Febvre, *The Problem of Unbelief in the Sixteenth Century: The Religion of Rabelais*, trans. Beatrice Gottlieb (Cambridge, Mass., 1982), p. 432. Although I will be taking issue with his argument about the medieval hierarchy of the senses, I do not want to leave the impression that this work is unimportant. To the contrary, it was among the first attempts to take seriously the challenging task of writing a history of the senses. For an appropriate acknowledgment by one of the more recent practitioners of this genre, see Alain Corbin, *Le miasme et la jonquille: L'odorat et l'imaginaire social 18ᵉ–19ᵉ siècles* (Paris, 1982), pp. ii and 271, where he also praises Mandrou.

organizes, classifies and orders was not the favored organ of a time that preferred hearing."[44] To buttress his argument, Mandrou adduces the Lutheran recourse to the Hebraic tradition of privileging the ear and analyzes the poetry of Pierre de Ronsard, Joachim Du Bellay, and Daniel Marot to the same effect. He concludes, "Until at least the eighteenth century, touch remained therefore the master sense; it tests, confirms what sight could only perceive. It assures perception, gives solidity to the impressions provided by the other senses that do not present the same security."[45]

In addition to a certain waffling about what the master sense of the early modern era actually was—hearing or touch—these generalizations are based on only a smattering of evidence. Nonetheless, they have enjoyed widespread currency. Roland Barthes, for example, reports in his essay on the Counter-Reformation theologian and founder of the Jesuit order Ignatius Loyola that "in the Middle Ages, historians tell us, the most refined sense, the perceptive sense *par excellence*, the one that established the richest contact with the world was hearing: sight came in only third, after touch. Then we have a reversal: the eye becomes the prime organ of perception (Baroque, art of the thing seen, attests to it)."[46] Many other commentators, English-speaking as well as French, echo this appraisal of the antivisual Middle Ages.[47]

In all these cases, there is an assumed contrast, sometimes explicitly stated, sometimes not, between medieval and modern visual cultures.

---

44. Robert Mandrou, *Introduction à la France moderne 1500–1640: Essai de Psychologie historique* (Paris, 1974), p. 76. Still another defense of this argument can be found in José Antonio Maravall, "La concepción dá saber en una sociedad tradicional," in *Estudios de historia del pensamiento español*, ser. 1: *Edad Media*, 2d ed. (Madrid, 1973).

45. Ibid., p. 79.

46. Roland Barthes, *Sade, Fourier, Loyola*, trans. Richard Miller (New York, 1976), p. 65.

47. See, for example, Donald M. Lowe, *History of Bourgeois Perception* (Chicago, 1982), p. 24; and Ian Hacking, *Why Does Language Matter to Philosophy?* (Cambridge, 1975), p. 32.

There is much to be said for emphasizing the ocularcentrism of modern Europe, although, as we will see, not for homogenizing its manifestations. It would be a mistake, however, to contrast it too rigidly to an ocularphobic Middle Ages. For medieval Christian culture was not as hostile to the eye as Febvre and Mandrou—on rather thin evidence—suggest.

Its Hellenic and Hebraic impulses, if we want to stay with that typology, were often in an uneasy balance. One of the major differences between Judaism and Christianity, after all, was the latter's faith in the corporeal incarnation of the divine in human form, which meant that the Mosaic taboo against graven images could easily be called into question.[48] In its place, there arose a very non-Jewish belief in the visible sacraments and the visible church. This tendency culminated in the late medieval practice of elevating the consecrated host for all worshipers to see.[49] Although the earliest Church fathers like Origen, Tertullian, and Clement of Alexandria distrusted the pagan residues in images and feared an overly anthropomorphic notion of the holy, their successors soon recognized the power of sight in making the Christian story available to the hoards of new believers from non-Jewish backgrounds. As early as the Hellenization of Christian doctrine begun by the converted Jew Philo of Alexandria in the first century, biblical references to hearing were systematically transformed into ones referring to sight.[50] The Gospel of Saint John had said that "God is Light," and medieval thinkers like the Pseudo Dionysus took the expression literally. "By the fourth century," the theologian Margaret Miles has recently argued, "there is abundant evidence of the importance of vision in worship."[51] Churches built by the converted

48. For recent accounts of the medieval Christian struggle over images, see Margaret R. Miles, *Image as Insight: Visual Understanding in Western Christianity and Secular Culture* (Boston, 1985); John Phillips, *The Reformation of Images: Destruction of Art in England, 1535–1660* (Berkeley, 1973), chap. 1; and Leo Braudy, *The Frenzy of Renown: Fame and Its History* (New York, 1986), chap. 4.

49. For a discussion of its implications and the reaction against it, see Heather Phillips, "John Wyclif and the Optics of the Eucharist," in *From Ockham to Wyclif,* ed. Anne Hudson and Michael Wilks (Oxford, 1987).

50. For a discussion see Hans Blumenberg, *The Legitimacy of the Modern Age*, p. 286.

emperor Constantine were filled with light, a residue of his earlier cult of the sun.

The neo-Platonic strain in medieval thought meant that the contrast between a higher *lumen* and an inferior *lux* was often redescribed in religious terms. Even a critic of ocular desire like Augustine still staunchly defended the higher light of God in which the pious man would ultimately stand bathed. "Thanks be to you, O Lord," he came to say near the end of the *Confessions*, "for all that we see!"[52] In his thirteenth-century treatise *De Luce*, Robert Grosseteste developed a complicated ocular metaphysics in which a divine primal light was contrasted to a lesser visible light available to human perception.[53] The distinctions between superior and inferior mirrors mentioned earlier paralleled this dichotomy.

The symbolic importance of the *speculum sine macula* became particularly keen with the spread of the Virgin's cult in the twelfth century. The positive value accorded to mirrors was so great that manuals for devotion were sometimes called specula because they were assumed to reflect the truth. Christian theologians in fact often resorted to the mirror to solve their most troubling questions: Why did a perfect God descend into an imperfect world of matter? How could He love a creature less perfect than Himself? According to Paul Zweig,

> The image of the mirror, and the corresponding vision of God's generosity as an act of self-delight, allowed these questions to be answered. God came down into the world as into a mirror. He

---

51. Miles, *Image as Insight*, p. 5.

52. Saint Augustine, *Confessions*, trans. R. S. Pine-Coffin (London, 1983), chap. 13, p. 343. The neo-Platonic residues in Augustine's thought have occasioned widespread discussion. For recent reassessments of their importance for the question of sight, which he understood as the intermingling of rays from and to the eye, see Margaret Miles, "Vision: The Eye of the Body and the Eye of the Mind in Saint Augustine's *De trinitate* and *Confessions*," *The Journal of Religion*, 63, 2 (April, 1983); and Georges Didi-Huberman, "Le paradoxe de l'être á voir," *L'Écrit du temps*, 17 (Winter, 1988), pp. 79–91.

53. Robert Grosseteste, *On Light (De Luce)*, trans. Clare C. Riedl (Milwaukee, 1942).

came down in order to possess an image of His own divinity. And He will allow man to be "saved," in order to save that fragment of His image captured in the divine soul.[54]

Here the power of specular sameness, which we have noted earlier, was given an ingenious twist: human salvation was but a device for the self-reflection of God.

In more secular terms, vision was also of great significance for medieval thought, especially when Aristotelian respect for the senses was restored in the thirteenth century. If optics had been one of the most developed of the Greek sciences, it continued to have pride of place among their medieval successors. The fourth-century translation of the first half of Plato's *Timaeus* by Chalcidius meant that most medieval theories of optics were strongly Platonic with overlays of Euclid's geometry and Galen's physiology of the eye. The story of the progress made in understanding how vision actually works, a story told in detail by Vasco Ronchi and David Lindberg,[55] shows how important the advances of medieval thinkers like Roger Bacon, John Peacham, John Dee, and especially the Islamic thinkers Al-Kindi and Alhazen were in preparing Kepler's great synthesis of the seventeenth century. Although the way to that achievement had to be cleared by dropping certain misconceptions from the Greek heritage, such as the alleged transmission of "visible species" from the object to the eye,[56] the continuities between the Hellenic science of optics and its me-

54. Paul Zweig, *The Heresy of Self-Love* (Princeton, 1980), p. 30. For other accounts of the medieval fascination with mirrors, see Benjamin Goldberg, *The Mirror and Man* (Charlottesville, Va., 1985), chaps. 6 and 7; and Herbert Grabes, *The Mutable Glass: Mirror-Imagery in Titles and Texts of the Middle Ages and the English Renaissance*, trans. Gordon Collier (Cambridge, 1982).

55. Vasco Ronchi, *Optics: The Science of Vision*, trans. Edward Rosen (New York, 1957); David C. Lindberg, *Theories of Vision from Al-Kindi to Kepler* (Chicago, 1976).

56. Normally, William of Ockham is credited with ending belief in "visible species." For a nuanced account of its stubborn persistence in the years after his efforts to undermine it, see Katherine H. Tachau, "The Problem of *Species in Medio* at Oxford in the Generation after Ockham," *Mediaeval Studies*, 44 (1982), pp. 394–443; "The

dieval successors cannot be underestimated. As Lindberg has put it, "all early natural philosophers acknowledged that vision is man's most noble and dependable sense, and the struggle to understand its workings occupied large numbers of scholars for some two thousand years."[57] The importance of this struggle in Christian culture has, in fact, led another commentator to argue that the fundamentally iconic basis of modern science itself can be traced to the privileging of vision in medieval thought.[58] Faith in beatific vision led to a belief, expressed by William of Ockham among others, in intellective cognition based on intuition (from the Latin *intueri*, "to look at"), which still remained potent in the innate idea doctrine of Descartes.[59]

In addition to the theological and scientific emphasis on sight, medieval religious practice also bore witness to its importance. The visionary tradition—based in part on a theatricalized interpretation of the injunction to imitate God (*imitatio Dei*) and in part on the neo-Platonic search for the colorless "white ecstasy" of divine illumination[60]—had numerous

---

Response to Ockham's and Aureol's Epistemology (1320–1340)," in *English Logic in Italy in the 14th and 15th Centuries*, ed. Alfonso Maierù (Naples, 1982); and *Vision and Certitude in the Age of Ockham: Optics, Epistemology and the Foundations of Semantics 1250–1345* (Leiden, 1988).

57. Lindberg, p. x. Tachau also notes with reference to the fourteenth century, "The prototypical sense was vision, and the prototypical formulation of this process [cognition as the abstraction from sense experience] was achieved by thinkers concerned specifically with explaining vision, namely, the perspectivists" ("The Problem of *Species in Medio*," p. 395). The perspectivists, it should be noted, included figures like Roger Bacon, John Peacham, and Witelo; only later did the term come to mean the Albertian model of vision rather than optics per se.

58. Steven Louis Goldman, "On the Interpretation of Symbols and the Christian Origins of Modern Science," *The Journal of Religion*, 62, 1 (January, 1982). He explicitly contrasts medieval Christian attitudes with those of Jewish thinkers of the period, who subordinated the visual imagination to discursive reasoning.

59. For an account of its importance, see Funkenstein, *Theology and the Scientific Imagination*, pp. 139, 185–186, 294.

60. The injunction to imitate God was, however, not exclusively mimetic in visual terms, but could also mean imitating His likeness in the more metaphorical sense of doing His work. See the discussion in W. J. T. Mitchell, *Iconology: Image, Text, Ideol-*

adepts, such as Meister Eckhardt.[61] In the *Divine Comedy*, Dante spoke of *abbaglio*, "the dazzling glare of paradise, which like the sun could only be stared at by a '*novella vista*.'"[62] Here the goal was often an unmediated vision of the divine without the interference of textuality. One can contend that such religious virtuosi were always a small minority, but their existence could allow later observers like Nietzsche to sarcastically characterize medieval humanity's highest aspirations in ocular terms. "Throughout the whole Middle Ages," he wrote in *Daybreak*, "the actual and decisive sign of the highest humanity was that one was capable of visions— that is to say, of a profound mental disturbance! And the objective of medieval prescriptions for the life of all higher natures (the *religiosi*) was at bottom to make one *capable* of visions!"[63] Indeed, the subtle refinement of visionary techniques continued up to and well beyond the dawn of the modern era, as shown by such works as Nicholas of Cusa's *On God's Vision* of 1413.[64]

For less exalted souls, the medieval Church also knew the power of visual stimulation. As Frances Yates has shown, the classical art of memory invented by Simonides, elaborated by Cicero and other rhetoricians, and important as late as the Renaissance, relied preeminently on visual aids, such as wheels, ladders, and theatrical plans.[65] During the High Middle Ages, even the Scholastics, with their penchant for abstract rea-

ogy (Chicago, 1986), pp. 31–36. The concept of "white ecstasy" seems to have been derived from the pure light that is not passed through a prism to produce the separate colors. For a recent meditation on its importance, see Michel de Certeau, "Extase blanche," *Traverse*, 29 (October, 1983).

61. For a discussion of Eckhardt's views, see Samuel Y. Edgerton, Jr., *The Renaissance Rediscovery of Linear Perspective* (New York, 1975), p. 60.

62. Claudio Guillén, *Literature as System: Essays Towards the Theory of Literary History* (Princeton, 1971), p. 286.

63. Friedrich Nietzsche, *Daybreak*, trans. R. J. Hollingdale (Cambridge, 1982), p. 68.

64. For an arresting examination of vision in Nicholas of Cusa, see Michel de Certeau, "Nicholas de Cues: Le secret d'un regard," *Traverses*, 30–31 (March, 1984), pp. 70–84.

soning and general distrust of "mere" metaphor, granted sight an important role. Thomas Aquinas, who called it the *"sensus magis cognoscitivus"* in his *Summa*,[66] defended the use of images by distinguishing between a good iconolatry and a bad idolatry. The former correctly venerated images, whereas the latter wrongly worshiped them.[67] In a society still overwhelmingly unable to read, the veneration of images was a useful tool in educating the faithful, as Gregory the Great recognized when he called statues "the books of the illiterate." The widespread use of stained glass, bas-reliefs, frescoes, altarpieces, wooden carvings, and so on, to tell biblical stories and to illuminate—often literally—the lives of saints and martyrs shows how popular it was.[68] So too does the visual spectacle of mystery plays designed to awaken devotion in the unlettered.[69] If we add the brilliant light suffusing the great Gothic cathedrals (a light whose metaphysical importance was stressed from the Abbot Suger on),[70] the cult of visual relics, and finally the vivid illumination of manuscripts, we can appreciate the vital role played by vision in the culture Febvre and Mandrou claim was more dependent on hearing or touch.

It has in fact been argued by Jacques Ellul that a great burst of idolatrous ocularcentrism came upon the Church in the fourteenth century in response to the crisis produced by the Avignon papacy and the Great

65. Frances A. Yates, *The Art of Memory* (Chicago, 1966). Interestingly, after these devices were rendered otiose by the invention of printing, they lingered in occult circles, such as Rosicrucianism, where seeing with the "third eye" was popular.

66. Thomas Aquinas, *Summa Theologiae*, I, 84, 2c, cited in Ong, p. 140.

67. For a discussion of the implications of the distinction, see Phillips, *The Reformation of Images*, p. 15. See also Michael Camille, *The Gothic Idol: Ideology and Imagemaking in Medieval Art* (Cambridge, 1989).

68. Ong claims (p. 51) that medieval glass was really more decorative than information-bearing, but gives no conclusive proof that this was the intention of the cathedral builders.

69. For a discussion of the mystery plays, see Rosemary Woolf, *The English Mystery Plays* (Berkeley, 1972).

70. For treatments of the metaphysics of light behind the construction of the cathedrals, see Otto von Simson, *The Gothic Cathedral* (London, 1956); and Erwin Panofsky, *Gothic Architecture and Scholasticism* (New York, 1967).

Schism. Following Georges Duby, he claims that the contest for the allegiance of the illiterate masses meant the unfortunate decision to resort to sensual seduction:

> During this period we see the profusion of images—of all images—and the cataclysmic appearance of visualization's effect on the people. Precisely when the Church is involved in its worst crisis, it falls back with all its weight on its institutionality, which it magnifies, and on the utterly idolatrous image utilized for every end.[71]

Whether or not Ellul's deeply antivisual account of the Church's fall into idolatry is accepted, it is clear that medieval Christendom was often intoxicated by what it saw. In fact, it is only the intensity of the ocular temptation that can explain the periodic rise of iconophobic movements in the Church: the Byzantine emperor Leo Isaurian's iconoclastic campaign in the eighth century, St. Bernard's Cistercian retreat from the abundance of images in the Clunaic order in the thirteenth century, John Wyclif and the English Lollards' debunking of visual spectacle in the fourteenth century, and finally the Protestant Reformation itself.

Although Martin Luther's followers were not above using visual aids such as cartoons and caricatures in their propaganda campaigns against the Church,[72] the Reformation tended to collapse the difference between iconolatry and idolatry, condemning them alike. As William Bouwsma has shown in the case of John Calvin, a virulent hostility to what was

71. Jacques Ellul, *The Humiliation of the Word*, trans. Joyce Main Hanks (Grand Rapids, Mich., 1985), p. 186. See also Georges Duby, *The Age of the Cathedrals: Art and Society, 980–1420*, trans. Eleanor Levieux and Barbara Thomson (Chicago, 1981). According to Margaret Miles, such attitudes betray an elitist hostility to the unlettered masses, and particularly women. See *Image as Insight*, p. 38. The cults of the Virgin and Mary Magdalene were often presented in visual form.

72. See R. W. Scribner, *For the Sake of Simple Folk: Popular Propaganda for the German Reformation* (Cambridge, 1981). In general, the German branch of the Reformation tended to be less programmatically iconophobic, which allowed artists like Dürer and Cranach to use the new print culture to good effect.

perceived as the hypertrophy of the visual was a key motivation in his return to the literal word of Scripture.[73] Physical blindness, Calvin contended, was spiritually valuable because it forced one to listen to the voice of God. A similar attitude permeated the English Reformation, whose desecration (or what its defenders would have called purification) of churches began with Henry VIII's dissolution of the monasteries and culminated in the Puritans' smashing of images of all kinds, which paralleled their hostility to the spectacle of the Mass and the illusions of the theatrical stage.[74]

Ironically, if we concentrate our attention on the iconophobic impulse of the Reformation and note as well the renewed interest in the sophistic arts of rhetoric and the recovery of classical texts in the Renaissance, it may well seem, contra Febvre and Mandrou, that vision was on the wane with the eclipse of the medieval world.[75] This reversed generalization, however, would be no more satisfactory than the one it replaces, for the Reformation helped spawn the Counter-Reformation, which was closely tied to a deeply visual baroque culture. And the Renaissance, for all its distrust of the medieval fetish of images (Erasmus, for example, played a role in their debunking),[76] was by no means predominantly suspicious of the visual. Indeed, its naturalist aesthetics, as David Summers has recently shown, were strongly dependent on a faith in the value of optical experi-

73. William J. Bouwsma, "Calvin and the Renaissance Crisis of Knowing," *Calvin Theological Journal*, 17, 2 (November, 1982), pp. 190–211.

74. The best account of the English iconoclasts is Phillips, *The Reformation of Images*, which shows how the Puritans were prepared by a long-simmering tradition of hostility. Barish, however, makes the astute observation that "Puritan repugnance to the visible and the tangible matters of faith did not prevent their clinging fiercely to it in matters of dress" (p. 166), for they were staunch supporters of sumptuary laws. It also should be noted that Dutch Calvinists were never as virulently iconoclastic as their English and Swiss counterparts, which helps explain the vital tradition of painting in Holland during the years of Calvinist hegemony.

75. The Renaissance Humanists were, to be sure, not as hostile to the eye as the Protestant Reformers. See Charles Trinkaus, *Likeness and Image: Humanity and Divinity in Italian Humanist Thought* (Chicago, 1973).

76. Phillips, pp. 35f.

ence.[77] Not only did Renaissance literature abound in ocular references,[78] not only did its science produce the first silvered glass mirror able to reproduce the world with far greater fidelity than before,[79] not only did some of its greatest figures like Leonardo da Vinci explicitly privilege the eye over the ear,[80] but also the Renaissance saw one of the most fateful innovations in Western culture: the theoretical and practical development of perspective in the visual arts, an epochal achievement whose importance we will examine shortly.

If one had to summarize the contribution of the medieval and early modern struggle over the proper role of the visual in the preparation of the modern ocularcentric culture that followed, three points should be stressed. First, the medieval metaphysics of light, in large measure a religious adaptation of Platonic residues, kept alive the assumption that vision was indeed the noblest of the senses, despite its potential for deception and the arousal of lascivious thoughts. Second, the lengthy dispute over the idolatrous implications of that metaphysics and the Church's visual practices led to a new awareness of the difference between representation and fetishism, the distinction Aquinas made between a venerating iconolatry and a worshiping idolatry. This in turn helped prepare the way for what might be called the secular autonomization of the visual as a realm unto itself. The early modern separation of the visual from the textual completed this differentiation, which was crucial in the preparation of the scientific worldview. It also made possible the liberation of art from

77. David Summers, *The Judgment of Sense: Renaissance Naturalism and the Rise of Aesthetics* (Cambridge, 1987).

78. Shakespeare, for example, revels in visual metaphors and references. For a recent account, see Joel Fineman, *Shakespeare's Perjured Eye: The Invention of Poetic Subjectivity in the Sonnets* (Berkeley, 1986). The great utopias of the Renaissance, Campanella's *City of the Sun*, and Andrae's *Christianopolis*, also abound in them, and could be used as well as occult memory systems based on sight. See Yates, *The Art of Memory*, pp. 377–378.

79. See Goldberg, chap. 8.

80. Leonardo da Vinci, *Treatise on Painting*, trans. A. Philip McMachon, 2 vols. (Princeton, 1956), vol. 1, p. 23.

the sacred tasks to which it had previously been bound. As John Phillips has noted, "the arts went their separate ways from religion because in great part Protestantism no longer really desired the assistance of visual aids in teaching the mysteries of faith."[81]

But, and this is the third general conclusion, if vision was relieved of its sacred function and allowed to pursue its own developmental path, the lessons that had been learned about its persuasive capabilities were never lost. In fact, they were immediately reapplied for political and social purposes. Whether or not these were enlightening or obscurantist is a question that is still heatedly debated. What can be said with some assurance, however, is that vision, aided by new technologies, became the dominant sense in the modern world, even as it came to serve new masters.

However, domination did not mean uniformity. Because of the multiple and often conflicting implications of these epochal transformations, the modern era emerged with a much more complicated attitude toward vision than is often assumed. As Jacqueline Rose has recently reminded us, "our previous history is not the petrified block of a singular visual space since, looked at obliquely, it can always be seen to contain its moment of unease."[82] That moment was largely perpetuated by the subterranean presence of what can be called the baroque ocular regime as the uncanny double of what we might call the dominant scientific or "rationalized" visual order (itself, as we will see, not fully homogeneous). Because much more time will be needed to explicate the latter, let us defy chronology and begin with a brief account of the former.

Baroque culture emerged in ways too complicated to spell out now in connection with the Catholic church's response to the challenge of Protestantism, the scientific revolution, and the explorations of the seven-

---

81. Phillips, p. 209.

82. Jacqueline Rose, *Sexuality in the Field of Vision* (London, 1986), pp. 232–233. As Peter de Bolla has suggested, the repeated affirmation of perspectival theory in eighteenth-century England implies that it was being tacitly challenged in practice. See his discussion in *The Discourse of the Sublime: History, Aesthetics and the Subject* (Oxford, 1989), chap. 8.

teenth century.[83] It also accompanied and abetted the rise of the absolutist state. Rejecting the Reformation's suspicion of vision and its trust only in the unmediated word of God, the baroque Church, after a moment of hesitation,[84] self-consciously resorted to sensual seduction in order to win back the masses (having already been somewhat successful in this endeavor in the fourteenth century). The unabashed naturalism first evident in Michelangelo da Caravaggio's stunning rejection of jejune Mannerist decoration was harnessed for spiritual ends. Whether the secular was transcendentalized or vice versa remains a point of contention. Whatever the religious implications, the aggrandizement of the eye was clearly encouraged. As Roland Barthes remarked in his essay on Ignatius Loyola, "We know that to these mistrustings of the image Ignatius responded with a radical imperialism of the image."[85]

This imperialism was not confined to religious propaganda, but appeared as well in the theatricalized splendor of the baroque court throughout Catholic Europe in the sixteenth and seventeenth centuries. The link between art and power, first systematically exploited in the Renaissance city-states and royal courts with their tournaments, fêtes, princely entries, firework displays, masques and water spectacles, reached new heights in the baroque.[86] According to the Spanish historian, José Antonio Maravall, its seductive use of spectacle was a deliberate ploy in a power struggle with disruptive social forces; in fact, he goes so far as to call it the first example of a cynical festering of mass culture by an authoritarian, centralizing state

83. For standard accounts, see John Rupert Martin, *Baroque* (New York, 1977); and Germain Bazin, *The Baroque: Principles, Styles, Modes, Themes* (London, 1968).

84. Martin notes that the Mannerism still in vogue immediately following the Council of Trent did not exploit heightened naturalist emotion for religious ends. Only in the late sixteenth century did the baroque come to dominate Catholic ecclesiastical and devotional art (p. 100).

85. Barthes, p. 66.

86. For accounts of their origins in the Renaissance, see Stephen Orgel, *The Illusion of Power: Political Theater in the English Renaissance* (Berkeley, 1975); Roy Strong, *Art and Power: Renaissance Festivals 1450–1650* (Woodbridge, Suffolk, England, 1984); and Christopher Pye, *The Regal Phantasm: Shakespeare and the Politics of Spectacle* (London, 1990).

for politically repressive purposes.[87] In the no less baroque Hapsburg Empire, it was not until the Reform Catholicism of Maria Theresa's reign (1740–1780) that critics of idolatrous popular devotion like Ludovico Antonio Muratori were able to turn the tide against visual seduction in favor of literate understanding.[88]

A far more positive reading of baroque visual culture has appeared in the recent works of the French philosopher Christine Buci-Glucksmann, *La raison baroque*, *La folie du voir*, and *Tragique de l'ombre*, which celebrate the disorienting, ecstatic, dazzling implications of the age's visual practices.[89] For Buci-Glucksmann, herself espousing many of the antiocularcentric discourse's conclusions, it is precisely the baroque's subversion of the dominant visual order of scientific reason that makes it so attractive in our postmodern age.[90] Anti-Platonic in its disparagement of lucid clarity and essential form, baroque vision celebrated instead the confusing interplay of form and chaos, surface and depth, transparency and obscurity. Sensitive to the interpenetration of the discursive and the figural—for example, in richly decorated emblem books—it registered an awareness of the impurities of both that was greatly in advance of its time. Resistant to any totalizing vision from above, the baroque explored what Buci-Glucksmann calls "the madness of vision,"[91] the overloading

---

87. José Antonio Maravall, *Culture of the Baroque: Analysis of a Historical Structure*, trans. Terry Cochran (Minneapolis, 1986). He also argues that it was essentially a bourgeois phenomenon, despite its ambivalence toward nationalization (p. 63).

88. See James Van Horn Melton, *Absolutism and the Eighteenth-Century Origins of Compulsory Schooling in Prussia and Austria* (Cambridge, 1988), chap. 3.

89. Christine Buci-Glucksmann, *La raison baroque: De Baudelaire à Benjamin* (Paris, 1984); *La folie du voir: De l'esthétique baroque* (Paris, 1986); and *Tragique de l'ombre: Shakespeare et le maniérisme* (Paris, 1990).

90. Here she differs radically from commentators like Martin, who connects the visually realistic dimension of the baroque with the scientific advances of the period (pp. 65f).

91. The term was first used by Maurice Merleau-Ponty in *The Visible and the Invisible*, ed. Claude Lefort, trans. Alphonse Lingis (Evanston, Ill., 1968), p. 75. It is also the subject of an essay by Michel de Certeau on Merleau-Ponty in *Esprit*, 66 (June, 1982), pp. 89–99, entitled "La folie de la vision."

of the visual apparatus with a surplus of images in a plurality of spatial planes. As a result, it dazzles and distorts rather than presents a clear and tranquil perspective on the truth of the external world. Seeking to represent the unrepresentable, and of necessity failing in this quest, baroque vision sublimely expresses the melancholy so characteristic of the period—that intertwining of death and desire trenchantly explored by Walter Benjamin.[92]

Significantly, the typical mirror of the baroque was not the flat reflecting mirror, which is often seen as vital to the development of rationalized perspective,[93] but rather the anamorphic mirror, either concave or convex, that distorts the visual image.[94] Anamorphosis, from the Greek *ana* (again) and *morphe* (form), also allows the spectator to reform a distorted picture by use of a nonplanar mirror. First developed by Leonardo in 1485 and popularized by Père Niceron's *La Perspective curieuse* in the early seventeenth century, such pictures were widely admired well into the eighteenth century. The most often remarked is Hans Holbein's *The Ambassadors* of 1533. A distorted skull lies at the feet of the sumptuously dressed figures staring out from the canvas, a reminder of an alternative visual order the solidity of their presence cannot efface, as well as the vanity of believing in the lasting reality of earthly perception. By combining two visual orders in one planar space, Holbein subverted and decentered the unified subject of vision painstakingly constructed by the dominant scopic regime.

Anamorphic painting was virtually forgotten except as a curiosity after the eighteenth century, only to be recovered by several contributors to the antiocularcentric discourse that is the subject of this study. Both Jacques Lacan and Jean-François Lyotard pondered its importance and, in fact, each reproduced the Holbein skull on the covers of one of his books.[95]

92. Walter Benjamin, *Origin of German Tragic Drama*, trans. John Osborne (London, 1977).

93. Edgerton, p. 134.

94. For a history of anamorphosis, see Fred Leeman, *Hidden Images: Games of Perception, Anamorphosistic Art and Illusions from the Renaissance to the Present*, trans. Ellyn Childs Allison and Margaret L. Kaplan (New York, 1976).

Here the pioneering efforts of Jurgis Baltrušaitis, a Latvian living in France, in rescuing the anamorphic tradition were crucial.[96] Thus, we might say that the discourse we will explore in this book is, at least on one level, a recovery of a subordinate, heterodox, and virtually obliterated visual practice—that of the baroque—from the initial moment of the modern era. Its later recovery may appear at times "antivisual" only because the dominant ocular regime of that era was so powerful and pervasive that it came to be identified with vision per se.

The arrival of that dominant regime was prepared by a constellation of social, political, aesthetic, and technical innovations in the early modern era, which combined to produce what has in retrospect been called "the rationalization of sight."[97] One of its sources was apparently the increasingly formalized and distant social space of the courtly societies of the era. In his account of the "civilizing process,"[98] the sociologist Norbert Elias has argued that the elaborate courtly rituals of display devised to mark the articulations of social hierarchy led to a devaluation of the more intimate senses of smell and touch in favor of a more remote vision. The political function of courtly spectacle, already alluded to in the case of the Spanish baroque described by Maravall, reached its crescendo in the Versailles of the Sun King, Louis XIV. As Jean-Marie Apostolidès has argued, the Apollonian splendor of Louis's court was soon transformed into a more

95. Jacques Lacan, *Le séminaire XI: Les quatre concepts fondamentaux de la psychanalyse* (Paris, 1973), not on the cover of the English translation; and Jean-François Lyotard, *Discours, Figure* (Paris, 1971). Lacan's fascination with the baroque is also shown in his "Du baroque," *Encore, le séminaire XX* (Paris, 1975), where he defines it as "the regulation of the soul by the corporeal gaze [*scopie corporelle*]" (p. 105).

96. Jurgis Baltrušaitis, *Anamorphoses: Ou Thaumaturgus Opticus* (Paris, 1984).

97. William W. Ivins, Jr., *On the Rationalization of Sight: With an Examination of Three Renaissance Texts on Perspective* (New York, 1973). For the rationalizers themselves, however, there was less an awareness of change than a belief in the discovery of an already inherent rational system. As Joel Snyder has noted, "For Alberti, there can be no issue that involves the 'rationalization' of vision, because what we see is established by rational processes." See his "Picturing Vision," *Critical Inquiry*, 6, 3 (Spring, 1980), p. 523.

98. Norbert Elias, *The Civilizing Process*, trans. E. Jephcott (New York, 1973), p. 203.

mechanical apparatus in which the power of the visual to control behavior was depersonalized:

> The image of the king, the image of his double body, invented at the time of courtly festivals, will detach itself from the private person and will function in an autonomous way. The machinist king is then succeeded by a king-machine whose unique body is confused with the machine of the State. At the end of the reign, the king's place becomes an empty space, susceptible of being occupied by anyone possessing the effective reality of power.[99]

It is, however, still a space assumed to be at the center of a vast network of visual channels through which the subjects are perpetually on view (a theme Foucault will elaborate in terms of a still later and more efficacious technology of surveillance).

The increased reliance on visually defined behavior in social and political terms reinforced that autonomization of the visual from the religious mentioned earlier. In the Middle Ages, as we have seen, there was a rough balance between textuality and figurality with occasional oscillations in one direction or another. As Norman Bryson has argued with reference to the great stained-glass windows of Canterbury Cathedral, their visual splendor was always in the service of the narratives they were meant to illustrate:

> The window displays a marked intolerance of any claim on behalf of the image to independent life. Each of its details corresponds to a rigorous programme of religious instruction. . . . Images are permitted, but only on the condition that they fulfil the office of communicating the Word to the unlettered. Their role is that of an accessible and palatable substitute.[100]

99. Jean-Marie Apostolidès, *Le roi-machine: Spectacle et politique au temps de Louis XIV* (Paris, 1981), p. 131.

100. Norman Bryson, *Word and Image: French Painting of the Ancien Régime* (Cambridge, 1981), p. 1.

The progressive, if by no means uniformly accepted, disentanglement of the figural from its textual task—the denarrativization of the ocular we might call it—was an important element in that larger shift from reading the world as an intelligible text (the "book of nature") to looking at it as an observable but meaningless object, which Foucault and others have argued was the emblem of the modern epistemological order.[101] Only with this epochal transformation could the "mechanization of the world picture"[102] so essential to modern science take place.

Full denarrativization was a long way off, only to be achieved in painting with the emergence of abstract art in the twentieth century. One way in which it was abetted, as Albert Cook has suggested in his discussion of Sandro Botticelli, Giorgione, Vittore Carpaccio, and Hieronymous Bosch, was by overloading the signs in a painting, producing a bewildering excess of apparent referential or symbolic meaning.[103] Without any one-to-one relationship between visual signifier and textual signified, images were increasingly liberated from their storytelling function.

The process of denarrativization was helped on its way even more powerfully by the great technical innovation of the Renaissance art, which is variously called the invention, discovery, or rediscovery of perspective, the technique for rendering three-dimensional space onto the two dimensions of the flat canvas.[104] For now it was possible to be concerned more with the rules and procedures for achieving the illusion of perspective

101. Michel Foucault, *The Order of Things: An Archaeology of the Human Sciences* (New York, 1973).

102. The classic study of this process is E. J. Diksterhuis, *The Mechanization of the World Picture*, trans. C. Dikshoorn (London, 1961).

103. Albert Cook, *Changing the Signs: The Fifteenth-Century Breakthrough* (Lincoln, Nebr., 1985). Cook notes, however, that the sixteenth-century successors to these painters, with the possible exception of Breughel, returned to a more controlled visual repertoire of readable images. He speculates that the post-Tridentine church may have been better at policing images than its immediate predecessor.

104. Bryson notes that "perspective strengthens realism by greatly expanding the area on the opposite side of the threshold to the side occupied by textual function, and we might even say by instituting into the image a permanent threshold of semantic neutrality" (*Word and Image*, p. 12). Whether or not its arrival was an invention or

than with the subject depicted. Space rather than the objects in it came to have increasing importance. Although Leon Battista Alberti—who first spelled out Filippo Brunelleschi's great breakthrough in his 1435 treatise *Della Pittura*,[105]—himself emphasized the importance of the painting's *istoria*, or ennobling story, his successors were not always willing to follow his lead. The early use of a figure in the painting literally pointing to its action was soon discontinued. With the differentiation of the aesthetic from the religious, which we've noted before as an outgrowth of the Reformation, perspective was free to follow its own course and become the naturalized visual culture of the new artistic order.

What makes it especially important is that it functioned in a similar way for the new scientific order. In both cases space was robbed of its substantive meaningfulness to become an ordered, uniform system of abstract linear coordinates. As such, it was less the stage for a narrative to be

---

discovery was first broached by Erwin Panofsky in a famous essay on "Die Perspektive als 'symbolische Form'," *Vorträge der Bibliothek Warburg, 1924–1925* (Leipzig, 1927), pp. 258–331. He contended that it was not natural and there to be discovered, but rather a symbolic form in Ernst Cassirer's sense. As the title of Edgerton's book suggests, he is cautious about seeing it as a complete invention and is equally circumspect about saying it was first discovered by the Renaissance. Ivins, who had a strong stake in differentiating the allegedly tactile Greeks from the visual moderns, emphasized the radical newness of the Albertian innovation. "The knowledge of perspective attributed to Agatharcus, Anaxagoras, and Democritus," he contended, "is a modern myth based on the utterly unwarranted reading into a casual remark by Vitruvius, who lived at least four hundred years later, of ideas that neither Vitruvius nor any Greek of the fifth century B.C. could possibly have had" (*Art and Geometry*, p. 40). For a different account, see John White, *The Birth and Rebirth of Pictorial Space* (Cambridge, Mass., 1987), chap. 16.

105. The work was also published in a Latin edition, which often leads it to be called *De Pictura*. Wendy Steiner has argued that *istoria* for Alberti already meant more of a spatial theme than a temporal narrative. See her discussion in *Pictures of Romance: Form Against Context in Painting and Literature* (Chicago, 1988), p. 23. Her book as a whole is concerned with the denarrativization of painting during the Renaissance and the complicated return of narrative in post-abstract twentieth-century painting. For an interesting account of the resistance to full denarrativization in the painting of Duccio, see Geoffrey Hawthorn, *Plausible Worlds: Possibility and Understanding in History and the Social Sciences* (Cambridge, 1991), chap. 4.

developed over time than the eternal container of objective processes. It was not until the time of Darwin that narrative regained a significant place in the self-understanding of science. More recently still, philosophers and historians of science have urged us to reconsider its role in all scientific explanations.[106] However, in the immediate aftermath of the scientific revolution, with its debt to the perspectival notion of space, narrative was banished from the cognitive method that produced "the truth" about external reality.

There is an enormous literature on the sources, development, and implications of perspectival vision which defies easy summary.[107] Several salient points are, however, worth stressing. First, the rapid and positive reception of the new technique was abetted by the late medieval metaphysics of vision with its positive evaluation of divine radiation. The Latin word *perspectiva* (from *perspicere*, to see clearly, to examine, to ascertain, to see through) was a synonym for optics itself. Painters like Lorenzo Ghiberti and Leonardo were conversant with and deeply influenced by ancient and medieval theories of optics, which often were imbued with religious meaning.[108] As Samuel Edgerton has noted, "Linear perspective . . . with its dependence on optical principles, seemed to symbolize a harmonious relationship between mathematical tidiness and nothing less

106. Alasdair McIntyre, "The Relationship of Philosophy to Its Past," in *Philosophy in History*, Richard Rorty, J. B. Schneewind, and Quentin Skinner, eds. (Cambridge, 1984), pp. 31–98.

107. In addition to the works by Edgerton, Ivins, White, and Panofsky mentioned above, the most important accounts would include M. H. Pirenne, *Optics, Painting and Photography* (Cambridge, 1970); Lawrence Wright, *Perspective in Perspective* (London, 1983); Michael Kubovy, *The Psychology of Perspective and Renaissance Art* (Cambridge, 1986); Richard Krautheimer, in collaboration with Trude Krautheimer-Hess, *Lorenzo Ghiberti* (Princeton, 1982), chap. 16; Claudio Guillén, *Literature as System*, chap. 8, which analyzes its metaphoric uses in literature; Karsten Harries, "Descartes, Perspective and the Angelic Eye," *Yale French Studies*, 49 (1973), pp. 28–42; and Hubert Damisch, *L'Origine de la perspective* (Paris, 1988).

108. Lindberg, 1, 152. For more on the religious background of perspective, see Michael Baxandall, *Painting and Experience in 15th Century Italy: A Primer in the Social History of Pictorial Style* (Oxford, 1971).

than God's will."[109] The visual microcosm was assumed to duplicate the invisible macrocosm created by the heavenly mathematician. Even when neo-Platonic theories of divine radiation based on the *lux/lumen* distinction no longer persuaded an increasingly secular world, the positive associations of geometrical order lingered.

Second, with the humanist turn of the Renaissance, an important shift occurred in the assumed point from which the rays emanated—or rather, to which they were now assumed to converge. For perspective meant not only an imagined visual cone (Euclid's word) or pyramid (Alberti's) with its apex the receding, centric (or as it was later called, vanishing) point in the scene on the canvas. It was also the reverse pyramid or cone whose apex was the beholder's eye (or the infinitesimal point that came to replace it in theoretical terms). The plane between the two symmetrical pyramids or cones was what Alberti in his famous metaphor called a transparent window, but in another sense it resembled more a mirror intersecting one pyramid, which then reflected that pyramid's apex back in the other direction.[110] The significance of this innovation was that the medieval assumption of multiple vantage points from which a scene could be painted, which at times meant no real vantage point at all, was replaced by one, sovereign eye. John Berger describes the implications of the change:

> The convention of perspective, which is unique to European art and which was first established in the early Renaissance, centers everything on the eye of the beholder. It is like a beam from a lighthouse—only instead of light travelling outward, appearances travel in. The conventions called those appearances *reality*. Perspective makes the single eye the center of the visible world. Everything converges on to the eye as to the vanishing point of infinity. The visible world is arranged for the spectator as the universe was once thought to be arranged for God.[111]

If the beholder was now the privileged center of perspectival vision, it is important to underline that his view*point* was just that: a monocular, unblinking fixed eye (or more precisely, abstract point), rather than the two active, stereoscopic eyes of embodied actual vision, which give us the experience of depth perception. This assumption led to a visual practice in which the living bodies of both the painter and the viewer were bracketed, at least tendentially, in favor of an eternalized eye above temporal duration.[112] Even when two-point perspective—*costruzione legittima*, as it was called—was introduced to portray objects at non–right angles to the window's plane, the assumption remained that each point was static and unchanging.

In Gibson's terms, the visual field now replaced the visual world. The ocular potential to privilege synchronic stasis, which we've seen Jonas claim was the key to Greek metaphysics, here achieved explicit visual expression. But now the participatory moment in *theoria*, the specular intertwining of likenesses in viewer and viewed, was lost as the spectator withdrew entirely from the seen (the scene), separated from it by Alberti's shatterproof window. No longer did the painter seem as emotionally in-

109. Edgerton, p. 24. The centric ray in particular was taken to be of great religious significance. It should be noted that we are talking only of linear perspective, not what is known as "atmospheric perspective." The latter recognized that distinct objects grew more indistinct the farther away they were. The latter was discovered at about the same time, but was not given any religious significance.

110. John White notes an alternative, if subordinate, perspectival tradition, which he calls "synthetic" and identifies with Paolo Uccello and Leonardo da Vinci. It relies on a concave rather than flat mirror, producing an effect of curved space closer to apprehensive visual experience. See White, chap. 12. The effect was not, however, as disorienting as the baroque anamorphism discussed by Buci-Glucksmann. For a recent consideration of the window metaphor, which challenges its centrality, see Joseph Masheck, "Alberti's 'Window': Art-historiographic Notes on an Antimodernist Misprision," *Art Journal*, 50, 1 (Spring, 1991).

111. John Berger, *Ways of Seeing* (London, 1972), p. 16.

112. For analyses, see Norman Bryson, *Vision and Painting: The Logic of the Gaze* (London, 1983); and Louis Marin, "Toward a Theory of Reading in the Visual Arts: Poussin's *The Arcadian Shepherds*," in *Calligram: Essays in New Art History from France*, ed. Norman Bryson (Cambridge, 1988). This bracketing of the body was not, however, confirmed in practical terms, as perspectival canvases could be viewed successfully from more than one point of observation by bodies in motion. See Kubovy, *The Psychology of Perspective and Renaissance Art*, on the "robustness" of perspectival beholding.

volved with the space he depicted; no longer was the beholder absorbed in the canvas.[113] The reduction of vision to the Medusan gaze (or often the male gaze contemplating the female nude)[114] and the loss of its potential for movement in the temporal glance was now ratified, at least according to the logic—if not always the actual practice[115]—of perspectival art.

The painter's own body, whose restoration we will see demanded by Merleau-Ponty and other twentieth-century critics of the dominant ocular regime, was effectively banished. Bryson summarizes the cost:

> In the Founding Perception, the gaze of the painter arrests the flux of phenomena, contemplates the visual field from a vantage-point outside the mobility of duration, in an eternal moment of disclosed presence; while in the moment of viewing, the viewing subject unites his gaze with the Founding Perception, in a perfect recreation of that first epiphany. Elimination of the diachronic movement of deixis creates or at least seeks, a synchronic instant of viewing that will eclipse the body, and the glance, in an infinitely extended Gaze of the image as pure idea: the image of *eidolon*.[116]

113. For an account, drawing on psychological object-relations theory, that suggests that perspectival space was a loss of affective involvement, see Peter Fuller, *Art and Psychoanalysis* (London, 1980), p. 87. See also Pierre Francastel, *Peinture et société* (Lyon, 1951), p. 87. For a discussion of the dialectic of absorption and distantiation, influenced by Merleau-Ponty, see Michael Fried, *Absorption and Theatricality: Painting and Beholder in the Age of Diderot* (Berkeley, 1980).

114. See Svetlana Alpers, "Art History and Its Exclusions," in *Feminism and Art History*, ed. Norma Broude and Mary D. Garrard (New York, 1982), where she discusses the famous print of Dürer's draftsmen drawing a woman's body through the screen of perspectival projection (p. 187). For another account, which reads it as an ironic warning against pure geometricalization, see Steiner, *Pictures of Romance*, pp. 45f.

115. For an analysis of the ways in which the mobile glance could still be invoked by Renaissance artists in a complex visual environment, alongside of the more static gaze (which he calls the "measured view") and the totalizing scan, see Randolph Starn, "Seeing Culture in a Room of a Renaissance Prince," in *The New Cultural History*, ed. Lynn Hunt (Berkeley, 1989).

116. Bryson, *Vision and Painting*, p. 94. Deixis refers to linguistic utterances that contain information about their locus of expression. In visual terms, this means the

The differentiation of the visual from the textual was thus intensified by the differentiation of the idealized gaze from the corporeal glance and the monocular spectator from the scene he observed on the other side of the window.

No less significant was the perspectivalists' assumption of what was visible in the perceptual field: a homogeneous, regularly ordered space, there to be duplicated by the extension of a gridlike network of coordinates (Alberti's "velo" or veil of threads extended from the centric point to the base and perpendicular to them).[117] The result was a theatricalized "scenographic" space, to use Pierre Francastel's widely adopted term.[118] It was this uniform, infinite, isotropic space that differentiated the dominant modern world view from its various predecessors, a notion of space congenial not only to modern science, but also, it has been widely argued, to the emerging economic system we call capitalism.

Making a strong case for a causal relationship between the invention of perspective and the rise of capitalism may be problematic, so it would be

---

concrete body of the painter positioned in the world. Bryson also makes the important point that the mobile glance introduces desire into the visual act, whereas the frozen gaze represses it (p. 122). With this in mind, Augustine's hostility to ocular desire might be reformulated as a critique of the glance in favor of the eternal images produced by the fixating gaze, which the Platonic tradition in general favors. Thus perspective can be understood as continuing the hostility of that tradition to the deceptive and dangerous illusions of desiring vision in its mobile mode.

117. For a discussion of its importance as an anticipation of Cartesian space, see James Bunn, *The Dimensionality of Signs, Tools and Models: An Introduction* (Bloomington, Ind., 1981). For accounts of the relationship of this visual regime and the development of modern science, see Giorgio de Santillana, "The Role of Art in the Scientific Renaissance," in *Critical Problems in the History of Science*, ed. Marshall Clagett (Madison, Wis., 1959); and David C. Lindberg and Nicholas H. Stenek, "The Sense of Vision and the Origins of Modern Science," in *Science, Medicine and Society in the Renaissance: Essays to Honor Walter Page*, ed. Allen G. Debus (New York, 1972).

118. Pierre Francastel, "The Destruction of a Plastic Space," in *Art History: An Anthology of Modern Criticism*, ed. Wylie Sypher (New York, 1963), p. 382. Perspective was, in fact, actually used in the construction of the Renaissance illusionist stage, with the king's box occupying the honored point of perfect vision. See Strong, *Art and Power*, pp. 32f.

better to fall back on the term Max Weber introduced in his celebrated account of the Protestant ethic and speak instead of an "elective affinity" between the two. A number of observers have suggested its various dimensions. According to Edgerton, Florentine businessmen with their newly invented technique of double-entry bookkeeping may have been "more and more disposed to a visual order that would accord with the tidy principles of mathematical order that they applied to their bank ledgers."[119] Brian Rotman has suggestively linked the invention of the vanishing point with the introduction of the Hindu number zero, vital for calculating mercantile trade, and the Renaissance invention of "imaginary money" without any anterior referent in valuable metals like gold.[120] Leonard Goldstein claims causal importance for the rational division of labor, to which he attributes similar changes in musical and poetic form.[121]

John Berger adds that more appropriate than the Albertian metaphor of the window on the world would be that of a "safe let into a wall, a safe in which the visible has been deposited."[122] For it was at the same time as the invention (or rediscovery) of perspective that the oil painting as a commodity to be sold and possessed came into its own. Separate from the painter and the viewer, the visual field depicted in perspectival paintings could become such a detached commodity available for capitalist circula-

119. Edgerton, p. 39.

120. Brian Rotman, *Signifying Nothing: The Semiotics of Zero* (New York, 1987). He sees all three as signaling an abandonment of the belief in signs as natural referents in favor of an understanding of them as representational conventions produced by a fictional metasubject.

121. Leonard Goldstein, *The Social and Cultural Roots of Linear Perspective* (Minneapolis, 1988). The most orthodox Marxist of these commentators, Goldstein goes so far as to claim that although the changes in musical and poetic form antedate any evidence for the capitalist division of labor by several centuries, since the causal relationship works for painting, it may also explain these earlier phenomena!

122. Berger, p. 109. For metaphoric support for this argument, see George Lakoff and Mark Johnson, *Metaphors We Live By* (Chicago, 1980), p. 31, where they contend that "we conceptualize our visual field as a container and conceptualize what we see as being inside it."

tion. Moreover, Raymond Williams contends, only the exaggerated capitalist separation of the spaces of production and consumption permitted a radical disjunction between working the land and merely viewing it from afar, as an aesthetically "pleasing prospect,"[123] which was the real estate version of perspectival art. Finally, to add a surmise of my own, the placement of objects in a relational visual field, objects with no intrinsic value of their own outside of those relations, may be said to have paralleled the fungibility of exchange value under capitalism.

However much weight one wants to give to arguments of this kind, there can be no doubt that the fortunes of both perspectivalism and the capitalist system prospered in the centuries that followed. Alberti's rules were refined and disseminated by later commentators like Jean Pelerin (known as Viator) and Albrecht Dürer to the point where they came to seem equivalent to natural vision.[124] Ivins points out the larger implications of this assumed unity between a technique of representation and vision itself:

> Either the exterior relations of objects, such as their forms for visual awareness, change with their shifts in location, or else their interior relations do. If the latter were the case there could be neither homogeneity of space nor uniformity of nature, and science and technology as now conceived would necessarily cease to exist.

123. Raymond Williams, *The Country and the City* (New York, 1973), p. 121. Williams is talking about the eighteenth-century division of a working field into a landscape to be appreciated for its picturesque beauty alone.

124. See Ivins, *On the Rationalization of Sight,* for discussions of their importance. Interestingly, he argues that Dürer was not fully in control of the technique he extolled. He describes the results in terms that unwittingly evoke Buci-Glucksmann's baroque "madness of vision": "The consistency with which he carried out these various distortions amounts almost to a methodological denial of the homogeneity of space. This fundamental contradiction of one of the great intuitive bases of experience produces a subtle psychological malaise in the beholder of his work. . . . It may also be that this basic contradiction is responsible for the fact that so many students of Dürer's work seem always to be working at some conundrum which, like squaring the circle, is incapable of solution" (pp. 42–43).

> Thus perspective, because of its logical recognition of internal
> invariances through all the transformations produced by changes
> in spatial location, may be regarded as the application to pictorial
> purposes of the two basic assumptions underlying all the great
> scientific generalizations, or laws of nature.[125]

Ivins, to be sure, was a champion of the rationalization of sight and the visual culture it promoted. He was prone to identify it with *all* art in the modern era.[126] However, it has recently been pointed out by Svetlana Alpers that at least the Dutch art of the seventeenth century followed a different course from its Italian counterpart.[127] Less insistent on a "monocular," static point of beholding, not as taken with the reverse pyramid on the other side of the window, and more skeptical of the importance of geometric form, northern painting sought instead to describe the textures and colors of a world of opaque and flat surfaces. Following an impulse to map that world in two dimensions rather than represent it in an illusory three,[128] and tolerant of the intrusion of verbal inscriptions into seemingly realistic images, Dutch art accepted the materiality of the canvas and the paint on it far more readily than did Italian. Rather than positing a privi-

125. Ibid., pp. 10–11.

126. In *Art and Geometry*, for example, he claims that "the history of art during the five hundred years that have elapsed since Alberti wrote has been little more than the story of the slow diffusion of his ideas through the artists and peoples of France" (p. 81).

127. Svetlana Alpers, *The Art of Describing: Dutch Art in the Seventeenth Century* (Chicago, 1983). By so sharply distinguishing between Dutch and Italian art, Alpers avoids the problem of trying to put painters as different as Vermeer and Cortona in the same category, which bedevils works like John Rupert Martin's *Baroque*. Martin, to be sure, admits that "the sober realism of the Dutch school bears no resemblance to the high-flown imagery of the Roman baroque, and neither shows any affinity to the noble classicism of the age of Louis XIV" (p. 26). But as a result, baroque becomes purely a period designation without any stylistic unity at all.

128. In discussing the mapping impulse in Dutch art, Alpers disputes Edgerton's claim that the recovery of Ptolemy's *Geography* with its grid of geometrical projections was important for Italian perspectival art. "Although the grid that Ptolemy proposed," she argues, "and those that Mercator later imposed, share this mathematical

leged beholder outside the painting gazing on a theatricalized scene from afar, it placed the viewer inside the scene as an ambulatory presence. It was thus far less hierarchical in its refusal to privilege deep focus over surface texture, far more "democratic" in its equal attention to the entire canvas.

The result, Alpers contends, was an even greater denarrativization and detextualization than took place, at least tendentially, in the south.[129] Rather than showing moments in mythical or religious stories, those *istoria* Alberti had called the necessary subject matter of perspectival art, it rested content with depicting a world of concretely rendered, precisely described objects. Although often imbued with allegorical meaning—still lifes could be mementi mori comparable to the *Vanitas* pictures of Catholic Spain and landscapes might serve as moralizing reminders of the inevitable passing of the seasons—Dutch art reveled in the concrete embodiment rather than the abstract lesson. When it focused on the human subject, it did so normally in the mode of the individual or group portrait, which emphasized the particular identity of the sitter or sitters rather than the putative universality of the more exalted southern subject.

Alpers's aim is to challenge the traditional supremacy of the southern tradition over the northern as the normative visual practice of Western art. "The Albertian picture," she complains, "has been so dominant in the Western tradition ever since the Renaissance that exceptions to it are rarely granted and attempts to analyze these exceptions are even rarer."[130] Although some of her particular claims have aroused controversy,[131]

---

uniformity of the Renaissance perspective grid, they do not share the positioned viewer, the frame, and the definition of the picture as a window through which an external viewer looks. . . . The projection is, one might say, viewed from nowhere. Nor is it looked through. It assumes a flat working surface" (p. 133).

129. Perhaps because of her desire to redress the balance and legitimate the value of descriptive over narrative art, Alpers tends to underplay the extent to which perspectival, southern art was also on the road to detextualizing the picture. And there were, of course, major figures in the north, such as Rembrandt, who, as she herself acknowledges, were certainly storytellers.

130. Alpers, p. 245.

131. See, for example, the review essay by Anthony Grafton and Thomas Da Costa Kaufmann, *Journal of Interdisciplinary History,* 16 (1985), pp. 255–266.

Alpers has successfully reopened the question of the multiplicity of visual cultures in modernity. Like the baroque "madness of vision," the Dutch "art of describing" remained available as a resource to be rediscovered by later critics of the dominant tradition. In fact, as we will see, photography has sometimes been construed in the same terms as the nonperspectival art Alpers finds in seventeenth-century Holland.

It is nonetheless clear that the rationalized art of the perspectivists was still the dominant visual practice, largely because of its close and symbiotic relationship to the new scientific world view of the day.[132] Alpers, to be sure, forges suggestive links between the scientific enthusiasms of Constantin Huygens, the optical discoveries of Kepler, and the Dutch fascination with lenses on the one hand and the art of describing on the other. The case of Kepler's importance, hitherto unremarked by art historians, is especially interesting, because of his characterization of the mechanics of vision in purely passive terms. Alpers summarizes his strategy as the deanthropomorphization of vision:

> He stands aside and speaks of the prior world picturing itself in light and color on the eye. It is a dead eye, and the model of vision, or of painting if you will, is a passive one. The function of the mechanism of seeing is defined as making a representation: representation in the dual sense that it is an artifice—in the very making—and that it resolves the rays of light into a picture.[133]

Kepler, she further points out, was the first to use the term *pictura* to describe images on the retina. Dutch art was thus in a certain sense "retinal" in its passive recording of what was actually seen, a characterization later applied to the Impressionists' very different paintings as well.

But this passive concept of optical experience was not really typical of the scientific revolution. Even in its understanding of visual experience, there was often a tendency to give some role to the activity of the mind in

132. See note 117.
133. Alpers, p. 36.

reading the images on the retina. Kepler prudently stopped when it came to explaining how those images, reversed and inverted, could be "seen" by the mind in their upright and correct order, but later thinkers like Descartes tried to make up the deficiency. In so doing, they were in accord with the visual tradition of Albertian painting, which went beyond merely recording what was projected on the retina. In both cases, the active potential in vision—its probing, penetrating, searching qualities—was given free rein.

One of the preconditions for the arrival of the scientific revolution, as Blumenberg has suggested,[134] was the long process of liberating human curiosity from its pejorative status as a frivolous distraction from man's meditation on the wisdom of the past, divinely or classically inspired. Augustine's hostility to ocular desire exemplified a general distrust of the temptations of "idle curiosity" and the appetite for dangerous new experiences it whetted. Once what Blumenberg calls the "trial of curiosity" was over and the defendant acquitted, the unleashing of the mastering, exploring, scrutinizing potential in sight meant that modern science could begin—for that science was a far more active and interventionist enterprise than the contemplation of the ancients. As such, it roughly paralleled those other great exploring ventures of the early modern era, the voyages to unknown lands, which were themselves fueled in large measure by visually charged curiosity.[135] The mapping impulse, which Alpers has linked to the Dutch art of describing because of its valorization of flatness, can also be seen as a more active search for controlling and dominating the earth, not very different from the imposition of the Albertian grid on visual space in paintings.[136]

The nonpassive dynamic of modern science was also defended by such

134. Blumenberg, *The Legitimacy of the Modern Age*, part 2.

135. For a recent critique of the visually impelled domination of the exotic "other," both by colonialists and more recent anthropologists, see Johannes Fabian, *Time and the Other: How Anthropology Makes Its Object* (New York, 1983), chap. 4.

136. Edgerton suggests a link between Columbus, perspectival art and the mapping impulse (p. 120), which may be less straightforward than he claims, but is not without merit.

empiricist advocates of the scientific method as Francis Bacon, who defiantly claimed that "I admit nothing but on the faith of the eyes."[137] Intersubjective visual witnessing was a fundamental source of legitimation for scientists like Robert Boyle, who championed the value of replicable experimentation.[138] And if Walter Ong is right, the pedagogically powerful tool of deductive Ramist logic, developed in the sixteenth century, meant the end of the Socratic dialogue and disputation in favor of a more visually active mode of reasoning. "The Ramist arts of discourse," he claims, "are monologue arts. They develop the didactic, schoolroom outlook which descends from scholasticism even more than do non-Ramist versions of the same arts, and tend finally to lose the sense of monologue in pure diagrammatics. This orientation is very profound and of a piece with the orientation of Ramism toward an object world (associated with visual perception) rather than toward a person world (associated with voice and auditory perception)."[139]

For Ong and other contemporary critics of the domination of this type of visual practice, modern science was thus tainted from its birth. More sympathetic observers like Blumenberg have replied that the new faith in the actively seeking eyes was a liberating event, allowing a proudly upright humanity to free itself from "blind obedience" to the voices of the past. No longer did humans have to bow their heads, bend their knees in supplication, and wait for instruction from the interpreters of sacred texts.[140]

However one judges its implications, the significance of the transformation cannot be doubted. The activist reevaluation of curiosity and the

137. Francis Bacon, *The Great Instauration* in *The Works of Frances Bacon*, James Spedding et al., eds., 14 vols. (London, 1857–1864), vol. 4, p. 30.

138. For an account of its importance, see Steven Shapin and Simon Schaffer, *Leviathan and the Air-Pump: Hobbes, Boyle, and the Experimental Life* (Princeton, 1985). They show that although Hobbes's challenge to Boyle's experimentalist assumptions may have initially failed, in the long run his understanding of the discursive, institutional construction of evidence has prevailed. Interestingly, they note the similarity between Boyle's approach and the Dutch "art of describing" discussed by Alpers.

139. Walter J. Ong, *Ramus, Method, and the Decay of Dialogue* (Cambridge, 1958), p. 287.

legitimation of probing vision were especially evident in the new confidence in the technical enhancement of the eye. Broadly speaking, the innovations of the early modern era took two forms: the extension of the range and power of our ocular apparatus and the improvement of our ability to disseminate the results in visually accessible ways. The former meant, inter alia, the perfection of the flat, silver-backed looking glass, most notably in sixteenth-century Venice; the invention of the microscope by Hans and Zacharias Jansen in the late sixteenth century; and the creation of the refracting telescope by several hands shortly thereafter. It also meant an increased fascination with the implications of the camera obscura, that "dark room" with a pinhole on one side projecting an inverted image on its far wall, used as early as the time of Leonardo to help artistic as well as scientific experimentation.[141] In all of these instances, technical advances were generally welcomed rather than shunned, as had so often been the case with the lenses and mirrors of an earlier era.[142] Philosophers like Baruch Spinoza, who ground lenses, Gottfried Wilhelm von Leibniz, who was fascinated by optical instruments, and Huygens, who was concerned with building telescopes, were all positively impressed by these innovations. Disciplining and enhancing normal perception, they remedied what Robert Hooke called the "infirmities" of the senses and led to the "enlargement of the[ir] dominion."[143]

Moreover, because the technical improvements in vision were far more

140. Blumenberg, "Licht als Metapher der Wahrheit," p. 443. From the religious point of view, this upright posture betokened hubris and arrogance. See the account in Bouwsma, "Calvin and the Renaissance Crisis of Knowing," p. 194.

141. The first published account appeared in 1521 in Cesariano's annotations to Vitruvius's *Treatise on Architecture*. See the discussion in Snyder, "Picturing Vision," p. 512.

142. The Pauline hostility to earthly mirrors has already been noted; perhaps the technical improvement in the mirror itself in the Renaissance helped change it. For an account of the reception of the microscope, see Catherine Wilson, "Visual Surface and Visual Symbol: The Microscope and Early Modern Science," *Journal of the History of Ideas*, 49, 1 (January–March, 1988), pp. 85–108. For its history, see Reginald S. Clay and Thomas M. Court, *The History of the Microscope* (London, 1932).

143. Robert Hooke, *Micrographia* (1665), as cited in Shapin and Schaffer, p. 36.

rapid than those of any other sense, they had the effect of intensifying its importance. Robert Innes has suggested two likely outcomes:

> Specifically instrumental auxiliaries of perception, which are assimilated to the systems of senses themselves, can either magnify the unaided sense-organ or power or they can reduce—through a kind of negative abstraction—the complex polymorphy of sense perception, which is its "natural" as well as "culturally induced" state, to a single mode of perception.[144]

In the case of the innovations of the early modern era, that single mode was visual.

The same effect was produced by the new technologies of dissemination, most famously the printing press and the invention of reproducible images through woodblocks and other more refined mechanical means. The impact of Gutenberg's revolutionary breakthrough, so sensationally trumpeted by Marshall McLuhan and Walter Ong, seems in fact to have been far greater than the mere dissemination of previous knowledge and practices. "The new intensity of visual stress and private point of view in the first century of printing," McLuhan claims, "were united to the means of self-expression made possible by the typographic extension of man. Socially, the typographic extension of man brought in nationalism, industrialism, mass markets, and universal literacy and education. For print presented an image of repeatable precision that inspired totally new forms of extending social energies."[145] As if these effects were not enough, he adds that "perhaps the most significant of the gifts of typography to man is that of detachment and noninvolvement. . . . It was precisely the power to separate thought and feeling, to be able to act without reacting, that split literate man out of the tribal world of close family bonds in private and social life."[146] Although, as we have seen while considering

144. Robert E. Innis, "Technics and the Bias of Perception," *Philosophy and Social Criticism*, 10, 1 (Summer, 1984), pp. 76–77.

145. Marshall McLuhan, *Understanding Media: The Extensions of Man* (London, 1964), p. 184.

Jonas's analysis of Hellenic metaphysics, this "gift" was perhaps already possessed by the Greeks, McLuhan is surely correct in stressing the impact of printing on multiplying the number of its beneficiaries.

Ong's claims are somewhat more circumspect, but far-reaching enough. "We are not suggesting that typographic man used his eyes more than earlier man had," he concedes. "Even primitive man is highly visual in the sense that he is a keen observer, detecting all sorts of minute visual clues in his environment which civilized man misses. What happened with the emergence of alphabetic typography was not that man discovered the use of his eyes, but that he began to link visual perception to verbalization to a degree previously unknown."[147] This in turn led, Ong contends, to modern individualism (the eye = I), the depersonalization of the external world, and the glorification of observation as the only valid way of knowing the world. "With the shift in the sensorium by print," he concludes, "the large-scale campaign for the 'clear and distinct' soon began, led by Ramus and focused by Descartes—a campaign for visually conceived cognitive enterprise."[148]

Some of these claims may well be hyperbolic, as the implications of printing were more complicated than McLuhan and Ong contend. The printed word could, after all, be taken as the recording of an aural event, which helps explain its importance for the Reformation. As Elizabeth Eisenstein has noted, "Printed sermons and orations did not remove preachers from their pulpits or speakers from their podiums. To the contrary, priests and orators both benefited from the way their personal charisma could be augmented and amplified by the printed word."[149] And the extension of print to other, more obvious aural phenomena like musi-

146. Ibid., p. 185.

147. Ong, *The Presence of the Word*, p. 50.

148. Ibid., p. 221.

149. Elizabeth L. Eisenstein, *The Printing Revolution in Early Modern Europe* (Cambridge, 1986), p. 92. In general, she is more circumspect in her claims than McLuhan or Ong, but she too emphasizes the importance of the new technology. For example, she argues that a unified historical perspective on the past needed more than Albertian notions of space: "How could the entire classical past be viewed 'from a

cal scores meant that hearing was also abetted by its dissemination. Still, while it would be wrong to conceptualize its impact in terms of a zero-sum game with the rise of sight necessarily leading to the debasing of the other senses, it does seem fair to conclude that visual primacy was aided by the invention of printing.

This generalization is even more securely grounded if we consider the impact of the mechanical reproduction of actual images. These were more explicitly visual than the graphic symbols on the printed page (which could, after all, be translated into acoustic equivalents by being read aloud). They too were revolutionized by technical advances in the early modern era.[150] Appearing slightly before Gutenberg's printing press, the invention of replicable prints of pictures and diagrams, first from wood cuts and then from engraved metal plates, had an incalculable effect on the standardization and dissemination of scientific knowledge (as well, we might add, as on artistic techniques like perspective, which was first transmitted in a printed book by Pelerin in 1504). Although for a long time limited by a still syntactical method of crosshatching, which Ivins called a "tyranny"[151] because of its failure to reproduce reality directly, the widespread appearance of the identical scientific plates and diagrams meant the unimpeded spread of knowledge across linguistic boundaries, knowledge whose reliability was far greater than the mere "heresay" of a pretypographic culture. Ivins thus concluded—showing that his capac-

---

fixed distance' until a permanent temporal location had been found for antique objects, place names, personages and events? The capacity to see the past in this way could not be obtained by new optical effects devised by Renaissance artists. It required a rearrangement of documents and artifacts rather than a rearrangement of pictorial space" (p. 117). Such an innovation could only be produced by the rationalization of records enabled by printing.

150. William M. Ivins, Jr., *Prints and Visual Communication* (Cambridge, Mass., 1953).

151. Ibid., p. 70. The "tyranny" of syntactical crosshatching was ended, he suggests, with the triumph of the photograph, which provides truthful representations of "how it actually was" (p. 94). This naive notion of the perfect imitative ability of the camera has been questioned by many recent students of its implications. See, for example, Snyder, "Picturing Vision."

ity for hyperbole was no less than that of McLuhan or Ong—"It is hardly too much to say that since the invention of writing there has been no more important invention than that of the exactly repeatable pictorial statement."[152]

Whether or not one gives greater weight to technical advances or social changes, it is thus evident that the dawn of the modern era was accompanied by the vigorous privileging of vision. From the curious, observant scientist to the exhibitionist, self-displaying courtier, from the private reader of printed books to the painter of perspectival landscapes, from the map-making colonizer of foreign lands to the quantifying businessman guided by instrumental rationality, modern men and women opened their eyes and beheld a world unveiled to their eager gaze.

⊙

The grip of modern ocularcentrism was perhaps nowhere as evident as in France, the culture whose recent reversal of attitudes is thus perhaps all the more worthy of study. No better evidence of its power can be offered than the stubborn hold Cartesian philosophy had on its major thinkers for so many years. As has often been remarked, Descartes was a quintessentially visual philosopher, who tacitly adopted the position of a perspectivalist painter using a camera obscura to reproduce the observed world.[153] "Cartesian perspectivalism," in fact, may nicely serve as a short-

152. Ivins, *Prints and Visual Communication*, p. 3. For an account of the later history of scientific atlases, which stresses the moral imperative behind the struggle for visual "truth," see Lorraine Daston and Peter Galison, "The Image of Objectivity," *Representations*, 40 (Fall, 1992), pp. 81–128.

153. See, for example, Jean-Joseph Goux, "Descartes et la perspective," *L'Esprit Créateur*, 25, 1 (Spring, 1985). Goux argues that the monocentric perspectivalism of Cartesian philosophy corresponded to the power of the absolute monarch, but it also opened the door for a democratic alternative by implying that anyone might occupy the perspectival point of view. For a discussion of the camera obscura as the emblematic visual apparatus of Cartesian perspectivalism, see Jonathan Crary, *Techniques of the Observer: On Vision and Modernity in the Nineteenth Century* (Cambridge, Mass., 1990), chap. 2.

hand way to characterize the dominant scopic regime of the modern era. It will therefore be useful to lower our high-flying balloon somewhat and focus our attention more closely on the text in which Descartes, more extensively than anywhere else, examines vision: *La Dioptrique* of 1637, one of the three scientific treatises he appended to his celebrated *Discourse on Method.*

For many commentators, Descartes is considered the founding father of the modern visualist paradigm. Thus, for example, Rorty claims that "in the Cartesian model, the intellect *inspects* entities modeled on retinal images. . . . In Descartes's conception—the one which became the basis for 'modern' epistemology—it is *representations* which are in the 'mind.'"[154] Hacking concurs that "the Cartesian world was thoroughly visual"[155] and adds, "The doctrine that we study our ideas with steadfast mental gaze was bequeathed by Descartes to the Port Royal *Logic*, and swallowed almost whole by the British disciples."[156] Gasché further contends,

> Although it is true that the Augustinian notion of *reditus in se ipsum*—a return upon and into oneself constituting the medium of philosophy—prefigures the modern concept of reflection, the philosophy of reflection is generally considered to have begun with Descartes's *prima philosophia*. . . . In Descartes the scholastic idea of the *reditus* undergoes an epochal transformation, whereby reflection, instead of being merely the medium of metaphysics, becomes its very foundation. With Cartesian thought, the self-certainty of the thinking subject—a certainty apodictically found in the *cogito me cogitare*—becomes the unshakable ground of philosophy itself.[157]

Descartes may thus not only be responsible for providing a philosophical justification for the modern epistemological habit of "seeing" ideas in the mind, but may also have been the founder of the speculative tradition of identitarian reflexivity, in which the subject is certain only of its mirror image.[158] In addition, he is also often seen as legitimating a mode of scientific investigation through visual observation of evidence (from the Latin *videre*), which could lead in a decidedly empirical direction. How these competing visual models could be derived from this thought will become apparent if we look closely at his treatise on optics.

La Dioptrique, or *Optics*, as it is usually translated, was only one of several meditations on vision written by Descartes, including a lengthy "treatise on light" as the first part of his *Treatise on the World*, left unpublished because of the Church's condemnation of Galileo in 1633, and *Meteorology*, another of the three studies appended to the *Discourse on Method*. The latter included discussions of lightning, the rainbow, and other visual phenomena. Descartes was very much an enthusiast of the new mechanical aids to vision; they had a particularly strong impact in Holland, where he spent a good part of his mature life. In fact, it was the invention of the telescope, which he attributed—we now know wrongly—to one Jacques Métius of the Dutch city of Alcmar, that sparked the writing of *La Dioptrique* itself. One of its major goals was the encouragement of the building of such devices, whose principles of construction he detailed with great precision.

The work begins with the famous encomium to vision and its technical enhancement we have used as one of the epigraphs of this chapter: "All the management of our lives depends on the senses, and since that of sight is the most comprehensive and the noblest of these, there is no doubt that the inventions which serve to augment its power are among the most useful that there can be."[159] Then Descartes adds the curious after-

154. Rorty, *Philosophy and the Mirror of Nature*, p. 45.

155. Hacking, *Why Does Language Matter to Philosophy?*, p. 31.

156. Ibid., p. 45.

157. Gasché, *The Tain of the Mirror*, p. 17.

158. The visual constitution of subjectivity was, to be sure, anticipated by earlier exponents of introspection, such as Montaigne, who wrote, "I turn my gaze inward, I fix it there and keep it busy. . . . I look inside myself; I continually observe myself" (Michel de Montaigne, *Essays*, trans. and ed. Donald Frame [New York, 1973], p. 273). Here the model is closer to the observation of an object by a subject than a purely specular subject looking at itself.

159. Descartes, *Discourse on Method, Optics, Geometry and Meteorology*, p. 65.

thought, "But to the shame of our sciences, this invention [the telescope], so useful and so admirable, was found in the first place only through experiment and good fortune."[160]

Descartes's "shame" expresses his chagrin that the purely inductivist tradition of experimentation and observation was lucky enough to discover what deduction should have ascertained without the need of experiential aids. His celebrated method was preeminently deductive, at least in intention.[161] And *La Dioptrique* was aimed at demonstrating how vision can be understood following that method and it alone, which was based on the prior existence of ideas innate in the mind.

Why then, it might be asked, should it be useful to construct telescopes, which could only help the sight of the actual eyes? What, to put it in somewhat different terms, was the relationship between seeing with the inner eye of the mind, the "steadfast mental gaze" looking at clear and distinct ideas, and the two technologically improved eyes of the body? To answer these questions, we have to compare Descartes's account of vision with that of the figure Alpers has argued best embodies in scientific terms the Dutch "art of describing": Kepler.

In *La Dioptrique*, there is a celebrated picture of Kepler gazing at a geometrically arranged cross-section of the eye.[162] Clearly, Descartes recognized his debt to his great predecessor. But there are a number of interesting and subtle differences between them. Kepler ended his analysis with the inverted and reversed image on the retina and refused to speculate on the difficult question of how the retinal "pictura" becomes our actual conscious experience of sight. It is for this reason that we have seen Alpers claiming that he deanthropomorphized vision, producing a dead and passive eye. In contrast, Descartes, like Plato before him, was never

160. Ibid. The metaphoric importance of the telescope for early modern theorists is discussed in Timothy J. Riess, *The Discourse of Modernism* (Ithaca, 1980), pp. 25ff.

161. The extent of Descartes's fidelity to the deductive method has often been a matter of dispute. Paul Olscamp, in the introduction to the English edition cited above, tries to establish the importance of induction in his work as well.

162. In the English edition of *Optics* cited above, the head of Kepler is missing, but the diagram remains (p. 92).

content with the sufficiency of mere sense experience, visual or otherwise. In the *Discourse on Method*, for example, he explicitly rejected the contention that "nothing is in the intellect that was not first in the senses," for "without the intervention of our understanding, neither our imagination nor our senses could ever assure us of anything."[163] Such assurance could only come from the indubitability of deductive reasoning beginning with innate ideas.

But despite its alleged function as an illustration of the superiority of that procedure, *La Dioptrique* in fact does not faithfully follow the Cartesian method. Descartes begins by conceding that he will not undertake to explain the "true nature"[164] of light, which he hints he has already accomplished in the still unpublished "Treatise on Light" in the *Treatise on the World*. In a letter composed shortly after the publication of *La Dioptrique*, he wrote, "Light, that is, *lux*, is a movement or an action in the luminous body, and tends to cause some movement in transparent bodies, namely *lumen*. Thus *lux* is before *lumen*."[165] *La Dioptrique* was, however, concerned primarily with *lumen*, the transmission of light, rather than *lux*, although certainly Descartes hoped to explicate the link between them. But he was never fully successful. Indeed, as he admitted in a famous letter to Marin Mersenne of May 27, 1638, he had not really worked out the relationship between deduction and the experiments he described in *La Dioptrique*, nor apparently the relationship between *lux* and *lumen*.[166]

Be that as it may, *La Dioptrique* asks its reader to consider light as "nothing else, in bodies that we call luminous, than a certain movement or action, very rapid and very lively, which passes toward our eyes through the medium of the air and other transparent bodies, in the same manner

163. Descartes, *Discourse on Method*, p. 31. Descartes did not, however, fully realize that the inversion of the retinal image was really a pseudoproblem, which was a discovery left to Bishop Berkeley. See Michael J. Morgan, *Molyneux's Question: Vision, Touch and the Philosophy of Perception* (Cambridge, 1977), p. 61 for a discussion.

164. Descartes, *Optics*, p. 66.

165. Descartes's letter to Morin, July 13, 1638, *Oeuvres*, ed. Charles Adam and Paul Tannery (Paris, 1897–1913), vol. 2, p. 205.

166. Descartes, *Oeuvres*, vol. 2, pp. 135–153.

that the movement or resistance of the bodies that this blind man encounters is transmitted to his hand through the medium of his stick."[167] Here, as many commentators have remarked, Descartes's reasoning was neither deductive nor inductive, but rather analogical, based on a comparative thought experiment that involved another sense. The analogy between sight and the touch of a blind man's stick was an old one, used as early as Simplicius's commentary on Aristotle's *De Anima*.[168] The point of the comparison is that both reveal an instantaneous transmission of the stimulus through pressure, either seen or felt, to the sensory organ. Descartes's physics was, in fact, grounded in the assumption that light passes without any lapse of time through an extended medium that filled the space between object and eye, no vacuum existing in nature. Nothing material passes from one to the other—just the pressure conveyed through the medium. Thus the medieval idea of actual images passing through the air—those "intentional" or "visible species" already called into question by William of Ockham—was mistaken.[169] Rays of light, for Descartes, were not even movements per se, but what he calls, somewhat vaguely, "an action or inclination to move."[170]

Descartes's next analogy was even less precise. In the second discourse of *La Dioptrique*, he introduces the example of tennis balls being hit through bodies of different density, which he claims explains the changes in the angle of their movement (those angles of refraction which are the subject of the book).[171] What makes this analogy problematic—as seven-

167. Descartes, *Optics*, p. 67.

168. Simplicius Cilicius, *Commentaria Semplicii in treis libros De Anima Aristotelis* (Venice, 1564).

169. For Descartes's general debt to Ockham, see Funkenstein, *Theology and the Scientific Imagination*, pp. 185f. It should be noted that he did hold on to the pre-Nominalist theory of extramission, but only for animals like the cat, which seemed to be able to see in the dark (*Optics*, p. 68).

170. Descartes, *Optics*, p. 70.

171. Descartes was far more interested in refracted than reflected light and apparently was soon aware of the tricks of anamorphic distortions from reading Jean-François Niceron's *La perspective curieuse* of 1638, which appeared shortly after the *Optics*. See the discussion in Leeman, pp. 105–108.

teenth-century critics of Descartes like Fermat were quick to point out—is the parallel between the transmission of light, which is allegedly an *instantaneous* pressure or inclination to move, and the actual movement of tennis balls, which have to take time when they pass through different media. The entire problem of the supposedly timeless transmission of light was, in fact, never solved by Descartes, which is one reason that his physics was ultimately replaced by that of Newton, who recognized the temporality of light waves.[172]

In the third discourse of *La Dioptrique*, Descartes turns from the refraction of light rays to the eye itself, which, like Kepler, he had personally examined by slicing through that of a cow. Unlike Kepler, however, he moved beyond the physical apparatus of the eye's lenses and vitreous humors to speculate about its link to human visual consciousness. In so doing, he made the celebrated claim that "it is the mind [*âme*] which senses, not the body."[173] "It is necessary," he continues, "to beware of assuming that in order to sense, the mind needs to perceive certain images transmitted by the objects to the brain, as our philosophers commonly suppose."[174] Even Kepler, he implies, was wrong to remain with the "pictura" focused on the retinal screen. For in so doing, he failed to address the crucial question of how we see upright, when the camera obscura of the eye can only receive reversed and inverted images. For sight in the mind is not dependent on the passive contemplation of such images, which resemble the objects they mirror. "We should consider that there are many other things besides pictures which can stimulate our thought, such as, for example, signs and words, which do not in any way

172. A recent attempt has been made by Stephen M. Daniel in "The Nature of Light in Descartes' Physics," *The Philosophical Forum*, 7 (1976), pp. 323–344, to defend him by claiming that the ambiguity of his theory meant it was more in line with twentieth-century physics than was Newton's. Light acts like an instantaneous wave when passing through the same medium, but like a moving particle when it passes through different media. Descartes, however, was not Heisenberg, so it is unlikely he would have himself felt happy with this equivocal solution.

173. Descartes, *Optics*, p. 87. *Âme* may be better translated as soul, but the standard version is mind.

174. Ibid., p. 89.

resemble the things which they signify. . . . There are no images that must resemble in every respect the objects they represent—for otherwise there would be no distinction between the object and its image—but that it is sufficient for them to resemble the objects in but a few ways."[175]

To clinch this point, Descartes invoked the evidence of perspectival art, which produces the experience of correct vision by devices that eschew perfect resemblance. Using the same example the twentieth-century psychologist James Gibson would adduce to distinguish between the "visual world" and the "visual field," he noted that "following the rules of perspective, circles are often better represented by ovals rather than by other circles; and squares by diamonds rather than by other squares."[176] The images formed in the brain, he contended, are the result of a similar process of reading signs that are not perfect reproductions of external reality. Thus, it is the mind, not the eye, that really "sees."

But the question still not answered is what the relationship between the physical art of seeing (through what we might call Kepler's cold eye) and our conscious vision might be. Is actual sight to be distrusted and mental representations considered the only true reality of which we have indubitable, because specular knowledge?[177] Is Descartes as hostile to the deceptions of actual sight as Plato? If so, why then the panegyric to the telescope, which aids only the latter?

That Descartes did, in fact, seek a positive link between what our physical organs sense and what the mind sees is demonstrated by his notorious reference to the pineal gland as the locus in the brain of that very interaction, a reference made yet more bizarre by his claim, "I could go even still further, to show you how sometimes the picture can pass from there through the arteries of a pregnant woman, right to some specific member

175. Ibid., pp. 89–90.

176. Ibid., p. 90.

177. For a strong argument to this effect, see Dalia Judovitz, "Vision, Representation and Technology in Descartes," in *Modernity and the Hegemony of Vision*, ed. David Michael Levin (Berkeley, 1993). Judovitz, following Merleau-Ponty's critique of Descartes, claims that he substitutes an entirely mathematical, disincarnated, logical simulacrum of sight for the real thing.

of the infant which she carries in her womb, and there forms these birth-marks which cause learned men to marvel so."[178] Although modern science now acknowledges that the pineal gland does in fact function as "the non-visual photoreceptor of an independent sensory system not a part of the eyes or any other sense,"[179] it could not bear the burden placed on it by Descartes. As the bridge between the *res cogitans* and the *res extensa*, it was soon discarded in favor of such equally problematic solutions as the "occasionalism" of Nicolas de Malebranche, which introduced God's intervention as the alleged link.

Another argument in *La Dioptrique* proved far more substantial. It was grounded in the distinction between two dimensions of vision: seeing location, distance, size, and shape on the one hand, and light and color on the other. In a more traditional philosophical vocabulary, this implied the difference between primary and secondary characteristics. In the modern terminology of scientific optics, it roughly approximated the difference between seeing with rods, which process contours and patterns, and seeing with cones, which give us sensitivity to color and brightness. Unlike Kepler, who claimed that all these characteristics resided in the object and then are transmitted to the waiting retina, Descartes claimed that color and light were merely a function of the physical apparatus of the eye, in particular the fibers of the optic nerve stimulated by the rotational velocities of light corpuscles.[180] No parallel could be assumed between what we experience in this way and a real world of extended matter confirmed by touch. Here deception and illusion are hard to avoid.

Distance, location, size, and shape are, however, *both* in the mind and

---

178. Descartes, *Optics*, p. 100.

179. Robert Rivlin and Karen Gravelle, *Deciphering the Senses: The Expanding World of Human Perception* (New York, 1984), p. 67. They further note that the pineal gland secretes a hormone called melatonin according to the level of light, a hormone that causes drowsiness and also sexual arousal (p. 207). For another, more popular account of the remarkable new research on the pineal gland, see "The Talk of the Town" column of *The New Yorker* of January 14, 1985. Still, no one holds that Descartes was correct about its role in vision.

180. Descartes, *Meteorology*, pp. 335f.

in the world. To make this case, Descartes once again resorted to an analogy from touch.

> Just as our blind man, holding the two sticks *AE*, *CE*, of whose length I am assuming that he is ignorant, and knowing only the interval which is between his two hands *A* and *C*, and the size of the angles *ACE*, *CAE*, can from that, as if by a natural geometry, know the location of the point *E*; so also when our two eyes, *RST* and *rst*, are turned toward *X*, the length of the line *Ss* and the size of the two angles *XSs* and *XsS* enable us to know the location of the point *X*.[181]

The crucial phrase here is "as if by a natural geometry," for Descartes was assuming that the intellectual process of geometrical triangulation underlying the blind man's capacity to feel distance by using his two sticks was somehow duplicated in our rationally constructed vision. We are thus not prone to be deceived about distance, location, shape, and size, because of a correspondence between our unconscious and innate geometrical sense and the geometrical reality of the world of extended matter. That we are not always perfectly certain, Descartes concedes, is due to the intervention of the brain between the mind and the world, or to the imperfect functioning of the nerves. These account for hallucinations of the insane and the illusions of dreams. But these physical impediments can be mitigated by the inventions that extend the power of empirical vision. The last four discourses of *La Dioptrique* are thus dedicated to a painstaking lesson in the construction of the telescope.

As Fermat, Bishop Berkeley, and a host of other critics were quick to point out, there was a major problem in Descartes's argument. His assumption of a natural geometry in the mind, which he identified with

181. Descartes, *Optics*, p. 106. Descartes shared the belief in a natural geometry with Leibniz, but later thinkers like Molyneux and Locke argued against them. See the discussion in Colin Murray Turbayne, *The Myth of Metaphor* (Columbia, S.C., 1970), pp. 109f.

Euclid's,[182] was not only problematic in itself, but was even more questionable when it was extended to the world without. Unable to anticipate the Copernican Revolution in philosophy later accomplished by Kant, Descartes posited a structure of the mind and then assumed it was congruent with the external world in a specular way.

Several recent commentators have suggested that Descartes's critique of a resemblance theory of knowledge in favor of one that introduced signs, which needed to be read by the mind, meant that he was at the forefront of that great epistemic shift Foucault has described in *The Order of Things* as the move from resemblances or similitudes to representations.[183] Images in the mind were thus perceptual *judgments*, not mere simulacra. They involved the intervention of language to read them correctly, an insight that was itself duplicated, doubtless unwittingly, in the rhetoric of *La Dioptrique* itself. For, as Michel de Certeau has remarked, Descartes oscillated between a self-referential "je dis" and a more objectivist "vous voyez."[184] In so doing, he reproduced the same tension that existed in *Discourse on Method*, where he employed the rhetoric of demonstration (I will "present my life here as in a painting") and the rhetoric of narration ("I am proposing only this work as, so to speak, a history—or if you prefer, a fable"), and often on the same page.[185] In other words, by moving

182. The analogy from touch suggests, if Ivins is right, that Descartes was still beholden to a Greek tactile tradition rather than a modern visual one. But Kepler, as Ivins himself notes in *Art and Geometry* (p. 101), argued that lines do ultimately meet at the point of infinity. Not only did Descartes follow Kepler in this respect, he was also a good friend of Gerard Desargues, who was the first to see that the conic section and perspective were alike.

183. John W. Yolton, *Perceptual Acquaintance: From Descartes to Reid* (Oxford, 1984); Joel Snyder, "Picturing Vision"; and Charles Lemore, "Descartes' Empirical Epistemology," in *Descartes: Philosophy, Mathematics and Physics*, ed. Stephen Gaukroger (Brighton, 1980).

184. Conversation with Michel de Certeau, Paris, March, 1985. For another discussion of the rhetoric of Descartes, see Ralph Flores, "Cartesian Striptease," *Sub-stance*, 39 (1983), pp. 75–88.

185. Descartes, *Discourse on Method*, p. 5.

from resemblances to representations, it can be argued, Descartes was subtly opening the door to a nonvisual, linguistically oriented epistemology of judgments.

But whereas many later theorists of representation would come to think of sign systems as conventional and self-referential, Descartes was still enough of an ontological realist with a strong correspondence theory of truth to believe that the mind's natural geometry—its intellectual sign system, if you will—was congruent with that in the natural world. Like the Albertian perspectivalists he so resembled, he had no qualms about naturalizing a particular visual practice and lifting it outside of history.

From the "vantage point of hindsight," it is easy to discern contradictions, insufficiencies, and "blind spots" in Descartes's account of vision. Not only was it based more on undefended analogical reasoning than on the deduction it was supposed to illustrate, but it also erred about the lack of light's temporality, the function of the pineal gland, and other more minor details such as the ability of Archimedes' giant mirror to burn distant ships (Descartes thought it couldn't; we now know otherwise).[186] These were mistakes that allowed many later commentators to dismiss his account as of little worth.

And yet, the Cartesian contribution to the dominant ocularcentric bias of the modern era, especially in his native France, was assuredly profound. A major source of that influence, it seems probable to assume, was the very ambiguity of his argument. If, as is often claimed, Descartes could become the warrant for rationalist and sensationalist philosophies, claimed by idealists and materialists alike, he was no less able to give encouragement to both speculative and empirical concepts of vision. Despite his avowed dualism, the specular element in his philosophy could foster an ultimately identitarian monism. Even if later readings of Descartes discovered their linguistic mediation, the innate ideas he posited were still most widely interpreted as being seen "clearly and distinctly" by the mind's eye. Not surprisingly, his more religious followers

186. Descartes, *Optics*, p. 147. For a rebuttal of his belief, see Goldberg, *The Mirror and Man*, p. 181.

like Malebranche were able to resurrect the spiritual metaphysics of light characteristic of earlier theologians like Grosseteste, while others were able to take his encomium to the telescope as a boost to their empiricist inclinations.

Cartesian dualism was, moreover, particularly influential because of its valorization of the disembodied eye—the "angelic eye," as Karsten Harries has called it[187]—shared by modern science and Albertian art. In either of its guises, speculative or observational, it justified a fully spectatorial rather than incarnate eye, the unblinking eye of the fixed gaze rather than the fleeting glance. Descartes himself anticipated this interpretation in *Discourse on Method*, with his celebrated thought experiment that he had no body, which allowed him to conclude that "this *me*—that is, the soul by which I am what I am—is completely distinct from the body: and is even easier to know than is the body."[188] The Descartes who had called his own philosophical quest a journey in which he tried "to be a spectator rather than an actor"[189] in the affairs of the world had reduced the visual world, in Gibson's sense, to a visual field and consigned the body to objecthood in it.

It was precisely over this issue that twentieth-century phenomenological critics of Cartesian perspectivalism like Heidegger and Merleau-Ponty would challenge his version of sight, and feminists like Irigaray would condemn the gender bias of his philosophy.[190] Building on Bergson's earlier critique of Descartes's bias for a spatial rather than temporal ontology, their polemics would inform the discourse that called many other dimen-

187. Harries, "Descartes, Perspective, and the Angelic Eye." Harries argues that such an eye, transcendental and beyond all perspectives, was not entirely without warrant for mere mortals, in that it expressed the very human ability to see something from the point of view of the other.

188. Descartes, *Discourse on Method*, p. 28.

189. Ibid., p. 24.

190. Luce Irigaray, *Speculum of the Other Woman*, trans. Gillian G. Gill (Ithaca, N.Y., 1985), p. 180. For another feminist critique of Descartes, informed more by object relations theory than French psychoanalysis, see Susan R. Bordo, *The Flight to Objectivity: Essays on Cartesianism and Culture* (Albany, N.Y., 1987).

sions of modern ocularcentrism into question. Included among these was the typical Cartesian gesture of refusing to listen to the voices of the past and trusting instead only to what one could "see with one's eyes." Insofar as the Enlightenment was premised largely on that same attitude, the antiocularcentric discourse often took on a self-consciously Counter-Enlightenment tone. Here, however, I am getting ahead of myself, for it will be necessary before analyzing the twentieth-century turn against vision to see more clearly what its target actually was. To do so, the role of ocularcentrism in the France so long beholden to its Cartesian point of departure must first be exposed to view.

CHAPTER TWO

Dialectic of EnLIGHTenment

If I could alter the nature of my being and *become a living eye*, I would voluntarily make that exchange.

WOLMAR IN JEAN-JACQUES ROUSSEAU'S *LA NOUVELLE HÉLOISE*[1]

The general system of the sciences and arts is a sort of labyrinth . . . . The encyclopedic arrangement of our knowledge . . . consists of . . . placing the philosopher at a vantage point, so to speak, high above this vast labyrinth, whence he can perceive the principle sciences and arts simultaneously. From there he can see at a glance the objects of their speculations and the operations which can be made on these objects. . . . It is a kind of world map which is to show the principal countries, their position and their mutual dependence, the road that leads directly from one to another.

JEAN LE ROND D'ALEMBERT[2]

If photography is allowed to deputize art in some of art's activities, it will not be long before it has supplanted or corrupted art altogether, thanks to the stupidity of the masses, its natural ally. . . . If once it be allowed to impinge on the sphere of the intangible and the imaginary, on anything that has value solely because man adds something to it from his soul, then woe betide us!

CHARLES BAUDELAIRE[3]

"What is an idea?" Voltaire asked in his *Philosophical Dictionary.* "It is an image," he immediately replied, "that paints itself in my brain. . . . The most abstract ideas are the consequences of all the objects I've perceived. . . . I've ideas only because I've images in my head."[4] In these simple propositions, delivered with Voltaire's characteristic self-assurance, both

1. Jean-Jacques Rousseau, *La nouvelle Héloise*, part 4, letter 12, in *Oeuvres complètes* (Paris, 1959), vol. 2, p. 491.

2. Jean le Rond D'Alembert, *Preliminary Discourse to the Encyclopedia of Diderot*, trans. Richard N. Schwab and Walter E. Rex (New York, 1963), pp. 46–47.

3. Charles Baudelaire, "The Modern Public and Photography," in *Classic Essays in Photography*, ed. Alan Trachtenberg (New Haven, 1980), p. 88.

4. Voltaire, *Philosophical Dictionary*, ed. and trans. Theodore Besterman (New York, 1972), p. 236.

the Enlightenment's debt to Descartes's ocularcentric theory of knowledge and its distance from it are readily apparent.

Like Descartes, Voltaire used "idea" to refer to an internal representation in human consciousness, an image in the eye of the mind. Ideas are no longer objective realities external to the subjective mind, like the Platonic *Eidos*. Voltaire thus shared with Descartes a dualism of consciousness and matter. He also agreed that the ultimate source of the truth of our ideas is God, but he admitted he had no way of knowing precisely how God acts to ensure that outcome. Voltaire furthermore shared Descartes's belief (although this specific passage does not explicitly say so) that ideas, if clear and distinct in the mind, can be expressed in lucid prose, especially in the language that the *philosophes* thought was the clearest possible: French.[5]

But unlike Descartes, Voltaire followed Francis Bacon, John Locke, and Isaac Newton and what has been called the sensationalist tradition in claiming that *only* the perception of external objects and never innate intuitions or deductions are the source of our ideas. Ian Hacking aptly summarizes the difference: "Cartesian perception is the active rendering of the object transparent to the mind. Positivist seeing is the passive blunting of light rays on opaque, impermeable 'physical objects' which are themselves passive and indifferent to the observer."[6] What we have

5. "What is not clear is not French," according to the famous treatise *De l'universalité de la langue française* written by Antoine Rivarol in 1784. A celebrated French proverb reads "ce qui se conçois bien s'exprime bien clairement." For discussions of the eighteenth-century obsession with clear prose, see Priscilla Parkhurst Clark, *Literary France: The Making of a Culture* (Berkeley, 1987), chap. 5; and Daniel Mornet, *Histoire de la clarté française: Ses origines, son évolution, sa valeur* (Paris, 1929). For a treatment of the continuing importance in the twentieth century of the French tongue as a "universal language" because of its putative clarity, see David C. Gordon, *The French Language and National Identity (1930–1975)* (The Hague, 1978). The modern fetish for clarity and distinctness has been traced by Walter J. Ong to the visual bias of Ramist logic. See his *Ramus, Method, and the Decay of Dialogue* (Cambridge, Mass., 1983), p. 280.

6. Ian Hacking, *Why Does Language Matter to Philosophy?* (Cambridge, 1975), p. 33. Here "positivist" is another way to say sensationalist. Hacking is drawing on Foucault's discussion of the shift away from Cartesianism in *The Birth of the Clinic*.

called the visual tradition of observation thus largely replaced that of speculation, once the residual active functions of the mind assigned by Locke to reflection were diminished, as they were by David Hume, Étienne Bonnet de Condillac, and other *philosophes*. Although all elements of the Cartesian attitude toward vision were not abandoned in eighteenth-century France—residues are evident in figures as diverse as Charles de Secondat, Baron de Montesquieu and Denis Diderot—they were fighting a losing battle with the more uncompromising sensationalism that gained ascendancy in the late Enlightenment.

Still, what also must be emphasized is the tacit continuation of an ocularcentric bias during the *siècle des lumières*. Both Descartes and the *philosophes* influenced by Locke remained beholden to a concept of the mind as a camera obscura.[7] Both could say with the Scottish philosopher Thomas Reid, "Of all the faculties called the five senses, sight is without doubt the noblest."[8] Both maintained a faith in the linkage between lucidity and rationality, which gave the Enlightenment its name. And both distrusted the evidence of the competing major sense organ, the ear, which absorbed only unreliable "hearsay." As one of its most illustrious interpreters has rightly concluded, "Such was the century of the Enlightenment which looked at things in the sharp clear light of the reasoning mind whose processes appear to have been closely akin to those of the seeing eye."[9]

These are the culminating words of a section called "The Art of Seeing" in a work entitled *The Invention of Liberty*. Their author is Jean Starobinski, whose explorations of the theme of vision no student of the eighteenth century can ignore. In a lifetime of influential books, most notably *Montesquieu par lui-même*, *The Living Eye*, *1789: The Emblems of Reason*, *Jean-Jacques Rousseau: Transparency and Obstruction*, and *The Invention of*

---

7. For Locke's use of the metaphor, see his *Essay Concerning Human Understanding*, ed. A. C. Fraser (Oxford, 1894), pp. 211–212.

8. Thomas Reid, *An Inquiry into the Human Mind on the Principles of Common Sense* (Edinburgh, 1801), p. 152.

9. Jean Starobinski, *The Invention of Liberty, 1700–1789*, trans. Bernard C. Swift (Geneva, 1964), p. 210.

Liberty,[10] Starobinski trenchantly probed every nuance of visual thematics in the literature, painting, architecture, and politics of the era. In fact, Starobinski has been so informative a cicerone that his own inevitable placement in the twentieth-century discourse about vision is sometimes forgotten. Recalling it now will serve not only to situate his analyses, but also to provide a cautionary counterexample to any overly totalizing argument about the antivisual inclinations of much recent French thought.

Starobinski was one of the most prominent members of the so-called Geneva School of literary criticism, whose other luminaries included Marcel Raymond, Albert Béguin, Georges Poulet, Jean-Pierre Richard, and Jean Rousset.[11] Sometimes known as genetic or phenomenological critics, they regarded the consciousness of the author as the primary object of inquiry, literature being understood as a form of consciousness. According to J. Hillis Miller, himself once associated with the School, the search for transparence is a fundamental aspect of their criticism. "Transparence is attained by seeing through an author, by bringing to light the intimate reason for each quality of the consciousness expressed in his work."[12] Starobinski, he notes, "has been haunted since his earliest writings by the dream of a perfect intellectualization of the body and of the world's density. In this transformation the mind becomes a limpid transparency open to a world made transparent."[13]

That such a goal set Starobinski apart from many of the intellectuals

10. Jean Starobinski, *Montesquieu par lui-même* (Paris, 1953); *The Living Eye*, trans. Arthur Goldhammer (Cambridge, Mass., 1989); *1789: The Emblems of Reason*, trans. Barbara Bray (Charlottesville, Va., 1982); *Jean-Jacques Rousseau: Transparency and Obstruction*, trans. Arthur Goldhammer (Chicago, 1988). For a full bibliography of his works, see *Pour un Temps/Jean Starobinski*, ed. Jacques Bonnet (Paris, 1985). For a discussion of their significance, see the essays collected there and Philippe Carrard, "Hybrid Hermeneutics: The Metacriticism of Jean Starobinski," *Stanford Literature Review*, 1, 3 (Fall, 1984).

11. For a discussion of the School, see Sarah Lawall, *Critics of Consciousness: The Existential Structures of Literature* (Cambridge, Mass., 1968).

12. J. Hillis Miller, "The Geneva School," in *Modern French Criticism: From Proust and Valéry to Structuralism*, ed. John K. Simon (Chicago, 1972), p. 294.

13. Ibid., p. 300.

who are the leading exponents of antiocularcentrism has not escaped notice.[14] Although by no means unaware of the dialectic of visual complexity in the Enlightenment, Starobinski has never displayed the deep suspicion of the gaze so often evident in his contemporaries. Thus, in the introductory essay of *The Living Eye*, he observed that *le regard* originally denoted "expectation, concern, watchfulness, consideration and safeguard," and concluded that "it is not easy to keep eyes open, to welcome the gaze that seeks us out. But surely for criticism, as for the whole enterprise of understanding, we must say: 'Look, so that you may be looked at in return.'"[15] Because Starobinski was more generously inclined toward the visual dimensions of the Enlightenment than many other contemporary French thinkers, it will be necessary to draw on other sources to balance our analysis, indebted as it nonetheless is to his pioneering efforts.

Any account of the *siècle des lumières* must begin with the reign of Louis XIV, the Apollonian Sun King. His court, at once theater and spectacle, was a dazzling display of superficial brilliance, bewildering to outsiders but legible to those who knew how to read its meaning. Here courtiers learned to decode the signs of power, distinction, and hierarchy in the gestures and accoutrements of bodies semaphorically on view.[16] Here the more elaborate the costume, the higher the powdered wig, the more arti-

14. Jean Molino, "La relation clinique ou Jean Starobinski dans la critique," in Bonnet, pp. 64–65, contrasts the Apollonian limpidity of his works with the darker philosophy of Sartre. It should be noted, however, that in certain respects, Starobinski follows Sartre. Thus, Lawall notes that "Starobinski's analysis of vision may embrace various literary attitudes, but it is typically existentialist in that it concentrates on being and seeming, choice and action, rather than on works or formal structures" (p. 184). Toward other figures in the mainstream discourse discussed in this book, Starobinski has kept his distance. Nowhere does he really engage with Foucault, Derrida, or even Lacan, which is striking in someone whose own work is heavily indebted to psychoanalysis.

15. Starobinski, *The Living Eye*, pp. 2, 13.

16. During the Italian Renaissance, Baldassare Castiglione had already primed the courtier to put himself on visual display. In *The Book of the Courtier*, trans. Charles Singleton (Garden City, N.Y., 1957), he advised him to use "proper devices, apt poses, and witty inventions that may draw on him the eyes of the onlookers as the magnet attracts iron" (p. 72).

ficial the painted face, the greater, it often seemed, the prestige. Here, as Louis Marin has demonstrated, the king—or rather his "second body"—was the focal point of a perspectival field of representations that drew on the Christian tradition of the Eucharist to confer sacramental presence on the royal image.[17]

In a century that also saw rapid material advances in the manufacture of plate glass, eyeglasses, and interior lighting, the very ability to look and to be seen in a social setting was markedly improved.[18] When Jean Baptiste Colbert smashed the Venetian monopoly on mirrors, the way was open for Louis XIV's unprecedented Galerie des Glaces at Versailles, as well as the so-called *glaces à répétition* or vista mirrors with their infinite reflections, which became a staple of aristocratic interior decoration.[19] Significantly, the great geometrical gardens of the era of French Classicism were designed to please the eye, not the still unappreciated nose.[20] At night, the gardens of Versailles were lit by 24,000 wax candles,[21] a spectacle exceeded only by the festive use of pyrotechnics for even more dazzling effects.

In addition to spectacle, the absolutist state also knew how to develop techniques of visual surveillance.[22] The thousands of new lanterns installed by public decree in Paris were, according to Wolfgang Schivelbusch, "attached to cables strung across the street so that they hung

---

17. Louis Marin, *Portrait of the King*, trans. Martha M. Houle, foreword by Tom Conley (Minneapolis, 1988). Marin shows that royal absolutism was grounded in the visual production of a "king-effect" through everything from portraits on medallions to geometers' maps of Paris. Even historical narratives of Louis XIV's reign culminated in iconic representations. The phrase "second body" refers to Ernst H. Kantorowicz's classic study, *The King's Two Bodies: A Study in Medieval Political Theory* (Princeton, 1957).

18. For a discussion of the material changes, see Philippe Perrot, *Le travail des apparences: Ou les transformations du corps féminin XVIIIe–XIXe siècle* (Paris, 1984), p. 63.

19. Benjamin Goldberg, *The Mirror and Man* (Charlottesville, Va., 1985), p. 173.

20. Alain Corbin, *Le miasme et la jonquille: L'odorat et l'imaginaire social 18e–19e siècles* (Paris, 1982), p. 95.

21. Wolfgang Schivelbusch, *Disenchanted Night: The Industrialization of Light in the Nineteenth Century*, trans. Angela Davies (Berkeley, 1988), p. 7.

exactly over the middle of the street, like small suns, representing the Sun King."[23] What he calls the "lighting of order" accompanied the "lighting of festivity."

The most accomplished literary recorder of the *éclat* of court life was Pierre Corneille, whose plays brilliantly captured what Starobinski called its *"puissance de voir."*[24] Corneille's heroes achieved their identity by gloriously fulfilling the images they created for themselves, and they did so with the whole world as their approving witness. At the center of the glittering Versailles spectacle was the king himself, whom Corneille famously described as both the God-like source of all light and the eye that could see everything, a figure of specular identity *par excellence*.

Less triumphantly affirmative than Corneille's theater was that of Jean Baptiste Racine. His Jansenist anxieties about being the object of the others' look created a theater of resentment in which being seen was less a mark of glory than of shame. Racine's characters lived in the shadows that prevented their achieving a stable and transparent identity. His use of the verb *voir* betrayed an awareness of the insatiable desire and the unresolvable dread that accompanies visual experience. The brightness of daylight for Racine signaled more than mere visibility; it meant as well what Starobinski calls—in a phrase that will be later applied to Sartre[25]—*le regard absolu* (the absolute gaze), the judging eye of God or the sun.

If the theater of the *ancièn regime* betrayed an oscillation between visual serenity and visual anxiety, so too did the theorizing of the *philosophes* during the eighteenth century. Montesquieu, Starobinski implies, resembled Corneille in his positive attitude toward visual experience, especially that which perceives its object from afar. Montesquieu,

22. The German absolutist states with their emphasis on policing the populace also developed methods of visual control, which were reinforced by the domination of sight in the reigning Rationalist philosophy of Christian Wolff. See the discussion in Howard Caygill, *Art of Judgement* (Cambridge, Mass., 1989), p. 182.

23. Schivelbusch, *Disenchanted Night*, p. 86.

24. Starobinski, *L'oeil vivant: Essais* (Paris, 1961) p. 43. The essays on Corneille and Racine are not included in the English translation.

25. François George, *Deux études sur Sartre* (Paris, 1976), pp. 303f.

who ironically died blind, sought pleasure from a panoramic, God's-eye view of as vast a scene as possible. For him, "evidence is a joy of the look. Rationality, clarity—classic virtues *par excellence*—are not only defined as a type of knowledge, but also as a type of happiness; they assure the distant deployment of sight and the seizure of forms until they are indistinct. . . . When it is a question of the look, Montesquieu no longer preaches moderation: happiness consists for our soul in 'fleeing limits,' in 'extending the sphere of its presence.'"[26] His method of understanding was based on an instantaneous take on the world, which brought him closer to Descartes, who mistakenly believed that light was transmitted at once, than to Newton. It is thus not surprising that Montesquieu came to be widely admired as the father of a disinterested social science, seeking the eternal forms of social and political life. From still another perspective, Montesquieu's unimpeded panoramic vision might be likened to the cultivated prospects of aristocratic country homes with their so-called *claire-voie* (what the English called a "ha-ha"), ditches rather than fences to keep livestock away from the house without obstructing the view.[27] For all the happiness he derived from his sovereign overview of the landscape, social as well as natural, Montesquieu remained a spectator only distantly involved with the objects of his gaze.

Or at least so he seemed in comparison with the very different figure who in a way deepened and complicated the Racinian tradition: Jean-Jacques Rousseau. Even more than those of Montesquieu, his ocular preoccupations evinced a passionate personal dimension. His search for transparency sought not merely to reveal the truth of the world, but also to make manifest his own internal truth, his own authentic self. In Starobinski's celebrated phenomenological description of Rousseau's consciousness, this struggle for crystalline limpidity is shown to take many forms and come up against many obstacles. Rousseau's initial impulse,

26. Starobinski, *Montesquieu par lui-même*, p. 35.

27. D. G. Charlton, *New Images of the Natural in France: A Study in European Cultural History 1750–1800* (Cambridge, 1984), p. 34.

derived perhaps from the Genevan Calvinist tradition of "holy watching," was to restore the transparency of men before God. Although the fall into opacity was deemed by Rousseau a fortunate one[28] because it made possible the joy of return, its reversal was complicated in a secular age; rather than visible to the eye of God, men must now become completely transparent to each other and each individual must become no less transparent to himself. Rousseau's desire to lift the veil of appearance and reveal an essential truth beneath was so intense that Starobinski does not hesitate to compare it with Plato's.[29]

In his efforts to achieve this goal, Rousseau considered many expedients. At times, he identified with the divine, omniscient eye, that *oeil vivant* Wolmar dreamed of becoming in *La nouvelle Héloise*. Here seeing everything accompanied a fantasy of total invisibility (similar to the transfigured role of Louis XIV at the end of his reign described by Jean-Marie Apostolidès).[30] At others times, Rousseau yearned to be the cynosure of all eyes, with his inner self fully visible to the judging gaze of others. This oscillation between complementary voyeuristic and exhibitionist tendencies, however, brought no real relief for Rousseau, who resembled Racine's characters in their anxiety before *le regard absolu*.[31]

Disgusted with what he saw as the mendacious superficiality of Parisian salon society dominated by women and frequented by other *philosophes*, Rousseau often sought solace in the lonely exploration of his "authentic" self or the solitary contemplation—better put, visionary projection—of

28. Starobinski, *Jean-Jacques Rousseau*, p. 135. On the ubiquity of the fortunate fall motif in late eighteenth- and early nineteenth-century thought, see M. H. Abrams, *Natural Supernaturalism: Tradition and Revolution in Romantic Literature* (New York, 1971).

29. Starobinski, *Jean-Jacques Rousseau*, p. 76.

30. Jean-Marie Apostolidès, *Le roi-machine: Spectacle et politique au temps de Louis XIV* (Paris, 1981), p. 128. He argues that the festivals of 1674 mark the change from the king on visible display to the king as absent center of a network of surveillance.

31. In *Jean-Jacques Rousseau*, p. 251, he uses this term, connecting it to the hope for divine absolution.

Arcadian natural beauty.[32] Turning on its head the metaphor of the camera obscura used by Descartes and Locke with reference to the external world, he applied it to knowledge of his own soul, whose dark corners he compulsively exhibited to the world. Never satisfied with withdrawal from society for very long, he dreamed no less fervently of a new social order in which humans would be utterly open to each other's gazes, a utopia of mutually beneficial surveillance without reprobation or repression.

Rousseau acknowledged that humanity lacked the full means to achieve that utopia. For following St. Augustine and Malebranche, he believed that man cannot be the source of his own light. This disability meant the necessity for Rousseau of linguistic mediation, the necessity of signs that interrupted the pure reciprocity of gazes. But here too he dreamed of the restoration of a primitive, natural language in which the conventional obstacles of modern speech, with its impersonal general concepts, would be overcome. Another means of achieving immediacy, Rousseau contended, was music, whose melodies in particular could directly reach the heart of its listeners. Thus other senses could come to the aid of sight in overcoming the obstacles to transparency.

Such music was an inherent component of the event Rousseau counterposed to the superficial and illusory theater he so disliked: the festival. As Starobinski puts it, "The theater is to the festival as opacity is to transparency."[33] Unlike the theater with its division between spectators and actors, the festival was a model of total participation. Whereas the theater trafficked in illusion and pandered to the senses, the festival provided a healthy moral experience in the open air. Rather than a mere representation—Rousseau was Platonic in his hostility to aesthetic as well as political representation—the festival was pure presence, an end in itself, a

32. As D. G. Charlton notes, for Rousseau, "'vision' is not only (or primarily) 'looking', *his* 'pastoral vision' also involves those other meanings of the word that imply imagination, insight, even dreaming of a prophetic kind. His concern is not with a 'return to nature', to a past in 'the Golden Age', but with the pastoral world as an 'image' of a possible, hoped-for future" (p. 40).

33. Starobinski, *Jean-Jacques Rousseau*, p. 95. For a discussion of Rousseau's critique of the theater, see Jonas Barish, *The Anti-Theatrical Prejudice* (Berkeley, 1981), chap. 9.

communion of souls without anything to mediate between them. Thus, the festival, most strikingly presented in the wine harvest in *La nouvelle Héloise*, had its counterpart in the patriotic community expressing the General Will developed in *The Social Contract*.

Rousseau's paean to the total transparency of the festival went so far that Jacques Derrida could stretch Starobinski's argument to claim that vision itself was no longer privileged there.

> It is the place where the spectator, presenting himself as spectacle, will no longer be either seer (*voyant*) or voyeur, will efface within himself the difference between the actor and the spectator, the represented and the representer, the object seen and the seeing object. . . . The open air is the element of the voice, the liberty of a breath that nothing breaks into pieces.[34]

That is, unless there is a gap between seeing subject and visible object, unless difference undermines specular unity, unless there is something to see in the infinite *glaces à répétition* of the festival, there is no real visual experience, only a problematic model of pure transparency, which Derrida claims is tacitly based on the alleged presence of the spoken word. In Rousseau, the Enlightenment's apotheosis of sight thus paradoxically turns into its opposite.

Whether or not Derrida's identification of perfect transparency with a covert privileging of the voice is fully persuasive, it helps to explain how ambivalent Rousseau actually was about sight (as he was about much else in the mainstream Enlightenment). Moreover, it is useful in making sense of what followed. For Rousseau's cult of pure presence inspired what Starobinski called "the festival of iconoclasm,"[35] in which the militants of the French Revolution acted out their own contradictory sentiments about images and their seductive power. The Jacobins, like the Puritans before them, were anxious to destroy the idolatrous worship of discred-

---

34. Jacques Derrida, *Of Grammatology*, trans. Gayatri Chakravorty Spivak (Baltimore, 1976), pp. 306 and 308.

35. Starobinski, *The Invention of Liberty*, p. 100.

ited symbols of authority, both religious and political.[36] They too ascetically bemoaned the distraction of the spectacle, most notably that surrounding the throne and altar of the ancien régime. Not for them was the superficial glitter of the female-dominated salons of prerevolutionary Paris.[37] Only when the decontexualization of religious and aristocratic works of art was made possible with the transformation of the Louvre into a public museum in August of 1793 did the national artistic patrimony have a chance to survive the Jacobins' fervor.

Inevitably, the iconoclastic festival, the communion of pure souls, was far more difficult to realize than the revolutionaries first believed. Rather than doing away with spectacle, rather than abolishing theater,[38] rather than restoring the pure presence of the voice, they found themselves creating a new revolutionary imaginary that was no less ocularcentric than the one they sought to overturn. The Apollonian Sun King was replaced by "the solar myth of the revolution."[39] Indeed, the monarch himself was now the victim of surveillance, an outcome that was brilliantly illustrated by Louis XVI's being recognized on the flight to Varennes by a patriot who knew his engraved portrait on paper currency. The smashed lanterns of the all-seeing *ancien régime* were soon in fact replaced by their revolutionary equivalents.[40] Diogenes, illuminating his search for truth with the light of a lantern, became a favorite symbol of the new order.[41] The result

36. Stanley J. Idzerde, "Iconoclasm During the French Revolution," *American Historical Review,* 60, 1 (October, 1954), pp. 13–16.

37. For an account of the rejection of the aristocratic salons, with their visual panache, in favor of a more verbally oriented bourgeois public sphere, see Joan B. Landes, *Women and the Public Sphere* (Ithaca, 1988). The Jacobin reaction to the "iconic specularity" of the *ancien régime,* she shows, was connected to their hostility to women in the public realm. For a similar argument, see Marie-Hélène Huet, *Rehearsing the Revolution: The Staging of Marat's Death,* trans. Robert Hurley (Berkeley, 1982).

38. In fact, theater thrived during the Revolution. See Beatrice F. Hyslop, "The Theater during a Crisis: The Parisian Theater during the Reign of Terror," *Journal of Modern History,* 17 (1945), pp. 332–355.

39. Starobinski, *1789: The Emblems of Reason,* pp. 40f.

was what one recent observer has called the revolution as *"theatrum mundi,"* a stage in which heroic actions were performed *"sous les yeux"* of the people.[42]

But what was to be presented on that stage was not immediately obvious. According to Apostolidès, the image of the prince was replaced by "pure abstractions, Justice, Fraternity, Liberty, Equality, which the revolutionaries put in their turn on display."[43] But how could abstractions be made visible? One rigorous student of Locke and Condillac, J. B. Salaville, denounced any attempt to create a symbolic imagery as pure idolatry.[44] But the impracticality of his argument persuaded no one and the Revolution quickly sought its own visual style. It found it primarily in the restoration of classical Greek and Roman models, which were masterfully manipulated by the great painter and Jacobin militant, Jacques Louis David.[45] As the impresario of Robespierre's Festival of the Supreme Being,

40. Schivelbusch, *Disenchanted Night*, p. 113. The same cycle of lantern-smashing and the revolutionary restoration of its own lighting took place in the 1830 revolution.

41. See Klaus Herding, "Diogenes als Bürgerheld," in *Im Zeichen der Aufklärung: Studien zur Moderne* (Frankfurt, 1989). For a different reading of Diogenes, which makes him into the founder of a tradition of body-affirming, anti-theoretical "kynicism," see Peter Sloterdijk, *Critique of Cynical Reason*, trans. Michael Eldred (Minneapolis, 1987). This Diogenes might well be accounted the forerunner of the transgressive antiocularcentrism of Georges Bataille, to be discussed in chapter 4.

42. Joseph Butwin, "The French Revolution as *Theatrum Mundi*," *Research Studies*, 43, 3 (September, 1975), pp. 141–152. For a more benign reading of the rise of what he calls "attestive" as opposed to "celebratory" visual politics in the democratic public sphere that emerged in the wake of the Revolution, see Yaron Ezrahi, *The Descent of Icarus: Science and the Transformation of Contemporary Democracy* (Cambridge, Mass., 1990), chapter 3.

43. Apostolidès, *Le roi-machine*, p. 159.

44. For an account of his protest, see E. H. Gombrich, "The Dream of Reason: Symbolism in the French Revolution," *The British Journal for Eighteenth-Century Studies*, 2, 3 (Autumn, 1979), p. 190.

45. The standard work on his role in the revolution is David Lloyd Dowd, *Pageant Master of the Republic: Jacques Louis David and the French Revolution* (Lincoln, Nebr., 1948). See also Jean Duvignaud, *"La fête civique": Histoire des spectacles* (Paris, 1965) and Mona Ozouf, *La fête révolutionnaire 1789–1799* (Paris, 1976).

he helped establish a new iconography for a new idol: Reason.[46] Even the oral moments of swearing fidelity to the revolution were given visual form by David in his paintings of founding oaths, both Roman (*The Oath of the Horatii*) and modern (*The Tennis Court Oath*).[47] Other visual symbols like the so-called eye of providence—the all-seeing eye in a triangle surrounded by rays, which had also been introduced into the Great Seal of the United States and is still on the back of a dollar bill—were adopted from the Masonic tradition, which had itself taken it from sources as ancient as Egyptian hieroglyphs.[48] In 1789, a revolutionary medallion with the eye was minted with the legend "Publicity is the Safeguard of the People"; another read "Liberty, your sun is the eye of the mountain" (the mountain referring to the most radical Jacobin faction, which sat in the highest seats in the assembly).

No less significant were attempts to provide a visual register of revolutionary ardor in dress, which preoccupied successive governments during the decade after 1789,[49] and the adoption of the new tricolor flag to replace the discredited fleur-de-lys.[50] The visual representation of revolutionary symbols like Marianne and Hercules was likewise a source of vigorous and lengthy contestation.[51] Even the most frightening dimen-

---

46. In addition to the deification of Reason, there were strong expressions of passion in the revolutionary imaginary, which sometimes took decidedly transgressive forms. As Claude Gandelman has shown, scurrilous, even scatological imagery was used in pamphlets and broadsheets to demean the discredited authorities of the *ancien régime*. See his "The Scatological Homunculus," in *Reading Pictures, Viewing Texts* (Bloomington, Ind., 1991).

47. For a discussion, see Starobinski, *1789: The Emblems of Reason*, pp. 101f.

48. On the "eye of providence," see Albert M. Potts, *The World's Eye* (Lexington, Ky., 1982), chap. 8. On its role in the revolutionary iconography, see Gombrich, p. 200. The politically militant offshoots of the Masons were significantly called the "Illuminati." For a recent defense of their role, see Margaret C. Jacob, *Living the Enlightenment: Freemasonry and Politics in Eighteenth-Century Europe* (New York, 1991).

49. See Lynn Hunt, *Politics, Culture, and Class in the French Revolution* (Berkeley, 1984), pp. 75f.

50. For a history of its adoption, see Raoul Girardet, "Les trois couleurs," in Pierre Nora, ed., *Les lieux de mémoire*, vol. 1, *La République* (Paris, 1984).

sion of the revolution expressed itself in visual terms with the so-called eye or *lunette* of the guillotine dominating the Terror, a period one historian has gone so far as to call that of "generalized visual paranoia."[52]

The Enlightenment and the Revolution it helped spawn may thus be justly said to have expressed that privileging of sight so often taken to characterize the modern era in general. But as in the case of Cartesian philosophy and Albertian perspectivalism, whose ambivalences we probed in the previous chapter, visual primacy was by no means without its complications. Certain of these will have already been evident in our recapitulation of Starobinski's analyses, especially those concerning Rousseau. Still others will become apparent if we pause now to examine more closely two of the era's most remarkable figures, Denis Diderot and Jacques Louis David.

Diderot's visual preoccupations were paramount throughout his extraordinary career. One of the first consequential modern critics of art, he wrote a series of *Salons* beginning in 1759 that helped establish the reputations of Jean Baptiste Greuze, Jean Baptiste Siméon Chardin, and Horace Vernet as painters of bourgeois life.[53] Himself a playwright of modest gifts, Diderot was closer to Jean le Rond d'Alembert than Rousseau on the issue of the theater, even if he shared the latter's nostalgia for festivals. His theorizing on the theater, moreover, emphasized its visual dimensions, defining effective scenes as realistic pictorial tableaux in which the essence of an action was intelligible at a glance. His belief in the visual representation of character in human physiognomy was serious enough to earn him a comparison with Johann Kasper Lavater and Franz Joseph Gall.[54] And the *Encyclopedia* he helped organize and edit was cel-

51. Maurice Agulhon, *Marianne au combat: L'Imaginarie et la symbolique républicaines de 1789 à 1880* (Paris, 1979); Hunt, *Politics, Culture and Class in the French Revolution*, chap. 3.

52. Norman Bryson, *Tradition and Desire: From David to Delacroix* (Cambridge, 1984), p. 96.

53. For an account of his activities as an art critic, see Anita Brookner, *The Genius of the Future: Essays in French Art Criticism* (Ithaca, 1988), chap. 2.

54. Starobinski, *The Invention of Liberty*, p. 136.

ebrated for its unprecedented use of plates, some three thousand in all, following his injunction that "a glance at the object or its representation says more than a page of discourse."[55]

Yet, it was also Diderot who wrote in 1765, anticipating the Jacobin destruction of images, "My friend, if we love truth more than fine arts, let us pray God for some iconoclasts."[56] Here he expressed a Rousseauist hostility to the seductive power of illusory images. Elsewhere in his work, other ambivalences about ocularcentrism can also be discerned. Perhaps most interestingly, they appear in his contribution to the debate over the so-called Molyneux Question and in his defense of what the art historian Michael Fried has called absorptive as opposed to theatrical modes of painting.[57] By examining these in turn, we can appreciate some of the countercurrents to Enlightenment ocularcentrism in its dominant form.

In a famous letter of 1693 to Locke, the Dublin lawyer William Molyneux had posed the question, Will a person born without sight, who has acquired knowledge of the world through other senses such as touch, be immediately able to distinguish objects if, by some miracle or a successful operation, he regains his ability to see? Will he be able to tell the difference by sight alone between a sphere and cube, whose shapes he knows only through his fingers? Put more generally, does the mind know before sense experience and if not, does each sense contribute a separate knowledge, which then has somehow to be coordinated into a unified sense of the world? Or perhaps even more fundamentally, is there intuitive knowledge prior to discursively constructed concepts, which are synthetic acts of understanding based on experience?[58]

Rather than a mere curiosity, Molyneux's question was, according to

55. Cited in Daniel Brewer, "The Work of the Image: The Plates of the *Encyclopédie*," *Stanford French Review*, 8, 2–3 (Fall, 1984), p. 235.

56. Diderot, *Magazin encyclopédique*, 3 (1795), pp. 52–53, originally in his *Salon* of 1765. Quoted in Idzerde, p. 13.

57. For a history of the debate unleashed by Molyneux, see Michael J. Morgan, *Molyneux's Question: Vision, Touch and the Philosophy of Perception* (Cambridge, 1977). Michael Fried's discussion of Diderot is in *Absorption and Theatricality: Painting and Beholder in the Age of Diderot* (Berkeley, 1980).

Foucault, "one of the two great mythical experiences on which the philosophy of the eighteenth century wishes to base its beginning."[59] A host of philosophers before Diderot had tackled the problem: Locke in his *Essay on Human Understanding,* Berkeley in his *Essay towards a New Theory of Vision,* Condillac in his *Essay on the Origin of Human Knowledge,* and Voltaire in his *Elements of the Philosophy of Newton,* to name the most prominent. Although they differed on a number of issues— Condillac, for example, criticized Locke's contention that first we sense something and then reflect on it, rather than do both simultaneously— virtually all agreed that the newly sighted would not immediately see the differences between objects they knew previously through other senses, because there were no innate ideas before sense impressions and no ideal space in the mind's eye. In 1728 a doctor named William Cheselden operated on the cataracts of a boy blinded since birth, who then had difficulties orienting himself after his sight was restored. Voltaire publicized the results widely ten years later in his book on Newton, and the *philosophes* thought they had a confirmation of their anti-innatist beliefs.[60]

Diderot was deeply interested in the Molyneux problem and sought in 1748, as it turned out in vain, to witness the removal of cataracts from the eyes of a blind girl by Antoine Ferchault, Seigneur de Réaumur. Instead, he pondered the records left by other such operations and the experiences

58. In these terms, the debate paralleled the famous dispute between the Newtonian Samuel Clarke and Leibniz over the characteristics of time and space. Whereas Leibniz claimed all perception was also conceptualization, Clarke argued that it contained an intuitive moment that was prior to the discursive act of conceptualization. For a brief discussion, see Amos Funkenstein, *Theology and the Scientific Imagination from the Middle Ages to the Scientific Revolution* (Princeton, 1986), pp. 107–108.

59. Michel Foucault, *The Birth of the Clinic: An Archaeology of Medical Perception,* trans. A. M. Sheridan (London, 1973), p. 65. The other was the foreign spectator in an unknown country. Both, Foucault claims, represented the freshness of the innocent gaze, which was linked with belief in the goodness of childhood. For an extensive account of the general fascination with blindness in this period, which deals at length with the debate over Molyneux's question, see William R. Paulson, *Enlightenment, Romanticism, and the Blind in France* (Princeton, 1987).

60. Today scientists are not so certain. See the discussion in Morgan, *Molyneux's Question,* p. 180.

of those who had suffered from blindness, most notably the celebrated Cambridge mathematician Nicholas Saunderson. The famous and controversial result was his *Letter on the Blind for the Use of Those Who See* of 1749.[61] Notorious for its bold dismissal of the claim for God's existence based on the universe's apparent design, which landed Diderot in prison for a while, it also contained a lengthy consideration of the Molyneux question. Diderot's innovation was not an argument that the newly sighted could in fact immediately distinguish shapes,[62] but rather his implicit challenge to the primacy of vision assumed by earlier students of the problem. Impressed by what the *Encyclopedia* article on the subject was later to call "the miracles of blindness,"[63] he offered two reasons for dethroning sight from the summit of the sensual hierarchy.

Diderot's first argument concerned the value of touch, which he claimed was as potent a source of knowledge as vision. One recent French commentator, Elizabeth de Fontenay, has gone so far as to say that in the *Letter,* "the great victor in this carnival of the senses established on the ruins of the castle of the eye and consciousness is touch."[64] Others, such as Geoffrey Bremner, are more cautious, pointing to Diderot's stress on the interdependence of the senses.[65] But what certainly comes through in his discussion is Diderot's deep respect for the powers of touch, which, as Saunderson's example illustrates, can even produce the most abstract forms of knowledge (largely because of the blind man's ignorance of color). For a materialist like Diderot, the dethroning of vision was especially appealing, for although he sarcastically calls idealism "an extrava-

---

61. A translation is available in Margaret Jourdain, ed., *Diderot's Early Philosophical Works* (Chicago, 1916).

62. This is the mistaken interpretation of Jeffrey Mehlman in *Cataract: A Study in Diderot* (Middletown, Conn., 1979), p. 13. Diderot explicitly accepts the results of the Cheselden experiment (p. 125).

63. Jourdain, *Diderot's Early Philosophical Works,* p. 227.

64. Elizabeth de Fontenay, *Diderot: Reason and Resonance,* trans. Jeffrey Mehlman (New York, 1983), p. 166.

65. Geoffrey Bremner, *Order and Chance: The Patterns of Diderot's Thought* (Cambridge, 1983), p. 37.

gant system which should to my thinking have been the offspring of blindness itself,"[66] he recognized the tendential linkage between privileging ideas in the mind and the putative superiority of vision. "If ever a philosopher, blind and deaf from birth, were to construct a man after the fashion of Descartes," he writes, "he would put the seat of the soul at the fingers' end, for thence the greater part of the sensations and all his knowledge are derived."[67] Diderot's rehabilitation of the other senses, most notably touch, thus anticipated one of the cardinal arguments of such twentieth-century critics of Cartesian ocularcentrism as Merleau-Ponty, who was also insistent on the imbrication of the senses.

So too did his second major challenge to conventional wisdom in the *Letter on the Blind*, his tentative exploration of the relations between perception in general and language. If there were no uniform, innate space underlying different perceptual experiences of the world, then how could such experiences be compared to one another at all? That translations from one to others did indeed take place Diderot did not doubt, as illustrated by his positive interest in the famous attempt by the Jesuit Pierre Louis Bertrand Castel to construct an ocular clavecin.[68] In conceptualizing how such translations took place, he borrowed an insight from Condillac that Molyneux's question was really divisible into two parts: What does the newly sighted man see, and would the mind be immediately able to *name* what it saw? Both Condillac and Diderot stressed the second question, which they answered negatively, as the crucial riposte to the doctrine of innate ideas. Translation occurred linguistically through conventional signs, which were learned, not inborn: "Our senses bring us back to symbols more suited to our comprehension and the conformation of our organs. We have arranged that these signs should be common prop-

66. Jourdain, *Diderot's Early Philosophical Works*, p. 104.

67. Ibid., p. 87.

68. Ibid., p. 171. Both Voltaire and Rousseau were far more skeptical about this device. Interestingly, Rousseau attacked it for confusing the natural successive order of sounds with the static order of vision, a distinction central to the aesthetics of other eighteenth-century thinkers like Lessing. See Rousseau's discussion in his *Essay on the Origin of Languages*.

erty and serve, as it were, for the staple in the exchange of our ideas."[69] Although at times Diderot dreamed of perfectly transparent signs, which he called hieroglyphs, he generally acknowledged an inevitable disparity between our sensual experience and its linguistic mediation.[70]

One implication Diderot drew from the interpenetration of the visual and the linguistic was developed in his discussion of linguistic inversion in the *Letter on the Deaf and Dumb* of 1751. Although he chauvinistically defended French as the language least disturbed by inappropriate inversions of mental activity, he nonetheless acknowledged an inevitable tension between the temporality of all language and the spatiality of mental pictures. "In the growth of language," he wrote, "decomposition was a necessity; but to *see* an object, to *admire* it, to *experience* an agreeable sensation, and to *desire* to *possess* it, is but an instantaneous emotion."[71] Thus, an epistemology based solely on the model of instantaneous vision was inadequate because it failed to register the inevitably temporal dimension of its linguistic mediation. However ocularcentric the Enlightenment in general may have been, at least one *philosophe* thus expressed doubts about its privileging of sight.

A similar challenge to the perspectivalist, scenographic tradition in painting may also be discerned in Diderot's art criticism. Remarking on Diderot's exhortation to place the spectator in a theater as if in front of a pictorial tableau, Fried contends that the normal interpretation of it as an "exaltation of vision" is wrong: "The primary function of the *tableau* as Diderot conceived it was not to address or exploit the visuality of the theatrical audience so much as to neutralize that visuality, to wall it off

69. Jourdain, *Diderot's Early Philosophical Works,* p. 89. Elsewhere, in his *Letter on the Deaf and Dumb,* Diderot speculated that the only shared understanding that might be prior to linguistic mediation would be geometry (Jourdain, *Diderot's Early Philosophical Works,* p. 165).

70. For a helpful discussion of Diderot's oscillating thoughts on this issue, see Norman Bryson, *Word and Image: French Painting of the Ancien Régime* (Cambridge, 1981), chap. 6. He points out a change in Diderot's attitude around 1765, when his earlier hopes for transparency diminish.

71. Jourdain, *Diderot's Early Philosophical Writings,* p. 191.

from the action taking place on stage, to put it out of mind for the dramatis personae and the audience alike."[72] In terms of painting itself, Diderot advocated what Fried calls the "supreme fiction" of a nonexistent beholder, unbeknownst to the subject of the painting, a subject entirely absorbed in its own thoughts, actions and emotions. This detheatricalization of the painting-beholder relationship also implies a collapse of the distance between observing eye and external scene, in a certain way similar to Rousseau's version of the festival.[73] Diderot's hostility to Cartesian dualism led to an aesthetic anticipation of that corporeal imbrication of the viewer and the viewed in the flesh of the world later defended by Merleau-Ponty. Although the theatricalized tradition reasserted itself after the mid-eighteenth century and continued into the nineteenth with such painters as Thomas Couture, Fried sees the absorptive alternative reasserting itself with Gustave Courbet.[74] His subtle analysis of its implications cannot be followed here, but suffice it to say that by probing its theoretical origins in the writings of Diderot, he provides strong confirmation of the heterodox character of that *philosophe's* attitude toward the mainstream scopic regime of the Enlightenment.

The power of Fried's interpretation is recognized by Bryson in his recent *Tradition and Desire: From David to Delacroix*, but he introduces one caveat: Fried's beholder may be in or out of the painting, spectatorially distant or completely absorbed, but "either way he remains an agent who simply sees, a viewing subject invited into the sphere of perception. Fried's subject is the same subject that is posited in the phenomenological reduction: monadic and self-enclosed, the subject sees the world from the world's center and in unitary prospect. . . . This leaves (at least) two things out: the presence of the other in vision which makes of *human* visuality (as opposed to the vision of the camera) a divided visuality, divided be-

72. Fried, *Theatricality and Absorption*, p. 96.

73. Fried makes the comparison explicitly on p. 221.

74. Michael Fried, "Thomas Couture and the Theatricalization of Action in 19th-Century French Painting," *Artforum*, 8, 10 (1970); "The Beholder in Courbet: His Early Self-Portraits and Their Place in His Art," *Glyph*, 4 (1978).

cause the subject is not alone in his perceptual horizon, but surrounded by the visualities of others with which it must interact, and secondly (a corollary of this) the permanent division of visual subjectivity in the visual *sign*."[75]

If Merleau-Ponty is the guiding spirit behind Fried's work, another participant in the twentieth-century French discourse on vision lurks behind Bryson's: Jacques Lacan, who stressed the failed reciprocity in the chiasmic intertwining of what he called the eye and the gaze.[76] Bryson claims that in the paintings of David, which are so often seen as the summa of the theatricalized, scenographic tradition of Enlightenment visuality, there can be found such a nonreciprocal, chiasmic tension. Of David's *Antoniochus and Stratonice*, for example, he writes, "The subjects represented as caught in the world of sight are divided, broken, in their habitation there: they see and they are seen, and how they see is distorted, violated, by how they are seen."[77] And in *The Oath of the Horatii*, he finds an irreconcilable tension between the three-dimensional space of its Albertian *veduta* and the flat, friezelike plane on which the characters stand.[78] The result resembles the visual complexity characteristic more of the baroque, as commentators like Buci-Glucksmann describe it, than of the dominant Cartesian perspectivalist tradition. It also introduces the return of the beholder's body, his or her incarnated glance rather than disembodied gaze, into the viewing process, for "just as the *veduta* promises the full intelligibility of the scene to a viewer placed at the center of monocular vision, so the frieze promises *its* intelligibility to a viewer mov-

75. Bryson, *Tradition and Desire*, p. 46.

76. Lacan's contribution to the critique of ocularcentrism is discussed in chapter 6. For an example of the type of belief in benign visual reciprocity that Lacan and Bryson challenge, see Starobinski's description of Chardin in *The Invention of Liberty*: "To emphasize sight and seeing Chardin does not need to depict human beings. With him things are not only seen, but see: they answer our own gaze" (p. 127).

77. Ibid., p. 49. Fried himself analyzes another picture by David, *Bélisaire*, in similar terms: "David turned those conventions [of Neoclassical painting] against the absolute dominance of the picture-plane which ordinarily they subserved. . . . He wielded and in a sense reinterpreted them so as to open the painting to a number of points of view other than that of the beholder standing before the canvas" (p. 159).

ing in binocular vision along a line."[79] Although conceding that later canvases by the politically repentant David, such as *The Intervention of the Sabine Women*, lose some of the visual complexity of the history paintings of the 1780s, Bryson shows that when looked at through the prism of twentieth-century musings on vision, even the master works of the *siècle des lumières* begin to oscillate before our eyes.

However controversial Bryson's specific analyses may be—and he has by no means convinced all art historians of their plausibility—it is thus necessary to acknowledge the complexity of the modern scopic regime, both in theoretical and practical terms, even at its moment of apparent triumph in the Enlightenment.[80] And yet, the general consensus—best expressed in Starobinski's oeuvre—that in comparison with other eras the

---

78. Compare his analysis with Starobinski's in *1789: The Emblems of Reason*, which sees only a thematic tension between the heroic, oath-taking men and the grieving women, the former representing fidelity to the state, the latter "sensitive femininity" (p. 110). Bryson links the visual heterogeneity of the scene to gender more subtly:

> For the males, visuality is dominated and blinded by signs: both as the signs of strength and virile possession they must project outwards, in constant strain, towards the gaze of the adversary; and inwardly, as a corrosion of sight where nothing may appear innocently or as itself, for everything has become the sign of another sign (in the *différance*, the deferral of vision). Theirs is essentially paranoid vision, if we take "paranoia" in its technical sense, as referring to a representational crisis in subjectivity; a crisis in which material life is invaded, devoured by signs, turned everywhere *into* the sign. For the females, visuality consists in being the blinded object of another's sight: the observed of all observers, the women are to be seen, not to see, and for them equally, visuality is the experience of Being becoming Representation. In David's painting both genders are portrayed as living under affliction, and it is this critical detachment from gender which renders the painting itself problematic. (p. 74–75)

Not only is the gender issue linked to the crisis of vision here, so too is the problem of the intertwining of language and perception, evident as well in Diderot's writings.

79. Bryson, *Tradition and Desire*, p. 78.

80. For yet another example of the complexities, see Mitchell Robert Breitweiser, "Jefferson's Prospect," *Prospects: An Annual Journal of American Cultural Studies*, 10 (1985). Breitweiser explores the implications of the view from Jefferson's hilltop estate at Monticello, which has often been compared to the Enlightenment, "that mental gaze at a world no longer mystified by the self-serving obscurities of priests, ministers and despots" (p. 316).

eighteenth century was an age that ratified the putative nobility of sight is difficult to gainsay. Certainly the Counter-Enlightenment, which can be said to have begun with German thinkers like Johann Georg Hamann at the end of that period, often chose to privilege the ear over the eye, placing its faith in the spoken word over the image.[81] Or as in the case of Johann Gottfried von Herder, its spokesmen subordinated sight, with its ability to see only surfaces, to touch as well as hearing.[82] In France, conservative anti-Lockeans like Louis de Bonald stressed the divine origins of language. The tradition of hermeneutics, which gained a new life in the early nineteenth century with Friedrich Schleiermacher, was also resolutely tied to aural experience. As one of its leading twentieth-century practitioners, Hans-Georg Gadamer has acknowledged that "the primacy of hearing is the basis of the hermeneutical phenomenon."[83]

According to Starobinski, two tendencies in the late eighteenth century contributed to the waning of the Enlightenment trust in sight. The first was the revival of a neo-Platonic desire for an ideal beauty that could not be perceived with the normal eyes of mundane observation. "A thirst for an intelligible Beauty, a reflection of the unity of Beauty, emerged strongly everywhere—in reaction . . . against the corrupting seduction of

81. For a classic account, see Isaiah Berlin, "The Counter-Enlightenment," in *Against the Current: Essays in the History of Ideas*, ed. Henry Hardy (New York, 1980). For an analysis of the religious underpinnings of the return to a sacramental notion of speech, see Harold Stahmer, *"Speak That I May See Thee": The Religious Significance of Language* (New York, 1968).

82. See, in particular, his discussion of sculpture in *Plastik, Werke*, 8 (Berlin, 1878). For Herder on hearing, see Michael Rosen, *Hegel's Dialectic and Its Criticism* (Cambridge, 1982), p. 95. For Herder on touch, see the discussion in Marshall Brown, *The Shape of German Romanticism* (Ithaca, 1979), p. 31. For a general account of his critique of the German Enlightenment's primacy of the visual, see Caygill, *Art of Judgement*, pp. 179f. Goethe also stressed the importance of touch, in particular its erotic implications, in his *Roman Elegies* of the late 1780s. See Sander L. Gilman, *Goethe's Touch: Touching, Seeing and Sexuality* (New Orleans, 1988).

83. Hans-Georg Gadamer, *Truth and Method* (New York, 1975), p. 420. For a discussion of this issue, see Martin Jay, "The Rise of Hermeneutics and the Crisis of Ocularcentrism," in *Force Fields: Between Intellectual History and Cultural Critique* (New York, 1993).

sensual pleasure. People aspired to an art that would no longer address itself to the eyes alone, but instead, through the inevitable mediation of sight, to the soul."[84] The second was a new valorization of darkness, as the necessary complement, even the source of light. Here Johann Wolfgang von Goethe's writings on color, which stressed the polarity of light and dark, and Francisco Goya's increasingly bleak paintings after 1800 are his main pieces of evidence.[85] The cause of the reversal, he speculates, was the changed course of the French Revolution.

> The solar myth of the Revolution delighted in the insubstantiality of darkness: Reason had only to appear, supported by will, and darkness disappeared . . . the myth was an illusion. France experienced the intensest moments of its Revolution in a symbolism by which the light of principle merged into the opacity of the physical world and was lost. Goya, at a greater distance from the source of revolutionary light, was in a better position to describe the grimacing face of what absolutely rejected light.[86]

One mark of the change was the replacement of passive sensation by a more active will as the mark of subjectivity in the philosophies dominating the early nineteenth century. Another was the revived interest in the aesthetics of the sublime rather than the beautiful, inaugurated by Edmund Burke and Immanuel Kant—the sublime being that "which evidences a faculty of mind transcending every standard of sense."[87] Still a third was the self-conscious Romantic thematics of the night as opposed

84. Starobinski, *1789: The Emblems of Reason*, p. 145.

85. When a strong source of light does appear in Goya's paintings, as in the celebrated "The Third of May 1808," it illuminates only the horror on the faces of the Spanish victims, while the French executioners—the agents of a supposedly Enlightened revolution—remain shrouded in darkness.

86. Ibid., p. 196.

87. Kant, *Critique of Aesthetic Judgment*, trans. J. C. Meredith (Oxford, 1911), p. 98. In the case of Burke, the sublime was specifically associated with words and beauty with images. See the discussion in W. J. T. Mitchell, *Iconology: Image, Text, Ideology* (Chicago, 1987), chap. 5.

to the day, Novalis's *Hymns to the Night* being only one of many familiar examples.[88] Indeed, once the Romantics jettisoned Locke's epistemology and the metaphor of the mind as the mirror of nature, once their initial enthusiasm for the revolutionary "dawn" had waned, they could speak, as William Wordsworth did in *The Prelude*, of "the bodily eye, in every stage of life the most despotic of the senses."[89]

But if the bodily eye of observation and induction no longer seemed worth praising, as it had during the Enlightenment, the neo-Platonic revival meant that the "third eye" of inspired revelation could still arouse enthusiasm. If the Romantics abandoned the mirror, they did so—to borrow the metaphor M. H. Abrams appropriated from William Butler Yeats—in order to light the lamp of inner inspiration.[90] Following Plotinus, they saw creation as emanation on the model of rays of light sent out from the sun; the mind was less a receptor of illumination than its expressive projector. A different way to conceptualize their quest is suggested by Geoffrey Hartman's phrase, "unmediated vision," a "pure representation, a vision unconditioned by the particularity of experience."[91]

88. A useful selection of German Romantic paeans to the night can be found in Hermann Glaser, ed., *The German Mind of the 19th Century: A Literary and Historical Anthology* (New York, 1981).

89. Wordsworth, *The Prelude*, ed., E. de Selincourt and Helen Darbishire, 2d ed. (Oxford, 1959), bk. 2, p. 127. The political metaphor of despotism, which Coleridge also used in describing the eye's domination in mechanical philosophy, was not accidental, as Wordsworth links his own subordination to it with his misguided support for the French Revolution.

90. M. H. Abrams, *The Mirror and the Lamp: Romantic Theory and the Critical Tradition* (Oxford, 1953). See also Jonathan Culler, *The Pursuit of Signs: Semiotics, Literature, Deconstruction* (Ithaca, 1981), chap. 8, for a further consideration of these metaphors. He concludes that although there is a difference between the mirror and the lamp, "both give us a system based on visibility, presence and representation, where the mind or author casts light upon that which he perceives and represents. . . . The economy of mimesis presupposes light; the lamp fits into that economy" (p. 163). It should be noted, however, that the image of the lamp was more English than French. According to Marguerite Iknayan, the French Romantics used the prism or the concave mirror rather than the lamp to symbolize expressivity. See *The Concave Mirror: From Imitation to Expression in French Esthetic Theory 1800–1830* (Saratoga, Calif., 1983), p. 151.

In British Romanticism, the metaphorics of inspired vision were especially evident. William Blake disdained "single vision and Newton's sleep" in the name of "four-fold vision," while Thomas Carlyle called for a new "spiritual optics,"[92] which would replenish the tired sight of mundane existence. The same visionary impulse can be discerned in the incandescent, luminous canvases of Joseph Mallord William Turner who, as John Ruskin noted, restored mystery to the visual arts.[93] Not surprisingly, his miraculous explorations of light have often invited comparison with the neo-Platonism of Percy Bysshe Shelley.[94]

German Romanticism, for all its nocturnal preoccupations and fascination with the musicalization of poetry, was not without a similar visual moment.[95] Philippe Lacoue-Labarthe and Jean-Luc Nancy have pointed to what they call "eidaesthetics" in the theory of the Jena Romantics, the yearning for a plastic representation of the Idea.[96] Georg Wilhelm Friedrich Hegel's defense of "imageless truth,"[97] his recognition that philo-

91. Geoffrey H. Hartman, *The Unmediated Vision: An Interpretation of Wordsworth, Hopkins, Rilke and Valéry* (New Haven, 1954), p.155.

92. Blake's reference to Newton comes in his poem "Of Happiness Stretched across the Hills" of November 22, 1802. For an analysis of the Romantic critique of Newton's optics, in particular his scientific reduction of the rainbow, see Abrams, *The Mirror and the Lamp*, pp. 303f. Carlyle's phrase is the title of an essay included in James Anthony Froude, ed., *Thomas Carlyle 1795–1835*, 2 vols. (New York, 1882), vol. 2, pp. 7–12. For a discussion, see Abrams, *Natural Supernaturalism*, pp. 356ff. The continuing power of visual images in Victorian literature and philosophy is treated in W. David Shaw, "The Optical Metaphor: Victorian Poetics and the Theory of Knowledge," *Victorian Studies*, 23, 3 (Spring, 1980), pp. 293–324.

93. John Ruskin, *Modern Painters*, ed. A. J. Finberg (London, 1927), pp. 236ff.

94. See, for example, Hugh Honour, *Romanticism* (New York, 1979), p. 100, and Wylie Sypher, *Rococo to Cubism in Art and Literature* (New York, 1963), p. 120.

95. For a discussion, see Brown, *The Shape of German Romanticism*, which deals with the spatial figures, especially the circle and the ellipse, in the poetry of the movement.

96. Philippe Lacoue-Labarthe and Jean-Luc Nancy, *The Literary Absolute: The Theory of Literature in German Romanticism*, trans. Philip Bernard and Cheryl Lester (Albany, N.Y., 1978), p. 53.

97. See Michael Rosen, *Hegel's Dialectic and Its Criticism*, chap. 4. Hegel, to be sure, did not contend that vision per se was inherently despotic. See the discussion in

sophical reflection need not be based on its visual counterpart, was in part a critique of this Romantic hope. And although there was no German Turner, the visionary power of Caspar David Friedrich's haunting land-scapes must also be acknowledged.[98]

Although less attention has been paid to the French Romantics' visual preoccupations, Rousseau's dialectic of transparency and opacity has been noted again in Victor Hugo, as has a fascination with the metaphorics of blindness.[99] So too the opposition between the fraudulent superficiality of the urban theater and the authentic transparency of the rural festival reappears in Gérard de Nerval's *Slyvie*.[100] And it is surely significant that Charles Baudelaire could find no higher praise for Honoré de Balzac than to call him a "passionate visionary," and Arthur Rimbaud still entitled his famous letters of 1871 to Paul Demeny "lettres du voyant."[101] Here too the waning of Enlightenment sensationalism did not mean a wholesale repudiation of ocular metaphors. In fact, to mention Balzac is to recall the stubborn persistence of a certain faith in the power of observation in "the literature of images"[102] that became known as realism.

Stephen Houlgate, "Vision, Reflection and Openness: The 'Hegemony of Vision' from a Hegelian Point of View," in *Modernity and the Hegemony of Vision*, ed. David Michael Levin (Berkeley, 1993). The issue of the visual in German Idealism as a whole is beyond our scope, but its exploration would doubtless contribute to an understanding of the roots of the twentieth-century interrogation of ocularcentrism.

98. See Honour, *Romanticism*, pp. 75–82.

99. Geoffrey Hartman, "Reflections on Romanticism in France," in *Romanticism: Vistas, Instances, Continuities*, ed. David Thorburn and Geoffrey Hartman (Ithaca, 1973), p. 50; Paulson, *Enlightenment, Romanticism, and the Blind in France*, chap. 6. For a discussion of the visual dimensions of French Romanticism, see Iknayan, *The Concave Mirror*. She points out that Saint-Martin and the Illuminists were far more interested in poetry and music than the visual arts (p. 89).

100. Gérard de Nerval, *Oeuvres complètes* (Paris, 1956), vol. 1, p. 268.

101. Baudelaire, *L'art romantique* (Paris, 1950), p. 169. Rimbaud, *Oeuvres complètes*, Rolland de Renéville and Jules Moquet, eds. (Paris, 1963), pp. 272–273.

102. Balzac used this phrase to describe his own *oeuvre*. Cited in Alan Spiegel, *Fiction and the Camera Eye: Visual Consciousness in Film and the Modern Novel* (Charlottes-ville, Va., 1976), p. 5. For a discussion of the importance of observation in realism, see Martin Turnell, *The Art of French Fiction* (London, 1959), chap. 1. Rosalind

Starobinski speaks of Stendhal's voyeuristic impulse to look, as it were, through a keyhole at his characters, a predilection that seems to have had its actual correlate in the intensified scopophilic activity recorded in houses of prostitution during this period.[103] No less telling was the novelist's frequent recourse to the metaphor of the mirror held up to the world, which he used to characterize his craft.[104] Later novelists were even more keenly concerned, as one critic has put it, "to place the reader in front of a spectacle."[105] Perhaps the most visually acute of their number was Gustave Flaubert, whose dispassionate, pitiless gaze has often been compared to that of a photographer or even a filmmaker, with his montage of successive perspectives.[106] The Flaubert who proudly confessed, "I

Krauss, however, argues that Balzac's faith in observation, strengthened by his interest in Lavater's physiognomical studies, was marked as well by a spiritualist fascination derived in part from Swedenborg's mysticism of light. See her "Tracing Nadar," *October*, 5 (Summer, 1978), pp. 38f. She sees a similar mixture present in the early reception of photography.

103. Starobinski, *L'oeil vivant*, p. 227. For an account of the *tableaux vivant* staged for hidden spectators in Parisian whorehouses, see Laure Adler, *La vie quotidienne dans les maisons closes, 1830–1930* (Paris, 1990), p. 130. According to Jann Matlock ("Censoring the Realist Gaze," *Gender and Realism*, ed. Margaret Cohen and Christopher Prendergast [Minneapolis, forthcoming]), realism's apparent affinity with the tabooed unveiling of the female body helps explain much of the resistance it met from critics in the 1830s, 1840s, and 1850s. Not only were unveiled women as objects of the salacious gaze a source of anxiety, so too were women as gazers, a threatening role evident in a number of representations of them looking voyeuristically through telescopes or lorgnettes. In short, even at the height of ocularcentric culture, one can find evidence of unease over its implications.

104. Stendhal used the metaphor in his prefaces to *Armance*, *Lucien Leuwen*, and *The Red and the Black*, where he credits it to Saint-Réal. That he may have used it with some irony, however, is conjectured by Raymond Tallis, who calls into question the literal reading of the ocular metaphors used by realists. See his *Not Saussure: A Critique of Post-Saussurean Literary Theory* (London, 1988), p. 101.

105. Turnell, *The Art of French Fiction*, p. 24.

106. Spiegel, *Fiction and the Camera Eye*, chap. 2. Flaubert had none of the superstitious fear of the camera shown by Balzac, who thought it would strip the subject of his layers of ghostlike skin. Nadar ridiculed Balzac for this belief in his *Quand j'étais photographe* (Paris, 1900). See the excerpt translated by Thomas Repensek as "My

derive almost voluptuous sensations from the mere act of seeing,"[107] was thus vulnerable to the charge of later critics like Sartre that he achieved a contrived transcendence through a *"principe de survol."*[108] Although Flaubert's linguistic innovations—such as his celebrated use of the free indirect style and his merciless exploration of the literary underpinnings of the mimetic effect—make it impossible to accept uncritically his famous claim, "I am an eye,"[109] at least in part, his novels do reflect the heightened visual sensibility of his age.

By the time of the Goncourt brothers and Émile Zola, it had become a commonplace to remark on novelists' "photographic" descriptions of the observed world.[110] The naturalists' fetishistic obsession with "scopic detailism," often of the woman's body, has continued to preoccupy critics

---

Life as a Photographer," *October*, 5 (Summer, 1978), p. 9. Nadar wryly notes that he believed Balzac was sincere, although he "had only to gain from his loss, his ample proportions allowing him to squander his layers without a thought."

107. Flaubert to Alfred Poitteven (1845) in *The Selected Letters of Gustave Flaubert*, ed. Francis Steegmuller (New York, 1957), p. 35; quoted in Spiegel, p. 5. The voluptuous element in Flaubert's visual experience was also expressed in the visionary richness of his imagination. The recurring figure of Saint Anthony in his work bears witness to the temptations of an almost hallucinatory visual impulse. Flaubert's self-imposed discipline of seeing with dispassionate coldness may have been a compensation for, or what Freud would call a "denegation" of, his visionary side.

108. Sartre, *L'Idiot de la famille*, 3 vols. (Paris, 1971–1972), cited in Dominick LaCapra, *"Madame Bovary" on Trial* (Ithaca, 1982), p. 99. Pierre Bourdieu, however, has argued that Flaubert's novels show a much less totalized vision than Sartre suggests. "Like Manet somewhat later," he writes, "Flaubert abandoned the unifying perspective, taken from a fixed, central point of view, which he replaced with what could be called, following Erwin Panofsky, an 'aggregated space,' if we take this to mean a space made of juxtaposed pieces without a preferred point of view." "Flaubert's Point of View," *Critical Inquiry*, 14 (Spring, 1988), p. 652.

109. Cited in César Graña, *Modernity and Its Discontents: French Society and the French Man of Letters in the Nineteenth Century* (New York, 1964), p. 131. For a probing analysis of the nonocular, linguistic basis of mimesis in realist fiction, which foregrounds Flaubert's exposure of its aporias, see Christopher Prendergast, *The Order of Mimesis: Balzac, Stendhal, Nerval, Flaubert* (Cambridge, 1986). He speculates that the recourse to ocular metaphors may have functioned as a way to fend off censorship, rather than as an authentic self-understanding of the novelist's craft (p. 60).

of their work to this day.[111] Wylie Sypher may thus well have been correct when he asserted that "the nineteenth century was among the most visual periods of Western culture, the most given to ideals of precise observation—a spectator-view shared by novelists, painters, scientists and, to an extent, by poets, who became 'visionary', although poetic vision did not always mean observation."[112]

⊙

The precise nature of visual experience and the implications drawn from it cannot be reduced, it bears repeating, to a simple formula. By the nineteenth century, what many have called the hegemonic scopic regime of the modern era, Cartesian perspectivalism, was beginning to waver as never before. The comparison between Flaubert's gaze and that of the camera mentioned above helps clarify one salient reason: the extraordinary changes in our capacity to see wrought by technology. Not only were these innovations often initiated in France, but their cultural meaning was nowhere as widely debated. If the remarkable impact of rapid urbanization on the visual experience of everyday life is also acknowledged, the sources of the intensified French interrogation of sight become clearer.

110. The Goncourts' visual preoccupations were noted by Paul Bourget in *Nouveaux essais de psychologie contemporaine* (Paris, 1883), pp. 137–198. See the discussion in Debora L. Silverman, *Art Nouveau in Fin-de-siècle France: Politics, Psychology, and Style* (Berkeley, 1989), pp. 33f. Zola himself was an enthusiastic devotee of the camera. See François Émile-Zola and Massin, *Zola Photographer*, trans. Liliane Emery Tuck (New York, 1988), and Jean Adhémar, "Émile Zola, Photographer," in *One Hundred Years of Photographic History: Essays in Honor of Beaumont Newhall*, ed. Van Deren Coke (Albuquerque, 1975). Paul Valéry later claimed that photography had a beneficial effect on realistic and naturalistic literature; see his 1939 essay, "The Centenary of Photography," in *Classic Essays on Photography*, ed. Trachtenberg, p. 193.

111. See, for example, Emily Apter, *Feminizing the Fetish: Psychoanalysis and Narrative Obsession in Turn-of-the-Century France* (Ithaca, 1991), p. 33. She follows the fascination with detail into the postnaturalist, decadent literature of *fin-de-siècle* writers like Joris-Karl Huysmans and Octave Mirbeau.

112. Wylie Sypher, *Literature and Technology: The Alien Vision* (New York, 1971), p. 74.

Although it is difficult to gauge the precise effects of these complex transformations, no account of the French discourse on vision in the twentieth century can ignore them.

To begin with changes in the urban landscape first, we have to acknowledge the central importance of Paris, the "capital of the nineteenth century," in Walter Benjamin's celebrated phrase,[113] in focusing the attention of French thinkers on visual issues. As a spectacle of incomparable variety and stimulation, Paris was and remains today the inevitable backdrop for many of the speculations about sight we will encounter in this narrative.

Unlike the court of Versailles, the Paris of the ancien régime presented a visual experience that defied easy intelligibility. Already in 1783, Louis-Sébastien Mercier was complaining about "the perpetual smoke rising from countless chimneys. . . . You can see a haze forming above the mass of houses and the city's transpiration, as it were, becomes perceptible."[114] It was not by chance that the scenes of tranquil transparency dreamed by Rousseau were set far away from the urban milieu, where Wolmar told Julie, "I see only phantoms that strike my eye, but disappear as soon as I try to grasp them."[115] Although there was no shortage of plans to construct "a geometrical city"[116] by architects like Étienne-Louis Boullée, Charles Nicholas Ledoux, and Pierre-Jules Delépine, not much was actually accomplished during the eighteenth century; even the Revolution constructed very little, making its mark instead by converting monuments like the church of St. Geneviève into the Pantheon. Utopian projects like that of Dondey-Dupré to build a lighting tower to illuminate all of Paris remained unrealized.[117]

113. Walter Benjamin, *Charles Baudelaire: A Lyric Poet in the Era of High Capitalism*, trans. Harry Zohn and Quintin Hoare (London, 1973), p. 155.

114. Mercier, *Tableaux de Paris* (Paris, 1783), cited in Louis Chevalier, *Laboring Classes and Dangerous Classes: In Paris During the First Half of the Nineteenth Century*, trans. Frank Jellinek (Princeton, 1973), p. 147.

115. Rousseau, *La nouvelle Héloise*, part 2, letter 17, cited in Marshall Berman, *All That Is Solid Melts into Air: The Experience of Modernity* (New York, 1982), p. 18.

116. Starobinski, *1789: The Emblems of Reason*, pp. 67f.

117. Schivelbusch, *Disenchanted Night*, p. 121.

Paris was still in many ways a medieval city well into the nineteenth century, lacking the rationalized grid of streets or open vistas of its modern counterpart. Although the glass-covered commercial arcades built during the Bourgeois Monarchy of Louis Philippe allowed the *flâneur* his leisurely stroll,[118] most street life was still unconducive to visual pleasure. In 1849, the writer Charles Henri Lecouturier could echo Mercier's eighteenth-century lament:

> If you contemplate Paris from the summit of Montmartre, the congestion of houses piled up at every point of a vast horizon, what do you observe? Above, a sky that is always overcast, even on the finest day. Clouds of smoke, like a floating black curtain, hide it from view. . . . One is reluctant to venture into this vast maze, in which a million beings jostle one another, where the air, vitiated by unhealthy effluvia, rising in a poisonous cloud, almost obscures the sun.[119]

Up closer, the visual experience of Paris seems to have been no less overwhelming in its phantasmagoric confusion.[120] Balzac's novels may have been based on the hope that the social world of the Restoration

118. The specifically male identity of the *flâneur* has been remarked by Janet Wolff in "The Invisible *Flâneuse*: Women and the Literature of Modernity," *Theory, Culture and Society*, 2, 3 (1985), pp. 37–46. In the public realm, respectable women were denied the right—or spared the imperative—to gaze covetously until the invention of the department store in the 1850s.

119. Cited in Chevalier, p. 374. Corbin adds that "the smoke became a preoccupation this time no longer because of its odor, but because, blackening and opaque, it attacked the lungs, blackened facades, obscured the atmosphere, while a concern for luminosity developed." *Le miasme et la jonquille*, p. 157.

120. The word *phantasmagoria*, it should be noted, was used as the name of one of the many machines of illusion concocted by the nineteenth century. It worked by projecting slides from behind a translucent screen to viewers on the other side. It was developed into a critical category by Walter Benjamin and Theodor W. Adorno in the twentieth century. For a recent discussion, see Terry Castle, "Phantasmagoria: Spectral Technology and the Metaphorics of Modern Reverie," *Critical Inquiry*, 15, 1 (Autumn, 1988), pp. 26–61.

could be made as transparently legible as that of the *ancien régime*, but the results often belied the expectation.[121] What one recent commentator has called the "environmentalist eye"[122] anxiously visualized the city as a dangerous, diseased and dirty place. Its hopes for clarity and intelligibility were projected onto a pictorially constructed version of sylvan nature outside the city's walls, promulgated by painters like those of the Barbizon School. The forest of Fontainebleau became a carefully cultivated refuge of *natura naturans* in which the bewildered city-dweller's eye could seek welcome relief.

The new urban crowd, whose characteristics were impressionistically traced by writers like E. T. A. Hoffmann and Edgar Allan Poe in the nineteenth century and more penetratingly analyzed by Georg Simmel and Benjamin in the twentieth, was, in fact, subject to sensory overload of a radically new kind. As Simmel put it in his classic study of "The Metropolis and Mental Life":

> The psychological basis of the metropolitan type of individual consists in the *intensification of nervous stimulation*, which results from the swift and uninterrupted change of outer and inner stimuli. . . . Lasting impressions, impressions which differ only slightly from one another, impressions which take a regular and habitual course and show regular and habitual contrasts—all these use up, so to speak, less consciousness than does the rapid crowding of changing images, the sharp discontinuity in the grasp of a single glance, and the unexpected onrushing impressions. These are the psychological conditions which the metropolis creates.[123]

Despite the attempts of slow-moving *flâneurs* to buck the increasingly frantic pace of the urban crowd, its turbulence and shocks to the senses

121. For an account of Balzac's novels that emphasizes the gap between his intentions and the results, see Prendergast, *The Order of Mimesis*, chap. 3. He concludes that Balzac's confidence in his ability to read visible signs of meaning in clothes, physiognomies and the like ultimately falters, which is "a sign of the developing opaqueness of the modern city" (p. 95).

seem to have provoked the protective reaction about which both Simmel and Benjamin movingly wrote.

Still more disruption ensued in the Second Empire, when the modernization of Paris began in earnest. In 1859, six years after becoming the Prefect of the Seine, Baron Georges-Eugène Haussmann began his massive rebuilding or, as more cynical contemporaries called it, "strategic beautification" of the capital.[124] Benjamin describes Haussmann's urban ideal as "one of views in perspective down long street-vistas. It corresponded to the tendency, which was noticeable again and again during the nineteenth century, to ennoble technical exigencies with artistic aims."[125] The uncompromising rectilinearity of the new boulevards, a result of Haussmann's military intentions, was based on the example of the railroad line, which imposed itself on the natural landscape. One of its ancillary goals was to render Paris less obscure, less opaque. As such, it was the physical correlate of the mid-century *enquêtes* about workers' conditions, whose self-proclaimed reliance on visual observation has been noted by historians.[126] Here, we might say, the Cartesian perspectivalist scopic regime seemed to find its perfect urban form—a judgment sym-

122. Nicholas Green, *The Spectacle of Nature: Landscape and Bourgeois Culture in Nineteenth-Century France* (Manchester, 1990), p. 66. He contrasts the "environmentalist eye" with the "consuming gaze," which derived pleasure from the new urban scene.

123. Georg Simmel, *The Sociology of Georg Simmel*, trans. and ed. Kurt H. Wolff (New York, 1950), pp. 409–410. For more on Simmel and the modern city, see David Frisby, *Fragments of Modernity: Theories of Modernity in the Work of Simmel, Kracauer and Benjamin* (Cambridge, Mass., 1986), chap. 2. For a discussion of his views about vision, see Deena and Michael Weinstein, "On the Visual Constitution of Society: The Contributions of Georg Simmel and Jean-Paul Sartre to a Sociology of the Senses," *History of European Ideas*, 5 (1984), pp. 349–362.

124. The best account is still David H. Pickney, *Napoleon III and the Rebuilding of Paris* (Princeton, 1958). See also J. M. and Brian Chapman, *The Life and Times of Baron Haussmann* (London, 1957), and Françoise Choay, *The Modern City: Planning in the Nineteenth Century* (New York, 1969).

125. Benjamin, *Charles Baudelaire*, p. 173.

126. See, for example, Michelle Perrot, *Enquêtes sur la condition ouvrière en France au XIXᵉ siècle* (Paris, 1972), pp. 11, 21, 26, 28.

bolically supported by the fact that only in 1853 was Paris as a whole surveyed and definitively mapped for the first time.

The results, however, were by no means to everyone's taste, and not only because of the dislocation it caused (mostly of workers) and its unorthodox financing. As early as 1865, critics like Victor Fournel were bemoaning the destruction of the Paris they loved.[127] According to Benjamin, "As far as the Parisians were concerned, [Haussmann] alienated their city from them. They no longer felt at home in it. They began to become conscious of the inhuman character of the great city."[128] Louis Chevalier adds,

> In destroying the old district of the Cité so thoroughly as to wipe it off the map of Paris, Haussmann destroyed far more than a tangle of slums and thieves' kitchens. . . . He destroyed the very images evoked and provoked by the district, the images attaching to it in the memory of the people of Paris. These images passed from this collective memory into another sort of memory, the picturesque tradition of the antiquarian, one of the most certain forms of oblivion.[129]

In a work devoted to the spatiotemporal shocks produced by railroad journeys, yet another commentator, Wolfgang Schivelbusch, remarks, "A comparable disorientation of the Parisians of the 1850s and 1860s can be understood as a result of their seeing, with their own eyes, one Paris intersecting and colliding with another in the process of demolition and reconstruction."[130]

What is most striking about the outcome of the Haussmannization of Paris was that, for all the rationality and clarity of the Baron's vision, the result was often to intensify visual uncertainty and confusion, at least in

127. Victor Fournel, *Paris nouveau et Paris futur* (Paris, 1865), pp. 218–229.

128. Benjamin, *Charles Baudelaire*, p. 174.

129. Chevalier, *Laboring Classes and Dangerous Classes*, p. 100.

130. Wolfgang Schivelbusch, *The Railway Journey: The Industrialization of Time and Space in the 19th Century* (Berkeley, 1986), p. 185.

the short run. As the art historian T. J. Clark has noted, the seemingly endless disruption of daily life produced by the massive reconstruction meant that "the city is rendered illegible,"[131] a new circumstance he claims was soon registered in the Impressionist demolition of three-dimensional space. The image of Paris in the mass media of the 1860s, Clark continues,

> was *parade*, phantasmagoria, dream, dumbshow, mirage, masquerade. Traditional ironies at the expense of the metropolis mingled with new metaphors of specifically visual untruth. They were intended to stress the sheer ostentation and flimsiness of the new streets and apartment blocks, and beyond that to indicate the more and more intrusive machinery of illusion built into the city and determining its use.[132]

One result seems to have been a weakening of the defenses of the urban viewer. As Fournel pointed out in 1858, the *flâneur* with his self-possessed observing skills was being replaced by the *badaud*, the mere gaper entirely taken in by what he sees. "The simple *flâneur*," he wrote, "is always in full possession of his individuality, whereas the individuality of the *badaud* disappears. It is absorbed by the outside world . . . which intoxicates him to the point where he forgets himself. Under the influence of the spectacle which presents itself to him, the *badaud* becomes an impersonal creature; he is no longer a human being, he is part of the public, of the crowd."[133]

The transformation of the *flâneur* into the *badaud* was abetted by the new commercial exploitation of the city's rapidly changing landscape. For the Paris that emerged from Haussmann's labors was not merely that of the grand boulevards with their fetishized straight lines, buildings all of the same height, and culminating squares. (Nor was it just that of the first

131. T. J. Clark, *The Painting of Modern Life: Paris in the Art of Manet and his Followers* (Princeton, 1984), p. 47.

132. Ibid., pp. 66–67.

133. Victor Fournel, *Ce qu'on voit dans les rues du Paris* (Paris, 1858), p. 263, cited in Benjamin, *Charles Baudelaire*, p. 69.

modern sewage system, whose beneficial impact on another sense, smell, was soon appreciated.)[134] It was also the Paris of the new department stores (*les grands magazins*) that began to line many of the most fashionable sidewalks in the 1860s.[135] Here the ocularcentric spectacle of desire was removed from the aristocratic court and given its bourgeois equivalent in the massive sheet glass windows displaying a wealth of commodities to be coveted and, if money allowed, consumed. Here the dandies' quest to distinguish themselves by nuances of fashion, visual signifiers of taste and style, became a tantalizing possibility for the masses (especially the new female consumers vividly portrayed in Zola's *Au bonheur des dames*).[136] Here the accelerated panoramic view of the railway journey was replicated as the customer faced a bewildering plethora of possible commodities to buy.[137] The bourgeois interior, filled to the bursting point with what one commentator has called the "visual cacophony"[138] of bric-a-bracomania, showed that many were in fact purchased. But not everyone was able to satisfy the commercially generated lust of their eyes. If in 1827 the bohemian poet Pierre-Jean de Béranger could write "*Voir, c'est avoir,*"[139] by the end of the century it became increasingly apparent that "just looking" was not the same thing as really possessing.[140]

Along with the direct stimulating of ocular desire in the department store itself went the indirect one produced by the explosion of advertising images in newspapers and journals. The lithograph, invented by the Ba-

134. Corbin shows how much of a struggle it actually was to separate the populace from the excrement in whose midst they were used to living. See *Le miasme et la jonquille,* pt. 3, chap. 5.

135. The first were the Bazaar de l'Hôtel de Ville and the Bon Marché. For an account, see Michael B. Miller, *The Bon Marché: Bourgeois Culture and the Department Store, 1869–1920* (Princeton, 1981).

136. Émile Zola, *Au bonheur des dames* (Paris, 1882); the most recent English edition, entitled *The Ladies Paradise* (Berkeley, 1992), has an introduction by Kristin Ross, which analyzes the appeal of the *grands magazins* in the terms of the spectacle theory developed by Henri Lefebvre and Guy Debord.

137. Schivelbusch, *The Railway Journey,* p. 189.

138. Apter, *Feminizing the Fetish,* p. 40.

varian Alois Senefelder in 1797 and brought to France during the Napoleonic invasions, was first used for limited aesthetic purposes by masters like Jean Auguste Dominique Ingres, Eugène Delacroix, and Théodore Géricault. After Delacroix's celebrated illustrations of Goethe's *Faust* in 1828, however, lithographs became immensely popular. Soon they were the mainstay of new journals like Charles Philipon's *Le Charivari* and *La Caricature* and Émile de Girardin's revolutionary *La Presse*, which began in 1836 as the first paper to be supported more by advertising than subscriptions.[141] Popular illustrators like Jean-Ignace-Isidore Grandville and Gérard Constantin Guys, the latter immortalized by Baudelaire as the "painter of modern life,"[142] had an enormous appeal. Even the realist novelists were influenced by their impact.[143] Significantly, the French government, stung by the satirical drawings of Daumier and other caricaturists who drew for Philipon, was moved to start its own illustrated journal, *La Charge*, the moment "at which the state seemed to discover the regulative force of administered culture."[144] Benjamin's "age of mechanical reproduction" had truly begun.

Soon after, the technique for reproducing images was enhanced still

139. Béranger, *Oeuvres complètes* (Paris, 1847), *Chansons,* p. 418. Cited in Dolf Sternberger, *Panorama of the 19th Century,* trans. Joachim Neugroschel (Oxford, 1977), p. 198.

140. For an analysis of the literary impact of this realization, see Rachel Bowlby, *Just Looking: Consumer Culture in Dreiser, Gissing and Zola* (New York, 1985). For an account of the debates spawned by the new commercial culture, see Rosalind H. Williams, *Dream Worlds: Mass Consumption in Late Nineteenth-Century France* (Berkeley, 1982).

141. For an account of the development and spread of lithography, see William M. Ivins, Jr., *Prints and Visual Communication* (Cambridge, 1985), chap. 5.

142. Charles Baudelaire, *The Painter of Modern Life and Other Essays,* trans. Jonathan Mayne (New York, 1965). Baudelaire's reaction to Grandville, it might be noted, was far less positive. See his essay on "Some French Caricaturists," in the same volume, pp. 181–182.

143. See M. Mespoulet, *Images et romans* (Paris, 1939).

144. Richard Terdiman, *Discourse/Counter-Discourse: The Theory and Practice of Symbolic Resistance in Nineteenth-Century France* (Ithaca, 1985), p. 158. Terdiman pro-

further by the development of the daguerreotype in 1839. The new invention became available for artistic and scientific books as well as for mass advertising when black and white photoengraving was perfected in the following decade (color could be added by hand). The result was what Baudelaire, who knew both its lures and its dangers, called "the cult of images."[145] Anonymous *imagiers* flooded the marketplace with what at its worst was a new form of visual pollution, the rise of what would soon be called—the word was coined in Munich in the 1860s, possibly as a corruption of the English "sketch"—kitsch.[146]

From another perspective, the cult of images could be interpreted as the democratization of visual experience, the extending down into the general population of those opportunities hitherto reserved for only the elite.[147] This conclusion is strengthened if we recognize the inclusion of previously scorned "low subjects" from everyday life in the canon of what could be reproduced, an extension that paralleled the literary realists' advances in incorporating similar themes in their novels.[148] Even death was now available as a popular spectacle for the masses, in either the literal

---

vides an acute account of the subversive quality of the journalistic image during the Bourgeois Monarchy.

145. Baudelaire, *Mon coeur mis à nu*, cited in Beatrice Farwell, *The Cult of Images: Baudelaire and the 19th-Century Media Explosion* (Santa Barbara, Calif., 1977), p. 7. Baudelaire claimed that glorifying the cult was "my single, great, original passion."

146. For an account of the concept's origins, see Matei Calinescu, *Faces of Modernity: Avant-Garde, Decadence, Kitsch* (Bloomington, 1977), p. 234.

147. Not all the visual innovations of the century were so quickly disseminated. In *France Fin de Siècle* (Cambridge, Mass., 1986), Eugen Weber notes that "in 1900 few homes had electric light, plate glass was associated primarily with the poshest stores, and large mirrors were reserved for the wealthy" (p. 165).

148. For a discerning analysis of what was and was not included in the expanded repertoire of images, see Raymond Grew, "Images of the Lower Orders in Nineteenth-Century French Art," in *Art and History: Images and Their Meaning*, ed. Robert I. Rotberg and Theodore K. Rabb (Cambridge, 1988). He argues that although many workers were shown in various poses, what was missing was any depiction of the social relations in which they were embedded. In addition, the worker was generally rendered as an artisan rather than as a laborer in a factory.

form provided by the Paris morgue with its glass display windows, or in wax simulacra at the Musée Grevin, founded in 1882.[149]

Other nineteenth-century innovations can be construed as having a comparable leveling effect. The progressive perfection of artificial illumination allowed virtually everyone to transcend the natural rhythms of light and dark.[150] After 1805, use of gas lamps in cities like Paris grew in frequency. In 1869 the introduction of brighter and safer kerosene furthered their efficiency, and finally, in the 1890s, Thomas Edison's invention of electrical lighting seemed to turn the night into day.[151] Not only did this mean the growing rationalization of time, as working hours could be regularized, but it also meant the opening up of new entertainment possibilities after work was done. Advances in theatrical lighting by Henri Duboscq at the Paris Opera were matched by the outdoor illumination of café concerts. Incandescent quicklime was borrowed from lighthouses,

149. For an account of these developments, see Vanessa Schwartz, "Popular Realism, Voyeurism and the Origins of Mass Culture in Fin-de-siècle Paris," Ph.D. diss., University of California, Berkeley (forthcoming). There had been an anatomical wax museum earlier in the century, the Musée Dupuytren, which was used by medical students but was not open to the general public.

150. See William T. O'Dea, *The Social History of Lighting* (London, 1958); and Schivelbusch, *Disenchanted Night*.

151. This metaphor, as Schivelbusch shows, was used for virtually all of the public lighting improvements from the seventeenth century on. Attempts to build immense lighting towers to illuminate an entire city, such as Sébillot's so-called Sun Tower proposed in the 1880s, were unsuccessful. See Schivelbusch, pp. 128–134.

The growing efficacy of artificial light had, however, an important consequence, which Hans Blumenberg has noted. Because of its power, it was no longer possible to contemplate the stars from an urban location. The city, he writes, "constitutes a secession from one of the most human possibilities: that of disinterested curiosity and pleasure in looking, for which the starry heavens had offered an unsurpassable remoteness that was an everyday phenomenon" ("Anachronism as a Need Founded in the Life-World: Realities and Simulation," *Annals of Scholarship*, 4, 4 [1987], p. 14). The planetarium was invented as a kind of compensation, but it served more as a "mausoleum of the starry heavens as the ideal of pure intuition" (p. 16). It also contributed, according to Blumenberg, to the confusion of real and simulacrum that is so much a part of contemporary visual experience, because it augmented rather than duplicated possible human sight.

where it had been invented in 1796 by the Englishman Thomas Drummond, to produce theatrical limelight in the 1850s. Soon after, the electrical age was inaugurated as the Eiffel Tower was topped by an electric beacon with a range of almost 120 miles in 1889, visible as far away as Orléans and Chartres.[152]

To mention the Eiffel Tower is to evoke still another unprecedented visual experience of nineteenth-century France: the great international expositions that took place in 1855, 1867, 1889, and 1900.[153] In addition to their providing yet another venue for the arousal and manipulation of ocular desire through the display of tantalizing commodities and luxurious exotica, they were also the locus of architectural experiments, in particular the great glass and steel enclosures first perfected by Joseph Paxton in 1851 as the Crystal Palace in London. Blinding in their admission of unprecedented amounts of evanescent light, they have been compared with everything from a Turner painting to the disorientation of railway journeys.[154] Not surprisingly, they have even been adduced, along with many other possible causes, as a source of the Impressionist challenge to Cartesian perspectivalism.[155]

Before evaluating the significance of that epochal event in the history of painting, it will be necessary to backtrack a bit and pause with the more general impact of the most extraordinary technical innovation in vision during the nineteenth century, indeed perhaps in all human history: the invention of the camera. There can be no doubt that the implications of photography for the twentieth-century French interrogation of sight were profound. An endless literature has been devoted to documenting its development and history, especially in France,[156] but only a few points can be pursued here.

---

152. See Joseph Harriss, *The Tallest Tower: Eiffel and the Belle Epoque* (Boston, 1975), p. 100.

153. See Raymond Isay, *Panorama des expositions universelles*, 3d ed. (Paris, 1937), and Philippe Hamon, *Expositions: Littérature et architecture au XIXe siècle* (Paris, 1989). The Eiffel Tower was built for the 1889 exposition.

154. For the first comparison, see Berman, *All That Is Solid Melts into Air*, p. 237; for the latter, see Schivelbusch, *The Railway Journey*, p. 47.

When the inventions of Joseph-Nicéphore and Isadore Nièpce, Louis-Jacques-Mandé Daguerre, and William Henry Fox Talbot—who all more or less simultaneously perfected methods to record images permanently in the 1830s[157]—became publicly known, the reaction in France as elsewhere was swift and vigorous. The *Gazette de France* reported on January 6, 1839, "This discovery partakes of the prodigious. It upsets all scientific theories on light and optics, and it will revolutionize the art of drawing."[158] Under the prodding of the distinguished astronomer and Republican member of the Chamber of Deputies, François Arago, the French government granted pensions to Daguerre and Isadore Niépce (his father had died in 1833) in exchange for their relinquishing claims to private patents. The techniques of photography, officially presented at a meeting of the Academy of Sciences on August 19, 1839, were thus immediately in the public domain.

The general reaction to the new optical miracle was overwhelmingly positive, producing in the 1840s what was called "Daguerreotypemania."[159] But among intellectuals, three issues soon emerged that continue to spark debate even today. The first concerned the relation between photographs and optical truth or illusion. The second introduced the

155. Schivelbusch, p. 49.

156. See, for example, Claude Nori, *French Photography: From Its Origins to the Present*, trans. Lydia Davis (New York, 1979); Gisèle Freund, *Photography and Society*, trans. Richard Dunn, Yong-Hee Last, Megan Marshall, and Andrea Perera (Boston, 1980); Beaumont Newhall, *The History of Photography: From 1839 to the Present Day* (New York, 1964); *Regards sur la photographie en France au XIXe siècle: 180 chefs-d'oeuvre de la Bibliothèque nationale* (Paris, 1980).

157. The elder Niépce is usually credited with the first fixation of an image on a pewter plate turned sensitive to light by bitumen, which he accomplished in 1826, but it was not until Daguerre and the younger Niépce perfected it in the late 1830s that it was ready to be revealed. Talbot's great contribution was his invention of the negative, which allowed multiple prints to come from the same picture.

158. "The Fine Arts: A New Discovery," reprinted in *Photography: Essays and Images*, ed. Beaumont Newhall (New York, 1980), p. 17.

159. See the 1840 lithograph with this title by T. H. Maurisset, reprinted in Freund, *Photography and Society*, p. 27.

vexed question, Is photography an art? It had as its corollary, what is the impact of photography on painting and vice versa? And the third addressed the impact on society of the new invention. In grappling with these issues, nineteenth-century thinkers helped prepare the way for the twentieth-century interrogation of vision in its wider senses.

Without a doubt the commonplace view of photography ever since its inception during the heyday of the Realist reaction to Romanticism is that it records a moment of reality as it actually appeared.[160] Daguerre's camera was immediately called a "mirror" of the world, a metaphor frequently repeated to this day.[161] Many of the first photographers in France, such as Hippolyte Bayard, Victor Regnault, and Charles Nègre, operated with a simple faith in the straightforward reproduction of the world; this earned them the sobriquet "primitive," even if their works could be appreciated by later generations in other ways.[162]

So powerful has the assumption of photography's fidelity to the truth of visual experience been that no less an observer than the great film critic André Bazin could claim that "for the first time an image of the world is formed automatically, without the creative intervention of man. . . . Photography affects us like a phenomenon in nature."[163] And even Roland Barthes could argue in his early essay on "The Photographic Message" that "certainly the image is not the reality but at least it is its perfect *analogon* and it is exactly this analogical perfection which, to common sense, defines the photograph. Thus can be seen the special status of the photographic image: *it is a message without a code.*"[164]

160. For a discussion of the Realist context of the initial reception of the new technology, see Victor Burgin, "Introduction" to Victor Burgin, ed., *Thinking Photography* (London, 1982), p. 10.

161. See Richard Rudisill, *Mirror Image* (Albuquerque, 1971).

162. See the catalogue *French Primitive Photography*, intro. Minor White, commentaries by André Jammes and Robert Sobieszek (New York, 1969).

163. André Bazin, "The Ontology of the Photographic Image," in *What Is Cinema?*, ed. and trans. Hugh Gray, foreword by Jean Renoir (Berkeley, 1967), p. 13. Bazin, of course, extended his realist aesthetic to the cinema as well.

The context in which photography earned this reputation is aptly summarized by Noël Burch.

> The 19th century witnessed a series of stages in the thrusting progress of a vast aspiration which emerges as the quintessence of the bourgeois ideology of representation. From Daguerre's Diorama to Edison's first Kinetophonograph, each state of the pre-history of the cinema was intended by its initiators—and seen by its publicists—as representatives of their class, as another step taken toward the "re-creation" of reality, toward a "perfect illusion" of the perceptual world.[165]

In this progress, each new improvement in the technology, like the stereoscope or color film, was seen as making up a deficiency in the previous ability to record what was "really" there.

Because of its rendering everlasting of the image cast by a camera obscura, it has often seemed, moreover, as if photography validated the perspectivalist scopic regime that was generally identified with vision itself after the Quattrocento.[166] The camera eye, as monocular as that of the peephole, produced a frozen, disincarnated gaze on a scene completely external to itself (an effect especially compelling before advances in film

164. Roland Barthes, *Image—Music—Text*, trans. Stephen Heath (New York, 1977), p. 17.

165. Noël Burch, "Charles Baudelaire versus Doctor Frankenstein," *Afterimage*, 8/9 (Spring, 1981), p. 5. In *The World Viewed: Reflections on the Ontology of Film* (Cambridge, Mass., 1979), Stanley Cavell adds that "so far as photography satisfied a wish, it satisfied a wish not confined to painters, but the human wish, intensifying in the West since the Reformation, to escape subjectivity and metaphysical isolation—a wish for the power to reach this world, having for so long tried, at last hopelessly, to manifest fidelity to another" (p. 21).

166. For examples of this assumption, see Ivins, *Prints and Visual Communication*, p. 138; Victor Burgin, "Looking at Photographs," in Burgin, *Thinking Photography*, p. 146; and Steve Neale, *Cinema and Technology: Image, Sound, Colour* (London, 1985), p. 20.

speed ended interminable sittings). As the "pencil of nature," to use Fox Talbot's famous phrase, the camera provided what Ivins would call "pictorial statements without syntax," direct images of the true surface *and* three-dimensional depth of the perceived world.[167] Such at least was the predominant belief when the invention first became known, some observers worrying that the little faces in the pictures were so real they could look back at them.[168] Even Baudelaire, whose keen hostility to the artistic pretensions of photography will be examined shortly, could acknowledge its alleged fidelity to nature.[169]

But if photography and its improvements, like the three-dimensional stereoscope which came into prominence in the 1860s, could be praised for providing ever more faithful reproductions of the seen world, a subcurrent of skepticism also began to emerge. The most prominent inventor of the camera had, after all, been known as a master of illusion. As Aaron Scharf notes,

> Well before his discovery Louis-Jacques-Mandé Daguerre had acquired a considerable reputation as a painter and inventor of illusionist effects in panoramas and, from 1816, as a designer of stage setting for the Paris opera. Almost at the same time as he invented the diorama, the most popular of all early nineteenth-century *trompe l'oeil* entertainments, Daguerre began to experiment with the photographic process.[170]

Significantly, his famous dioramas were called "miracle rooms"[171] because of their displays of illusionistic virtuosity. Because of the physical

167. Fox Talbot, *The Pencil of Nature* (London, 1844); Ivins, *Prints and Visual Communication,* chap. 6. The syntax to which Ivins refers is the cross-hatching or dots used to render light and dark in traditional prints. For a similar analysis, which stresses the realism of screen half-tone prints of photographs in the mass media in the 1890s, see Estelle Jussim, *Visual Communication and the Graphic Arts: Photographic Technologies in the Nineteenth Century* (New York, 1974), p. 288.

168. See the comment of the photographer Dauthendey, cited in Walter Benjamin, "A Short History of Photography," *Screen* (Spring, 1972), p. 8.

imprinting of light waves on the plate of the camera, that materially causative link between object and visual sign which modern linguists have
call "indexicality,"[172] it might seem as if now the *oeil* was not *trompé* in
Daguerre's new invention. But doubts nonetheless soon arose.

In the mid-1840s, photographers discovered that they could retouch
their photos or even combine two to make a composite, techniques that
were revealed to the astonished French public at the 1855 Universal Exposition by a Munich photographer named Hampfstängl.[173] Soon it became the norm in portraits to help nature rather than merely record it.
Some commentators used the ability to combine images to defend the
artistic potential of the new medium.[174] But it was also clear that the
doctoring of "true" resemblances of the surface of the world was an abiding possibility. Thus, in the so-called spirit photography foisted on a

169. See his letter to his mother of 1865, where he encourages her to go to a studio,
even if he worries that the photographer will catch all of her wrinkles and faults.
Baudelaire, *Correspondance* (Paris, 1973), vol. 2, p. 554.

170. Aaron Scharf, *Art and Photography* (London, 1983), p. 24.

171. Sternberger, *Panorama of the 19th Century*, p. 9. For an analysis of panoramas
and dioramas as anticipations of the panopticon and the society of the spectacle, see
Éric de Kuyper and Émile Poppe, "Voir et regarder," *Communications*, 34 (1981),
pp. 85–96.

172. The term "index" was introduced by C. S. Peirce to denote signs with a direct or
"motivated" link to a referent; he used the term "symbol" to denote those that were
entirely conventional and artificial, and "icon" to mean those that resembled their
referent. See his "Logic as Semiotic: The Theory of Signs," in *The Philosophy of Pierce:
Selected Writings*, J. Buckler, ed. (London, 1940), pp. 98–119. Historians of photography have often pointed to its indexical character, for example Rosalind Krauss in
"Tracing Nadar," p. 34, where she argues that Nadar was aware of its importance.
Krauss has developed the idea of indexicality to describe certain kinds of modernist
art as well. See her "Notes on the Index, Parts I and II," in *The Originality of the
Avant-Garde and Other Modernist Myths* (Cambridge, Mass., 1985). Peirce himself
saw photography as combining indexical with iconic features. See the discussion in
Mitchell, *Iconology*, pp. 56–63.

173. Freund, *Photography and Society*, p. 64.

174. See the discussion in James Borcoman, "Notes on the Early Use of Combination
Printing," in Van Deren Coke, ed., *One Hundred Years of Photographic History: Essays
in Honor of Beaumont Newhall* (Albuquerque, 1975).

gullible public by an American charlatan, W. H. Mumler, in the 1860s, ghostly presences were registered by double exposures. Only when amateur photographers with their mass-produced Kodaks in the 1880s achieved the same results by forgetting to advance their film was the hoax decisively undone. Yet as late as the Dreyfus Affair, it was still necessary to warn the naive viewer against concocted images, as shown by the front-page article devoted to "The Lies of Photography" in *Le Siècle* in 1899.[175]

Of still greater importance was the realization that even unretouched photos could be understood to provide something less than perfect verisimilitude, either of objects or of the human perception of them. As early as 1853, Francis Wey was commenting on the limitations of what he called "heliography": "First of all, the accuracy of perspective is only relative: we have corrected it, but we have not completely rectified it. Secondly, heliography deceives us with regard to the relationship among tones. It pales blue tints, pushes green and red toward black and has difficulty capturing delicate shades of white."[176]

Although it is difficult to reconstruct the stages of disillusionment, which the examples of Bazin and the early Barthes show was never total, by the late twentieth century the realist paradigm was practically obliterated. A host of contemporary critics testify to its disappearance. Umberto Eco, consciously rejecting Barthes in favor of a purely semiotic analysis, confidently claims that "everything which in images appears to us still as analogical, continuous, non-concrete, motivated, natural, and therefore 'irrational,' is simply something which, in our present state of knowledge and operational capacities, *we have not yet succeeded in* reducing to the discrete, the digital, the purely differential."[177] He then proceeds to enumerate no fewer than ten categories of codes that can be applied to the

175. "Les mensonges de la photographie," *Le Siècle*, January 11, 1899; reprinted in Norman L. Kleeblatt, ed., *The Dreyfus Affair: Art, Truth and Justice* (Berkeley, 1987), p. 212. The paper printed eighteen composite photos of enemies in the Affair appearing to be friends.

176. Cited in Elizabeth Anne McCauley, *A. E. E. Disdéri and the Carte de Visite Portrait Photograph* (New Haven, 1985), p. 194.

177. Umberto Eco, "Critique of the Image," in Burgin, *Thinking Photography*, p. 34.

photographic message, which has no claim to being a simple reproduction of "the real."

Joel Snyder, no less hostile to the mimetic claims of the photographic image, summarizes the differences that separate the photographic image from the human experience of sight.

> To begin with, our vision is not formed within a rectangular boundary; it is, per Aristotle, unbounded. Second, even if we were to close one eye and place a rectangular frame of the same dimensions as the original negative at a distance from the eye equal to the focal length of the lens (the so-called distance point of perspective construction) and then look at the field represented in the picture, we would still not see what is shown in the picture. The photograph shows everything in sharp delineation from edge to edge, while our vision, because our eyes are foveate, is sharp only at its "center." The picture is monochromatic, while most of us see in "natural" color (and there are some critics who maintain that the picture would be less realistic if it were in color). Finally, the photograph shows objects in sharp focus in and across every plane, from the nearest to the farthest. We do not—because we cannot—see things this way.[178]

According to James E. Cutting, "The eye has neither shutters nor exposure time, yet the visual system allows us to see a moving object clearly, whereas a still camera would register blur. In addition, the shape of the projection surfaces are different. . . . The photograph, the canvas, and the sketch pad are flat; the retina conforms nearly to a section of a sphere."[179] And Craig Owens adds the further objection that "the argument that the properties of the photographic image are derived not from the characteristics of the medium itself but from the structure of the real, registered

178. Joel Snyder, "Picturing Vision," *Critical Inquiry*, 5, 3 (Spring, 1980), p. 505.
179. James E. Cutting, *Perception with an Eye for Motion* (Cambridge, 1986), pp. 16–17.

mechanically on a light-sensitive surface, may describe the technical procedures of photography. But it does not account for the photograph's capacity to internally generate and organize meaning."[180]

Although it is doubtful that many nineteenth-century commentators were as clear as these writers on the distinctions between photographs and "natural" visual experience, not everyone was seduced by the realist claims of its early proponents. Even if the dream of technical improvements leading to greater and greater verisimilitude never died, each new innovation seemed to raise as many questions as it laid to rest,[181] a process that was only intensified with the invention of the cinema. The photographic camera thus paradoxically played a key role in discrediting the camera obscura model of visual experience.

One suggestive interpretation of the unsettling effect of these technical innovations concerns the rediscovery of a visual tradition at odds with the scopic regime based on the camera obscura, the Dutch "art of describing" analyzed by Svetlana Alpers. It may not have been by chance that a renewed interest in Jan Vermeer, Frans Hals, and their compatriots took place in the 1860s, shortly after the impact of the camera.[182] According to Alpers, "Many characteristics of photographs—those very characteristics that make them so real—are common also to the northern descriptive mode: fragmentariness; arbitrary frames; the immediacy that the first practitioners expressed by claiming that the photograph gave Nature the

180. Craig Owens, "Photography *en abyme*," *October*, 5 (Summer, 1978), p. 81.

181. The invention of the stereoscope, for example, could have a complicated effect on the assumption of the materially causative or indexical nature of the photographic image. For its three-dimensional effect was produced nowhere but in the mind. Moreover, as Jean Clair has noted, it thwarted the fetish of the permanent image with its commercial possibilities: *"Because it has no material reality it does not permit symbolic exchange.* As a virtual image, an immaterial imitation, a totally transparent, all-too-perfect delusion of reality, it does not permit one to trade the substance for the shadow, unlike the material document on paper" ("Opticeries," *October*, 5 [Summer, 1978], p. 103). He goes on to argue that Duchamp's antiretinal art was indebted to his fascination with stereoscopic images and their descendants known as anaglyphs.

182. The link is suggested by Anne Hollander in "Moving Pictures," *Raritan*, 5, 3 (Winter, 1986), p. 100.

power to reproduce herself directly unaided by man. If we want historical precedence for the photographic image it is in the rich mixture of seeing, knowing, and picturing that manifested itself in seventeenth-century images."[183] It is therefore the ghost of Kepler rather than that of Descartes or Alberti who hovers over the birth of the camera. The dead image on the retina that he had called a *pictura* was thus now given its mechanical fixation without the intervention of the rationalized space added by Cartesian perspectivalism (yet another example of the multiplicity of scopic regimes so often assumed to be unified in the modern period).[184]

Regardless of whether photographs are more properly included in the northern rather than southern pictorial tradition, what is incontestable is their extraordinary expansion of the range of human visual experience. As Benjamin noted, "Photography makes aware for the first time the optical unconscious, just as psychoanalysis discloses the instinctual unconscious."[185] The layers of this unconscious were peeled away with new technical advances like artificial illumination in the 1850s and stop-action chronophotography in the 1870s and 1880s. The most celebrated developers of the latter were Eadweard Muybridge in Britain and Étienne-Jules Marey in France. By revealing aspects of movement hitherto undetectable by the unaided eye, they helped to denaturalize conventional visual experience and uncouple vision from its association with static form.[186] As Aaron Scharf notes, "Not only did the Muybridge pho-

183. Svetlana Alpers, *The Art of Describing: Dutch Art in the Seventeenth Century* (Chicago, 1983), pp. 43–44. See also Carl Chiarenza, "Notes on Aesthetic Relationships between Seventeenth-Century Dutch Painting and Nineteenth-Century Photography," in Coke, ed., *One Hundred Years of Photographic History.*

184. It is also important to recall that perfect resemblances between objects and their mental representations was not an assumption of Descartes's optics. The soul, he insisted, saw, not the eye, and as such, it provided a natural geometry not mechanically sensed by the physical apparatus of sight. The absence of that natural geometry in photographic images helped undermine Cartesian perspectivalism.

185. Benjamin, "A Short History of Photography," p. 7.

186. For thoughts on Marey's importance for a new association of vision with speed, see Paul Virilio, *The Aesthetics of Disappearance*, trans. Philip Beitchman (New York, 1991), p. 18.

tographs contradict many of the most accurate and up-to-date observations of artists, but phases of locomotion were revealed which lay beyond the visual threshold. The meaning of the term 'truth to nature' lost its force: what was true could not always be seen, and what could be seen was not always true."[187]

Yet another unsettling effect occurred when the increased speed of film allowed completely spontaneous moments of seeming evanescence to be caught forever. Here the implications were varied. One was the apparent robbing of life's flowing temporality by introducing a kind of visual rigor mortis, which forged a link between the camera and death, a link noted as early as 1841 by Ralph Waldo Emerson and still potent in recent French thought.[188] Although the so-called pictorialist photographers of the late nineteenth century may have been trying to reintroduce time in their images by softening their focus, the hard-edged violence of the snapshot seems more characteristic of the medium. A further implication drawn from the freezing of evanescence was the calling into question of the fiction of a transcendental subject looking at the same scene through eternity. As John Berger has suggested,

> The camera isolated momentary appearances and in so doing destroyed the idea that images were timeless. Or, to put it another way, the camera showed that the notion of time passing was inseparable from the experience of the visual (except in paintings). What you saw depended upon where you were when. What you saw was relative to your position in time and space. It was no longer possible to imagine everything converging on the human eye as on the vanishing point of infinity.[189]

Or put in Bryson's terms, the camera helped restore the rights of the incarnated glance over the disincarnated gaze, and in so doing reintroduced an awareness of the "deictic" temporality of all seeing.[190]

It did so, however, by creating a temporality of pure presentness in which the historical becoming of narrative time was stripped away. As Siegfried Kracauer recognized in 1927, the spatializing impact of the photograph was a barrier to true memory, however much it may have seemed to be its aid. "In the illustrated newspapers," he noted, "the world is turned into a photographable present and the photographed present is completely eternalized. It seems to be snatched from death; in reality, it surrenders itself to it."[191] That is, by violently stopping the flow of time, it introduced a memento mori into visual experience. Bergson's criticism of photography and the cinema, as the next chapter will make clear, anticipated this analysis. Barthes's ruminations on the links between the camera and death, to be explored in chapter 8, elaborated it still further.

In the long run, the invention of the camera may well have helped un-

187. Scharf, *Art and Photography*, p. 211. Thierry de Duve adds that "with the onset of motion photography, artists who were immersed in the ideology of realism found themselves unable to express reality and obey the photograph's verdict at the same time. For Muybridge's snapshots of a galloping horse demonstrated what the animal's movements were, but did not convey the sensation of their motion" ("Time Exposure and Snapshot: The Photography as Paradox," *October*, 5 [Summer, 1978], p. 115).

188. Ralph Waldo Emerson, *Journals of Ralph Waldo Emerson, 1841–1844*, ed. Edward Waldo Emerson and Waldo Emerson Forbes (Boston, 1912), vol. 6, pp. 100–101. Perhaps the most poignant recent exploration of the link is Roland Barthes, *Camera Lucida: Reflections on Photography*, trans. Richard Howard (New York, 1981). See also Thierry de Duve, "Time Exposure and Snapshot: The Photograph as Paradox." As Steve Neale has noted, the invention of the cinema seemed to hold out hope for the revitalizing of the image, the reversal of the rigor mortis of the still photograph. See his discussion in *Cinema and Technology*, p. 40.

189. John Berger, *Ways of Seeing* (London, 1972), p. 18.

190. Norman Bryson, *Vision and Painting: The Logic of the Gaze* (New Haven, 1983), chap. 5. He is talking about art, not science, which still remained for a long time reliant on an objectivist, disincarnated subject. Deixis, the recognition of the contingent here and now of every visual act, had been, he claims, repressed in the dominant Western pictorial tradition. Roger Scruton also notes that the main difference between the photograph and the painted portrait lies in the attempt of the latter to capture a representative version of the sitter over time, not a momentary glimpse of him or her. See his *The Aesthetic Understanding: Essays in the Philosophy of Art and Culture* (London, 1983), p. 110. Unlike Bryson, he uses this argument to deny artistic status to photography, which he sees as a causal (indexical) rather than intentional (symbolic) medium.

191. Siegfried Kracauer, "Die Photographie," in *Das Ornament der Masse: Essays* (Frankfurt, 1963), p. 35.

dermine confidence in the authority of the eyes, which helped prepare the way for the interrogation of sight in twentieth-century French thought. Rather than confirming the eye's ability to know nature and society, photography could have the exact opposite effect. For, as we will remark when examining the Surrealist fascination with photography, the pencil of nature could draw some remarkably unnatural things.

The second great controversy unleashed by the invention of the camera concerned the relationship between photography and art.[192] Here the questions were manifold and often had legal as well as theoretical significance.[193] Were photographs really works of art, despite the seeming absence of an artistic hand in their production? If they were, was traditional painting now relieved of its time-honored mission to render the world faithfully on canvas? If it still tried to register visual experience in some way or another, how did the optical unconscious revealed by photography affect that effort? And what, finally, was the effect of photographic reproductions of works of art in other media?

In an often cited statement uttered just as photography was made public for the first time, the painter Paul Delaroche proclaimed, "From this day on, painting is dead."[194] In a literal sense, he was mistaken, although hoards of miniaturists were put out of business.[195] But there can be no question that painting was radically changed by the new medium. Many artists, from obscure portrait painters to masters like Delacroix and Ingres, eagerly used photos to help them in their work. Some were appar-

192. The best summary of the debate is in Scharf, *Art and Photography.* See also, Paul C. Vitz and Arnold B. Glimcher, *Modern Art and Modern Science: The Parallel Analysis of Vision* (New York, 1984).

193. In an important decision called *Mayer and Pierson* v. *Thiebault, Betbeder, and Schwabbé* in 1862, the French courts decided that photography was in fact an art in order to protect the copyright of the image. For an exploration of the implications of this decision, see Bernard Edelman, *The Ownership of the Image: Elements of a Marxist Theory of Law,* trans. E. Kingdom (London, 1979).

194. Cited and discussed in Gabriel Cromer, "L'original de la note du peintre Paul Delaroche à Arago au sujet du Daguerréotype," *Bulletin de la Sociétè Française de Photographie et de Cinématographie,* 3d ser., 17 (1930), pp. 114ff.

195. Freund, *Photography and Society,* p. 10.

ently affected by what they saw. Thus, for example, the harsh tonal divisions produced by artificial lighting have been seen as influencing Edouard Manet, and the blurred images of moving objects resulting from slow film have been credited with inspiring Jean-Baptiste-Camille Corot's proto-Impressionism of the 1840s.[196] So too the flattening of space in Impressionism, which has sometimes been interpreted as reflecting the impact of the new interest in Japanese art, has also been derived from the breakdown of perspectivalism in photography.[197] Edgar Degas's ephemeral images of dancers or horses caught in motion have often been compared with the snapshots that became possible with the perfection of faster film. The later impact of Muybridge and Marey's dissection of movement has been noted on the heterogeneous "fractured space" evident in Manet, Paul Cézanne, and Marcel Duchamp.[198] Even the brazen nudes staring out at the viewer in Manet's *Dejeuner sur l'herbe* and *Olympia* have sometimes been linked to the Second Empire's pornographic photographs.[199]

What makes all of these putative influences so ironic is that the Impressionists themselves, indebted as they often were to the reigning positivist ideology of the era, generally claimed to be passive recorders of what they saw. Even Cézanne could protest that "being a painter I attach myself first of all to visual sensation."[200] A further irony lies in the fact that the same naturalist pretense of passive neutrality on the part of early exponents of the camera was precisely what led to its denunciation by artists hostile to the ideology of realistic mimesis. As early as three weeks after Daguerre

196. Scharf, *Art and Photography*, pp. 62 and 89.

197. Vitz and Glimcher, *Modern Art and Modern Science*, p. 50. For a more skeptical interpretation of the importance of photography for Impressionism, see Kirk Varnedoe, "The Artifice of Candor: Impressionism and Photography Reconsidered," *Art in America*, 68 (January, 1980).

198. Vitz and Glimcher, *Modern Art and Modern Science*, pp. 118 and 123; Scharf, *Art and Photography*, p. 255.

199. McCauley, *A. A. E. Disdéri*, p. 172.

200. Cited from a conversation with Émile Bernard in Herschel B. Chipp, *Theories of Modern Art: A Source Book by Artists and Critics* (Berkeley, 1968), p. 13.

addressed the French Academy of Science, a writer in *Le Charivari* contended that "considered as art, the discovery of M. Daguerre is perfect silliness, but considered as the action of light on bodies, the discovery of M. Daguerre realizes an immense progress."[201] Daumier later complained that "photography imitates everything and expresses nothing. It is blind in the world of spirit."[202] And the poet Alphonse de Lamartine called it "this chance invention which will never be art, but only a plagiarism of nature through a lens."[203]

But no one was as famously contemptuous of the artistic pretensions of photography as Baudelaire, who loudly lamented the triumph of naturalist idolatry in his Salon review of 1859.[204] Although granting to the new technology its scientific and industrial uses, he fulminated mightily against its incursions into the realm of "the intangible and the imaginary."[205] Of the vulgar masses' desire for the perfect reproduction of nature, he wrote, "An avenging God has heard the prayers of this multitude. Daguerre was his messiah. . . . It was not long before thousands of pairs of greedy eyes were glued to the peep-holes of the stereoscope, as though they were the sky-lights of the infinite."[206] Although it is hard to disentangle Baudelaire's contempt for the masses from his distaste for their new toy, it is clear that he deeply distrusted the implications of photography for art. This attitude was so deeply ingrained that even later when photographers self-consciously eschewed naturalism for artistic embellishments of the image, writers like Marcel Proust could still echo Baudelaire's suspicions.[207]

201. Cited in Heinrich Schwarz, *Art and Photography: Forerunners and Influences*, ed. William E. Parker (Chicago, 1987), p. 141.

202. Cited in ibid., p. 140.

203. Cited in Freund, *Photography and Society*, p. 77. This remark was made in 1858; a short time later, Lamartine reversed himself after seeing the very expressive work of Antoine Samuel Adam-Salomon.

204. Baudelaire, "The Modern Public and Photography." André Jammes points out, however, that until 1859, Baudelaire was not explicitly critical of photography. In fact, he willingly posed for Nadar, to whom he dedicated a poem in *Fleurs du Mal*, as he did one to Maxime du Camp, the first French photographer of the Middle East. See Jammes's essay in the *French Primitive Photography* catalogue.

Such complaints were fundamentally misplaced in one important respect: the imaginative arts could never be annihilated by the camera because the latter's vision of reality was itself never straightforwardly mimetic or entirely indexical. Recent commentators like Heinrich Schwarz and Peter Galassi have convincingly shown that the predecessors of photography were not merely optical instruments like the camera obscura, but also certain traditions in painting itself.[208] The landscapes of John Constable, for example, demonstrate a "new and fundamentally modern pictorial syntax of immediate, synoptic perceptions and discontinuous, unexpected forms. It is the syntax of an art devoted to the singular and contingent rather than the universal and stable. It is also the syntax of photography."[209] Rather than being conceptualized as the realistic antithesis of artifical image making, the photographic image can thus be understood, at least in part, as an aesthetic way station between earlier non-Albertian art (best exemplified by the Dutch "art of describing" or Constable's landscapes) and the definitive break with perspective in the Impressionist and post-Impressionist era.

The Baudelairean disdain for the corrupting effect of photography on art was mistaken in one more way. The mass reproduction of paintings and other art works, begun by Adolphe Braun in 1862, anticipated, as many critics have noted, André Malraux's famous idea of the "imaginary museum," in which access to the art of the world was universalized.[210]

205. Baudelaire, p. 88.

206. Ibid., p. 87.

207. For a discussion of the attempt to make photos look like everything from oil paintings to lithographs, see Freund, *Photography and Society*, p. 88. For Proust's critical reaction to the medium, see Susan Sontag, *On Photography* (New York, 1978), p. 164.

208. Schwarz, *Art and Photography*; Peter Galassi, *Before Photography: Painting and the Invention of Photography* (New York, 1981).

209. Galassi, *Before Photography*, p. 25. Krauss, however, cautions against accepting Galassi's argument when it comes to stereoscopic photos, like those of Timothy O'Sullivan, which sought to be perspectival. See *The Originality of the Avant-Garde and Other Myths*, pp. 134f.

210. André Malraux, *The Voices of Silence* (Princeton, 1978).

One result was the stimulus to artistic experimentation produced by the photographic records of artifacts from exotic cultures which supplemented the actual objects on display in the ethnographical museums that were established in the nineteenth century. Thus, the invention of the camera can be credited with helping educate Western eyes to new aesthetic possibilities.[211]

From another perspective, however, the extension of the range of Western aesthetic experience could be interpreted as an example of the dominating anthropological gaze at the "other" trenchantly examined by recent critics like Johannes Fabian and Stephen Tyler.[212] As early as the 1850s, what has been called "photographic orientalism"[213] began with Maxime du Camp's series on Egypt, Nubia, Palestine, and Syria and Louis de Clercq's remarkable portraits of Jerusalem. Other reproduced images of exotic scenes, individuals, or objects soon followed. Extending the world's fair logic of gazing curiously at the other, the new technology abetted what one historian has called seeing "the world as exhibition."[214] Mass tourism based on the visual appropriation of exotic locales and the no less photogenic natives (or fauna) inhabiting them was not far behind.[215]

Another effect was evident in the sphere of esoteric Western art. The very aestheticization of "primitive" artifacts meant removing them from their original context—functional, ritual, or whatever—and appreciating

211. Ivins, *Prints and Visual Communication*, p. 147. It also might be noted that exposure to images of different ethnic types could have a liberalizing effect. Thus, for example, McCauley claims that Lavater's physiognomic works allowed the appreciation of beauty in forms other than that mandated by the Hellenic model of Winckelmann. See her *A. A. E. Disdéri*, p. 168.

212. Johannes Fabian, *Time and the Other: How Anthropology Makes Its Object* (New York, 1983); Stephen A. Tyler, "The Vision Quest in the West or What the Mind's Eye Sees," *Journal of Anthropological Research*, 40, 1 (1984), pp. 23–40.

213. Sobieszek, "Historical Commentary," *French Primitive Photography*, p. 5.

214. Timothy Mitchell, "The World as Exhibition," *Comparative Studies in Society and History*, 31 (1989). See also his *Colonizing Egypt* (Cambridge, 1988). For another account of the visual appropriation of the exotic other, which emphasizes its gender dynamics, see Malek Alloula, *The Colonial Harem*, trans. Myrna and Wlad Godzich (Minneapolis, 1986).

only their abstract form. No account of the prehistory of Modernism can ignore the impact of this revaluation of primitivism, which often drew on an older, Romantic belief in the power of "innocent" vision. But its political ambiguities have also become harder to gainsay in recent years.[216]

If the photographic appropriation of the exotic "other" did not, however, much trouble nineteenth-century sensibilities, neither did other social consequences of the new technology—at least at first. What, in fact, was the impact on society of this remarkable extension of our visual experience? On one level, the photographer might be understood as merely continuing visual practices already in place. Thus, for example, Susan Sontag has claimed that "photography first comes into its own as an extension of the eye of the middle-class *flâneur*, whose sensibility was so accurately charted by Baudelaire. The photographer is an armed version of the solitary walker reconnoitering, stalking, cruising the urban inferno, the voyeuristic stroller who discovers the city as a landscape of voluptuous extremes."[217] Like the naturalist novelist fascinated by the exotica of the "lower depths," the photographer could both expose and revel in the hitherto hidden corners of "picturesque" slums. The remarkable documentary potential of the new technology was immediately appreciated in comparison with the more costly and cumbersome procedures that it replaced. And, of course, photography, as already noted, could also be employed to extend the visual impact of advertising already revolutionized by lithography during the post-Napoleonic era.

But more novel uses of the new medium were also possible. In 1854, an enterprising portraitist by the name of A. A. E. Disdéri invented the

215. For a critique, see Kenneth Little, "On Safari: The Visual Politics of a Tourist Representation," in *The Varieties of Sensory Experience: A Sourcebook in the Anthropology of the Senses*, ed. David Howes (Toronto, 1991).

216. For a recent discussion of these ambiguities, see James Clifford, *The Predicament of Culture: Twentieth-Century Ethnography, Literature and Art* (Cambridge, Mass., 1988), chap. 9.

217. Sontag, *On Photography*, p. 55. This comparison was already made in the 1850s by Victor Fournel, who called the *flâneur* a "mobile and impassioned daguerrotype." *Ce qu'on voit dans les rues de Paris*, p. 261.

personal *carte de visite* by reducing the normal size of a picture and printing the negative cheaply a dozen times.[218] The innovation, which made Disdéri a rich man before he was bankrupted by intense competition from a multitude of new studios, had apparently egalitarian effects.[219] Everyone from the emperor to the *filles de joie* of the Second Empire's *demimonde* sat for his camera. He thus anticipated the democratization of the camera only fully realized with the second wave of technological innovations begun by the American George Eastman and his Kodak in the 1880s. When the picture postcard came of age in the *belle epoque,* the visual pleasure of owning scenes of Paris and other sites of beauty was generalized as never before.[220]

But there were other, less benign implications of Disdéri's invention. What began as a private calling card could soon become a public document, used for licenses, passports and other state regulated forms of identification and surveillance. As John Tagg, writing from a Foucaultian perspective, has contended, the standardized image it fostered was a leading example of the disciplined and normalized subject produced by modern techniques of power: "The body made object; divided and studied; enclosed in a cellular structure of space whose architecture is the file-index; made docile and forced to yield up its truth; separated and individuated; subjected and made subject. When accumulated, such images amount to a new representation of society."[221] Anne McCauley finds equally sinister implications:

> The acceptance of the carte portrait as an item of exchange, a collectable, by the middle class and the subsequent adoption of

218. McCauley, *A. A. E. Disdéri*; see also Freund, *Photography and Society,* pp. 55f.

219. The egalitarianism produced by the camera can be interpreted in positive or negative terms, depending on one's attitude toward the society it depicted. For those who stress the still class-riven structure of that society, photographic democratization is only ideological. For an argument of this kind, see Neale, *Cinema and Technology,* p. 23. Similar worries appeared much earlier as well. For an interesting account of their various forms in the American context, see Neil Harris, "Iconography and Intellectual History: The Half-Tone Effect," in John Higham and Paul K. Conkin, *New Directions in American Intellectual History* (Baltimore, 1979).

the practice by the workers themselves represent the insidious transformation of the individual into a malleable commodity. Direct human intercourse was in a sense supplemented by the interaction with a machine-generated and therefore irrefutably exact alter-ego, a fabricated "other." The creation and popularization of the carte de visite during the Second Empire therefore represents an early step toward the simplification of complex personalities into immediately graspable and choreographed performers whose faces rather than actions win elections.[222]

No less ominous was the use of photos for police purposes, which began in earnest in the aftermath of the Paris Commune in 1871.[223] Combined with a questionable anthropology that pretended to be able to identify criminals and anarchists by their physiognomies, the techniques perfected by Alphonse Bertillon in the 1880s had political implications as well, implications that would continue to trouble recent commentators like Berger, Sontag, and Tagg.[224] Moreover, in a population still largely only semiliterate, political propaganda was also abetted by the skillful use of the new medium, which came into its own with the tendentious composite reconstructions of incidents during the Commune by Eugène Appert.[225] Later political movements like that supporting General Boulanger expanded the demagogic use of photographic propaganda.

220. For an account of the importance of the postcard, see Naomi Schor, "*Carte Postales*: Representing Paris 1900," *Critical Inquiry*, 18, 2 (Winter, 1992). Her argument is directed against the strongly Foucaultian reading of the camera in the work of John Tagg and others influenced by the antiocularcentric discourse.

221. John Tagg, *The Burden of Representation: Essays on Photographies and Histories* (London, 1988), p. 76.

222. McCauley, *A. A. E. Disdéri*, p. 224.

223. Donald E. English, *Political Uses of Photography in the Third French Republic 1871–1914* (Ann Arbor, Mich., 1984).

224. Berger, *About Looking*, pp. 48f.; Sontag, *On Photography*, p. 5; Tagg, *The Burden of Representation*, chap. 3.

225. Nori, *French Photography*, p. 21.

Still another exploitation of the camera's eye was its use to record alleged visual representations of insanity. First attempted by Hugh Welch Diamond at the Surrey Asylum in England, the technique came into its own with Albert Londe at Charcot's clinic Salpêtrière in the 1880s.[226] Here the older tradition of picturing the insane, which had been developed by artists as prominent as Charles Le Brun in the seventeenth century and Géricault in the nineteenth, were quickly surpassed as the stop-action chronophotography of Marey was used to freeze every detail of the appearance of madness.[227] The result was what one commentator has called "the invention of hysteria," that quintessentially visual pathology enacted by women, often miming religious poses of devotional ecstasy, in the ocularcentric world of Jean-Martin Charcot's amphitheater. Attracting a broad public, including writers like Guy de Maupassant, these displays of visible illness could become objects of mass cultural appropriation through their dissemination in photographed form (allowing them as well to be rediscovered by the Surrealists a generation later). Significantly, the introduction of psychoanalysis into France, which was to play such a role in the antiocularcentric discourse we are tracing, meant an explicit rejection of Charcot's faith in the theatrical representation of madness; the "talking cure" needed no Albert Londe to depict the symptoms of the wounds it hoped to heal.

More "normal" subjects of the dissecting photographic gaze could also have their movements broken down in ways that abetted their control. The innovations of Muybridge and Marey not only led to Duchamp's *Nude Descending a Staircase*; they also helped in the rationalization of the

226. See Sander L. Gilman, ed., *The Face of Madness: Hugh W. Diamond and the Origins of Psychiatric Photography* (New York, 1976); Georges Didi-Huberman, *Invention de l'hysterie: Charcot et l'iconographie photographique de la Salpêtrière* (Paris, 1982); and Elaine Showalter, *The Female Malady: Women, Madness and English Culture, 1830–1980* (New York, 1985). Charcot also worked with an artist, Paul Richer, to depict hysterical postures. See Apter, *Feminizing the Fetish*, p. 28. It should be noted that the camera was used even earlier to record nervous maladies like epilepsy.

227. For an account of the tradition of attempts to picture insanity, see Sander L. Gilman, *Seeing the Insane: A Cultural History of Psychiatric Illustration* (New York, 1982).

work process through time and motion studies. Marey, in fact, was one of the pioneers of the European "science of work," which sought to combat fatigue and promote efficiency.[228] Its American counterpart, developed by Frederick Winslow Taylor, also understood the value of photography. His disciple, Frank B. Gilbreth, invented the "cyclegraph," in which lights would be attached to parts of subjects' bodies and by means of long time exposures their movements could be charted and their inefficiencies remedied.[229]

A final social use of the camera, which might be seen as the realization of that *principe de survol* valorized by thinkers from Montesquieu to Flaubert and then attacked by later ones like Merleau-Ponty, is suggested by one of the exploits of the greatest photographer of the nineteenth century, Gaspard-Félix Tournachon, known as Nadar.[230] In 1856, Nadar, who had already descended into the earth to record the catacombs of Paris using artificial illumination, ascended into the sky to view it from above in a hot air balloon. The first aerial photographs were such a success that he commissioned the construction of a larger airship known as *Le Géant* in 1863. Although it cost him a fortune and had only mixed results because of technical difficulties, it marked the beginning of a tradition of high altitude surveillance of the works of humanity and nature that culminated in the first pictures of earth by the American astronauts in 1968.

More immediate uses were recognized by the French government, which offered Nadar fifty thousand francs to photograph troop movements dur-

228. For an account of Marey's role in this movement, see Anson Rabinbach, *The Human Motor: Energy, Fatigue, and the Origins of Modernity* (New York, 1990), chap. 4. He stresses the difference between the European "science of work," which sought to maximize efficiency, and the American "scientific management" associated with Frederick Winslow Taylor, which was more explicitly interested in maximizing profits.

229. For a discussion, see Stephen Kern, *The Culture of Time and Space 1800–1918* (Cambridge, Mass., 1983), p. 116.

230. Among the many studies of Nadar, see especially Jean Prinet and Antoinette Dilasser, *Nadar* (Paris, 1966); Nigel Gosling, *Nadar* (London, 1976); Philippe Néagu et al., *Nadar*, 2 vols. (Paris, 1970); and Roger Greaves, *Nadar ou le paradox vital* (Paris, 1980).

ing the conflict with Italy in 1859. This request Nadar refused, but during the Prussian siege of Paris in 1870, he was less reluctant to support the war effort. Along with the use of photography to make maps from the ground, which began in 1859, and the assignment of photographers to every army regiment, started on the suggestion of Disdéri in 1861, aerial photography showed the military potential of the new medium.

Nadar in his high-flying balloon was also the subject of a celebrated lithograph by Daumier published in 1863 in Étienne Carjat's newly founded *Le Boulevard*. Humorously captioned "Nadar raising photography to the height of art," it pictures the photographer precariously perched in the swaying cabin of his balloon, his top hat caught by the wind, as he snaps a city of photography studios beneath him. As Heinrich Schwarz observes of its manifold implications,

> It deals with aerial photography, which, together with the intrusion of Japanese art, was to have a decisive influence upon the new optical approach—the bird's-eye view—of the Impressionist painters; it satirizes an actual personality among the early French photographers and his passion for showmanship; it ridicules the rapid growth of the photographic profession and in a sarcastic way raises the serious question whether photography should be considered an art or a purely mechanical procedure.[231]

Daumier's drawing might also be interpreted, with a little license, as emblematic of the state of ocularcentrism itself in the late nineteenth century. The unmoving gaze from afar that the Enlightenment—exceptions like Diderot aside—could identify with dispassionate cognition was beginning to be shaken by the force of new cultural winds. The widespread dissemination of new visual experiences brought about by social as well as technological changes had introduced uncertainties about the truths and illusions conveyed by the eyes. Although the dominant ethos until the 1890s was still the observationally oriented approach called positivism,

231. Schwarz, *Art and Photography*, p. 141.

with its literary correlate naturalism, a new attitude was visible on the horizon. The hegemony of what we have called Cartesian perspectivalism was beginning to unravel, leading initially to explorations of alternative scopic regimes (including those waiting to be recovered from earlier eras), and finally to a full-fledged critique of ocularcentrism in the twentieth century, a critique that could take on an explicitly Counter-Enlightenment pathos. Its first unmistakable signs can be discerned in the evolution of French painting from Impressionism to Post-Impressionism, in the development of modernist literary theory and practice, and in the new philosophy of Henri Bergson. It is to these transitional phenomena that we must turn in the next chapter, before exploring in detail the more recent interrogation of sight in twentieth-century French thought.

CHAPTER THREE

The Crisis of the Ancien Scopic Régime: From the Impressionists to Bergson

> We maintain that the brain is
> an instrument of action, and not
> of representation.
>
> HENRI BERGSON[1]

"The second half of the nineteenth century lives in a sort of frenzy of the visible," wrote the French filmmaker and theoretician Jean-Louis Comolli. "It is, of course, the effect of the social multiplication of images."[2] But ironically, as we have already noted, the impact of that frenzy was to undercut the self-confidence of the human viewer:

> At the very same time that it is thus fascinated and gratified by
> the multiplicity of scopic instruments which lay a thousand views
> beneath its gaze, the human eye loses its immemorial privilege;
> the mechanical eye of the photographic machine now sees *in its*
> *place*, and in certain aspects with more sureness. The photograph
> stands as at once the triumph and the grave of the eye. There is

1. Henri Bergson, *Matter and Memory*, trans. N. M. Paul and W. S. Palmer (New York, 1988), p. 74.
2. Jean-Louis Comolli, "Machines of the Visible," in *The Cinematic Apparatus*, eds. Teresa de Lauretis and Stephen Heath (New York, 1985), p. 122.

> a violent decentering of the place of mastery in which since the
> Renaissance the look had come to reign. . . . Decentered, in panic,
> thrown into confusion by all the new magic of the visible, the hu-
> man eye finds itself affected with a series of limits and doubts.[3]

Comolli, one of the editors of the *Cahiers du Cinéma*, writes from within the antiocularcentric discourse we are examining in this study, so his
generalizations may seem extreme. But there is ample evidence to demonstrate that the waning years of the nineteenth century did see an accelerated interrogation of the privileged scopic regime of the modern era, that
which we have called Cartesian perspectivalism. And, as we have tried to
demonstrate, technological innovations such as the camera contributed
to the undermining of its privileged status.

In the wake of these events, however, there appeared not only doubt,
but also the courage to explore new visual experiences. An explosion of
artistic experiments restored earlier visual cultures—photography, as already noted, may have helped revive the Dutch "art of describing"—and
developed new ones. In the visual arts and in literature, these innovations
contributed to that extraordinary aesthetic efflorescence we call Modernism. In philosophy, it abetted bold attempts to replace Cartesian and
other discredited "spectatorial" epistemologies with alternatives that explored the embodied and culturally mediated character of sight.

But in many of these cases—and here Comolli's intuition about a crisis
in confidence is correct—the initially euphoric exploration of new visual
practices ultimately led to a certain disillusionment, which fed the more
radically antiocular discourse that came into its own in late twentieth-
century France. Here the dethroning of the dominant scopic regime came
to mean a more fundamental denigration of the visual *tout court*. This
chapter will attempt to trace, with no pretense to comprehensiveness, this
crucial transitional process in the visual arts, literature, and philosophy in
France during the years before and just after the First World War. Beginning with the developments in painting that led to the "antiretinal" art of

3. Ibid., p. 123.

Marcel Duchamp, it will turn to changes in literary attitudes toward the visual best expressed in the novels of Marcel Proust, and then conclude with an account of the philosophy of Henri Bergson, whose explicit devaluation of vision was to have a profound, if not always explicitly acknowledged, effect on twentieth-century French thought.

⊙

As the art historian Jonathan Crary has recently demonstrated,[4] nineteenth-century science shifted its attention away from the geometricalized laws of optics and the mechanical transmission of light to the physical dimensions of human sight. As early as the 1820s and 1830s, he writes, "the visible escapes from the timeless incorporeal order of the camera obscura and becomes lodged in another apparatus, within the unstable physiology and temporality of the human body."[5] In the terms of the medieval distinction noted before, *lumen*, whether understood as divine radiation or natural illumination, is supplanted by *lux*, perceived light in the eye of the concrete beholder, as the focus of interest. In fact, in the 1820s, the development of a wave theory of light by Augustin Jean Fresnel undermined the rectilinear notion of *lumen* itself.

One significant implication of this shift—or perhaps even one of its causes—was the renewed prestige of color, which Descartes had relegated to the uncertain workings of the fallible human eye and denigrated in relation to pure form. Goethe's *Farbenlehre* challenged Newton's optics, and chemists like E. M. Chevreul investigated color with scientific precision. Through the popularization of writers like Charles Blanc, whose *Grammar of Painting and Engraving* was published in 1867, these findings had a strong impact on French painting.[6] So too did the research of

---

4. Jonathan Crary, *Techniques of the Observer: On Vision and Modernity in the Nineteenth Century* (Cambridge, Mass., 1990).

5. Ibid., p. 70.

6. See the discussion in Paul C. Vitz and Arnold B. Glimcher, *Modern Art and Modern Science: The Parallel Analysis of Vision* (New York, 1984), p. 36. It might be thought that a renewed stress on color over form would contribute to the triumph of

physiologists and psychologists like Joseph Plateau, Jean Purkinje, Gustav Fechner, Johannes Müller, and Hermann Helmholtz, who analyzed such visual phenomena as after images and binocular fusion. Inventions like the stereoscope also sparked debates about the nature of vision that went well beyond those unleashed by Molyneux's question in the eighteenth century. By removing the verification of touch—its three-dimensional images were only in the perception of the viewer—the stereoscope called into question the assumed congruence between the geometry of the world and the natural geometry of the mind's eye. Nor was it possible to privilege any longer a monocular point of view, as the role of both physical eyes in vision was evident in the stereoscopic experience.

The return of the body meant as well a greater sensitivity to the temporal dimension of sight, the glance as opposed to the gaze in Norman Bryson's suggestive terminology. The flux of sensations in experienced time began to dislodge the frozen "take" of a transcendental, atemporal viewing subject. Philosophers like François-Pierre Maine de Biran emphasized the role of the will and the active body in determining inward experience. Here the complicated impact of photography, producing static and fixed representations of what were nonetheless fleeting moments of evanescence, must also be taken into account. Although it would be premature to speak of an explicit awareness of the desiring, sexualized body as a source of visual experience—such an awareness would have to await Duchamp and other twentieth-century artists—the importance of internal physiological stimulations with their own rhythms, established by the work of Müller in particular, was now for the first time acknowledged as a determinant of sight.

Another, more politically inflected interpretation of these changes em-

---

pure vision because only the eye can register color, whereas touch also provides a sense of form. But paradoxically, the lack of that very tactile verification could undermine the authority of the visual by showing its dependence on the physiological apparatus of the viewer alone, thus severing the experience of sight from any objective reality "out there." Once the problematic status of that experience was made explicit, the epistemological stature of sight was shaken. The emphasis on color seems to have contributed to that result, or at least been symptomatic of it.

phasizes the relationship between scientific and economic reification in late capitalism. In a discussion of Joseph Conrad's "Impressionist" style, the Marxist literary critic Fredric Jameson has tied the "deperceptualization of the sciences" with the intensification and penetration of market relations, which combine to have an impact on visual experience. He argues,

> The very activity of sense perception has nowhere to go in a world in which science deals with ideal quantities, and comes to have little enough exchange value in a money economy dominated by considerations of calculation, measurement, profit and the like. This unused capacity of sense perception can only reorganize itself into a new and semi-autonomous activity, one which produces its own specific objects, new objects that are themselves the result of a process of abstraction and reification, such that older concrete unities are now sundered into measureable dimensions on one side, say, and pure color (or the experience of purely abstract color) on the other.[7]

In painting, the impact of these scientific, technological, and economic developments seems to have been only slowly and imperfectly registered until the 1870s and 1880s. Color, to be sure, had been increasingly liberated from its subservience to line by such Romantic artists as Delacroix. In fact, Baudelaire, in his 1846 Salon, explicitly recognized its importance for Delacroix's depiction of movement and atmosphere and compared colorists to epic poets.[8] It is also true that Turner's resurrection of Leonardo's *sfumato* can be accounted a challenge to the geometricalized

7. Fredric Jameson, *The Political Unconscious: Narrative as a Socially Symbolic Act* (Ithaca, 1981), p. 229. Jameson also notes the utopian implications of the liberation of color as a protest against the grayness of a desacralized market system. See his remarks on p. 237.

8. Charles Baudelaire, "The Salon of 1846," in *The Mirror of Art*, trans. Jonathan Mayne (New York, 1956). For a discussion, see Elisabeth Abel, "Redefining the Sister Arts: Baudelaire's Response to the Art of Delacroix," *Critical Inquiry*, 6, 3 (Spring, 1980), pp. 363–384.

optics of the perspectivalist tradition.[9] And Courbet's self-portraits may well have been attempts to overcome Cartesian dualism and, in the words of Michael Fried, "evoke within the painting his intense absorption in his own live bodily being."[10] But it was not until the advent of the "new painting"[11] that we know as Impressionism that the dominant scopic regime really began to be subjected to the "violent decentering" of which Comolli speaks.

This is obviously not the place to hazard a full-scale account of the history and implications of that much-studied movement, but several general points, familiar to every cultural historian, must be made. Rather than painting theatricalized scenes in an idealized, geometricalized space on the other side of the canvas/window as seen from afar, the Impressionists sought to reproduce the experience of light and color on the retinas of their eyes. Rejecting the traditional transformation of the direct sketch done from nature into the "licked" canvas completed in a studio, they followed the lead of the Barbizon School of the 1820s and left their work seemingly unfinished, their brush strokes still evident, the contours of their forms blurred, their colors often juxtaposed rather than smoothly blended. Learning from the examples of the photograph and the Japanese print, they de-emphasized three-dimensionality, chiaroscuro modeling, and hierarchized composition in favor of flattened or foreshortened space, a heightened attention to autonomous details, and a relative democratization of subject matter.

In fact, *what* was painted often seemed less important than *how* it was painted, as the experience of sight rather than persons, narratives, or natural objects became the subject of their art. As in the celebrated case of Monet's multiple versions of haystacks or the facade of the Rouen cathedral, the external model became little more than an occasion for the

9. Crary makes this point in the discussion following his "Modernizing Vision," in *Vision and Visuality*, ed. Hal Foster (Seattle, 1988), p. 47.

10. Michael Fried, "The Beholder in Courbet: His Early Self-Portraits and Their Place in his Art," *Glyph*, 4 (1978), p. 97.

11. *The New Painting: Impressionism 1874–1886,* catalogue by Charles S. Moffett, Ruth Berson, Barbara Lee Williams, and Froma E. Wissman (San Francisco, 1986).

stimulus of their retinas. Although recent commentators like T. J. Clark have prudently reminded us of the continued importance of their subject matter—in many cases, the spectacle of modern life[12]—the Impressionists can nonetheless be understood as a way station to the pure, self-referential art that is so often identified with high modernist formalism. At the same time, however, their emphasis on the fleeting, temporalized, evanescent glance meant they retained a certain awareness of the corporeally situated quality of vision, which high modernism, as we will see shortly, sometimes forgot. In fact, their work seemed at times to restore an almost tactile dimension to painting, which was in tension with the cool, spectatorial distance of their observing eye.[13] No less a challenge to the privilege of that dispassionate eye was the shocking return of the viewer's gaze in the work of Manet, most notably the nudes in *Déjeuner sur l'herbe* and *Olympia*, which problematized the unidirectional subject-object relation in traditional perspectivalist painting.[14]

To understand this mixed legacy, we have to pause for a moment with the complicated reaction to the Impressionist breakthrough that is loosely called Post-Impressionism. Roughly speaking, its successors took Impressionism to be grounded in a naive sensationalist epistemology, comparable to the then hegemonic positivism defended by Hippolyte Taine,

12. T. J. Clark, *The Painting of Modern Life: Paris in the Art of Manet and His Followers* (Princeton, 1984).

13. Pierre Francastel, for example, writes of Renoir that "he draws close to the model, touches, feels it with his eye and hand; he clings to it, more sensitive to the qualities of contact than, like Degas, to the usual aspects of contour." "The Destruction of a Plastic Space," in *Art History: An Anthology of Modern Criticism*, ed. Wylie Sypher (New York, 1963), p. 394.

14. Interestingly, during the Quattrocento itself, this unidirectionality was not yet established. Often a "demonstrator" figure pointing to significant events on the canvas looked directly at the beholder. Only after 1500 was this device no longer deemed necessary and, save for certain exceptions such as Caravaggio's seductive boys, the beholder's gaze was rarely returned until Manet. For an interesting discussion of the "demonstrator," see Claude Gandelman, "The 'Scanning' of Pictures," *Communication and Cognition*, 19, 1 (1986), pp. 18ff. For a recent discussion of the visual dynamics of *Olympia*, see Mieke Bal, "His Master's Eye," in *Modernity and the Hegemony of Vision*, ed. David Michael Levin (Berkeley, 1993).

Émile Littré, and other descendants of Auguste Comte. Like positivism in the 1880s and 1890s, it generated a fierce reaction. One alternative, represented by Georges Seurat, accepted the scientific intentions of the Impressionist movement, but attempted to realize them with a more precise application of Chevreul's color theories, as developed by David Sutter and Charles Henry in the 1880s.[15] The seeming spontaneity of the Impressionist glance was jettisoned in favor of a labored juxtaposition of dots of discrete color intended to produce a more faithful representation of visual experience. But Neo-Impressionism, Divisionism, or Pointillism, as it was variously known, failed to retain its hold for very long. As one commentator has recently remarked, Seurat "was caught in the contradiction between two fundamentally opposed ways of seeing, the one fluctuating and inconstant, the other constant and permanent—the two contradictory courses could not function together, combined into *one* logical visual conception."[16]

Another alternative rejected more vigorously the sensationalist pretensions of the Impressionists, either complaining that their work in fact betrayed a disturbance of vision—Joris-Karl Huysmans invoked Charcot's idea of a "malady of the retina"[17]—or arguing that painting in any case should focus on ideas, not mere surface appearances. This latter critique, which inspired the painters normally called Symbolists, was exemplified in Paul Gauguin's dismissive characterization of the Impressionists: "They heed only the eye and neglect the mysterious center of thought, so falling into merely scientific reasoning. . . . When they speak of their art, what is it? A purely superficial art, full of affectations and purely material. There is no thought there."[18]

Precisely what constituted the thought to be depicted was by no means

15. David Sutter, "Les phémenomènes de la vision," *L'Art*, 1 (1880); Charles Henry, *Cercle Chromatique* (Paris, 1888), *Rapporteur esthétique* (Paris, 1888); *Eléments d'une théorie générale de la dynamogénie autrement dit du contraste, du rythme, de la mésure avec application spéciales aux sensations visuelle et auditive* (Paris, 1889).

16. John Alsberg, *Modern Art and Its Enigma: Art Theories from 1800 to 1950* (London, 1983), p. 125.

17. Joris-Karl Huysmans, *L'art moderne* (Paris, 1975), p. 103.

self-evident. While some Symbolists yearned to evoke occult or other mysterious truths, putting, as Odilon Redon famously wrote, "the logic of the visible at the service of the invisible,"[19] other Post-Impressionists returned to an interest in the purely geometric representation of ideal linearity, shorn however of its mimetic implications. Here, interestingly, a certain continuity existed with the dominant pedagogy of drawing in the French schools associated with the figure of Eugène Guillaume, who dominated Third Republic artistic education from 1881 to 1909.[20] Guillaume's nonretinal stress on geometric form as a visual language fit nicely with the needs of industrial technological design as well as with the Republican ideology of universal rationalism. That strain in modernism which privileged grids—"flattened, geometricized, ordered . . . antinatural, antimimetic, antireal," as Rosalind Krauss has described them[21]— could gain sustenance from this conceptualist reaction to the fleeting glance of Impressionist visual experience.

In the immediate aftermath of the "new painting," however, this path was by no means the only one open. An attempt could be made to combine the subjectivist awareness of the Impressionists with a recognition of

18. Paul Gauguin, *Diverses Chose, 1896–97,* reprinted in *Theories of Modern Art: A Source Book by Artists and Critics,* ed. Herschel B. Chipp (Berkeley, 1975), p. 65. The contention that the Impressionists were merely passive "eyes" has not gone uncontested. See, for example, the spirited defense of Monet as a "complete man" by Roger Shattuck in *The Innocent Eye: On Modern Literature and the Arts* (New York, 1984), pp. 221f. Recognizing the corporeal implications of Monet's practice, he writes, "Such vision is so intense as to resemble a form of audition or even touch, linking us closely to the physical world of our own body" (p. 234).

19. Odilon Redon, *À Soi-même: Journal (1867–1915),* cited in Chipp, p. 119. Redon's own fascination with the eye as a powerful symbol—in, for example, his lithograph "Vision" in the 1879 series *Dans le rêve*—would repay close study. Such enucleated eyes, like the decapitated heads of John the Baptist he so often painted in the same period, perhaps express the same castration anxiety evoked by the *femmes fatales* like Salomé, whose Medusan gaze so fixated the Decadents.

20. For a general history of Third Republic art policy, see Miriam R. Levin, *Republican Art and Ideology in Late Nineteenth-Century France* (Ann Arbor, Mich., 1986).

21. Rosalind E. Krauss, *The Originality of the Avant-Garde and Other Modernist Myths* (Cambridge, Mass., 1985), p. 9.

the material thingness of the objects painted, and to do so without losing the newly won sensitivity to the lived body of the artist and the beholder. The initiator of this impossible project was Cézanne, whose "doubt" about accomplishing it is the subject of a famous essay by Merleau-Ponty.[22]

From the Impressionists, Cézanne, as Merleau-Ponty read him, derived a "devotion to the visible world" and a belief in painting as "the exact study of appearances."[23] But he soon abandoned their naive belief in unmediated perception, seeking instead to rediscover the objects they had dissolved. For Cézanne, "the object is no longer covered by reflections and lost in its relationships to the atmosphere and to other objects: it seems subtly illuminated from within, light emanates from it, and the result is an impression of solidity and material substance."[24] Rejecting the Impressionists' limited palette of seven primary colors, he added earth tones, white, and black, which restored the density of the objects represented on the canvas. But he did so without also restoring the fiction of a distanced spectator able to see such objects in a perspectivalized space from afar. Like the non-Euclidean mathematicians of the nineteenth century, he realized the multiplicity of spatial orders in the world.[25] He also

22. Maurice Merleau-Ponty, "Cézanne's Doubt," in *Sense and Non-sense*, trans. Hubert L. Dreyfus and Patricia A. Dreyfus (Evanston, Ill., 1964). For a discussion of it in the context of Cézanne criticism, see Judith Wechsler, *The Interpretation of Cézanne* (Ann Arbor, Mich., 1981).

23. Merleau-Ponty, "Cézanne's Doubt," p. 11.

24. Ibid., p. 12.

25. The first non-Euclidean geometry was developed independently by N. I. Lobachevsky and Farkas Bolyai in the 1830s, but its importance was not realized by philosophers and scientists until near the end of the century. An important statement of the new awareness was Henri Poincaré's *La Science et l'hypothèse* (Paris, 1902). There were also literary popularizers like Gaston de Pawlowski, the author of *Voyage au pays de la quatriéme dimension* (Paris, 1912). The Cubists and Duchamp were both very interested in the concept of four- (or even n-) dimensional space suggested by non-Euclidean geometry. For a thorough account of its influence and reception, see Linda Dalrymple Henderson, *The Fourth Dimension and Non-Euclidean Geometry in Modern Art* (Princeton, 1983). She shows that the importance of these ideas antedated the reception of Einstein's relativity theory, with which they are sometimes conflated.

discovered, Merleau-Ponty claims, "what recent psychologists have come to formulate: the lived perspective, that which we actually perceive, is not a geometric or photographic one."[26] This lived perspective was in fact rooted in an experience prior to the artificial isolation of the senses and the hegemonic autonomy of sight. Thus, Cézanne tried to present objects that were present to all the senses at once: "We *see* the depth, the smoothness, the softness, the hardness of objects. Cézanne even claimed that we see their odor."[27] In so doing, Cézanne wanted to overcome the very distance between viewer and viewed, thus shattering the window's glass separating beholder from the scene on the other side. His task, therefore, was the recapturing of the very moment when the world was new, before it was fractured into dualisms of subject and object or the modalities of separate senses.

Not surprisingly, so ambitious a project could never be successfully accomplished. To render reality in all its sensual manifestations in a medium that remained stubbornly visual proved an intractable problem. Merleau-Ponty concludes that "Cézanne's difficulties are those of the first word. He considered himself powerful because he was not omnipotent, because he was not God and wanted nevertheless to portray the world, to change it completely into a spectacle, to make *visible* how the world *touches* us."[28] However partial his triumph, Cézanne's doubt was enormously stimulating to later painters. As Clark has noted, "Doubts about vision became doubts about almost everything involved in the act of painting: and in time the uncertainty became a value in its own right: we could say it became an aesthetic."[29] That aesthetic was what we call modernism, which in such movements as Cubism, Futurism, and Vorticism further explored Cézanne's demolition of the received visual order.

26. Merleau-Ponty, "Cézanne's Doubt," p. 14. The psychologists in question are those associated with the Gestalt school, but Merleau-Ponty could also have been talking about James Gibson, whose distinction between "visual field" and "visual world" fits his argument nicely.

27. Ibid., p. 15.

28. Ibid., p. 19.

29. Clark, *The Painting of Modern Life*, p. 12.

Modernist aesthetics, to be sure, has traditionally been construed as the triumph of a pure visuality, concerned solely with formal optical questions.[30] The most authoritative and influential exponent of this position has been the American critic Clement Greenberg, who purged Cézanne of precisely those corporeal and omnisensual dimensions Merleau-Ponty celebrated in his work.[31] For Greenberg, Cézanne fought the Impressionist stress on experienced light and color in the name of pure spatial form. The Cubists may have thought they were introducing tactile and other sensual values, but according to Greenberg, "Cubism ended up with an even more radical denial of all experience not literally accessible to the eye. The world was stripped of its surface, of its skin, and the skin was spread flat on the flatness of the picture plane. Pictorial art reduced itself entirely to what was visually verifiable, and Western painting had finally to give up its five hundred years' effort to rival sculpture in the evocation of the tactile."[32] Even modernist sculpture, he argued, "turned out to be almost as exclusively visual in its essence as painting itself."[33]

If Greenberg's formalist version of the modernist priviliging of the visual were the whole story, we would be confronted with the paradox that the antivisual discourse of the twentieth century was utterly at odds with the dominant artistic practice of the same era. However, recent critics of Greenberg—such as Leo Steinberg, Rosalind Krauss, Victor Burgin, Hal Foster, Thierry de Duve, and P. Adams Sitney—have reopened the question of the purity of the visual in modernism.[34] By stressing the importance of a hitherto undervalued countertendency, they have revealed the origins within the modernist project of an explicitly antivisual impulse

30. This interpretation is at least as old as Clive Bell's influential *Art* (New York, 1958), which first appeared in 1913. Of Cézanne, he wrote, "Everything can be seen as pure form, and behind pure form lurks the mysterious significance that thrills to ecstasy" (p. 140).

31. Clement Greenberg, "Cézanne," in *Art and Culture: Critical Essays* (Boston, 1965).

32. Greenberg, "On the Role of Nature in Modernist Painting," *Art and Culture*, p. 172.

33. Greenberg, "The New Sculpture," in *Art and Culture*, p. 142.

that ultimately prepared the way for what has become known as post-modernism. Rejecting Greenberg's injunction always to render substance entirely optical, they have explicitly questioned what Krauss calls "the modernist fetishization of sight."[35] Instead, they emphasize that impulse to reinstate the living body, which we have seen evident in both Impressionism and Cézanne, as Merleau-Ponty read him.[36] At its most extreme, this revisionist art historiography, itself influenced by the French antivisual discourse of our era, has sought to pit the body *against* the eye, producing a paradoxical project for painting, to say the least.

In fact, the paradox is so great that at times it seems as if only the end of painting as it has traditionally been conceived would resolve it. In the work (or "antiwork") of Duchamp, which has explicitly been called "a reaction *against* modern art,"[37] the outer limits of that self-cancellation were most rigorously explored. For many years, Duchamp was relegated by critics like Greenberg to a marginal role in the history of modernism, once the scandal of his *Nude Descending a Staircase* at the 1913 Armory

34. Leo Steinberg, *Other Criteria* (New York, 1972); Krauss, *The Originality of the Avant-Garde and Other Modernist Myths*; Victor Burgin, *The End of Art Theory: Criticism and Postmodernity* (London, 1986); Hal Foster, *Recodings: Art, Spectacle, Cultural Politics* (Port Townsend, Wash., 1985); Thierry de Duve, *Pictorial Nominalism: On Marcel Duchamp's Passage from Painting to the Readymade*, trans. Dana Polan (Minneapolis, 1991); P. Adams Sitney, *Modernist Montage: The Obscurity of Vision in Cinema and Literature* (New York, 1990). For more political critiques, of Greenberg, see Serge Guilbaut, *How New York Stole the Idea of Modern Art: Abstract Expressionism, Freedom, and the Cold War*, trans. Arthur Goldhammer (Chicago, 1984), and Craig Owens, *Beyond Recognition: Representation, Power, and Culture* (Berkeley, 1992).

35. Krauss, "Antivision," *October*, 36 (Spring, 1986), p. 147. See also her contribution to the discussion of "Theories of Art after Minimalism and Pop," in *Discussions in Contemporary Culture*, 1, ed. Hal Foster (Seattle, 1987).

36. The living body is understood here not as the subject of the work, but as an aspect of the creation/reception process. The nonfigural, antimimetic impulse of modernism at its most abstract generally meant the denial of the human figure as a worthy subject. As a result, some commentators have even talked of the "iconoclastic" impulse in modernism. See, for example, José Ortega y Gasset, *The Dehumanization of Art*, trans. Helene Weyl (Princeton, 1968), p. 40.

37. Octavio Paz, *Marcel Duchamp: Appearance Stripped Bare*, trans. Rachel Phillips and Donald Gardner (New York, 1978), p. 174.

Show in New York was recounted. Recently, however, he has been celebrated as the most subversive presence in that tradition because of the radical challenge in his later work to its notions of a postperspectivalist renewal of vision. That challenge took a number of different forms that culminated in his restoration of the desiring body.

One of his earlier provocations attacked the traditional status of the artwork itself. Rather than an ontological view of art, he proposed a "pictorial nominalism" in which arbitrary designation replaced aesthetic essentializing. Taking to an extreme the incorporation of materials from everyday life in Cubist collages, Duchamp's "readymades" questioned the difference between representation and presentation, while at the same time mocking the traditional auratic notion of a "work of art" from the hand of an individual genius. Mass-produced objects like bicycle wheels or urinals were given putative aesthetic status by the artist's signature, a kind of self-parodying fiat that sought to undercut the very institution of art.[38] It did so by decontexualizing the object from everyday life and recontextualizing it in the museum, where only certified "great works" were displayed. In so doing, the boundary between avant-garde and kitsch, which Greenberg saw as fundamental to the modernist project, was implicitly problematized.[39]

Because of the importance of its nonvisual contextual frame, the readymade was not a purely visual phenomenon. As Duchamp told Pierre Cabanne when asked about which objects he chose, "In general one had to defend oneself against the 'look.' It is very difficult to choose an object because after a couple of weeks you come to like it or detest it. You have to achieve something so indifferent to you that you have no aesthetic emotion. The choice of ready-mades is always based on visual indifference as

38. For a discussion of the Dadaist project to call into question the institution of art, to which Duchamp's readymades contributed, see Peter Bürger, *Theory of the Avant-Garde*, trans. Michael Shaw (Minneapolis, 1984), pp. 51f.

39. Greenberg, "Avant-garde and Kitsch," in *Art and Culture*. For an interesting discussion of Duchamp's effacing the boundary, see Matei Calinescu, *Faces of Modernity: Avant-Garde, Decadence, Kitsch* (Bloomington, 1977), pp. 254–255.

well as on the complete absence of good or bad taste."[40] According to Rosalind Krauss, it owed something to the photograph, or more specifically, the snapshot: "The readymade's parallel with the photograph is established by its process of production. It is about the physical transposition of an object from the continuum of reality into the fixed condition of the art-image by a moment of isolation, or selection."[41] In both cases, what you see is *not* what you get, because of the insufficiency of the decontextualized image by itself.

Duchamp's provocations, like those of other artists in the Dadaist camp, could quickly be recuperated by the ideological and commercial pressures of the institution he tried to subvert. It is now in fact commonplace to note that museums proudly exhibit the "originals" of his readymades, as indeed he himself knew they would.[42] Duchamp's more radical gesture then was the virtual abandonment of artistic production itself after 1924 in favor of chess, a game he played with considerable success. His deliberately uncompleted *Large Glass* (also known as *The Bride Stripped Bare by Her Bachelors, Even*), damaged in transit after its exhibition in Brooklyn in 1926, came to be seen as symbolic of this rejection. Or at least so it seemed until the posthumous installation of his remarkable *Etant donnés: 1° la chute d'eau, 2° le gaz d'éclairage (Given: 1. The Waterfall, 2. The Illuminating Gas* in its English translation) at the Philadelphia Museum of Art in 1969, a surprising revelation that he had in fact been working on something for the previous twenty years.

Not merely a challenger to conventional notions of the artwork and the institution of art, Duchamp must also be understood as one of the most persistent and imaginative explorers of the conundrums of the visual produced by the technical and artistic breakthroughs of the late nineteenth century. He was, for example, fascinated with the implications of the stereoscope and later devices of three-dimensional illusion

40. Pierre Cabanne, *Entretiens avec Marcel Duchamp* (Paris, 1967), pp. 83–84.
41. Krauss, *The Originality of the Avant-Garde*, p. 206.
42. See his remarks to Cabanne, *Entretiens avec Marcel Duchamp*, p. 139.

such as the anaglyph, which produced optical effects in the brain without any material reality behind them.[43] He also mastered the techniques of anamorphic perspective, which had been virtually forgotten since their heyday three centuries before, and was fascinated with the implications of non-Euclidean geometry. And along with Frantisek Kupka, Robert Delaunay, and the Futurists, he drew—most notably in the *Nude Descending a Staircase*—on the chronophotographic experiments of Muybridge and Marey.[44]

Duchamp himself, however, distanced his work from that of these other artists by claiming that "futurism was an impression of the mechanical. It was strictly a continuation of the Impressionist movement. I was not interested in that. I wanted to get away from the physical act of painting. I was much more interested in recreating ideas in painting. For me the title was very important. . . . I was interested in ideas—not merely visual products. I wanted to put painting once again at the service of the mind."[45] For rather than trying to find a still more faithful representation of visual experience, in motion or at rest, Duchamp rejected "the retinal shudder"[46] of conventional art, which included Impressionism and Post-Impressionism (with the salient exception of Surrealism). In its place, he put an art that self-consciously undermined the primacy of visual form itself.

Duchamp's critique of the fetishism of sight thus provides an important

43. For a discussion of his interest in stereoscopes and anaglyphs, see Jean Clair, "Opticeries," *October*, 5 (Summer, 1978), pp. 101–112. He notes that the immateriality of the stereoscopic image, unlike that of the photograph, fit well with Duchamp's mocking of the commercially valuable "work of art," because it resisted becoming an exchangable commodity.

44. See, for example, Vitz and Glimcher, *Modern Art and Modern Science*, p. 127. Interestingly, Merleau-Ponty, echoing Bergson's critique of the cinema, thought they were all failures at showing real movement. "They give a Zenonian reverie on movement," he remarked, referring to Zeno's paradoxes. "Eye and Mind," in *The Primacy of Perception*, ed. James M. Edie (Evanston, Ill., 1964), p. 185.

45. Duchamp, "Painting . . . at the service of the mind," in Chipp, *Theories of Modern Art*, pp. 393–394.

46. Duchamp to Cabanne, *Entretiens avec Marcel Duchamp*, p. 74.

counterexample to the Greenbergian construction of modernism (significantly, his name is entirely absent from Greenberg's *Art and Culture*). It drew on several nonvisual sources, which might be broadly divided into literary and psychological. Duchamp acknowledged the importance of two writers whose "delirium of imagination"[47] he found inspirational: Jean-Pierre Brisset and Raymond Roussel. In both cases, the delirium was essentially linguistic, a recognition of the power of puns, anagrams, and the like to undermine the purely communicative function of language. Such works as Duchamp's *Large Glass* have been interpreted as transpositions of their method into a visual register—or more correctly, a visual *cum* linguistic one.[48] So too the spatial effect of his film *Anémic Cinéma* has been compared by Jean Clair to the "tropological" space Foucault was to find in Roussel: "a flat space in which words and figures rotate indefinitely, with neither end nor beginning, a space wholly subject to the infinitely glittering effect of meaning, in the definite absence of all meaning."[49]

Stressing the complicated relation between titles and works,[50] playing with the artist's name and identity (most outrageously in the persona of Rrose Sélavy),[51] producing rebuses that both invited and resisted semantic decoding, Duchamp problematized not only the representations of

47. Duchamp, "Painting . . . at the service of the mind," p. 394. For a discussion of the theme of *délire* in twentieth-century French literature which treats Brisset and Roussel, see Jean-Jacques Lecercle, *Philosophy Through the Looking-Glass: Language, Nonsense, Desire* (London, 1985), pp. 17–27.

48. Paz, *Marcel Duchamp*, p. 11.

49. Jean Clair, "Opticeries," p. 112.

50. Perhaps the most notorious example is his Mona Lisa with a mustache called *LHOOQ*, which is an obscene pun in French. For a general appreciation of the importance of titles in Duchamp and Surrealists like Miró and Magritte, see Laurie Edson, "Confronting the Signs: Words, Images, and the Reader-Spectator," *Dada/Surrealism*, 13 (1984), pp. 83–93.

51. Rrose Sélavy, with its deliberate confusion of gender, was a pun for "Eros, c'est la vie." Duchamp went so far as to be photographed in drag by Man Ray. He also called himself Belle Haleine. See the discussion by Arturo Schwartz, "Rrose Selavy: Alias Marchand de Sel alias Belle Haleine," *l'Arc*, 59 (1975).

sensations (retinal art) but also that of ideas. At times, he seemed to suggest that a picture was in need of a thousand words, and even then it didn't translate easily into a meaningful object. Only René Magritte, the Belgian Surrealist, would equal his invention of visual puns and semantically opaque metaphors, but Duchamp went even further in his hostility to painterly painting.

Duchamp's disdain for pure opticality—the art of both the Impressionists and their formalist successors, both of which he insisted was "retinal"—appeared not only in his introduction of linguistic frames and mediations but also in his preoccupation with the ways in which the desiring body enters the pictorial landscape. "Instead of being a M. Teste," his friend the Italian painter Gianfranco Baruchello once remarked, "Duchamp, in a way, was a kind of M. Corps."[52] There is of course nothing oxymoronic about the concept of ocular desire; indeed, Bryson goes so far as to claim that "the life of vision is one of endless wanderlust, and in its carnal form the eye is nothing but desire."[53] It was, however, by and large the decarnalized eye that characterized the Cartesian perspectivalist scopic regime.[54] Its conventional depiction of the nude, for example, was one in which desire was kept at bay, which accounts for the shock of works like Manet's *Déjeuner sur l'herbe* and *Olympia* in the 1860s.

High modernism, read in formalist terms, continued this inclination. Even as it allowed the body to reestablish its importance, in the way Merleau-Ponty claims it did in Cézanne, that body tended to remain de-eroticized. As Meyer Schapiro has noted, "Cézanne reduced the intensity of perspective, blunting the convergence of parallel lines in depth, setting the solid objects back from the picture plane and bringing distant objects nearer, to create an effect of contemplativeness in which desire has been suspended."[55]

52. Gianfranco Baruchello and Henry Martin, *Why Duchamp? An Essay on Aesthetic Impact* (New York, 1985), p. 95.

53. Norman Bryson, *Tradition and Desire: From David to Delacroix* (Cambridge, 1984), p. 209.

54. Typically does not mean exclusively. Bryson, for example, shows in *Tradition and Desire* the introduction of desire in Delacroix and Ingres.

In Duchamp, however, the presence of desire complicated still further the visual "noise" produced by the interruption of linguistic signs. He forced the idealized nude of traditional painting off her pedestal and down the staircase, where she could arouse more explicitly erotic responses. But in so doing, he also decomposed her form as an object of desire, mocking the attempt to derive direct sensual pleasure from her contemplation. If he identified with Rrose Sélavy (*Eros, c'est la vie*), the life Duchamp suggested by his pun was certainly not one of erotic plenitude. The ocular desire introduced into his work was not that of straightforward erotic stimulation producing satisfaction; as many commentators have noted, he was the great master of the uncompleted work, the unachieved climax, the masturbatory gesture of repetition without real release. As Octavio Paz observes, "Duchamp set up a vertigo of delay in opposition to the vertigo of acceleration."[56] Infinite deferral prevents any action from being triumphantly carried out. The "bride" in the *Large Glass* remains forever in the process of being stripped bare.

In fact, the two sections of the work—the upper that of the "bride," the lower that of the "bachelors"—were rendered through two incommensurable spatial projections that defy visual unity. So too does the disparity between the perspectivalist or anamorphic lines etched on the glass and the "real world" visible through the work's transparent "canvas." The result is a denial of visual plenitude, which reinforces the pattern of endless sexual excitation and frustration explicit on a thematic level.

Duchamp's fascination with optical machines of all kinds included the so-called roto-reliefs, those revolving discs with spirals or eccentric circles first investigated by the scientist Plateau in 1850.[57] They played a significant role in his 1924–1926 film anagrammatically entitled *Anémic Cin-*

55. Meyer Schapiro, *Modern Art 19th and 20th Centuries: Selected Papers* (New York, 1982), pp. 87–88. These remarks come in an essay on Van Gogh which establishes the deeply emotional quality of his painting, but which doesn't stress erotic desire as one of its components.

56. Paz, *Marcel Duchamp*, p. 2.

57. See the discussion in Vitz and Glimcher, *Modern Art and Modern Science*, pp. 196f.

éma, which also included verbal puns rotated on wheels. The hypnotic repetition of their patterns, according to Krauss, evoked "the beat of desire . . . a desire that makes and loses its object in one and the same gesture, a gesture that is continually losing what it has found because it has only found what it has already lost."[58] Moreover, the desire invoked was not gender-specific, but irreducible to sexual difference instead.[59] Just as the nude descending Duchamp's famous staircase is decomposed into forms and shapes that resist retinal pleasure, so the evocation of desire in Duchamp's "precision optics" leads to little erotic satisfaction. What it does do, however, is introduce a temporalizing disruption into the dream of timeless, eternal form, which underlay the modernist fetish of the optical in its more decarnalizing moments.

No less disturbing were the implications of Duchamp's parting gift to the art of the twentieth century, his *Etant donnés* first shown in Philadelphia a year after his death in 1968. The visitor unceremoniously enters a small, dark room, at the end of which is a rough-hewn door surrounded by an arch of bricks with two eye holes through which a startling scene can be observed. Although no verbal description (or photograph for that matter) does justice to it, Paz's comes close:

> First of all, a brick wall with a slit in it, and through the slit, a wide open space, luminous and seemingly bewitched. Very near the beholder—but also very far away on the "other side"—a naked girl, stretched out on a kind of bed or pyre of branches and leaves, her face almost completely covered by the blond mass of her hair, her legs slightly open and slightly bent, the pubes strangely smooth in contrast to the splendid abundance of her hair, her right arm out of the line of vision, her left slightly raised, the hand, grasping a

58. Rosalind Krauss, "The Im/pulse to See," *Visions and Visuality,* ed. Hal Foster, p. 62. See also her "The Blink of an Eye," in *Nature, Sign, and Institutions in the Domain of Discourse*, Program in Critical Theory, University of California, Irvine (Berkeley, 1989).

59. For an analysis of this issue, see Dalia Judovitz, "Anemic Vision in Duchamp: Cinema as Readymade," *Dada/Surrealism*, 15 (1986), p. 48.

small gas lamp made of metal and glass. . . . On the far right, among some rocks, a waterfall catches the light. Stillness, a portion of time held motionless. The immobility of the naked woman and the landscape contrasts with the movement of the waterfall and the flickering of the lamp. The silence is absolute. All is real and verges on banality; all is unreal and verges—on what?[60]

To its detractors, the *Etant donnés* is little more than another of Duchamp's hoaxes, "the ultimate bluff against art and its whole super-structure, an obscene diorama pawned off on a reputable museum because of the reputation of the 'artist' and the brilliant literary apparatus lending it prestige."[61] To those less hostile, it represents Duchamp's most profound exploration of the troubled confluence of vision and desire. The viewer is turned into an explicit voyeur at a peep show, a theme Duchamp had in fact already probed in the *Large Glass*, where "ocular witnesses" watch the "bride" being stripped bare by her "bachelors." Now, however, the beholder is directly turned into a scopophilic viewer, caught in the embarassing act that underlies all visual pleasure. Or more precisely, that act is put in quotations marks, for as Dalia Judovitz observes, "the problem with the scene is its 'hyperreality,' its excessive realism, which stages eroticism as a 'too' obvious spectacle. The diorama-like character of the scene is further emphasized by the presence of an almost blinding light, an excess of illumination."[62] Moreover, the hairless genitals of the splayed model are almost too blatantly open to the viewer's gaze, as if Courbet's once-shocking *Origin of the World* with its naked vagina is trumped by a kind of hypernakedness mocking the scopophilic urge to look. Through the eyeholes of the door, the voyeur stares at the female "hole" at the center of the scene, a vanishing point in which there is "nothing to see."

The installation also subverts the traditional identification of subjectivity with either a monologic, spectatorial gaze or a dialogic specularity.

60. Paz, *Marcel Duchamp*, p. 96.

61. Shattuck, *The Innocent Eye*, p. 291.

62. Dalia Judovitz, "Rendez-vous with Marcel Duchamp: *Given*," *Dada/Surrealism*, 16 (1987), p.187.

Rather than the picture returning the gaze of the beholder in the manner of, say, Manet's *Olympia*, which suggests the possibility of reciprocity, the viewer becomes the uneasy object of a gaze from behind—that of those waiting to stare at the peep show. The door, as Paz notes, is like the hinge of a chiasmic visual scene, which turns the gazing beholder into the object of the other's look. As a result, the equation of the "I" with the sovereign "eye" becomes itself unhinged.

Without necessarily intending it, Duchamp here instantiates the visual interaction explored in existential and psychological terms by major contributors to the French antivisual discourse like Sartre and Lacan. Not surprisingly, his work was also explicitly praised by a later contributor, Lyotard, who shared his fascination with the crossings of discourse, figurality, and desire.[63] For Lyotard, Duchamp's various transformations of incommensurable spaces and his resistance to visual plenitude even had healthy political implications.[64] Still other recent commentators would see his *Large Glass* prefiguring, as it were, Derrida's *Glas* and anticipating the French feminist critique of the dominating male gaze.[65]

To allude to these figures is obviously to get ahead of the story. Before attempting to trace their complicated variants of the antiocularcentric discourse, it is necessary more firmly to establish its origins. If the history of modernist painting, broadly construed, can be understood as a laboratory of postperspectivalist optical experimentation, with a subcurrent of outright antiretinalism culminating in Duchamp, roughly parallel developments can be discerned as well in the literary experiments of the French avant-garde. And without forcing the congruences too brutally, certain further parallels may become apparent in French philosophy as well.

63. Jean-François Lyotard, *Les transformateurs Duchamp* (Paris, 1977).

64. Ibid., p. 31. He also explicitly praises Duchamp's dissolution of visual unity and his ascetic rejection of totalization as an improvement over Merleau-Ponty's more hopeful search for a new visual order beyond Cartesianism (p. 68).

65. Carol P. James, "Reading Art Through Duchamp's *Glass* and Derrida's *Glas*," *Substance*, 31 (1981), pp. 105–128; Judovitz, "Rendez-vous with Marcel Duchamp: *Given*," p. 200, n. 11.

⊙

Ever since the Renaissance Humanists rediscovered Horace's proclamation in his *Art of Poetry* that *ut pictura poesis* (as is painting, so is poetry), the relationship between literature and the visual arts has been a topic of lively and sustained aesthetic interest.[66] In France in particular, it has been especially popular from the time the salons of seventeenth-century *précieuse* hostesses like Mlle de Scudéry brought together writers and artists.[67] To attempt a recapitulation of its history, or even more ambitiously of the variations in actual artistic practice, is obviously beyond the scope of this discussion. Indeed, it would be impossible to do justice to the full range of innovations during the aesthetic modernist moment in that story without posing a host of complicated questions, whose answers would require extended consideration. What, for example, is the relationship between literary and poetic "images" or "figures"?[68] Can perspective in painting be compared with "point of view" in literature?[69] Is there a parallel between spatial form in the visual arts and literature, which came into its own in modernism?[70] Can the "colors of rhetoric" be compared with

66. For histories of the debate, see Rensselaer W. Lee, "*Ut Pictura Poesis*: The Humanistic Theory of Painting," *Art Bulletin*, 22 (1940), pp. 197–269; and Mario Praz, *Mnemosyne: The Parallel Between Literature and the Visual Arts* (Princeton, 1967). Horace's point was that despite their different means, both arts shared the aim of instruction by depicting noble acts.

67. See Helen Osterman Borowitz, *The Impact of Art on French Literature* (London, 1985), for an account of this interaction.

68. For very different attempts to answer this question, see P. N. Furbank, *Reflections on the Word 'Image'* (London, 1970) and W. J. T. Mitchell, *Iconology: Image, Text, Ideology* (Chicago, 1986), chap. 1.

69. It was Henry James who first broached this issue. For more recent discussions, see Percy Lubbock, *The Craft of Fiction* (New York, 1957); and David Carroll, *The Subject in Question: The Languages of Theory and the Strategies of Fiction* (Chicago, 1982).

70. Here the seminal text is Joseph Frank, "Spatial Form in Modern Literature," reprinted in *The Avant-Garde in Literature*, ed. Richard Kostelanetz (Buffalo, N.Y., 1982), pp. 43–77, which has spawned a minor industry in response.

the perceived colors in a work of visual art?[71] Is there a modernist version of the time-honored tension between poetry written for the ear on the poet's "Aeolian harp" and poetry written for the eye through the "prism" of his or her imagination?[72] What is the role of specular, concave, or anamorphic mirroring in literary texts, especially after the *mise en abyme* became a self-conscious staple of modernist reflexivity?[73] Are there literary parallels to modernist movements in the visual arts such as Impressionism and Cubism?[74] What are the literary reflections of new visual technologies such as photography and the cinema?[75] What are the implications of the deliberate confusion or integration of the senses through techniques of synesthesia, which aspire to the creation of a *Gesamtkunstwerk?* Finally, can the critic transfer the hermeneutics or semiotics of literary analysis to the "reading" of visual artifacts and vice versa?

Rather than try to tackle so formidable a list of questions or others that could easily be invented, it will be more useful to single out only a few strands in a very complicated story and look for parallels, if they exist, with comparable developments in the visual arts themselves and in the philosophy of the same era. In so doing, we may get a clearer sense of the sources of the antivisual discourse that will come into its own a generation or so later. For as in the case of the experiments in painting

71. The phrase "colors of rhetoric" goes back to Chaucer. For an insightful discussion of its contemporary significance, see Wendy Steiner, *The Colors of Rhetoric: Problems in the Relation Between Modern Literature and Painting* (Chicago, 1982).

72. For a learned history of this debate, see John Hollander, *Vision and Resonance: Two Senses of Poetic Form*, 2d ed. (New Haven, 1985).

73. It was André Gide who first thematized the *mise en abyme*. For recent considerations of its importance, see Lucien Dällenbach, *Le récit speculaire* (Paris, 1977); and Linda Hutcheon, *Narcissistic Narrative: The Metafictional Paradox* (New York, 1980).

74. For such an argument, see Wylie Sypher, *From Rococo to Cubism in Art and Literature* (New York, 1960).

75. See, for example, Alan Spiegel, *Fiction and the Camera Eye: Visual Consciousness in Film and the Modern Novel* (Charlottesville, Va., 1976); Bruce Morrissette, *Novel and Film: Essays in Two Genres* (Chicago, 1985); Ralph F. Bogardus, *Pictures and Texts: Henry James, A. L. Coburn, and New Ways of Seeing in Literary Culture* (Ann Arbor, Mich., 1984).

discussed above, the liberation of literature from its alleged mimetic function led to a burst of creative energy in which the relations between vision and text were boldly explored. But also as in the case of painting, a certain uneasiness over the implications of these new experiments began to surface. Here Stéphane Mallarmé and Marcel Proust will be our main witnesses.

Nineteenth-century realist fiction, as already remarked in the previous chapter, called on the author's visual acuity to create its effect of represented reality, the novel's "holding a mirror to nature," in Stendhal's famous phrase.[76] Zola's Naturalist injunction to follow the model of the positivist physiologist Claude Bernard and "replace novels of pure imagination by novels of observation and experimentation"[77] can in retrospect be understood as both the apotheosis of this inclination and the harbinger of its coming crisis. For like the Impressionists with whom they are so often compared, the Naturalists relied on a vision that privileged the raw description of surface appearances over the more penetrating gaze revealing deep structures preferred by Realists.[78] That is, even as Zola talked of the novelist's experiment as a "forced observation"[79] rather than merely

76. According to Anita Brookner, "The concept was taken up and popularized by George Sand and was fully realized by Flaubert." *The Genius of the Future: Essays in French Art Criticism* (Ithaca, 1971), p. 53. Stendhal also emphasized the expressive character of art as well as the mimetic. See the discussion in Marguerite Iknayan, *The Concave Mirror: From Imitation to Expression in French Esthetic Theory* (Saratoga, Calif., 1983), pp. 49ff.

77. Émile Zola, "The Experimental Novel," in *Documents of Modern Literary Realism,* ed. George J. Becker (Princeton, 1963), p. 172.

78. This contrast between a phenomenalist naturalism and an essentialist realism was classically defended by Georg Lukács in *Studies in European Realism* (New York, 1964). Although Lukács's Hegelian Marxist defense of Realism has been subjected to considerable criticism, it continues to be compelling in terms of the issue of surface versus depth perception. For a recent discussion of Impressionism and Naturalism, which draws on his argument about their reification of surface, see Jameson, *The Political Unconscious.* For an alternative reading of the Realism/Naturalism relationship which seeks to go beyond the ocular metaphor, see Christopher Prendergast, *The Order of Mimesis: Balzac, Stendhal, Nerval, Flaubert* (Cambridge, 1986).

79. Zola, "The Experimental Novel," p. 163.

the passive registering of sensations, his method often seemed indiscriminately descriptive—too "retinal" in its fidelity to the experienced world.

And as in the case of Impressionism, an emphasis on raw experience, scientifically controlled or otherwise, could lead to a fetishistic preoccupation with the sensibility of the describer rather than with the object described. As early as Paul Bourget's 1883 *Nouveaux essais de psychologie contemporaine*, the Goncourt brothers' obsessive attention to visual detail was linked with their hyperaesthetic, elitist self-absorption.[80] Significantly, the famous "Manifesto of the Five against *La Terre*," an 1887 declaration of revolt by Zola's former disciples, could complain: "'A corner of nature seen through a temperament' has been transformed with respect to Zola into 'a corner of nature seen through a *morbid sensory apparatus*.'"[81]

Whether morbid or not, the emphasis on the author's sensory apparatus in Naturalism meant a heightened attention to surface effects, which could among other things produce that preference for color over form we have already noted in Impressionism. Thus the not yet Decadent Joris-Karl Huysmans, in his laudatory review of Zola's *L'Assommoir* in 1876, could proudly claim, "We make use of all the colors of the palette, of black as well as blue, we admire Ribera and Watteau without distinction."[82] "It is characteristic of Zola, in the manner of the Impressionist painters whom he admired," a later critic would agree, "to shift the emphasis of his visualization away from those qualities that inhere in the object itself to those qualities that are largely determined by the receiving apparatus of the observer. (Color, for instance, is not a property of the object itself. The experience of color is subjective.)"[83]

---

80. Bourget, *Nouveaux essais de psychologie contemporaine* (Paris, 1883), pp. 137–198. For a more recent discussion of the Goncourts' visual preoccupations and their links with aestheticism, see Debora L. Silverman, *Art Nouveau in Fin-de-Siècle France: Politics, Psychology and Style* (Berkeley, 1989), pp. 33f.

81. "Manifesto of the Five against *La Terre*," in Becker, *Documents of Modern Literary Realism*, p. 349.

82. Huysmans, "Émile Zola and *L'Assommoir*," in Becker, *Documents of Modern Literary Realism*, p. 233.

Significantly, the literary rediscovery of color as opposed to form was not confined to Naturalism. Baudelaire, as already noted, praised its resurrection in the paintings of Delacroix, and in turn has been lauded for his own use of its evocative potential. Roger Shattuck, speculating on the possible influence on him of Chevreul, claims that "like the most extreme of the Impressionists at the height of their scientific experiments, Baudelaire yearns to obliterate the contours of objects in order to convey the pervasive vibration of molecules and light."[84] His fascination with color was anything but Naturalist, linked as it was with his complicated theory of correspondences between sensual and transcendental phenomena. But what he shared with the later Naturalists was a withdrawal of confidence in the author's ability to represent in language the formal regularities of a "real" world in Cartesian perspectivalist space, the world in which the Realists had felt more firmly secure.

The implications of the restoration of color were even more evident in the case of Symbolist poetry. Here an emphasis on the senses could paradoxically lead in an antipositivist direction, as the relationship between perceived sensation and external object, already under some strain in late positivism, virtually collapsed. As Françoise Meltzer has contended, "Color leads to the heart of what symbolism is, for it is the paradigmatic literary expression of a general spiritual crisis—a crisis in epistemology."[85] This crisis meant not only a loss of faith in the ability to depict what Locke would have called primary qualities (those formal regularities of the Cartesian perspectivalist scopic regime), but also the secondary ones, which the Naturalists still believed themselves capable of describing with verisimilitude.

Objects were not entirely absent from the Symbolist aesthetic, but they tended to be prized for their connotative, associative power, rather than as

83. Spiegel, *Fiction and the Camera Eye*, p. 42.

84. Shattuck, *The Innocent Eye*, p. 143.

85. Françoise Meltzer, "Color as Cognition in Symbolist Verse," *Critical Inquiry*, 5, 2 (Winter, 1978), p. 254.

referential anchors. Although the young Mallarmé had appreciated the Impressionists' stress on an "aspect" of reality caught on their retinas,[86] when he came to value that famous "flower absent from all bouquets," the stimulus of actual sight seemed left far behind. Color became less a property of observed objects than a verbal effect. While contending that Mallarmé never completely jettisoned the ontological priority of the natural world, Paul de Man conceded that he "may well be the nineteenth-century poet who went further than any other in sacrificing the stability of the object to the demands of a lucid poetic awareness."[87]

The Symbolists' fascination with color over form and their hostility to the mimetic residue left in Impressionism and Naturalism was paralleled by their celebration of the musicality of poetry.[88] Here they sought to realize an inclination already embryonically apparent in Romanticism, despite its adoration of the seer's "unmediated vision." Indeed, they went even further in seeking the systematic "derangement of the senses."

The Symbolists' devotion to Richard Wagner, which began with Baudelaire's defense of *Tannhäuser* in 1861 and culminated with the *Revue wagnérienne* in 1885–1888,[89] expressed their apotheosis of sound and concomitant deprivileging of sight. As Meltzer notes, "Color, with its

86. See his 1876 review of the Impressionists, reprinted as "The Impressionists and Edouard Manet" in *The New Painting*, where he writes, "I content myself with reflecting on the clear and durable mirror of painting, that which perpetually lives yet dies every moment, which only exists by the will of Idea, yet constitutes in my domain the only authentic and certain merit of nature—the Aspect" (p. 34).

87. Paul de Man, *The Rhetoric of Romanticism* (New York, 1984), p. 8.

88. The Impressionists too were deeply interested in musical effects. As Wylie Sypher notes, "The chromatic art of the Impressionists easily slid over into auditory effects: witness the last harmonies of Monet and Whistler, where geometric perspective doesn't matter. In his late coloristic technique, Monet salvages the auditory values that had never been really excluded from the culture McLuhan considers visual." *Literature and Technology: The Alien Vision* (New York, 1971), p. 113.

89. See Gerald D. Turbow, "Art and Politics: Wagnerism in France," in *Wagnerism in European Culture and Politics*, ed. David C. Large and William Weber (Ithaca, 1984). Although the ideal of the *Gesamtkunstwerk* was opposed to pure music and thus entailed a corresponding elevation of the visual to a role of unwonted significance in musical performances, Wagner's preference was for atmosphere and color over form

dominance in symbolist verse, may be seen as the poetic equivalent and linguistic analogy of music, for it too has no prescribed *signifié* but rather moves directly from the *signe* to connotation."[90] They valued in music less its underlying formal structure, however, than its sensual effects on the listener. Paul Verlaine advised poets to remember "de la musique avant tout chose" and Mallarmé announced that "Music and Literature constitute the moving facet—now looming toward obscurity, now glittering unconquerably—of that single, true phenomenon which I have called Idea."[91] What they meant was what might be called the auditory version of *lux* rather than *lumen*, a distinction in fact already made by Boethius when he contrasted *musica humana* with *musica mundana* in the sixth century.[92]

Not surprisingly, their stress on the suggestive effects of verbal color and music was accompanied by a deliberate retreat from the communicative norm of linguistic clarity, which had so long dominated French letters. Verlaine's influential injunction to "take eloquence and wring its neck" meant not only a call to abandon the hackneyed clichés of the past. It also signaled a preference for hermetic obscurity over easy accessibility. Ironically, in their zeal to purify the language the Symbolists separated purity from clarity, and in so doing, helped pave the way for the belief that when a visual dimension of the text was present to consciousness, it should produce meaningless opacity rather than communicative transparency.

In fact, for all its emphasis on the musicalization of poetry, Symbolism

---

or line. In the music itself, color also predominated, which contributed to its phantasmagoric effect. See the discussion in Theodor W. Adorno, *In Search of Wagner*, trans. Rodney Livingstone (London, 1981). In such works as *Tristan*, with its famous dousing of the torch by the lovers in Act 2, the Counter-Enlightenment implications of Wagner's project are most apparent.

90. Meltzer, "Color as Cognition in Symbolist Verse," p. 259.

91. Verlaine, *"Art poétique"*; Mallarmé, "Music and Literature," reprinted in *Modern Continental Literary Criticism*, ed. O. B. Hardison, Jr. (New York, 1962), p. 183. Mallarmé's stress on the Idea may have expressed the Platonic impulse in his thought, but it is important to note that unlike Plato, he valorized its sensual rather than intellectual manifestations.

92. For a discussion, see Hollander, *Vision and Resonance*, p. 13.

itself did at times probe the visual dimension of literature in precisely this way. Synesthesia, after all, meant the creative confusion of the senses, not the overthrowing of one hierarchy in the name of another. In the later Mallarmé in particular, a renewed appreciation of another of poetry's visual aspects can be discerned. Here, however, it was not so much the exploration of correspondences between color and sonority, the attempt to "see" the tints of musically resonating vowels, as a sensitivity to the actual appearance of the printed text on the page, its material reality as a non-representational entity in its own right. Here in fact was an early version of the typical modernist contention that poetry should not mean, but be.[93]

Visual poetry was not an invention of the modernist period, having as ancient a pedigree as the Greek Simmias of Rhodes (c. 300 B.C.).[94] It had flourished during Carolingian era when acrostics were a favored form, was popular among the anti-iconic Islamic poets, and returned in the Renaissance and Baroque, when Villon, Rabelais, and others played with its possibilities. During the eighteenth century it fell out of favor as too frivolous for high art, although it never entirely disappeared as a popular pastime. Its revival as a serious form, however, had to await the publication in 1897 of Mallarmé's "Un coup de dés jamais n'abolira le hasard" (A Throw of the Dice Will Never Abolish Chance).

One of his most enigmatic works, "Un coup de dés" has inspired elaborate interpretative efforts, but only a few points can be developed here.[95] Mallarmé did not ape the visible form of an object in his arrangement of words, as had, say, Rabelais with a bottle-shaped drinking song in *Gargantua and Pantagruel*. Instead, he varied the typeface of different words,

---

93. This injunction appeared, for example, in Wallace Stevens's "Opus Posthumous," in the lines: "The poem is the cry of the occasion / Part of the res itself and not about it."

94. See Richard Kostelanetz, ed., *Visual Literary Criticism: A New Collection* (Carbondale and Edwardsville, Ill., 1979); "Visual Poetics," special isssue of *Dada/Surrealism*, 12 (1983); and Hollander, *Vision and Resonance*, chap. 12.

95. Probably the most exhaustive study is Robert Greer Cohn, *Un coup de dés jamais n'abolira le hasard* (Paris, 1952).

which were dispersed over both pages of an open book surrounded by large expanses of open space. Spatial relations rather than normal syntax functioned to tie the words together. The effect was not to reinforce the semantic meanings of the words, as in traditional visual poetry, but rather to intersect with and perhaps even disturb them. Slowing down the normal linear rush through a poem's lines, it created a necessary delay in the realization of its meaning. According to Lyotard, an admirer of Mallarmé's devaluation of communication, "When the word is made thing, it is not to copy a visible thing, but to render visible an invisible, lost thing: it gives form to the imaginary of which it speaks."[96] This form, however, is opaque rather than transparent; if the materiality of the word on the page can be said to mirror the meaning of the text, it does so through an anamorphic glass, which reflects only chiasmically. The result is a hybrid "discourse/figure" that "expresses through its blanks, its body, the folds of its pages."[97]

Mallarmé's goal, to be sure, was to arouse in the reader an openness to that mysterious Idea his work always sought to evoke. Thus the material dimension of his work never willingly undercut its auratic, cultic aspirations. Nor did Mallarmé challenge the institution of art itself with its transcendental, autotelic pretensions in the way that Duchamp with his readymades did. His work was thus never quite the literary equivalent of Duchamp's "antiretinal" painting, even if it problematized the communicative function of language.

But one possible direction implied by "Un coup de dés" was the so-called *chosiste* or "concrete poetry" of later modernism.[98] Here words tended to be reduced to nothing but their material thingness on the page, virtually without any communicative, representational, or even aural potential (they were impossible to read aloud). A further way station on the road to this exclusively visual poetry were the patterned *calligrames* of the

96. Jean-François Lyotard, *Discours, Figure* (Paris, 1985), p. 69.
97. Ibid., p. 68.
98. See Augusto de Campos, "Points—Periphery—Concrete Poetry," in Kostelanetz, ed., *The Avant-Garde Tradition in Literature*, as well as many of the essays in Kostelanetz, ed., *Visual Literary Criticism*.

"painter-poet" Guillaume Apollinaire, which were influenced by the antinarrative simultanism of the Cubist and Futurist painters.[99] Futurist poets like F. T. Marinetti, Dadaists like Tristan Tzara, Hugo Ball, and Raoul Hausmann, and a host of other writers through the twentieth century developed still other variations of the visual poetry whose revival was begun by Mallarmé. Even the visually self-conscious novels of Alain Robbe-Grillet were to manifest the anticommunicative opacity of "Un coup de dés," albeit without its unconventional typography.

In fact, it is only by realizing the power of Mallarmé's model that we can begin to understand what might well seem like a non sequitur: the contribution of an often visually obsessed modernist literature—other examples could easily be drawn from non-French traditions like Anglo-American Imagism[100] or Italian Futurism—to the antiocular discourse we are examining in this study. The contradiction is resolved, however, if we remember the radical difference between, on the one hand, a Realism that sought to describe in transparent words a visible reality there to be observed by an all-seeing narrator, or even a Naturalism that tried to be faithful to the fleeting appearances of that still objective world, and on the other, the experiments in antimimetic multiperspectivalism, anamorphosis, self-reflecting *mise en abyme*, discourse/figure chiasmus, and concrete poetics that we call modernism. Writing about the aftermath of Victorian English literature, the critic W. D. Shaw makes an observation that applies as well to its continental counterpart.

> After 1870, the rise of a formalist tradition, founded upon a theory of symbolic fictions in the philosophy of science and religion, treats the images of the artist as material realities in their own right. Instead of likening these images to shadows, to the mere copies of an original, formalism becomes a potent means

99. Apollinaire is called the "painter-poet" in Roger Shattuck's discussion of him in *The Banquet Years: The Origins of the Avant-Garde in France 1885 to World War I* (New York, 1968), chap. 10. For his art criticism, see the collection edited by LeRoy C. Breunig, *Apollinaire on Art: Essays and Reviews 1902–1918*, trans. Susan Suleiman (New York, 1972).

for turning the tables on reality—for turning *it* into a shadow. The disappearance of dimensions of depth (the spatial depth of a stereopticon and the temporal depth of a time-lapse photograph) brings into being a new region of copresence, which resembles the merely two-dimensional surface of kaleidoscopes.[101]

Is it any surprise that, as in the case of Modernist painting, an explosion of ocular experimentation could produce visual spleen as well as visual euphoria?

The potential for this disillusionment is evident in Marcel Proust, whose visual interests, even obsessions, have been remarked by a wide variety of commentators. His essays on the 1890s on Chardin, Monet, Rembrandt, Gustave Moreau, and Jean Antoine Watteau, as well as his appreciation of Ruskin's art criticism, have been plumbed for their effect on his fiction.[102] Virtually every ocular experience and every attitude toward vision of his era has been discerned in his work. His "multiple vision" focusing on psychological, social, and even preternatural experience has been praised as a summa of the detached observational techniques of modern French fiction.[103] His "intensely—even morbidly—ocular" preoccupations have been compared both to telescopic and microscopic voyeurism.[104] His fascination with the evocatory power of sensory impressions—as the famous madeleine shows, not only visual

100. In France, the Imagist aesthetic was perhaps best expressed by Remy de Gourmont, who turned in the late 1890s from the evocative musicality of Symbolism to a stress on less emotive visual metaphors. For a discussion of his influence on poets like Pound and Eliot, see Sanford Schwartz, *The Matrix of Modernism: Pound, Eliot, and Early 20th-Century Thought* (Princeton, 1985).

101. W. D. Shaw, "The Optical Metaphor: Victorian Poetics and the Theory of Knowledge," *Victorian Studies*, 23, 3 (Spring, 1980), p. 320.

102. See, for example, Borowitz, *The Impact of Art on French Literature*.

103. Martin Turnell, *The Art of French Fiction* (London, 1959), pp. 13–14.

104. Harry Levin, *The Gates of Horn: A Study of Five French Realists* (New York, 1966), p. 387. For another discussion of his voyeurism, see Dennis G. Sullivan, "On Vision in Proust: The Icon and the *Voyeur*," *Modern Language Notes*, 84, 4 (May, 1969), pp. 646–661.

ones—has earned him a comparison with the Impressionists or Division-ists,[105] just as his sensitivity to the kaleidoscope of multiple perspectives has led to one with the Cubists.[106] The retrospective totalization at the end of *Remembrance of Things Past* has been interpeted as the triumph of atemporal spatialized form, produced by a God's-eye view from afar of juxtaposed rather than successive moments in time.[107] His enlargements of those microscopically examined instances has been likened to cin-ematic close-ups.[108] Even Proust's exquisitely discriminating "optics of clothes" has been dissected as a major element in his work.[109]

These and countless other arguments and comparisons have been ad-duced to demonstrate the indisputable centrality of Proust's visual preoc-cupations. But what is sometimes not fully appreciated is the extent to which he incorporated many of the doubts and uncertainties about ocularcentrism, which we have seen emerging in the Modernist era. To-ward the new visual technologies of the nineteenth century, for example, Proust maintained a certain ambivalent skepticism. Like Baudelaire be-fore him, he worried about the camera, whose alienating coldness he deeply distrusted.[110] According to Susan Sontag, "Whenever Proust men-

105. See, for example, J. Theodore Johnson, Jr., "Proust's 'Impressionism' Reconsid-ered in the Light of the Visual Arts of the Twentieth Century," in *Twentieth Century French Fiction,* ed. George Stambolian (New Brunswick, N.J., 1975) and Eloise Knapp Hay, "Proust, James, Conrad and Impressionism," *Style,* 22, 3 (Fall, 1988). Both of these essays begin by noting Proust's Impressionist moments and then dis-cuss others closer to Post-Impressionist movements like Cubism. In *Remembrance of Things Past,* the artist Elstir is a composite of various Impressionist painters with a strong residue of Chardin.

106. See, for example, Claude Gandelman, "Proust as Cubist," *Art History,* 2, 3 (Sep-tember, 1979); and Stephen Kern, *The Culture of Time and Space 1880–1918* (Cam-bridge, Mass., 1983), p. 148.

107. Frank, "Spatial Form in Modern Literature," pp. 52ff.; for a more extensive exploration of this theme, see Georges Poulet, *L'Espace proustienne* (Paris, 1963).

108. Siegfried Kracauer, *History: The Last Things Before the Last* (New York, 1969), p. 161.

109. Diana Festa-McCormick, *Proustian Optics of Clothes: Mirrors, Masks, Mores* (Saratoga, Calif., 1984).

tions photographs, he does so disparagingly: as a synonym for a shallow, too exclusively visual, merely voluntary relation to the past, whose yield is insignificant compared with the deep discoveries to be made by responding to cues given by all the senses—the technique he called 'involuntary memory.'"[111] And like many other intellectuals of his day, such as Remy de Gourmont,[112] he deeply distrusted the implications of the cinema.[113]

Proust's involvement with voyeurism, while not as ironically detached as Duchamp's was to be in *Etant donnés*, also exposes its ambiguous links to desire and domination. The voyeuristic gaze in *Remembrance of Things Past* might be understood to have a sinister implication, for, as one critic put it, "the subject defined by vision is also defined by violence, and the Albertine constituted as an icon is also constituted as a prisoner. . . . Vision, within this context, achieves the status of an *act*. It is situated with all modalities of immediacy for Proust, within the category of aggression."[114] Here we have anticipated the cruel dialectic of "le regard" later explored by Sartre in *Being and Nothingness*. Not for Proust was the benign reciprocity of lovers' glances.

Nowhere, however, were Proust's ambivalences about vision as evident as in his profound explorations of the relationship between time and sight. The issue of vision's alleged spatiality and resistance to temporality

110. See the treatment of the camera in *The Guermantes Way, Remembrance of Things Past*, trans. C. K. Scott-Moncrieff (New York, 1934), 1, pp. 814–815; and 3, pp. 332 and 897–898. For a discussion of the first of these passages, see Alan Spiegel, *Fiction and the Camera Eye*, pp. 83ff.

111. Susan Sontag, *On Photography* (New York, 1978), p. 164.

112. Remy de Gourmont, "L'image," *Le Film* (May 22, 1924); reprinted in *Intelligence du cinématographe*, ed. Marcel L'Herbier (Paris, 1946). A change in the French intellectuals' attitudes came only after World War I with the work of Louis Delluc. See the discussion in Stuart Liebman, "French Film Theory," *Quarterly Review of Film Studies*, 8, 1 (Winter, 1983), pp. 1–23.

113. Proust, *Remembrance of Things Past*, 2, pp. 1003–1004; and 3, p. 917. Despite his disdain, critics have found cinematic techniques in his work; see, for example, Johnson, Jr., "Proust's 'Impressionism'," pp. 44ff.

114. Sullivan, "On Vision in Proust," pp. 660–661.

has been long and inconclusively debated. In the *ut pictura poesis* tradition, it was most famously developed by Gotthold Ephraim Lessing in *Laokoön* (1766), in which the stasis of painting was contrasted absolutely with the dynamism of poetry.[115] This rigid opposition was often tacitly or explicitly challenged, and Proust was himself clearly unimpressed by it. In *Remembrance of Things Past*, time was developed in specifically ocular terms.

As Shattuck has demonstrated, that model of temporalized vision was fundamentally binocular rather than monocular.[116] The stereoscope rather than the single photograph was the key to a liberating visual experience for Proust. Rather than reducing sight to a single but flat image which could then only be followed by a bewildering chaos of others, the stereoscope created depth by combining two images through a meaningful juxtaposition.

> The *stereoscopic principle* abandons the portrayal of motion in order to establish a form of arrest which resists time. It selects a few images or impressions sufficiently different from one another not to give the effect of continuous motion, and sufficiently related to be linked in a discernible pattern. This stereoscopic principle allows our binocular (or multiocular) vision of mind to hold contradictory aspects of things in the steady perspective of recognition, of relief in time.[117]

Proust's binoculars were thus a means to deal with the breakdown of Cartesian monocular certainty without succumbing to the vertigo of Impressionist evanescence or Post-Impressionist kaleidoscopic fragmentation. The technique, however, gives both time and space their due, for the

115. For recent treatments of Lessing, see Jeoraldean McClain, "Time in the Visual Arts: Lessing and Modern Criticism," *The Journal of Aesthetics and Art Criticism*, 44, 1 (Fall, 1985) and Mitchell, *Iconology*, chap. 4.

116. Roger Shattuck, *Proust's Binoculars: A Study of Memory, Time and Recognition in À la recherche du temps perdu* (Princeton, 1983).

117. Ibid., p. 51.

coordination of the two images requires a minute delay in perception. Writing explicitly against Joseph Frank's single-minded stress on spatial form, Shattuck contends that *Remembrance of Things Past* affirms both a temporal and spatial perspective: "On the one hand it insists on the lived temporal order of things, which combines individual development with a sense of the gradual modulation of reality itself. On the other it focuses on occasional resurrections revealing a glimpse of the past outside of contingent time and creating patterns so convincing as to be called essences."[118]

But how successful, we may ask, is this integration of two (or more) perspectives? How well does binocular vision really compensate for the confusions and uncertainties of the post-Cartesian scopic regime? How synoptic is the "high altitude" retrospective totalization at the end of the novel's own temporality? Shattuck himself is generally positive in his answers to these questions.

> Marcel and the reader, after the opening glimpse of paradise in Combray, move on into the world with only one eye open. Relief in time, binocular vision of reality, come only in moments of mysterious pleasure provoked by an unfamiliar setting (carriage, train, hotel) or by music. Then suddenly at the end, the other eye opens when we are sure it has atrophied, and Marcel attains both the wholeness of vision to recognize himself and his world, and the final certainty of his vocation.[119]

But he also acknowledges that that vocation is to be an artist, which means the resolution Marcel achieves is an entirely aesthetic one within a work of art, not something "in life." Significantly, in one of his long footnotes, Shattuck acknowledges that such a solution remains problematic.

> Light is the most important single factor in the knowledge of the universe. Yet, as is clear on every page of Proust, this medium of

118. Shattuck, *Proust* (London, 1974), p. 119. For his somewhat less critical treatment of Frank in *Proust's Binoculars*, see pp. 112–113.

119. Shattuck, *Proust's Binoculars*, p. 96.

> observation ultimately becomes a barrier to final knowledge. . . .
> The binocular nature of human vision (which requires that we see
> double and cross-eyed) introduces into the seat of our conscious-
> ness the principle of essential discrepancy, of meaningful error.
> This illusion of relief in three dimensions would scarcely suffice if
> we could not move through space and explore the nature of that
> error in order to make sense of it.[120]

Read against the grain, Proust's seemingly triumphant stereoscopic integration of spatiality and temporality, vision and the word, appears far
less secure— for his contemplative, aesthetic totalization lacks precisely
such a kinesthetic confirmation. As in the case of other modernist successors to a discredited Cartesian perspectivalism, his experiments in a new
visual order could not really provide a way to tame the bewildering
"frenzy of the visible" that led to the antiocular discourse of the twentieth
century.

⊙

Proust's optics of temporality have often been compared with the recovery of experienced time, *durée*, by Henri Bergson.[121] It is in his work that
we will encounter the initial frontal attack on ocularcentrism in modern
French philosophy. In fact, if Hannah Arendt is correct, Bergson was the
first modern philosopher anywhere to dispute the nobility of sight.[122] Although Nietzsche must also be considered a rival for this honor, his influence on the antiocularcentric discourse we are tracing came far later in
France than did Bergson's, whose critique was also more explicitly hostile.

The development of Western philosophy cannot be understood, it

120. Ibid., pp. 143–145.

121. See, for example, Floris Delattre, "Bergson et Proust: Accords et Dissonances,"
Les Études Bergsoniennes, 1 (1948), pp. 13–127. For a dissenting point of view, see
Gandelman, "Proust as Cubist," p. 361. He claims that Proust's notion of time is
more constructivist than Bergson's.

122. Hannah Arendt, *The Life of the Mind: Thinking* (New York, 1978), p. 122;
Jacques Ellul, in *The Humiliation of the Word*, trans. Joyce Main Hanks (Grand Rapids, Mich., 1985), p. 37, claims that Kierkegaard was the first.

bears repeating, without attending to its habitual dependence on visual metaphors of one sort or another. From the shadows playing on the wall of Plato's cave and Augustine's praise of the divine light to Descartes's ideas available to a "steadfast mental gaze" and the Enlightenment's faith in the data of our senses, the ocularcentric underpinnings of our philosophical tradition have been undeniably pervasive. Whether in terms of speculation, observation, or revelatory illumination, Western philosophy has tended to accept without question the traditional sensual hierarchy. And if Rorty's argument about the "mirror of nature" is right, modern Western thinkers in particular have built their theories of knowledge even more resolutely on a visual foundation.

Although alternative traditions such as a hearing-centered hermeneutics can be discerned during the heyday of ocularcentrism, at least at the margins of philosophical discourse, it was only during the waning years of the nineteenth century that a concerted challenge to the hegemony of the visual was successfully launched. As in the case of painting and literature, its animus was first directed against the domination of the ancien scopic régime we have called Cartesian perspectivalism, and then it was broadened to include all variants of ocularcentrism. In France more explicitly than elsewhere, the interaction of all these assaults seems to have produced that widely shared suspicion of sight, at least among intellectuals, which might be called, with apologies to Comolli, a frenzy of the antivisual.

In the case of philosophy, three changes must be singled out for special mention. The first concerns what can be termed the detranscendentalization of perspective; the second, the recorporealization of the cognitive subject; and the third, the revalorization of time over space. In all of these ways, the status of visual primacy was brought into question. Although certain subsequent philosophers such as Merleau-Ponty sought to retrieve a more viable notion of vision from the wreckage of the older one, the act of demolition, as we hope to show in subsequent chapters, was too decisive to be reversed. Still obsessed with visual questions to our day, most French thinkers have nonetheless decisively jettisoned the ocularcentric assumptions of the Western tradition.

One of the ironies of the story leading to that outcome is the coincidence at the end of the nineteenth century of the dissolution of the perspectival grid in painting and the authorial or narrative point of view in literature, on the one hand, and the emergence of a self-conscious "perspectivism" in philosophy, on the other. Here the initial step was taken in Germany, where the term was coined by Gustav Teichmüller in his *Die wirkliche und die scheinbare Welt* of 1882.[123] Unlike the earlier monadological perspectivism of Leibniz, this version did not assume a preestablished harmony among different points of view. Teichmüller was much admired by Nietzsche, who wrote in *The Genealogy of Morals*, "Let us beware of the tentacles of such contradictory notions as 'pure reason,' 'absolute knowledge,' 'absolute intelligence.' All these concepts presuppose an eye such as no living being can imagine, an eye required to have no direction, to abrogate its active and interpretative powers, precisely those powers that alone make of seeing a seeing of *something*. All seeing is essentially perspective, and so is all knowing."[124]

In such works as *Beyond Good and Evil* and *The Gay Science*, Nietzsche would apply perspectivism to normative as well as cognitive issues. Indeed, as Gary Shapiro has noted, he would even apply it to vision itself, arguing against any single version, benign or malevolent, as essential.[125] Later thinkers like José Ortega y Gasset would popularize the view that modernist philosophy was essentially perspectivalist.[126]

The seeming irony produced by the rise of philosophical perspectivism

123. For a discussion of the origins of philosophical perspectivism, see Claudio Guillén, *Literature as System: Essays Toward the Theory of Literary History* (Princeton, 1971), pp. 318f.

124. Nietzsche, *The Genealogy of Morals,* trans. Francis Golfing (New York, 1956), p. 255.

125. Gary Shapiro, "In the Shadows of Philosophy: Nietzsche and the Question of Vision," in *Modernity and the Hegemony of Vision*, ed. David Michael Levin (Berkeley, 1993).

126. Ortega y Gasset, *The Modern Theme*, trans. James Cleugh (New York, 1961), chap. 10; see Guillén for a discussion, pp. 334f. He cites a work on Ortega by Antonio Rodriguez Huéscar, which lists some thirteen meanings of the term "perspective" in his vocabulary.

at the time of its collapse elsewhere will dissolve, however, if we remember the inherently transcendental premises of the Cartesian perspectivalist scopic regime. That is, Descartes assumed that the clear and distinct ideas available to anyone's mental gaze would be exactly the same because of the divinely insured congruence between such ideas and the world of extended matter. Individual perspectives did not, therefore, matter, as the deictic specificity of the subject could be bracketed out in any cognitive endeavor. The same assumption informed the Albertian concept of painterly perspective; all beholders would see the same grid of orthogonal lines converging on the same vanishing point, if they gazed through, as it were, the same camera obscura. Perspective in this sense was atemporal, decorporealized, and transcendental.

Significantly, a detranscendentalized interpretation of perspective first achieved prominence in the area of knowledge Descartes had scorned as inferior to philosophy—that is, in history.[127] Since at least the time of Chladenius in the eighteenth century, the uniqueness of the individual historian's angle of vision on the past was acknowledged as a crucial determinant of the narrative he or she constructed.[128] The assumption remained of an actual history "in itself" prior to the perspectivalist reconstruction by later historians. Although the dream of obtaining an omniscient view of it did not completely die, as Hegel's philosophy of history demonstrates, at least some distance was opened between partial perspectives and such a putatively total one.

Nietzsche's more radical gesture was to deny the premise of a historical reality "in itself" and extend that denial beyond the "soft" realm of historical knowledge to the allegedly "hard" ones of philosophy and science.

127. There were, to be sure, anticipations in other areas. Montaigne's essays and Nicholas of Cusa's cosmological speculations display an awareness of the implications of finite, localized perspective. Descartes's transcendentalization of perspective can, in fact, be interpreted as a defensive reaction against the relativist threat posed by such uses of perspective. See Karsten Harries, "Descartes, Perspective and the Angelic Eye," *Yale French Studies*, 49 (1973), p. 29.

128. See Reinhard Koselleck, *Futures Past: On the Semantics of Historical Time*, trans. Keith Tribe (Cambridge, Mass., 1985), pp. 130f.

All that was left was an irreducibly nontranscendental riot of interpretations without an external object to serve as the standard by which their veracity could be measured. The death of God meant the end of a God's-eye view.[129] The very distinction between an illusory appearance present to the fallible senses of the observing subject and a deeper, essential truth available to the intellect or reason (there to be "seen" by the "mind's eye") collapsed. So too did the distance between subjective consciousness and a mimetically reproduced object, that dualism which began, as we have seen Hans Jonas argue, with the ancient Greek privileging of sight. Plato's singular sun of truth illuminating a reality of forms was replaced by a thousand and one suns shining on a multitude of different realities.[130]

Not surprisingly, Nietzsche's detranscendentalized perspectivism would be much admired by later contributors to the antiocularcentric discourse. Sarah Kofman, for example, endorsed his dethroning of the camera obscura model as a way to discern truth from falsehood, the model that underlay theories of ideology such as Marx's.[131] She applauded as well his frank acknowledgment that metaphors, often those of vision, inevitably informed the most denotatively neutral philosophical language.[132] Lyotard would compare Duchamp's transformations of incommensurable spatial projections with Nietzsche's destruction of a master point of view.[133]

Nietzsche's critique also extended to the putatively disinterested purity of even the partial perspectivalist gaze, which was assumed by positivists

---

129. It is not even clear that a profane, individual view was left in its place. As Lars-Henrik Schmidt has noted, "Nietzsche's 'perspective' is a paradoxical category of process: it formulates in itself the paradox that there is no center for perspectives in perspectivism. Yet the concept of perspective in itself demands a center, from which perspectivalism occurs. This paradoxical relationship is true of all of Nietzsche's 'categories' and refers to the fact that using words is already too much; it is already a lie. The paradoxical category refers to its own impossibility" (*Immediacy Lost: Construction of the Social in Rousseau and Nietzsche* [Copenhagen, 1988], p. 147).

130. For a discussion of the metaphor of multitudinous suns in Nietzsche, see Bernard Pautrat, *Versions du soleil: Figures et système de Nietzsche* (Paris, 1971), pp. 288f.

131. Sarah Kofman, *Camera obscura: de l'idéologie* (Paris, 1973).

and their aesthetic correlates, the Impressionists and Naturalists. Himself plagued by failing eyesight from the age of twelve on, he knew of the pitfalls of relying on visual experience alone.[134] Mocking what he sarcastically dubbed the doctrine of "immaculate perception,"[135] Nietzsche insisted that every viewpoint was always value-laden, never detached. Vision was thus as much projective as receptive, as much active as passive. What in aesthetic terms was the creative mingling of the Apollonian dream of individuated, pure form with the blind forces of self-dissolving Dionysian energy, in cognitive terms meant the disruption of the speculative or observational ideal of neutrality by the insistent voice of life-affirming instincts. These appeared in shadows as well as light, or in the dim twilight of dawn before the glare of the midday sun.[136]

Another way to register the disruption of the ideal of neutrality was to acknowledge the existence of the concrete body underlying the putatively disincarnated subject of knowledge. Nietzsche was not, to be sure, the first to remark its importance; Ludwig Feuerbach, and after him, Marx had developed a materialist notion of the practical rather than contemplative subject, which meant in part situating theory in the context of lived bodily experience. In France, François-Pierre Maine de Biran had also stressed the importance of the willing body in his psycho-physiological corrective to the sensationalism of Condillac and the Ideologues Pierre Cabanis and Antoine Louis Claude Destutt de Tracy, while resisting a strictly materialist reading of that body.[137] It was not, however, until Bergson that the rights of the body were explicitly set against the tyranny

132. Sarah Kofman, *Nietzsche et la métaphore* (Paris, 1983).

133. Lyotard, *Les transformateurs Duchamp*, pp. 49 and 154.

134. Ronald Hayman, *Nietzsche: A Critical Life* (New York, 1980), p. 24.

135. Friedrich Nietzsche, *Thus Spake Zarathustra*, trans. R. J. Hollingdale (London, 1961), p. 149.

136. Gary Shapiro remarks on the importance of these metaphors in such works as *The Wander and His Shadow, The Twilight of the Idols*, and *Daybreak*.

137. For a discussion of Maine de Biran's relation to Bergson, see Henri Gouhier, "Maine de Biran et Bergson," *Études Bergsoniennes*, 1 (1948), pp. 131–173.

of the eye. Going beyond the residually visual implications of perspectivism,[138] he developed a fundamental critique of ocularcentrism that outdistanced even that of Nietzsche.

To interpret Bergson as a defender of the body against the eye may seem improbable to those who recall his acknowledged debt to "spiritualist" thinkers like Félix Ravaisson,[139] his attraction to Catholicism, and his easy incorporation into the religiously inflected antimaterialism that came to be called Bergsonism. So too his positing of a creative rather than naturalist evolution, his belief in the immortality of the soul, and his distrust of the positivist reduction of mind to brain may suggest an unlikely candidate for champion of the body. And certainly, there is little evidence that he thought very deeply about the body as a gendered, libidinally charged source of desire in the manner of his Viennese contemporary, Sigmund Freud.[140]

And yet, in certain fundamental ways, Bergson helped redirect philosophical inquiry back toward the body as intertwined with consciousness before the separation of mind from matter. In *Matter and Memory*, first published in 1896, he challenged the positivist image of the body as an object to be analyzed from the outside, as merely one of innumerable "things" in the material world. Instead, he claimed that it was the ground of all of our perceptions: "As my body moves in space, all the other images vary, while that image, my body, remains invariable. I must, therefore, make it a center, to which I refer all the other images. . . . *My body* is that which stands out as the center of these perceptions."[141]

Rather than construing the body as an object of contemplation, Bergson claimed, we should understand it instead as the ground of our

138. In the index to his collected works compiled in *Les Études Bergsoniennes*, 6 (1961), there is no entry for perspective or perspectivism.

139. Bergson, "The Life and Work of Ravaisson," *The Creative Mind*, trans. Mabelle L. Andison (Totowa, N.J., 1975).

140. Bergson was not entirely ignorant of psychoanalysis, as shown by the occasional reference to Freud, e.g., in *The Creative Mind*, p. 75, but he seems never to have incorporated it into his work.

141. Bergson, *Matter and Memory*, pp. 46–47.

acting in the world: "Our body is an instrument of action, and of action only. In no degree, in no sense, under no aspect, does it serve to prepare, far less to explain, a representation."[142] A fundamental truth of the lived body, as opposed to the body as object of contemplation, is its movement in the world, its ability to be a vehicle of human choice. Because of this movement, the body provides us with perceptions that are necessarily informed by recollection and anticipation, rather than mere instantaneous receptions of external stimuli. Memory for Bergson consists both of images available to voluntary recall by the intellect and corporeally inscribed habits "which accumulate within the body."[143] Whereas the former are like pictures in the mind, the latter are actions that are repeated without any intervening images. "To *picture*," Bergson insisted, "is not to *remember*."[144]

What Bergson liked to call "true memory" was irreducible to bodily habits, for it also involved the restoration into consciousness of recollections that are stored somewhere else. But although that ill-defined "somewhere else" was not reducible to the body, without the latter, memories could not come into consciousness.

> The bodily memory, made up of the sum of the sensori-motor
> systems organized by habit, is then a quasi-instantaneous memory
> to which the true memory of the past serves as base. Since they
> are not two separate things, since the first is only . . . the pointed
> end, ever moving, inserted by the second in the shifting plane of
> experience, it is natural that the two functions should lend each
> other mutual support. . . . It is from the present that the appeal to
> which memory responds comes, and it is from the sensori-motor
> elements of present action that a memory borrows the warmth
> which gives it life.[145]

142. Ibid., p. 225.
143. Ibid., pp. 81–82.
144. Ibid., p. 135.
145. Ibid., pp. 152–153.

The body that can evoke memory in this second way is one in which all the senses are equiprimordial. Auditory, tactile, gustatory, and olfactory memories play as vital a role as do visual ones. Positivist psychologists like Théodul Ribot were wrong in claiming that "the mechanism of consciousness is comparable, without metaphor, to that of vision"[146] and then linking memory to the visual constitution of the self. Thus, while Bergson's preferred example was the smell of a rose,[147] Proust was not betraying his intentions by invoking Marcel's childhood with the taste of a madeleine. The very experience of being in the world, Bergson contended synesthetically, was prior to the dissociation of the senses. Explicitly rejecting the Sensationalist answer to the Molyneux problem (there was no innate knowledge of space before each sense individually experienced it), he contended that contemporary psychology, especially the work of Paul Janet and William James, had shown otherwise.[148] "The truth," he insisted, "is that space is no more without us than within us, and that it does not belong to a privileged group of sensations. *All* sensations partake of extensity; all are more or less deeply rooted in it."[149]

With these arguments Bergson hoped to overcome the false premises of both Idealism and Materialism. The former believed in the ontological priority of images in the mind, the latter in one central image: that of the body as a material thing. For Bergson, each was too cognitive, each too trusting in images of the intellect, each not sensitive enough to that vital substratum of concrete, lived reality available only to the holistic understanding of the intuition.[150] In short, Idealists and Materialists alike were

146. Théodul Ribot, *Les maladies de la mémoire* (Paris, 1881), p. 83.

147. Bergson, *Time and Free Will: An Essay on the Immediate Data of Consciousness*, trans. F. L. Pogson (New York, 1960), p. 161.

148. Bergson, *Matter and Memory*, pp. 215 and 259.

149. Ibid., p. 216.

150. Bergson sometimes defined the notoriously imprecise term "intuition" as a kind of internal vision, comparable to that of the seer. For example, in *La pensée et le mouvant* (Paris, 1934), he calls it "the direct vision of spirit by spirit" (p. 35). But then he immediately adds that it is so close to its object that it is in direct contact with it, thus suggesting a tactile rather than visual definition (ibid.).

unable to appreciate the priority of lived action over contemplative understanding based on the questionable apotheosis of sight.

Entailed in Bergson's defense of action over contemplation was his celebrated restoration of the philosophical importance of experienced time, a restoration explicitly directed against the hypertrophied role of vision. Although as we have noted earlier, it is wrong strictly speaking to equate sight with stasis—the eye's saccadic jumps, scanning of images, ability to glance as well as gaze, and so on, all contradict the equation—vision more than any other sense seems to betray an affinity for synchronicity, which our culture has often exploited by freezing the glance into the gaze.

Paradoxically, it was within the realm of the seemingly most diachronic, the measurement of time, that this affinity manifested itself. With the development of mechanical aids to keeping time in the later Middle Ages,[151] natural temporal rhythms and the eccentric temporalities of personal experience were subordinated to that relentlessly uniform series of points on a unidirectional line we now so automatically identify with time *per se*. Publically visible on the face of a clock, measured by the mechanical movement of its hands around a geometrically precise circle, time was thus expressed in essentially spatial terms.

The successful extension of this spatialization of time, often linked to the dissemination of the same bourgeois practices that fit so well with the triumph of Albertian perspective, reached its apogee in the nineteenth century. Despite the Romantics' attempt to imbue time with personal emotional pathos, often melancholic, it remained in thrall to the exigencies of capitalist industrialization. As Richard Glasser has observed, "time was spatialized in order to satisfy the general need for security. Future possibilities were directed into a restricted number of channels. This conception of things, which determined the future both as regards time and space with the greatest exactitutde, might be symbolized as a railway system and a timetable."[152] Not surprisingly, Marxist theoreticians like

151. David S. Landes, *Revolution in Time: Clocks and the Making of the Modern World* (Cambridge, Mass., 1983), chap. 3.
152. Richard Glasser, *Time in French Life and Thought*, trans. C. G. Pearson (Totowa, N.J., 1972), p. 288.

Georg Lukács would include the spatialization of time in their analysis of capitalist reification, in particular of the workers' labor power, which was even more rigorously controlled through the introduction in the twentieth century of Taylorist methods of performance regulation.[153]

Lukács was well acquainted with Bergson's critique.[154] Although Romantic poets like Alfred de Vigny had already protested against the spatialization of time,[155] it was only with Bergson that its links with the domination of vision were made explicit. In his 1889 doctoral thesis, *Time and Free Will: An Essay on the Immediate Data of Consciousness*, he argued that the very reduction of temporality to number, or extensive magnitude, privileges sight, for "every clear idea of number implies a visual image in space."[156] Such an image, moreover, is one of quantitative rather than qualitative difference, for each number is an abstract unit exchangeable with any other. The bias for quantity over quality, Bergson contended, already appears in the very notion of a uniform spatiality, which characterized philosophies like Kant's: "The more you insist on the difference between the impressions made on our retina by two points of a homogeneous surface, the more do you thereby make room for the activity of the mind, which perceives under the form of extensive homogeneity what is given it as qualitative heterogeneity."[157] Granting that activity too much power led to what Bergson called "Kant's great mistake":[158] conceiving time itself as a homogeneous medium. Here others had preceded him, as demonstrated by Zeno's paradoxes, which Bergson famously refuted by rigorously distinguishing between indivisible movement in time and the homogeneously divisible space in which it took place. (Zeno's

---

153. Georg Lukács, *History and Class Consciousness*, trans. Rodney Livingstone (Cambridge, Mass., 1968), p. 90.

154. In fact, he was attacked by other Marxists for absorbing too much from the "anti-scientific" Bergson. See, for example, Lucio Colletti, *Marxism and Hegel*, trans. Lawrence Garner (London, 1973), chap. 10.

155. See Glasser, *Time in French Life and Thought*, p. 292.

156. Bergson, *Time and Free Will*, p. 79.

157. Ibid., p. 95.

158. Ibid., p. 232.

arrow, he argued, is never at rest at a spatial point, but is always moving, which is why it can hit its target.)

Bergson's insistence on the qualitative irreducibility of experienced time meant that it was not easily available to vision. Other senses were more likely to make it manifest to us: "When, with our eyes shut, we run our hands along a surface, the rubbing of our fingers against the surface, and especially the varied play of the joints, provide a series of sensations, which differ only by their *qualities* and which exhibit a certain order in time."[159] Perhaps even more than touch, hearing provides the experience of temporal duration, a salient example being a melody, which intertwines past, present and future in a meaningful whole.

Such a holistic unity, Bergson also contended, was the basis of the true self, "a self in which *succeeding each other* means *melting into one another* and forming an organic whole. . . . In order to recover this fundamental self, as the unsophisticated consciousness would perceive it, a vigorous effort of analysis is necessary, which will isolate the fluid inner states from their image, first refracted, then solidified into homogeneous space."[160] Our mistake is to identify our selves with the external images available to others in the social world, rather than with the internal experience of individually endured time, the private reality of *durée*.

For Bergson, the stakes of this differentiation were extraordinarily high, for human freedom as he interpreted it depended on the irreducibility of temporality to spatiality and the dethronement of the imperial eye. "Freedom," he argued, "is the relation of the concrete self to the act which it performs. This relation is indefinable, just because we *are* free. For we can analyze a thing, but not a process; we can break up extensity, but not duration."[161] Thus the scientific dream of prediction based on the putative knowledge of causal patterns in human behavior is misguided: "There cannot be any question either of foreseeing the act before it is performed or of reasoning about the possibility of the contrary act once

159. Ibid., p. 99.
160. Ibid., pp. 128–129.
161. Ibid., p. 219.

the deed is done, for to have all the conditions given is, in concrete duration, to place oneself at the very moment of the act and not to foresee it."[162] Foresight, like other inappropriate uses of vision, is inimical to human freedom. The representation of time in spatial terms is only adequate for time already flown, but not for the actual flowing of time—for, in other words, death, but not for life.

Bergson's vitalist bias for "life," his implicit linking of the domination of the eye with deathlike rigor mortis, was most compellingly expressed in *Creative Evolution*, the 1907 book that reached his largest audience. Here he developed his notoriously imprecise idea of an *élan vital*, that instinctual life drive giving direction to a process Darwin had ascribed only to the blind mechanism of natural selection. The pantheistic cosmological implications of his argument have not fared well in subsequent years, save for their occasional resurrection in the heterodox theology of a Teilhard de Chardin.[163] Ultimately of more importance was Bergson's introduction of a new metaphor to characterize the spatializing intellect and its limitations, a metaphor taken from the technological innovations in visual experience of his own era. Redescribing the mistaken premises underlying Zeno's paradoxes, he argued,

> Instead of attaching ourselves to the inner becoming of things, we place ourselves outside them in order to recompose their becoming artificially. We take snapshots, as it were, of the passing reality, and, as these are characteristic of the reality, we have only to string them on a becoming, abstract, uniform and invisible, situated at the back of the apparatus of knowledge, in order to imitate what there is that is characteristic of this becoming itself. Perception, intellection, language so proceed in general. . . . The *mechanism of our ordinary knowledge is of a cinematographical kind.*[164]

The cinema served as a potent metaphor for the misleading cognition of temporality because it combines still images of immobile sections with the impersonal, abstract "becoming" of the apparatus, integrating them to create a simulacrum of real time. It is as if the chronophotography of

Muybridge and Marey with its reduction of temporality to discrete moments is deceptively reanimated by the spatialized time of the machine.

In invoking this metaphor, Bergson seems to be making especially extreme claims about the tyranny of the eye. Not only intellection, but *all* perception through whatever sense, he appears to be arguing, is inherently cinematographic in its "ordinary" cognitive modes. As Gilles Deleuze has recently observed,[165] this assertion may mean that Bergson, unlike the later phenomenologists, refused to contrast a healthy natural perception to a distorted artificial one. But in the context of his other discussions of nonvisual perception, which he always described in noncinematographic terms, it seems hard to interpret this one passage so categorically. In later works such as *The Creative Mind*, he continued to invoke heard melodies as examples of nonspatial perception, which in no way could be construed as comparable to the cinema.[166] The one sense that cannot avoid being cinematographic is vision, and here Deleuze's point may be right, as will be evident when we examine Merleau-Ponty's consciously non-Bergsonian attempt to develop a new ontology of sight.

Less disputable is the fact that Bergson believed cinematographic modes of thought antedated the invention of the moving picture. It was already evident, he argued, in Greek philosophy—in particular in the Platonic doctrine of Ideas: "*Eidos* is the stable view taken of the instability of things. . . . We end in the philosophy of Ideas when we apply the cinematographical mechanism of the intellect to the analysis of the real."[167] Be-

162. Ibid., p. 239.

163. For a comparison of their ideas, see Madeleine Madaule-Barthélémy, *Bergson et Teilhard de Chardin* (Paris, 1963).

164. Bergson, *Creative Evolution*, trans. Arthur Mitchell (London, 1919), pp. 322–323. Emphasis in original. Bergson had already used the metaphor of the photograph to describe spatialized perception in *Matter and Memory* (p. 38). What was new here was his introduction of the cinema.

165. Deleuze, *Cinema 1: The Movement-Image*, trans. Hugh Tomlinson and Barbara Habberjam (London, 1986), p. 57.

166. Bergson, *The Creative Mind*, p. 147.

167. Bergson, *Creative Evolution*, p. 332.

cause of modern science's dependency on the language of abstract signs, it too has not escaped the cinematographical trap.[168] Indeed, all modes of intellection, based as they are on symbolization, are susceptible to this tendency, for language, rather than being an alternative to visual perception, shares with it a weakness for atemporal abstractions. Only a prelinguistic grasp of fluid, creative, vital reality will take us beyond the camera eye.[169] Only a sympathy for the formless flow of time will allow us to transcend the implications of our ocularcentric bias, for *"form is only a snapshot view of transition."*[170]

According to Deleuze's recent reading of Bergson's reaction to the cinema, the postulation of a rigid contradiction between the deceptive movement of images on the screen and real duration was, in fact, a step backward from the earlier argument in *Matter and Memory*, composed before the invention of the cinema, that "image-movements" do in fact exist. For Deleuze, the explanation may be the limited technology of the first movies: "On the one hand, the viewpoint [*prise de vue*] was fixed, the shot was therefore spatial and strictly immobile; on the other hand, the apparatus for shooting [*appareil de prise de vue*] was combined with the apparatus for projection, endowed with a uniform abstract time."[171]

168. Ironically, at the same time Bergson was damning science for its reliance on vision and abstract language, an explicitly antivisual revolution was occurring in physics, which reached its culmination in the quantum mechanics of Werner Heisenberg and Niels Bohr in the 1920s. For a full account, see Arthur I. Miller, *Imagery in Scientific Thought: Creating 20th-Century Physics* (Boston, 1984). In addition, even geometry was being redescribed in non-representational terms. The weakening of faith in the role of visual observation in theoretical physics may well have had a subterranean influence on the crisis of ocularcentrism itself, although it was rarely stressed by the French thinkers we are examining.

169. Bergson's own inevitable dependence on language to convey his thoughts has been widely remarked. See for example, Leszek Kolakowski, *Bergson* (Oxford, 1985), p. 33. Bergson was well aware of this paradox and tried to find an artistically evocative way of expressing himself that would minimize the damage.

170. Ibid., p. 319. Emphasis in original. Bergson frequently used the metaphor of the snapshot with its implications of a violent interruption of time. See, for example, *The Creative Mind*, p. 16. He also challenged other visual metaphors of cognition, such as the mind as mirror of nature. See his discussion of William James in *The Creative Mind*, p. 211.

Thus, although there are several qualifications in the argument of *Creative Evolution*, which Deleuze claims are often ignored, he concludes that "because Bergson only considered what happened in the apparatus (the homogeneous abstract movement of the procession of images) he believed the cinema to be incapable of that which the apparatus is in fact, most capable, eminently capable of: the movement image—that is, pure movement extracted from bodies or moving things."[172] Deleuze himself ingeniously finds in *Matter and Memory* and in certain of Bergson's other works an analysis of movement-images and the immanent luminosity of things prior to the light that is shined on them, which he claims brilliantly characterizes the cinema as it really is. Be that as it may, there can be little doubt that when Bergson chose the term "cinematographic" to damn the ocularcentric bias of Western metaphysics, modern science, and even ordinary language itself, he was expressing a suspicion of visual primacy that extended as well to its new technological manifestations.

Indeed, in one sense, Bergson went even further than Nietzsche in his critique of that primacy. The latter's radical perspectivalism implied, after all, a certain inescapability of visual mediation, however partial. As art in *The Birth of Tragedy* could not arise from Dionysian frenzy alone, but required the discipline of Apollonian form, so cognition and perhaps ethical judgment as well could not dispense entirely with the point of view of the situated subject. Bergson, however, was anxious to escape the relativistic implications of this argument in order to reestablish metaphysical contact with true reality. Thus, he contended that "philosophers agree in making a distinction between two ways of knowing a thing. The first implies going all around it, the second entering into it. The first depends on the viewpoint chosen and the symbols employed, while the second is taken from no viewpoint and rests on no symbol. Of the first kind of knowledge we shall say that it stops at the *relative*; of the second that, wherever possible, it attains the *absolute*."[173]

171. Deleuze, *Cinema 1*, p. 3.
172. Ibid., p. 23.
173. Bergson, *The Creative Mind*, p. 159.

It was, moreover, impossible to reach the absolute by harmonistically combining partial viewpoints into a unified whole (a ploy suggested by later thinkers like Karl Mannheim, whose "relationism" sought to overcome relativism in precisely this way). "Though all the photographs of a city taken from all possible points of view indefinitely complete one another," Bergson protested, "they will never equal in value that dimensional object along whose streets one walks. . . . A representation taken from a certain point of view, a translation made with certain symbols still remain imperfect in comparison with the object whose picture has been taken or which the symbols seek to express. But the absolute is perfect in that it is perfectly what it is."[174] Only intuition, he lamely concluded, can provide the sympathetic entry into the interiority of the object, which is blocked by intellectual analysis, linguistic symbolization and visual representation.

There is, to be sure, one sense in which Bergson, despite his hostility to ocularcentrism, may appear to rely on it implicitly. In his hostility to the conceptual abstraction of language at its most scientific, he often called on verbal images as a possible antidote. In *Time and Free Will*, for example, he wrote, "The poet is he with whom feelings develop into images, and the images themselves into words which translate them while obeying the laws of rhythm. In seeing these images pass before our eyes we in our turn experience the feeling which was, so to speak, their emotional equivalent."[175] But then he added, very much in the manner of the Symbolists with their praise for poetry's musicality, "We should never realize these images so strongly without the regular movements of the rhythm by which our soul is lulled into self-forgetfulness, and, as in a

174. Ibid., pp. 160–161.

175. Bergson, *Time and Free Will*, p. 15. Compare this passage, however, with the claim in *Matter and Memory* that sympathetic thoughts between two consciousnesses must be *prior* to the verbal images that communicate them: "I shall never be able to understand it if I start from the verbal images themselves, because between two consecutive verbal images there is a gulf which no amount of concrete representations can ever fill. For images can never be anything but things, and thought is a movement" (p. 125).

dream, thinks and sees with the poet."[176] Art, moreover, suggests feelings to us and "willingly dispenses with the imitation of nature when it finds some more efficacious means."[177]

Thus, the widely remarked influence of Bergson on the Imagist poetry of the modernist movement, transmitted by T. E. Hulme to Anglo-American poets like T. S. Eliot, Ezra Pound, and William Carlos Williams,[178] should be construed as impelling them away from mimetic representation and toward the immediate presentation or evocation of lived experience through the arresting juxtaposition of verbal images. According to Bergson, "No image can replace the intuition of duration, but many diverse images, borrowed from very diverse orders of things, may, by the convergence of their action, direct consciousness to the point where there is a certain intuition to be seized."[179] Because of the temporalizing implications of this action, Imagism may have gone beyond the embrace of spatialized form so often assumed to be its goal and introduced a certain open-endedness, which implies mobility.[180]

Moreover, as W. J. T. Mitchell has recently stressed,[181] the very term "image" can imply more than a verbal description of a purely visual experience; it can also mean the metaphoric, ornamental, rhetorically figurative use of language as opposed to its literal use. Although the Imagists sought to employ concrete, unornamented visual descriptions in their

176. Bergson, *Time and Free Will*, p. 15.

177. Ibid., p. 16.

178. For recent accounts, see Schwartz, *The Matrix of Modernism*; and Paul Douglass, *Bergson, Eliot and American Literature* (Lexington, Ky., 1986). Douglass cites Williams's Bergsonian lament from *In the American Grain* of 1925: "Men are trained never to possess fully but just to SEE. This makes scientists and it makes masochists. . . . Our life drives us apart and forces us on science and invention—away from touch" (p. 167).

179. Bergson, *An Introduction to Metaphysics*, trans. T. E. Hulme (London, 1949), pp. 15–16.

180. See Douglass, *Bergson, Eliot and American Literature* for a critique of Joseph Frank along these lines.

181. Mitchell, *Iconology*, chap. 1.

poetry, Bergson's usage—when he used the term honorifically[182]—often seems to have been more traditionally rhetorical, which helps account for the hostility of such rationalist defenders of clear prose and crisply defined concepts as Julien Benda. In fact, according to Émile Bréhier, Bergson's images "are rarely visual; most of the time, they are images of operations, actions, movements, efforts, images that one can call dynamic."[183] In short, however much Bergson may have invoked images as an antidote to concepts, he did so by striving to minimize their linkages to the static, spatializing power of sight.

Was it also possible to apply Bergsonian ideas to the visual arts themselves? Although he rarely wrote about painting,[184] Bergson did mention Turner and Jean Baptiste Camille Corot in his 1911 Oxford lecture on "The Perception of Change," and he did discuss Leonardo da Vinci's *Treatise on Painting* in his essay on Ravaisson.[185] Of great artists, he wrote, "If we accept them and admire them, it is because we had already perceived something of what they show us. But we had perceived without seeing. . . . The painter has isolated it; he has fixed it so well on the canvas that henceforth we shall not be able to help seeing in reality what he himself saw."[186] Approving of Leonardo's reliance on mental rather than perceptual images as the basis of his art, he further contended that "true art aims at portraying the individuality of the model and to that end it will seek behind the lines one sees the movement the eye does not see."[187] As for Ravaisson's own views on art pedagogy, Bergson applauded

182. Romeo Arbour distinguishes three separate usages of the term in Bergson: "image-sensations," "internal images," and "verbal expressions." See his *Henri Bergson et les lettres françaises* (Paris, 1955), p. 121. The first of these is the most negatively inflected.

183. Émile Bréhier, "Images plotiniennes, images bergsoniennes," in *Les Études Bergsoniennes*, 2 (1949), p. 113. In the discussion that followed his paper, Bréhier admitted the paradoxical quality of dynamic images: "The image is dynamic because, as we know, it is we who are dynamic, not the image" (p. 221).

184. There are only two references in the index to his collected works.

185. Bergson, *The Creative Mind*, pp. 135–136, 229ff.

186. Ibid., p. 136.

his preference for teaching the graceful curves of the human body rather than the geometric rules of perspective, which were defended by Eugène Guillaume. Although the eye was tendentially mechanistic and static, at least the subject matter of painting could be organic and lifelike.

Such ruminations on painting are, to be sure, without much profundity; it is thus to the indirect implications of Bergson's thought for the visual arts that we have to go to answer our question. As in the case of Proust's ambitious attempt to reconcile temporal *durée* and spatial form, certain modernist painters can be interpreted as attempting the same for their work. Thus, for example, Cézanne has been credited with going beyond the Impressionists' goal of capturing one fleeting moment in a still spatialized time and achieving instead "with varying intensity and success the pictorial realization of time as duration rather than as instantaneous succession."[188] Although there is no evidence that the painter had read the philosopher, Cézanne's carefully constructed works can be understood as an attempt less to catch flux on the canvas than to reanimate in the beholder the experience of the artist's own endured time. Moreover, if Merleau-Ponty was right about Cézanne's heroic search for a means to render the world's being prior to the dissociation of the senses and the split between subject and object, then here too a possible parallel can be drawn with Bergson's own insistence on the equiprimordiality of the senses in the apprehension of the world.

Even more evidence exits to suggest the importance of Bergson for Cubism.[189] The Symbolist poet Tancrède de Visan introduced his ideas to

187. Ibid., p. 230.

188. George Hamilton Heard, "Cézanne, Bergson and the Image of Time," *College Art Journal,* 16, 1 (Fall, 1956), p. 6.

189. See Robert Mark Antliff, "Bergson and Cubism: A Reassessment," *Art Journal,* 47, 4 (Winter, 1988); and Christopher Green, *Léger and the Avant-Garde* (New Haven, 1976). Bergson himself was not, however, taken with their work, which he saw as too spatially simultaneous in inspiration. See Edward F. Fry, ed., *Cubism* (New York, 1966), p. 67. One might also explore the importance of Bergson for Futurist art, for example that of Giacomo Balla or Umberto Boccioni, which sought to depict motion on the canvas or in sculptural form. For an analysis of the myriad ways in which twentieth-century sculpture tried to break down the space/time antithesis, see

Albert Gleizes and Jean Metzinger around 1910. Their advocacy in the influential 1912 treatise *Cubism* of an omnisensual perception of space, which derived as well from the theories of Henri Poincaré, helped justify the abandonment of linear perspective in favor of a more qualitative, intuitively derived notion of spatial representation. The viewer's creative intuition, they also argued, was necessary to complete the experience begun by the artist, an experience that was true to the dynamism of duration.

A less sanguine interpretation of the feasibility of that outcome will emerge, however, if Duchamp rather than Cézanne or the Cubists is the artist compared to Bergson. In a recent analysis of *The Large Glass,* Lucia Beier has suggested that the more logical implication of Bergson's thought for painting is the impossibility of depicting duration on the canvas. Duchamp, who was far more likely to have actually read Bergson than Cézanne, deliberately left *The Large Glass* unfinished in recognition of the futility of what he himself had tried to accomplish in *Nude Descending a Staircase.* According to Beier,

> The *Nude* was "a static image of movement"; by melting one
> physical position into another using simultaneous images he was
> employing what Bergson described as the cinematographic
> method in *Creative Evolution.* I believe Duchamp read this account
> in which Bergson claimed that the representation of movement as
> such was a function of the intellect and not intuition. In his desire to
> use the intuitive method in art, Duchamp turns aside from the
> depiction of objective movement and incorporates the spectator's
> perception of potential movement, or motion, into his new piece,
> the *Large Glass.*[190]

She interprets the "Bachelors" as representing Bergson's viewing Intellect and the "Bride" as the Intuition, with the unreconciled tension between their respective geometricality and vitality as emblematic of

---

Rosalind E. Krauss, *Passages in Modern Sculpture* (Cambridge, Mass., 1977). Bergson's influence on artists like Jean Arp, Barbara Hepworth, and Henry Moore is discussed on p. 141.

Duchamp's retreat from the project of a visual art that adequately represents temporality. "Duchamp," she concludes, "is contending that it is in fact impossible to capture the experience of duration in the work of art and he is mocking the attempt to do so. As it were he answers the question Bergson never really completely made up his mind about."[191]

Whether or not one seeks to establish direct relations of influence between Bergson and artists like Proust, Eliot, Cézanne, or Duchamp, it is abundantly apparent that his trenchant critique of ocularcentrism had a profound and widespread effect in the decades that followed. Even after his reputation was eclipsed during the interwar era, damaged by the charges of irrationalism leveled by Julien Benda and Jacques Maritain and weakened by the change of mood after the war, Bergson continued to enjoy considerable subterranean influence.[192] Although the phenomenologists and existentialists disdained his metaphysical yearnings, rejected his optimistic cosmology, and scorned his indifference to history and politics, they embraced many of his arguments against the fallacies of a visually constituted subjectivity.[193] The Surrealists, despite their preference for Freud's version of the unconscious and their insistence on a libidinally charged notion of desire ignored by Bergson, shared his rejection of the Intellect with its fetish of clear and distinct ideas and bias for

190. Lucia Beier, "The Time Machine: A Bergsonian Approach to the 'Large Glass' *Le grand verre*," *Gazette des Beaux-Arts*, 88 (November, 1976), p. 196.

191. Ibid., p. 199. Another way to interpret the contrast between the Bride and her Bachelors is to see the latter as existing in conventional, three-dimensional space, whereas the former is in the four-dimensional alternative Duchamp had absorbed from his reading in non-Euclidean geometry. See Henderson, *The Fourth Dimension and Non-Euclidean Geometry in Modern Art*, p. 156.

192. There is a considerable literature on the permeation of his ideas in many fields. See, for example, Thomas Hanna, ed. *The Bergsonian Heritage* (New York, 1962); Shiv K. Kumar, *Bergson and the Stream of Consciousness Novel* (New York, 1963); and Anthony Pilkington, *Bergson and His Influence: A Reassessment* (Cambridge, 1976).

193. See Jeanne Delhomme, "Le problème de l'intériorité: Bergson et Sartre," *Revue internationale de philosophie*, 48, 2 (1959), pp. 201–219; Jean Hyppolite, "Henri Bergson et l'existentialisme," *Les Études Bergsoniennes*, 2 (1949), pp. 208–212; Augustin Fressin, *La perception chez Bergson et chez Merleau-Ponty* (Paris, 1967).

abstract form.[194] And even the poststructuralists of a still later era, with all of their contempt for his celebration of vitalist immediacy, reveal an affinity for Bergson's stress on both the importance of temporal deferral as opposed to spatial presence, and the qualitatively heterogeneous rather than the quantitatively homogeneous.[195]

Bergson, to be sure, also bequeathed a host of unanswered questions to subsequent generations. Although his sensitivity to the acting body as opposed to the contemplative eye was an advance over many earlier philosophers, his description of that body and its relationship to consciousness still left a great deal—literally—to be desired. So too his account of the relation between vision and language would soon seem based on naive and outdated linguistic assumptions. The vacillation in his work between damning images as inherently static and deathlike, on the one hand, and possessing a genuine ability to move, or at least to arouse the experience of movement when skillfully employed by artists, on the other, was matched by other ambiguities. Was all visual perception tendentially cinematographic, as he claimed in *Creative Evolution*, or could it be synesthetically reunited with the other senses to recapture an equiprimordial sensual experience prior to its elevation to a dominating role? Was the tyranny of the eye a function of bad habits, as he sometimes implied,[196] or was there

194. For a discerning comparison of Bergson and the Surrealists, see Arbour, *Henri Bergson et les lettres françaises*, pp. 317ff.

195. The most explicit Bergsonian among the poststructuralists is Deleuze, who emphasized the importance of difference in Bergson's philosophy. See *Bergsonism*, trans. Hugh Tomlinson and Barbara Habberjam (New York, 1991). It is not hard to hear an anticipation of Derrida in such descriptions of *durée* as the following from *Time and Free Will*: "a wholly qualitative multiplicity, an absolute heterogeneity of elements which pass over into one another" (p. 229).

196. For example, in *The Creative Mind*, p. 147. At moments like this, Bergson seems to be falling for the contrast between conventional sight and the fresh and innocent vision that was characteristic of Romantic thought. For a gloss on the latter, see Simon Watney, "Making Strange: The Shattered Mirror," in *Thinking Photography*, ed. Victor Burgin (London, 1982), p. 156. What perhaps separated the two was Bergson's unsentimental indifference to a putative childhood visual innocence.

something more fundamentally problematic about its way of perceiving the world?

However one judges the complicated impact of Bergson's critique of ocularcentrism, the First World War and its aftermath seems to have both disseminated it more widely and imbued it with an urgency that was not apparent before. Like much else in the cultural life of the interwar era, the denigration of sight was expressed with an intensity that often bordered on violence. Indeed, as we will see in the next chapter, in the cases of Georges Bataille and the Surrealists, that border was often deliberately transgressed and the noblest of the senses subjected to explicit rituals of violent degradation.

CHAPTER FOUR

The Disenchantment of the Eye: Bataille and the Surrealists

It is time to abandon the world
of the civilized and its light.

GEORGES BATAILLE[1]

I have discarded clarity as
worthless. Working in darkness,
I have discovered lightning.

ANDRÉ BRETON[2]

If, as it is often claimed, the First World War challenged and in certain cases toppled the traditional hierarchies of European life, the "noblest of the senses" was by no means impervious to its impact.[3] The interrogation of sight hesitantly emerging in certain prewar works of philosophy and art was given an intense, often violent inflection by the war, which also helped disseminate an appreciation of its implications. The ancien scopic régime, which we've called Cartesian perspectivalism, lost what was left of

1. Georges Bataille, "The Sacred Company," in *Visions of Excess: Selected Writings, 1927–1939*, ed. Allan Stoekl, trans. Allan Stoekl, Carl R. Lovitt, and Donald M. Leslie, Jr. (Minneapolis, 1985), p. 179.

2. André Breton, written in collaboration with Jean Shuster, "Art Poétique" (1959); in Breton, *What Is Surrealism?: Selected Writings*, ed. Franklin Rosemont (London, 1969), p. 299.

3. According to Paul Virilio, "1914 was not only the physical deportation of millions of men to the fields of battle, it was also, with the apocalypse of the deregulation of perception, a diaspora of another kind, the moment of panic in which the American and European masses no longer believed their eyes." *La Machine de la vision* (Paris, 1988), p. 38.

its hegemony, and the very premises of ocularcentrism themselves were soon being called into question in many different contexts. In certain cases, the crisis of visual primacy expressed itself in direct terms; in others, it produced compensatory vindications of an alternative scopic order to replace the one that seemed lost. For some, the critique of ocularcentrism was carried out in the spirit of a radicalized Enlightenment, still hopeful of an emancipatory outcome; for others, it meant a Counter-Enlightenment abandonment of the project of illuminating reason itself.

These effects were nowhere as evident as in interwar France, where the visual preoccupations we have noted in the nineteenth century were given a new intensity. As a result, many intellectuals from a wide variety of different camps experienced a palpable loss of confidence in the eye, or at a very minimum, in many of its time-honored functions. While in this chapter the complicated responses of Georges Bataille and the Surrealists will provide an avenue of entry into the new, more violent interrogation of vision after the war, the next will follow the more directly philosophical expression of the same impulse in the phenomenology of Sartre and Merleau-Ponty. The groundwork will then have been laid for the exploration of the myriad varieties of antiocular thought in the decades from the end of World War II to the present day, to which the remainder of this narrative will be devoted.

⊙

To generalize about the effects on visual experience and the discursive reflection on that experience stimulated by the First World War is very hazardous. Recent commentators such as Paul Fussell, Eric J. Leed, Stephen Kern, Modris Eksteins, Kenneth Silver, and Sidra Stich have made, however, a suggestive start.[4] The western front's interminable trench warfare, they point out, created a bewildering landscape of indistinguishable, shadowy shapes, illuminated by lightning flashes of blinding intensity, and then obscured by phantasmagoric, often gas-induced haze. The effect was even more visually disorienting than those produced by such nineteenth-century technical innovations as the railroad, the camera, or the cinema.

When all that the soldier could see was the sky above and the mud below, the traditional reliance on visual evidence for survival could no longer be easily maintained. The invention of camouflage and the disappearance of differences in uniform between men and officers added to the experience of war as at once a frightening reality and a not so grand illusion. According to Leed, "The invisibility of the enemy, and the retirement of troops underground, destroyed any notion that war was a spectacle of contending humanity. . . . The invisibility of the enemy put a premium upon auditory signals and seemed to make the war experience peculiarly subjective and intangible."[5]

One reaction was a compensatory exaltation of the aerial perspective of the flyer, those "knights of the sky" able to rise above the confusion of the earth-bound—and often earth-bespattered—combatants. Nadar's balloonist became Antoine de Saint-Exupéry's aviator, heroically embodying the ancient myth of Icarian freedom.[6] From the air, the labyrinth of trenches could seem like a patterned carpet. Perhaps this was the perspective that earned Gertrude Stein's appellation, "the Cubist war."[7] Cubism,

4. Paul Fussell, *The Great War and Modern Memory* (London, 1975); Eric J. Leed, *No Man's Land: Combat and Identity in World War I* (Cambridge, 1979); Stephen Kern, *The Culture of Time and Space: 1880–1918* (Cambridge, Mass., 1983); Modris Eksteins, *Rites of Spring: The Great War and the Birth of Modern Age* (New York, 1989); Kenneth E. Silver, *Esprit de Corps: The Art of the Parisian Avant-Garde and the First World War, 1914–1925* (Princeton, 1989); Sidra Stich, *Anxious Visions: Surrealist Art* (New York, 1990).

5. Leed, *No Man's Land*, p. 19.

6. Saint-Exupéry himself, as Leed notes, was too young to have flown in the war, but his writings of the 1920s drew on many actual accounts of aerial combat. Eksteins explains the astonishing response to Charles Lindbergh's flight across the Atlantic in 1927 as a delayed reaction to the war. See *Rites of Spring*, chap. 8. The Icarian parallel, of course, holds as well for the outcome that many flyers suffered. Some fifty thousand airmen died by the end of the war. See J. M. Winter, *The Experience of War* (London, 1988), p. 108.

7. Gertrude Stein, *Picasso* (New York, 1959), p. 11. The precise formulation "Cubist war" is actually a paraphrase of this passage by Stephen Kern, *The Culture of Time and Space: 1880–1918* (Cambridge, Mass., 1983), p. 288. As John Welchman has noted, the analogy between aerial photography and Cubism (as well as Futurism) was made

which was in fact on the wane in Paris, grew increasingly popular among artists with experience at the front.[8] But whereas from the perspective of the ground it expressed the decomposition of spatial order, from the air it suggested a landscape with unexpected intelligibility. Within the internal history of Cubism itself, the shift may have been reflected in the transition from its analytical to synthetic phases.

Another escape was provided by focusing on the one thing that remained visible from the trenches, at least when the gas or smoke was not interfering: the boundless sky, whose dreamy beauty could be ironically juxtaposed to the brutal reality of earthly combat. Such a sky could also become the locus for a projected, split vision in which the victim could somewhere become the distanced observer of his or her own fate. "The sky," Leed writes, "is charged with intense significance: It *must* be the residence of the observer watching himself struggle through the nightmare of the war, for only then will the eye survive the dismemberment of the body."[9]

Still another reaction, manifest in the avant-garde visual arts themselves, was the willed return to visual lucidity and clarity, which Silver has shown accompanied a new nationalist-inflected classicism in the arts as a whole. The new mood in Paris was evident in the waning popularity of Cubism, the reevaluation of Cézanne in non-Bergsonian terms, the revival of interest in Seurat's serene canvases, and the newly sober preoccupations of artists like Robert Delaunay, Pablo Picasso, and Juan Gris. It culminated in the uncompromising Purism of Amédée Ozenfant and Le

---

during the war itself in training manuals for pilots. See his "Here there and otherwise," *Artforum International* (September, 1988), p. 18. After the war, Ernest Hemingway made a similar comparison. See his remarks in "A Paris to Strasbourg Flight," in *By-Line Ernest Hemingway* (New York, 1968), p. 38. Other Modernist movements also appropriated the visual experience of the war for their own purposes. Constructivists like El Lissitzky and Suprematists like Kasimir Malevich were fascinated by the implications of aerial photographs. As late as 1939, Italian Futurists like Tullio Crali were painting vertiginous scenes of pilots diving over geometrically rendered urban landscapes.

8. Silver, *Esprit de Corps*, p. 79.

9. Leed, *No Man's Land,* p. 137.

Corbusier (Charles Édouard Jeanneret) in the late teens.[10] Postwar reconstruction would require, they reasoned, the restoration of a unified scopic regime, which would be compatible with the disciplined collectivist society they saw emerging from the ashes of the conflagration. Here the precarious "recall to order" of the 1920s found one of its origins, as certain modernists sought to contain the more explosive and disintegrative implications of their predecessors' work.

But despite such compensatory myths and exercises in nostalgic purification, the actual impoverishment of normal visual experience also produced more directly disturbing effects. For, to cite Leed again,

> the deterioration of the visual field experienced by many in
> trench warfare removed those visual markers that allow an
> observer to direct his attention to what comes first and what later.
> . . . The constriction of vision eliminated most of those signs that
> allow individuals to collectively order their experience in terms of
> problems to be solved in some kind of rational sequence. . . .
> Naturally, this chaotic world was judged entirely on the basis of
> the individual's own perspective, a perspective that mobilized
> deeply layered anxieties, animistic images, and surprising and
> unbidden associations.[11]

"The Cubist war" could thus also mean the practical collapse of that transcendental notion of a shared perspective already theoretically undermined by Nietzsche. And with it could come the return of all the demons seemingly repressed by the "civilizing process," which was grounded to a significant extent in the domination of the dispassionate gaze.

10. Kenneth E. Silver, "Purism: Straightening Up After the Great War," *Artforum* (March, 1977). "Instead of indeterminacy, simultaneity, the mutability of time and space, the Purists will substitute something stable and durable. In place of Cubist complexity Jeanneret and Ozenfant will provide images with a freshly starched spiritual and moral rectitude, showing the certainty and direction of 'the great collective current,'" (p. 57).

11. Leed, *No Man's Land*, pp. 130–131.

No figure during the subsequent decades expressed both the trauma and the ecstasy of that liberation as powerfully as did Georges Bataille. Certainly none tied it as explicitly to the dethronement of the eye as did he. Bataille's own wartime experiences have, however, rarely been given their due in the now voluminous literature on him, and one can indeed only conjecture about their direct impact. Perhaps, as his friend Pierre Andler contended, they left him with a visceral pacifism that undermined his willingness to endorse violent means even against fascism.[12] Yet on a deeper level, the war seems to have exercised a certain positive fascination. It is striking that many of Bataille's obsessive themes would betray an affinity for the experiences of degradation, pollution, violence, and communal bonding that were characteristic of life in the trenches. None of those themes was as dramatically intertwined with the war's impact as that of the eye.

According to his own testimony (which not all commentators have accepted with equal trust), Bataille, who was born in 1897, fled the invading German army in 1914, was called up in January, 1916, and fell seriously ill and was discharged a year later.[13] Although there is little to indicate he had any combat experience, it is significant that two decades later, on the eve of another war, he could exult in the risking of life in battle as a joyous release from petty, selfish concerns.[14] "Conflict is life," he insisted. "Man's value depends upon his aggressive strength. A living man regards death as the fulfillment of life; he does not see it as a misfortune."[15]

In seeking to evoke the mystical experience of "joy before death," Bataille turned to typical images from the First World War of the all-

12. Andler's personal recollections are discussed in Rita Bischoff, *Souveränität und Subversion: Georges Batailles Theorie der Moderne* (Munich, 1984), p. 292.

13. Georges Bataille, "Autobiographical Note," *October,* 36 (Spring, 1986), p. 107.

14. Georges Bataille, "The Threat of War," *October,* 36 (Spring, 1986), originally written in 1936; and "The Practice of Joy Before Death," in *Visions of Excess,* originally written in 1939. In notes written in 1941, however, Bataille contended that his personal relation to war was always that of an outsider, who had never experienced ecstatic release at the front. "In war what is arresting for me," he wrote, "is a means of agonized contemplation. For me that is still connected to a nostalgia for ecstatic states, yet this nostalgia today seems dubious and lugubrious to me: It never had, I

encompassing sky and blinding light. His sky, however, participated in the general destruction, rather than served as an escape from it: "I imagine the earth turning vertiginously in the sky, I imagine the sky itself slipping, turning and lost. The sun, comparable to alcohol, turning and bursting breathlessly. The depth of the sky like an orgy of frozen light, lost."[16] "I MYSELF AM WAR," he proclaimed, and added, "There are explosives everywhere that will soon blind me. I laugh when I think that my eyes persist in demanding objects that do not destroy them."[17]

Bataille's deeply charged summoning of blindness had another likely source, which has been remarked by virtually all of his commentators: his blind and paralyzed father, who died insane in November, 1916. Here too, however, the experience of the war seems to have played a role, for Bataille and his mother had abandoned the father to his fate when the Germans invaded Rheims in August, 1914. The son returned two years later to find only the sealed coffin of his dead father, with whom he at least partly came to identify.[18] "Today," he would write in 1943, "I know I am 'blind,' immeasurable, I am man 'abandoned' on the globe like my father at N. No one on earth or in heaven cared about my father's dying terror. Still, I believe he faced up to it as always. What a 'horrible pride,' at moments, in Dad's blind smile."[19]

---

must say, any active value. I never fought in any of the wars in which I might have been involved." Cited in Denis Hollier, ed., *The College of Sociology (1937–1939)*, trans. Betsy Wing (Minneapolis, 1988), p. 139.

15. Bataille, "The Threat of War," p. 28.

16. Bataille, "The Practice of Joy Before Death," p. 238.

17. Ibid., p. 239.

18. According to Rita Bischoff, Bataille's disgust with the war was also directed against the paternal order which spawned it, an order represented by his own father. Thus the pseudonym used in his first published work was in part a repudiation of his patronym. His strong identification with certain maternal values, those of the "earth" as opposed to those of the heavens, may reveal the force of this choice. See Bischoff, *Souveränität und Subversion*, p. 293. Although Bataille was certainly no friend of paternal authority in its traditional guises, when it came to his father's blindness, it is hard not to discern an ultimate identification with him as well.

19. Bataille, "W.C. Preface to *Story of the Eye*," appended to *Story of the Eye*, trans. Joachim Neugroschel (New York, 1982), p. 123.

Before Bataille came to identify with his father, however, he seems to have felt closer to his mother instead. The first essay he published, in 1920, was a lyrical reflection on the cathedral of Notre-Dame de Rheims, which had been destroyed during the German invasion.[20] According to Denis Hollier,[21] the cathedral functioned for Bataille as a visual metaphor of maternity, a regressive symbol of continuity and repose. Significantly, it was also linked to images of illumination. "Joan of Arc's vision," the young Bataille wrote, "still so thrilling to myself four years later, is the light I offer up to your desires, the vision of Notre-Dame de Rheims bathed in sunlight."[22] Shortly thereafter, for reasons that remain murky, Bataille repudiated this maternal identification, and with it his celebration of visions of clarity. "All of Bataille's writings would be aimed at the destruction of this cathedral," Hollier concludes; "to reduce it to silence he would write against this text."[23] In fact, he would write "against architecture" of any kind, because it represented visual order and legible space, covering over tomblike the subterranean disorder it abhorred.

Whatever the personal sources of Bataille's subsequent lucubrations, at once tormented and triumphant, on death, violence, eroticism, religious transgression,[24] and blindness, the results would slowly find an appreciative audience able to understand their implications for the traditional privileging of vision. The first attempt he made to reach that audience came in 1926 with the composition of a short book written under the pseudonym Troppman and called *W.C.* "Of violent opposition to any form of dignity,"[25] it was never finished, its fragments burned by the author. Significantly, it contained a drawing of an eye, the eye of the scaf-

20. Lost until after his death, it is reprinted in Denis Hollier, *Against Architecture: The Writings of Georges Bataille*, trans. Betsy Wing (Cambridge, Mass., 1989), pp. 15–19.

21. Ibid., p. 19.

22. Ibid., p. 16.

23. Ibid., p. 15.

24. In 1917, he thought of becoming a monk, and in 1920, he went to stay with a Benedictine order on the Isle of Wight, only to lose his faith "because his Catholicism has caused a woman he has loved to shed tears" (*Autobiographical Note*, p. 107).

25. Ibid., p. 108.

fold, which he called in tribute to Nietzsche "the Eternal Return." "Solitary, solar, bristling with lashes," he would later recall, "it gazed from the lunette of a guillotine."[26] This lunette, he confided, was mixed up in his mind with that of the toilet seat on which his blind father sat to void his bowels. A symbol of terrorist surveillance, it thus also stood for the liberating blindness through which the expended waste Bataille was to celebrate as *dépense* could explosively pass.

A year later, a slim volume published under the pseudonym Lord Auch appeared in a private edition of 134 copies, accompanied by eight lithographs drawn by Bataille's friend André Masson. It was called *Histoire de l'oeil* (*Story of the Eye*) and was so transgressively pornographic that it never appeared under Bataille's name during his lifetime.[27] After his death and then with its republication in 1967, however, it became a widely discussed classic, eliciting commentaries by Roland Barthes, Michel Foucault, Susan Sontag, and a host of scholarly interpreters.[28] There can, in

26. Bataille, "W.C. Preface to *Story of the Eye*," p. 120.

27. There were two other changed editions published when he was alive, in 1940 and 1943, both in Paris, although giving Burgos and Seville as places of publication. In the *Oeuvres* published by Gallimard in 1967, five years after his death, the 1928 and the later editions appear as separate texts. The English translation is made from the 1928 edition. In 1943, Bataille explained the provenance of his pseudonym: "Lord Auch [pronounced *osh*] refers to a habit of a friend of mine; when vexed, instead of saying 'aux chiottes!' [to the shithouse], he would shorten it to 'aux ch.'" *Lord* is English for God (in the Scriptures): Lord Auch is God relieving himself" (W.C. Preface to *Story of the Eye*, p. 120).

28. Roland Barthes, "The Metaphor of the Eye," in *Critical Essays* (Evanston, Ill., 1972), first publication in 1963; Michel Foucault, "A Preface to Transgression," in *Language, Counter-Memory, Practice: Selected Essays and Interviews*, ed. Donald F. Bouchard, trans. Donald F. Bouchard and Sherry Simon (Ithaca, N.Y., 1977); Susan Sontag, "The Pornographic Imagination," in *Styles of Radical Will* (New York, 1981); among the more scholarly commentaries, see Michele H. Richman, *Reading Georges Bataille: Beyond the Gift* (Baltimore, 1982), chap. 3; Brian T. Fitch, *Monde à l'envers / texte réversible: la fiction de Georges Bataille* (Paris, 1982), chaps. 4 and 5; Peter B. Kussel, "From the Anus to the Mouth to the Eye," *Semiotext(e)*, 2, 2 (1976), pp. 105–119; Paul Foss, "Eyes, Fetishism, and the Gaze," *Art & Text*, 20 (February–April, 1986), pp. 24–41; Susan Rubin Suleiman, "Pornography, Transgression and the Avant-Garde: Bataille's *Story of the Eye*," in *The Poetics of Gender*, ed. Nancy K. Miller (New York, 1986).

fact, be few works of this genre since those of the Marquis de Sade that have generated so much earnest exegesis.

Story of the Eye is a pivotal text for our own story of the eye's interrogation for a variety of reasons. Whatever else it may be, the eye in this story is, to borrow Brian Fitch's phrase, *l'oeil qui ne voit pas.*[29] Bataille finishes his tale with the enucleated eye of a garroted priest inserted in the anus and then the vagina of the heroine, as the narrator realizes that he finds himself "facing something I imagine I had been waiting for in the same way that a guillotine waits for the neck to slice. I even felt as if my eyes were bulging from my head, erectile with horror."[30] Enucleation is, in fact, a central theme of the story, which reproduces an actual episode Bataille witnessed in 1922: the ripping out of the matador Granero's eye by a bull's horn in Seville. Until he saw the famous scene of the slit eyeball in the Surrealist masterpiece *Un chien andalou* by Dali and Buñuel in 1928, about which he wrote enthusiastically in the pages of *Documents,*[31] he had no more vivid image to express his obsessive fascination with the violent termination of vision. The enucleated eye was a parodic version of the separation of sight from the body characteristic of the Cartesian tradition; no longer able to see, it was then thrust back into the body through vaginal or anal orifices in ways that mocked in advance Merleau-Ponty's benign reembodiment of the eye in the "flesh of the world."

The novel challenges the primacy of sight in more subtle ways as well. As Barthes pointed out in an essay that in any other context could innocently be called seminal, Bataille's narrative can be read not merely as a sado-masochistic erotic reverie, but also as a linguistic adventure. That is, the tale is motivated less by the increasingly bizarre couplings of its ostensible protagonists than by the metaphoric transformations of the objects on which they fetishistically focus. The most notable series is that linked to the eye itself, which is enchained with images of eggs, testicles, and the sun. A second train is composed of the liquids associated with them

29. Fitch, *Monde á l'envers,* chap. 4.
30. Bataille, *Story of the Eye,* p. 103.
31. See his 1929 essay "The Eye," reprinted in *Visions of Excess,* pp. 17–19.

(tears, egg yolks, sperm) and other liquids like urine, blood, and milk. According to Barthes, none of these terms is given any privilege, none has any foundational priority: "It is the very equivalence of ocular and genital which is original, not one of its terms: the paradigm *begins* nowhere. . . . Everything is given on the surface and without hierarchy, the metaphor is displayed in its entirety; circular and explicit, it refers to no secret."[32] Thus, the time-honored function of the penetrating gaze, able to pierce appearances to "see" the essences beneath, is explicitly rejected.

Bataille furthermore links the two metaphoric chains to each other in metonymic ways, so that signifiers from one (e.g., eggs) are coupled with signifiers from others (e.g., urination). The result, Barthes concludes, are typically Surrealist images produced through radically decontexualized juxtapositions (e.g., suns that cry, castrated or pissing eyes, eggs that are sucked like breasts). Thus, what is transgressed is not merely normal sexual behavior, but also the rules of conventional language. Because in French, words like *couille* are near anagrams of *cul* and *oeil*, the effect of linguistic promiscuity is as strong as that of its more obvious sexual counterpart.

Barthes's structuralist reading, with its strongly textualist rather than experiential bias, may have its flaws,[33] but it points to one important implication of the novel: that whether understood literally or metaphorically, the eye is toppled from its privileged place in the sensual hierarchy to be linked instead with objects and functions more normally associated with "baser" human behavior.[34] This is, indeed, the most ignoble eye imaginable.

32. Barthes, "The Metaphor of the Eye," p. 242.

33. For critiques, see the work cited above by Suleiman, Kussel, and Fitch. Suleiman contends that its blindspot is the importance of the view of the body, in particular the female body, in the story, which she connects to Bataille's castration anxiety produced by looking at his mother's genitals. Kussel claims that Barthes underplays the real fear of blindness in Bataille, which is underlined by the autobiographical information about his father that he provides in his later prefaces. Fitch, however, argues that it is less a case of an object than a word, "l'oeil," that is at issue; he claims Barthes is too interested in objects in fictions, rather than words in texts.

34. Bataille's valorization of base and transgressive human behavior is continuous with a long tradition that Peter Sloterdijk traces back to the "kynicism" of Diogenes.

To understand fully the depths of that ignobility, we have to recall the speculative claim Freud was advancing at virtually the same time in *Civilization and Its Discontents*.[35] Human civilization, Freud conjectured, only began when hominids raised themselves off the ground, stopped sniffing the nether regions of their fellows, and elevated sight to a position of superiority. With that elevation went a concomitant repression of sexual and aggressive drives and the radical separation of "higher" spiritual and mental faculties from the "lower" functions of the body.

Bataille was himself in analysis with Dr. Adrien Borel when he wrote *Story of the Eye*. He later contended that "by August 1927, it put an end to the series of dreary mishaps and failures in which he had been floundering, but not the state of intellectual intensity, which still persists."[36] Nor would his fascination with Freudian ideas end, as he continued to draw on them throughout his life. Although there is no evidence that he knew of Freud's specific conjectures about the connections between elevated vision and repression—indeed, the chronology of their respective publications suggests otherwise, even if it is likely that Freud's ideas were in circulation among analysts before coming into print—*Story of the Eye* can be read as a tacit plea for the reversal of this most fateful of human developments. Bataille's later defense of what he called a "general" as opposed to a "restricted" economy, one based on *dépense* (waste or expenditure), loss, transgression, and excess, rather than production, exchange, conservation, and instrumental rationality, was closely tied to this critique of the primacy of vision.[37] The only light cast by the potlatch ceremonies he found so fascinating was produced by the flames consuming the wealth

---

See his *Critique of Cynical Reason*, trans. Michael Eldred (Minneapolis, 1987). Curiously, Bataille is missing from his account of the tradition, which pits disruptive kynicism against the status-quo-affirming cynicism that he claims is prevalent today.

35. Sigmund Freud, *Civilization and Its Discontents*, trans. James Strachey (New York, 1961), pp. 46–47. The earliest record of this speculation is his letter of November 14, 1987, to Wilhelm Fleiss. See Sigmund Freud, *The Origins of Psychoanalysis, Letters to Willian Fleiss, Drafts and Notes: 1887-1902*, ed. Marie Bonaparte, Anna Freud, and Ernst Kris, trans. Eric Mosbacher and James Strachey (New York, 1954), pp. 230-231.

36. Bataille, "Autobiographical Note," p. 108.

destroyed. So too Bataille's critique of absolute knowledge—most notably that sought by Hegel—in favor of a "non-knowledge" or "un-knowing," which always defeats the ability to think it clearly and distinctly, drew on the same impulse.[38] If, as Robert Sasso puts it, Bataille wanted to go "*du savoir au non-savoir*,"[39] he certainly understood the importance of *voir* for *savoir*. It could be undermined only through the explosive sound of laughter or the blurred vision produced by tears.[40]

No less subversive of traditional ocularcentrism was Bataille's unprecedented transfiguration of the familiar metaphor of the sun. In a short piece entitled "The Solar Anus," written in 1927 and published with drawings by Masson four years later, he identified himself with the sun, but one of violent aggression rather than benign illumination—a "filthy parody of the torrid and blinding sun."[41] It was a sun that loves the night and seeks to copulate with it: "I want to have my throat slashed," Bataille wrote, "while violating the girl to whom I will have been able to say: you are the night."[42] Such a sun could thus be conflated with an anus, the darkest of possible holes.

In another brief essay written in 1930, Bataille invoked the "rotten sun" as an antidote to the elevated sun of the dominant Western tradition.[43]

37. For a short presentation of these concepts, see "The Notion of Expenditure" in *Visions of Excess*. For a good summary of their roots in Bataille's reading of anthropology, especially that of Marcel Mauss, see Richman, *Reading Georges Bataille*. The distinction between the two economies has had a widespread impact in poststructuralist thought. See, for example, Jacques Derrida's influential essay "From Restricted to General Economy: A Hegelianism without Reserve," in *Writing and Difference*, trans. Alan Bass (Chicago, 1978).

38. See, for example, his remarks on Hegel's search for transparency in *L'expérience intérieure*, in his *Oeuvres complètes*, vol. 5 (Paris, 1973), p. 141; and his three essays on "Un-knowing" in *October*, 36 (Spring, 1986).

39. Robert Sasso, *Georges Bataille: Le Système du Non-Savoir* (Paris, 1978), chap. 4.

40. Bataille, "Un-Knowing: Laughter and Tears," *October* 36 (Spring, 1986), pp. 89–102.

41. Bataille, "The Solar Anus," in *Visions of Excess*, p. 9.

42. Ibid.

43. Bataille, "Rotten Sun," in *Visions of Excess*.

The latter was based on the prudent refusal to stare directly into it, the former with the self-destructive willingness to do so. The Platonic tradition of rational heliocentrism could thus be subverted by a mythic alternative, which he identified with the Mithraic cult of the sun.

> If we describe the notion of the sun in the mind of one whose weak eyes compel him to emasculate it, that sun must be said to have the poetic meaning of mathematical serenity and spiritual elevation. If on the other hand one obstinately focuses on it, a certain madness is implied, and the notion changes meaning because it is no longer production that appears in light, but refuse or combustion, adequately expressed by the horror emanating from a brilliant arc lamp. In practice the scrutinized sun can be identified with mental ejaculation, foam on the lips, and an epileptic crisis. In the same way that the preceding sun (the one not looked at) is perfectly beautiful, the one that is scrutinized can be considered horribly ugly.[44]

The two ways of conceiving the sun are represented in the myth of Icarus, who seeks the sun of elevated beauty, but is destroyed by the vengeful sun of combustion. In a sense, Bataille's Icarus might be called "inverted," as one commentator has noted,[45] because he falls into the sun rather than back to earth.

Bataille furthermore linked the ability to stare at the "rotten sun" with artistic creativity. This essay was itself written as a brief tribute to Picasso, whose decomposition of forms challenged the search in academic painting for elevated beauty. Later, in a celebration of Blake, Bataille would write of *The Tyger*, "Never have eyes as wide open as these stared at the sun of cruelty."[46] But it was in two essays of 1930 and 1937 on Vincent Van Gogh that he made the connections between looking at the sun, self-destruction, and aesthetic creativity most explicit.[47]

44. Ibid., p. 57.
45. Jonathan Strauss, "The Inverted Icarus," *Yale French Studies*, 78 (1990).

Drawing on a case study of an automutilator called Gaston F., written up by Borel and two collaborators, he pondered the implications of the painter's own automutilation.[48] The patient had torn off one of his fingers after staring at the sun, symbolically instantiating the psychoanalytic link between blindness and castration. For Bataille, Van Gogh's sun paintings and his severed ear enacted a similar sacrificial mutilation: "The eagle-god who is confused with the sun by the ancients, the eagle who alone among all beings can contemplate while staring 'at the sun in all its glory,' the Icarian being who goes to seek the fire of the heavens is, however, nothing other than an automutilator, a Vincent Van Gogh, a Gaston F."[49] Such a sacrifice, according to the logic of Bataille's general economy, was an act of deindividuating freedom, an expression of ecstatic and "sovereign" heterogeneity. At the moment Van Gogh introduced the sun into his work, "all of his painting finally became *radiation, explosion, flame*, and himself, lost in ecstasy before a source of *radiant* life, *exploding, inflamed*."[50]

If the sun could thus be split into an elevating, ennobling, rational source of light, not to be looked at directly, and an aggressive, dismembering, sacrificial source of destruction, joyously blinding those who dare to stare at it unflinchingly, so too the eye itself could have several conflicting meanings for Bataille. In a 1929 essay for *Documents* simply entitled "Eye," he explored examples of the fears and anxieties engendered by the experience of ocular surveillance.[51] Citing such instances of the "eye of conscience" as Grandville's lithograph "First Dream: Crime and Expiation," Hugo's poem "La Conscience," and the illustrated weekly *The Eye*

46. Bataille, *Literature and Evil*, trans. Alastair Hamilton (New York, 1973), p. 73.

47. Bataille, "Sacrificial Mutilation and the Severed Ear of Vincent Van Gogh," in *Visions of Excess*; "Van Gogh as Prometheus," *October*, 36 (Spring, 1986).

48. H. Claude, A. Borel, and G. Robin, "Une automutilation révélatrice d'un état shizomaniaque," *Annales médico-psychologiques*, vol 1 (1924), pp. 331–339. Bataille notes that Borel told him of this case after he first thought to link Van Gogh's automutilation and his solar obsessions.

49. Bataille, "Sacrificial Mutilation," p. 70.

50. Bataille, "Van Gogh as Prometheus," p. 59.

51. Bataille, "Eye," in *Visions of Excess*.

of the Police, he emphasized the sadistic implications of being the object of the punishing gaze. The slitting of the eye in *Un chien andalou*, "this extraordinary film"[52] by Luis Buñuel and Salvador Dali, showed, he claimed, how the eye could be related to cutting, both as its victim and as its perpetrator. But such violence, Bataille concluded, was not without its positive implications: "If Buñuel himself, after filming of the slit-open eye, remained sick for a week . . . how then can one not see to what extent horror becomes fascinating, and how it alone is brutal enough to break everything that stifles?"[53] For Bataille, submission to the aggressive power of the "cutting" gaze, like that to the blinding power of the sun, could be a source of liberating subversion.

In two other essays written around 1930, Bataille turned to another concept, that of the "pineal eye," which had played a central role in Descartes's philosophy.[54] Strictly speaking, Descartes had known it only as a gland, not as a vestigial eye, which was understood only by nineteenth-century science. Significantly, however, he had accorded it a pivotal role in the transformation of the visual experience of the two physical eyes into the unified and coherent sight of the mind or soul. The pineal gland was thus the very seat of rational intellection. In contrast, Bataille concocted a phantasmatic anthropology which pitted the pineal gland against both the two eyes of everyday sight and the rational vision of the mind's eye.

Interestingly, he did so by subtly reversing the axes of verticality and horizontality posited by Freud as connected, respectively with civilization and bestiality. Normal sight, he claimed, was a vestige of humanity's originally horizontal, animal status. But it was a burden rather than a blessing: "The horizontal axis of vision, to which the human structure has remained strictly subjected, in the course of man's wrenching rejection of

52. Ibid., p. 19.
53. Ibid.
54. Bataille, "The Jesuve" and "The Pineal Eye," both in *Visions of Excess*; for a comparison of his usage with that of Descartes, see David Farrell Krell, "Paradoxes of the Pineal: From Descartes to Bataille," in *Contemporary French Philosophy*, ed. A. Phillips Griffiths (Cambridge, 1987).

animal nature, is the expression of a misery all the more oppressive in that it is apparently confused with serenity."[55]

In contrast, the pineal eye yearns to burst out from its confinement and blind itself by staring at the sun, that destroying sun ignored by rational heliocentrism: "The eye, at the summit of the skull, opening on the incandescent sun in order to contemplate it in sinister solitude, is not a product of the understanding, but is instead an immediate existence; it opens and blinds itself like a conflagration, or like a fever that eats the being, or more exactly, the head."[56] This version of verticality is not, *pace* Freud, an escape from humanity's "lower" functions, but is intimately linked with them. Its volcanic eruptions are "discharges as violent and as indecent as those that make the anal protuberances of some apes so horrible to see"; its bursting through the skull is like an erection "which would have vibrated, making me let out atrocious screams, the screams of a magnificent but stinking ejaculation."[57]

The sun that it seeks to reach through these explosions is at once a solar anus and a fecal or bronze eye. Here the distancing function of normal sight and the elevating tradition of rational heliocentrism are undone as eye, sun, and anus are all indiscriminately mingled in a general economy of ecstatic heterogeneity. Here blindness and castration are less to be feared than welcomed as the means to liberate the mundane self from its enslavement in a restricted economy based on the fastidious discriminations of servile sight.

Bataille's radical devaluation of conventional visual experience and its metaphorical appropriation continued to be manifest throughout his career. Thus, for example, during his most Marxist phase, around 1930, he defended a version of "base" materialism very different from the conventional philosophical kind, linking it to the Gnostic principle of darkness that was opposed to the Hellenic worship of clarity and light.[58] Like

55. Bataille, "The Pineal Eye," p. 83.

56. Ibid., p. 82.

57. Bataille, "The Jesuve," p. 77.

58. Bataille, "Base Materialism and Gnosticism," in *Visions of Excess*, p. 47.

Bergson, although without acknowledging the similarity, he rejected a materialism based on a visual image of matter in favor of one derived from the bodily experience of materiality. Likewise, he repudiated the classical—and also high modernist—fetish of form, which was so dependent on visual distance. Instead, he privileged the "*informe*," that formlessness apparent in phlegm and putrefaction.[59] As Rosalind Krauss has shown, the same sentiment generated the fascination shown by Bataille and other contributors to *Documents* for primitive art.[60] Unlike most modernists who saw in primitive artifacts models of universal, abstract form, the group around Bataille appreciated instead their links with sacrificial rituals of mutilation and waste.

Later in the 1930s, Bataille adopted the image of the headless, "acephalic" man as the central symbol for the community he and his friends Michel Leiris and Roger Caillois wanted to create around the Collège de sociologie.[61] *Acéphale,* their journal, published four issues between 1936 and 1939.[62] Here the explosion of the pineal eye was understood to have taken with it the head, that symbol of reason and spirituality based on the hegemony of the eyes. The gruesome work of the guillotine was also invoked as still haunting the Place de la Concorde. Today that square was dominated, Bataille wrote, by "eight armored and acephalic figures" with helmets "as empty as they were on the day the executioner decapitated the king before them."[63] Even the bull's head affixed to another symbol beloved by Bataille's circle, the Minotaur, was gone.[64]

The sacred community he wanted to resurrect would only come when "man has escaped from his head just as the condemned man has escaped

59. Bataille, "Formless," in *Visions of Excess.*

60. Rosalind E. Krauss, *The Originality of the Avant-Garde and Other Modernist Myths* (Cambridge, Mass., 1985), pp. 67ff.

61. For a history of the group, see Hollier, ed., *The College of Sociology.*

62. For its program, see *October*, 36 (Spring, 1986), p. 79; and the essay "The Sacred Conspiracy" in *Visions of Excess.* The latter is accompanied by a picture by Masson of an acephalic man, holding a sword in one hand, a flaming sacred heart in the other, his labyrinthine bowels open to view and a skull in the place of his genitals.

63. Bataille, "The Obelisk," *Visions of Excess.*

from prison. . . . He reunites in the same eruption Birth and Death. He is not a man. He is not a god either. He is not me but he is more than me: his stomach is the labyrinth in which he has lost himself, loses me with him, and in which I discover myself as him, in other words as a monster."[65] Rather than seeking a way out of the labyrinth through aerial flight, that compensatory myth sustaining so many veterans of the trenches on the western front, Bataille urged instead a joyous entanglement in its coils.[66] The labyrinth, as Hollier has noted, served as the antidote to the pyramid, that architectural symbol of solidity and substance, which was homologous to the optical cone.[67] Its valorization also signaled Bataille's repudiation of the Enlightenment, which, as d'Alembert's *Pre-*

64. *Minotaure* was a journal to which Bataille's friends often contributed in the 1920s and 1930s. The marvelous photograph by Man Ray published in vol. 7 (1935) of a torso with its head in shadows transformed into a bull's head suggests that even this symbol could somehow be acephalic. The prevalence of the image during this period is shown by its frequent adoption by Picasso after 1937.

65. Bataille, "The Sacred Conspiracy," p. 181.

66. The labyrinth, in fact, was a frequent image used by other modernist writers from Joyce to Borges. Guy Davenport goes so far as to call it "a life-symbol of our century." See his *The Geography of the Imagination* (San Francisco, 1981), p. 51. Its coils evoke those of the ear from whose power Icarus tried to escape by privileging the eye. Many years later, Jacques Derrida would spell out the connection. See *The Ear of the Other: Otobiography, Transference, Translation,* ed. Christie McDonald, trans. Peggy Kamuf and Avital Ronell (Lincoln, Nebr., 1985), p. 11. Still another evocation of the image appeared in the work of Luce Irigaray, who speculated that its etymology may have been the same as that for "lips," *labra,* whose self-touching was emblematic of women's sexuality. See her essay "The Gesture in Psychoanalysis," in *Between Feminism and Psychoanalysis,* ed. Teresa Brennan (London, 1989), p. 135. It should also be noted that even earlier it was a favorite symbol of Nietzsche, who wrote, "We are especially curious to explore the labyrinth, we try to make acquaintance with Mr. Minotaur, about whom they tell such terrible things . . . you wish to save us with the aid of this thread? And we—we pray earnestly, lose this thread!" *Werke,* ed. Alfred Kröner, 2d ed., 20 vols. (Leipzig, 1901–1913, 1926), vol. 16, pp. 439–440. Ariadne was one of Nietzsche's heroines as well, and seems to have been identified with Cosima Wagner. For a general account of the labyrinth in world literature, see Gustav René Hocke, *Die Welt als Labyrinth* (Reinbeck, 1957).

67. Hollier, *Against Architecture,* p. 72.

liminary Discourse to the Encyclopedia made clear, sought to place the philosopher high above the labyrinth of knowledge.[68]

Even after the Second World War, when the ambiguous political implications of Bataille's interwar fantasies had a certain sobering effect on him, he continued to criticize the ocularcentric traditions of our culture in a variety of ways. Taking issue with Sartre's still-Enlightenment-inspired defense of pellucid prose as the clear passage of ideas from one subjectivity to another, he contended that true communication at the deepest level demands obscurity. "Communication, in my sense," he wrote in *Literature and Evil*, "is never stronger than when communication, in the weak sense, the sense of profane language or, as Sartre says, of prose which makes us and the others appear penetrable, fails and becomes the equivalent of darkness."[69] Like Maurice Blanchot, with whom he became friends in 1940, Bataille came to see literature—prose no less than poetry—as the privileged locus of obscure communication, the guilty repository of sovereign and transgressive Evil.

There were visual manifestations of the same phenomenon as well, for Bataille was deeply taken with the possibility of what one commentator has called an anti-idealist "iconography of the heterogeneous."[70] Fascinated by the primitive cave paintings discovered at Lascaux,[71] Bataille invidiously contrasted the visual tradition that emerged when men left the cave and sought to paint in the clarity of sunlight with one in which darkness and obscurity still reigned supreme. Even his book of 1955 on Manet, in many ways a conventional appreciation of modernist optical-

68. See the remarks of d'Alembert used as an epigraph to chap. 2.

69. Bataille, *Literature and Evil*, p. 170.

70. Bischoff, *Souveränität und Subversion*, chap. 1, which provides a thorough survey of Bataille's visual preoccupations. Hollier also remarks on Bataille's interest in painting as "the defacement of the human figure," which he contrasts with Bataille's distaste for architecture. "The space of painting," he writes, "is space where someone who has torn his eyes like Oedipus feels his way, blinded. Thus it is not to the eye but to the missing-eye that painting corresponds. . . . Automutilation needs to be thought of as a pictorial act, even *the* pictorial act, par excellence. For painting is nothing if it does not attack the architecture of the human body" (pp. 79–80).

71. Bataille, *Lascaux ou la naissance de l'art* (Paris, 1955).

ity, contained, as Krauss has noted, a short paean to Goya, whose art of excess and violence provided a countermodel comparable to those he had celebrated in Van Gogh and Picasso during the interwar years.[72] In short, when Bataille was discovered in the 1960s by a generation of post-structuralist thinkers eager to follow his philosophical, literary, and anthropological lead, his counter-Enlightenment critique of vision was also readily available as a vital inspiration to their own ruthless interrogation of the eye.

⊙

Bataille's obsessive visual concerns may well have had a personal source, as his own reminiscences of his blind father imply. But the frequency of themes in his work that can be traced to the wartime experiences of so many others of his generation suggest that they were by no means uniquely his own. The group of artists and writers who came to be called Surrealists were themselves deeply disturbed by those experiences. As their first historian, Maurice Nadeau, observed, "Breton, Éluard, Aragon, Péret, Soupault were profoundly affected by the war. They had fought in it by obligation and under constraint. They emerged from it disgusted; henceforth they wanted nothing in common with a civilization that had lost its justification, and their radical nihilism extended not only to art but to all its manifestations."[73] Was ocularcentrism one of the manifestations they chose to reject? If, as Sidra Stich has argued, the traumas of the war were reproduced in the "anxious visions" of Surrealist art, did they also lead to an anxiety about vision itself? And if so, were the mainstream Surrealists as violently hostile to the hegemony of the eye as Bataille?

To answer these questions is no simple task, as the Surrealists were a large and heterogeneous group of artists with countless internal quarrels and many reversals of opinion over the long duration of the movement

72. Bataille, *Manet*, trans. Austryn Wainhouse and James Emmons (Geneva, 1955); Rosalind Krauss, "Antivision," *October*, 36 (Spring, 1986), p. 152. Jean Starobinski's use of Goya in *1789: The Emblems of Reason*, it may be remembered, was similar.

73. Maurice Nadeau, *The History of Surrealism*, trans. Richard Howard, intro. Roger Shattuck (London, 1987), p. 45.

(which has not entirely given up the ghost even today). Despite all the best efforts of their "pope," André Breton, to keep order, they remained an unruly and obstreperous assemblage of individuals radically unwilling to submit to discipline for very long. However much the Surrealists wanted to suppress the traditional idea of the artistic genius and work collectively, the narcissism of small differences often interfered. Moreover, the many visual artists associated with them—painters, photographers, cinematographers, and those who invented their own media of expression—developed clearly disparate and individual styles; no one can confuse an Ernst with a Dali or a Miró with a Magritte. And although there is no shortage of verbal statements of their intentions in manifestoes, memoirs, interviews, and exhibition catalogues, the visual results cannot be assumed to correspond with or merely exemplify their avowed purposes. Thus, to pretend to have located a monolithic Surrealist attitude toward the visual would indeed be foolish.

Still, what allows historians (and allowed its adherents) to call Surrealism a relatively coherent phenomenon suggests that at least some recurrent patterns can be discerned, which with due caution can be called typical. One way to approach them would be to focus for a moment on the quarrel between Bataille and Breton, which involved, inter alia, a difference of opinion about vision.[74] As Bataille would remember it, contact began around 1925, but was almost immediately followed by a falling out which came to a head in 1929. A cautious rapprochement occurred, however, in 1935 with their joint membership in a political group called *Counterattack*.[75]

Part of the tension was caused by Breton's suspicion that Bataille wanted to challenge his leadership and set up a rival group, which became a self-fulfilling prophecy when he did become the figure around whom disaffected Surrealists like Caillois, Leiris, Masson, Robert Desnos, Roger Vitrac and Georges Limbour could rally. Another part was due to Breton's

74. For a general overview of the dispute, see Richman, *Reading Georges Bataille*, pp. 49ff.
75. Bataille, "Autobiographical Note," *October*, 36 (Spring, 1986), pp. 108–109.

personal distaste for Bataille's perverse pornographic and excremental obsessions,[76] as well as for the hypocritical contradiction he saw between Bataille's advocacy of violence and his professional career as a librarian at the Bibliothèque Nationale. But issues of substance were also involved, which bear on their different attitudes toward vision.

Breton's rejection of Bataille was made public in the *Second Manifesto of Surrealism* of 1930, where he defended himself against what he called Bataille's "absurd campaign against . . . 'the sordid quests for every integrity.'"[77] Bataille, he claimed, was interested only in the vilest and most corrupt things, was indifferent to anything useful, and had returned to an old antidialectical notion of materialism, which was simply the reverse of idealism. Moreover, his wholesale repudiation of the homogenizing powers of rationality produced a performative contradiction, insofar as he had to engage in communicative rationality to express it (a charge that would be repeated against Bataille many years later by Jürgen Habermas):[78]

> M. Bataille's misfortune is to reason: admittedly, he reasons like someone who "has a fly on his nose," which allies him more closely with the dead than the living, but *he does reason*. He is trying, with the help of the tiny mechanism in him which is not completely out of order, to share his obsessions: this very fact proves that he cannot claim, no matter what he may say, to be

76. Salvador Dali noted the limits of Breton's tolerance for the scatological and perverse phenomena that so obsessed Bataille: "Blood was acceptable. Even a little excrement. But not excrement alone. I could portray sexual organs, but not anally oriented optical illusions. The arsehole was frowned upon! Lesbians were welcomed, but not homosexuals." *Journal d'un génie* (Paris, 1964), p. 23.

77. André Breton, *Manifestoes of Surrealism,* trans. Richard Seaver and Helen R. Lane (Ann Arbor, Mich., 1972), p. 180.

78. Jürgen Habermas, *The Philosophical Discourse of Modernity: Twelve Lectures,* trans. Frederick Lawrence (Cambridge, Mass., 1987), pp. 235–236. A similar complaint was made earlier by Raymond Queneau in 1939, who contended that "there is no antipathy between reason and that which exceeds it, whereas antireason only cures myopia with enucleation and headaches with the guillotine." Cited in Hollier, ed., *The College of Sociology,* p. 161.

opposed to any system, *like an unthinking brute.* What is paradoxical and embarrassing about M. Bataille's case is that his phobia about the "idea," as soon as he attempts to communicate it, can only take an ideological turn."[79]

Bataille's response came in two pieces written around 1930, although not immediately published: "The Use Value of D. A. F. Sade (An Open Letter to My Current Comrades)" and "The 'Old Mole' and the Prefix *Sur* in the Words *Surhomme* [Superman] and Surrealist."[80] The former, which was one salvo in an ongoing war over the correct reading of Sade involving many other combatants,[81] contains little directly bearing on the issue of vision.[82] The latter, however, drew on and expanded Bataille's earlier ruminations on the contrast between ennobling vision and baser forms of knowledge (or non-knowledge). Here the metaphor he introduces pitted the eagle against the "old mole," the latter derived from Marx's celebrated image of the Revolution in *The Eighteenth Brumaire.*

The eagle, Bataille points out, is more glamorous and virile a symbol

79. Breton, *Manifestoes of Surrealism*, p. 184. The irony of this charge is that Breton was normally anxious to transcend the confinements of the very logical consistency that he here invoked against Bataille.

80. Both are translated in Bataille, *Visions of Excess.*

81. Along with Lautréamont and Rimbaud, Sade was the great example of the *poète maudit* so beloved by Surrealism. See the issues of *Le Surréalisme au service de la révolution* from October, 1930, on. The great Sade scholar of the era was Maurice Heine, with whom Bataille was close friends. He asked him to verify the story he had told in an earlier essay, whose veracity Breton had attacked, concerning Sade's dipping rose petals in liquid manure. Heine could not. The battle over Sade's legacy continued after the war; see Pierre Klossowski, *Sade, mon prochain* (Paris, 1947), and the chapter on Sade in Bataille's *Literature and Evil.* For a good account of the stakes in the controversy, see Carolyn Dean, "Sadology," in *History of French Literature*, ed. Denis Hollier (Cambridge, Mass., 1989).

82. It does include, however, a kind of answer to Breton's charge of performative contradiction: "*As soon as the effort at rational comprehension ends in contradiction, the practice of intellectual scatology requires the excretion of unassimilable elements,* which is another way of stating vulgarly that a burst of laughter is the only imaginable and definitely terminal result—and not the means—of philosophical speculation" ("The Use Value of D. A. F. Sade [An Open Letter to My Current Comrades]," p. 99).

than the mole. With its hooked beak, it has "formed an alliance with the sun, which castrates all that enters into conflict with it (Icarus, Prometheus, the Mithraic bull)."[83] As such, it might be expected that Bataille would interpret the eagle as an ambivalent figure, like the sun, at times Platonic and at times "rotten," with whom it allies itself. But because of the polemical intent of the essay, it is only its unattractive implications that he chose to stress: "Politically the eagle is identified with imperialism, that is, with the unconstrained development of individual authoritarian power, triumphant over all obstacles. And metaphysically the eagle is identified with the *idea*, when, young and aggressive, it has not yet reached a state of pure abstraction."[84] Breton's desire to ride the eagle on a revolutionary flight would thus be disastrous: "Revolutionary idealism tends to make of the revolution an eagle above eagles, a *supereagle* striking down authoritarian imperialism, an idea as radiant as an adolescent eloquently seizing power for the benefit of utopian enlightenment. The detour naturally leads to the failure of the revolution and, with the help of military fascism, the satisfaction of the elevated need for idealism."[85] Even Nietzsche, Bataille concedes, fell prey to the same temptation with his concept of the Superman, despite his understanding of the base roots of the "highest" ideas.

Instead, the Revolution must look to the bowels of the earth, where the blind mole burrows. Its materialism must reject any Icarian strategy of idealizing that base world. "The passage from Hegelian philosophy to materialism (as from utopian or Icarian socialism to scientific socialism)," he insisted, "makes explicit the necessary character of such a rupture."[86] Although Bataille's own engagement with Hegel would grow more complex after his attendance at Alexander Kojève's famous lectures in the

83. Bataille, "The 'Old Mole' and the Prefix *Sur*," p. 34.

84. Ibid.

85. Ibid.

86. Ibid., p. 43. For a discussion of Bataille's identification of the eye with the circular nature of Hegelian dialectics, see Allan Stoekl, *Agonies of the Intellectual: Commitment, Subjectivity, and the Performative in the 20th-Century French Tradition* (Lincoln, 1992), p. 288.

mid-1930s, his disdain for the Surrealist appropriation of the Hegelian themes of transcendence and sublation would remain constant. The identification of the eagle with Hegel, which is especially compelling in French because both words sound alike, would also have a long future in the antivisual discourse Bataille helped disseminate; it would reappear in spectacular fashion in Derrida's *Glas* in 1974.

How justified, it must be asked, was Bataille's characterization of Surrealism as an Icarian movement that sought out heterogeneous, transgressive material only to transfigure it in an idealist direction? How bewitched were its adherents by a positive notion of visual sublimity? Or did even the Surrealist search for new visual experience, for what may well be called visionary redemption, paradoxically contribute to the crisis of ocularcentrism?

⊙

The tenacious hold of ocularcentrism over Western culture, it bears repeating, was abetted by the oscillation among models of speculation, observation, and revelation. When one or another faltered, a third could be invoked as the foundation of a still visually privileged order of knowledge. In the case of Surrealism, it is readily apparent that speculative reason, bathing in the light of clear and distinct ideas mirrored in the mind's eye, and mimetic observation, trusting in the reflected light of objects apparent to the two physiological eyes, were both explicitly scorned. It is no less evident that the third tradition, that of visionary illumination, was elevated in their place to a position of honor.

Once the more nihilistic and destructive impulses of Dadaism, out of which Surrealism emerged in the early 1920s, were overcome (or at least so it seemed), the movement sought to realize the avant-garde's optimistic project of transforming daily existence by infusing it with the redemptive power of art. Although often employing provocative verbal violence comparable to Bataille's,[87] the Surrealists were never as willing to celebrate waste, expenditure, and destruction as ends in themselves. Combining, as Breton famously put it, Rimbaud's injunction to "change life" with

Marx's call to "transform the world,"[88] they hoped to revolutionize more than just aesthetic fashions.

This ambition not only led them into a series of tragicomic alliances with Communist and Trotskyist parties,[89] but also permitted them to adopt the self-image, as old as the earliest prophetic religions and as recent as Rimbaud's "Lettres du voyant," of the seer. One of Breton's first manifestos, written in 1925, was in fact called "A Letter to Seers," and in 1934 he would still insist, "'I say that we must be *seers*, make ourselves seers': for us it has only been a question of discovering the means to apply this watchword of Rimbaud's."[90] As Blaise Cendrars put it in 1931, "Let us open this third eye of Vision; let us surnaturalize."[91] Max Ernst would add in 1936, "Blind swimmer, I have made myself a seer. *I have seen.*"[92] Indeed, as late as 1943, Benjamin Péret would embrace Novalis's dictum, "the man who really thinks is the seer."[93]

The Surrealist adoption of the visionary model was evident in both their verbal and their plastic creations. Indeed, virtually from its inception, Surrealism would be fascinated by the interaction of the eye and the text.[94] Mallarmé's "Un coup de dés" was one of their most admired poems. Apollinaire's *Calligrames* were no less revered. Indeed, Apollinaire,

87. See for example, their diatribes against the corpse of Anatole France in 1924, collected in Nadeau, pp. 233ff. What suggests an important difference between them and Bataille, however, is their respective attitudes toward war; he glorified the experience of sacrifice, whereas they were almost all pacifists.

88. Breton, "Speech to the Congress of Writers" (1935), in *Manifestoes of Surrealism*, p. 241.

89. For an account of their political affiliations, see Helena Lewis, *The Politics of Surrealism* (New York, 1988).

90. Breton, "Surrealist Situation of the Object," *Manifestoes of Surrealism*, p. 274.

91. Blaise Cendrars, *Aujourd'hui* (Paris, 1931), p. 31.

92. Max Ernst, *Au-delà de la peinture* (Paris, 1936), excerpted in Patrick Waldberg, *Surrealism* (New York, 1971), p. 98.

93. Benjamin Péret, "A Word from Péret," in *Death to the Pigs and Other Writings*, trans. Rachel Stella et al. (Lincoln, Nebr., 1988), p. 197.

94. For an exploration of this theme, see Mary Ann Caws, *The Eye in the Text: Essays on Perception, Mannerist to Modern* (Princeton, 1981).

who had coined the term Surrealism for his 1917 drama, *Mamelles de Tirésias*, was instrumental in redirecting French poetry away from its Symbolist stress on musicality.[95] "Until the beginning of the twentieth century," the editors of *Surréalisme* wrote in 1924, "the *ear* had decided the quality of poetry: rhythm, sonority, cadence, alliteration, rhyme; everything for the ear. For the last twenty years, the *eye* has been taking its revenge. It is the century of the film."[96] Breton's personal distaste for music has been widely acknowledged,[97] and indeed there was little, if any, explicitly Surrealist musical composition. Surrealism, as Breton put it in *Mad Love*, sought instead to recover the virginal sight, the *jamais vu*, that would be the uncanny complement of the *déjà vu*.[98]

This visionary project would involve following two trails already blazed by Rimbaud: self-conscious sensual derangement and the suppression of the mundane, rational ego. Breton explicitly contended in 1925 that "to aid the systematic derangement of all the senses, a derangement recommended by Rimbaud and continuously made the order of the day by the Surrealists, it is my opinion that we must not hesitate to *bewilder sensation*."[99] The Surrealist painter Paul Nougé added that the production of radically new experiences in the viewer could only be brought about by creating forbidden images—"bewildering objects."[100]

95. For an analysis of the visual dimensions of Apollinaire's poetry, see Timothy Mathews, *Reading Apollinaire: Theories of Poetic Language* (Manchester, 1987), especially chap. 2.

96. "Manifeste du surréalisme," *Surréalisme*, 1 (October, 1924), p. 1. This was the only issue of a journal edited by Ivan Goll, who ultimately had little to do with the group around Breton. The manifesto was followed by a short piece on the cinema, which extolled the virtues of its French versions over its American or German.

97. René Held, for example, speaks of Breton's "aversion towards music." See his *L'oeil du psychanalyste: Surréalisme et surréalité* (Paris, 1973), p. 164. After World War II, however, Breton and the Surrealists came to appreciate American jazz, in part because of its black roots. See his "Silence Is Golden" (1946), in André Breton, *What Is Surrealism?*

98. Breton, *Mad Love*, trans. Mary Ann Caws (Lincoln, Nebr., 1987), p. 90. *Jamais vu* was used by Breton as early as his appreciation of Francis Picabia in the early 1920s. See *What Is Surrealism?*, p. 14.

The suppression of the rational self was to be sought through the celebrated and controversial technique of automatic writing, which allowed free association to produce arresting images unobtainable by conscious creative effort.[101] Chance, which Mallarmé had realized could never be abolished by the throw of the dice, was thus preferable to deliberate manipulation.[102] Other techniques included the game that became known as "exquisite corpse,"[103] which involved the stringing together of arbitrarily chosen phrases by different poets unaware of what preceded or followed, and Raymond Roussel's method of writing a novel by beginning with one sentence and ending with its homophonic, but semantically distinct double. Although the precise proportion of chance to contrivance in all of these techniques continues to spur debate, the results were often strikingly unexpected images, unlike virtually any in previous Western literature.

The nature of Surrealist images, verbal and pictorial, has been the subject of extensive critical reflection, only a few of whose conclusions can be advanced here.[104] As in the case of Bergson, "image" was a counterterm to "concept," the latter being identified with the stifling logic of the ratio-

99. Breton, "The Surrealist Situation of the Object," p. 263.

100. Paul Nougé, *Histoire de ne pas rire* (Brussels, 1956), p. 239.

101. The origins of automatic writing have been variously attributed to the "mental automatism" examined by the French psychiatrist Pierre Janet, the nineteenth-century debates over sleep-walking and hysteria, and the literary experiments of the German writer Ludwig Börne, whom Freud later acknowledged as one of the forerunners of free association.

102. Man Ray produced a film in the late 1920s entitled *Le mystère du Château de Dés*, which explicitly drew on Mallarmé's poem. See the discussion in Steven Kovács, *From Enchantment to Rage: The Story of Surrealist Cinema* (London, 1980), p. 143.

103. The term comes from a phrase in the first game they played: "the exquisite corpse will drink new wine." Americans who grew up in the 1950s will remember the introduction of a related game called "Madlibs," which involved the insertion of arbitrarily chosen words in blanks in a narrative. The results were often hilarious, but rarely approached what Walter Benjamin had called the "profane illuminations" of Surrealism.

104. For a helpful account, see J. H. Matthews, *The Imagery of Surrealism* (Syracuse, 1977).

nalism Surrealism generally denigrated.[105] Also reminiscent of Bergson, when he used the term honorifically, was the Surrealists' refusal to identify "image" with a mental representation of an external object, a thing in the world, a mimetic sensation. It referred instead to the revelation of an internal state, a psychological truth hidden to conscious deliberation, what Mary Ann Caws has called an "inscape" rather than an "outlook."[106]

The often-cited classic example of the quintessential Surrealist image was Isadore Ducasse, le Comte de Lautréamont's "chance meeting of an umbrella and a sewing machine on a dissecting table" from his *Chants de Maldoror*. What made it so arresting for Breton and his collaborators was the effect produced by the juxtaposition of two incongruous and seemingly unrelated objects in a space utterly unlike their normal context (although they may well have also liked its scarcely veiled sexual connotation). As Breton put it, images of this kind were "incandescent flashes linking two elements of reality belonging to categories that are so far removed from each other that reason would fail to connect them and that require a momentary suspension of the critical attitude in order for them to be brought together."[107] The relationship between the two objects is not, strictly speaking, metaphorical because the principle of paradigmatic similarity does not work to create a unified symbol. Nor do such images signify through metonymic linkages along a syntagmatic chain, as is the case with realist prose. Instead, their ineffable effect is produced by their very resistance to such traditional modes of signification. Their power, when they succeed, is produced by their evocation of that uncanny "convulsive beauty" Breton would call "the marvelous." They are, he claimed, "endowed with a persuasive strength rigorously proportional to the violence of the initial shock they produced. Thus it is that close up, they are destined to take on the character of things *revealed*."[108]

105. The qualifier has to be added, for, as noted in examining Breton's critique of Bataille, Surrealism could employ rational arguments when it needed them.

106. Caws, *The Eye in the Text*, chap. 6.

107. Breton, "On Surrealism in Its Living Works" (1953), in *Manifestoes of Surrealism*, p. 302.

Because of the Surrealists' fascination with psychoanalysis and F. W. H. Myers's "gothic psychology" of the subliminal,[109] what was revealed was often understood as a direct manifestation of unconscious desire.[110] Reversing Augustine's anxiety about the "lust of the eyes," they reveled in the fact that, as Breton put it, "as far as the eye can see, it recreates desire."[111] More precisely, the Surrealist image sought to duplicate the mysterious workings of dreams, which allowed desire to be expressed, without conscious intervention, in plastic and verbal form. Rejecting Bergson's metaphysical belief in *durée* as the locus of human volition, the Surrealists claimed that the onrush of oneiric images evinced a kind of causality of desire that overwhelmed the conscious will. Although the Surrealists contrived mechanisms that could be manipulated to produce "the marvelous," once it came, conscious volition was left far behind. Breton may have denied the resemblance to a spiritualist who is merely a vessel for external voices,[112] but the Surrealist poet nonetheless succumbed to powerful forces beyond his or her conscious control. Citing Baudelaire on the effects of drugs, Breton claimed, "It is true of Surrealist images as it is of

108. Breton, *Mad Love*, p. 88.

109. Breton, "The Automatic Message," in *What is Surrealism?*, p. 100. Myers, an English psychologist of the paranormal, wrote *The Human Personality and its Survival of Bodily Death* (London, 1903). For an account of its importance for Breton, see Jennifer Munday, "Surrealism and Painting: Describing the Imaginary," *Art History*, 10, 4 (December, 1987), p. 501.

110. The belief that language could somehow serve as the transparent medium for the revelation of desire was at odds with the often hermetically obscure nature of Surrealist poetry and prose. In fact, because of their sensitivity to the arbitrary, nonrepresentational quality of language, they have sometimes been praised for understanding what more systematic linguists like Saussure and his followers were discovering at roughly the same time. Not surprisingly, the two intellectual currents could later mingle in thinkers like Lacan.

111. Breton, *Mad Love*, p. 15.

112. Breton, "The Automatic Message" (1933) in *What Is Surrealism? Selected Writings,* ed. Franklin Rosemont (London, 1978), p. 105, where he writes, "Contrary to what spiritualism proposes—that is, the dissociation of the subject's psychological personality—surrealism proposes nothing less than the *unification* of that personality."

opium images that man does not evoke them; rather they 'come to him spontaneously, despotically. He cannot chase them away, for the will is powerless now and no longer controls the faculties.'"[113] This process corresponded to what in life Breton called the law of "objective chance," in which serendipitous meetings—like that he describes with Nadja in *Mad Love*—produce the "marvelous."

Surrealism began by stressing poetic language as the medium through which its images could best be expressed, but soon its emphasis shifted to include the visual arts as well. Breton himself noted that automatic writing could induce visual hallucinations.[114] The unconscious could also be visually manifest in hysterical symptoms, which Breton and Aragon, sounding more like Charcot than Freud, celebrated in 1928 as "the greatest poetic discovery of the later nineteenth century."[115] Was it also possible to achieve convulsive beauty by more conventional visual means, such as painting? Could one make visible—*donner à voir*, in Paul Eluard's phrase[116]—the lightning flash of profane illuminations? Not all Surrealists were immediately convinced. In the third issue of *La Révolution surréaliste*, Pierre Naville, fearing that it would become just another art journal and betray its revolutionary mission, claimed that "everyone knows that there is no *surrealist painting*."[117] Even when Naville's objections were brushed aside, Breton could still call painting a "lamentable expedient" and confess his boredom in art museums in the essays that became *Surrealism and Painting*.[118] But the title essay of that book did

113. Breton, "Manifesto of Surrealism," p. 36.

114. Breton, "The Automatic Message," p. 108.

115. Editorial entitled "The Fiftieth Anniversary of Hysteria," *La Révolution surréaliste*, 11 (1928), in *What Is Surrealism?*, p. 320. The original was accompanied by six plates from Albert Londe's *Iconographie photographique de la Salpêtrière*. Other Surrealists would also draw on the iconography of hysteria, for example Dali in his "Phénomène de l'ecstase" in *Minotaure* (December, 1933).

116. Paul Eluard, *Donner à voir* (Paris, 1939).

117. Pierre Naville, "Beaux-Arts," *La Révolution surréaliste*, 1, 3 (April, 1925), p. 27. The quarrel over painting was part of a larger political dispute, which ultimately led to a break with Naville in 1929.

appear in 1928, thus ratifying what was already clear in practice: Surrealism was as much a visual as verbal phenomenon. In a few years, Breton could proclaim that "at the present time there is no fundamental difference between the ambitions of a poem by Paul Eluard or Benjamin Péret and the ambitions of a canvas by Max Ernst, Miró, or Tanguy."[119] Breton himself even tried his hand at fashioning collages and what he called "poem-objects," integrating readymades and poetry. He and his collaborators sat for or composed innumerable portraits, individual and group, which presented their images to the world.[120]

What in part allowed the visual in through the side door, as Nadeau has remarked, was the trick of defining what the Surrealists championed as being "beyond painting"[121] or "painting defied."[122] And indeed, like Duchamp, whose work they so much admired, Surrealism sought to challenge many of the received truths about the creation of visual beauty. Even their self-portraits problematized the narcissistic premises of the genre, relentlessly displacing, as Martine Antle has put it, "the 'who I am' toward the 'whom I haunt,' the visible toward the invisible, the 'figural' toward the 'spectral' elements."[123]

If the Surrealists radically defied visual conventions, they did so, at least initially, in the hope of restoring the Edenic purity of the "innocent eye," an ideal which had been defended by the Romantics, if not earlier.[124] By violently disturbing the corrupted, habitual vision of everyday

---

118. Breton, *Surrealism and Painting*, trans. Simon Watson Taylor (London, 1972), p. 3. It is often pointed out that rather than referring to Surrealist painting, Breton still uneasily linked them together as two distinct categories.

119. Breton, "Surrealist Situation of the Object," p. 260.

120. See Martine Antle, "Breton, Portrait and Anti-Portrait: From the Figural to the Spectral," *Dada/Surrealism*, 17 (1988), pp. 46–58.

121. Nadeau, *The History of Surrealism*, p. 110. *Beyond Painting* was, in fact, the title of a book by Max Ernst, trans. Dorothea Tanning (New York, 1948). He had used it as early as the announcement of one of his exhibitions in 1920.

122. Aragon, *La peinture au défi* (Paris, 1926).

123. Antle, "Breton, Portrait and Anti-Portrait," p. 48.

124. For a discussion of its history and revival among twentieth-century photographers, including the Surrealists, see Simon Watney, "Making Strange: The Shattered

life, the visionary wonder of childhood, so they believed, might be recaptured. "The eye," Breton began *Surrealism and Painting* by announcing, "exists in its primitive state."[125] Unlike the music he generally denigrated, painting could therefore provide spiritual illuminations: "Auditive images, in fact, are inferior to visual images not only in clearness but also in strictness, and with all due respect to a few melomaniacs [passionate lovers of music], they hardly seem intended to strengthen in any way the idea of human greatness. So may night continue to fall upon the orchestra, and may I, who am still searching for something in this world, may I be left with open or closed eyes, in broad daylight, to my silent contemplation."[126]

How did painting (or going "beyond" it) provide the occasion for stimulating the eye to regain its innocence? Revitalizing a metaphor seemingly discredited by modernist abstraction, Breton admitted that "it is impossible for me to consider a picture as anything but a window, in which my first interest is to know what it *looks out on*, or, in other words, whether, from where I am, there is a 'beautiful view,' for there is nothing I love so much as that which stretches away before me and *out of sight*. Within the frame of an *unnamed figure, land- or seascape*, I can enjoy an enormous spectacle."[127] But rather than revealing an external world situated in Cartesian perspectivalist space, the window opened "out" on the psychic

---

Mirror," in *Thinking Photography*, ed. Victor Burgin (London, 1982). The idea of the "oeil sauvage" included the connotation of savagery, as well as innocence. The Surrealist eye was never very remote from the cruel potential in vision, perhaps most explicitly thematized in the work of Artaud and Bataille.

125. Breton, *Surrealism and Painting*, p. 1. The phrase *l'état sauvage* was a reference to an earlier description of the visionary Rimbaud by Paul Claudel. See the discussion in Mundy, "Surrealism and Painting," p. 498. Later, in an interview in 1946, Breton would continue to defend the Surrealist interest in non-European art by claiming that "the European artist in the twentieth century can ward off the drying up of the sources of inspiration swept away by rationalism and utilitarianism only by resuming so-called primitive vision, which synthesizes sensory perception and mental representation" ("Interview with Jean Duché," in Breton, *What Is Surrealism?* p. 263).

126. Breton, *Surrealism and Painting*, pp. 1–2.

127. Ibid., pp. 2–3.

world within: "the plastic work of art, in order to respond to the undisputed necessity of thoroughly revising all real values, will refer to a *purely interior model* or cease to exist."[128]

Windows, as Susan Harris Smith has recently shown,[129] were, in fact, an abiding preoccupation of the Surrealists, and unpacking their complicated meaning can help explicate the implicit tensions in their visionary celebration of the innocent eye. The epiphanous experience Breton himself underwent before hitting on automatic writing as the royal road to the unconscious was produced by an image that suddenly came to him, "a phrase . . . *which was knocking at the window,*" of a man being cut in two by a window.[130] Many Surrealist painters would later play on the theme of the window as a transitional or liminal plane between reality and imagination, foreground and background, external and internal worlds. Often deploying it to suggest yearning for the beyond, they also used the window as an aperture through which a face could look into the shadowy room of the unconscious.

More unsettling, however, were the uses to which Surrealists like Magritte could put windows. In a number of his works, such as *La Condition Humaine I* (1933), *The Domain of Arnheim* (1949), or *Euclidean Walks* (1955), he used them to create visual paradoxes or puns, incommensurable spatial orders which were disjunctively combined to challenge the viewer's faith in his eyes.[131] At times, the Surrealists could also play on the

128. Ibid., p. 4.

129. Susan Harris Smith, "The Surrealists' Windows," *Dada/Surrealism*, 13 (1984), pp. 48–69. Windows were also a favored metaphor of French poets much admired by the Surrealists, such as Baudelaire and Apollinaire. For a discussion of the former's use, see Sima Godfrey, "Baudelaire's Windows," *L'Esprit Créateur*, 22, 4 (Winter, 1982), pp. 83–100. For an extensive analysis of Apollinaire's "Les Fenêtres" of 1913, which was written in connection with Robert Delaunay's Cubist canvases on the same theme, see Mathews, *Reading Apollinaire*, pp. 132ff.

130. Breton, "Manifesto of Surrealism," p. 21. Italics in original.

131. Describing *The Human Condition*, Magritte wrote: "I placed in front of a window, seen from inside a room, a painting representing exactly that part of the landscape which was hidden from view by the painting. Therefore, the tree represented the real tree situated behind it, outside the room. It existed for the spectator, as it

theme of the shattered window, literally embodied in Duchamp's *Large Glass*, or the opaque window, as in his *Fresh Widow* (1920), thus problematizing the notion of the transparency of visual experience, even when it pretended to be that of the seer.

These last uses alert us to some of the ways in which Surrealist painting could defy the high modernist ethic of pure opticality. Even as they self-consciously sought to renew vision, the Surrealists were calling into question many of the assumptions underlying that very project. They did so in part by rehabilitating subject matter and resisting the lures of nonrepresentational abstraction based on the dream of complete visual presence and self-sufficient form. The rehabilitation of subject matter did not mean restoring naive mimesis, but rather wrenching objects out of their original contexts and allowing them to follow the uncanny logic of the Surrealist image. Representation was resurrected only to call it into question, thus exposing the arbitrary nature of the visual sign. As Magritte put it in "Words and Images" in *La Révolution surréaliste* in 1929, "Everything points to the fact that scarcely any relationship exists between the object and that which represents it."[132] In relation to the conventions of realist art, Surrealist painting thus could seem to be, following the title of one of Magritte's most famous works, "the betrayal of images."

In fact, titles themselves played a key role in this effort. Often chosen with the goal of disrupting or contesting the apparent meaning of the image, titles could also be introduced directly into the picture, as in Miró's *Un oiseau poursuit une abeille et la baisse* (1941).[133] Or words could be introduced into the painting calling its apparent visual meaning into

---

were, simultaneously in his mind, as both inside the room in the painting, and outside in the real landscape. Which is how we see the world: we see it as being outside ourselves even though it is only a mental representation of it that we experience inside ourselves." Cited in Suzi Gablik, *Magritte* (London, 1970), p. 184.

Lacan was to invoke Magritte's windows in his discussion of phantasy in his 1962 *Séminaire*. See David Macey, *Lacan in Contexts* (London, 1988), p. 45.

132. Magritte, "Les mots et les images," *La Révolution surréaliste*, 12 (December 15, 1929), p. 32. Magritte's close relations with the Paris Surrealists lasted only three years, from 1927 to 1930, and he ultimately came to regret his connection. But his work was always admired by Breton.

question, the most famous example being Magritte's "ceçi n'est pas une pipe" under the image of a pipe painted in 1928.[134] As in the case of Duchamp, the discursive was thus allowed to undermine the self-sufficiency of the figural in radical ways. "Painting the impossible," as Magritte liked to call it, meant giving "precedence to poetry over painting."[135] As Breton recognized, Magritte "put the visual image on trial, stressing its weakness and demonstrating the subordinate character of figures of speech and thought."[136] The eye should not only be in the text, the Surrealists seem to be saying; the text must also be in the eye.[137]

In a very different register, Surrealist experiments in producing arresting visual effects by techniques such as collage, frottage, decalcomania, fumage, coulage, and étréticissements[138] also challenged the integrity of optical experience. Their tactility invoked the hegemony of touch over vi-

133. For a discussion of the function of titles in Surrealism, see Laurie Edson, "Confronting the Signs: Words, Images and the Reader-Spectator," *Dada/Surrealism*, 13 (1984), pp. 83–93.

134. On the incorporation of words into images, see John Welchman, "After the Wagnerian Bouillabaisse: Critical Theory and the Dada and Surrealist Word-Image" in *The Dada and Surrealist Word-Image*, ed. Judi Freeman (Cambridge, Mass., 1990) and Georges Roque, "Magritte's Words and Images," *Visible Language*, 23, 2/3 (Spring, Summer, 1989). For an earlier reflection on this theme, see Michel Butor, *Les mots dans la peinture* (Geneva, 1969).

135. Magritte in a letter to James Thrall Soby, May, 1965, cited in Matthews, *The Imagery of Surrealism*, p. 34. Apparently, it was the sight of de Chirico's *The Song of Love*, with its surgeon's rubber glove combined with an antique statue, that led to his decision to paint the impossible. See the discussion in Gablik, *Magritte*, p. 25.

136. Breton, "Genesis and Perspective of Surrealism in the Plastic Arts," in *What Is Surrealism?*, p. 226.

137. For these reasons, it is hard to accept Mundy's contention that surrealist painting is essentially an affair of transparent internal perception in which "the image must simply be seen" ("Surrealism and Painting," p. 499).

138. Collage involved the chance juxtaposition and reassembling of different found objects on a canvas, without the goal of creating *trompe l'oeil* effects as in cubist *papier collé*. Frottage meant rubbings of textures such as the grain of wood or the veins of leaves. Decalcomania meant spreading color on a sheet of paper, placing another sheet on top of it, then separating them to reveal a chance pattern. Fumage functions with the traces of smoke. Coulages were paint drippings on a canvas, anticipating the

sion, which Diderot had defended during the Enlightenment.[139] Ernst, who was the pioneer in developing certain of these methods, saw them as the visual equivalent of automatic writing, and Breton compared them to a graphic version of the "exquisite corpse" game.[140] One Surrealist painter, Romanian-born Victor Brauner, took them to an extreme by drawing with his eyes entirely closed. Such techniques problematized the adequacy, self-sufficiency and, in Brauner's case, even the necessity of perception in general, and of vision in particular. Collage, for example, provided a kind of metalanguage about the visual that makes explicit the differential play of presence and absence, presentation and representation, which high modernism sought to efface. As Krauss has argued,

> Collage operates in direct opposition to modernism's search for perceptual plenitude and unimpeachable self-presence. Modernism's goal is to objectify the formal constituents of a given medium, making these, beginning with the very ground that is the origin of their existence, the objects of vision. Collage problematizes that goal, by setting up discourse in place of presence, a discourse founded on a buried origin, a discourse fueled by that absence.[141]

Other techniques like frottage and fumage generated whatever meaning they did by a combination of indexical signification, produced by the

---

technique of Jackson Pollock. Étrécissements, developed in the 1960s by Marcel Mariën, are commercial photographs with parts of the original cut off (the word comes from *rétrécissements* with the first letter snipped off).

139. Breton explicitly praised Diderot for inspiring "the possibility of a purely tactile art which would aim at apprehending the object by primitive means and reject all that might be tyrannical and decadent in the realm of *sight*" ("Genesis and Perspective of Surrealism in the Plastic Arts" [1942], in *What Is Surrealism?*, p. 220). Here the connection was made with Futurism, but it would work as well with certain Surrealist practices too.

140. Ernst, *Au-delà de la peinture*, in Waldberg, *Surrealism*, p. 98; Breton, *Le Cadavre Exquis: Son Exaltation*, in idem, p. 95.

physical residue of their material source, and the pattern "discovered" in them by their viewers. As such they were related to another medium to which the Surrealists turned for help in their search for "the marvelous": photography.[142] For despite its more iconical character, its signification by resemblance, the indexical quality of the photograph was often explicitly foregrounded by its Surrealist practitioners.

The importance of this medium for the Surrealist project has only recently come, as it were, into focus. It has often been noted that the movement's first journal, *La Révolution surréaliste*, lacking the typographic fireworks of its Dadaist predecessors, would have seemed like an austere scientific journal if not for the presence of photographs by Man Ray as well as sketches by other Surrealist artists.[143] It has also been remarked that many other Surrealist texts, such as Breton's *Les vases communicants* (1932), *Mad Love* (1937), and *Nadja* (1938), had accompanying photos by Jean-André Boiffard, Brassaï, and Man Ray. And the Surrealists' discovery of Eugène Atget, then virtually unknown, has also not gone unnoticed.[144]

But in general, the putative mimetic or iconic imperative of the medium—acknowledged by Breton himself when he credited photography

141. Krauss, *The Originality of the Avant-Garde and Other Modern Myths*, p. 38.

142. For a wide selection of Surrealist photographs with excellent annotations, see Edouard Jaguer, *Les mystères de la chambre noire: le surréalisme et la photographie* (Paris, 1982).

143. Pierre Naville, who with Bernard Péret was the initial editor, deliberately sought to emulate a scientific journal, thus conceding nothing to "the pleasure of the eyes" (Nadeau, *The History of Surrealism*, p. 98).

144. Walter Benjamin, "A Short History of Photography," *Screen*, 3 (Spring, 1972), p. 20; and Watney, "Making Strange: The Shattered Mirror," p. 171. Four of his works were reprinted in *La Révolution surréaliste* in 1926. In the 1930s, Man Ray's assistant Berenice Abbot brought Atget's work to the United States and helped stimulate Surrealist photography in America. In a different light, however, Atget can also be seen as a forerunner of the *neue Sachlichkeit* sensibility of the German New Vision of the 1920s. However he is understood, Atget's work represented a kind of voyeuristic capturing of urban life, often in danger of disappearing, which fit well with the Surrealists' fascination with wandering through the modern city.

with undermining realist painting[145]—seemed to make it an unlikely tool for Surrealist purposes. Thus, Simon Watney articulated a widespread assumption when he claimed that "photography proved by and large to be resistant to the surrealist imagination, and Man Ray's photographs have far more to do with a Modernist aesthetic derived from Cubist painting than with Surrealism. . . . In the majority of cases the long-term influence of Surrealism meant little more than the creation of the extended sense of the picturesque."[146] Even when the links between Surrealist photography and the politically motivated defamiliarization effects sought by other modernist artists such as the Russian Futurists are acknowledged, its ultimate impact has seemed limited. For as a tool of radical social enlightenment, it had little direct success.

In the different context of our narrative of the interrogation of vision, however, the Surrealists' experiments with the medium can be deemed of greater importance. As Krauss has suggestively demonstrated,[147] Surrealist photography presented a dual challenge to the high modernist attempt to wrest a new visual order from the wreckage of Cartesian perspectivalism. First, it introduced into the photographic image a kind of temporal deferral or "spacing,"[148] which might be called internalized montage. Second, it often drew on the explicitly antivisual implications of Bataille's work, rather than on the search for an "innocent eye" in Breton.

Despite the extraordinary heterogeneity of Surrealist photographic practice, ranging from Jacques-André Boiffard's close-ups of big toes to Man Ray's solarizations, Krauss finds a common theme in all of them.

---

145. Breton, "Max Ernst," in *What Is Surrealism?*, p. 7; and "The Surrealist Situation of the Object," in *Manifestoes of Surrealism*, p. 272. Breton, to be sure, did appreciate the nonmimetic potential of the medium as well, as shown by his enthusiasm for Man Ray's rayographs. He also saw its resemblance to automatic writing, which he calls "the true photography of thought" in the piece on Ernst.

146. Watney, "Making Strange: The Shattered Mirror," pp. 170–171. These claims are part of a larger argument that challenges the political sufficiency of estrangement and defamiliarization as a means to expose social contradictions. He contends that different contexts of reception have to be taken into account as well, because certain contexts more easily absorb shocks than others. The history of Surrealism's refunctioning for advertising purposes bears out his warning.

Implicitly introducing the principle of Dadaist photomontage into a seemingly intact and undoctored image, they undercut the temporal instantaneity of the traditional snapshot.

> Without exception the surrealist photographers infiltrated the body of this print, this single page, with spacing. . . . More important than anything else is the strategy of doubling. For it is doubling that produces the formal rhythm of spacing—the two-step that banishes the unitary condition of the moment, that creates *within* the moment an experience of fission. For it is doubling that elicits the notion that to an original has been added its copy.[149]

A famous example of the technique was Man Ray's portrait of *La Marquise Casati* of 1922, which seems to have two or maybe three sets of eyes superimposed on each other.

The importance of spacing is that it destroys the fateful linkage of vision with pure synchronous presence and introduces the interruption of discursivity, or in the Derridean terminology Krauss adopts, *écriture*. The photograph is particularly adept at instantiating the deferral and doubling of writing because of its dual status as indexical and iconic sign, signifying both by the physical trace left by light waves and by the resemblance its image bore to the object off which those waves bounced:

> Surreality *is*, we could say, nature convulsed into a kind of writing. The special access that photography has to this experience is its

147. Krauss, "The Photographic Conditions of Surrealism" in *The Originality of the Avant-Garde and Other Modernist Myths*; "Corpus Delicti," *October*, 33 (Summer, 1985), pp. 31–72; with Jane Livingston, *L'Amour Fou: Surrealism and Photography* (New York, 1985).

148. The term is Derrida's and it suggests an interplay of absence and presence, the sequential temporality lurking in even the most apparently static spatiality, that defeats "the metaphysics of presence."

149. Krauss, "The Photographic Conditions of Surrealism," p. 109. The recent montage photographs of David Hockney, in which sections of an original image are dissected and then resynthesized, would seem to take the technique of spacing to an extreme.

> privileged connection to the real. The manipulations then available
> to photography—what we have been calling doubling and
> spacing—appear to document these convulsions. The photographs
> are not *interpretations* of reality, decoding it, as in Heartfield's
> photomontages. They are presentations of that reality as config-
> ured, or coded, or written.[150]

Conventional notions of Surrealist imagery as wholly independent of external reality and based solely on the imagination were thus explicitly called into question by the mixed quality of photography. Rather than allowing the "innocent eye" of the seer to look inward into his unconscious to "see" images of the marvelous, Surrealist photographs were often as much creations of the darkroom as windows on reality, internal or external. They thus showed, even more than its painting, the composite quality of internal and external objects as well as the imbrication of the figural and the discursive, and thus the impure status of vision itself.

Even more disruptive of the assumption that Surrealism merely celebrated visionary optics is Krauss's demonstration that Bataille rather than Breton may best be seen as the inspiration for much of its photography. Noting that a number of visual artists excommunicated by Breton, such as Masson, Desnos, and Boiffard, gravitated into Bataille's orbit around the journal *Documents*, she remarks that even before their break with mainstream Surrealism, they—and others like Man Ray—were already exponents of Bataille's notion of *informe*, the anti-idealizing distortion of the body's integral form. Bataille's influence was also apparent in the photographs in *Minotaure*, launched in 1933, with their degrading transformations of the human body into animallike images and their confusion of organs, such as mouths and anuses. Such photographers as Boiffard, Bellmer, and Raoul Ubac subjected the body to a series of violent visual assaults reminiscent of *Story of the Eye*, producing images "of bodies dizzily yielding to the force of gravity; of bodies in the grip of a distorting perspective; of bodies decapitated by the projection of shadow; of bodies

150. Ibid., p.113.

eaten away by either heat or light."[151] Their often fetishistic, sexually charged displacements of familiar human forms was accompanied by an uncanny denaturalization of the spatial order in which they were situated. The results exemplified the nonreciprocal chiasmic intertwining of the eye and the gaze, each the apex of a different visual cone, that Lacan was beginning to explore at the same time and in the same milieu.[152]

As a result, Surrealist photography proved a scandal for what can be called the dominant tradition of "straight photography," with its assumed spectator still the unified subject of the Cartesian perspectivalist tradition. "That subject," Krauss concludes, "armed with a vision that plunges deep into reality and, through the agency of the photograph, given the illusion of mastery over it, seems to find unbearable a photography that effaces categories and in their place erects the fetish, the *informe*, the uncanny."[153] Thus Surrealist photography, long in the shadow of its other visual practices, must be seen as one of the movement's most consequential contributions to the twentieth century's crisis of ocularcentrism.

Can the same be said of another realm of Surrealist optical experimentation, the cinema?[154] Eschewing the skepticism we have observed in

---

151. Krauss, "Corpus Delicti," p. 44. The gender dimension of this attack on the body, most obvious in Bellmer's dismembered dolls, has been the subject of considerable controversy. Krauss has argued against its importance, but other commentators are not convinced. See, for example, Steve Edwards, "Gizmo Surrealism," *Art History*, 10, 4 (December, 1987), pp. 511ff. His critique is situated in a larger defense of the value of Breton over Bataille because of their respective political implications. See also Hal Foster, "L'Amour Faux," *Art in America*, 74, 1 (January, 1986).

152. To be precise, the chiasmic intertwining she evokes was really only spelled out in Lacan's later work, *The Four Fundamental Concepts of Psycho-analysis*, but in the 1930s, his theory of the mirror stage was already developed and available to the group around Bataille. In fact, *Minotaure* published an essay in 1938 by Pierre Mabille, entitled "Miroirs," which discussed it.

153. Ibid., p. 72.

154. The literature on the Surrealist cinema is now very extensive. Among the most helpful treatments are J. H. Matthews, *Surrealism and Film* (Ann Arbor, Mich., 1971); Steven Kovács, *From Enchantment to Rage: The Story of Surrealist Cinema* (Rutherford, N.J., 1980); Linda Williams, *Figures of Desire: A Theory and Analysis of Surrealist Film* (Urbana, Ill., 1981); and the special issue of *Dada/Surrealism*, 15

Bergson, the Surrealists avidly embraced the new medium. One of its earliest French champions had, in fact, been Apollinaire, who introduced cinematic effects into such poems as "Zone" and even tried his hand at writing a film script. As early as 1917, Philippe Soupault had written "cinematographic poems" based on montagelike transitions and the sudden transfiguration of objects; he too composed films scripts. Jacques Vaché, the absurdist whose life (and self-inflicted death) so inspired the Surrealists, was also spellbound by film. The year Breton spent with Vaché in Nantes in 1916 turned him as well into a passionate convert, who with his friends would hop from movie house to movie house seeing snatches of as many films as they could. Robert Desnos, who was the Surrealists' most serious film critic, spoke for many of them when he gushed, "For us and only for us had the Lumière brothers invented the cinema. There we were at home. That darkness was the darkness of our rooms before going to sleep. Perhaps the screen could match our dreams."[155]

The 1920s in France were especially congenial to experimental cinema, partly because the widespread *ciné-club* movement allowed the easy distribution of noncommercial films.[156] Dada artists like Francis Picabia and René Clair exploited the new medium's capacity for trick photography in such works as *Entr'acte*, which owed more to the visual prestidigitation of Georges Méliès than to the realism of the Lumière brothers. Others drew on film's completely nonmimetic, mechanical potential, often producing nonnarrative, illogical effects, like those developed in Duchamp's *Anémic Cinéma*. Man Ray's first film, *Le retour à la raison* of 1921, for example, included animated rayographs. But the Dadaists soon came to distrust the cinema's spectaclelike closeness to the nineteenth-century

---

(1986), which has a full bibliography. For Surrealist writings on film, see Paul Hammond, ed., *The Shadow and Its Shadow: Surrealist Writings on Cinema* (London, 1978).

155. Robert Desnos, *Cinéma*, ed. André Tchernia (Paris, 1966), p. 154; cited in Kovács, p. 15.

156. For histories of French cinema, see Richard Abel, *French Cinema: The First Wave, 1915–1929* (Princeton, 1984); Roy Armes, *French Cinema* (New York, 1985); and Alan Williams, *The Republic of Images: A History of French Filmmaking* (Cambridge, Mass., 1992).

ideal of synesthesia and the *Gesamtkunstwerk*, which rendered the audience overly passive.[157]

The Surrealists, on the other hand, admired precisely that result. They restored narrative, character, and optical realism, but imbued them with the oneiric effects they sought elsewhere through poetic and plastic means. As early as 1911, the critic Jules Romains had noted a link between films and dreams in his discussion of the cinema audience: "The group dream now begins. They sleep; their eyes no longer see. They are no longer conscious of their bodies. Instead there are only passing images, a gliding and rustling of dreams."[158] Not surprisingly, the affinity between Surrealism and the film would be quickly recognized. Its classic statement came in a widely cited essay by Jean Goudal, not himself a member of the movement, in 1925.[159] The cinema, he contended, promotes conscious hallucinations in which the ego is suppressed: "Our body itself undergoes a sort of temporary depersonalization which robs it of the sense of its own existence. We are nothing more than two eyes riveted to ten meters of white screen."[160] Cinema, he claimed, also brilliantly realizes the Surrealist project of generating meaning without recourse to the logical entailments of conventional language. It could even more vividly produce profane illuminations through visual juxtapositions than the verbal images in Surrealist poems.

How successful were the Surrealists in producing films of their own to realize this promise? Much of their talent was, in fact, spent in devising scenarios rather than in shooting actual films—that is, in verbal rather than visual endeavors. Often published as *ciné-romans* in film journals,

157. For an account of their disillusionment, see Thomas Elsaesser, "Dada/Cinema?" in *Dada/Surrealism*, 15 (1986), pp. 13–27.

158. Jules Romains, "La Foule au cinématographe," *Puissances de Paris* (Paris, 1911), p. 120. Linda Williams has more recently argued that it was less the content of dreams that Surrealist cinema sought to represent than the process of dreamwork itself, which it sought to evoke. See her *Figures of Desire*, pp. 17ff.

159. Jean Goudal, "Surréalisme et cinéma," *Revue Hebdomadaire*, 34, 8 (February 21, 1925), pp. 343–357, in English in Hammond, ed., *The Shadow and Its Shadow*.

160. Ibid., p. 308.

their scripts tried to transgress the stabilizing, conventionalizing function of the typical *film racontés* available on the mass market.[161] As a result, some of them are of considerable interest—for example, certain of Antonin Artaud's, which play with the theme of high-altitude flight so popular in the aftermath of World War I.[162]

But the inability, for financial as well as aesthetic reasons, to transform most of them into actual films soon took its toll. The invention of talkies made production costs prohibitive for esoteric experiments without a mass audience. By the early 1930s, the Surrealists' infatuation with the cinema had begun to cool down. Breton himself had done little beyond his expression of youthful exuberance to sponsor its production. It was one thing to enjoy watching films, but quite another to make them. Few Surrealists became as explicitly bitter as the frustrated Artaud, who proclaimed in a 1933 essay called "The Premature Senility of the Film," "The world of the cinema is a dead world, illusory and truncated. . . . We must not expect of the cinema to restore to us the Myths of the man and the life of today."[163] But most would come to share the later lament of Benjamin Péret: "Never had a means of expression witnessed as much hope as the cinema. . . . And yet never has one observed such disproportion between the immensity of possibilities and the derisory results."[164]

Although the number of its successes was small, Surrealism did produce two universally acclaimed masterpieces before its interest waned: *Un*

161. For an account, see Richard Abel, "Exploring the Discursive Field of the Surrealist Scenario Text," *Dada/Surrealism*, 15 (1986), pp. 58–71.

162. Kovács, *From Enchantment to Rage*, p. 170. In a note on p. 180, he posits a connection between films and flight, which draws on Freud's speculations about their common links to sexuality, but he neglects the specific postwar context in which the aviator's vision was glorified.

163. Antonin Artaud, "La vieillesse précose du cinéma," *Les cahiers jaunes,* 4 (1933), in *Oeuvres complètes* (Paris, 1970), pp. 104 and 107; for an account of his disillusionment, see Kovács, *From Enchantment to Rage,* chap. 5, and Sandy Flitterman-Lewis, "The Image and the Spark: Dulac and Artaud Reviewed," *Dada/Surrealism*, 15 (1986), pp. 110–127. The latter focuses on his disastrous collaboration with Germaine Dulac in the making of *The Seashell and the Clergyman* in 1927.

164. Benjamin Péret, cited in Kovács, *From Enchantment to Rage*, p. 250.

chien andalou (1929) and *L'age d'or* (1930). Both were by the Spanish artists Luis Buñuel and Salvador Dali, who in this period were very much part of the Parisian avant-garde community. An enormous amount of critical attention has been devoted to both of these works, discussing everything from the relative role of the two collaborators to the shift in the political implications from one film to the other.[165] Rather than rehearse all of its conclusions, I want to probe the meaning of only one of these films' central episodes, which has special significance for the Surrealist contribution to the crisis of ocularcentrism: the celebrated slitting of the eye in *Un chien andalou.*

The film consists of a series of loosely linked, rebuslike scenes that powerfully evoke the Surrealists' fascination for the world of dreams. According to Buñuel, "The plot is the result of a CONSCIOUS *psychic automatism* and, to that extent, it does not attempt to recount a dream, although it profits by a mechanism analogous to that of dreams."[166] Bataille, one of the work's most enthusiastic supporters, described its power as follows: "Several very explicit facts appear in successive order, without logical connection it is true, but penetrating so far into horror that the spectators are caught up as directly as they are in adventure films. Caught up and even precisely caught by the throat, and without artifice; do these spectators know, in fact, where they—the authors of this film, or people like them—will stop?"[167]

Another source of *Un chien andalou*'s fascination was its defiance of attempts to interpret it, even as it insistently solicited such attempts. Buñuel claimed that "NOTHING in the film SYMBOLIZES ANYTHING,"[168] but admitted that psychoanalysis might help make sense of it. Its most widely interpreted episode occurs at the beginning, in what is

165. For an extensive selection, see the entries under Buñuel and Dali in Rudolf Kuenzli's bibliography of works on Dada and Surrealist film in *Dada/Surrealism*, 15 (1986).

166. Luis Buñuel, "Notes on the Making of *Un chien andalou,*" *Art in Cinema,* ed. Frank Stauffacher (New York, 1968), p. 29.

167. Bataille, "Eye," *Visions of Excess*, p. 19.

168. Buñuel, "Notes on the Making of *Un chien andalou,*" p. 30.

sometimes called the film's prologue. Introduced by the caption, "Once upon a time," invoking mythic temporality, a cloud slices across the moon, to be followed by the slow, deliberate, and unresisted slashing of a woman's eyeball with a razor. According to Bataille, Buñuel told him that it had been devised by Dali, "to whom it was directly suggested by the real vision of a narrow and long cloud cutting across the lunar surface."[169] Years later, Buñuel would say he had dreamed it himself.[170] Whatever its provenance, it was realized with stunning efficacy, as the dead cow's eye substituted for the woman's by the magic of montage burst apart with devastatingly gruesome horror.

Variously interpreted, inter alia, as a simulacrum of sexual cruelty against women, a symbol of male castration anxiety, the conception of an infant, an indication of homosexual ambivalence, and an extended linguistic pun,[171] the act's literal dimension has sometimes been overlooked.[172] That is, the violent mutilation of the eye, that theme so obsessively enacted in Bataille's pornographic fiction, is here paradoxically given to the sight of those with the courage not to avert their eyes from what appears on the screen. There is little visual pleasure, to put it mildly, in the result, which mocks that seductive lure of the cinema critics like Christian Metz were so vehemently to denounce.

In fact, a recent commentator armed with Metz's arguments, Linda Williams, has provocatively interpreted Surrealist cinema precisely as an attempt to subvert the dominant regime of cinematic pleasure. In the Lacanian terminology adopted by Metz, which will be examined in a subsequent chapter, she claims that although the Surrealist poets first turned to film because it seemed to offer an escape from what they felt to be the

169. Bataille, "The 'Lugubrious Game,'" *Visions of Excess*, p. 29.

170. Carlos Fuentes, "The Discreet Charm of Luis Buñuel," *New York Times Magazine* (March 11, 1973), p. 87, cited in Kovács, *From Enchantment to Rage*, p. 191.

171. Buñuel himself seems to have been satisfied with none of these interpretations. See his remarks to François Truffaut in "Rencontre avec Luis Buñuel," *Arts* (July 25, 1955), p. 5, cited in Kovács, *From Enchantment to Rage*, p. 245.

172. One recent exception is Mary Ann Caws, "Eye and Film: Buñuel's Act," in *The Art of Interference: Stressed Readings in Verbal and Visual Texts* (Princeton, 1989).

rigidities of codified language, their exploitation of the filmic image soon became a very sophisticated attempt to expose the viewer's own misrecognition of the image. Thus, their cultivation of what Lacan calls the Imaginary aims ultimately at the revelation of the ways in which the image, too, is structured by processes similar to those at work in language.[173] In Williams's reading of *Un chien andalou,* the slitting of the eye is thus a figure for the rupture of the visual pleasure accompanying experiences of imagistic wholeness.

The eye was, in fact, a central Surrealist image in more than its cinema, and indeed can be discerned in much twentieth-century visual art.[174] Anticipated by Odilon Redon's haunting images of single eyes as balloons, flowers, or Cyclops staring toward heaven, artists like Giorgio de Chirico, Ernst, Dali, Man Ray, and Magritte developed a rich ocular iconography. In most cases, the eyes (or often the single eye) were enucleated, blinded, mutilated, or transfigured, as in *Story of the Eye,* into other shapes like eggs, whose liquid could easily be spilled. Ernst's *Two Ambiguous Figures* (1919), with its transparent heads fitted with opaque goggles, Man Ray's *Object of Destruction* (original version, 1923), with its eye cut from a photograph of a lover and mounted on a metronome, Dali's *The Lugubrious Game* (1929), with its chilling mixture of images of castration and enucleation, and Alberto Giacometti's *Suspended Ball* (1930–1931) with its globe erotically/sadistically split by a crescent wedge[175] all typify the violent denigration of the visual that culminated in Buñuel's slashing razor.

Here the third eye of the seer is deprived of its spiritualizing, elevating function and compelled to reveal its affinity with sadistic and erotic impulses instead. The Icarian flights of Breton's seer end in the bowels of

173. Williams, *Figures of Desire,* p. 41.

174. For discussions, see Jeanne Siegel, "The Image of the Eye in Surrealist Art and Its Psychoanalytic Sources, Part One: The Mythic Eye," *Arts Magazine,* 56, 6 (1982), pp. 102–106 and "Part Two: Magritte," 56, 7 (1982), pp.116–119; and Gerald Eager, "The Missing and Mutilated Eye in Contemporary Art," *The Journal of Aesthetics and Art Criticism,* 20, 1 (Fall, 1961), pp. 49–59.

175. For an analysis of this sculpture, which links it to *Story of the Eye* and *Un chien andalou,* see Krauss, *The Originality of the Avant-Garde,* p. 58.

Bataille's labyrinth.[176] Indeed, if Jeanne Siegel is right, the explicit link between the third eye and transgressive sexuality argued by the psychoanalyst Rudolf Reitler in 1913 may have directly influenced Max Ernst and through him other Surrealists.[177] Whatever the source, there can be little doubt that the eye seemed to many Surrealist artists less an object to be revered, less the organ of pure and noble vision, than a target of mutilation and scorn, or a vehicle of its own violence. It is largely on the basis of an analysis of Surrealist eye imagery that the art historian Gerald Eager could generalize about all twentieth-century painting,

> whose eyes are not moist or movable, they are not alive and do not suggest the power to look back and see. When the viewer looks at them, they do not have the power to look back and see. So the individual or divine spark of contact does not exist in the missing or mutilated eye. In place of contact there is rejection; instead of sight, there is complete blindness.[178]

Although this analysis of the implications of Surrealist painting, photography, and cinema might well be construed as demonstrating the triumph of Bataille over Breton, it should be noted in conclusion that the latter also came to evince doubts about the privileging of the visual. In "The Automatic Message" of 1933, he admitted that "verbal inspiration is infinitely richer in visual meaning, infinitely more resistant to the eye, than visual images properly so called."[179] Such a belief, he then confessed, "is the source of my unceasing protest against the presumed 'visionary' power of the poet. No, Lautréamont and Rimbaud did not *see* what they described; they were never confronted by it *a priori*. That is, they never

---

176. For a reading of *L'age d'or* that also interprets it in terms of Bataille's worldview, see Allen Weiss, "Between the Sign of the Scorpion: *L'Age d'or*," *Dada/Surrealism*, 15 (1986), pp. 159–175.

177. Siegel, "The Image of the Eye in Surrealist Art," p. 106. Reitler's essay was "On Eye Symbolism," *Internationale Zeitschrift für Ärztliche Psychoanalyse*, 1 (1913).

178. Eager, "The Missing or Mutilated Eye in Contemporary Art," p. 59.

179. Breton, "The Automatic Message," p. 107.

described anything. They threw themselves into the dark recesses of being; they heard indistinctly."[180] It is thus no surprise to find Breton, like Bataille, availing himself of the metaphor of the labyrinth as the enfolded, convoluted, unilluminated space where the Surrealist confronts the unconscious.[181]

Whether or not Breton's protest against the "visionary" model of poetic creation was quite as unceasing as he claimed—as already noted, he approvingly cited Rimbaud's "lettres du voyant" again in his 1935 "Surrealist Situation of the Object"—he clearly revealed his priorities when he insisted that "I believe as fully today as I did ten years ago—I believe blindly . . . blindly with a blindness that covers all visible things—in the triumph *auditorily* of what is unverifiable visually."[182] Thus, when the painters ultimately failed Breton by remaining dogged egotists rather than submitting themselves to the discipline of collective work—even the much-admired Ernst was excommunicated for accepting the Grand Prix at the Venice Biennale in 1953—he could fall back on his original distrust of the "lamentable expedient" that was the direct visual expression of the marvelous.[183]

In short, the provocative slitting of the cow/woman's eye in *Un chien andalou* is a far cry indeed from the serene dissection of the *oeil de boeuf* in Descartes's *Dioptrique*. That founding document of the Cartesian perspectivalist tradition became, in fact, a subject of other, more explicit critiques as the antivisual discourse spread into other regions of French intellectual life. In the philosophical movement that became known as

180. Ibid.

181. For a discussion of the various uses of the metaphor in Breton, see John Zuern, "The Communicating Labyrinth: Breton's 'La Maison d'Yves'," *Dada/Surrealism*, 17 (1988). He notes that Breton identified himself more with Theseus than the Minotaur, but adds, "The surrealist Theseus, the revolutionary, does not free the world from tyranny by entering the labyrinth and destroying the beast, but by taking the entire world into the labyrinth with him, where, confounded with the liberated unconscious, the world is transformed" (p. 118).

182. Breton, *"The Automatic Message,"* p. 107.

183. For Breton's disillusionment with painters, see "Against the Liquidators" (1964) in *What is Surrealism?*

phenomenology, it provided a convenient target for French critics of ocularcentrism. In the work of Jean-Paul Sartre and Maurice Merleau-Ponty in particular, as the following chapter hopes to demonstrate, the interrogation of the eye and its gaze expanded into new and eagerly explored territories of investigation.

CHAPTER FIVE

Sartre, Merleau-Ponty, and the Search for a New Ontology of Sight

> But all of a sudden I hear footsteps in the hall. Someone is looking at me! What does this mean?
>
> JEAN-PAUL SARTRE[1]

> I would like to see more clearly, but it seems to me that no one sees more clearly.
>
> MAURICE MERLEAU-PONTY[2]

Despite the challenge of Bergson before the First World War and the Surrealists' embrace of Hegel after it, mainstream French philosophy remained in the thrall of neo-Kantian and positivist tendencies until well into the 1930s. In fact, in the broadest sense, it had never been able to throw off many of the fundamental assumptions bequeathed to it by Cartesianism.[3] Among the most stubbornly persistent was its spectatorial and intellectualist epistemology based on a subjective self reflecting on an objective world exterior to it. Here the most zealous guardian of the flame

---

1. Jean-Paul Sartre, *Being and Nothingness: An Essay on Phenomenological Ontology*, trans. Hazel E. Barnes (New York, 1966), p. 319.

2. Maurice Merleau-Ponty, *The Primacy of Perception*, ed. James M. Edie (Evanston, Ill., 1964), p. 36.

3. Indeed, even today, Descartes is still a figure to be reckoned with in France. See Vincent Carraud, "The Relevance of Cartesianism," in *Contemporary French Philosophy*, ed. A. Phillips Griffiths (Cambridge, 1987).

was Léon Brunschvicg, whose dominance at the Sorbonne stretched from 1909 until the German occupation of Paris in 1940.[4]

The story of how a group of young, restless and extraordinarily gifted thinkers in the interwar years—including Gabriel Marcel, Paul Nizan, Jean Wahl, Jean Hyppolite, Claude Lévi-Strauss, Simone de Beauvoir, and most notably Jean-Paul Sartre and Maurice Merleau-Ponty—rebelled against the hegemony of Brunschvicg and the orthodoxies of Third Republic philosophy has been told too often to repeat here.[5] Their tutelage in Hegelian dialectics in the lectures of Alexander Kojève, rediscovery of history and politics, impatience with Eurocentric models of culture, and search for a philosophy of the concrete to replace the stale abstractions of neo-Kantianism are all now widely appreciated.

Less well known, however, is their radical questioning of the ocular-centric bias of the dominant tradition, which complemented in important ways the critiques examined in previous chapters. From a position very different from those of Bataille and the Surrealists, whose work in fact they often maligned,[6] Sartre and Merleau-Ponty in particular conducted a probing interrogation of the visual that must be understood as a central episode in this narrative. Although diverging on a number of basic points, Sartre and Merleau-Ponty shared a deep-seated suspicion of the Cartesian perspectivalist gaze, which often extended to the primacy of vision itself.

4. On Brunschvicg's role, see Colin Smith, *Contemporary French Philosophy* (London, 1954) and Jacques Havet, "French Philosophical Tradition between the Two Wars," in *Philosophic Thought in France and the United States*, ed. Marvin Farber (Albany, N.Y., 1950).

5. See Mark Poster, *Existentialist Marxism in Postwar France* (Princeton, 1975), and Vincent Descombes, *Modern French Philosophy*, trans. L. Scott-Fox and J. M. Harding (Cambridge, 1980).

6. Sartre in particular was critical of Surrealism. See his hostile review of Bataille's *L'expérience intérieure*, "Un nouveau Mystique" in *Situations I* (Paris, 1947), and his critique of Surrealism in *What Is Literature?*, trans. Bernard Frechtman (New York, 1949). For a general account of his attitude, see Michel Beaujour, "Sartre and Surrealism," *Yale French Studies*, 30 (1964). Merleau-Ponty seems to have been less engaged with their ideas. But see footnote 19.

They also shared a debt no less profound to German critics of ocular-centrism, whose ideas they helped disseminate, if often in creatively garbled form, in France. German philosophy, ever since the Reformation, seems to have been less positively inclined toward vision than the French. In general, German thinkers have tended to privilege aural over visual experience, as indicated by their tendency to draw on poetry or music rather than painting in their work.[7] Schopenhauer, Nietzsche, and Adorno are three salient examples of German philosophers who heard in music the quintessential art form, either because it purported to express the will more directly than painting or because its nonrepresentational quality insulated it against too naturalist a mimesis of the given world.[8] Hermeneutic thinkers from Schleiermacher and Wilhelm Dilthey to Gadamer have trusted more in the word than the image. Philosophers of Life like Ludwig Klages have linked the primacy of the optical to the domination of rigid intellectual concepts over the flowing vitality of the soul.[9] Even Marxists like the members of the Frankfurt School appreciated the force of the taboo on images (*Bilderverbot*) explicitly derived from the ancient Jewish interdiction but implicitly in accordance with a long-standing German inclination.

For the generation of Sartre and Merleau-Ponty, however, the main inspiration from across the Rhine came from the movement known as phenomenology, in particular the philosophy of Edmund Husserl and Martin Heidegger. The Husserl discovered by Sartre and Merleau-Ponty in the early 1930s might not, at first glance, seem very much like a critic of ocularcentrism. In such works as the *Cartesian Meditations* of 1931,[10] he

7. There were, of course, exceptions to this rule. Friedrich Schiller, for example, stressed the importance of sight in his aesthetics. See *On the Aesthetic Education of Man in a Series of Letters,* trans. Reginald Snell (New York, 1965), p. 126.

8. It is a cliché of cultural history that German musical culture has been more advanced than French. For an attempt to account for this superiority, see Marcel Beufils, *Comment l'Allemagne est devenue musicienne* (Paris, 1983).

9. Ludwig Klages, *Der Geist als Widersacher der Seele,* 2 vols., 3d ed. (Munich, 1954), vol. 1, chap. 30. Similar sentiments can be found in Oswald Spengler, *The Decline of the West,* vol. II, trans. Charles Francis Atkinson (New York, 1950), pp. 6ff.

10. Edmund Husserl, *Cartesian Meditations,* trans. D. Cairns (The Hague, 1970).

defined phenomenology as a kind of neo-Cartesianism, concerned with the rigorous scientific investigation of ideas in all their conceptual clarity and distinctness. Husserl, moreover, defended the need to purify philosophy of the psychological residues he saw lurking even in Descartes in order to become genuinely transcendental. Phenomenology should be what he called an "eidetic science," able to gain intuitive insights into essences. Intuition, contrary to Bergson's use of the concept, could reveal more than the interior experience of lived temporality. The phenomenological "reduction" (or *epoché* as he often called it) led back (the Latin word *reducere*) to the source of existence and meaning. By bracketing the "natural standpoint," which takes for granted normal perceptual experience and identifies reality with the ensemble of empirical "facts," and then painstakingly describing the data of the consciousness that remained, the phenomenologist could gain access to a more fundamental level of reality.

That Husserl chose to call the eidetic intuition a *Wesenschau* (literally a look into essences) suggests the persistence of ocularcentric premises in his thought. As Joseph J. Kockelmans has put it, "Husserl seeks the ultimate foundation of all our rational assertions in an immediate vision, i.e., an original intuition of the things themselves concerning which we want to make a statement."[11] Indeed, despite the many shifts in his position over the years, concerning for example the proper relationship between psychology and phenomenology, many of his commentators have remarked on the privilege he consistently gave to sight. Thus, for example, in his introductory study *La phénomenologie*, Lyotard writes, "in reality, the ultimate ground for every rational affirmation is in 'sight' (*Sehen*) in general, that is, in the originary foundational consciousness (*Ideen*)."[12] And Quentin Lauer adds that for Husserl, "philosophy, then, is either a seeing, or it is no science at all."[13]

11. Joseph J. Kockelmans, "What Is Phenomenology?" in *Phenomenology: The Philosophy of Edmund Husserl and Its Interpretation*, ed. Joseph J. Kockelmans (Garden City, N.Y., 1967), p. 29.

12. Jean-François Lyotard, *La phénoménologie* (Paris, 1954), p. 12; this work, his first book, was written when Lyotard was a phenomenologist himself.

In fact, the apparently central role of vision in Husserl's thought has been the target of certain French critics, who more explicitly reject the assumption of its putative nobility. As early as 1930 in one of the first French appreciations of his work, Emmanuel Levinas's *Theory of Intuition in Husserl's Phenomenology*,[14] his reliance on ocular metaphors in describing intuition and theory was singled out for critique. More recently, in *Speech and Phenomena*, published in 1967, Derrida criticized Husserl's privileging of the *Augenblick*, the timeless blink of an instant in which the "scene of ideal objects" appears to consciousness, as complicitous with the Western metaphysics of presence.[15] And in 1976, Marc Richir, a follower of Merleau-Ponty, claimed that Husserl's great mistake was the "installation of pure seeing in the position of an absolute overview (*survol*) vis-à-vis the world."[16]

How then, it must be asked, did Husserl help furnish Sartre and Merleau-Ponty with arguments against ocularcentrism? Two reasons are paramount. First, however much Husserl may have retained a visual bias in the idea of *Wesenschau*, however steeped his rhetoric may have been in visual metaphors of clarity, he radically undermined the spectatorial distance between viewing subject and viewed object in the Cartesian epistemological tradition. Although he wanted to make phenomenology a science, he was careful to avoid equating science with its Galilean version.

13. Quentin Lauer, "On Evidence," in Kockelmans, ed., *Phenomenology*, pp. 155–156.

14. Emmanuel Levinas, *The Theory of Intuition in Husserl's Phenomenology*, trans. André Orianne (Evanston, 1973).

15. Jacques Derrida, *Speech and Phenomena and Other Essays on Husserl's Theory of Signs*, trans. David B. Allison (Evanston, 1973). Derrida also credits Husserl's succumbing to the metaphysics of presence to his belief in the immediacy of the voice, as opposed to writing. For discussions of his critique, see Rudolf Bernet, "Is the Present Ever Present? Phenomenology and the Metaphysics of Presence," and Leonard Lawler, "Temporality and Spatiality: A Note to a Footnote in Jacques Derrida's *Writing and Difference*," in John Sallis, ed., *Husserl and Contemporary Thought* (Atlantic Highlands, N.J., 1983).

16. Marc Richir, *Au-delà du renversement copernicien: La question de la phénoménologie et de son fondement* (The Hague, 1976), p. 8.

For consciousness was not independent of its object, nor was an object a thing standing apart to be viewed from afar; consciousness was always *of* something. The complicated notion of intentionality, which Husserl had adopted from Franz Brentano, may have been cast as a ray or a beam emanating from a subject, but it nonetheless suggested that traditional philosophical notions of representation had to be revised.

The mind was not completely distanced from a world which was represented to it as images in its metaphorical eye. Nor was it sufficient to trust the physiological experience of seeing one aspect of an object, for the intended object transcended any of its specific profiles or representations. Even Bergson's distinction between intuited experiences of internal *durée* and intellectual knowledge of objects in external space failed to register the primordial oneness of all consciousness prior to its dissociation. Husserl's famous call to return to "the things themselves" meant regaining the experience of the intertwining of subject and object, which was lost in all dualistic philosophies.

Second, although Husserl's early work sought to defend the concept of the transcendental ego, which might be construed as a residual version of the Cartesian *cogito*, his later work, most notably *The Crisis of the European Sciences and Transcendental Phenomenology* of 1936,[17] put the stress on the prereflective *Lebenswelt* (lifeworld) instead. Here both the cultural/historical variations of everyday life (the *doxa* of opinion prior to the *episteme* of science) and the lived body played a central role. Although most commentators deny that the *Lebenswelt* simply replaced the transcendental ego in Husserl's thinking, Merleau-Ponty in particular was able to seize on it as the means to strip phenomenology of its Cartesian residues.[18] Now phenomenology could mean something besides searching for pure essences through eidetic intuition; it could mean as well exploring impure existence, which resisted reduction to the object of a gaze, phenomenological or otherwise.

That Merleau-Ponty was able to interpret Husserl in this way was in

17. Edmund Husserl, *The Crisis of the European Sciences and Transcendental Phenomenology,* trans. D. Carr (Evanston, 1970).

part made possible by the more explicit critique of visual primacy already present in Heidegger's phenomenology, which also entered the French debates in the 1930s. The complex history of the French reception of his thought, marked by the now notorious misreading of him as an "existentialist" and "humanist," cannot be recounted here. Nor can a full presentation be attempted of the visual theme as it was developed in the vast corpus of Heidegger's work, which is still only partially in print. Only certain central motifs can be highlighted before turning to Sartre's and Merleau-Ponty's contributions to the anti-ocularcentric discourse.

In one sense, Heidegger's thought, for all its fascination with certain Hellenic models, can be construed as recovering the Hebraic emphasis on hearing God's word rather than seeing His manifestations. Noting his appeal to Christian theologians, Hans Jonas has observed,

> He brings to the fore precisely what the philosophical tradition ignored or withheld—the moment of call over against that of form, of mission over against presence, of being grasped over against surveying, of event over against object, of response over against the pride of autonomous reason, and generally the stance of piety over against the self-assertion of the subject. At last . . . the suppressed side of "hearing" gets a hearing after the long ascendancy of "seeing" and the spell of objectification which it cast upon thought.[19]

Whether or not Heidegger's restoration of hearing can truly be derived from Old Testament taboos on graven images—his general attitude toward the Jews was, to put it mildly, less than admiring—he was certainly critical of many of the aspects of Greek thought that allow it to be called the fount of Western ocularcentrism. The Apollonian impulse in Greek

18. For an account of Merleau-Ponty's use of the later Husserl, see James Schmidt, *Maurice Merleau-Ponty: Between Phenomenology and Structuralism* (London, 1985), pp. 35ff.

19. Hans Jonas, *The Phenomenon of Life: Toward a Philosophical Biology* (Chicago, 1982), p. 240.

art, with its privileging of beautiful form, and the visually oriented concept of *theoria* were among his favorite targets.[20] His hostility to the heliocentric rationalism of Platonism was no less explicit, as was his rejection of the dualism of subject and object entailed by privileging vision. Like Bergson, Heidegger bemoaned the neglect of temporality in Western metaphysics since Heraclitus in favor of a spatializing ontology based on the synchronicity of the fixating gaze.

Heidegger's critique of the ocularcentrism of post-Socratic Greek thought extended as well to the dominant Western philosophical and scientific traditions. "In *theoria* transformed into *contemplatio*," he wrote, "there comes to the fore the impulse, already prepared in Greek thinking, of a looking-at that sunders and compartmentalizes. A type of encroaching advance by successive interrelated steps toward that which is to be grasped by the eye makes itself normative in knowing."[21] A further step

20. In "The Origin of the Work of Art" (1935) he wrote, "Form and content are the most hackneyed concepts under which anything and everything may be subsumed. And if form is correlated with the rational and matter with the irrational; if the rational is taken to be the logical and the irrational the alogical; if in addition the subject-object relation is coupled with the conceptual pair form-matter; then representation has at its command a conceptual machinery that nothing is capable of withstanding." In Martin Heidegger, *Basic Writings*, ed., David Farrell Krell (New York, 1977), p. 158.

In "Science and Reflection" (1954) he wrote, "The word 'theory' stems from the Greek *theorein*. The noun belonging to it is *theoria*. Peculiar to these is a lofty and mysterious meaning. The verb *theorein* grew out of the coalescing of two root words, *thea* and *horao*. *Thea* (cf. theater) is the outward look, the aspect, in which something shows itself. Plato names this aspect in which what presences shows what it is, *eidos*. To have seen this aspect, *eidenai*, is to know [*wissen*]. The second root word in *theorein, horao*, means: to look at something attentively, to look it over, to view it closely." In Martin Heidegger, *The Question Concerning Technology and Other Essays*, ed. William Lovitt (New York, 1977), p. 163. Heidegger, however, did acknowledge an alternative Greek usage of *theoria* as "the reverent paying heed to the unconcealment of what presences" (p. 164), but he claimed it was lost when the Romans translated the word into *contemplatio*.

21. Heidegger, "Science and Reflection," p. 166. The Latin *contemplari*, he claimed, comes from *templum*, the place which can be seen from any point and from which any point is visible.

occurred when *theoria* was conflated with observation, which in German (*Betrachten*) contains residues of the Latin *tractare*, to manipulate and work over. The science based on visual manipulation was thus anything but disinterested.

Contrasting the early Greek attitude of wonder, which lets things be, with that of curiosity, which is based on the desire to know how they function, Heidegger linked the latter with the hypertrophy of the visual. In *Being and Time*, he wrote, "The basic state of sight shows itself in a peculiar tendency of Being which belongs to everydayness—the tendency towards 'seeing.' We designate this tendency by the term 'curiosity,' which characteristically is not confined to seeing, but expresses the tendency towards a peculiar way of letting the world be encountered by us in perception."[22] The ultimate triumph of curiosity over wonder was an essential component in the hegemony of the technological world view in the modern era.[23]

Technology was deeply problematic for Heidegger because it carried to an extreme the distancing of subject and object, which had come into its own in modern philosophy with Descartes. It drew on the mode of relating to Being he called *Vorhandenheit* (presence-at-hand), which posited something in front to be seen, rather than *Zuhandenheit* (readiness-to-hand), which meant using something practically without visualizing it first. Even Nietzsche, Heidegger contended, was complicitous with the modern technological world view, because of his doctrine of the will to power and his perspectivalist definition of values.[24]

22. Heidegger, *Being and Time*, trans. John Macquarrie and Edward Robinson (New York, 1962), p. 214. For a very different analysis of the emancipation of curiosity, see Hans Blumenberg, *The Legitimacy of the Modern Age*, trans. Robert M. Wallace (Cambridge, Mass., 1983).

23. For useful accounts of his views on the subject, see Harold Alderman, "Heidegger's Critique of Science and Technology," in *Heidegger and Modern Philosophy*, ed. Michael Murray (New Haven, 1978); and Michael E. Zimmerman, *Heidegger's Confrontation with Modernity: Technology, Politics, Art* (Bloomington, Ind., 1990).

24. Heidegger, "The Word of Nietzsche 'God is Dead'" (1943), in *The Question Concerning Technology and Other Essays*, where he notes that "the essence of value lies in its being a point-of-view. Value means that upon which the eye is fixed" (p. 71).

For Heidegger, the tendency latent in Plato's doctrine of Being as *Eidos* became fully manifest in what he called the modern "age of the world picture." So fateful was this development that he could claim that "the fundamental event of the modern age is the conquest of the world as picture."[25] It was so profoundly significant because it facilitated the birth of the modern humanist subject, who stood apart from a world he surveyed and manipulated. Even when the sophist Protagoras had declared that "man was the measure of all things," he was still operating with a concept of truth that was not yet representational, not yet based on the correspondence of object and mental image. Only the modern age had allowed what Heidegger called Enframing (*Ge-stell*) to gain full sway, turning the world into a "standing reserve" for arrogant human domination. What such an attitude forgot was that "world is never an object that stands before us and can be seen. World is the ever-nonobjective to which we are subject as long as the paths of birth and death, blessing and curse transport us into Being."[26]

Heidegger's critique of the primacy of vision is so sweeping that many commentators have been led, as noted above, to stress his privileging of the ear instead. John D. Caputo, for example, writes that "Heidegger turns to acoustical and aural metaphors . . . ocular metaphors presuppose distance and detachment, and Heidegger is constantly replaying them in aural terms, which stress the *belonging* of Dasein to Being. Hence Heidegger frequently invokes the kinship between *Hören, Horchen* and *Gehören*: hearing, hearkening to and belonging."[27] There can be no doubt that in many ways this claim is valid, especially if we recall his growing fascination with poetry, especially Hölderlin's, in the 1930s, but it is not the

---

25. Heidegger, "The Age of the World Picture" (1938), in *The Question Concerning Technology and Other Essays*, p. 134.

26. Heidegger, "The Origin of the Work of Art" (1935), in *Basic Writings*, p. 170.

27. John D. Caputo, "The Thought of Being and the Conversation of Mankind: The Case of Heidegger and Rorty," in *Hermeneutics and Praxis*, ed. Robert Hollinger (Notre Dame, Ind., 1985), p. 255. See also David Michael Levin, *The Listening Self: Personal Growth, Social Change and the Closure of Metaphysics* (London, 1989). One might add the word *Gehorsam*, which means obedience.

entire story. For at times, Heidegger also employed visual metaphors of his own to evoke his alternative to the dominant metaphysical/scientific tradition, metaphors which have even encouraged some commentators to place him in the Romantic lineage of visionary innocence.[28]

Heidegger's debt to Husserl's "phenomenological seeing"[29] meant that the road to ontology, the revelation of Being, was through an uncovering of what was hidden. "Because *logos* lets something be seen," he wrote in *Being and Time*, "it can *therefore* be true or false. But everything depends on staying clear of any concept of truth construed in the sense of 'correspondence' or 'accordance'."[30] If such a concept of truth as revelation or unhiddenness (*aletheia*) rather than correspondence could be defended, so too could a more attractive notion of *techne* than that associated with the modern technological world view. "There was once a time when it was not technology alone that bore the name *techne*," Heidegger claimed. "Once that revealing which brings forth truth into the splendor of radiant appearance was also called *techne*. . . . The poetical brings the true into the splendor of what Plato in the *Phaedrus* calls *to ekphanestaton*, that which shines forth most purely."[31]

Such a shining forth took place in what Heidegger came to call a "*Lichtung*" or forest clearing, in which Being discloses itself. "What is light in the sense of being free and open," Heidegger cautioned, "has

28. See, for example, Allan Megill, *Prophets of Extremity: Nietzsche, Heidegger, Foucault, Derrida* (Berkeley, 1985), p. 156. For more sustained considerations of Heidegger's differentiated attitude toward vision, which stresses its positive moments, see David Michael Levin, "Decline and Fall: Ocularcentrism in Heidegger's Reading of the History of Metaphysics," in *Modernity and the Hegemony of Vision*, ed. David Michael Levin (Berkeley, 1993), and Zimmerman, *Heidegger's Confrontation with Modernity*, pp. 95ff., where he discusses Heidegger's thoughts on Hölderlin's suggestion that Oedipus "has an eye too many."

29. In his 1947 "Letter on Humanism," Heidegger even claimed that the language of *Being and Time* was "still faulty insofar as it does not yet succeed in retaining the essential help of phenomenological seeing and in dispensing with the inappropriate concern with 'science' and 'research'." In *Basic Writings*, p. 235.

30. Heidegger, Introduction to *Being and Time*, in *Basic Writings*, p. 80.

31. Heidegger, "The Question Concerning Technology," in *Basic Writings*, p. 315–316.

nothing in common with the adjective 'light' which means 'bright,' neither linguistically nor factually. . . . Still, it is possible that a factual relation between the two exists. Light can stream into the clearing, into its openness, and let brightness play with darkness in it. But light never first creates openness. Rather, light presupposes openness."[32] Here the thinking subject does not cast his light, the searchlight of curiosity, on to mute and opaque objects, but rather Being is allowed to manifest itself to *Dasein*. Traditional philosophy, he complained, "does speak about the light of reason, but does not heed the opening of Being. The *lumen naturale*, the light of reason, throws light only on openness. . . . No outward appearance without light—Plato already knew this. But there is no light and no brightness without the opening."[33]

A key difference between these two modes of vision, one which might be called epistemological, the other ontological, concerns the spectatorial distance of the former in comparison with the embeddedness of the later. David Michael Levin captures Heidegger's argument about the shortcomings of epistemological vision when he writes,

> The visible deeply *objects* to our habitual objectification; it will not fully give itself, will not wholly yield itself, to our desire. The most extreme evidence in which this is visible appears when we engage in an exercise in intensive staring: "a fixed staring at something that is purely present-at-hand (*vorhanden*)." In German, the word which we translate as "re-presentation" is *Vorstellung*. Now, this word signifies a gesture of setting down (*stellen*) in front (*vor*), a gesture which corresponds to the "frontal" ontology of our modern, nihilistic world. I submit that the concealed essence of "re-presentation" begins to appear through this interpretation, and that it is, in a word, *staring*.[34]

32. Heidegger, "The End of Philosophy and the Task of Thinking" (1966), *Basic Writings*, p. 384. He added that the clearing is also the place where echoes and resonances can be made present.

33. Ibid., p. 386.

The more benign version of sight, which refuses to stare aggressively at its objects, is dependent on a primordial opening to Being which is prior to the very differentiation of the senses. After the differentiation, it is maintained by what in *Being and Time* Heidegger calls "*Umsicht,*" pre-reflective, circumspect vision. Here the viewer is situated within a visual field, not outside it; his horizon is limited by what he can see around him. Moreover, his relation to the context in which he is embedded is nurturant, not controlling: "Letting something be encountered is primarily circumspective; it is not just sensing something, or staring at it. It implies circumspective concern."[35]

One way to define the opposition between the two visual modes in Heidegger is suggested by Levin's distinction between the "assertoric" and "aletheic gaze."[36] The former is abstracted, monocular, inflexible, unmoving, rigid, ego-logical and exclusionary; the latter is multiple, aware of its context, inclusionary, horizonal, and caring. Although Heidegger deeply regretted the power of the former in Western thought and practice, he nonetheless held out some hope for the reinstatement of the latter. He was never simply hostile to vision *per se*, but only to the variant that had dominated Western metaphysics for millennia.

In the French reception of his ideas, complicated by the spotty availability of his texts, both dimensions of Heidegger's thought were not always equally appreciated. While Merleau-Ponty favored what might be called an "aletheic gaze," Sartre was far more hostile to any redemptive notion of vision. Indeed, if the antiocularcentric discourse we are tracing can be said to have had a quintessential articulation, it would have to be in the uncompromisingly relentless demonization of *le regard* throughout the long course of his remarkable career.

⊙

34. David Michael Levin, *The Opening of Vision: Nihilism and the Postmodern Situation* (New York, 1988), p. 68.

35. Heidegger, *Being and Time*, p. 176.

36. Levin, *The Opening of Vision*, p. 440.

Sartre's critique of ocularcentrism was especially powerful because he conflated many of the complaints expressed by other critics into one relentless, overwhelming indictment. Not only, he claimed, does the hypertrophy of the visual lead to a problematic epistemology, abet the domination of nature, and support the hegemony of space over time, but it also produces profoundly disturbing intersubjective relations and the construction of a dangerously inauthentic version of the self. Sartre's interrogation of the eye thus included social, psychological, and indeed existential dimensions, which he invariably described in the most frighteningly negative terms.

Sartre, who once admitted, *"I think with my eyes,"*[37] was profoundly curious in the sense of that term defined by Heidegger in *Being and Time*: he passionately wanted to penetrate the world's secrets and reveal them to his pitiless gaze. One commentator went so far as to call him "the most many-sided voyeur of the century."[38] But Sartre was no less sensitive to the dangers of visually incited curiosity, both for the gazer and the object of the gaze. The result was a personal and intellectual dialectic of attraction and repulsion, avowal and denial, rivaling that of the Rousseau portrayed by Starobinski.

Sartre's obsessive hostility to vision—by one estimate, there were over seven thousand references to "the look" in his work[39]—was so unremitting that it has been tempting to account for it as a personal problem. As in the case of Bataille, whose scatalogical and violent preoccupations also invite speculations of this kind, Sartre's ocularphobia has been interpreted in biographical terms, including even the impact of his physical makeup. And far more than Bataille, whose career was followed in relative obscurity, Sartre solicited such interpretations by deliberately exposing himself to public view.

37. Sartre, *The War Diaries of Jean-Paul Sartre: November 1939/March 1940*, trans. Quinton Hoare (New York, 1984), p. 15 (italics in original).

38. William F. Redfern, *Paul Nizan: Committed Literature in a Conspiratorial World* (Princeton, 1973), p. 214.

39. See Alain Buisine, *Laideurs de Sartre* (Lille, 1986), p. 103. He attributes the figure to an unnamed American psychoanalyst.

As early as 1952, Sartre's phenomenology of sight was subjected to a psychoanalytic reading by René Held, who claimed that his celebrated treatment of "the look" in *Being and Nothingness,* about which more later, disclosed less about its ostensible subject matter than about its author.[40] Sartre's frightening description of visual interaction, he charged, demonstrated extreme castration anxiety, a narcissistic fear of splitting the body from the self, and masochistic fantasies about enslavement to dominating figures. Sartre's exaggerated account of the mortifying power of the gaze of the Other recalled for Held the magical theory behind the primitive belief in the evil eye. Although he agreed that the psychological implications of sight were profound, and cited the work of other analysts like Daniel Lagache to prove it, Held claimed that Sartre's account was pathologically one-sided.

In 1976 François George, less beholden than Held to the Freudianism Sartre himself so distrusted, probed what he called "le regard absolu" in Sartre's work.[41] The term, it will be recalled, had been coined by Starobinski in his discussion of Racine, although George did not acknowledge its provenance. The "absolute look" was that of an omniscient God able to observe and then judge all human behavior. George, having the benefit of reading Sartre's childhood reminiscences, *The Words,* which had appeared in 1964, was able to discern the paternal behind the divine eye. Or more precisely, he was able to see the residue of the dead father's gaze—Jean-Baptiste Sartre having died when his son was only fifteen months old—in the imagination of the orphan. An orphan, he noted, feels especially guilty in the sight of his absent parents. "It is a question of an imaginary look, of a look supposed to be cast on the child by the father, condemning him at the same time to abandonment."[42] Although Sartre loudly denied that his father's death was traumatic,[43] its residues

40. René Held, "Psychopathologie du regard," *L'evolution psychiatrique* (April–June, 1952), p. 228.

41. François George, *Deux études sur Sartre* (Paris, 1976), pp. 303–339.

42. Ibid., p. 307.

43. Sartre, *The Words,* trans. Bernard Frechtman (New York, 1964), p. 11, where he claims it gave him freedom and no superego. He also asserted that his father was "not

were obvious to George: "The look is always absolute, it emanates from a pitiful, dead transcendence, which makes reciprocity unthinkable."[44]

The Words in fact provides considerable material for such interpretations of Sartre's visual obsessions. "For several years," Sartre recalled, "I was able to see above my head a photograph of a frank-looking little officer with a round, baldish head and a thick moustache. The picture disappeared when mother married."[45] Unlike Baudelaire with his anguished feeling of betrayal when his mother married General Aupick, Sartre passed over this event, which took place when he was ten, in virtual silence. Indeed, his stepfather, a naval engineer named Mancy, remained a shadowy figure in *The Words*. But Sartre was far less reticent to describe the role of his maternal grandfather, Charles Schweitzer, with whom he and his mother came to live when his father died. Here the absolute gaze no longer emanating from his dead father found another source, who, remembered Sartre, "so resembled God the Father that he was often taken for Him."[46]

Not only does Sartre remark on the bearded old man's apparent resemblance to the divinity, but he also notes his grandfather's weakness for self-display: "He had the good and bad fortune to be photogenic. The house was filled with photos of him. Since snapshots were not practiced, he had acquired a taste for poses and *tableaux vivants*. Everything was a pretext for him to suspend his gestures, to strike an attitude, to turn to stone."[47] Bizarrely, the camera's medusan power would intervene in the relations between grandfather and grandson: "As soon as he saw us, however far away, he would 'take his stance' in obedience to the behests of an invisible photographer. . . . At this signal, I would stop moving, I would lean forward, I was a runner getting set, the little birdie about to spring from the camera."[48]

---

even a shadow, not even a gaze" (p. 12). For a thorough analysis of this issue, see Robert Harvey, *Search for a Father: Sartre, Paternity, and the Question of Ethics* (Ann Arbor, Mich., 1991).

44. George, *Deux études sur Sartre*, p. 307.

45. Sartre, *The Words*, p. 12.

46. Ibid., p. 13.

Here the young Sartre played the role of the camera eye turning the other into stone. More often, he seems to have felt defined by such moments of being caught in a field of gazes. "My truth, my character, and my name," he recalled, "were in the hands of adults. I had learned to see myself through their eyes. . . . When they were not present, they left their gaze behind, and it mingled with the light. I would run and jump across that gaze, which preserved my nature as a model grandson."[49] So bewitched was he by the experience, Sartre even believed that he was the handsome boy his family insisted he was. "Dozens of photos are taken of me, and my mother retouches them with colored pencils. . . . My mouth is puffed with hypocritical arrogance: I know my worth."[50]

The disillusionment that soon followed created in him, so it seems, a lifelong distrust for the illusions of sight and the treachery of definition by the gaze of others. His actual ugliness, he ruefully concluded, was "my negative principle, the quicklime in which the wonderful child was dissolved."[51] Its implications have recently been probed with great finesse in the most extensive biographical account of his visual obsessions, Alain Buisine's *Laideurs de Sartre* (*Sartre's Uglinesses*).[52] Divided into three sections, "the public philosopher," "the squinting (*louche*) philosopher,"[53] and "the blind philosopher," the book examines a series of variations on the ocular theme in Sartre. The first concerns his drive to be fully transparent to his audience, which recalls the exhibitionist openness to the multitude sought by Rousseau two centuries earlier. "I try to be as translucid as possible," Buisine quotes Sartre as saying, "because I believe that all of that dark region we have in ourselves, at once dark for us and for

47. Ibid., p. 15.

48. Ibid. For an analysis of the implications of posing, see Owens, "Posing" in *Beyond Recognition*. He draws on Lacan and Barthes, but neglects Sartre.

49. Ibid., p. 52.

50. Ibid., p. 17.

51. Ibid., p. 158.

52. See note 39.

53. *Louche*, which also means suspicious-looking, equivocal, even weird, was one of Sartre's own favorite words.

others, can only be illuminated for ourselves in trying to make it clear for others."[54]

Sartre's desire for perfect transparency, like that of Rousseau's, was thwarted by obstacles he could not fully overcome. "There reigned in my spirit," Sartre masochistically confessed, "a pitiless clarity; it was an operating theater, hygienic, without shadows, without dark corners, without microbes under a cold light. And yet, as intimacy doesn't allow itself to be completely banished, there was nonetheless beyond, or rather in the sincerity of public confession, a type of bad faith in me."[55] Even while he was struggling to reveal himself to the world, the reputation of Sartre as master intellectual, celebrity, even institution, got in the way. Buisine concludes that Sartre came to understand that the very project of total transparency was inherently unrealizable, for if all subjects were totally transparent to each other, then there would be nothing strictly speaking left to see. Indeed, Sartre's early decision to dedicate himself to writing, to words, was a dim anticipation of this realization. As he put it in his autobiography, "I was born of writing. Before that, there was only a play of mirrors."[56] Although Sartre came to bemoan the sterility of mere writing in comparison with the action he advocated during his most militant period, he never wanted to return to the hall of mirrors in which he had been trapped as a child.

Mirrors, in fact, were fraught with danger for Sartre because they provided reminders of the bad faith involved in accepting the look of the other as true. "The mirror had taught me," he confessed, "what I had always known: I was horribly natural. I have never gotten over that."[57] In the second section of his book, Buisine explores the implications of Sartre's wall-eyed squint, which developed after he left the paradise of his family's idealizing gaze. Not only would looking in the mirror disabuse one of the mistake of identifying with the other's gaze, but it would also

54. Buisine, *Laideurs de Sartre*, p. 29.
55. Cited in ibid., p. 37.
56. Sartre, *The Words*, p. 95.
57. Ibid., p. 69.

provide evidence of the meaninglessness of one's own corporeal existence. Commenting on the scene in Sartre's novel *Nausea*, in which the hero Roquentin examines his face, Buisine notes that for Sartre, "regarding oneself for a long time in the glass, the petrified subject assists in the obscene return of a flesh which is beyond sense, a literally insignificant return of the organic and even the inorganic, of the geologic, of the primitive, of an upsurge of the aquatic in the reflection of the face."[58] As in the case of Bataille, the eye is identified by Sartre with liquid images of the fetus or the womb, which links it to the mother, but in repellent ways. "To regard oneself in the mirror in Sartre's milieu is a *periscopic immersion* . . . to see myself in a mirror is to plunge into the depths of an abyss."[59]

In his final section, Buisine speculates about the implications of Sartre's near blindness at the end of his life. Discussing his works on painters like Tintoretto and Titian, he contends that Sartre's disgust for color is due to its being an experience only available to the eyes. He further argues that Sartre's disdain for abstract painting, for example that of Picasso, was due to its lack of tactility, of weight. And he concludes that "probably never has a critic of art denied and denigrated the power of the eye as much as Jean-Paul Sartre."[60] His final image is that of the elderly Sartre, now almost totally sightless, sitting in a hotel in Venice, the most visually stimulating of cities, comforting himself by listening to music on the radio. "Music," he writes, "has the power to deliver him from the anguish of castration. . . . Finally with music the 'aesthetic' categories of beautiful and ugly lose their pertinence, because its disincarnation undoes all identificatory projects, forbids all (auto)-mimetic reference."[61]

The persuasiveness of these psychological and biographical treatments of Sartre's highly charged attitude toward vision depends not only on the plausibility of psychoanalytic explanations, but also on the trustworthiness of Sartre's own recollections. The author of *The Words* may well have

58. Buisine, *Laideurs de Sartre*, p. 96.
59. Ibid., p. 98.
60. Ibid., p. 133.
61. Ibid., p. 162.

projected his later theories back on to his childhood experiences. But however their origins are understood, there can be no doubt that the results mightily stimulated the discourse discussed in this book. For as in the case of Bataille, what may have been originally private obsessions found a ready audience already primed to be suspicious of the hegemony of the eye. Many subsequent contributors to the denigration of vision, such as Lacan, Foucault, and Irigaray, cannot, for all their obvious differences, be understood without recognizing the residues of Sartre's critique in theirs.

What precisely was the nature of that critique? It took, in fact, many forms. Although Sartre was deeply indebted to Husserl's phenomenology, he immediately detected problems with the idea of a transcendental ego, which he interpreted in visual terms. In Sartre's first major work, *The Transcendence of the Ego*, written in 1936, he complained that Husserl's strong notion of an "I" introduced opacity into consciousness. By positing a self-reflecting ego, "one congeals consciousness, one darkens it. Consciousness is then no longer a spontaneity; it bears within itself the germ of opaqueness."[62] Instead, true consciousness was pure translucence, unburdened by positivity. Other attempts to fill it with opaque thingness, like psychoanalysis, were equally pernicious.[63] Although the later Sartre would nuance his categorical opposition between transparent consciousness and the alien opacity introduced into it from without, in the first phase of his work, it reigned supreme.

If, however, pure consciousness were understood as transparency rather than opacity, how can we say Sartre was simply antivisual? Wasn't he merely contrasting a good vision, which sees through things, with a bad one which reaches no further than their opaque surfaces? The answer appeared in his next two works of philosophy, which dealt with the issue of images and the imagination, *Imagination: A Psychological Critique*

62. Sartre, *The Transcendence of the Ego: An Existentialist Theory of Consciousness*, trans. Forrest Williams and Robert Kirkpatrick (New York, 1957), pp. 41–42.

63. See Sartre's remarks on psychoanalysis's introduction of the point of view of the other into subjective consciousness in *Being and Nothingness*, trans. Hazel E. Barnes (New York, 1966), p. 699.

(1936) and *The Psychology of Imagination* (1940).[64] Here Sartre posited a radical difference between sense perception and the imagination. Like Bergson, he criticized the belief that images were only likenesses of external objects reflected in consciousness. "We pictured consciousness," he wrote, "as a place peopled with small likenesses and these likenesses were the images. No doubt but that this misconception arises from our habit of thinking in space and in terms of space. This we shall call: *the illusion of immanence.*"[65] Philosophers like Hume, who confused images with sense data, were wrong, for the former were best understood as acts which intend an object that is either absent or doesn't exist. Here Husserl was a better guide than Bergson, who lacked a positive understanding of intentionality.[66]

For Sartre, although images may draw on analogies with objects of perception, they themselves are unreal. In fact, imagination is precisely the active function of consciousness that transcends or nihilates the reality of the perceived world. As such, it serves as a model for the negation and lack that Sartre would soon identify with the "for-itself" in *Being and Nothingness.* What is vital for understanding his larger argument is that Sartre distinguished images from perception, visual or otherwise, and identified them with the intentionality of action instead. As a result, he was able to describe consciousness less in terms of visual transparency than in those of pure nihilating action. Although nonperceptual images

64. Sartre, *Imagination: A Psychological Critique*, trans. Forrest Williams (Ann Arbor, Mich., 1962), and *The Psychology of Imagination*, trans. Bernard Frechtman (New York, 1948). For helpful analyses of these works, see Hide Ishiguro, "Imagination," in Mary Warnock, ed., *Sartre: A Collection of Critical Essays* (Garden City, N.Y., 1971); Thomas R. Flynn, "The Role of the Image in Sartre's Aesthetic," *The Journal of Aesthetics and Art Criticism*, 33 (1975), pp. 431–442; and Eugene F. Kaelin, "On Meaning in Sartre's Aesthetic Theory," in *Jean-Paul Sartre: Contemporary Approaches to His Philosophy*, ed. Hugh J. Silverman and Frederick A. Elliston (Pittsburgh, 1980).

65. Sartre, *The Psychology of Imagination*, p. 5.

66. Ibid., p. 85. Interestingly, Merleau-Ponty defended Bergson against Sartre in his review of the book in the *Journal de Psychologie Normale et Pathologique*, 33 (1936), p. 761.

teach us nothing about the external world, their very "no-thing-ness" or invisibility suggests a critical link to human freedom, as Sartre interpreted it. In short, the Sartre who could escape from the play of mirrors and the defining power of adult gazes by immersing himself in words—"imaginary child that I was," he wrote in his autobiography, "I defended myself with my imagination"[67]—now posited a radical break between sight and consciousness, which directly challenged the ocularcentric tradition's equation of the "I" and the "eye."

Before Sartre spelled out the full ontological implications of this new view of consciousness in *Being and Nothingness*, he anticipated certain of its arguments in *Nausea*, the literary work published in 1938 that elevated him from an esoteric philosopher to a full-fledged culture hero.[68] Here too visual themes play a prominent role. Implicitly drawing on Heidegger's distinction between *Zuhandenheit* and *Vorhandenheit*, Sartre contrasted tactile with visual experience. As Alain Robbe-Grillet notes in his essay on the novel, "The first three perceptions recorded at the beginning of the book are all gained by the sense of touch, not that of sight. The objects which provoke revelation are, in effect, respectively, the pebble on the beach, the bolt of a door, the hand of the Self-Taught Man."[69] Sartre thus anticipated his later political defense of "dirty hands" against the clean hands of the nonengaged, contemplative observer above the fray.[70] But now what made such hands superior was their ability to reveal existential truths unavailable to the eye, rather than political ones.

Sartre's critique of visual distance is most notably expressed in the celebrated scene in which Roquentin confronts the source of his existential nausea by understanding the meaningless thingness of the root of a chestnut tree. "Even when I looked at things," Roquentin muses, "I was miles

67. Sartre, *The Words*, p. 71.

68. Sartre, *Nausea*, trans. Lloyd Alexander (New York, 1949).

69. Alain Robbe-Grillet, "Nature, Humanism, Tragedy" in *For a New Novel: Essays on Fiction*, trans. Richard Howard (New York, 1965), p. 65.

70. Sartre, "Dirty Hands," in *No Exit and Three Other Plays*, trans. Lionel Abel (New York, 1949).

from dreaming that they existed: they looked like scenery to me. I picked them up in my hands, they served me as tools, I foresaw their resistance. But all that happened on the surface."[71] In touching and smelling the black root, he realizes that vision by itself is insufficient: "I did not simply *see* this black; sight is an abstract invention, an idea that has been cleaned up, simplified, one of man's ideas. That black there, amorphous, weakly presence, overflowed sight, smell and taste."[72]

His epiphanous experience leaves Roquentin with the feeling that "there was nothing more, my eyes were empty and I was spellbound by my deliverance."[73] But then sight once again intrudes, as he notices the movement of the tree's branches: "No more than three seconds and all my hopes were swept away. Viewing these hesitant branches groping around like blind men, I could not succeed in grasping the process of coming into existence."[74] Even shutting his eyes doesn't help, since "the images, fore-warned, leaped up and filled my closed eyes with existences: existence is a fullness from which man can never get away. Strange images. They represent a multitude of things. Not real things; other things which looked like real things."[75] Here not even the derealizing power of the imagination serves to release Roquentin from his torment. For the imagination, he realizes, is parasitic on the prior existence of meaningless matter, which comes to us primarily through sight. "To imagine nothingness," Roquentin laments, "you had to be there already, in the midst of the World, eyes wide open and alive; nothingness was only an idea in my head, an existing

71. Sartre, *Nausea*, p. 171. Here picking things up with the hands doesn't suffice, because objects are still understood in the mode of *Vorhandenheit*, as tools for visualized purposes.

72. Ibid., p. 176. Interestingly, Robbe-Grillet notices this passage, but claims it shows that "sight remains, in spite of everything, our best weapon . . . the most effective operation" ("Nature, Humanism, Tragedy," p. 74). This interpretation tells us more about Robbe-Grillet than Sartre, although his work too can be seen as only ambiguously pro-visual.

73. Ibid., p. 177.

74. Ibid., p. 178.

75. Ibid., p. 180.

idea floating in this immensity; this nothingness had not come *before* existence."[76]

One reading of Roquentin's struggle to make sense of his nausea might conclude that the most basic prereflective level of human interaction is essentially tactile or visceral, as we blindly muck about in the slimy, viscous reality in which we are immersed (as in the mud implied by calling Roquentin's town Bouveille). Visual reflection, consciousness in the mode of *Vorhandenheit*, then tries to master this experience by turning it into conceptual ideas, finding essences where there is nothing but brute existence. These efforts, however, fail to overcome the meaningless, absurd thingness of the world. Shifting metaphors, Sartre is thus able to claim that ideas cannot "digest" reality; hence the nausea of existence.

But another reading, which recalls Roquentin's experience in the mirror mentioned above, would claim that sight too can be an organ capable of disabusing us of the fallacies of essentializing conceptualization. For if we can see our ugliness or the sheer thingness of our bodies, we are prevented from accepting the idealizing images foisted on us by the flattering gaze of others. Rather than being only the means of essentializing an absurd existence, vision can also reveal the excess of "thatness" over the "whatness" that is the source of human anguish. However construed, vision thus provides us with no way out of the dilemmas of our alienated existence.

Thus far, three main manifestations of Sartre's critique of sight have been identified. The first is his rejection of an opaque transcendental ego intruding into the translucency of pure, active consciousness. The second is his radical separation of perception, visual or otherwise, from the derealizing, nihilating imagination, which proves in *Nausea* not to be so radically pure after all. And the third is the failed attempt of vision to impose concepts and ideas on the recalcitrant meaninglessness of the material world, which is more directly available to our other senses, or better put, is a primordial reality prior to the very differentiation of the senses. Vision is thus insufficient as a means to conceive the subject, or what he will call the "for-itself," and no less problematic in its attempts to conceptualize the object, or the "in-itself."

The opposition between "for-itself" and "in-itself" was most clearly developed in *Being and Nothingness: An Essay on Phenomenological Ontology* (1943), where Sartre reprised all of these themes and fleshed them out by offering the detailed ontology absent from his earlier work. In addition, he provided a profoundly troubling discussion of intersubjective and intrasubjective interactions based on the exchange of gazes. Here Hegel's celebrated master-slave dialectic, interpreted by Kojève to maximize its reciprocal violence rather than the mutual recognition stressed by others, was recast in the register of sight, with the horrifying results that invited the psychological explanations detailed above.

For Sartre, the domination of the object world by a distant subject, facilitated by the hegemony of sight, became a model as well for intersubjective relations. Departing from Husserl, whose treatment of interpersonal interaction depended on reciprocal empathy, Sartre emphasized the hostile contest of wills between competing subjects.[77] Explicitly rejecting Heidegger's irenic notion of *Mit-sein* (co-being) in favor of conflict as the original meaning of being-for-others,[78] Sartre elevated his own experience as the victim of the look—or what he recalled as such—into something very much like a universal human condition. Addressing the hoary philosophical question of how we know the existence of other selves, other interiorities, Sartre contended that "my apprehension of the Other in the world as *probably being* a man refers to my permanent possibility of *being-seen-by-him*; that is, to the permanent possibility that a subject who sees me may be substituted for the object seen by me. 'Being-seen-by-the-Other' is the *truth* of 'seeing-the-Other.' "[79] There is always an oscillation between these two modes of relating to the Other. Although it can be produced by other perceptual experiences, such as the sound of footsteps

76. Ibid., p. 181.
77. For a comparison of the two thinkers on this issue, see Frederick A. Elliston, "Sartre and Husserl on Interpersonal Relations," in Silverman and Elliston, eds., *Jean-Paul Sartre: Contemporary Approaches to His Philosophy.*
78. Sartre, *Being and Nothingness*, p. 525.
79. Ibid., p. 315.

or the movement of a curtain, "what *most often* manifests a look is the convergence of two ocular globes in my direction."[80]

When this happens, the uncanny experience of being looked at completely blots out the possibility of returning the gaze. Significantly, Sartre distinguishes between the eye as the object of a look and the look itself (a distinction repeated by Lacan). "It is never when eyes are looking at you that you can find them beautiful or ugly, that you can remark on their color," he writes. "The Other's look hides his eyes; he seems to go *in front of them*."[81] This inability is tied, Sartre claims, to the incommensurability between perception and imagination, which he had examined in *The Psychology of Imagination*. "This is because to perceive is to *look at*, and to apprehend a look is not to apprehend a look-as-object in the world (unless the look is not directed upon us); it is to be conscious of *being looked at*."[82] But now, perception is understood as an act in the sense that it transforms the object of the gaze, whereas imagination is identified less with derealizing freedom than with the paralyzing internalization of the other's gaze.

The nonreciprocity between look and eye, between being the subject and object of the gaze, is in fact related to a fundamental struggle for power. For the one who casts the look is always subject and the one who is its target is always turned into an object. Or at least, objectification is the telos of the look, even if it comes up against the ultimate barrier of the "for-itself's" constitutive nothingness. That fundamental property of the subject is, however, threatened when the self identifies with the other's look. Here the Cartesian self-reflecting *cogito* is replaced by a self that is constituted by the gaze of the other: "*l'Autre me voit, donc je suis*," as François George nicely puts it.[83]

Taking into itself the opacity of an object that contradicts its pure transparency, the self becomes like the mistaken notion of the transcendental

80. Ibid., p. 316.
81. Ibid., pp. 316–317.
82. Ibid., p. 317.
83. George, *Deux études sur Sartre*, p. 321.

ego posited by Husserl. Sartre describes the process in his celebrated vignette of the voyeur caught looking through the keyhole, which, as already noted, was later instantiated in Duchamp's *Etant donnés*. Whereas, before being caught, the viewer is a pure, acting consciousness unselfconsciously experiencing the emotions, such as jealousy, that accompany it, once seen, he is turned into something else: "First of all, I now exist as *myself* for my unreflective consciousness. . . . I see *myself* because *somebody* sees me."[84] Second, the result is colored by a new emotion, that of shame, which is "the *recognition* of the fact that I *am* indeed that object which the Other is looking at and judging."[85] Shame can be called the transcendental emotional a priori of Sartre's universe of threatening gazes, so pervasive is it in his description of the result of being seen.

But the stakes are higher than mere embarrassment or humiliation, for it is human freedom itself that is undermined by the look of the Other. "I grasp the Other's look at the very center of my *act* as the solidification and alienation of my own possibilities. . . . The Other as a look is only that— my transcendence transcended. Of course I still *am* my possibilities in the mode of non-thetic consciousness (of) these possibilities. But at the same time the look alienates them from me."[86] Like Bergson, Sartre sees the loss of human freedom partly in terms of visual spatialization: "The Other's look confers spatiality upon me. To apprehend oneself as looked-at is to apprehend oneself as a spatializing-spatialized."[87] Even when he adds that it is temporalizing as well, he claims that the time it imposes on the "for-itself" is that of simultaneity, which denies the forward thrust of individual potentiality.

The sinister dialectic of gazes also plays itself out with reference to our corporeal self-consciousness. When the body is on display to the gaze of the Other, it becomes a fallen object, which is the original meaning of our sense of shame at being caught naked. "To put on clothes," Sartre con-

84. Sartre, *Being and Nothingness*, p. 319.
85. Ibid., p. 320.
86. Ibid., p. 322.
87. Ibid., p. 327.

tends, "is to hide one's object-state: it is to claim the right of seeing without being seen; that is, to be pure subject. That is why the Biblical symbol of the fall after the original sin is the fact that Adam and Eve 'know that they are naked'."[88] Here too, the internalization of the Other's shame-engendering look produces a disastrous outcome, as the body loses its primary function as the agency of human action (once again, a point made earlier by Bergson). Instead, one's own body is turned into an object of the other's vision for oneself as well.

The acceptance of such self-reification, Sartre argues, was at the root of the typical Cartesian problem of wondering how inverted and reversed images on the retina can be turned into normal sight. The camera obscura version of sight assumed by this question was based on a fallacious attempt to reconcile the eye as an object, whose functioning could be compared to a camera lens and screen, and the subjective experience of seeing. For Sartre, the mistake was that "we have considered a dead eye in the midst of the visible world in order to account for the visibility of this world. Consequently, how can we be surprised later when consciousness, which is absolute interiority [for Descartes], refuses to allow itself to be bound to this object?"[89]

Such philosophical mistakes could presumably be remedied by abandoning Descartes's discredited dualism, but the social interactions promoted by vision as Sartre understood it were far less easy to overcome. A salient example was the inability to create a meaningful community, which in the Hegelian terminology he adopted at the same time as he was learning phenomenology, was called the project of totalization. Indeed, from *Being and Nothingness* to the *Critique of Dialectical Reason* (1960), if not to the very end of his life, Sartre was haunted by the question of achieving a totalistic knowledge of reality (or at least of the social world), and the concomitant possibility of a normative totalization overcoming the various alienations of human existence.[90] Totalizing cognition and totalizing action were closely related, as dialectical sides of the same coin, although how closely Sartre did not realize until his embrace of Marxism after the war.

The primary impediment to knowing the whole, as Heidegger had also pointed out in his discussion of *Umsicht*, was the situated nature of our individual vantage point, which could not see beyond a limited horizon of knowledge. It is impossible to transcend this specificity, Sartre insisted, "because I exist as myself on the foundation of this totality and to the extent that I am engaged in it."[91] Indeed, not even a God's-eye view would provide a perspective on the whole.

> No consciousness, not even God's, can "see the underside"—that is, apprehend the totality as such. For if God is consciousness, he is integrated in the totality. And if by his nature, he is a being *beyond consciousness* (that is, an in-itself which would be its own foundation) still the totality can appear to him only as *object* (in that case he lacks the totality's internal disintegration as the subjective effort to reapprehend the self) or as subject (then since God *is not* this subject, he can only experience it without knowing it). Thus no point of view on the totality is conceivable; the totality has no "outside," and the very question of the meaning of the "underside" is stripped of meaning.[92]

Not even in his most Marxist moments in the 1950s and 1960s did Sartre find a way to overcome this pessimistic conclusion; no metasubject able to totalize the whole and see its totalization, such as the proletariat posited by Hegelian Marxists like Lukács, was ever possible. Without even Heidegger's faith in alethic vision, the revelation of the truth of Being in a primal *Lichtung*, Sartre resolutely refused to posit a redemptive notion of the visual.

88. Ibid., p. 354.
89. Ibid., p. 374.
90. For an account of Sartre's attempt to resolve this issue in the context of the general Western Marxist search for a viable concept of totality, see Martin Jay, *Marxism and Totality: The Adventures of a Concept from Lukács to Habermas* (Berkeley, 1984), chap. 11.
91. Sartre, *Being and Nothingness*, p. 370.
92. Ibid.

If such an outcome was denied on the "macroscopic" level of knowing the totality, it was no less rejected on the "microscopic" level of human relations at their putatively most reciprocal: the interaction of lovers. Not even their mutual glances of tenderness, captured in the ambiguous meaning of the word "regard," can overcome the frightening dialectic of subject and object posited by Sartre.[93] Desire, he claims, is always the yearning to possess the subjectivity of the other, appropriating him or her as flesh. Even the most seemingly "I-thou" relationship, to borrow Martin Buber's familiar terminology, is at root an "I-it" interaction. Although the expression of desire is often tactile, coming through the caress, it has an inevitably visual component as well. "I am possessed by the Other," Sartre writes; "the Other's look fashions my body in its nakedness, causes it to be born, sculptures it, produces it as it *is*, sees it as I shall never see it. The Other holds a secret—the secret of what I am."[94] Lovers, for Sartre, are engaged in a mutual dialectic of possession, which goes beyond the Hegelian master-slave interaction because "the lover wants the beloved's freedom *first and foremost*,"[95] wants, that is, to have it entirely for himself.

The result is a series of moves and countermoves, which can only be described in terms of sado-masochism acted out through a contest of gazes. Whatever triumph the lover may have in possessing the freedom of the beloved through the look is always short-lived, however, as the ultimate subjectivity of the "for-itself" cannot be completely extinguished through objectification. Summing up his argument about the frustrations of mutual desire, Sartre concludes,

> In the primordial reaction to the Other's look I constitute myself as a look. But if I look at his look in order to defend myself against the Other's freedom and to transcend it as freedom, then both the freedom and the look of the Other collapse. I see eyes; I see a

93. For a useful comparison of Simmel's notion of reciprocal visual interaction with Sartre's, which focuses on the issue of regard, see Deena Weinstein and Michael Weinstein, "On the Visual Constitution of Society: The Contributions of Georg Simmel and Jean-Paul Sartre to a Sociology of the Senses," *History of European Ideas*, 5, 4 (1984), pp. 349–362. They conclude that both positions tell us something about the way in which vision contributes to social interaction.

being-in-the-midst-of-the-world. Henceforth the Other escapes me. I should like to act upon his freedom, to appropriate it, or at least, to make the Other's freedom recognize my freedom. But his freedom is death; it is no longer absolutely *in the world* in which I encounter the Other-as-object, for his characteristic is to be transcendent to the world.[96]

The sado-masochistic dialectic of the look is thus doomed to failure for both lovers, as there is no way to reconcile human freedom with the desire to possess. To make his point, Sartre invokes the passage from Faulkner's *Light in August* in which the castrated and dying Negro, Christmas, looks at his executioners "with his eyes open and empty of everything save consciousness. . . . For a long moment, he looked up at them with peaceful and unfathomable and unbearable eyes."[97] And he concludes, "Here once more we are referred from the being-in-the-act-of-looking to the being-looked-at; we have not got out of the circle."[98]

That Sartre never felt we can get out of the circle is amply demonstrated by the many other invocations of the visual in his subsequent work. His own literary creations were replete with references to it. For example, in his play of 1943, *The Flies*, King Aegisthus laments, "*I have come to see myself only as they see me.* I peer into the dark pit of their souls and there, deep down, I see the image that I have built up. I shudder, but I cannot take my eyes off it. Almighty Zeus, who am I? Am I anything more than the dread that others have of me?"[99] In his 1945 novel *The Reprieve,* the homosexual character Daniel anguishes, "*They* see me—no, not even that: *it* sees me. He was the *object* of looking. . . . I am *seen.* Transparent, transparent, transfixed. But by whom?"[100]

94. Sartre, *Being and Nothingness*, p. 445.
95. Ibid., p. 452.
96. Ibid., p. 481.
97. Ibid., p. 496.
98. Ibid., p. 497.
99. Sartre, *The Flies*, trans. Stuart Gilbert (London, 1946), p. 71.
100. Sartre, *The Reprieve*, trans. Eric Sutton (New York, 1947), p. 135.

Sartre's literary criticism was no less frequently focused on visual issues. His 1939 essay on "François Mauriac and Freedom" criticized the technique of the omniscient narratorial point of view and concluded that "there is no room for a privileged observer."[101] In his 1947 *Baudelaire*, Sartre disapprovingly contended that the poet "tried all his life *to turn himself into a thing* in the eyes of other people and his own. He wanted to take up his stand at a distance from the great social fête like a statue, like something definitive and opaque which could not be assimilated."[102] As late as his massive, unfinished study of Flaubert, Sartre could still express his rage at the novelist's adoption of the disinterested position of *survol,* that putative God's-eye view, whose deliberate denial he had applauded in other figures like Kierkegaard.[103]

Sartre's political writings also often drew on his critique of the gaze. Thus, for example, in his 1948 preface to an anthology of African texts edited by Leopold Senghor, he told his French readers,

> I want you to feel, as I, the sensation of being seen. For the white man has enjoyed for three thousand years the privilege of seeing without being seen. It was a seeing pure and uncomplicated; the light of his eyes drew all things from their primeval darkness. The whiteness of his skin was a further aspect of vision, a light condensed. The white man, white because he was a man, white like the day, white as truth is white, white like virtue, lighted like a torch all creation; he unfolded the essence, secret and white, of existence. Today, these black men have fixed their gaze upon us and our gaze is thrown back into our eyes. . . . By this steady and corrosive gaze, we are picked to the bone.[104]

101. Sartre, "M. François Mauriac et la liberté," *Situations I* (Paris, 1947), p. 46.

102. Sartre, *Baudelaire,* trans. Martin Turnell (New York, 1950), p. 79.

103. Sartre, *The Family Idiot: Gustave Flaubert, 1821–1857,* trans. Carol Cosman (Chicago, 1981), vol. 2, chap. 11. For his appreciation of Kierkegaard's rejection of "overview thought," see "Kierkegaard: The Singular Universal," *Between Existentialism and Marxism,* trans. John Matthews (New York, 1974), pp. 154–155.

104. Sartre, *Black Orpheus,* trans. S. W. Allen (Paris, 1976), pp. 7–11.

Here Sartre anticipated the analysis of the power of the gaze in sustaining imperialist and racist domination later detailed by Edward Said in *Orientalism.*[105]

Perhaps the most sustained and imaginative use of his phenomenology of vision, however, appeared in his remarkable 1952 study of the writer Jean Genet, *Saint Genet: Actor and Martyr.*[106] The original, defining moment in Genet's personal formation is described in the terms of the voyeur at the keyhole in *Being and Nothingness*. As the ten-year-old boy unself-consciously reaches into a drawer, he is suddenly *"caught in the act. Someone has entered and is watching him. Beneath this gaze the child comes to himself. He who was not yet anyone suddenly becomes Jean Genet. . . . A voice declares publicly: 'You're a thief'."*[107] Although the labeling is verbal, Sartre leaves no doubt what came first: "Pinned by a look, a butterfly fixed to a cork, he is naked, everyone can see him and spit on him. The gaze of the adults is a *constituent power* which has transformed him into a *constituted nature.*"[108]

Not only is Genet condemned to his identity as a thief by the look of the other, so too is his sexual self-image fixed by visual objectification, indeed penetration: "Sexually, Genet is first of all a raped child. This first rape was the gaze of the other, who took him by surprise, penetrated him, transformed him forever into an object."[109] Ultimately, Genet came to take on these objectifications willingly, even heroically, as his own identity. "What he desires is to be manipulated passively by the Other so as to become an object in his own eyes."[110] Although on one level a surrender, on another, this decision allowed Genet to come to the same bleak con-

---

105. Edward W. Said, *Orientalism* (New York, 1979), pp. 239ff. Said contrasts synchronic essentializing vision with particularizing narrative, and links the former with the Western appropriation of the Eastern "other."

106. Sartre, *Saint Genet: Actor and Martyr*, trans. Bernard Frechtman (New York, 1963).

107. Ibid., p. 17.

108. Ibid., p. 49.

109. Ibid., p. 79.

110. Ibid., p. 81.

clusion reached by Sartre himself in *Being and Nothingness*: "Exhausted but not appeased, Genet gazes at the beautiful, tranquil appearance which has taken shape again beyond his reach, and he concludes: 'Love is despair.' But we now know that this despair is willed and that he first rejected the only chance of salvation through love: reciprocity."[111] His homosexual relationships may have once been an attempt to communicate with other men, but Genet, according to Sartre, realizes the failure of such efforts: "He has gone out of himself, he has gone toward his fellow man and encountered only appearances. He now returns to himself. He is alone beneath the fixed light which has not ceased to traverse him."[112]

Genet is thus far superior to those like the Surrealists who seek visionary redemption. "Breton hopes, if not to 'see' the superreal, at least to merge with it in a unity wherein vision and being are one and the same. Genet knows that enjoyment of it is denied him on principle. . . . The high and the low cease to be perceived as contradictory and the greatest Evil is at the same time the greatest Good. . . . Breton's superreal, perceived as the inaccessible and substantial reverse of existence, is Genet's Saintliness."[113]

Although not himself seduced by the Saintliness of evil, Sartre clearly identified with Genet's attempt to deal with the dilemmas of his existence through words, through exercising the same literary imagination to which the young Sartre himself had turned for relief. "The glamorous word repeats, while effacing it, the original crisis: it too hits him in the face and reveals the existence of Another, of a Gaze directed at Genet; but this Other is kindly, for it is the I-who-is-Another, it is Genet himself."[114] Significantly, the poetry Genet writes has nothing to do with the tradi-

111. Ibid., p. 114. Presumably, the chance to achieve such salvation through reciprocity was not taken very seriously by Sartre.

112. Ibid., p. 137.

113. Ibid., p. 244. It is hard not to see parallels between Bataille and Genet, as Sartre describes him here. In fact, a few pages later Sartre will say, "I reject Saintliness wherever it manifests itself, among the canonized saints as well as Genet, and I smell it, even beneath their secular disguises, in Bataille, Gide and Jouhandeau" (p. 246).

114. Ibid., p. 298.

tional apotheosis of formal beauty: "Fall, void, night of unknowing: it is not a matter of an Apollonian poetry sparkling with brilliant, visible images. . . . In Genet, the image is rarely visual; it remains a secret cleft in words."[115] For Sartre, "Genet's art does not aim, will never aim, at making us see. . . . The avowed aim of his magnifying attempts is to annihilate the real, to disintegrate vision."[116] Thus, he is the opposite of Breton, who tries to use words to give us a revelatory vision of The Word; Genet instead uses language to nihilate the real, to deny the very possibility of any higher reality to be revealed. "Genet has no poetic *intuition*. The surrealist is filled with his images. . . . Genet's poems flee from him into the consciousness of the Other, he writes them blindly, in the darkness. They deserve, much more than do those of Henri Thomas, to be called 'Blind Man's Work'."[117]

"Blind Man's Work" might also be the motto for Sartre's own relentless critique of the gaze. Not all French phenomenologists, however, were as ruthlessly hostile as he, even if they shared his rejection of the discredited Cartesian perspectivalist scopic regime. Paradoxically, Sartre's radical distinction between the "for-itself" and the "in-self," as well as his categorical opposition between perception and imagination, came themselves to be faulted as expressions of a residual debt to Descartes's dualism. Instead, Heidegger's notion of a Being prior to the split between subject and object and his belief in a social *Mitsein* more fundamental than the interminable conflicts posited by Sartre found a ready hearing. Could they be reconciled with a more benign notion of vision than that found in Sartre's playhouse of disillusioning mirrors and cross fire of wounding gazes? Could a new ontology of vision replace the pernicious spectatorial epistemology, that all phenomenologists found so wanting? Answers to these questions were sought and sought again in the work of Maurice Merleau-Ponty. In fact, if any serious philosophical attempt to check the

115. Ibid., pp. 298–300.

116. Ibid., p. 440.

117. Ibid., p. 514. Thomas, born in 1912, is a French poet and novelist, who published *Travaux d'aveugle* in 1941.

momentum of the antiocularcentric discourse in France can be located, it would thus be his remarkable exploration of what he called the "madness of vision."[118]

⊙

Lacking Sartre's compulsive need for confessional self-transparency, Merleau-Ponty left no autobiographical reflections comparable to *The Words*.[119] Despite the loss of his father during the First World War, when Merleau-Ponty was six, he seems to have had a relatively secure and happy childhood, free from the visually induced mortifications apparently suffered by the young Sartre.[120] If his personal sense of being victimized and objectified by the gaze of others was less intense than Sartre's, it is not surprising that his work presented a far less bleak analysis of vision's ontological as well as social implications. In fact, Merleau-Ponty's meditations on the visual, every bit as obsessive and incessant as Sartre's, came to conclusions that seem diametrically opposed to those of his friend. His version of phenomenology may thus plausibly be called a heroic attempt to reaffirm the nobility of vision on new and firmer grounds than those provided by the discredited Cartesian perspectivalist tradition.

And yet, even in his case, it can be demonstrated that the suspicions and doubts plaguing other twentieth-century French critics of ocularcentrism ultimately surfaced. Although many later contributors to the discourse examined in this book explicitly condemned him for being too hopeful about redeeming the visual, certain anticipations of their qualms can be discerned in his work as well. Merleau-Ponty thus occupies a piv-

118. Maurice Merleau-Ponty, *The Visible and the Invisible*, ed. Claude Lefort, trans. Alphonso Lingis (Evanston, Ill., 1968), p. 75.

119. The most extensive biography of the early Merleau-Ponty can be found in Theodore F. Geraets, *Vers une nouvelle philosophie transcendentale: La genése de la philosophie de Maurice Merleau-Ponty jusqu'à la Phénoménologie de la perception* (The Hague, 1971). See also Barry Cooper, *Merleau-Ponty and Marxism: From Terror to Reform* (Toronto, 1979) and Schmidt, *Maurice Merleau-Ponty*.

120. Sartre himself claimed that Merleau-Ponty's childhood was happy. See "Merleau-Ponty," *Situations*, trans. Benita Eisler (New York, 1965), p. 296.

otal place in this narrative. Registering the collapse of the dominant scopic regime, he attempted to defend an alternative philosophy of the visual, which would have beneficial social implications as well. But his project, cut short by his untimely death at the age of fifty-three, was never satisfactorily completed. That it was almost universally read as a failure by the generation that followed suggests how powerful the accumulated force of the antiocularcentric discourse had become by the time of his departure from the scene in 1961.

Merleau-Ponty's fascination with perception in general and vision in particular was evident at the very outset of his career, even before the impact of Husserl on his thought. In 1933, he drew up a thesis proposal called "On the Nature of Perception," which disputed Brunschvicg's contention that the world of sensible perception was ultimately reducible to intellectual relations and scientific knowledge.[121] Here his main theoretical inspiration came from Gestalt psychology, recently introduced to France by Aron Gurwitsch, and Anglo-American philosophical "Realism," rather than from the phenomenology to which he was so decisively drawn shortly thereafter. That event took place when he encountered Husserl's *Crisis of the European Sciences and Transcendental Phenomenology* in 1936, which led him to devour the rest of Husserl's published work and seek out unpublished manuscripts in the newly created archive in Louvain, Belgium. At about the same time, he became familiar with Heidegger's version of phenomenology, which would have an increasingly powerful impact on his ruminations about the visual, and much else as well, in the decades to come.

Although Merleau-Ponty's preoccupations remained obstinately consistent throughout his career, justifying Sartre's remark that he was "always digging at the same place,"[122] his development is generally divided into two major phases.[123] The first, whose most notable achievements

121. For a discussion, see Geraets, pp. 9–10.

122. Sartre, "Merleau-Ponty," p. 322.

123. Other periodizations would emerge if Merleau-Ponty's political odyssey were examined, but here the only criterion is his attitude toward perception.

were *The Structure of Behavior*, published in 1942, and *Phenomenology of Perception*, which appeared three years later, expressed his most optimistic hopes in the possibility of a post-Cartesian philosophy grounded in perception.[124] After an interregnum, filled principally by his meditations on history, Marxism and contemporary politics,[125] Merleau-Ponty returned to his earlier philosophical concerns. In several of the essays appearing in *Signs* in 1960, in "The Eye and the Mind" of 1961, and in the posthumously published, uncompleted manuscript known as *The Visible and the Invisible*, he deepened and problematized the analysis of the issues he had treated in the 1930s and early 1940s.[126]

In a report he wrote for his candidacy to the Collège de France in 1952, Merleau-Ponty himself distinguished between the phases of his development in the following terms: "My first two works sought to restore the world of perception. My works in preparation aim to show how communication with others, and thought, take up and go beyond the realm of perception which initiated us to the truth."[127] To what extent, it must be asked, was his recognition that the mere restoration of perception alone would not provide access to "the truth" a subtle departure from the assumption that the nobility of sight could be renewed after the collapse of Cartesianism? What effect did his interest in intersubjective communication and what he called the "prose of the world"[128] have on his

---

124. Merleau-Ponty, *The Structure of Behavior*, trans. Alden L. Fisher (Boston, 1963); *Phenomenology of Perception*, trans. Colin Smith (London, 1962). The essay on "Cézanne's Doubt," discussed earlier, was also from this period, its first publication coming in 1945.

125. The most important results of these efforts were *Humanism and Terror*, trans. J. O'Neill (Boston, 1969); *Sense and Non-Sense*, trans. H. L. Dreyfus and P. A. Dreyfus (Evanston, 1964); and *The Adventures of the Dialectic*, trans. J. Bien (Evanston, 1973).

126. Merleau-Ponty, *Signs*, trans. Richard C. McCleary (Evanston, 1964); "The Eye and the Mind," in *The Primacy of Perception*, trans. James M. Edie (Evanston, 1964); *The Visible and the Invisible*, ed. Claude Lefort, trans. Alphonso Lingis (Evanston, 1968).

127. Merleau-Ponty, "An Unpublished Text by Merleau-Ponty: *A Prospectus of His Work*," in *The Primacy of Perception*, p. 3.

earlier celebration of perception? How significant were his assimilation of psychoanalytic and linguistic motifs, which were to become even more influential in France after his death, in the decline of his faith in a phenomenology of perception as a sufficient foundation for a new ontology? Did, in short, the ambiguities that were never resolved in his thought work against his apparent intentions and inadvertently contribute to the continuing crisis of ocularcentrism?

Merleau-Ponty's first sustained effort to grapple with the enigmas of perception, *The Structure of Behavior*, was published during the war, but completed in 1938, when he had only haltingly entered the world of Husserl and Heidegger. It was written largely within the universe of discourse of experimental psychology, whose scientific approach to the mind was precisely what phenomenologists had spurned as "psychologism." Rather than adopting this hostility, Merleau-Ponty sought to draw on the insights of contemporary psychological research, while criticizing its unreflective and reductionist ontological assumptions.

Carefully examining such competing schools as Pavlovian reflexology and atomistic behaviorism, Merleau-Ponty concluded that the most promising approach was that of Wolfgang Koehler, Max Wertheimer, Adhémar Gelb, Kurt Goldstein, and Kurt Koffka, the Gestaltists. Their emphasis on the structural component of perception and the formal determination of reflex behavior meant that they were sensitive to the ways in which the mind was active without being beholden to the intellectualist categories posited by transcendental philosophies like neo-Kantianism. Unidirectional causal explanations of perception informing sensationalist epistemologies, including psychoanalysis,[129] were equally surpassed because the Gestaltists registered the circular, interactional nature of sense experience. As the Gestaltists had demonstrated, figures needed grounds and vice versa. The human retina was thus more than a

128. This was the projected title for a work never completed, whose fragments were published in 1969.

129. According to Merleau-Ponty, Freud was guilty of adopting one-directional causal categories because of his use of metaphors of energy rather than structure. *See The Structure of Behavior*, p. 220.

passive screen registering impressions from without. In fact, whatever the object to be investigated, whether it be the nonvital physical world, the biological order, or the realm of human symbolic exchange, relational structuralism was the most appropriate approach.

Moreover, Merleau-Ponty insisted, the structural dimension of perception was fully compatible with the meaningfulness that we perceive in the world. Unlike the later Structuralists of the 1960s, he believed that at least in the human order formal structure and subjective meaning were intertwined, not opposed. For, and here the effect of Husserl was evident, structuration was an intentional phenomenon. "The natural 'thing', the organism, the behavior of others and my own behavior exist only by their meaning," he insisted. And then he added, "This meaning which springs forth in them is not yet a Kantian object; the intentional life which constitutes them is not yet a representation; and the 'comprehension' which gives access to them is not yet an intellection."[130] Prior to all of these ways of conceptualizing phenomena and our relation to them was a primordial order of signification, which tied together what transcendental and sensationalist philosophies had torn asunder.

Gestalt psychology was useful in reaching this understanding, but it had not gone far enough in rejecting what Merleau-Ponty called the realist epistemology of "the outside spectator,"[131] who believed the structures he saw were wholly independent of his constitutive powers. In fact, as Bergson had recognized, perception was active, rather than contemplative, although he wrongly confined such action to the sphere of vitality alone.[132] "Life" was an insufficient category to capture the richness of the "orders of signification" in which humanity was embedded, and which played a central role in constituting perceptual experience.

In his account of that experience, Merleau-Ponty reached several arrest-

130. Ibid., p. 224.

131. Ibid., p. 162.

132. Ibid., pp. 164–165. For a comparison of the two thinkers' attitudes toward perception, see Augustin Fressin, *La perception chez Bergson et chez Merleau-Ponty* (Paris, 1967).

ing conclusions about its visual component. *The Structure of Behavior* began with an account of the distinction between the scientific understanding of light, which he called "real light" and which the medieval world knew as *lumen*, and the qualitative experience of light in naive consciousness, which he termed "phenomenal light" and the medieval thinkers *lux*. Rather than accepting the radical cleavage between the two, Merleau-Ponty contended that the Gestaltist nature of nonscientific perception meant that a continuum existed between them. Science thus grew out of natural perception, rather than being its antithesis or corrective. As he was to put it a short time later, "The perceived world is the always presupposed foundation of all rationality, all value and all existence. This thesis does not destroy either rationality or the absolute. It only tries to bring them down to earth."[133] Thus the seeming inconsistency between two notions of light did not mean that vision was self-contradictory and even in some sense "irrational," but rather that subjective visual experience and its scientific redescription were ultimately part of the same order of signification.

Second, Merleau-Ponty discussed the implications of the inevitably perspectivalist dimensions of all seeing. Against both the transcendentalists, who feared that this acknowledgment would mean cognitive relativism, and the Nietzscheans, who reached the same conclusion but welcomed it, he followed Husserl in arguing that multiple profiles (*Abschattungen*) indicated the existence of an actual "thing" in the world transcending all of its aspects. "Perspective does not appear to me a subjective deformation of things," he argued, "but, on the contrary, to be one of their properties, perhaps their essential property. It is precisely because of it that the perceived possesses in itself a hidden and inexhaustible richness, that it is a 'thing'."[134] Rather than shutting humans off in a little camera obscura of their own, nontranscendental perspectivalism reunited

133. Merleau-Ponty, "The Primacy of Perception and Its Philosophical Consequences," *The Primacy of Perception*, p. 13. This text was written in 1946, shortly after the publication of *Phenomenology of Perception*.

134. Ibid., p. 186.

them with the objective world. "Far from introducing a coefficient of subjectivity into perception, it provides it on the contrary with the assurance of communicating with a world which is richer than what we know of it, that is, of communicating with a real world."[135]

Third, Merleau-Ponty directly challenged the Cartesian account of vision, critically examining, as he would on several subsequent occasions, *La Dioptrique*. Descartes was right, he concluded, in abandoning the medieval notion of "intentional species" flying through the air from object to eye, and with it, the resemblance theory of vision. For if such entities existed, the different perspectival profiles of perception would be impossible. But Descartes still remained too beholden to the realist paradigm, which turned vision into a view *on* the world, rather than *in* it. His struggle to explain how the reversed and inverted images on the retinas were somehow translated into the unified images in the mind, which led him to the desperate expedient of the pineal gland, bore witness to his inability to leave the old spectatorial concept of vision. Even today, Merleau-Ponty charged, the same assumption lingered in the so-called association zones of experimental psychology, which were the functional equivalent of the pineal gland.[136]

Descartes's critique of intentional species also erred in giving too constructive a role to the intellect, the *cogito*, with its projection of natural geometry onto the observed world. Playfully taking liberties with Descartes's celebrated claim that it is not the eyes but the soul that really sees, he reinterpreted the spiritual category in his own terms and opposed it to something else: "It is the soul which sees and not the brain; it is by means of the perceived world and its proper structures that one can explain the spatial values assigned to a point of the visual field in each particular case."[137] The "soul" did not see intelligible essences, but rather things with existential or real presence. "The universe of consciousness revealed by the *cogito* and in the unity of which even perception itself seemed to be

135. Ibid.
136. Ibid., p. 192.
137. Ibid., pp. 192–193.

necessarily enclosed," he charged, "was only a universe of thought in the restricted sense: it accounts for the thought of seeing, but the fact of vision and the ensemble of existential knowledges remain outside of it."[138]

If the Cartesian account of vision was thus deficient because of its inattention to the existential presence of the objects on view, what of the explicitly Existentialist alternative being developed simultaneously by Sartre? Even though the fully worked out account we have described above was still in the making, Merleau-Ponty had encountered enough of his friend's early work to become suspicious of certain of its implications. Although he shared Sartre's distaste for Husserl's transcendental ego, approved of his stress on the "lived body," and even anticipated his critique of Surrealism,[139] Merleau-Ponty distanced himself from his friend on two fundamental issues.

First, whereas Sartre had invidiously compared the derealizing imagination with the mundane world of perceptual observation, Merleau-Ponty refused to separate the two realms so categorically. As he noted in a later treatment of the same theme, Sartre himself had acknowledged certain confusions between the two in his discussion of illusions, and thus "necessarily suggests the possibility of a situation anterior to the clear distinction between perception and imagination which was made at the

138. Ibid., p. 197.

139. Of the Surrealist detachment of objects from their context of human use value in order to liberate their "marvelous" potential, he wrote, "In adults, ordinary reality is a human reality and when use-objects—a glove, a shoe—with their human mark are placed among natural objects and are contemplated as things for the first time, or when events on the street—a crowd gathering, an accident—are seen through the panes of a window, which shuts out their sound, and are brought to the condition of pure spectacle and invested with a sort of eternity, we have the impression of acceding to another world, to a surreality, because the involvement which binds us to the human world is broken for the first time, because a nature 'in itself' (*en soi*) is allowed to show through" (p. 167).

In *The Visible and the Invisible*, however, he cited approvingly a passage from Max Ernst claiming that "the painter's role is to circumscribe and to project forth what sees itself within him" (p. 208). Here Surrealism was understood less as observing a spectacle than as a willingness to suspend the active subject in order to allow vision, like language for the poet of automatic writing, to "see" the painter.

start."[140] Perception, Merleau-Ponty implied, was intertwined not only with the scientific and rational intellect, but also with the artistic imagination. As we have noted in our earlier account of his essay on Cézanne, for Merleau-Ponty, the great artist does not negate perception; he or she renews it by returning us to that primordial experience before the split between imagination and sensation, expression and imitation.

If Merleau-Ponty resisted Sartre's distinction between perception and imagination, he also subtly distanced himself from the unreciprocal social relations to which Sartre's still dualist ontology inevitably led. More faithful than his friend to the dialectic of recognition in Hegel and the analysis of *Mitsein* in Heidegger, he emphasized the potential for communication through shared signification, which was evident on the prereflective level of perception.

> The behavior of another expresses a certain manner of existing before signifying a certain manner of thinking. And when this behavior is addressed to me, as may happen in dialogue, and seizes upon my thoughts in order to respond to them . . . I am then drawn into a *coexistence* of which I am not the unique constituent and which founds the phenomenon of social nature as perceptual experience founds that of physical nature.[141]

Intersubjective relations are not thus constituted by a duel of objectifying gazes; indeed, they cannot be reduced to their visual component alone. Nor could perception as a whole. In a telling footnote near the end of his text, Merleau-Ponty pondered Heidegger's claim that we have a primordial perception of the "world" prior to sight. Reserving judgment about its full implications, he nonetheless concluded that "what is certain is that the perceived is not limited to that which strikes my eyes. When I am sitting at my desk, the space is closed behind me not only in

140. Merleau-Ponty, "Phenomenology and the Sciences of Man," in *The Primacy of Perception*, p. 74. He made a similar point in *The Visible and the Invisible*, pp. 39 and 266.

141. Merleau-Ponty, *The Structure of Behavior*, p. 222.

idea but also in reality."[142] Sight, in other words, had to be integrated with the other senses in order for us to "make sense" of our experience of the world.[143]

If *The Structure of Behavior* concentrated on the attempts of experimental psychology and certain philosophies to conceptualize perceptual experience, Merleau-Ponty's next work turned directly to that experience itself. A much more thickly textured, arduously labored, convoluted book than its predecessor—perhaps because it strove to emulate the ambiguities of perception rather than master them with categorical distinctions—*Phenomenology of Perception* has spawned a small cottage industry of interpretation, culminating in a full-length book devoted entirely to its paraphrase.[144] This is not the place for yet another rehearsal of its complex arguments; instead, only certain salient points warrant emphasis.

Setting out to provide no less than an "inventory of the perceived world,"[145] Merleau-Ponty proceeded by systematically criticizing classical prejudices about perception, which he grouped in two camps called "empiricist" and "intellectualist." The former assumed that sensations were produced by the impingement of stimuli entirely from without on the passive receptive apparatus of the sensorium. It thus reduced vision to the tradition of observation. The latter posited an absolute subjectivity,

142. Ibid., p. 249.

143. The multiple meanings of sense (*sens*) in French include the idea of direction, which fits well with the emphasis on intentionality in Merleau-Ponty. For a later discussion of the word's various meanings, see Jacques Rollande de Renéville, *Itinéraire du sens* (Paris, 1982).

144. Monika M. Langer, *Merleau-Ponty's Phenomenology of Perception: A Guide and Commentary* (London, 1989). Other useful treatments can be found in Gary Brent Madison, *The Phenomenology of Merleau-Ponty: A Search for the Limits of Consciousness* (Athens, Ohio, 1981); Remy C. Kwant, *The Phenomenological Philosophy of Merleau-Ponty* (Pittsburgh, 1963); Garth Gillan, ed., *The Horizon of the Flesh: Critical Perspectives on the Thought of Merleau-Ponty* (Carbondale, Ill., 1973); Samuel B. Mallin, *Merleau-Ponty's Philosophy* (New Haven, 1979); Albert Rabil, Jr., *Merleau-Ponty: Existentialist of the Social World* (New York, 1967); and Schmidt, *Maurice Merleau-Ponty: Between Phenomenology and Structuralism*.

145. Merleau-Ponty, *Phenomenology of Perception*, p. 25.

which constituted the world it perceived entirely out of the subject's own interiority. Here speculation, in which the subject only sees a mirror image of itself, was dominant.

For Merleau-Ponty, both traditions were equally at fault for factoring out the actual phenomenon of perception itself, empiricism because it turned the subject into an object in the world like all others, intellectualism because it made the cognitive subject all-powerful, turning perception into a mere function of thought, an effect of judgment. In both cases the world was construed as a spectacle to be observed from afar by a disembodied mind. It was necessary instead to delve into the experience of perception prior to the constitution of the body as object and the *cogito* as rational subject. Although his own philosophical tools were inevitably reflective, Merleau-Ponty sought to explore the prereflexive phenomenal field he called "being in the world."[146] He did so by drawing on the results of psychological examinations of perceptive disorders, which revealed the suppressed assumptions of "normal" perception. These abnormalities he then interpreted through phenomenological descriptions, which, however, explicitly spurned Husserl's goal of escaping the imperfect world of existence for the purer world of eidetic essences.

If Merleau-Ponty rejected the visual traditions we have called observation and speculation, can it be said that he adopted the third alternative, that of revelatory illumination, which the Surrealists in certain moods were seeking to revive at around the same time? If the goal of the seer is understood to be the attainment of perfect transparency, fusion with the divine light, or clairvoyant purity, then obviously Merleau-Ponty with his celebration of the interminable ambiguities of visual experience was not of their number. Contrary to certain interpretations,[147] he never sought a

146. Ibid., p. xiii.

147. See, for example, Eugenio Donato, "Language, Vision and Phenomenology: Merleau-Ponty as a Test Case," *Modern Language Notes*, 85, 6 (December, 1970), which argues that for Merleau-Ponty, "vision partakes of the undivided unity of Subject and Object, Self and Other, whereas the universe of discourse is one of contradictions" (p. 804). Claude Lefort is correct to claim instead that "nowhere did he recommend the intuition, the coincidence or the fusion with things, which would

mystical unity in which all shadows were dissolved in a flash of unearthly brilliance. Although he may have wanted to redeem the primacy of perception and spoke of a primordial sensorium prior to the differentiation of the senses, he never believed perception was the realm of redemption in the mystical sense of perfect reconciliation.

Still, in two ways, certain residues of the visionary tradition may be discerned in Merleau-Ponty, which became even more evident in his later work. First, his insistence on mingling the viewer with the world on view meant an ecstatic decentering of the subject, an acknowledgment that however active perception may be, it also meant a kind of surrender of the strong ego, a willingness to let things be, which has invited comparison with the ideas of Meister Eckhart.[148] Second, contact with the visible world did not produce nausea in Merleau-Ponty as it did in Sartre, but a sense of wonder instead. Never fully throwing off the Catholicism of his early training,[149] he reveled in the richness of created, incarnated Being available to the eyes.

By and large, there is little in *Phenomenology of Perception* to sustain an explicitly visionary interpretation of Merleau-Ponty's restoration of perception. After a lengthy introductory section devoted to demolishing the classical prejudices, the book begins with a detailed examination of the lived body in its physiological, psychological, sexual, and expressive

---

suppress interrogation and would discredit language. The philosophy of coincidence like that of reflection, the intuition of Being like that of the overview (*survol*) of Being could only be in his eyes two forms of positivism, two ways of not knowing our inherence in the world." *Sur une colonne absente; Écrits autour de Merleau-Ponty* (Paris, 1978), p. 26.

148. Michel de Certeau, "The Madness of Vision," *Enclitic*, 7, 1 (Spring, 1983), p. 28. He claims the filiation is through Heidegger's notion of *Gelassenheit*. Such passages as the following from "Eye and Mind" suggest the validity of this interpretation: "The thinking that belongs to vision functions according to a program and a law which it has not given itself. It does not possess its own premises; it is not a thought altogether present and actual; there is in its center a mystery of passivity" (p. 175).

149. For a discussion of his complicated and ambivalent relationship to religion, see Rabil, *Merleau-Ponty: Existentialist of the Social World*, chap. 9.

modes. The second part of the book examines the perceived world, focusing on sensing, space, the natural world, and the human world. The final part treats being-for-itself and being-in-the-world, with special attention paid to the issues of the *cogito*, temporality and human freedom.

In many ways, his arguments deepened the conclusions he had already reached in *The Structure of Behavior*. Thus, for example, he frequently emphasized the imbrication of the senses, each of which creates its own perceived world and at the same time contributes to an integrated world of experience. Unlike Bataille, he refused to degrade vision and connect it with allegedly baser human functions, but he certainly sought to level the traditional sensual hierarchy and question the elevation of sight above the other senses. In particular, the role of touch needed emphasis, Merleau-Ponty going so far as to claim that it even played a role in our perception of color, which was dependent on light cast on the textured surface of objects in the world.[150]

Recognizing the existence of a primordial, prereflexive perceptual relation to the world helped resolve such time-honored puzzles as that posed by Molyneux in his famous letter to Locke concerning the implications of a newly sighted blind man. The empiricist solution—that each sense was utterly distinct—and the intellectualist alternative—that a transcendental knowledge of space exists prior to sense experience—were both inadequate, because they failed to register the primary layer of intersensory experience in the body anterior to the differentiation of the senses and their resynthesis on the level of reflected thought. Instead, Merleau-Ponty claimed, the unification was like the merging of binocular into monocular vision, produced by a kind of bodily intentionality before mind distinguished itself from matter. "The senses," he contended, "translate each other without any need of an interpreter, and are mutually comprehensible without the intervention of any idea."[151]

Because of the importance of the intentional component in perception, Merleau-Ponty echoed Bergson in stressing temporality as one of its con-

150. Merleau-Ponty, *Phenomenology of Perception*, pp. 209ff.
151. Ibid., p. 235.

stituent elements. The lived body was irreducible to a static image observed from without. Thus, Zeno's paradoxes, at least those that applied to human movement, were based on a false reduction of motion to an intellectual judgment about a succession of static states, like the stop-action frames of chronophotography.[152] Although Merleau-Ponty did not share Bergson's distrust of the cinema, he agreed that "the lived perspective, that which we actually perceive, is not a geometric or photographic one."[153] Thus, in "The Eye and the Mind," he would take the side of painters like Géricault against photographers like Marey in their depiction of movement, and cite approvingly Rodin's verdict that "it is the artist who is truthful, while the photograph is mendacious; for in reality, time never stops cold."[154]

If the phenomenal field linking, but not fully uniting, lived body and natural environment was based on the communication of the senses, so too the human *Lebenswelt* entailed reciprocity rather than conflict. Indeed, the very bodily experience of being at once viewer and viewed, toucher and object of the touch, was an ontological prerequisite for that internalization of otherness underlying human intersubjectivity. The hoary philosophical problem of other minds was thus poorly posed, because the primary experience of sympathetic understanding was prereflexive and corporeal. Contrary to Sartre, and here the hints of a disagreement in *The Structure of Behavior* became a full-fledged critique, the "inhuman gaze"[155] of mutual objectification exists only on the level of thought, not on the level of interactive presence. For all his talk of situating consciousness in bodily experience, Sartre had thus missed the existence of the intersubjective (or intercorporeal) dimension that always subtends the seemingly self-contained subject. A Cartesian despite himself, Sartre

152. Ibid., p. 268.

153. Merleau-Ponty, "Cézanne's Doubt," in *Sense and Non-sense*, p. 14. For his attitude toward the cinema, see "The Film and the New Psychology" in the same collection. He claims, *contra* Bergson, that "a film is not a sum total of images, but a temporal *gestalt*" (p. 54).

154. Merleau-Ponty, "The Eye and the Mind," pp. 185–186.

155. Merleau-Ponty, *Phenomenology of Perception*, p. 361.

failed to acknowledge the dialectical interplay of bodily intentionalities prior to the duel of wounding gazes.

As a result, the only way Sartre could conceptualize a community was through the gaze of a third person external to the fragile collective subject it creates from without. In contrast, Merleau-Ponty more optimistically posited a cooperative, complementary world of intersubjectivity in which mutual regard is a visual as well as emotional phenomenon. What he would call "tele-vision"[156] meant a kind of transcendence of the isolated subject and a sympathetic entry into the subjectivity of others. Although the ambiguities of communal existence meant the realization of its full potential was still a historical task, which Merleau-Ponty in his more Marxist moments assigned to the proletariat, he was careful to distance himself from Sartre's a priori dismissal of the possibility of *Mitsein*. The objectifying look of the other was unbearable, he insisted, only "because it takes the place of possible communication," but "the refusal to communicate . . . is still a form of communication."[157]

Phenomenology of Perception thus concluded with a far more hopeful account than Sartre's of vision's role in the nurturance of human freedom. Despite the divisions between them, the two managed to work together on *Les Temps Modernes* after the Liberation. But in the years that followed, their friendship foundered as political disputes compounded theoretical ones. Only near the end of Merleau-Ponty's life did a hesitant rapprochement begin. Significantly, their differing attitudes toward vision permeated their political disagreements. Merleau-Ponty's lengthy attack on Sartre's "ultra-Bolshevism" in *The Adventures of the Dialectic* of 1955 is a case in point. Sartre's fellow-traveling support of the Communist Party, Merleau-Ponty charged, revealed his identification of it with a pure, transcendental subject gazing from afar at a recalcitrant, opaque object entirely external to it. That object was the proletariat, which was robbed of its own subjectivity as a result. "For Sartre," Merleau-Ponty complained, "the relationships between classes, the relationships within the proletariat, and finally those of the whole of history are not articulated relationships, including tension and the easing of tension, but are the immediate or magical relationships of our gazes."[158] Sartre may protest that he was subordinating his own gaze to that of the Party, thus identifying with the accusing gazes of the most oppressed victims of society, but in fact the result was a kind of visual solipsism: "Despite appearances, the Other is less accepted than neutralized by a general concession. The *cogito* empties like a container through the gap opened by the Other's gaze; but since there is no meaning visible in history, Sartre finds himself caught in no perspective other than his own, a perspective in which he would have to confront himself."[159] The institutional interworld that made up the recalcitrant stuff of history was thus lost, as Sartre once again failed to find a mediation between the nihilating, objectifying gaze and its opaque, meaningless object.

Ultimately, Sartre came to see the power of much of Merleau-Ponty's criticism and sought in *The Critique of Dialectical Reason* to wean himself from the Cartesian residues in his thought. How successful his efforts actually were has been a point of dispute ever since.[160] Although he abandoned his indifference to the interworld of mediations between subject and object and distanced himself from the existentialist despair of his early work, nowhere did Sartre explicitly repudiate his harsh description of the objectifying power of the gaze.

Merleau-Ponty, in contrast, returned with fresh eyes, as it were, to his initial formulations about the primacy of perception and was in the process of a major revision of his thought when his work was abruptly cut short in May of 1961. The earliest effort to realize his project, the unfinished manuscript written before 1952 called *The Prose of the World,* produced one lengthy article entitled "Indirect Language and the Voices of Silence," published in his lifetime.[161] In 1960, "Eye and the Mind" pre-

156. The term appears in various places throughout his work, for example, in *Signs*, p. 16, and *The Visible and the Invisible*, p. 273.

157. Merleau-Ponty, *Phenomenology of Perception*, p. 361.

158. Merleau-Ponty, *The Adventures of the Dialectic*, p. 153.

159. Ibid., p. 195.

160. For an analysis of his success, see Jay, *Marxism and Totality*, chap. 11.

161. It appeared in *Signs*.

sented what appeared to be a preliminary statement of his general conclusions. After his death, Claude Lefort collected the first part of his manuscript and the notes for the second as *The Visible and the Invisible*.

Fragmentary, uncompleted, and often obscure, this body of work is not easy to interpret in an unequivocal way. From one perspective, it may well appear to lend weight to the contention that Merleau-Ponty continued his search for a redemption of sight, even for a new ocularcentric ontology. Rather than talking of perception in general, with its implicit leveling of the hierarchy of the senses, he now concentrated on the sense of sight more than any other. Leaving behind his reliance on Gestalt psychology, whose spectatorial epistemological foundations he could no longer abide, Merleau-Ponty plunged more deeply than ever before into the enigmas of visibility and invisibility as the privileged avenue of entry into the question of Being. And he did so while still defending the special role of painting as opposed to other arts like music, which he never analyzed with any seriousness.[162]

The text that best supports this interpretation is "Eye and the Mind," which begins with an invidious comparison between science and painting. Whereas the former looks on things from above, the latter immerses the viewer in the world on view. The painter does not depict representations in his mind, but rather paints with his body, which is mingled with the perceived world. The self revealed by painting is thus "not a self through transparence, like thought, which only thinks its object by assimilating it, by constituting it, by transforming it into thought. It is a self through confusion, narcissism, through inherence of the one who sees in that which he sees."[163]

The "narcissism of sight" is thus an appropriate phrase because "the world is made of the same stuff as the body."[164] And yet, although at one with the world, the painter is also apart from it, which is the paradoxical, enigmatic "madness" of vision: "Painting awakens and carries to its high-

162. For a critique of Merleau-Ponty's neglect of music, see Claude Lévi-Strauss, "Musique, peinture, structure," *L'esprit*, 66 (June, 1982), pp. 76–77.
163. Merleau-Ponty, "Eye and Mind," pp. 162–163.

est pitch a delirium which is vision itself, for to see is *to have at a distance*; painting spreads this strange possession to all aspects of Being, which must in some fashion become visible in order to enter into the work of art."[165] It is precisely the revelation of the oneness and multiplicity of Being that makes painting so remarkable. Thus, with a sunny optimism that might have made Bataille shudder, Merleau-Ponty concluded, "The eye accomplishes the prodigious work of opening the soul to what is not soul—the joyous realm of things and their god, the sun."[166]

Interestingly, in presenting his defense of painting, Merleau-Ponty not only drew on modernists like Cézanne, Henri Matisse, and Paul Klee, but also on Dutch art, that "art of describing" Svetlana Alpers calls an alternative to Albertian perspectivalism. Citing Paul Claudel's description of the "digestion" of empty interiors by the "round eye of the mirror" in many Dutch paintings, Merleau-Ponty remarked that "this prehuman way of seeing things is the painter's way. More completely than lights, shadows, and reflections, the mirror anticipates, within things, the labor of vision. . . . The mirror appears because I am seeing-visible [*voyant-visible*], because there is a reflexivity of the sensible; the mirror translates and reproduces that reflexivity."[167] The curved mirror was especially powerful in this regard because its tactile dimension helps collapse the seemingly unbridgeable distance between the Albertian painter's disembodied eye and the scene before him on the other side of the windowlike canvas.

This "defenestration" of the painter's eye, as Marc Richir has noted, was also extended by Merleau-Ponty to the philosopher's as well.[168] "Eye and Mind," in fact, turns directly from a consideration of Dutch painting to an analysis of Descartes's *Dioptrique*, "the breviary of a thought that wants

---

164. Ibid., p. 163. On this theme, see David Michael Levin, "Visions of Narcissism: Intersubjectivity and the Reversals of Reflection," in *Merleau-Ponty Vivant*, ed. M. Dillon (Albany, 1990), pp. 47–90.

165. Merleau-Ponty, "Eye and Mind," p. 166.

166. Ibid., p. 186.

167. Ibid., p. 168.

168. Marc Richir, "La défenestration," *L'Arc*, 46 (1971).

no longer to abide in the visible and so decides to construct the visible according to a model-in-thought."[169] Among Descartes's failings was his inability to appreciate the ontological importance of painting, which "for him is not a central operation contributing to the definition of our access to Being; it is a mode or variant of thinking, where thinking is canonically defined according to intellectual possession and evidence."[170] Symptomatically, Descartes deemphasized color in favor of spatial design and denigrated texture in favor of form. Although he was correct to try to liberate space from the empiricists' fetish of surface appearance, "his mistake was to erect it into a positive being, outside all points of view, beyond all latency and all depth, having no true thickness."[171] In our post-Euclidean world, Merleau-Ponty insisted, we are now aware that space is no longer what it seemed to Descartes, with his geometer's eye outside and above the scene it surveyed. "It is, rather, a space reckoned starting from me as the zero point or degree zero of spatiality. I do not see it according to its exterior envelope; I live it from the inside; I am immersed in it. After all, the world is all around me, not in front of me."[172]

"Eye and Mind" would thus seem like an apotheosis of vision, understood in terms closer to Heidegger's horizonal *Umsicht* than Descartes's *pensée au survol.* And yet, read alongside the other fragments of his uncompleted project, it may betoken a less enthusiastic endorsement of the visual—understood in any of its conventional senses—than appears at first glance. In fact, in three ways, Merleau-Ponty's later work can be interpreted as anticipating some of the themes of later contributors to the antiocularcentric discourse. First, his new emphasis on the "flesh of the world" rather than the lived, perceiving body meant that the notion of vision itself began to assume a post-humanist inflection, comparable to Heidegger's, which made it less obviously a term referring to what is normally thought of as human beings looking at the world. Second, Merleau-Ponty's increasingly sympathetic interest in psychoanalysis, especially the work of Lacan, meant that he came to acknowledge certain of the problematic implications of the visual constitution of the self. And finally, his growing fascination with language, fueled in part by an enthusiastic, if garbled, reading of Saussure, would introduce a potential tension between perception and expression, figurality and discursivity, which later thinkers would explicitly develop in antiocularcentric directions.

The post-humanist implications of Merleau-Ponty's concept of the flesh of the world were anticipated in several ways before *The Visible and the Invisible*. In a 1951 essay entitled "Man and Adversity," Merleau-Ponty had written,

> If there is a humanism today, it rids itself of the illusion Valéry designated so well in speaking of "that little man within man whom we always presuppose." Philosophers have at times thought to account for our vision by the image or reflection things form upon our retina. This was because they presupposed a second man behind the retinal image who had different eyes and a different retinal image responsible for seeing the first.[173]

Such an assumption was false, so if humanism can be said to exist, it cannot be based on a notion of a disembodied observer, seeing with the mind's eye.

If the Cartesian I/eye was ruled out by Merleau-Ponty as a basis for humanism, so too was the existentialist alternative famously defended in 1946 by Sartre in "Existentialism Is a Humanism."[174] Merleau-Ponty, as already noted, distrusted his friend's identification of the subject with a nihilating "for-itself" opposed to being as the imagination was opposed to perception. In the introduction to *Signs*, he contended that "it would be better to speak of 'the visible and the invisible,' pointing out that they are not contradictory, than to speak of 'being and nothingness'."[175] And

169. Merleau-Ponty, "Eye and Mind," p. 169.

170. Ibid., p. 171.

171. Ibid., p. 174.

172. Ibid., p. 178.

173. Merleau-Ponty, "Man and Adversity," *Signs*, p. 240.

174. Sartre, "Existentialism Is a Humanism," in *Existentialism from Dostoevsky to Sartre*, ed. Walter Kaufmann (Cleveland, 1963).

175. Merleau-Ponty, *Signs*, p. 21.

he added in *The Visible and the Invisible* that "the analytic of Being and Nothingness is the seer who forgets that he has a body and that what he sees is always beneath what he sees, who tries to force the passage toward pure being and pure nothingness by installing himself in pure vision, who makes himself a visionary, but who is thrown back to his own opacity as a seer and to the depth of being."[176]

Even Husserl's phenomenological version of the subject, Merleau-Ponty came to realize, was too beholden to a visually constituted humanism, still too much an idealist philosophy of consciousness and reflection.[177] The very concept of intentionality presupposed a too centered intending subject. "Through the conversion to reflection, which leaves nothing but ideates, *cogitata*, or noemata subsisting before the pure subject we finally leave the equivocations of the perceptual faith."[178] Any philosophy of reflection, including Husserl's, was thus inadequate: "We reproach the philosophy of reflection not only for transforming the world into a noema, but also for distorting the being of the reflecting 'subject' by conceiving it as 'thought'—and finally for rendering unthinkable its relations with other 'subjects' in the world that is common to them."[179]

Finally, the collective metasubject of history, which he had tentatively supported in his militant Marxist period, seemed no less problematic as a source of a viable humanism. No retrospective total knowledge of history

176. Merleau-Ponty, *The Visible and the Invisible*, p. 88.

177. The precise extent of Merleau-Ponty's repudiation of Husserl is a matter of debate. See the exchange between Madison and Geraets at the end of Madison, *The Phenomenology of Merleau-Ponty*; Jacques Taminiaux, "Phenomenology in Merleau-Ponty's Late Work," in *Life-world and Consciousness: Essays for Aron Gurwitsch*, ed. Lester E. Embree (Evanston, Ill., 1972); and Frederic L. Bender, "Merleau-Ponty and Method: Toward a Critique of Husserlian Phenomenology and Reflective Philosophy in General," *Journal of the British Society for Phenomenology*, 14, 2 (May, 1983), pp. 176–195.

178. Merleau-Ponty, *The Visible and the Invisible*, p. 30. The term *noemata* refers to Husserl's distinction between noesis and noema, the former indicating a particular act of perception, the latter the intended total meaning of the perceptual act, which unites discrete profiles into a thing. Noemata is plural for noema.

179. Ibid., p. 43.

would ever be possible, no sovereign, God's-eye survey of the whole would ever be granted to the proletariat or any other pretender to the role of subject/object of history. The flesh of history is as unsurveyable as the flesh of the natural world; we are always in the middle of a multilayered process best understood in terms of the figure of speech known as chiasmus. The visible and the invisible was like a fold in Being, a crossing over, a hinge, not a flat landscape to be observed from afar.

Merleau-Ponty's dethroning of the observing subject, whether Cartesian, Sartrean, Husserlian, or Marxist, went so far that at times he seemed to deny not only the link between vision and the mind, but also between vision and the lived body. In *The Visible and the Invisible* he would write, "There is here no problem of the *alter ego* because it is not *I* who sees, not *he* who sees, because an anonymous visibility inhabits both of us, a vision in general, in virtue of that primordial property that belongs to the flesh, being here and now, of radiating everywhere and forever, being an individual, of being also a dimension and a universal."[180] It is precisely because of this remarkable anonymity that Merleau-Ponty began to talk of "the visible and the invisible," those utterly impersonal phenomena, rather than the viewer and the viewed. He thus contested the assumption that representation by itself could adequately capture the world, and contended that "what I want to do is to restore the world as a meaning of Being absolutely different from the 'represented,' that is, as the vertical Being which none of the 'representations' exhaust and which all 'reach,' the wild Being."[181]

Wild Being, the flesh of the world, thus became the fundamental category for Merleau-Ponty, grounding both subject and object, viewer and viewed, mind and body. But although ultimately one, thus allowing the narcissism of vision, the flesh is not a specular unity or Idealist identity. Instead, it contains internal articulations and differentiations, which Merleau-Ponty struggled to capture with terms like dehiscence, separation (*écart*), latency, reversibility, and circularity. Neither purely transpar-

180. Ibid., p. 142.
181. Ibid., p. 253.

ent nor completely opaque, the flesh is an interplay of dimensionalities of light and shadow. Consciousness can never have a completely positive vision of reality as full presence, because it inevitably has a blind spot (*punctum caecum*): "*What* it does not see is what makes it see, is its tie to Being, its corporeity, are the existentials by which the world becomes visible, is the flesh wherein the *ob*ject is born. It is inevitable that the consciousness be mystified, inverted, indirect, in principle it sees the things *through the other end*, in principle it disregards Being and prefers the object to it."[182] Despite the apparent polarity one might infer from this passage, Being was not the simple obverse of objectness, as black to white, but rather the larger context in which the object was situated. What consciousness misses in Being is the invisible inextricably intertwined with the visible in a chiasmic exchange that never achieves dialectical sublation. Being is in the interplay of the visible and invisible, which no humanist subject can ever truly see.

If Merleau-Ponty's meditations on the flesh of the world thus undermined traditional notions of a coherent viewing subject and raised invisibility to the same ontological status as visibility, so too did his cautious embrace of psychoanalysis. The changes in his attitudes toward Freud are too complex to detail here, but it is clear that near the end of his career he began to be more sympathetic to certain psychoanalytic ideas. Rather than construing Freudianism merely as a version of the causal psychology he damned in *The Structure of Behavior*, he began to appreciate its substantive contribution to the philosophical problems he so obsessively explored. As Gary Brent Madison has correctly noted, "A direct consequence of the change in Merleau-Ponty's perspective and of his discovery of the flesh—a discovery which forces him to revise completely the 'prereflective *cogito*' of the *Phenomenology*—is an increased sympathy for psychoanalysis and, in particular, its notion of the *unconscious*."[183]

One aspect of the unconscious which Merleau-Ponty found especially congenial complemented his earlier interests in the cognitive development of children, the role of the so-called mirror stage in creating the knowing self. In his 1960 essay "The Child's Relations with Others," Merleau-Ponty drew on psychologists like Henri Wallon and Paul Guillaume, who had discussed the cognitive implications of specular images.[184] What he called "autoscopy," or the external perception of a self, was responsible, among other things, for an ideal, uniform notion of space, which is assumed to be the same wherever the image of the child appears. It also has profound affective implications that purely cognitive psychology fails to explain.

Here psychoanalysis, in particular the work of Jacques Lacan, provided a useful corrective. Having recently read Lacan's seminal papers, "The Psychic Effects of the Imaginary Mode" and "The Mirror Stage as Formative of the Function of the I," Merleau-Ponty noted that they accounted for an aspect of specularity that Wallon had noted but neglected to address: the child's jubilation on seeing itself for the first time. "Lacan's answer," he approvingly writes, "is that, when the child looks at himself in the mirror and recognizes his own image there, it is a matter of *identification* . . . until the moment when the specular image arises, the child's body is a strongly felt but confused reality. To recognize his image in the mirror is for him to learn that *there can be a viewpoint taken on him*."[185] It thus makes possible narcissistic pleasure.

But in addition to registering the positive emotional implications of the mirror stage, Merleau-Ponty followed Lacan, as he read him, in discerning negative ones as well. "Thereupon I leave the reality of my lived *me* in order to refer myself constantly to the ideal, fictitious, or imaginary *me*, of which the specular image is the first outline. In this sense I am torn from myself, and the image in the mirror prepares me for another still more serious alienation, which will be the alienation by others. For others have only an exterior image of me, which is analogous to the one seen in the mirror."[186] One result is the conflict between the internal and external

182. Ibid., p. 248.

183. Madison, *The Phenomenology of Merleau-Ponty*, p. 192.

184. Merleau-Ponty, "The Child's Relations with Others," in *The Primacy of Perception*, pp. 125ff. He distinguished between the "specular image," which is a psychological phenomenon, from the "image in the mirror," which is merely physical.

185. Ibid., p. 136.

186. Ibid.

senses of the self, which leads to aggressive feelings as well as narcissistic jubilation. Another is the creation of the "specular I," which is different from the "introceptive *me*."

In adopting Lacan's account so enthusiastically, Merleau-Ponty almost readmitted Sartre's bleak version of the dialectic of vision (which, in fact, directly influenced Lacan) through the back door. But in one telling way, *pace* Madison, he held on to a residue of his earlier phenomenological belief in the existence of a prereflective ego prior to its constitution by sight. "The personality before the advent of the specular image," he wrote, "is what psychoanalysts call, in the adult, the ego (*soi*), i.e., the collection of confusedly felt impulses. . . . With the specular images appears the possibility of an ideal image of oneself—in psychoanalytic terms, the possibility of a super-ego."[187] This equation of the mirror stage with the creation of the ego ideal or the super ego was not, however, what Lacan had meant; he identified it squarely with the ego itself and thus explicitly jettisoned Merleau-Ponty's phenomenological notion of an ego prior to the *cogito*. For all his appreciation of Merleau-Ponty's positive appropriation of his work, Lacan thus carefully distanced himself from his interpretation of it in the tribute he wrote after the philosopher's death and in later statements.[188]

The issue of vision in Lacan will be addressed in a later chapter; what is important to note now is that Merleau-Ponty, however imperfectly he may have understood Lacan's convoluted arguments, took from him the recognition that the mirror stage could well be the source of an alienated self and conflict between visually constituted selves. He also seems to have been deeply impressed by Lacan's emphasis on the linguistic dimension of the unconscious, as demonstrated by his approving citation of the famous claim that it was "structured like a language."[189] Here too his grasp of the intricacies of Lacan's linguistics of *délire*, to borrow Jean-Jacques

187. Ibid.

188. Jacques Lacan, "Maurice Merleau-Ponty," *Les Temps Modernes*, 184–185 (1961), pp. 245–254; see also the confirmation of this judgment in *Four Fundamental Concepts of Psycho-analysis*, ed. Jacques-Alain Miller, trans. Alan Sheridan (New York, 1981), p. 119.

Lecercle's term,[190] may have been unsure, but by stressing the role of language, he was subtly distancing himself from his earlier celebration of perception. As he put it in his posthumously published prospectus, "The study of perception could only teach us a 'bad ambiguity,' a mixture of finitude and universality, of interiority and exteriority. But there is a 'good ambiguity' in the phenomenon of expression."[191]

Merleau-Ponty had emphasized from the beginning the importance of signification, claiming that the world was replete with meaning and that perception was the ground of communication. But now at the end of his career, he hesitatingly started to explore the ways in which language worked at cross-purposes with perception. The extent of his shift away from his original position is not absolutely certain, for as in many other respects, his final work is tantalizingly incomplete and fragmentary. Moreover, his appropriation of linguistic theory, especially that of Saussure, seems to have been partial and often based on misunderstandings.[192] Still, several generalizations can be hazarded with some assurance.

For all his fascination with the power of painters to evoke the primordial perceptual experience prior to the differentiation of the senses, Merleau-Ponty came to acknowledge that the meanings they conveyed remained mute.[193] Thus language is necessary to bring the meanings of perception into explicit speech. "In a sense the whole of philosophy, as Husserl says, consists in restoring a power to signify, a birth of meaning, or a wild meaning, an expression of experience by experience, which in particular clarifies the special domain of language. And in a sense, as

189. Merleau-Ponty, *The Visible and the Invisible*, p. 126. Sartre claimed that Merleau-Ponty agreed with Lacan on this issue. See "Merleau-Ponty," p. 306.

190. Jean-Jacques Lecercle, *Philosophy Through the Looking-Glass: Language, Nonsense, Desire* (London, 1985). He defines *délire* as "reflexive delirium."

191. Merleau-Ponty, "An Unpublished Text by Maurice Merleau-Ponty: *A Prospectus of His Work*," p. 11.

192. For an account of the confusions in his reading of Saussure, see Schmidt, *Maurice Merleau-Ponty*, pp. 105ff.

193. Merleau-Ponty, "Eye and Mind," p. 169, and "Indirect Language and the Voices of Silence," p. 81.

Valéry said, language is everything, since it is the voice of no one, since it is the very voice of the things, the waves and the forests."[194] For Merleau-Ponty, literary language in particular provides the demonstrative stories that inscribe the invisible in the visible.[195] Here the celebrated Heideggerian contention that language is the "house of Being" found its echo, as Merleau-Ponty came to see that sense and the senses were not mutually entailing.

At other times Merleau-Ponty turned to what he saw as the healing power of communicative language as an antidote to the inadequacies of visual interaction. Thus, in the introduction to *Signs*, where he talked of the enigma of "tele-vision," he asked the Sartrean question, "What is it like when one of the others turns upon me, meets my gaze, and fastens his own upon my body and my face?"[196] His answer was that "unless we have recourse to the ruse of speech, putting a common domain of thoughts between us and a third party, the experience is intolerable. There is nothing left to look at but a look. Seer and seen are exactly interchangeable. The two glances are immobilized upon one another. . . . Vision produces what reflection will never understand—a combat which at times has no victor. . . . Speech . . . would interrupt this fascination."[197]

But elsewhere, he recognized that language, spoken or not, could be less a supplement to perception than at odds with it, at least potentially. For all the interaction between the two, "there is all the same this difference between perception and language, that I *see* the perceived things and that the significations on the contrary are invisible. The natural being is at rest in itself, my look can stop on it. The Being whose home is language cannot be fixed, looked at."[198] Still, the two were not to be conceptualized in terms of an opposition or a negation. "Meaning is *invisible*, but the invisible is not the contradictory of the visible: the visible itself has an invisible

194. Merleau-Ponty, *The Visible and the Invisible*, p. 155.

195. This argument is developed by de Certeau, "The Madness of Vision," p. 30.

196. Merleau-Ponty, *Signs*, p. 16.

197. Ibid., pp. 16–17.

198. Merleau-Ponty, *The Visible and the Invisible*, p. 214.

inner framework (*membrure*), and the in-visible is the secret counterpart of the visible."[199] If perception is a mute version of language, needing it to come into full speech, so too language bears within it the residue of its silent predecessor, which inaugurated the drama of meaningfulness that is our destiny.

In short, the precise relationship between vision and language remained very much to be worked out by Merleau-Ponty, whose journey away from his original phenomenological restoration of perception never reached a final destination. Its abrupt truncation is poignantly illustrated by a detail disclosed by Claude Lefort. When Merleau-Ponty died suddenly on May 3, 1961, an open book was found on his desk: Descartes's *Dioptrique*, still the stimulus to fresh thoughts on the theme that had obsessed him for so many years.

Perhaps the "good ambiguity" that he claimed defined the relationship between perception and language could never be conclusively resolved. But perhaps also, the ambiguity may not have been so good after all, at least for the reception of Merleau-Ponty's thought. After his death, his star rapidly waned, and not merely because a later generation would grow impatient with his political vacillations.[200] Faithful disciples like Richir and Lefort aside, French intellectuals lost interest in phenomenology, with its stress on meaning and expression, and read the lessons of Saussure in a manner very different from Merleau-Ponty. So too, the very project of grounding philosophy in perception or in Being seemed problematic to thinkers disdaining any version of foundationalist thought.

But perhaps the main source of criticism for many of those disenchanted with Merleau-Ponty's legacy was their belief that his work remained far too ocularcentric, despite all the countertendencies we have discerned in his later writings. Rather than celebrating the mutual imbrication of the discursive and the figural in the flesh of the world, they would question any positive resolution of the conflict between them,

199. Ibid., p. 215.

200. For a good account of the radical shift in climate, political and theoretical, around 1960 in France, see Descombes, *Modern French Philosophy*.

even one lacking the full dialectical sublation explicitly denied by Merleau-Ponty. Thus, Lyotard, himself an early defender of phenomenology, spoke for many when he condemned Merleau-Ponty's defense of Cézanne for

> remaining hostage to a philosophy of perception that grants to vision the rediscovery in the Cézannian disorder of a true order of the sensible and the lifting of the veil which Cartesian and Galilean rationalism has thrown over the world of experience. We have no reason to believe that the *curvature* of Cézannian space, its intrinsic disequilibrium, the passion that the painter experienced for the baroque organization of plastic space . . . is any more exempt [than that of other painters] from the marks of desire and better able to restore us to the phenomenality of the sensible.[201]

Elsewhere, he would chide Merleau-Ponty for ignoring artists like Duchamp or the Cubists, whose work explored the alterity and heterogeneity Lyotard claimed was lost in phenomenological aesthetics.[202]

René Magritte, whose contempt for figural plenitude has already been discussed, likewise complained that "Eye and Mind" turned the visible world into an overly meaningful, homogeneous, expressive realm robbed of its ineradicable enigmas. In a 1962 letter to Alphonse de Waelhens he wrote, "The only kind of painting Merleau-Ponty deals with is a variety of serious but futile divertissement, of interest only to well-intentioned humbugs. The only painting worth looking at has the same *raison d'être* as the *raison d'être* of the world—mystery."[203]

201. Jean-François Lyotard, *Des dispositifs pulsionnels* (Paris, 1980), pp. 77–78. For a comparison of the two, see Jean-Loup Thébaud, "Le chair et l'infini: J. F. Lyotard and Merleau-Ponty," *Esprit*, 66 (June, 1982), pp. 158–162.

202. Jean-François Lyotard, "Philosophy and Painting in the Age of Their Experimentation: Contribution to an Idea of Postmodernity," *The Lyotard Reader*, ed. Andrew Benjamin (Oxford, 1989), p. 189.

203. René Magritte, Letter to Alphonse de Waehlens, April 28, 1962; reprinted in Harry Torczyner, *Magritte: Ideas and Images*, trans. Richard Miller (New York, 1977), p. 55.

Similarly, Luce Irigaray would attack the "labyrinthine solipsism" produced by the ungendered nature of Merleau-Ponty's musings on the narcissism of vision and conclude that he had "accorded an exorbitant privilege to vision—or rather, he expressed the exorbitant privilege of vision in our culture."[204] Foucault would include Merleau-Ponty's search for lost origins in perception in the category of "transcendental narcissism," which he condemned in *The Archaeology of Knowledge*.[205] And Christian Metz, damning as bedfellows the phenomenological account of perception and the experience of being seduced by the movies, would claim that it was "no accident that the main form of idealism in cinematic theory has been phenomenology."[206]

Although such critics perhaps underplayed the doubts that were developing in Merleau-Ponty himself about the primacy of perception in general and vision in particular, they certainly reflected the wholesale denigration of "the noblest of the senses" which characterized the era after his death. His effort to provide a more nuanced and less hostile account of vision than that found in Sartre was widely regarded as unsuccessful. By the 1960s, at a time when earlier critics of vision like Bataille were coming into their own, the antiocularcentric discourse became a pervasive, if not always coherently or self-consciously articulated feature of French intellectual life. Fueled by a politically inflected indictment of the dominant intellectual traditions and cultural practices of Western culture, it coalesced into a full-fledged attack not merely on ocularcentrism, but often

204. Luce Irigaray, *Éthique de la différance sexuelle* (Paris, 1984), pp. 148 and 163. For another feminist analysis of Merleau-Ponty, see Judith Butler, "Sexual Ideology and Phenomenological Description: A Feminist Critique of Merleau-Ponty's *Phenomenology of Perception*," in *The Thinking Muse: Feminism in Modern French Philosophy*, ed. Jeffner Allen and Iris Marion Young (Bloomington, Ind., 1989).

205. Foucault, *The Archaeology of Knowledge and the Discourse on Language*, trans. A. M. Sheridan Smith (New York, 1972), p. 203. For an excellent comparison of the two on the question of painting, see Stephen Watson, "Merleau-Ponty and Foucault: De-aestheticization of the Work of Art," *Philosophy Today*, 28, 2/4 (Summer, 1984), pp. 148–166.

206. Christian Metz, "The Imaginary Signifier," *Screen*, 16, 2 (Summer, 1985), p. 54.

on visuality in any and all of its forms. Even when the radical politics of the generation of 1968 waned, the interrogation of sight persisted as a powerful theme in French thought. Indeed, it remains so to this day.

CHAPTER SIX

Lacan, Althusser, and the Specular Subject of Ideology

"During the night before my father's funeral," Freud wrote in *The Interpretation of Dreams*, "I had a dream of a printed notice, placard or poster—rather like the notices forbidding one to smoke in railway waiting rooms—on which appeared either "You are requested to close the eyes," or, "'You are requested to close an eye.'"[4]

1. Jacques Lacan, *The Four Fundamental Concepts of Psycho-analysis*, ed. Jacques-Alain Miller, trans. Alan Sheridan (New York, 1981), pp. 118–119.

2. Lacan, "The Topic of the Imaginary," in *The Seminar of Jacques Lacan*, Book I, *Freud's Papers on Technique, 1953–1954*, ed. Jacques-Alain Miller, trans. John Forrester (New York, 1991), p. 76.

3. Louis Althusser and Étienne Balibar, *Reading Capital*, trans. Ben Brewster (London, 1970), p. 21.

4. Sigmund Freud, *The Interpretation of Dreams*, trans. James Strachey (New York, 1965), p. 352. This dream of November 23, 1896, was also reported to Freud's friend

In his exegesis, Freud dwelt on the ambiguity manifested in the dual formulation of the request, which he used to illustrate the willingness of the dream-work to tolerate undecidability or even outright contradiction.

With a certain amount of license, this ambiguity can be interpreted as expressing as well the complicated psychoanalytic attitude toward vision. For at times, Freud seems to suggest that understanding the workings of the unconscious requires shutting both our eyes, while at others he relents and allows one eye to remain open. But even the latter may have an antivisual implication, if we interpret it, as Freud did in *The Interpretation of Dreams*, as implying "winking at" or "overlooking" an unpleasant visual experience.

Whatever the degree of hostility to the visual in Freud's work, an appreciation of its importance seems to have played a role in the long-delayed French reception of psychoanalysis, for it was only when the antiocular discourse came into its own in the 1960s that psychoanalytic thought began to permeate the general intellectual climate in France.[5] Here the major figure was undoubtedly Jacques Lacan, whose celebrated dictum that the unconscious was structured like a language meant, among many other things, that the hope of understanding the constitution of the subject through a philosophy of perception alone was moribund. Lacan absorbed many of the negative lessons of the failure of that project, which he combined with others he had derived from the interwar Surrealist interrogation of the visual. The result was a radical recasting of Freud's thought, which focused attention as never before on the issue of sight.

Wilhelm Fliess in a letter a few days later. For an extensive discussion of its significance, see Marthe Robert, *From Oedipus to Moses: Freud's Jewish Identity*, trans. Ralph Manheim (New York, 1976), chap. 4.

5. The most extensive history of the French reception is Elisabeth Roudinesco, *La Bataille de cent ans: Histoire de la psychanalyse en France*, vol. 1, 1885–1939 (Paris, 1982), vol. 2, 1925–1985 (Paris, 1986); for a critique of its teleological reading of that history as a prelude to Lacan, see Paul Bercherie, "The Quadrifocal Oculary: The Epistemology of the Freudian Heritage," *Economy and Society*, 15, 1 (February, 1986), pp. 23–70. See also Sherry Turkle, *Psychoanalytic Politics: Freud's French Revolution* (New York, 1978); and Marion Michel Oliner, *Cultivating Freud's Garden in France* (Northvale, N.J., 1988).

Lacan's revision, as it were, of psychoanalysis profoundly influenced a wide variety of French intellectuals from Marxist political theorists like Louis Althusser to film critics like Christian Metz. And even when feminists like Luce Irigaray challenged the gender implications of his work, they retained—indeed, intensified—his critique of the visual constitution of subjectivity. This chapter will explore Lacan's seminal contribution to the antiocular discourse and examine one of its major offshoots, Althusser's analysis of ideology. Following a discussion in the next chapter of the work of Foucault and Debord on surveillance and the spectacle, Lacan's impact on film theory and feminism will be analyzed.

Although it was only with Lacan's linguistic turn that psychoanalysis became self-consciously antivisual, there were tendencies in Freud's own work that lent themselves to a similar interpretation. Before proceeding to Lacan, then, it will be necessary to pause with the ways in which classical psychoanalysis also implicitly requested that we close an/the eye(s). Significantly, several of these ways were first explicitly thematized by other contemporary French critics of ocularcentrism.

"The invention of hysteria," to borrow once again Georges Didi-Huberman's phrase, took place in the theatricalized amphitheater and photographic studio of Charcot's clinic at Salpêtrière. Freud, whose scientific curiosity was mightily aroused by what he witnessed during his stay there, later admiringly spoke of Charcot's observational skills.

> He was, as he himself said a "*visuel*," a man who sees. . . . He used to look again and again at the things he did not understand, to deepen his impression of them day by day, till suddenly an understanding of them dawned on him. In his mind's eye the apparent chaos presented by the continual repetition of the same symptoms then gave way to order. . . . He might be heard to say that the greatest satisfaction a man could have was to see something new—that is, to recognize it as new; and he remarked again and again on the difficulty and value of this kind of "seeing."[6]

6. Sigmund Freud, "Charcot" (1893), *The Standard Edition of the Complete Psychological Works of Sigmund Freud*, vol. 3 (London, 1962), pp. 12–13.

Freud's own intellectual curiosity remained insatiable, and he stead-fastly continued to value clinical observation. But he gradually distanced himself from Charcot's ocularcentric method. He came to believe that the very desire to know (*Wisstrieb*), rather than being innocent, was itself ul-timately derived from an infantile desire to see, which had sexual origins.[7] Sexuality, mastery, and vision were thus intricately intertwined in ways that could produce problematic as well as "healthy" effects. Infantile scopophilia (*Schaulust*) could result in adult voyeurism or other perverse disorders such as exhibitionism and scopophobia (the fear of being seen).[8] Some of his most celebrated case studies, such as that of the Rat Man, centered on obsessional visual fantasies, and he came to interpret obscene jokes partly in terms of displaced scopophilic desire. *Witz* (wit) and *Wissen* (knowledge) thus revealed a common root, as Samuel Weber has ob-served, in *videre* (to see).[9]

Freud also explored the powerful symbolic resonance of the eyes. Blind-ness, for example, could imply castration, as in the Oedipus legend or in E. T. A. Hoffmann's story, "The Sandman." Freud's discussion of the lat-ter appeared in his celebrated essay of 1919 on "The Uncanny," which he followed Friedrich Schelling in defining as "the name for everything that ought to have remained secret and hidden but has come to light."[10] The

7. Freud, "Five Lectures on Psychoanalysis," *Standard Edition*, vol. 11, p. 44.

8. For a recent psychoanalytic discussion, see David W. Allen, *The Fear of Looking: Or Scopophilic-exhibitionist Conflicts* (Charlottesville, Va., 1974). He notes that the translation of *Schaulust* is sometimes scoptophilia, but says that scopophilia is prefer-able.

9. Samuel Weber, *The Legend of Freud* (Minneapolis, 1982), p. 172. Weber, drawing on recent French thought, has many pertinent observations about Freud's critique of vision.

10. Freud, "The Uncanny," *Standard Edition*, vol. 17, p. 224. This essay has occa-sioned enormous critical attention. See, for example, Samuel Weber, "The Sideshow, or: Remarks on a Canny Moment," *MLN* (1973), pp. 1102–1113; Neil Hertz, "Freud and the Sandman," *Textual Strategies*, ed. Josué V. Harari (Ithaca, 1979), pp. 296–321; Bernard Rubin, "Freud and Hoffmann: 'The Sandman'," and Françoise Meltzer, "The Uncanny Rendered Canny: Freud's Blind Spot in Reading Hoffmann's 'Sandman'," both in *Introducing Psychoanalytic Theory*, ed. Sander L. Gilman (New

sadistic implications of the penetrating "phallic" stare were also evident in such phenomena as the "gaze of Medusa."[11] Here the eye was the source of castration rather than the symbol, when enucleated, of its enactment. And finally, the absorption of the self in its mirror image was a basic characteristic of the varieties of narcissism, primary and secondary, which Freud examined from 1910 on and which psychoanalysts have never tired of trying to interpret since.[12]

On an even more speculative level, Freud explained the phylogenesis of the species as the triumph of the eye over the nose. In *Civilization and Its Discontents*, he famously conjectured that civilization was "a consequence of man's raising himself from the ground, of his assumption of an upright gait; this made his genitals, which were previously concealed, visible and in need of protection, and so provoked feelings of shame in him." Humans' erect posture led to "the devaluation of olfactory stimuli and the isolation of the menstrual period to the time when visual stimuli were paramount and the genitals became visible, and thence to the continuity of sexual excitation, the founding of the family and so to the threshold of human civilization."[13] Civilization was thus based on the shame produced by the visibility of the genitalia and the need to distance ourselves from the "dirtiness" and unpleasant odors of our nether regions. Bataille's

---

York, 1982). Among the French theorists who have written about it are Hélène Cixous, "Fiction and Its Phantoms: A Reading of Freud's *Das Unheimliche* (The Uncanny)," *New Literary History,* 7 (1976), pp. 525–548; and Jacques Derrida, *Dissemination*, trans. Barbara Johnson (London, 1982).

11. Freud, "Medusa's Head" (1922), *Standard Edition*, 18. For a critical analysis of Freud's use of the Medusa legend, see Tobin Siebers, *The Mirror of Medusa* (Berkeley, 1983), chap. 5.

12. For a recent summary of the debates, see C. Fred Alford, *Narcissism: Socrates, the Frankfurt School, and Psychoanalytic Theory* (New Haven, 1988). See also Kathleen Woodward, "The Look and the Gaze: Narcissism, Aggression, and Aging," *Working Papers of the Center for Twentieth-Century Studies* (Fall, 1986), no. 7, for a defense of a benign version of narcissism based on the idealizing gaze of older people rather than the desiring look of younger ones.

13. Freud, *Civilization and Its Discontents*, trans. James Strachey (New York, 1961), pp. 46–47.

implicit response to this argument in *Story of the Eye* has already been discussed; soon so too will Irigaray's explicit critique.

Freud, to be sure, was no Bataille or Irigaray, and eschewed any hope for the radical undoing of the ocularcentric civilization produced by the assumption of an upright stance, despite its manifold discontents. In many ways, in fact, he remained very much a man of the Enlightenment, if a more sober and disillusioned one than his eighteenth-century predecessors. The metaphors he frequently used of casting light on the dark recesses of the mind or illuminating the "dark continent" of feminine sexuality were of a piece with his hope to map the unchartered topography of the psyche.[14]

And yet, Freud's stoic commitment to the enlightened values of the scientific tradition was often tempered by a realization, sometimes explicit, sometimes not, of the limits of its ocularcentric premises. His thought was thus enough of a departure from that of the *visuel* Charcot's for later French thinkers to find him an ally in their critique of visual hegemony. Most obviously, his stress on the interpretation of verbally reproduced phenomena such as dreams or slips of the tongue, as opposed to the mere observation of hysterical symptoms or physiognomies, meant that listening was more important than seeing.[15] Although there were visual representations in dreams, they had to be rearticulated in linguistic form before they could become available for analysis.[16] In addition, Freud admitted that even the most thorough exegesis of dreams confronted a blind spot, which he called its "navel": a place "which has to be left obscure . . . the spot where it reaches down into the unknown."[17]

Still more evidence of Freud's turn away from the visual could be found in his insistence on the couch as a way to avoid direct eye contact between patient and analyst. Not only did this device diminish the perceptual

14. For an analysis of these metaphors, see David Macey, *Lacan in Contexts* (London, 1988), chap. 6.

15. For a good discussion of this issue, see Weber, *The Legend of Freud*, pp. 17ff.

16. The centrality of language to Freud's work is powerfully demonstrated in John Forrester, *Language and the Origins of Psychoanalysis* (New York, 1980).

17. Freud, *The Interpretation of Dreams*, p. 564.

stimuli interfering with the patient's free association in the "talking cure," it also thwarted the scopophilic-exhibitionist potential in a more face-to-face therapy. In addition, it abetted the blankness of the analyst so crucial to the transference process. If some visual interaction did occur, as it inevitably would, Freud insisted that "the doctor should be opaque to his patients and, like a mirror, should show them nothing but what is shown to him."[18]

French admirers of Freud often praised precisely these antivisual implications. Michel de Certeau, for example, applied the notion of a novel, which Freud introduced in *Moses and Monotheism*, to all of his work. "To adopt the style of the novel," he concluded, "is to abandon the 'case study' as it was presented and practiced by Charcot in his Tuesday sessions (*ses Mardis*). These latter consisted of 'observations,' that is to say coherent charts or pictures, composed by noting the facts relevant to a synchronic model of an illness."[19] Similarly, Derrida approvingly noted the movement from optical metaphors of the psyche ("a compound microscope, or a photographic apparatus") in *The Interpretation of Dreams* to more scriptural ones in his later work, such as what Freud called a "mystic writing pad" (a transparent piece of celluloid over a wax slab, which erases but keeps traces of what disappears).[20] Here the temporality, spacing, and difference that had been banished from Descartes's famous ball of wax was restored as Freud "performs for us the scene of writing,"[21] an *écriture* that combined absence with presence and defeats any direct visual representation.

18. Freud, "Recommendations to Physicians Practicing Psychoanalysis" (1912), *Standard Edition*, vol. 12, p. 118.

19. Michel de Certeau, *Heterologies: Discourse on the Other*, trans. Brian Massumi, foreword by Wlad Godzich (Minneapolis, 1986), p. 20.

20. Derrida, "Freud and the Scene of Writing," in *Writing and Difference*, trans. with intro., Alan Bass (Chicago, 1978). Derrida notes that prior to *The Interpretation of Dreams* in his 1895 *Project for a Scientific Psychology*, Freud had already introduced a model of articulated deferral that was more graphic than purely optical. For Lacan's gloss on the optical metaphor in *The Interpretation of Dreams*, see "The Topic of the Imaginary," pp. 75ff.

21. Ibid., p. 227.

No less indicative of the French appreciation of Freud's antivisual implications was an increasingly frequent willingness to acknowledge in a positive way his Jewish background. Whereas in its early years psychoanalysis was often stigmatized by being called a "Jewish science,"[22] in recent French thought the attribution has instead been a source of explicit praise. A major reason for the shift was the growing appreciation of the Jewish taboo on graven images, which Freud was assumed to share.

In 1965, André Green exhorted his listeners in Lacan's seminar to attend "to Freud's interest, at the end of his life, in Moses—not only as Jew, but also because monotheism appears to be closely tied to the forbidding of idolatry."[23] In 1970, Jean-François Lyotard published an essay entitled "Jewish Oedipus," psychoanalytically interpreting *Hamlet* in terms of the Hebraic ethics of unrepresentability.[24] Marthe Robert followed with an entire book dedicated to exploring "Freud's Jewish identity."[25] A few years later, Jean-Joseph Goux wrote an article on "Moses, Freud: The Iconoclastic Prescription," which claimed that Freud's critique of Michelangelo's statue of Moses grew out of his hostility to the positive depiction of the very figure who brought God's commandment against idolatry to humankind.[26] Colloquia on the themes *Is Psychoanalysis a Jewish Story?* and *The Interdiction on Representation*[27] brought together a wide range of Jewish and gentile scholars to discuss the theme in 1980 and 1981.

In virtually all of these cases, the famous question Freud himself posed,

22. For a discussion of its impact on the French reception, see Roudinesco, vol. 1, pp. 395ff.

23. André Green, "The Logic of Lacan's *objet (a)* and Freudian Theory: Convergences and Questions," in *Interpreting Lacan*, ed. Joseph H. Smith and William Kerrigan (New Haven, 1983), p. 188.

24. Jean-François Lyotard, "Jewish Oedipus," *Driftworks*, ed. Roger McKeon (New York, 1984); the original appeared in *Critique*, 277 (June, 1970). Lyotard returned to the same theme in the 1984 essay "Figure Foreclosed," in *The Lyotard Reader*, ed. Andrew Benjamin (Cambridge, Mass., 1989).

25. See note 4.

26. Jean-Joseph Goux, *Les iconoclastes* (Paris, 1978).

27. Adélie and Jean-Jacques Rassial, eds., *La psychanalyse est-elle une histoire juive?* (Paris, 1981); *L'interdit de la représentation* (Paris, 1985).

why was psychoanalysis created by an "entirely atheist Jew?" was answered with reference to the issue of vision. Lyotard's version was the most compelling.

> It was necessary to wait for it to be a Jew because it had to be someone for whom religious reconciliation ("sublimation") was prohibited, for whom art, re-presentation itself, was unable to fill the Greek function of truth: it was necessary *to wait*, because it was necessary that this someone belong to a people for whom the beginning is the end of Oedipus and the end of the theatre; a people who had renounced the desire to see to the point that it wants to *do* before it wants to *hear* (because there is still too much seeing in hearing). . . . And it was necessary that this Jew be an atheist in order that the renounced desire to see could change into a desire to know . . . but in discourse alone, its back turned, without looking, without even the third eye, with only the third ear.[28]

A fuller exploration of the implications of the French appropriation of the Jewish taboo will have to await a later chapter. What is important to note now is the firm association between the reception of psychoanalysis and Jewish iconoclasm, which emerged in the 1970s. What must next be demonstrated is how this outcome was prepared by the linguistically inflected "return to Freud" initiated by Lacan, who in the words of one commentator, took "to their utmost extreme the antivisual and antimimetic aspects of Freud's thought."[29]

⊙

28. Lyotard, "Jewish Oedipus," p. 53.
29. Susan A. Handelman, *The Slayers of Moses: The Emergence of a Rabbinic Interpretation in Modern Literary Theory* (Albany, N.Y., 1982), p. 155. Handelman tries to situate Lacan in the tradition of heterodox rabbinic hermeneutics she sees repeated in much recent French thought. Jean-Joseph Goux also attributes Lacan's attempt to be *"more iconoclastic than the iconoclasts"* to the Mosaic taboo. See his "Lacan Iconoclast," in *Lacan and the Human Sciences*, ed. Alexandre Leupin (Lincoln, Nebr., 1991), p. 115. In contrast, Michel de Certeau stresses Lacan's debts to his education

The story begins with a famous crime. After a winter thunderstorm in February of 1933 in Le Mans, the wife of a lawyer named Lancelin and her daughter Geneviève returned to their home to find it in darkness. Blaming their maids, the sisters Christine and Léa Papin, for a power failure clearly not their fault, they touched a nerve whose gruesome consequences were vividly described in an essay in the Surrealist journal *Minotaure* in December.

> [The sisters] each grab an adversary, and tear out her eyes from the socket while she is still alive—something which is, they say, unheard of in all the annals of murder. Then, using whatever comes to hand—a hammer, a pewter jug, a knife—they fling themselves on the bodies of their victims, smashing in their faces, exposing their genitals, lacerating their thighs and buttocks, and daubing them with each other's blood. They then wash up the instruments they used for their atrocious rites, clean themselves up and go to sleep in the same bed.[30]

Not surprisingly, the two sisters became instantaneous heroines to the Surrealists, whose fantasies of enucleation were now actually realized by victims of apparent social oppression.[31] This was, they exulted, beauty at

---

in Benedictine Catholicism. See his discussion in "Lacan: An Ethics of Speech," in *Heterologies: Discourse on the Other*, trans. Brian Massumi, foreword Wlad Godzich (Minnesota, 1985), pp. 58ff. For Lacan's own thoughts on the Jewish dimension of Freud's thought, see his remarks on the importance of Midrash in his interview with Jeffrey Mehlman in *Yale French Studies*, 48 (1975), pp. 32ff. Mehlman returns to the question of Lacan and the Jews in *Legacies of Anti-Semitism in France* (Minneapolis, 1983), chap. 2, where he ponders the ambiguous implications of Lacan's citation of Léon Bloy's anti-Semitic *Le salut par les Juifs*. For more information on Lacan's relations to Jews, including his wife Sylvie Maklès Bataille, and Jewish themes, see Roudinesco, vol. 2, p. 161. She reports that, although he didn't belong to the Resistance, he helped Jewish refugees obtain papers to escape to the Vichy section of France during the early years of the war.

30. Jacques Lacan, "Motifs du crime paranoïaque: le crime des soeurs Papin," *Minotaure*, 3/4 (December, 1933), p. 25. For discussions of the episode and its implications, see Roudinesco, vol. 2, pp. 138ff.; Macey, *Lacan in Contexts*, pp. 69ff.

its most convulsive. Years later the horror of the act would still continue to haunt the French collective psyche, as evidenced by the sisters' reappearance as Claire and Solange Lemercier in Genet's play *The Maids* in 1947.[32]

What makes it of exceptional importance for the story this book is telling, however, is that the writer of the article in *Minotaure* was thirty-three-year-old Jacques Lacan, and the lessons he wrested from the obscurity—both metaphorical and literal—of the Papin sisters' crime were of prime importance in the development of the most powerful concept in the French reception of Freud: the "mirror stage" in which the role of vision in the constitution of the self was given a hitherto unimagined prominence.

Lacan had already been drawn to another celebrated instance of savage crime committed by a woman, the attempted knifing of an actress by a railway clerk called Aimée. Diagnosed as a paranoiac, she was the main case discussed in his doctoral dissertation, directed by Gaëtan Gatian de Clérambault in 1932.[33] Lacan's interest in the visual dimension of paranoia was likely stimulated by Clérambault, whose own visual preoccupations were extraordinarily intense.[34] In his clinic, Elisabeth Roudinesco reports, "the cult of the gaze reached its paroxysm. In Clérambault, the art of observation was mixed with a story of the eye reviewed by Charcot and corrected by Roussel. . . . Without a private clientele, he passed his life perfecting his eagle's gaze; he manipulated and observed sickness without

31. Macey, *Lacan in Contexts*, p. 69.

32. For a discussion of the similarities and dissimilarities between the two sets of sisters, see Philip Thody, *Jean Genet: A Study of His Novels and Plays* (New York, 1970), pp. 164ff. Sartre also comments on Genet's appropriation of the crime in *Saint Genet: Actor and Martyr*, trans. Bernard Frechtman (New York, 1963), pp. 617ff.

33. Lacan, *De la psychose paranoïaque dans ses rapports avec la personnalité* (Paris, 1932).

34. For example, he staged and collected some forty thousand photographs of draped figures during his trips to Morocco. Some are reproduced in the special issue on Clérambault in *Tumult: Zeitschrift für Verkehrwissenschaft*, 12 (1988). For an imaginative attempt to interpret these photographs using Lacanian categories, see Joan Copjec, "The Sartorial Superego," *October*, 50 (Fall, 1989), pp. 55–95.

ever hearing it."[35] Clérambault, however, reserved his most dramatic visual act for the last. Having lost his eyesight through cataracts, he decided on November 17, 1934, to end his life. Sitting in an armchair in front of a mirror, he shot himself in the mouth. In a document found after his death, he invited any interested colleague to examine his eyes.

Lacan, who had worked with Clérambault from 1928 on and who called him his only master in psychiatry, was thus already sensitized to the links between vision and aggression which the criminal episodes he pondered only reinforced. He drew on a wide variety of sources in his efforts to interpret them, including the then fashionable theories of autopunishment, erotomania, and mental automatism.[36] The Surrealist musings of Salvador Dali on the links between paranoia and hallucinatory images were also in evidence.[37] But what brought his analysis together was his adoption of Freud's explanation of paranoia as an unsuccessful defense against repressed homosexual desire.[38]

According to Freud, the defense failed because it entailed a disavowal of the anxiety-producing wish and a projection of it onto an allegedly persecuting other, who was often felt to be watching the self. Such hallucinatory "delusions of observation,"[39] as Freud called them, were complicated by the paranoid's confusion of the projected persecutor with his loved

35. Roudinesco, vol. 2, pp. 120–121. See also Emily Apter, *Feminizing the Fetish: Psychoanalysis and Narrative Obsession in Turn-of-the-Century France* (Ithaca, 1991), p. 106, for a discussion of his contribution to the theory of female fetishism.

36. See Carolyn Dean, "Law and Sacrifice: Bataille, Lacan, and the Critique of the Subject," *Representations*, 13 (Winter, 1986), pp. 42–62, and *The Self and Its Pleasure: Bataille, Lacan, and the History of the Decentered Subject* (Ithaca, 1992).

37. Roudinesco, vol. 2, p. 125.

38. Freud, "Psychoanalytic Notes on an Autobiographical Account of a Case of Paranoia (Dementia Paranoides)" (1911), in *Standard Edition*, vol. 12, trans. James Strachey (London, 1953–1974).

39. Although primarily visual, these delusions could be auditory, as also in the case of Sartre's notion of "the look" in *Being and Nothingness*. For a psychoanalytic treatment of auditory delusions of observation, see Otto Isakower, "On the Exceptional Position of the Auditory Sphere," *International Journal of Psychoanalysis*, 20, 3/4 (July–October, 1939), p. 346. Lacan, to be sure, seems to have stressed the visual rather than auditory dimension of the cases he studied.

object, which ultimately reflected a narcissistic failure to distinguish self from other.

In the case of the Papin sisters, who were emotional Siamese twins, Lacan emphasized their inability to endure separation. When compelled to live in different prison cells, they had enormous difficulty; Christine in fact wildly hallucinated and attempted to tear her own eyes out. In the case of Aimée, the inseparability was with a string of different figures, including the assaulted actress, who were all surrogates for a strong primary identification with her mother. In both instances, psychosis followed from too intense and close an identification with another and the concomitant inability to escape a kind of narcissistic doubling. Or rather, the only way to "escape" was through the violent destruction of the double, a kind of self-punishment akin to self-castration. "They plucked out their victims' eyes," Lacan noted of the Papin sisters, "as the Bacchantes castrated their victims."[40] But here the victim was ultimately the self, punished because its narcissistic identification with the projected persecuting other implied intolerable homosexual desire.

Lacan's complicated explanation of the crimes to which he was so drawn is of special importance because it provided the kernel of a more ambitious argument whose impact on the antivisual discourse proved enormously powerful. Just as Freud had found clues to the workings of the "normal" psyche in his studies of hysteria, so Lacan's analysis of paranoid psychosis led him to posit a universal stage through which all humans pass, a stage displaying marked similarities to the pathological crimes of specular violence committed by the Papin sisters and Aimée.

On August 3, 1936, Lacan read a paper to the Fourteenth Congress of the International Psychoanalytic Association, which met in Marienbad with Ernest Jones presiding. It was entitled "The Mirror Stage. Theory of a Structuring and Genetic Moment in the Constitution of Reality, Conceived in Relation to Psychoanalytic Experience and Doctrine."[41] Al-

40. Lacan, "Motifs du crime paranoïaque," p. 28.

41. The paper was indexed as "The Looking-Glass Phase" in *The International Journal of Psycho-Analysis*, 18 (1937), p. 78, but contrary to the claim of the editors of

though unpublished, it was the predecessor of a later version delivered to the Sixteenth Congress in 1949 and included in *Écrits*, the immensely influential collection of Lacan's work which appeared in 1966.[42] Although the precise relation between the two versions remains a source of some conjecture among students of Lacan's often enigmatic *oeuvre*, the main rudiments of the "mirror stage" argument seem to have been in place by the mid-1930s.[43]

The universalization and normalization of the mirror stage—his greatest heresy against conventional psychoanalysis, according to Didier Anzieu[44]—was abetted by Lacan's absorption of several other influences, some narrowly psychological, others more generally cultural. Among them were scientific studies of imitation in animals, especially pigeons and locusts, and Roger Caillois's remarkable comparison of insect with human behavior in the pages of *Minotaure*.[45] These works seemed to have alerted Lacan to the importance of visual fusion with the other through morphological mimicry. According to Caillois, however, such a fusion was accompanied by a loss of psychic energy. Borrowing a term from Pierre

---

Écrits: A Selection, trans. Alan Sheridan (New York, 1977), p. xiii, it was not published in English translation. For an interesting discussion of the mysterious history of this text and its citations, see Jane Gallop, "Lacan's 'Mirror Stage': Where to Begin," *SubStance*, 37/38 (1983), pp. 118–128.

42. The title was now "The Mirror State as Formative of the Function of the I as Revealed in Psychoanalytic Experience."

43. In 1936, Lacan published a paper entitled "Au-delà du 'Principe de réalité,'" *Evolution psychiatrique*, 3 (1936), pp. 67–86, in which the mirror-stage theory was indirectly adumbrated. It appears more explicitly in his 1938 essay "Les complexes familiaux en pathologie," republished in *Les complexes familiaux dans la formation de l'individu. Essay d'analyse d'une fonction en psychanalyse* (Paris, 1984).

44. Cited in Anthony Wilden's prefatory note to Lacan, *The Language of the Self*, p. xiii. What makes this claim especially interesting is Anzieu's identity, which Wilden does not mention. According to Roudinesco, vol. 2, p. 135, he was the son of Aimée, who was then analyzed by Lacan many years later without Lacan's knowing (or repressing) who he was! Anzieu subsequently became an analyst himself.

45. Roger Caillois, "Mimétisme et Psychasthénie Légendaire," *Minotaure*, 7 (June, 1935); for suggestive analyses of its relevance to Lacan's argument, see Rosalind Krauss, "Corpus Delicti," *October*, 33 (Summer, 1985), pp. 46ff.; and Paul Foss, "Eyes, Fetishism, Text," *Art and Text*, 20 (February–April, 1986), pp. 27ff.

Janet, Caillois called this condition "psychasthenia," which meant a drop in ego strength.[46] Here visual experience meant a crisis of the boundaried well-formed self, which invites comparison with Bataille's notion of *informe*.[47]

Lacan, however, was interested as much in the precarious formation of that self as in its dissolution, as much in the energetics of the ego as in its entropic decline, and he turned to child psychology for part of the explanation. In 1931, the French psychologist Henri Wallon had published a paper entitled "How the Child Develops the Notion of His Own Body."[48] Although the published version of Lacan's "mirror stage" essay mentions Wallon only in passing, it is clear that he was deeply influenced by the argument in this piece, as well as by the lectures by Wallon he attended from 1928 to 1934.[49] Wallon had experimented on the differences between animal and human infant behavior in front of a mirror, demonstrating that whereas the former failed to take its reflection for itself, the latter did so. Thus was born a visually constituted notion of the self. Wallon also noted that children often identified very closely with the feelings of others, for example crying when another child felt pain. This phenomenon, known as "transitivism" and investigated by other child psychologists like Charlotte Bühler and Elsa Köhler, suggested that the temporary confusion of self-image and the image of the other could be understood as functional in the creation of a healthy self.

46. For an analysis of this argument, see Denis Hollier, "Mimesis and Castration, 1937," *October*, 31 (Winter, 1985), pp. 3–16.

47. Krauss, "Corpus Delicti," p. 49.

48. Henri Wallon, "Comment se développe chez l'enfant la notion du corps propre," *Journal de Psychologie* (November–December, 1931), pp. 705–748. It was later republished in his *Les Origines du caractère chez l'enfant* (Paris, 1949), whose influence on Merleau-Ponty we have already noted.

49. Macey claims that the slighting of Wallon in the presentation of the mirror stage was typical of Lacan's deliberate self-mythification, which underplayed the importance of his predecessors. (See *Lacan in Contexts*, p. 4.) For a defense of Lacan's honest "plagiarism" as a performative instantiation of his claim that the self was always constituted by the incorporation of the other, see Mikkel Borch-Jacobsen, *Lacan: The Absolute Master*, trans. Douglas Brick (Stanford, 1991), p. 2.

Whereas Wallon conceived of these experiences in essentially positive terms as advances in the maturation of consciousness, Lacan interpreted them more darkly. Roudinesco nicely summarizes the difference:

> If one compares the Wallonian point of view with Lacan's, one perceives that the latter radically transformed a psychological experience into a theory of the imaginary organization of the human subject. From whence the change in terminology: experience [*épreuve*] becomes a stage [*stade*], and one passes therefore from a description of a concrete experience to the elaboration of a doctrine. . . . Lacan separates himself from Wallon's perspective in describing the process from the angle of the unconscious and no longer from the conscious, and in affirming that the specular world, in which the primordial identity of the self is expressed, does not contain the other. Lacan keeps the notion of the imaginary, but he defines it under the category of negativity.[50]

Before exploring the implications of that negativity, let us be clear about the description of the mirror stage posited by Lacan in its final formulation in the 1949 essay. Born before it has overcome its organic insufficiency, the human infant is initially in a state of postnatal "fetalization." Between the ages of six and eighteen months, however, the infant achieves a compensatory sense of selfhood through visual identification with its image in a mirror. What Freud had called primary narcissism was thus achieved through taking an image for the reality of a coherent self, an image which compensates for its still dependent and immature body.[51] This *gestalt* of corporeal wholeness also anticipates the child's later upright posture, which recapitulates on an individual level that fateful step in the history of the species Freud identified with the privileging of sight over smell or touch. Because the child experiences this new sense of wholeness

50. Roudinesco, vol. 2, p. 157.

51. For Lacan's gloss on narcissism, see his two seminars, "On Narcissism" and "The Two Narcissisms," in *The Seminar of Jacques Lacan*, Book 1, *Freud's Papers on Technique, 1953–1954*, ed. Jacques-Alain Miller, trans. John Forrester (New York, 1991).

as an overcoming of "motor incapacity and nursling dependence,"[52] he enjoys what Lacan calls a "jubilant assumption of his specular image."[53] Although this image might be understood as the source of the Ideal-I, the term Freud introduced in his 1914 essay "On Narcissism," or the super-ego, coined nine years later in *The Ego and the Id*,[54] Lacan was careful to claim that it was the ego itself that was at stake. The sight of a specular image, he wrote, "situates the ego, before its social determination, in a fictional direction, which will always remain irreducible for the individual alone."[55]

How, it must now be asked, was the mirror stage related to the psychotic violence shown in the cases of the Papin sisters and Aimée? How did Lacan transform Wallon's positive description of specular identification in a negative direction? The answer lies in Lacan's absorption of the analysis of Hegel's master-slave interaction presented in Alexandre Kojève's lectures at the École des Hautes Études in the mid-1930s.[56] Kojève's influential anthropological reading of *The Phenomenology of Spirit* as a dialectic of desire, violence, and intersubjective recognition left a strong mark on Lacan, as it did on an entire generation of French intellectuals.

According to Kojève, human consciousness emerges over time in response to a primordial desire to overcome a lack, a felt sense of incompleteness on the part of the biological proto-subject. But what defines human as opposed to animal desire is that its realization must entail an interaction with the desire of the other, an interaction which is the basis

52. Lacan, "The Mirror Stage as Formative of the Function of the I as Revealed in Psychoanalytic Experience," *Écrits*, p. 2.

53. Ibid. For a critique of the empirical validity of this claim of jubilation, and much else in the mirror-stage argument, see Raymond Tallis, *Not Saussure: A Critique of Post-Saussurean Literary Theory* (London, 1988), pp. 142ff.

54. Merleau-Ponty, it will be recalled, had interpreted it this way in "The Child's Relation with Others."

55. Lacan, "The Mirror State," p. 2.

56. For an account of their impact on him see, Roudinesco, vol. 2, pp. 149ff. See also, Wilfried Ver Eecke, "Hegel as Lacan's Source for Necessity in Psychoanalytic Theory," and Edward S. Carey and J. Melvin Woody, "Hegel, Heidegger, Lacan: The Dialectic of Desire," both in Smith and Kerrigan, *Interpreting Lacan*.

of history. The initial attempt to achieve a coherent sense of selfhood is made by reducing the other to an image of the self in a manner similar to the projective transitivism noted by child psychologists like Wallon. This violent derealization of the other, however, proves unsatisfactory, for only when the other is truly separate from the self can the self benefit from its recognition. A second stage of the dialectic thus entails acknowledgment of the ineradicable otherness of the nonself, which resists reduction to a specular double. In Kojève's terms, a "higher" self is constituted by a dialectic of desire in which achieving the other's recognition supplants solipsistic visual projection. This negative dialectic, however, resists the ultimate *Aufhebung* of difference in Hegel's system as it is normally understood; otherness remains unsublatable in a grand unity of subject and object.[57]

The role of language in preserving otherness and thwarting specular identity was essential to Lacan, and will be discussed momentarily.[58] But first, it is necessary to make clear the extent of Lacan's critique of the visual constitution of the self. Here a comparison with another member of Kojève's audience, Sartre, will be useful, for the similarities in their attitudes toward the gaze have been widely acknowledged.[59] In the 1949 article Lacan specifically criticized Sartre, as he would Merleau-Ponty fifteen years later, for positing an irreducible core of subjective autonomy, a "self-sufficiency of consciousness"[60] prior to the intersubjective dialectic

57. Roudinesco notes that the difference between Wallon and Lacan can be understood in part as a contrast between a more optimistic Hegelian version of the unity of the self and a pessimistic Kojèvian one (vol. 2, p. 157).

58. For Kojève, who was a Marxist, labor was even more crucial than language, but Lacan ignored its role.

59. See, for example, Macey, *Lacan in Contexts*, p. 103; Anthony Wilden, notes to Lacan, *The Language of the Self: The Function of Language in Psychoanalysis*, trans. Anthony Wilden (New York, 1968), pp. 160ff.; Leo Bersani, *Baudelaire and Freud* (Berkeley, 1977), p. 112; and Fredric Jameson, "Imaginary and Symbolic in Lacan: Marxism, Psychoanalytic Criticism, and the Problem of the Subject," *Yale French Studies*, 55/56 (1977), p. 379. Jameson goes on, however, to endorse Jeffrey Mehlman's claim that Sartre's *Saint Genet* is itself too Hegelian and thus beholden to the Imaginary (p. 380).

of desire. The residual Cartesian *cogito* latent in phenomenology, he implied, must be sternly rejected. But what Lacan did not spurn was Sartre's radical demolition of the transcendental ego created by the internalized look of the other. As Macey has noted, "The parallel [in Sartre] with the ego of the mirror stage is startling; in both cases the ego is viewed as an illusory representation, as a source and focus of alienation. Both authors make use of optical metaphors, and both relate their theorizations to Rimbaud's formula [*Je est un autre*]."[61]

Sartre and Lacan also shared a deep distrust of the spatialized self created by the reifying look, a distrust traceable to the revaluation of temporality in Bergson and Heidegger.[62] Both posited a desiring subject, whose primordial lack could never be filled either by internalizing the look of the other or by accepting the "misrecognition" of the mirror.

The term *méconnaissance*, also translatable as *misprision*, was introduced by Lacan specifically with reference to the constitution of the ego.[63]

60. Lacan, "The Mirror Stage," p. 6.

61. Macey, *Lacan in Contexts*, p. 103. The Rimbaud formula seems to have been taken to mean that the "I" was the product of the internalization of the other's look. In Lacan's fluid vocabulary, however, the "je" often meant as well the speaking subject. For its complicated relations to the "moi" in his thought, see Ellie Ragland-Sullivan, *Jacques Lacan and the Philosophy of Psychoanalysis* (Urbana, 1987), pp. 58ff. Roudinesco points out that the splitting of Freud's *Ich* into the *je* and the *moi*, which she identifies with the subject of the unconscious and imaginary self, was anticipated by Edouard Pichon (vol. 2, p. 311).

62. See Lacan's remarks on the contemporary significance of Bergson in *Écrits*, p. 28. See also his very Bergsonian contention that the "*malaise* of modern man does not exactly indicate that this precision [of the mechanical clock] is in itself a liberating factor for him" (p. 98). Ragland-Sullivan, however, notes his distaste for other Bergsonian ideas, such as *élan vital*. See *Jacques Lacan and the Philosophy of Psychoanalysis*, p. 197. His debts to Heidegger have been more widely remarked. See, for example, William J. Richardson, "Psychoanalysis and the Being-question," in Smith and Kerrigan, *Interpreting Lacan*. An example of Lacan's debt to Heidegger's critique of vision in particular is the remark in "The Topic of the Imaginary" that "the whole of science is based on reducing the subject to an eye, and that is why it is projected in front of you, that is to say objectivated" (p. 80).

63. Lacan, "The Mirror Stage," p. 6. *Méconnaissance*, it might be noted, was first used with reference to Aimée's ego formation. Surprisingly, Lacan, who reveled in the

Insisting that the ego was nothing more than an illusory construct based on a false faith in a mirror image of corporeal wholeness, Lacan set himself resolutely against ego psychology, one of whose leading advocates had in fact been his own analyst, Rudolph Loewenstein.[64] "The *mirror stage*," he wrote,

> is a drama whose internal thrust is precipitated from insufficiency to anticipation—and which manufactures for the subject, caught up in the lure of spatial identification, the succession of phantasies that extends from a fragmented body-image to a form of its totality that I shall call orthopaedic—and, lastly, to the assumption of the armor of an alienating identity, which will mark with its rigid structure the subject's entire mental development.[65]

The therapeutic goal of a strong, integrated ego, therefore, is misguided, for rather than proving an escape from the vicissitudes of alienation, it is itself the greatest alienation of all. Produced by identification with a specular mirage, a dead image of a body like a film "suddenly stopped in mid-action,"[66] it is nothing less than an instantiation of what Sartre called "bad faith."[67] Indeed, from a clinical point of view, Lacan claimed, "The ego represents the center of all the *resistances* to the treatment of symptoms."[68]

---

play of language, neglected to tie *voir* and *non-savoir*. The reason may have been that *connaissance* has the connotation of knowledge as recognition, which fits better with the Kojèvean dialectic of recognition.

64. Loewenstein came to Paris in 1925, but ultimately emigrated to the United States, where along with Heinz Hartmann and Ernst Kris, he established the hegemony of ego psychology. Lacan would strongly identify ego psychology with America, but its origins were clearly in Europe. Lacan's analysis with Loewenstein seems to have begun in 1932. According to Roudinesco, it played little role in his intellectual development, and relations with his analyst were far cooler than with Clérambault. See vol. 2, pp. 132ff.

65. Lacan, "The Mirror Stage," p. 4. The language of armoring may suggest Wilhelm Reich, but Lacan distinguishes their positions in a later essay "The Function and Field of Speech and Language in Psychoanalysis," *Écrits*, pp. 101 and 109.

66. Lacan, "Aggressivity in Psychoanalysis," *Écrits*, p. 17.

It is now easier to understand the link between Lacan's work on paranoid violence and his discussion of the mirror stage. If specular identification meant the rigid, "orthopaedic"[69] constriction of the psyche, failing to move beyond the mirror stage could lead to a repetition of its aggression. That is, if the self were narcissistically projected on to the other, who was then construed as of the same sex, self-punishment for disavowed homosexual desires could produce violence toward the projected source of those desires. Once the idealized other lost its ideal status, the unity of the self based on identification with the ideal would be threatened, and aggression could be unleashed "outward." Aimée could knife the actress and the Papin sisters kill their employers, acts that seem to be intersubjective, but in fact were intrasubjective instead.

Such a dynamic is not confined to psychotics, Lacan reasoned, but is also evident in everyone's passage through the mirror stage because of such virtually universal experiences as sibling rivalry, which he dubbed the "intrusion complex."[70] As a result, what Lacan called "the Imaginary,"[71] the dimension or realm of images, perceived or imagined, conscious or not, is a constant dimension of the human psyche,[72] which can never permit unimpeded access to "the Real," the realm of raw, unrepresentable

67. Ibid., p. 15. Lacan, it should be noted, shared much of Sartre's pessimism about being able to escape "bad faith" for very long. He never contrasted a fully successful "recognition" or "cognition" to the "misrecognition" of the mirror stage.

68. Ibid., p. 23.

69. For an interesting discussion of the implications of the orthopaedic, see Catherine Clément, *The Lives and Legends of Jacques Lacan*, trans. Arthur Goldhammer (New York, 1983), p. 90.

70. Lacan, "La Famille," *Encyclopédie Française*, 8 (Paris, 1938), p. 840. For a discussion, see Alphons De Waelhens, *Schizophrenia* (Pittsburgh, 1978), pp. 76–79.

71. Perhaps his best account is in the seminars grouped under the rubric "The Topic of the Imaginary" in *The Seminar of Jacques Lacan*, Book 1.

72. Ellie Ragland-Sullivan persuasively contends that "in that many Lacanian commentators have taken the Imaginary to refer only to the alien imagos with which an infant initially identifies, they have reduced this order to the neurotic function of engaging adults in the closure of narcissistic relations. Condemned to the limitations of neurosis or child-like fantasy, the Imaginary is seen as a phase to be transcended on

fullness prior to the organization of the drives. But there is nonetheless a difference between normal and psychotic behavior which depends on the partial transition from the Imaginary to a further stage, which Lacan termed "the Symbolic." Coincident with the resolution of the Oedipus complex, the Symbolic meant the child's entry into language.

Lacan's clear preference for the Symbolic over the Imaginary has been widely recognized. Antoine Vergote, for example, has written, "It recalls the negative theology which broke idolatrous images. An iconoclast of the mirrors of Narcissus, Lacan awakens an anthropology trapped in the snare of specular duplication."[73] Michel de Certeau adds that the ethical dimension of Lacan's theory was due precisely to his rejection of the "alienating imagination"[74] in the name of interminable speech. However much his celebrated public seminars may have resembled Charcot's theatricalized presentations of hysteria,[75] however indebted he may have been to Clérambault's psychiatry of the gaze,[76] however fascinated he may have become with topographical representations of the unconscious in his later years,[77] Lacan thus remained preeminently a critic of ocularcentrism. Even in his most scientistic moments, he resolutely rejected the residues of disinterested observation still lurking in Freud.[78] And for all

---

the road to psychic awareness and freedom. My reading of Lacan's texts lends far greater scope to the Imaginary. By connecting the unconscious to conscious life through a variety of invisible joins, the Imaginary places affective value on Symbolic order conventions and thereby infers a heterogeneity into discourse. As the purveyor of active, albeit repressed, representations and identificatory 'knowledge,' the Imaginary judges people and experiences 'intuitively,' in light of invisible resonances. Like the *moi*, the Imaginary also functions to blot out the unconscious knowledge to which its very existence gives silent witness" ("Counting from 0 to 6: Lacan and the Imaginary Order," *Working Papers of the Center for Twentieth Century Studies*, Fall, 1984, p. 8).

73. Vergote, Foreword to Anika Lemaire, *Jacques Lacan*, trans. David Macey (London, 1977), p. xix.

74. de Certeau, "Lacan: An Ethics of Speech," p. 61.

75. For the comparison, see Macey, *Lacan in Contexts*, p. 15.

76. Roudinesco, vol. 2, p. 142, claims that he "always preserved that ethic of the look learned from Clérambault."

his debts to the structuralist linguistics of Saussure and Roman Jakobson, he never assumed the coolly detached vantage point of the disinterested spectator able to reduce the *délire* of linguistic practice to neatly opposed binary oppositions.[79] If there was any *clarté* in Lacan's own language, it was, as one commentator has remarked, that of Magritte's deceptively lucid canvases, replete with visual puns.[80]

This is not the place to hazard yet another heroic explication of Lacan's complicated, ambiguous, and slippery analysis of the Symbolic. Nor is it possible to disentangle the web of disparate sources from the Surrealists and Heidegger to Saussure and Jakobson, which allowed him to posit the linguistic workings of the unconscious. Suffice it to say that for Lacan, only when the illusory *dyadic* specularity of the mirror stage is surpassed by the *triadic* interaction of the Oedipal drama can a nonnarcissistic intersubjectivity become possible, an intersubjectivity in which the alterity of the nonself is preserved rather than destroyed. The creation of the superego through the *introjection* of the prohibition of the father against incest creates a secondary identification, which supplants the primary identification based on specular *projection*.

Only, that is, when the desire for fusion (either with the image of the self in the mirror or even earlier with the mother) is replaced by the acceptance of the prohibition of that desire, represented by the father's "no,"

77. Goux argues that the mathematical and topographic musings of the later Lacan merely reinforced his hostility to vision: "Lacanian thought is a *technological iconoclasm*. . . . In an era conditioned by the triumph of technology, with the machine mastering *nature* and informing *matter*, Lacan decrees a supericonoclasm, grounded in mechanographic functions bespeaking a symbolic order that transcends human subjects" ("Lacan Iconoclast," p. 116).

78. For a discussion of the differences, see Shoshana Felman, *Jacques Lacan and the Adventure of Insight: Psychoanalysis in Contemporary Culture* (Cambridge, Mass., 1987), pp. 61ff.

79. For accounts that stress Lacan's poetic rather than scientific approach to language, see Macey, *Lacan in Contexts*, chap. 5, and Jean-Jacques Lecercle, *Philosophy Through the Looking-Glass: Language, Nonsense, Desire* (London, 1985), chap. 4.

80. William Kerrigan, "Introduction," in Smith and Kerrigan, *Reading Lacan,* p. xxiv.

can a healthy subject replace the "misrecognized" subject of the mirror stage. Because the father's "no" is a speech act, and one which in French is conveniently homophonic with his name (the "*non-du-père*" and the "*nom-du-père*"), the introjection is a fundamentally linguistic phenomenon, which is why entrance into the Symbolic is related to the Oedipus complex. The healthy subject thus produced, however paradoxical it may seem, is thus split, decentered, and, to recall Bataille's metaphor for the headless body, "acephalic."[81] It accepts the condition of infinite desiring which the mirror stage tried to overcome through primary narcissistic identification with the image of wholeness in the glass. Or more precisely, it leaves behind mirror-stage primary desire for the secondary "metonymic" desire that Lacan called "demand."[82]

The splitting of the ego helps to defuse the aggressive potential in the mirror stage which is still evident in paranoid psychosis. It does so because the split self is no longer in danger of projecting its ideal of wholeness on to another, which it confuses with itself. Nor is it prone to punish itself in that other when it feels threatened by the transgressive homosexual desires it has projected outward. The resolution of the Oedipus complex means the overcoming of castration anxiety, as the child introjects the father's phallus as a symbolic signifier, rather than trying to *be* the imaginary phallus that will complete the mother's "castrated" body. "Having" the phallus as an internalized object of linguistic desire is thus superior to confusing the self with the image of it. This secondary identification with a word rather than an image means that the self-castration evident in such acts as tearing out the eyes of the specular double is no longer a threat. In sum, only when the unconscious functions like a language and not like a mirror can the mature subject, split and introjecting the other rather than projecting itself onto it, be achieved.

81. The term is used by Lacan himself. See *The Seminar of Jacques Lacan*, Book II, *The Ego in Freud's Theory and in the Technique of Psychoanalysis 1954–1955*, ed. Jacques-Alain Miller, trans. Sylvia Tomaselli (New York, 1991), p. 167.

82. According to Lemaire, "In Lacan, demand appears to be a generic term designating the symbolic, significant site in which the primordial desire is gradually alienated" (*Jacques Lacan*, p. 165).

But what if the unconscious could never completely transcend its nonlinguistic, visual dimension, even when the subject successfully negotiated passage through the mirror stage? What if the persistence of the eye in the mind/psyche remained, even in the midst of the Symbolic? What, in other words, if instead of experiencing two distinct temporal stages in a developmental process, the unconscious was structured synchronically without any absolute break between before and after the resolution of the Oedipal phase?

⊙

The answers to these questions were spelled out elsewhere in Lacan's work, for his animadversions on the dangers of visual primacy did not end with his influential characterization of the mirror stage and the Imaginary. In at least two other moments, Lacan returned to the theme of vision: when he integrated the concept of "scotomization" into his analysis of psychosis and when he critically appropriated Merleau-Ponty's chiasmic ontology of the visible and the invisible, which he redescribed in terms of "the eye" and "the gaze."[83] In both cases, Lacan interrogated the implications of vision, variously understood, in the constitution of the self and its vicissitudes. These two arguments, moreover, were related, for as Emily Apter has noted, "the scotomized Lacanian subject is caught in a contentious struggle for mastery between the eye and the gaze that parallels Charcot's dialectic between scopophilia and scotomization."[84]

Scotomization was a term first borrowed by Charcot from ophthalmology in the 1880s to describe hysterical vision, and then revived by the French analysts René Laforgue and Edouard Pichon in the 1920s.[85] Tech-

---

83. Still a third appeared in his late seminar on television, which has been translated as "Television" by Denis Hollier, Rosalind Krauss, and Annette Michelson in *October*, 40 (Spring, 1987). For an analysis of its relation to his other work on vision, see Shoshana Felman, "Lacan's Psychoanalysis, or the Figure in the Screen," *October*, 45 (Summer, 1988).

84. Apter, *Feminizing the Fetish*, p. 149.

85. For discussions, see Roudinesco, vol. 1, pp. 388ff., Macey, pp. 35ff., Apter, pp. 147ff., and Dean, pp. 107 ff.

nically referring to a retinal lesion producing a visual blindspot, the term (from the Greek *skotos* for darkness) was used by them to designate a mode of psychotic unawareness that was different from repression as Freud had defined it. Whereas repression meant denying an instinct or its mental derivative any access to consciousness, scotomization was a "a process of psychic depreciation, by means of which the individual attempts to deny everything which conflicts with his ego. . . . Contrary to what happens in normal repression, the mind in spite of outward appearances is really simply trying to evade a situation in which it has to endure frustration and which it apprehends as a castration."[86]

In a series of exchanges, public and private, with Laforgue, Freud rejected this distinction, claiming that "'scotomization' seems to me particularly unsuitable, for it suggests that the perception is entirely wiped out, so that the result is the same as when a visual impression falls on the blind spot in the retina."[87] Although Freud apparently won the immediate argument and the term was dropped from orthodox psychoanalytic parlance, it seems to have had a sustained impact on Lacan. As early as 1938, Pichon noted its residue in Lacan's work, and the term would explicitly resurface in such texts as "Aggressivity in Psychoanalysis" ten years later, where Lacan tellingly referred to Freud's failure to recognize the ego's ability to scotomize as a *méconnaissance*.[88]

Lacan had also adopted in the interim another technical term from Pichon which did much of the same work as scotomization, "foreclosure."[89] *Forclusion* was proposed as the French translation of Freud's *Verwerfung*, which was different from repression (Freud's *Verdrängung*, translated into French as *refoulement*). The difference consisted in the nonintegration of foreclosed signifiers into the unconscious, their "cast-

86. Laforgue, "Scotomization in Schizophrenia," *International Journal of Psychoanalysis*, 8 (1927), p. 473, cited in Macey, p. 35.

87. Freud, "Fetishism," *Standard Edition*, 21, pp. 153–154.

88. Pichon's observation is cited in Macey, p. 37; Lacan's use appears in "Aggressivity in Psychoanalysis," p. 22.

89. For a helpful account, see John P. Muller, "Language, Psychosis and the Subject in Lacan," in Smith and Kerrigan, *Reading Lacan*.

ing out" in the literal meaning of *ver-werfen*, which prevented them from reappearing as neurotic symptoms. Instead, they resurfaced in the realm of the real, most often as hallucinations, the classic case being that of Schreber.[90] Thus, foreclosure rather than repression is the defense mechanism of psychosis, especially paranoia.

Another way to describe the difference is to note that whereas repression translates perceptual experience into the realm of the Symbolic—there must first have been an "affirmation" (*Bejahung*) of that experience, which actually exists prior to its repression—scotomization and foreclosure do not. For in their case, what is denied may or may not have existed in the first place. Psychosis can thus be triggered by the failure to resolve the traumatic experience of castration anxiety produced by the child's perception of the mother's visible lack of a penis, a resolution that could only take place through the introjection of the father's linguistic prohibition. The child remains instead in a dyadic union with the mother, in which he or she identifies with the assumed object of maternal desire, the imaginary phallus. This identification during the mirror stage is abetted by that jubilation the child feels when it sees its erect and plenitudinous image in the mirror, as one Gestalt of tumescence slides into another. Striving, as we have noted earlier, to *be* that object which seems able to fulfill the mother's apparent lack, the child never comes to accept the law against incestuous coupling laid down by the father. The name-of-the-father, representing Symbolic castration, is thus a signifier whose integration into the unconscious is thwarted. As a result, the child never really enters the Symbolic, where the phallus operates as a signifier of unfulfillable desire, splitting the ego, remaining instead trapped in an Imaginary relationship in which image and reality are conflated.

The ultimate source of psychosis seems to be the mother's attitude, her insistence on the child serving as the fulfillment of her lack. In Anika Lemaire's summary of Lacan's argument, "If the mother treats the child as the complement of her own lack, as the phallus with which the child is in

90. For Lacan's treatment of it, see "On a Question Preliminary to Any Possible Treatment of Psychosis," *Écrits*.

any case trying to identify, if, therefore, the child is everything to her and merges with her in a diffuse union, then the child cannot dispose of his own individuality."[91]

Based on the assumption that desiring, "castrated" mothers feel such a lack, Lacan's account of the origin of psychosis could be construed as expressing a gender bias, which his feminist critics would come to question. What they were less willing to dispute, however, was his devaluation of visual experience evident in the residues of scotomization still present in the concept of foreclosure. Scotomization, it will be recalled, suggests that an actual blindspot occurs when something is too threatening to be seen. Foreclosure goes further in suggesting that the "sight" of the mother's apparent castration triggers a casting out of the rejected image, or more precisely, an inability to integrate it in symbolic, linguistic terms and its reappearance as a hallucination—sometimes aural (hearing voices) as well as visual—in the order of the Real. In both cases, psychosis appears to be connected to a disturbance in sight, whereas health is identified with linguistic introjection. Or put more precisely, it is the disturbance of the linguistic or Symbolic realm by the interruption of the visual or Imaginary that causes psychological damage.

But Lacan's argument is more complicated than it first appears. That such a disturbance may well be more than the mere return of an earlier phase, as the chronologically sounding stage argument would suggest, is shown by the hidden premise behind the child's alleged visual perception of a lack in his or her mother's body. For vision alone cannot produce a sense of a lack, which is always already a symbolic concept.[92] Therefore the synchronic imbrication of the verbal and the visual is implied by Lacan's conflation of scotomization and foreclosure.[93] With this in mind,

91. Anika Lemaire, *Jacques Lacan*, trans. David Macey (London, 1970), p. 234. Lacan also explains perversions in a similar way. "The whole problem of the perversions," he writes, "consists in conceiving how the child, in relation to the mother, a relation constituted in analysis not by his vital dependence on her, but by his dependence on her love, that is to say, by the desire for her desire, identifies himself with the imaginary object of this desire insofar as the mother herself symbolizes it in the phallus" ("On a Question Preliminary to Any Possible Treatment of Psychosis," *Écrits*, p. 198).

it might be possible to reformulate the misrecognition of the mirror state precisely as the occlusion of the linguistic moment that is always intertwined with the visual.

The synchronic argument cuts both ways: even after the "entrance" into the Symbolic, the Imaginary, with all of its attendant problems, remains potent. No less suggestive of this conclusion than his argument about scotomization, and even more influential on the subsequent antiocular discourse in France, were Lacan's remarkable ruminations on the chiasmic intertwining of "the eye" and "the gaze" in four seminars he gave in 1964. These were included by his son-in-law Jacques-Alain Miller nine years later in the collection called *The Four Fundamental Concepts of Psycho-analysis* under the rubric, "Of the Gaze as *Objet Petit a*." Because of their importance, it will be necessary to unpack their complicated argument with some care.

Lacan began the first seminar, "The Split Between the Eye and the Gaze," by paying tribute to Merleau-Ponty's pioneering interrogation of vision, in particular the recently published *The Visible and the Invisible.*

92. It is only by tacitly reading the two stages synchronically that allows Lacanians like Shoshana Felman to claim that "the mirror thus epitomizes perception as a visual centering anchored in the misperception—in the denial—of one's castration: the apparent fullness of the image in the mirror is an objectification of the gaze which, in substantifying the image as an object, elides from it the very insufficiency experienced by the subject" ("Lacan's Psychoanalysis, or the Figure in the Screen," p. 103). That is, only when the Symbolic and the Imaginary are assumed to overlap can the sense of incompleteness produced by the infant's motor incapacities be turned into castration anxiety and its overcoming in a visual Gestalt of wholeness be understood as a denial.

93. Still another moment in Lacan's work in which the synchronicity of the two stages is suggested can be found in his various discussions of the celebrated "fort-da" children's game Freud analyzed in *Beyond the Pleasure Principle*. According to Freud's account, the child gains a sense of mastery by moving his image in and out of a mirror while shouting "Fort!" (gone!) and "Da" (there!), just as he does with a spool on a thread which he can move in an out of his visual field. Some of his commentators (e.g., Ragland-Sullivan, *Jacques Lacan and the Philosophy of Psychoanalysis*, p. 171) interpret Lacan's discussion as the paradigm for the Symbolic order. Others (e.g., Tobin Siebers, *The Mirror of Medusa*, pp. 163–164) read it as still emblematic of the Imaginary.

Praising it for going beyond Merleau-Ponty's earlier *Phenomenology of Perception* because of its rejection of the constitutive, form-giving powers of the intentional subject, Lacan nonetheless reinterpreted its significance in his own terms.

> You will see that the ways through which he will lead you are not only of the order of visual phenomenology, since they set out to rediscover—this is the essential point—the dependence of the visible on that which places us under the eye of the seer. But this is going too far, for that eye is only the metaphor of something that I would prefer to call the seer's "shoot" (*pousse*)—something prior to the eye. What we have to circumscribe, by means of the path he indicates for us, is the pre-existence of a gaze—I see only from one point, but in my existence I am looked at from all sides.[94]

Merleau-Ponty was, in other words, right in dividing the scopic field. But he was mistaken in interpreting it as a chiasmus of visibility and invisibility; it would be better instead, Lacan claimed, to conceptualize it in terms of the eye and the gaze.

To explain what he meant by these terms, Lacan drew once again on one of his co-contributors to *Minotaure*, Roger Caillois. In a work concerning animal mimicry entitled *Méduse et compagnie*, Caillois had raised the question of whether the imitated eyes, *ocelli*, employed by certain animals to frighten predators or victims, achieve their effect because they resemble real eyes or vice versa. That is, do real eyes fascinate on their own terms or because they imitate their simulacrum? Whatever the answer to this question, the implication was that the real eye should be understood as being crossed in the scopic field by the "gaze" of a fake one. Caillois's example was thus "valuable in marking the pre-existence to the seen of a given-to-be-seen."[95]

Returning to his critique of the Imaginary, Lacan went on to explain

94. Lacan, *The Four Fundamental Concepts of Psycho-analysis*, p. 72.
95. Ibid., p. 74.

that the problem of remaining hostage to the mirror stage, a problem that characterized Western philosophical ocularcentrism as a whole, was due precisely to its inflation of the role of the eye at the cost of recognizing that of the gaze. That is, it fails to register what Merleau-Ponty had pointed out: "that we are beings who are looked at, in the spectacle of the world. That which makes us consciousness institutes us by the same token as *speculum mundi*."[96] This failure can also be understood if we contrast waking and sleeping experience. Whereas awakened consciousness only operates with a looking eye, in our dreams, images show themselves to our unconscious. "In the final resort, our position in the dream is profoundly that of someone who does not see. The subject does not see where it is leading, he follows. . . . In no case will he be able to apprehend himself in the dream in the way in which, in the Cartesian *cogito*, he apprehends himself in thought."[97] Because of the privilege normally given to wakened consciousness, it is necessary in analysis to bring to the surface the crossing of eye and gaze, avoiding the alibi of visual plenitude and mastery. "It is not, after all, for nothing," Lacan noted, "that analysis is not carried out face to face. The split between eye and gaze will enable us, you will see, to add the scopic drive to the list of the drives."[98]

96. Ibid., p. 75. Commenting on this passage, Alexander Gelley writes, "Man as mirror or image of the universe—this might be taken as the humanist sense of the phrase. But Lacan underscores the disabling ambiguity implicit in derivatives of the Latin root *species*: (1) that which is seen, the view; (2) the spectacle in the sense of theatrical illusion, mere effect; and (3) the mirroring or reflecting back on itself of the viewing instance" (*Narrative Crossings: Theory and Pragmatics of Prose Fiction* [Baltimore, 1987], p. 27).

97. Lacan, *The Four Fundamental Concepts of Psycho-analysis*, p. 75.

98. Ibid., p. 78. Freud had suggested oral, anal, and genital drives but also wrote about a scopophilic drive in the *Three Essays on Sexuality*, Standard Edition, vol. 7, pp. 191–192. Lacan nonetheless claimed that he was adding it to the more familiar drives. He also posited an invocatory drive related to the voice. According to Lacanian theory, "the drives represent the cause of sexuality in the psychic; they do so only partially and yet they constitute the only link of sexuality to our experience" ("The Phallic Phase and the Subjective Import of the Castration Complex," in *Feminine Sexuality: Jacques Lacan and the École Freudienne*, eds. Juliet Mitchell and Jacqueline Rose, trans. Jacqueline Rose [New York, 1982], p. 119. This article was an

To explore the implications of that drive, Lacan turned in the next seminar to the theme of anamorphosis, whose importance had been brought home to him by Jurgis Baltrusaitis's influential study.[99] Before treating it directly, he began by commenting on Paul Valéry's *La Jeune Parque*, in which the main character talks of seeing himself seeing. The problem with this formulation, Lacan suggested, was that it remained indebted to a still Cartesian notion of the subject as constituted by the eye alone: "The privilege of the subject seems to be established here from that bipolar reflexive relation by which, as soon as I perceive, my representations belong to me."[100] Merleau-Ponty's phenomenological alternative, with its depriviliging of the Cartesian subject, was superior, but according to Lacan, it lacked the courage to take its chiasmic conclusions to their nonreciprocal end. Merleau-Ponty, he charged, had fallen back on an alleged substratum prior to reflection: "For him, it is a question of restoring . . . of reconstituting the way by which, not from the body, but from something that he calls the flesh of the world, the original point of vision was able to emerge . . . what I would like to call the function of *seeingness* (*voyure*)."[101]

Psychoanalysis, however, calls into question the search for a primordial *voyure*, anterior to the split between the eye and the gaze. It does so, he contended, because it regards "consciousness as irremediably limited, and institutes it as a principle, not only of idealization, but of *méconnaissance*, as—using a term that takes on new value by being referred to a visible

---

unsigned contribution to Lacan's journal *Scilicet* in 1968.) The importance of construing vision as a scopic drive is that it then must seek an erotic object outside of itself for fulfillment; this is the role of the gaze. For Lacan, drives cannot be realized, which is why the eye and the gaze are shown in perpetual disharmony. For a useful gloss on Lacan's drive theory, see Juliet Flower MacCannell, *Figuring Lacan: Criticism and the Cultural Unconscious* (Lincoln, Nebr., 1986), pp. 161ff.

99. Jurgis Baltrušaitis, *Anamorphoses: ou Perspectives curieuses* (Paris, 1955); the third edition (Paris, 1984), mentions Lacan's appropriation, as well as others by contemporary intellectuals such as Roland Barthes, Jean Cocteau, and Jean-François Lyotard.

100. Lacan, *The Four Fundamental Concepts of Psycho-analysis*, p. 81.

101. Ibid., pp. 81–82.

domain—*scotoma*."[102] Here Lacan reintroduced the visually inflected category Freud had banished as superfluous, and now not merely as an explanation for psychosis, but as a dimension of the psyche per se. Blind spots, he implied, were incurable. The misprision of visually constituted consciousness operates, as Lacan had earlier claimed with reference to the mechanism of foreclosure, by seeking to overcome its sense of incompleteness through identification: "The interest the subject takes in his own split is bound up with that which determines it—namely, a privileged object, which has emerged from some primal separation, from some self-mutilation induced by the very approach of the real, whose name, in our algebra, is the *objet a*."[103]

The *objet a* (object small a) was Lacan's term for the object of lack or the missing object that will seemingly satisfy the drive for plenitude, "a" being the first letter of the French word for "other" (*l'autrui*).[104] At its most fundamental level, it is the phallus which the child (of whatever sex, according to Lacan) wishes to be in order to make up for the mother's alleged lack, her apparent castration. It can then be transformed into the Symbolic register as the metonymic object of desire which motivates the split subject's interminable search for a unity it can never achieve. But it operates as well in the realm of the Imaginary, where "the object on which depends the phantasy from which the subject is suspended in an essential vacillation is the gaze. . . . From the moment that this gaze appears, the subject tries to adapt himself to it, he becomes that punctiform object, that point of vanishing being with which the subject confuses his own failure."[105]

102. Ibid., pp. 82–83.

103. Ibid., p. 83.

104. The fact that it is a letter should not go unremarked. As Goux has noted, the letter as opposed to the image is privileged in Lacan's analysis of dreamwork, even when dreams employ visual rebuses. See his "Lacan Iconoclast," pp. 110–111. Lyotard, as a later chapter will show, attempted to restore a certain notion of the visual to the unconscious by opposing the line to the letter.

105. Lacan, *The Four Fundamental Concepts of Psycho-analysis*, p. 83.

To explicate his cryptic assertion that in scopic relations the gaze functions as the *objet a*, Lacan turned to the "brilliant passages"[106] in Sartre's *Being and Nothingness* in which the reifying power of the gaze was explored. Although he challenged Sartre's claim that the eye cannot see the eye that looks at it, he agreed that the gaze had the quality of being unseen: "The gaze I encounter—you can find this in Sartre's own writing— is, not a seen gaze, but a gaze imagined by me in the field of the Other."[107] It is for this reason that *le regard* can include nonvisual phenomena like the rustling of the leaves. More important, the unseen character of the gaze meant it was not necessarily that of another subject looking threateningly at the original subject, but might rather be understood as a function of the desire of the original subject, the desire for the *objet a*, or perhaps even for the large "A" that subtends such desire.[108]

For further help in explicating this relationship, Lacan turned to anamorphosis, as exemplified by Hans Holbein's *The Ambassadors*, a painting that was on the cover of the French edition of *The Four Fundamental Concepts of Psycho-analysis*.[109] Normal perspective, he noted, correspond-

106. Ibid., p. 84.

107. Ibid. This passage nuances Ragland-Sullivan's otherwise accurate observation that "existentialist philosophers demonstrated that the *regard* is always 'out there.' Lacan connects it to dreams and shows that it is also always 'in here': the gaze of the Other (A)." *Jacques Lacan and the Philosophy of Psychoanalysis*, p. 44.

108. Stressing the differences between Lacan and Sartre on this issue, Stephen Melville suggestively contends that the gaze is "not that of another person: it is *outside*: outside not only Lacan but outside the fisherman as well, *there*, in the glinting of light off the sardine can. This gaze belongs not to the (small o) other but to the Other— language, world, the fact of a movement of signification beyond human meaning. The opposed points of the double dihedron Lacan puts on the board are thus not two opposed eyes, but represent more nearly an opposition of the eye to itself, of the visual to itself" ("In the Light of the Other," *Whitewalls*, 23 [Fall, 1989], p. 20).

109. It was, David Macey points out (*Lacan in Contexts*, p. 46), a favorite painting of the Surrealists. Significantly, Lyotard would also put it, or rather the distorted skull at the Ambassadors' feet, on the cover of one of his books, *Discours, Figure*, 4th ed. (Paris, 1985), which was in part a critique of Lacan. According to Christine Buci-Glucksmann, Lacan's fascination with anamorphosis is of a piece with his Gongorian rhetoric, both of which suggest his affinity for the Baroque. See her "Une archéologie de l'ombre: Foucault et Lacan," *L'écrit du temps*, 17 (Winter, 1988), p. 34.

ed to the Cartesian subject's geometrical mapping of space, a geometricalization that could be based, as Diderot had noted in his *Letter on the Blind*, on a sightless man's touch. Such a rigid and linear reduction of vision invited comparison, Lacan suggested, with an erect penis, or more precisely, that which appeared as the lack-fulfilling phallus in the mother's Imaginary: "How can we not see here, immanent in the geometral dimension—a partial dimension in the field of the gaze, a dimension that has nothing to do with vision as such—something symbolic of the function of the lack, of the appearance of the phallic ghost?"[110]

In *The Ambassadors*, this phallic gaze, that of the dominant Cartesian perspectivalist scopic regime, was challenged by another, which was expressed by the distorted skull at the bottom of the canvas, a skull whose natural shape could be restored only by an oblique glance from the painting's edge. Such an object, which Lacan compared to such Surrealist images as Dali's soft watches,[111] expressed another kind of desire than that which seeks phallic plenitude. Instead, it suggested the desire of the Symbolic realm in which the subject is decentered, split, and comes to terms with its own incompleteness. "Holbein makes visible for us here something that is simply the subject as annihilated—annihilated in the form, that is, strictly speaking the imaged embodiment of the *minus-phi* [− ø] of castration, which for us, centers the whole organization of the desires through the framework of the fundamental drives."[112]

Rather than an image in the phallic eye of the geometricalized subject, the anamorphic skull thus is to be found in the impersonal, diffuse "gaze as such, in its pulsatile, dazzling and spread out function, as it is in this picture."[113] Or to put it differently, the eye is that of the specular, Cartesian subject desiring specular plenitude and phallic wholeness, and believing it can find it in a mirror image of itself, whereas the gaze is that of

110. Lacan, *The Four Fundamental Concepts of Psycho-analysis*, p. 88.

111. A number of Dali's paintings introduced anamorphic shapes. For a discussion of their impact on Lacan, see Allen S. Weiss, "An Eye for an I: On the Art of Fascination," *SubStance*, 51 (1986), pp. 87–95.

112. Lacan, *The Four Fundamental Concepts of Psycho-analysis*, pp. 88–89.

113. Ibid.

an objective other in a field of pure monstrance. To believe that these two chiasmically crossing dimensions of the scopic field could ever be reconciled harmoniously in something like Merleau-Ponty's *voyure* is to forget the lesson that Lacan had absorbed in Kojève's lecture hall: true reciprocity is only an illusion. There is no way, to put it in the terms of traditional optics, to reconcile *lumen* and *lux*, no way to combine Newton's light with Goethe's color.[114]

In his next seminar, entitled "The Line and the Light," Lacan reformulated and expanded his argument, using triangulated schemas to illustrate the chiasmic intertwining of eye and gaze. The first, that of the eye, signified Cartesian perspectivalist vision, in which the viewer's monocular eye was at the apex and the object at the far wall of the triangle. The image was on another line parallel to that wall, but halfway between it and the eye/apex. The second schema, that of the gaze, put a point of light at the apex, the picture at the far wall, and what Lacan called the screen halfway between. Here the subject is placed not at the apex, but at the midpoint, as if it were an image on a screen in a generalized perceptual field, not a seeing eye. This subject, Lacan contended, "is caught, manipulated, captured in the field of vision."[115] Holbein's anamorphosed skull with its invocation of the nothingness of death expresses this subject trapped in a visual field it cannot master. Indeed, Lacan insisted, "In this matter of the visible, everything is a trap. . . . There is not a single one of the divisions, a single one of the double sides that the function of vision presents, that is not manifested to us as a labyrinth."[116] The labyrinth, that potent figure Bataille and the Surrealists (and later Derrida and Irigaray) used to challenge the putative clarity of a God's-eye view of the world, here reappears as Lacan posits a visual field in which light "may travel a straight line, but . . . is refracted, diffused, it floods, it fills—the eye is a sort of a bowl—it flows over too, it necessitates, around the ocular bowl, a whole series of organs, mechanisms, defenses."[117]

114. See Melville for a discussion of Lacan and Goethe, pp. 26ff.
115. Lacan, *The Four Fundamental Concepts of Psycho-analysis*, p. 92.
116. Ibid., p. 93.

Yet another figure introduced by one of Lacan's friends on *Minotaure*, Roger Caillois, resurfaced in his attempt to clarify the relation between eye and gaze, that of the dihedron, the intersection of two planes. Caillois had used it in his 1935 essay on "Mimétisme et psychasthénie légendaire" to explain animal mimicry, a piece whose impact on Lacan's "mirror stage" has already been mentioned.[118] Lacan used the dihedron to superimpose his two visual triangles in inverted form. The chiasmic interposition of the two planes created a new figure in which the middle sections of both triangles, the image in that of the eye, the screen in that of the gaze, coincided in the form of a divided subject. At its center was an opaque line very different from the transparent window typical of the Albertian subject's view on the world.[119]

To clarify its implications, Lacan moved from the realm of visual schemas to that of narration and offered an anecdote, which he claimed was true. Years ago when he was fishing off Brittany, a friend pointed to a sardine can in the water and said laughingly, *"You see that can? Do you see it? Well, it doesn't see you!"*[120] Ruminating on the lesson his friend had drawn from the floating can, Lacan concluded that it was mistaken, for the can "was looking at me, all the same. It was looking at me at the level of the point of light, the point of light, the point at which everything that looks at me is situated—and I am not speaking metaphorically."[121] Lacan, in other words, felt that he was indeed in the center of a conflictual visual field, at once the eye looking at the can and the screen in an impersonal field of pure monstrance. His subjectivity was thus split between the apex at the end of the triangle of the eye and the line in the middle of the

117. Ibid., p. 94.

118. *Minotaure*, 7 (June, 1935). For discussions of its importance, see Hollier, "Mimesis and Castration, 1937," pp. 3–16, and Rosalind Krauss, "Corpus Delicti," pp. 31–72.

119. The distinction is made by Kaja Silverman, "Fassbinder and Lacan: A Reconsideration of Gaze, Look and Image," *Camera Obscura*, 19 (January, 1989), p. 74.

120. Lacan, *The Four Fundamental Concepts of Psycho-analysis*, p. 95. Italics in original.

121. Ibid.

triangle of the gaze. He was both the viewer of Holbein's painting and the smeared skull in its visual field.

Another variation on this unsublated dialectic was evident in fact in the realm of painting, to which Lacan turned at the end of this seminar and that which followed, entitled "What Is a Picture?" It was by looking at the art of painters like Cézanne, he reminded his audience, that Merleau-Ponty had overthrown the traditional identity of eye and mind. In pictures, something of the gaze is always manifested, he argued, but the spectator is invited by the artist to "lay down his gaze there as one lays down one's weapons. This is the pacifying Apollonian effect of painting. Something is given not so much to the gaze as to the eye, something that involves the abandonment, the *laying down*, of the gaze."[122] There is, however, a certain duplicity in all of this, which Lacan suggested with the concept of the "lure" (*leurre*, which also means enticement, decoy, and bait, and was tied by Lacan to *méconnaissance*). In *trompe l'oeil* painting in particular, the gaze in fact triumphs over the eye. The result is similar to the negative dialectic of lovers described by Sartre: "When in love, I solicit a look, what is profoundly unsatisfying and always missing is that—*You never look at me from the place from which I see you.* Conversely, *what I look at is never what I wish to see....* The relation ... between painter and the spectator is a play of *trompe l'oeil*, whatever one says."[123] The defeat of the mastering eye in *trompe l'oeil* art Lacan dubbed "dompte-regard."

After some cryptic and hasty remarks on icons, the Jewish taboo on images,[124] and the role of painting in communal settings, Lacan concluded by returning to the link between desire and vision, which he called the "appetite of the eye." "Modifying the formula I have of desire as unconscious—*man's desire is the desire of the Other*—I would say," he explained, "that it is a question of a sort of desire *on the part of* the Other, at the end of which is the *showing* (*le donner-à-voir*)."[125] That is, the gaze can

122. Ibid., p. 101.

123. Ibid., p. 103.

124. For more on Lacan's fascination with the Jewish God and his stress on language over images, see MacCannell, *Figuring Lacan*, p. 16.

be thought of as brought about by the Other's desire to show itself, a desire that is matched only by the eye's desire to see. But showing and seeing do not harmoniously complement each other or overcome the split in the subject. The violence of their struggle is revealed in the ubiquitous existence of myths of the evil eye, which Lacan interpreted as showing that "the eye carries with it the fatal function of being in itself endowed—if you will allow me to play on several registers at once—with the power to separate."[126] The Latin word for envy, *invidia*, with its derivation from the verb to see (*videre*), suggests the yearning to overcome this separation. True envy, Lacan claimed, "makes the subject pale before the image of a completeness closed upon itself, before the idea that the *petit a*, the separated *a* from which he is hanging, may be for another the possession that gives satisfaction."[127] Such satisfaction is not only impossible, but the fury unleashed by the apparent attempt to attain it may also have a deadly result. For the evil eye operates as the *fascinum*, "that which has the effect of arresting movement and, literally, of killing life."[128] This power may be metaphorical, but it captures the aggressive potential of vision, a potential to which Lacan was sensitive ever since his earliest studies of the links between paranoia and the mirror stage in the 1930s. Significantly, the transcription of this last seminar on vision ends with a question from Jacques-Alain Miller, who wondered if anything in Lacan's critique of Merleau-Ponty's celebration of a healthy visual ontology had been changed by the publication of *The Visible and the Invisible* with its acknowledgment of the nondialectical chiasmus in sight. "Absolutely nothing," replied the intransigent Lacan.

Although it is impossible to summarize Lacan's complicated dialectic of the eye and the gaze in any simple formula, it is clear that his thinking had moved beyond his early discussion of the mirror stage. First, whereas in the mirror-stage argument, vision was involved in an imaginary identifi-

125. Lacan, *Four Fundamental Concepts of Psycho-analysis*, p. 115.
126. Ibid., p. 115.
127. Ibid., p. 116.
128. Ibid., p. 118.

cation with a gestalt of corporeal wholeness, an identification due to a specular projection of narcissistic sameness, now it was connected as well with desire for the other. As Jacqueline Rose has noted, Lacan understood Freud "in terms of the gradual intrusion of the axis of desire on to the axis of identification, an intrusion which can be measured against the shift from the drives of demand (oral, anal) to those of desire (scopic, invocatory) in which the physical distance of the object reveals the relation between subject and object to be necessarily disjunct."[129] That is, the *objet a* Lacan called the gaze is not a mirror image of the subject; it is chiasmically crossed with the subject's eye. The dyad of specular projection is replaced by a dual and inverted triangulation, even more complicated than the triadic introjection of the father's name associated with the resolution of the Oedipus complex.

Not only have we moved beyond the Imaginary realm of specular doubling into that of the disjunction between desiring subject and its unattainable object, but we are also now on the threshold of explicitly intersubjective relations.[130] That is, vision, as Lacan's evocation of Sartre makes clear, may be understood as a conflictual field in which the looker is always a body to be observed. Even though on one level the impersonal gaze is a function of the split subject's internal dynamics, his desire for the *objet a* as a way to compensate for a lack, on another, it expressed the unsublated dialectic of intersubjective gazes, that dihedron of superimposed visual triangles Lacan had borrowed from Caillois and used to redescribe Kojève's dark version of Hegel.

As such, vision necessarily enters the realm of the Symbolic in which language is paramount.[131] A lack, after all, is precisely that which cannot

129. Rose, *Sexuality in the Field of Vision*, p. 182. For a discussion of the difference between demand and desire in Lacan's vocabulary, see Lemaire, *Jacques Lacan*, pp. 166ff.

130. One might argue that for Lacan some level of intersubjectivity exists in the psyche from the very beginning, but it achieves greater significance with the entry into the Symbolic. Lacan's recognition of the importance of intersubjectivity has earned him an unexpected comparison with Jürgen Habermas, who also tries to get beyond the philosophy of the subject. See Peter Dews, *Logics of Disintegration: Poststructuralist Thought and the Claims of Critical Theory* (London, 1987), pp. 234ff.

be seen; it must exceed the realm of the visual. Indeed, one recent commentator, Joan Copjec, has contended that the two triangles in the dihedron can be understood as counterposing optics and semiotics. As a result, she argues,

> semiotics, not optics, is the science that clarifies for us the structure of the visual domain. Because it alone is capable of lending things sense, the signifier alone makes vision possible. There is and can be no brute vision, no vision totally devoid of sense. Painting, drawing, all forms of picture-making, then, are fundamentally graphic arts. And because signifiers are material, that is, because they are opaque rather than translucent, because they refer to other signifiers rather than directly to a signified, the field of vision is neither clear nor easily traversable. It is instead ambiguous and treacherous, full of traps.[132]

Copjec's claim is made in the service of a critique of French film theory's appropriation of Lacan, which she faults for conflating his mirror stage theory with his later work on the gaze. The legitimacy of that critique will be addressed in a later chapter's discussion of such film theorists as Christian Metz, Jean-Louis Baudry and Jean-Louis Comolli. What is important to note now is that however correctly Lacan's often cryptic work was understood, it was invariably taken as a powerful weapon in the dismantling of ocularcentrism.

Although his office may have had the most recent issues of the French art magazine *l'Oeil* on display,[133] although his lustful visual enjoyment of Giovanni Lorenzo Bernini's statue of Saint Theresa may have aroused

131. According to Juliet Flower MacCannell, Lacan "reduces the drive to its minimal equation in the passion of the signifier to become the signified—of the image to become the concept" (*Figuring Lacan*, pp. 67–68).

132. Joan Copjec, "The Orthopsychic Subject: Film Theory and the Reception of Lacan," *October*, 49 (Summer, 1989), p. 68.

133. So Stuart Schneiderman reported in *Jacques Lacan: The Death of an Intellectual Hero* (Cambridge, Mass., 1983), p. 130.

some feminist ire,[134] Lacan's fundamental suspicion of the gaze was widely appreciated. Even when he resorted to complicated topological examples, such as Klein bottles, Möbius strips, and Borromean knots, to describe the workings of the unconscious, Lacan was rarely read as anything but a critic of ocularcentrism who gave a "paranoid coloration" to vision that produced an iconoclasm "even more radical than Freud's."[135] No better example of this generalization can be provided than the work of the Marxist theoretician Louis Althusser, whose appropriation of Lacan brought him into the mainstream of 1960s French radicalism.

⊙

Lacan's argument about the mirror stage had already begun to have an impact during the heyday of phenomenology and existentialism in

134. A picture of the statue is on the cover of *Séminaire* 20. For a feminist response, see Clément, *The Lives and Legends of Jacques Lacan*, pp. 65ff.

135. For the characterization of paranoia, see Norman Bryson, "The Gaze in the Expanded Field," in *Vision and Visuality*, ed. Hal Foster (Seattle, 1988), p. 104. For the comparison with Freud, see Goux, "Lacan Iconoclast," p. 114. For another example of this reading of Lacan's use of topology, see Juan-David Nasio, "Topologerie," *L'interdit de la représentation*. He argues that rather than a straightforward use of visual images of space, Lacan's topographical devices were attempts to go beyond the Imaginary to provide fantasmatic renderings of the Real. He thus coins the term "topolologerie" to distinguish what Lacan is doing from normal topology, just as the neologism "linguisterie" is sometimes used to set his work apart from normal linguistics.

Significantly, when Lacan discussed his use of these diagrams, he acknowledged that they bore a relationship to Surrealist painting, presumably to that of Magritte, whose visual conundrums and puns he so admired. See his remarks in the discussion following "Of Structure as an Inmixing of an Otherness Prerequisite to Any Subject Whatever," *The Structuralist Controversy: The Languages of Criticism and the Sciences of Man*, eds. Richard Macksey and Eugenio Donato (Baltimore, 1970), p. 197.

Perhaps the one major exception to the rule of reading Lacan as a critic of ocularcentrism can be found in Gilles Deleuze and Félix Guattari's *Anti-Oedipus: Capitalism and Schizophrenia*, trans. Robert Hurley, Mark Seem, and Helen R. Lane (Minneapolis, 1983). They contend that psychoanalysis in any form succumbs to the domination of images and theatricality because of its privileging of the Oedipus Complex. For a defense of Lacan against their reading, see Ragland-Sullivan, *Jacques Lacan and the Philosophy of Psychoanalysis*, p. 272.

France. Not only did Merleau-Ponty draw on it in his discussions of the child's relation with others, so too did Simone de Beauvoir in her pioneering feminist analysis of *The Second Sex*.[136] But it was not really until the widely remarked dethronement of phenomenology by the loosely integrated movement known as Structuralism that Lacan's interrogation of sight reached its widest audience. Although Structuralism was by no means unequivocally hostile to vision—Claude Lévi-Strauss's anthropology can be interpreted as profoundly ambivalent[137]—its general stress on language over perception fit well with the larger trend traced in this book.

Lacan was himself often called a structuralist, reflecting the interest in Saussure he absorbed from Lévi-Strauss in 1946 and his later reading of Jakobson in the 1950s.[138] The designation was later challenged and with good reason, for his fascination with language turned out to be more with a delirious version he called *lalangue* than with the scientific variety known as *la langue*.[139] But in the 1960s, before the distinction was clear, Lacan was able to make common cause with the major exponent of what was then known as Structuralist Marxism, Louis Althusser.[140]

136. Simone de Beauvoir, *Le deuxième sexe* (Paris, 1949), vol. 1, pp. 287–288.

137. Lévi-Strauss's preference for musical over visual analogies is well-known, as is his hostility to the observational norm in science and his cerebral indifference to the perceptual dimension of intepretation. But his work nonetheless often expressed a faith in a synoptic overview well captured in the title of one of his recent collections, *A View from Afar*. Poststructuralist critics have frequently argued that structuralism in general was beholden to a geometricalized formalism that bespoke its adherence to Western ocularcentrism. See, for example, Derrida's remarks in *Writing and Difference*, trans. Alan Bass (Chicago, 1978), pp. 15ff.

138. On Lacan's reading of these linguists, see Françoise Gadet, *Saussure and Contemporary Culture* (London, 1986), p. 153. For a representative analysis of Lacan's structuralist credentials, see Edith Kurzweil, *The Age of Structuralism: Lévi-Strauss to Foucault* (New York, 1980), chap. 6.

139. The difference is spelled out in Jacques-Alain Miller, "Theorie de lalangue (rudiment)," *Ornicar?*, 1 (Paris, 1975).

140. For general accounts of Althusser's career, see Ted Benton, *The Rise and Fall of Structural Marxism: Althusser and His Influence* (London, 1984); Gregory Elliott, *Althusser: The Detour of Theory* (London, 1987); and Robert Paul Resch, *Althusser and the Revival of Marxist Social Theory* (Berkeley, 1992).

The initial contact seems to have come from Althusser, whose interest in psychoanalysis had a personal as well as an intellectual impetus.[141] According to Roudinesco, "In Althusser's eyes, the work of Lacan occupied a strategic position of first importance. Not only did it permit him to criticize the Pavlovian grid through which the Communist movement had denounced Freudianism as a 'bourgeois science,' but it also contested the adaptive ideas of the American school [ego psychology]."[142] Knowing of Lacan's difficulties with the orthodox psychoanalytic hierarchy, Althusser offered him space at the École Normale Supérieure to hold his seminar in January, 1964. As a result, Lacan, whose earliest political sympathies had tended vaguely to the Right,[143] suddenly became a guiding spirit of the French Left. By 1966, Lacan himself was publically endorsing Althusser's version of Marxism against Sartre's.[144]

For his part, Althusser had even earlier made a strong declaration of support for Lacan. In January, 1964, he published a polemical intervention in the French Communist Party journal *La Nouvelle Critique* entitled "Freud and Lacan" that was designed to reverse the Party's long-standing condemnation of psychoanalysis dating from the days of Georges Politzer.[145] His full understanding of Lacan has been questioned,[146] but he clearly grasped the importance of Lacan's critique of ocularcentrism. For

141. Althusser suffered from serious manic-depressive episodes that culminated in the tragic murder of his wife Hélène in 1980. For a discussion, see Roudinesco, vol. 2, pp. 384ff. She notes that he was not personally analyzed by Lacan, as is sometimes rumored.

142. Ibid., p. 386. The anti-American dimension of this alliance seems to have been significant. According to Turkle, "In 1964, Lacan went so far as to blame the Soviet Union's rejection of psychoanalysis on the fact that the Americans had distorted it, a position which made it easier for the Communist Party's rapprochement with psychoanalysis to be via Lacan and his school" (*Psychoanalytic Politics*, p. 92).

143. In his youth he was drawn to the Action Française and Charles Maurras. Other French analysts who were his friends, such as Laforgue and Pichon, were also on the Right. By the late 1930s, however, there were signs of his disenchantment with some of their positions. See Elisabeth Roudinesco, "M. Pichon devant la famille," *Confrontations* (Spring, 1980).

144. See the piece entitled "Lacan juge Sartre," in *Le Figaro littéraire*, December 29, 1966, p. 4.

Althusser, it was the key to a new theory of ideology which radically departed from the traditional Marxist identification of it with a "false consciousness" that would be overcome under communism.[147]

"Freud and Lacan" was one of Althusser's most influential texts, enjoying still greater international renown when it was translated by the *New Left Review* in 1969.[148] It struck a blow not only against the residues of phenomenological and existentialist Marxism but also against the older Western Marxist valorization of Hegel. For with the help of Lacan's concept of the Imaginary, it was now possible to damn Hegel's identitarian philosophy of reflection as an expression of the Mirror Stage writ large.[149] The Hegelian Absolute Subject or its Marxist surrogate, the proletariat as Subject-Object of history, was thus no less a *méconnaissance* than the ego psychologists' centered ego. Thus, Hegel, whose notion of truth other commentators have called resolutely imageless,[150] could be assimilated to the discredited Western tradition of ocularcentric speculation.

Marxism was itself beholden to that tradition insofar as it adopted a

145. It is reprinted in Althusser's *Lenin and Philosophy and Other Essays*, trans. Ben Brewster (New York, 1971), with the corrections he made in February, 1969. Politzer's attack was first made in 1924 and remained Party dogma well into the 1960s. See Turkle, *Psychoanalytic Politics*, pp. 88ff.

146. Macey writes that "for all his insistence on the need to read *Capital*, Althusser shows little sign of having read Lacan in any great detail" (*Lacan in Contexts*, p. 18).

147. Althusser also borrowed other concepts from Lacan, such as the idea of metonymic causality, which he used in *Reading Capital*, written with Étienne Balibar, trans. Ben Brewster (London, 1970), p. 188. He also praised Lacan for providing an "exemplary reading lesson" (p. 16), which was a model for his own "symptomatic" reading of Marx.

148. For an account of its British impact, see Elliott, *Althusser: The Detour of Theory*, pp. 334ff.

149. See, for example, Jameson, "Imaginary and Symbolic in Lacan," p. 391. The difference between Lacan's version of reflexivity and the tradition of self-reflection is explored in Felman, *Jacques Lacan and the Adventure of Insight*, pp. 60–61. A parallel critique of Hegel from a Derridean position can be found in Rodolphe Gasché, *The Tain of the Mirror: Derrida and the Philosophy of Reflection* (Cambridge, Mass., 1986).

150. See, for example, Michael Rosen, *Hegel's Dialectic and Its Criticism* (Cambridge, 1982), chap. 4.

notion of ideology that was counterposed to either a speculative notion of truth—the subject has true knowledge when it understands the objective world as a specular double of itself—or an observational notion of truth—the mind is a mirror in which the external world can be reflected. Marx himself had given some warrant for these visual interpretations of truth in his adoption of the camera obscura metaphor in *The German Ideology*, where he contended, "If in all ideology men and their circumstances appear upside-down as in a camera obscura, this phenomenon arises just as much from their historical life-processes as the inversion of objects on the retina does from their physical life-processes."[151]

The precise implications of this optical metaphor have been widely discussed in Marxist circles,[152] and would continue to provide a lightning rod for controversy in the French antivisual discourse.[153] Althusser's departure from the dominant tradition was two-fold. First, he jettisoned the distinction between an occluded and a clear vision, and identified ideology with a reliance on sight of any kind. Whatever science may have meant for Althusser—and there is no shortage of commentary trying to figure it out[154]—it did not mean a correspondence between a perceptually observed object and its mental representation. Real objects, he insisted, are not to be confused with objects of knowledge. Marx's method of "symptomatic reading," moreover, was not equivalent to correcting the "oversights" of earlier writers, who failed to see through a problem. As he put it in *Reading Capital*, "We must completely reorganize the idea we have of knowledge, we must abandon the mirror myths of immediate vision and reading, and conceive of knowledge as a production."[155]

Second, Althusser pessimistically concluded that there was no real es-

151. Karl Marx and Friedrich Engels, *The German Ideology*, ed. C. J. Arthur (London, 1970), p. 47. For recent considerations of the metaphor, see W. J. T. Mitchell, *Iconology: Image, Text, Ideology* (Chicago, 1986), chap. 6; and Martin Jay, "Ideology and Ocularcentrism: Is There Anything Behind the Mirror's Tain?" in *Force Fields: Between Intellectual History and Cultural Critique* (New York, 1993).

152. For an account of the debates surrounding reflection in Marxism, see Raymond Williams, *Marxism and Literature* (Oxford, 1977), pp. 95–100.

153. See, for example, Sarah Kofman, *Camera obscura: de l'idéologie* (Paris, 1973).

cape from the ideological misrecognitions produced by our inevitable formation by the Imaginary. Arguing that *The German Ideology* was really a pre-Marxist document,[156] he drew on Lacan to claim that ideology is a human constant, no matter how perfect the society. Defining it as "the imaginary relationship of individuals to their real conditions of existence,"[157] he claimed that its constitutive category was that of the subject, which could function under other names such as God or the Platonic soul. The formation of the subject had a linguistic dimension, which Althusser called interpellation or hailing, the "Hey, you there!" that was anticipated by the family name already in place prior to birth. But the basic mechanism of ideological subjecthood was the misrecognition of the mirror stage. "The structure of all ideology, interpellating individuals as subjects in the name of a Unique and Absolute Subject," he claimed, "is *speculary*, i.e., a mirror-structure, and *doubly* speculary: this mirror duplication is constitutive of ideology and ensures its functioning."[158] What made it double was the subjection of the subject not only to his mirror image, but also to a meta-Subject like God, whose imitation was then valorized.

Any philosophy that posited a centered subject was thus ideological. "Hegel is (unknowingly) an admirable 'theoretician' of ideology insofar as he is a 'theoretician' of Universal Recognition who unfortunately ends up in the ideology of Absolute Knowledge. Feuerbach is an astonishing 'theoretician' of the mirror connection, who unfortunately ends up in the ideology of the Human Essence."[159] Only Spinoza, Marx, and Freud, read through Lacan's "intransigent and lucid—and for many years isolated

154. See, for example, Alex Callinicos, *Althusser's Marxism* (London, 1976), where he concludes that, for Althusser, "*There is no general criterion of scientificity*" (p. 59).

155. Althusser and Balibar, *Reading Capital*, p. 24.

156. Althusser, "Ideology and Ideological State Apparatuses," *Lenin and Philosophy*, p. 158.

157. Ibid., p. 162.

158. Ibid., p. 180.

159. Ibid., p. 181.

theoretical effort,"[160] had fully appreciated that the "real subject is de-centered, constituted by a structure which has no 'center' either, except in the imaginary misrecognition of the 'ego', i.e. in the ideological forma-tions in which it 'recognizes' itself."[161]

Although a science based on their writings might avoid the lure of the Imaginary and be able to dissolve the subject in a system of structural relations, for the normal human being, ideology was inevitable. Rather than being an aspect of consciousness and thus amenable to enlighten-ment, ideology, Althusser insisted, "is profoundly *unconscious*, even when it presents itself in reflected form (as in pre-Marxist 'philosophy'). . . . Men 'live' their ideologies as the Cartesian 'saw' or did not see—if he was not looking at it—the moon two hundred paces away: *not at all as a form of consciousness, but as an object of their 'world'*—as their *'world'* itself."[162] Although a few theoreticians and artists—such as Brecht[163]—were able to avoid "living" entirely in the world of the Imaginary, the vast majority of humanity, Althusser implied, were not. Instead, they will remain trapped, like unwitting Cartesians or Hegelians, trapped in a hall of ideological mirrors.

The tension between so gloomy a prognosis and the redemptive im-pulse in Marxism, which Althusser never completely abandoned, may well have contributed to the growing crisis in his work during the 1970s. Whatever its cause or causes, by the end of that decade his earlier system was in a shambles and the school he had founded was in disarray. Apolo-gizing for his "theoreticist tendency," he conceded that by accident "the young pup called structuralism slipped between my legs."[164] Among its residues that he now wanted to exorcise was Lacanian psychoanalysis. In an essay of 1976 entitled "The Discovery of Dr. Freud,"[165] Althusser took back much of the praise of "Lacan and Freud."

160. Althusser, *Reading Capital*, p. 16. Intransigent and even at times isolated Lacan may have been, but lucid he never was!

161. Althusser, "Freud and Lacan," pp. 218–219.

162. Althusser, *For Marx*, trans. Ben Brewster (New York, 1970), p. 233.

163. Ibid., p. 144.

In truth, Althusser had never really probed very deeply into Lacan's work. Never, for example, did he draw on the *Four Fundamental Concepts of Psycho-analysis* for a richer understanding of the dialectic of vision and language. What he did do was provide a bridge between Lacan's critique of ocularcentrism and Marxism, thus lending a certain antivisual pathos to much Marxist thought in France in the 1960s and 1970s. Others like Jean-Joseph Goux would find Lacan's categories of the Imaginary and the Symbolic useful tools in their versions of Marxism.[166]

Even without the influence of Lacan, the French radical discourse of the 1960s drew on the critique of ocularcentrism. At virtually the same moment as the publication of *Écrits*, two powerful works appeared that raised still higher the stakes of the Western privileging of the visual: Michel Foucault's *Les mots et les choses*, translated as *The Order of Things*, and Guy Debord's *The Society of the Spectacle*. In these works and others produced by these theorists and their collaborators in the 1960s and 1970s, the social and political implications of ocularcentrism were probed with new urgency. Now the gaze was tied not only to the psychological lures of the

164. Althusser, *Essays in Self-Criticism*, trans. Grahame Lock (London, 1976), p. 124.

165. Althusser, "La découverte du Dr. Freud," in *Dialogue Franco-Soviétique sur la Psychanalyse*, ed. Léon Chertok (Toulouse, 1984). For discussions of the circumstances of its publication and its significance, see Roudinesco, vol. 2, pp. 645–647, and Elliot, *Althusser: The Detour of Theory*, p. 321.

166. In "Le temple d'Utopie," in *Les iconoclastes*, Goux contended that whereas Feuerbach's critique of religion was based on an Imaginary restitution of alienated wholeness, Marx's was grounded in a Symbolic critique of exchange value as a specular doubling. "To denounce fetishism," he wrote, "is to find behind an imaginary formation a structurally symbolic relation" (p. 38).

Not all Althusserians, to be sure, were as unequivocally critical of visual images. The literary critic Pierre Machery, for example, tried to find some virtues in Lenin's reflectionist notion of literature. See his 1964 essay, "Lenin, Critic of Tolstoy," in *A Theory of Literary Production*, trans. Geoffrey Wall (London, 1978). For Machery, the literary text mirrored not a world of objects, but one of contradictions, whose ideological occlusion it exposed.

It must also be acknowledged that not every French leftist identified the Imaginary with alienation and ideology. A salient counterexample was Cornelius Castoriadis, whose "*L'institution imaginaire de la société* (Paris, 1975) emphasized the creative potential of the Imaginary instead.

Imaginary and the interpersonal dialectics of the Look but also to the social institutions of surveillance and the spectacle. The evil eye emerged from the realm of superstition to become the ruling metaphor of social control and political oppression at its most insidious.

⊙

The story of the role of anti-ocularcentrism in the development of Structuralist Marxism has a fascinating epilogue. In 1992, two years after Althusser's death and twelve since his incarceration in a mental institution for the murder of his wife, Hélène, the French intellectual world was stunned by the unexpected appearance of two remarkable autobiographical texts, *L'avenir dure longtemps*, composed in 1985, and *Les faits*, dated 1976.[167] With ruthless, self-lacerating honesty, Althusser movingly revealed the life of psychological torment that had led to the inexplicable crime. He also lay bare the psychological as well as intellectual sources of his turn from the Catholicism of his youth to Marxism, which he dated in 1947. Admitting that he was really familiar with only a few of Marx's texts—most scandalously, only the first volume of the *Capital* he had instructed his followers how to read correctly—he also described his attraction to Marx in terms that will now seem familiar.

Attributing an early horror for close human contact to his mother's fear of intimacy, Althusser explained that in the place of touch, he had unwittingly privileged the eye.

> The eye is passive, at a distance from its object, it receives its image without having to work, without engaging the body in any process of approach, of contact, of manipulation (dirty hands, dirtiness was a phobia of my mother and it is why I have a sort of complacency for dirtiness). The eye is thus the speculative organ par excellence, of Plato and Aristotle to St. Thomas and beyond.

167. Louis Althusser, *L'avenir dure longtemps suivi de Les faits*, ed. Olivier Corpet and Yann Moulier Boutang (Paris, 1992).

As a child, I would never have "put my hand on the cunt" of any little girl, but I was somewhat of a voyeur and remained one for a long time. . . . I was thus a child of the eye, without contact, without body, because it is by the body that all contact occurs.[168]

Yearning to regain contact with his own body and those of others, Althusser explained how he sought all types of physical exercise and struggled to master his repugnance for female flesh (including its odor). On an intellectual level, the same desire to get beyond the alienating distancing of the eye led first to Spinoza and then to Marxism.

When I "encountered" Marxism, it was by my body that I adhered to it. Not only because it represented the radical critique of all "speculative" illusion, but also because it permitted me to live by the critique of all speculative illusion in a true rapport with naked reality, and gave me the power henceforth to live the physical rapport (the contact, but especially the work on social or other matter) *in thought itself.* In Marxism, in Marxist *theory,* I found a thought that takes into account the primacy of the active and laboring body over passive and speculative thought, and thought that rapport as materialism itself. . . . It was not by accident that I thought, in Marxism, all categories under the primacy of practice.[169]

Whether or not Althusser's embrace of Marxism provided a successful resolution of his psychological problems—*L'avenir dure longtemps* is, after all, the confession of a violent criminal still considered irresponsible for his acts—his choice of explanations for that embrace testifies to the con-

168. Ibid., pp. 205–206. The echoes of the phenomenological valorization of the body against the eye are especially striking in this passage, which shows little trace of the Lacanian critique of wholeness. Elsewhere in his text, Althusser praised Merleau-Ponty, although not Sartre, as a "great philosopher, the last France had before the giant who is Derrida" (p. 170).
169. Ibid., pp. 207–208.

tinuing power of the antiocularcentric discourse well into the 1980s. However idiosyncratic his personal history, however unique the sources of his psychological disintegration, it is striking to find Althusser evincing the same suspicion of the visual that animated so many of his less troubled compatriots. If, as several commentators on the autobiographies noted, one of their implicit models was the remarkable confession of an earlier "insane" murderer edited by Foucault, *I, Pierre Rivière...*,[170] Althusser also seems to have appreciated the dangers, for the "subject" as well as for society, to be found in what Foucault was darkly to call "the empire of the gaze."

170. Michel Foucault, ed., *I, Pierre Rivière, having slaughtered my mother, my sister and my brother...*, trans. Frank Jellinek (New York, 1975).

CHAPTER SEVEN

From the Empire of the Gaze to the Society of the Spectacle: Foucault and Debord

> Our society is not one of spectacle, but of surveillance. . . . We are neither in the amphitheatre, nor on the stage, but in the panoptic machine, invested by its effects of power, which we bring to ourselves since we are part of its mechanism.
>
> MICHEL FOUCAULT[1]

> The entire life of societies in which modern conditions of production reign announces itself as an immense accumulation of *spectacles*. Everything that was directly lived has moved away into a representation.
>
> GUY DEBORD[2]

In February, 1973, the psychoanalyst Jacques-Alain Miller, Lacan's son-in-law and the editor of *Ornicar?*, wrote an essay entitled "Jeremy Bentham's Panoptic Device" which was published two years later.[3] Analyzing Bentham's 1791 treatise on a model prison, Miller noted that its intention was to provide a general guide for a "polyvalent apparatus of surveillance, the universal optical machine of human groupings."[4] Bentham had envisioned a circular arrangement of cells visible to a jailor in a tower in its center, who was himself hidden by a system of shutters from their returning gaze. The result, Miller implied, was the sinister embodiment

---

1. Michel Foucault, *Discipline and Punish: The Birth of the Prison*, trans. Alan Sheridan (New York, 1979), p. 217.

2. Guy Debord, *Society of the Spectacle* (Detroit, 1977), par. 1.

3. Originally entitled "La despotisme de l'utile: la machine panoptique de Jeremy Bentham" and published in *Ornicar?* 3 (May, 1975), pp. 3–36, it appeared in English translation in *October*, 41 (Summer, 1987), where the date of composition is noted. The following quotations are from the English text.

4. Ibid., p. 3.

in stone and metal of the unreciprocal visual dialectic posited in Lacan's theory of the eye and the gaze, the antithesis of Merleau-Ponty's more benign interaction of the visible and the invisible in the flesh of the world.

> This configuration sets up a brutal dissymmetry of visibility. The enclosed space lacks depth; it is spread out and open to a single, solitary central eye. It is bathed in light. Nothing and no one can be hidden inside it—except the gaze itself, the invisible omni-voyeur. Surveillance confiscates the gaze for its own profit, appropriates it, and submits the inmate to it.[5]

Miller's evocation of the Panopticon not only implicitly challenged the phenomenologists' attempt to rescue a healthy dialectic of the visual, but also struck at the older Enlightenment project of linking reason and illumination. "The Panopticon," he wrote, "is the temple of reason, a temple luminous and transparent in every sense: first because there are no shadows and nowhere to hide: it is open to constant surveillance by the invisible eye; but also, because totalitarian mastery of the environment excludes everything irrational: no opacity can withstand logic."[6] Even the jailor is subjected to the controlling gaze of the public, which provides the ultimate moral sanction against deviance from the norm.

In addition to the manipulative force of surveillance, Bentham, so Miller noted, retained as a reserve instrument of control the older practice of analogous punishments, imprinting on the body of the criminal an appropriate sign of his crime. "One of the merits of analogous punishments," according to Miller, "was that the spectacle of its application immediately evoked its cause—thereby giving it immediate legitimacy—and, conversely, that the perpetration of the crime would also bring to mind the eventual punishment for it—intensifying the latter's dissuasive power."[7] Thus, alongside of surveillance, the spectacle of symbolic signifi-

5. Ibid., p. 4.
6. Ibid., pp. 6–7.
7. Ibid., p. 13.

cation could still serve as a potent mechanism of social control in the name of enlightenment.

Miller was not the first to criticize the coercive implications of Bentham's panoptic dream, which had already drawn attention outside of France.[8] Nor was his critique the most influential, that honor going to Michel Foucault's more extensive discussion in *Discipline and Punish*, also published in 1975.[9] But it merits recalling now to reinforce the point made at the end of the previous chapter's discussion of Althusser: the psychological analysis of vision in Lacan could easily be absorbed into a social and political critique in which *voir* was linked with both *savoir* and *pouvoir*. For not only could vision be damned for its role in the construction of an ideological notion of the ego, it could also be deemed complicitous in the complementary apparatuses of surveillance and spectacle so central to the maintenance of disciplinary or repressive power in the modern world.

Among French intellectuals in the 1960s and 1970s, it was Michel Foucault who most explicitly interrogated the gaze of surveillance and Guy Debord and his Situationist International collaborators who explored the vision of the spectacle. Together, they provided a panoply of arguments

8. For an earlier analysis that comes to similar conclusions, see the essay by the American historian Gertrude Himmelfarb, "The Haunted House of Jeremy Bentham," *Ideas in History*, eds. Richard Herr and Harold T. Parker (Durham, N.C., 1965). Miller never cites this piece, nor does Foucault in his account of the Panopticon.

9. Foucault, *Discipline and Punish*, where Miller's essay is not cited. In general, there was little overt exchange between Foucault and the École Freudienne. Lacan himself only rarely referred to Foucault, one exception being the essay "De Rome 53 à Rome 67: La psychanalyse raison d'un échec," *Scilet*, 1 (1968), pp. 42–50. It may, however, be the case that his analysis of the eye and the gaze was in part a critical response to Foucault's account of representation. For an argument to this effect, see Pierre-Gilles Guégen, "Foucault and Lacan on Velázquez: The Status of the Subject of Representation," *Newsletter of the Freudian Field*, 3, 1 and 2 (Spring, Fall, 1989). For his part, Foucault denied that he had "an in-depth experience of [Lacan's] teaching." Foucault, *Remarks on Marx: Conversations with Duccio Trombadori*, trans. R. James Goldstein and James Cascaito (New York, 1991), p. 73. Despite his association with Lacan in the popular press as one of the stars of "structuralism," he seems to have been little influenced by the experience.

against the hegemony of the eye which augmented and extended those already encountered in this narrative and others still to come. With their work, the ocularcentrism of those who praised the "nobility of sight" was not so much rejected as reversed in value. Vision was still the privileged sense, but what that privilege produced in the modern world was damned as almost entirely pernicious. This chapter will enter the territories Foucault called "the unimpeded empire of the gaze"[10] and Debord the "society of the spectacle"[11] to explore the reasons for that judgment.

⊙

After Foucault's death in 1984, the philosopher Gilles Deleuze characterized his friend's work as a dual investigation of articulable statements and fields of "visibilities." Although admitting that Foucault had come increasingly to stress the former, Deleuze insisted that he "continued to be fascinated by what he saw as much as by what he heard or read, and the archaeology he conceived of is an audiovisual archive. . . . Foucault never stopped being a *voyant* at the same time as he marked philosophy with a new style of statement."[12] Michel de Certeau was no less insistent on the visual character, the "optical style," of Foucault's oeuvre: "The works are studded with tables and illustrations. The text is also cadenced by scenes and figures. . . . The entire discourse proceeds in this fashion from vision to vision. The step that marks the rhythm of the discourse's forward march, in which that march finds support and from which it receives its impulse, is a visual moment."[13] For Christine Buci-Glucksmann, Fou-

10. Foucault, *The Birth of the Clinic: An Archaeology of Medical Perception*, trans. A. M. Sheridan (London, 1973), p. 39.

11. Debord, *Society of the Spectacle*. The first French publication was in 1967, but the term was used much earlier. See for, example, Debord's 1957 essay, "Toward a Situationist International," in *Situationist International Anthology*, ed. and trans. Ken Knabb (Berkeley, 1981), p. 25.

12. Gilles Deleuze, *Foucault*, trans. and ed. Sean Hand (Minneapolis, 1988), p. 50.

13. Michel de Certeau, "The Laugh of Michel Foucault," in *Heterologies: Discourse on the Other*, trans. Brian Massumi (Minneapolis, 1986), p. 196.

cault's writings, along with those of Lacan, could be called an "archaeology of the shadow" that recalled the Baroque "madness of vision."[14] Indeed, the centrality of the visual to Foucault's work led a fourth commentator, John Rajchman, to celebrate it as a veritable "art of seeing" and a fifth, Thomas Flynn, to credit it with inaugurating the spatializing logic of postmodernism.[15]

Foucault, like so many other French thinkers in this century, was unquestionably fascinated by visual issues and relatively indifferent to auditory ones.[16] In addition to the frequent tableaux and illustrations alluded to above, his book on Magritte and his unfinished manuscript on Manet testify to his profound involvement with the history of visual representation.[17] So too, his "obsessive" concern for the modern institutionalization of power in spatial terms and stress on the neglected importance of geography in relation to history[18] show a keen awareness of the value of

14. Christine Buci-Glucksmann, "Une archéologie de l'ombre: Foucault et Lacan, *L'Écrit du Temps*, 17 (Winter, 1988), pp. 21–37. The Merleau-Pontyan term "madness of vision" recalls the title of her earlier book, *La folie du voir: De l'esthéthique baroque* (Paris, 1986).

15. John Rajchman, "Foucault's Art of Seeing," *October*, 44 (Spring, 1988); Thomas Flynn, "Foucault and the Eclipse of Vision," in *Modernity and the Hegemony of Vision*, ed. David Michael Levin (Berkeley, 1993).

16. As Pierre Boulez observed, there is scarcely a word about music in any of Foucault's works, although he enjoyed listening to it. See "Quelques souvenirs de Pierre Boulez," *Critique*, 471–472 (August–September, 1986), p. 747. Boulez notes with regret that very few contemporary French intellectuals are seriously interested in musical issues.

17. Foucault, *This Is Not a Pipe*, trans. and ed. James Harkness (Berkeley, 1982); *Le noir et le couleur*, written in Tunisia in 1967, but destroyed. See the reference in "Michel Foucault: A Biographical Chronology," in *Philosophy and Social Criticism*, 12, 2–3 (1987), p. 273. During his years in Uppsala, Sweden in 1955–1956, he organized discussions at the Maison de France of Manet, the Impressionists, and Giacometti. See Jean Piel, "Foucault à Uppsala," *Critique*, 471–472 (August–September, 1986), p. 749.

18. See, for example, "The Question of Geography," in *Power/Knowledge: Selected Interviews and Other Writings 1972–1977*, ed. Colin Gordon, trans. Colin Gordon et al. (New York, 1980), where he admits his "spatial obsessions" (p. 69), and "Space, Knowledge, Power," in *The Foucault Reader*, ed. Paul Rabinow (New York, 1984). See

visual analysis. One recent commentator, Allan Megill, has claimed that in his earlier, more structuralist moments, Foucault was himself intent on portraying a "lucent, Apollonian world"[19] within which ocularcentrism was neutrally accepted, although he abandoned the attempt in his late writings. Yet even Foucault the genealogist would call for a method that "corresponds to the acuity of a glance that distinguishes, separates and disperses . . . the kind of dissociating view that is capable of decomposing itself."[20]

But if Foucault was keenly appreciative of the importance of sight, his work provided ample indications of his wariness about its innocence. Initially, he seems to have been drawn to an understanding of the centrality of vision through an exposure to phenomenology, not only in the Hegelian version promoted by his mentor Jean Hyppolite, but also that associated with Heidegger, Merleau-Ponty and the psychologist Ludwig Binswanger. One of his first published works, an introduction to the French translation of Binswanger's *The Dream and Existence* written in 1954, chastised traditional psychoanalysis, including Lacan, for privileging language over vision in its account of the unconscious.[21]

But the vision that should be incorporated into psychoanalysis, Foucault insisted, had to be understood phenomenologically, taking into account the lived spatial experience that emerged from the body's inter-

---

also his discussion of "heterotopias" in "Of Other Spaces," *Diacritics*, 16 (1986), pp. 22–27. For an appreciation of Foucault's role in stimulating new thinking on geography, see Edward W. Soja, *Postmodern Geographies: The Reassertion of Space in Critical Social Theory* (London, 1989), pp. 16ff. For an analysis of his spatial concerns, see Paul Rabinow, "Ordonnance, Discipline, Regulation: Some Reflections on Urbanism," *Humanities in Society*, 5, 3/4 (Summer/Fall, 1982), pp. 267–278.

19. Allan Megill, *Prophets of Extremity: Nietzsche, Heidegger, Foucault and Derrida* (Berkeley, 1985), p. 218. The inspiration for Megill's characterization comes from Derrida's critique of *Madness and Civilization* in *Writing and Difference*, trans. Alan Bass (Chicago, 1978).

20. Foucault, "Nietzsche, Genealogy, History," in *Language, Counter-memory, Practice: Selected Essays and Interviews*, ed. Donald F. Bouchard (Ithaca, 1977), p. 153.

21. Foucault, "Introduction" to Ludwig Binswanger, *Le rêve et l'existence*, trans. Jacqueline Verdeaux (Paris, 1954), p. 27.

twining with the world. "Authentic" versions of that experience were undermined, he claimed, if vision were reduced to its traditional Cartesian spectatorial role based on the dualism of subject and object. One of Binswanger's patients, Foucault noted in terms that echoed Merleau-Ponty, was disturbed because of her fear of falling into the world and her neurotic hope of living *"une existence de survol."*[22] It was also wrong, he warned, to reduce the imagination revealed in dreams to mere images. Approvingly citing Sartre's strictures against this fallacy,[23] he claimed that dreams transcend their visual content, pointing to an ontological truth that is beyond sense experience.

Although Foucault continued to be wary of "high altitude" thinking and the fetish of pure images, he soon jettisoned many of the phenomenological premises evident in this early work,[24] including the search for subjective authenticity and ontological truth. As Deleuze has noted, although inspired by Heidegger and Merleau-Ponty's notion of the "fold of Being," with its doubling of vision and language, he came to doubt the harmonious intertwining of the two posited by phenomenology: "In Heidegger and Merleau-Ponty, Light opens up a speaking no less than a seeing, as if signification haunted the visible which in turn murmured meaning. This cannot be so in Foucault, for whom the light-Being refers only to visibilities, and language-Being to statements."[25] While he may ultimately have overemphasized his distance from Merleau-Ponty,[26] Fou-

22. Ibid., p. 101.

23. Ibid., p. 107.

24. According to Denis Hollier, even in the introduction to Binswanger, there is evidence of Foucault's interest in nonphenomenological writings on visual themes, most notably Roger Caillois's essay on mimicry, which was also important for Lacan. The result was that already in this work Foucault was putting in place "a labyrinthine series of facing mirrors within which the vital difference begins to wander." Hollier, "The Word of God: 'I am Dead'," *October,* 44 (Spring, 1988), p. 77.

25. Deleuze, *Foucault,* p. 111.

26. See Richard A. Cohen, "Merleau-Ponty, The Flesh and Foucault," *Philosophy Today,* 28, 4, 4 (Winter, 1984), for a critique of Foucault's exaggerated rejection of phenomenology.

cault came to condemn the phenomenology of perception as a final variant of the very "transcendental narcissism" it claimed to overcome.[27]

Although Foucault's renunciation of phenomenology has often been assimilated to the French structuralist turn in the 1960s, with its debt to Saussure, his disillusionment was actually rooted much earlier in soils of very different composition. One was the French tradition of the philosophy of science associated with Jean Cavaillès, Gaston Bachelard, and Georges Canguilhem;[28] the other that of modernist, post-Nietzschean literary experimentation exemplified by Bataille, Blanchot, Brisset, and Roussel. From these two sources far more than from linguistics, Foucault learned to distrust the phenomenological search for an incarnated ontology of sight.

As early as his introduction to Binswanger, Foucault showed an interest in Bachelard's analysis of imagination.[29] Later, as many commentators have noted, he would draw on the French philosophy of science's insistence on ruptures, discontinuities, dispersions, and the importance of error in the history of knowledge.[30] But it was its radically antiempiricist separation of the epistemological development of science from any

27. Foucault, *The Archaeology of Knowledge and the Discourse of Language*, trans. A. M. Sheridan (New York, 1972), p. 203. Merleau-Ponty, it will be recalled, had written of the "fundamental narcissism of all vision" in *The Visible and the Invisible*, ed. Claude Lefort, trans. Alphonso Lingis (Evanston, Ill., 1968), p. 139, but he did not consider it transcendental.

28. In his 1978 introduction to Canguilhem's *The Normal and the Pathological*, trans. Carolyn R. Fawcett and Robert S. Cohen (New York, 1989), Foucault would write of the division in French thought between "a philosophy of experience, of sense and of subject and a philosophy of knowledge, of rationality and the concept. On the one hand, one network is that of Sartre and Merleau-Ponty; and then another is that of Cavaillès, Bachelard and Canguilhem" (p. 8). The latter, he contended, was more influential in the crisis of the 1960s and its aftermath.

29. Foucault, Introduction to Binswanger, p. 116. He refers to Bachelard's *L'air et les songes*, which was one of a series of remarkable texts that investigated the imagination and poetry rather than the history of science. One of the most important of these was *The Poetics of Space*, trans. Maria Jolas (Boston, 1964), where Bachelard insisted that a modern metaphysics had to be discursive: "It should beware of the privileges of evidence that are the property of geometrical intuition. Sight says too many things at the same time. Being does not see itself. Perhaps it listens to itself" (pp. 214–215).

ground in the perceptual observation of the natural world that most influenced Foucault's critique of the hegemony of sight. For if the history of science could be treated as a series of conceptual constructs—"problematics" or "veridical discourses" in Bachelard's vocabulary—with no real verification by sense data, then the role of the transcendental, observing eye of Baconian science was nugatory. But so too was that of the perspectival eye embedded in the flesh of the world in Merleau-Ponty's sense of the term.

One of the major implications of the history of science tradition was, in fact, the retreat from ontology back into epistemology, but epistemology shorn of any reflective or speculative moment linking thoughts in the mind with their putative objects in the "real world." Scientific "evidence," as understood by Bachelard, Canguilhem, and later Foucault, would no longer be connected innocently to its root in *videre*, the Latin verb "to see." For what we see is mediated by the cultural construction of our apparently natural perception. As Rajchman has noted, Foucault often wrote ironically of "self-evidence" to emphasize the artifice in our visual experience; what was self-evident, taken for granted as natural, was precisely what had to be called into question.[31]

In 1957, Canguilhem gave a course at the Sorbonne on the role of vision as the model of Western cognition.[32] Although Foucault was teaching in Uppsala, Sweden at the time, it is likely that he soon came to know

30. See, for example, Charles C. Lemert and Garth Gillan, *Michel Foucault: Social Theory and Transgression* (New York, 1982), pp. 14ff.; and J. G. Merquior, *Foucault* (London, 1985), p. 39. For an Althusserian reading of the relationship, see Dominique Lecourt, *Marxism and Epistemology: Bachelard, Canguilhem, Foucault*, trans. Ben Brewster (London, 1975). Another account can be found in Mary Tiles, "Epistemological History: The Legacy of Bachelard and Canguilhem," in *Contemporary French Philosophy*, ed. A. Phillips Griffiths (Cambridge, 1987). It should be noted that Foucault was never as beholden to the idea of an epistemological break as was Althusser. See his exchange with Jacques-Alain Miller in the interview, "The Confession of the Flesh," in *Power/Knowledge: Selected Interviews and Other Writings, 1972–1977*, ed. Colin Gordon (New York, 1980), p. 211.

31. Rajchman, "Foucault's Art of Seeing," pp. 93ff.

32. Sarah Kofman mentions this course in *Camera obscura: de l'idéologie* (Paris, 1987), p. 17.

of its contents. For it was at this time that he began the work on the history of madness in the "classical" Age of Reason, which was to be officially sponsored for his *doctorat d'état* by Canguilhem in 1961.[33] *Madness and Civilization*—or to give it its original French title, *Folie et déraison. Histoire de la folie à l'âge classique*[34]—showed the extent of Foucault's appreciation of the role of vision or, more precisely, specific visual regimes, in constituting cultural categories. It demonstrated no less vividly his resistance to the totalizing claims of an Enlightenment that had elevated its ocularcentric notion of Reason to a universal truth.[35]

The modern category of insanity, Foucault contended, was predicated on the dissolution of the medieval and Renaissance unity of word and image, which liberated a multitude of images of madness and deprived them of any eschatological significance. As a result, madness became a pure spectacle, a theater of unreason: "During the classical period, madness was shown, but on the other side of bars; if present, it was at a distance, under the eyes of reason that no longer felt any relation to it and that would not compromise itself by too close a resemblance. Madness had become a thing to look at."[36] For the "classical" mind, the essence of insanity was either blindness, a term referring "to the night of quasi-sleep which surrounds the images of madness, giving them, in their solitude, an

33. Following an abortive first effort at the University of Uppsala, Foucault took the manuscript to Hyppolite, who recognized that it could not be accepted as a dissertation in philosophy. He then sent Foucault to Canguilhem, who enthusiastically endorsed it in the history of science. See Alan Sheridan, *Foucault: The Will to Truth* (London, 1980), p. 6.

34. The original French work was published in Paris in 1961. The English translation by Richard Howard (New York, 1965) was made of the abridged edition, which appeared in 1964.

35. Interestingly, when Foucault returned to the question of the Enlightenment in the late 1970s, he noted that the Enlightenment, or at least Kant, had at times itself understood the historical specificity of its philosophizing. See his "What Is Enlightenment?" in *The Foucault Reader*, ed. Paul Rabinow (New York, 1984), p. 38. In his introduction to Canguilhem, he contended that the French philosophy of science, like the Frankfurt School's Critical Theory, was true to this self-critical aspect of the dialectic of Enlightenment (pp. 10–12). In his earlier work, however, the Age of Reason was not treated in as differentiated a way.

invisible sovereignty,"[37] or dazzlement, which means that "the madman sees the daylight, the same daylight as the man of reason (both live in the same brightness); but seeing this same daylight, and nothing but this daylight, he sees it as void, as night, as nothing."[38]

The concept of illuminating reason opposed to blind or dazzled madness was most explicit in Descartes's philosophy. Although distrusting the evidence of the actual senses, Cartesianism nonetheless betrayed an ocular bias that worked to exclude the insane.

> Descartes closes his eyes and plugs up his ears the better to see the true brightness of essential daylight; thus he is secured against the dazzlement of the madman who, opening his eyes, sees only the night, and not seeing at all, believes he sees when he imagines. . . . Unreason is in the same relation to reason as dazzlement to the brightness of daylight itself. And this is not a metaphor. We are at the center of the great cosmology which animates all classical culture.[39]

There was, as well, an institutional expression of the visual definition of insanity in the birth of the asylum, where "madness no longer exists except as *seen*. . . . The science of mental disease, as it would develop in the asylum, would always be only of the order of observation and classification. It would not be a dialogue."[40] For the leading psychiatrist of the postclassical era, the reformer Philippe Pinel, the patient was no longer merely the object of another's scrutiny, but even more a victim of ocular control. For Pinel turned the patient into a self-reflective mirror so that

36. Foucault, *Madness and Civilization*, p. 70. By "the classical period," Foucault seems to have meant the years roughly from Descartes to the end of the Enlightenment. Identifying them with classicism shows how central French history was for his general analysis.

37. Ibid., p. 106.

38. Ibid., p. 108.

39. Ibid., pp. 108–109.

40. Ibid., p. 250.

"madness would see itself, would be seen by itself—pure spectacle and absolute subject."[41] And even though Freud introduced a linguistic dimension into his psychoanalysis, he never abandoned entirely the ocular bias of the psychiatric tradition. "It would be fairer to say," Foucault contended, "that psychoanalysis doubled the absolute observation of the watcher with the endless monologue of the person watched—thus preserving the old asylum structure of non-reciprocal observation but balancing it, in a non-symmetrical reciprocity, by the new structure of language without response."[42] In fact, only in the nonpsychiatric discourse of artists such as de Sade, Goya, and Artaud were the marginalized claims of darkness and the night allowed to reassert themselves in the modern world, thus providing a prototype for the recovery of "unreason" in art, the reverse side of madness.

The Birth of the Clinic, published in 1963, has been called an "extended postscript"[43] to *Madness and Civilization*, which is an especially apt description if its concentration on the complicity of visual domination with the rise of modern medicine is acknowledged. In this "archéologie du regard médical," as it was subtitled, Foucault drew on all of the negative connotations surrounding "le regard" since Sartre's discussion of it in *Being and Nothingness*, if not earlier.[44] Although Foucault later came to regret his choice of words, because he felt "the gaze" connoted a unified subject rather than the "enunciative modalities" that manifest its dispersion,[45] his analysis was grounded in the contention that the medical innovations of the classical age betokened an intensified faith in visual evidence.

According to Foucault, medical experimentation in the clinic came to be identified with the "careful gaze" in which the "eye becomes the de-

41. Ibid., p. 262.

42. Ibid., pp. 250–251.

43. Sheridan, *Michel Foucault*, p. 37.

44. Foucault's generally critical relation to Sartre has been explored by Mark Poster. See his *Foucault, Marxism and History: Mode of Production versus Mode of Information* (Cambridge, 1984), chap. 1. The English translation of the subtitle misleadingly renders *regard* as "perception" rather than "gaze" or "look."

positary and source of clarity; it has the power to bring a truth to light that it receives only to the extent that it has brought it to light; as it opens, the eye first opens the truth: a flexion that marks the transition from the world of classical clarity—from the 'enlightenment'—to the nineteenth century."[46] The new medical gaze differed from the Cartesian privileging of internal vision at the cost of the actual senses, and rejected its belief in a transcendent, ideal Spectator. Instead, it emphasized the totality of observers, whose "sovereign power of the empirical gaze"[47] played over the solid and opaque surfaces of the body. "No light could now dissolve them in ideal truths; but the gaze directed upon them would, in turn, awaken them and make them stand out against a background of objectivity. The gaze is no longer reductive, it is, rather, that which establishes the individual in his irreducible quality."[48]

But what this individualizing gaze "sees" is not, in fact, a given, objective reality open to an innocent eye, like that of the naive child so highly valued by the Enlightenment and the Romantics alike.[49] Rather, it is an epistemic field, constructed as much linguistically as visually. The constitutive role of language, however, was occluded by the assumption that language and vision were one, "the great myth of a pure Gaze that would

45. Foucault, *The Archaeology of Knowledge*, trans. A. M. Sheridan Smith (London, 1972), p. 54. Responding to this self-critique, Deleuze writes, "Foucault believes more and more that his earlier books do not show the primacy of the systems of the statement over the different ways of seeing or perceiving. This is his reaction against phenomenology. But for him, the primacy of statements will never impede the historical irreducibility of the visible—quite the contrary, in fact" (*Foucault*, p. 49).

46. Foucault, *The Birth of the Clinic*, p. xiii.

47. Ibid.

48. Ibid., p. xiv.

49. The cult of the child, Foucault noted, was linked with the privileging of the eye: "What allows man to resume contact with childhood and to rediscover the permanent birth of truth is this bright, distant, open naivety of the gaze. Hence the two great mythical experiences on which the philosophy of the eighteenth century had wished to base its beginning: the foreign spectactor and the man born blind restored to light [the Molyneux problem]. But Pestalozzi and the *Bildungsromane* also belong to the great theme of the Childhood-Gaze. The discourse of the world passes through open eyes, eyes open at every instant as for the first time" (p. 65).

be pure Language: a speaking eye."[50] The result, according to Foucault, was no more or less close to the "truth" than the epistemic regime it had replaced. "In its sovereign exercise, the gaze took up once again the structures of visibility that it had itself deposited in its field of perception."[51]

Although an initial eighteenth-century focus on visible surfaces and symptoms gave way in what Foucault called "the age of Bichat"[52] to a more penetrating gaze into the internal organic landscape through the dissection of corpses, the search was still for an "invisible visibility."[53] The unexpected result of the ever more curious visual penetration of the body, Foucault suggested, was a focus not on the vitality of the patient, but rather on his or her mortality:

> That which hides and envelops, the curtain of night over truth, is, paradoxically, life; and death, on the contrary, opens up to the light of day the black coffer of the body: obscure life, limpid death, the oldest imaginary values of the Western world are crossed here in a strange misconstruction that is the very meaning of pathological anatomy. . . . Nineteenth-century medicine was haunted by that absolute eye that cadaverizes life and rediscovers in the corpse the frail, broken nervure of life.[54]

What made this development in the seemingly limited field of medical experimentation so fateful for Foucault was its function as a model for future investigations in all of the "sciences of man." "It will no doubt remain a decisive fact about our culture," he grimly concluded, "that its

50. Ibid., p. 114.

51. Ibid., p. 117.

52. Marie-François-Xavier Bichat was the leader of a new generation of physicians who came to dominate French medicine around 1800. See the discussion in John E. Lesch, *Science and Medicine: The Emergence of Experimental Physiology, 1790–1855* (Cambridge, Mass., 1984), chap. 3.

53. Foucault, *The Birth of the Clinic*, p. 165.

54. Ibid., p. 166.

first scientific discourse concerning the individual had to pass through this stage of death."[55] Just as psychology was born of the visually constructed notion of the Insane, so too the modern science of the individual emerged from the visual penetration of the dead body. And because the importance of perception, sight in particular, in this cadaverization of life was so great, it would be impossible, Foucault added, to turn to it for an antidote to positivist reification, as the phenomenologists had naively hoped. In a passage covertly directed against Merleau-Ponty, he wrote,

> When one carries out a vertical investigation of this positivism, one sees the emergence of a whole series of figures—hidden by it, but also indispensible to its birth—that will be released later, and, paradoxically, used against it. In particular, that with which phenomenology was to oppose to it so tenaciously was already present in its underlying structures: the original powers of the perceived and its correlation with language in the original form of experience.[56]

If the history of modern scientific experimentation thus showed Foucault that the privileging of vision and the suppression of the linguistic led to a problematic epistemology whose inadequacies phenomenology could not remedy, perhaps modernist literary experimentation might provide a viable alternative. The complicated interlacing of language and vision was, in fact, a central theme in the work of Raymond Roussel, the writer to whom Foucault devoted a very different kind of study at the

55. Ibid., p. 197. The relation between vision and death was a theme that preoccupied other French thinkers admired by Foucault, such as Maurice Blanchot. See, for example, his "The Two Versions of the Imaginary," in *The Space of Literature*, trans. Ann Smock (Lincoln, Nebr., 1982). Here Blanchot suggests similarities between images and cadavers as resemblances at one remove from their original objects. Blanchot, to be sure, did not privilege originality and the immediacy of life over the ambiguous doubling and distancing of images or death. Nor, in fact, did Foucault. The main difference between them seems to be that Blanchot's meditations on the theme lack the historical specificity of Foucault's.

56. Foucault, *The Birth of the Clinic*, p. 199.

same time that he explored the birth of the clinic.[57] Often neglected because of its seeming irrelevance to Foucault's more central concerns,[58] *Death and the Labyrinth*—to give the book its English title—demonstrates the complexity of his fascination with visual issues.

That he thought them fundamental to Roussel's work is demonstrated by his publishing a short piece specifically on saying and seeing in Roussel a year before the book's appearance.[59] In the longer study, he expanded his analysis to cover the entire oeuvre of a writer whose experimental prose and troubled life—long depressed and unheralded as a writer, he committed suicide in 1933 at the age of sixty-six—had intrigued French intellectuals from the Surrealists to Robbe-Grillet.[60] Roussel was most celebrated for his "method" (*procédé*) of beginning a novel with a sentence that was

57. Foucault, *Raymond Roussel* (Paris, 1963); an English translation appeared as *Death and the Labyrinth: The World of Raymond Roussel*, trans. Charles Ruas (New York, 1986). The following quotations are from the original text. According to Allan Stoekl, it remains "the most thorough commentary on this writer's work." See Stoekl, *Politics, Writing, Mutilation: The Cases of Bataille, Blanchot, Roussel, Leiris, and Ponge* (Minneapolis, 1985), p. 37. In 1970, Foucault also published a tribute to Jean-Pierre Brisset, whose elaborate experiments with language have often been compared with Roussel's. See Foucault, "Sept propos sur le 7e ange," preface to Brisset, *La grammaire logique* (Paris, 1970). Significantly, Roussel and Brisset's "delirium of the imagination" was also much admired by Marcel Duchamp, who attributed the inspiration for his "Large Glass" to the former. See his 1946 interview, "Painting . . . at the service of the mind," reprinted in *Theories of Modern Art: A Source Book by Artists and Critics*, ed. Herschel B. Chipp (Berkeley, 1975), pp. 394–395.

58. A recent exception is Deleuze's book on Foucault, in which the importance of *Raymond Roussel* is understood. Another is Hollier's "The Word of God: 'I am Dead'," where he remarks that it should be understood as the twin of *The Birth of the Clinic* (p. 83).

59. Foucault, "Dire et voir chez Raymond Roussel," *Lettre ouverte*, 4 (Summer, 1962), pp. 38–51; with some changes, it served as the opening chapter in the book.

60. There are many positive references to Roussel scattered throughout Surrealist writings, e.g., in André Breton's texts collected as *What Is Surrealism?: Selected Writings*, ed. Franklin Rosemont (London, 1978). For Robbe-Grillet's appreciation, see his "Enigma and Transparency in Raymond Roussel," in *For a New Novel: Essays on Fiction*, trans. Richard Howard (New York, 1965). Although this essay was actually a review of Foucault's book, written for *Critique*, 199 (December, 1963), Robbe-Grillet oddly never mentions his name.

phonetically repeated at its end, with only one element changed to make the meaning of the two sentences utterly different.[61] His deliberate disdain for the communicative, representational, or referential functions of language made Roussel an obvious candidate for praise on the part of thinkers who wanted to privilege complete linguistic self-referentiality or its polysemic, catachrestic undecidability.[62]

But significantly for Foucault, Roussel had also revealed a preoccupation with vision, expressed even in the titles of certain of his works, such as *La vue* and *La poussière de soleil*. After reading Foucault's text, Robbe-Grillet was to note that "*sight*, the privileged sense in Roussel, rapidly achieves an obsessive acuity, tending to infinity."[63] But if vision were present in his texts, it was introduced as a further impediment to meaning, not as a way to compensate for the meaninglessness of the words. Unlike the Surrealists, who were bent on seeking a hidden significance beneath the surface of Roussel's mysterious prose, Foucault insisted that his work "systematically imposes an unformed, divergent, centrifugal uneasiness, oriented not towards the most reticent of secrets, but towards the redoubling and transmutation of the most visible forms."[64] It was thus like an endless labyrinth in which no thread led to an "outside" of clarity and illumination, a verbal equivalent of Bataille's *informe*.

In places, Foucault seemed to appropriate Merleau-Ponty's terms in describing the "interlacing" of the visible and the invisible in "exactly the same tissue, the same indissoluble substance,"[65] or in claiming *La vue* presented a universe without perspective or, more precisely, one "combining

---

61. Roussel revealed his method in a work intended to be published posthumously called *Comment j'ai écrit certains de mes livres* (Paris, 1963).

62. According to Hayden White, Foucault was among those who admired Roussel for his foregrounding catachresis. See his "Michel Foucault," in *Structuralism and Since: From Lévi-Strauss to Derrida*, ed. John Sturrock (Oxford, 1979), pp. 87ff. For another analysis that deals with Foucault's admiration for the similar linguistic *délire* of Jean-Pierre Brisset, see Jean-Jacques Lecercle, *Philosophy Through the Looking-Glass: Language, Nonsense, Desire* (London, 1985), chap. 1.

63. Robbe-Grillet, "Enigmas and Transparency in Raymond Roussel," p. 86.

64. Foucault, *Raymond Roussel*, pp. 19–20.

65. Ibid., p. 132.

the vertical point of view (which permits everything to be embraced as in a circle) and the horizontal point of view (which places the eye at ground level and gives to sight only the first dimension) so well that everything is seen in perspective and yet each thing is envisaged in its complete context."[66] Deleuze, in fact, claimed that Foucault found in Roussel a practical embodiment of the phenomenological belief in the fold of vision: "an ontological Visibility, forever twisting itself into a 'self-seeing' entity, on to a different dimension from that of the gaze or its objects."[67]

But what prevented Roussel from wholeheartedly embracing Merleau-Ponty's ontology, according to Foucault, was his resolute lack of faith in the meaningfulness of the world, a world that contained only "images visibly invisible, perceptible but not decipherable, given in a lightning flash and without possible reading, present in a radiance that repelled the gaze."[68] Although Foucault noted a shift between the early and late Roussel—the works up to *La vue* were illuminated by a dazzling, homogeneous light, the light of a sun too bright to permit any nuanced shadows, whereas everything written after, most notably *Nouvelles impressions de l'Afrique*, was cloaked in the darkness of a "closed-in sun" (*soleil enfermé*)—the implication was the same: the visual in Roussel provided only "a blank lens" (*lentile vide*) incapable of focusing on a clear and distinct world.[69] Genuine transparency, in the sense of a medium that completely dissolved to reveal an unequivocal truth or unambivalent meaning, was thus denied to both language and perception. While the modern discourse of science sought to efface language in favor of the empirical gaze, thus fostering a mistaken belief in the veracity of observation, modernist literature exemplified by Roussel restored the unsublatable dialectic of saying and seeing in which neither overcame the "muteness of objects."[70]

66. Ibid., p. 138.

67. Deleuze, *Foucault*, p. 111.

68. Foucault, *Raymond Roussel*, p. 75.

69. "*Le soleil enfermé*" is the title of chap. 8 of the book; "*La lentille vide*" is that of chap. 7.

70. Foucault, *Raymond Roussel*, p. 154.

It was, in fact, Foucault's constant awareness of the visually opaque dimension of language itself, which he called its rebuslike character,[71] that makes it problematic to characterize him primarily as a structuralist, even of a heterodox kind.[72] Whatever doubts he may have had about the phenomenological residues in his positing of a medical gaze, however much he may have wanted to undercut the humanist fiction of a constitutive subject, Foucault never sought to put a *langue*-like diacritical structure in their place. There was for him no surface enigma to be decoded by finding a pattern beneath, no spatial coherence to be mapped out in two-dimensional terms.

Roussel was not the only debunker of this dream to whom Foucault was drawn; the Belgian Surrealist painter René Magritte was another. In an essay written in 1968 and then expanded into a little book five years later, Foucault explored a more explicitly visual version of the interaction he had discerned in Roussel.[73] Describing Magritte's canvases as the opposite of *trompe l'oeil* because of their undermining of the mimetic conventions of realistic painting, he also referred to them as "unraveled

71. Ibid. A similar stress on the rebus appeared in Jean-François Lyotard's *Discours/figure* (Paris, 1971), pp. 295ff.

72. Perhaps because he does not treat *Raymond Roussel*, Allan Megill is able to claim in chap. 5 of *Prophets of Extremity* that the spatial preoccupations of the early Foucault, most obvious in *The Order of Things*, allow him to be justly called a structuralist *malgré lui* in the special sense of the term Megill derives from Derrida. He cites, for example, Foucault's statement about "the table upon which . . . language has intersected space" in the preface to that book (p. xviii), but he neglects to note that Foucault begins his sentence with a reference to Roussel and his catachrestic use of the "table" as an imaginary space where Lautréamont's famous sewing machine and umbrella meet. It is not so much, in other words, a question of the homology between spatial form and linguistic structure as the tension between them. As Foucault says in *Raymond Roussel*, "This discourse forms a tissue where the texture of the verbal is already crossed with the chain of the visible" (p. 148).

73. Foucault, *This Is Not a Pipe*. For a useful discussion, see Guido Almansi, "Foucault and Magritte," *History of European Ideas*, 3 (1982), pp. 305–309. In a letter to Foucault of June 4, 1966, appended to the book, Magritte wrote, "I am pleased that you recognize a resemblance between Roussel and whatever is worthwhile in my own thoughts. What he imagines evokes nothing imaginary, it evokes the reality of the world that experience and reason treat in a confused manner" (p. 58).

calligrams" because they refused to close the gap between image and word. In the terms he had introduced in *The Order of Things*, written between the Roussel and Magritte studies, the Surrealist had discarded art's claim to provide representative "resemblances" of the external world in favor of repetitive "similitudes" that circulate a series of visual and linguistic signs without any external referent.[74] Whereas resemblances always affirmatively assert the irreducible sameness of image and object based on the original status of the latter, similitude, Foucault argued, "multiplies different affirmations, which dance together, tilting and tumbling over one another."[75] The orders of the visible and sayable, most explicitly at odds in the similitudinous discordance between Magritte's images and their mysterious titles, thus demonstrate a "non-relation."[76]

Foucault's celebration of the heterogeneous interference between the discursive and figural in Roussel and Magritte was no less evident in his contribution to *Critique*'s 1963 homage to its recently deceased founder.[77] Noting the "obstinate prestige to the Eye . . . as a figure of inner experience"[78] accorded by Bataille, he stressed the difference between vision in a

74. Although the terms are the same in *The Order of Things* and *This Is Not a Pipe*, the meaning has shifted somewhat. In the former, "resemblances" and "similitudes" are used as virtual synonyms, denoting the allegedly inherent relationship between a signifier and a signified. As such, they are contrasted with "representations" in which the arbitrary nature of that link is stressed. In the book on Magritte, however, Foucault writes, "Resemblance serves representation, which rules over it; similitude serves repetition, which ranges across it. Resemblance predicates itself upon a model it must return to and reveal; similitude circulates the simulacrum as an indefinite and reversible relation of the similar to the similar" (p. 44). Ironically, in a letter of May 23, 1966, appended at the end of the book (p. 57), Magritte himself chastised Foucault for distinguishing between resemblances and similitudes, claiming that only thought resembles objects in the world, whereas things either do or do not have similitude with one another. For a suggestive attempt to unravel their relationship, see Silvano Levy, "Foucault on Magritte and Resemblance," *The Modern Language Review*, 85, 1 (January, 1990).

75. Foucault, *This Is Not a Pipe*, p. 46.

76. Ibid., p. 36. Deleuze (p. 140) notes a certain parallel here with Blanchot's "Speaking Is Not Saying" in *L'entretien infini* (Paris, 1969).

77. The English translation appeared as "A Preface to Transgression," in *Language, Counter-Memory, Practice*.

Cartesian philosophy of reflection or a science of observation, on the one hand, and Bataille's transgressive vision of *dépense* on the other. Whereas the "former sought pure transparency and truth,"

> the latter reverses this entire direction: sight, crossing the globular limit of the eye, constitutes the eye in its instantaneous being; sight carries it away in this luminous stream (an outpouring foundation, streaming tears, and, shortly, blood), hurls the eye outside of itself, conducts it to the limit where it bursts out in the immediately extinguished flash of its being. Only a small white ball, veined with blood, is left behind, only an exorbitated eye to which all sight is now denied. . . . In the distance created by this violence and uprooting, the eye is seen absolutely, but denied any possibility of sight; the philosophical subject has been dispossessed and pursued to its limit.[79]

So too has the phenomenological subject, who sought meaning in lived experience and the imbrication of the eye in the flesh of the world. Instead, as Hollier has pointed out,[80] the living eye for Bataille and Foucault is negated in favor of an anonymous visual field ironically seen by no one.

According to Foucault, moreover, the upturned, unseeing eye in Bataille also marks the limit of language's ability to signify, "the moment when language, arriving at its confines, overleaps itself, explodes and radically challenges itself in laughter, tears, the overturned eyes of ecstasy, the mute and exorbitated horror of sacrifice."[81] It thus suggests a link between human finitude, language's limits, which cannot be dialectically overcome, and the death of God, "a sun that rotates and the great eyelid that closes upon the world."[82]

78. Ibid., p. 44.
79. Ibid., pp. 45–46.
80. Hollier, "The Word of God: 'I am Dead'," p. 84.
81. Foucault, "A Preface to Transgression," p. 48.
82. Ibid.

The eclipse of the solar divinity was linked for Foucault, as it had been for Bataille, with the decline of his secular analogue, the humanist concept of Man. Hostility to traditional notions of visual primacy and the critique of humanism were intricately linked in the work that most vividly established Foucault's credentials as an antihumanist, *Les mots et les choses* of 1966, translated as *The Order of Things*.[83] Significantly, the work begins with one of Foucault's most celebrated visual tableaux, his description of Velázquez's *Las Meninas*, and ends with a no less frequently cited visual metaphor of Man's face etched in the sand being erased by the waves at the edge of the sea.

Rather than focusing on these now widely discussed framing moments in the text—there is a small cottage industry devoted just to Foucault on Diego Velázquez[84]—I want to explore instead the arguments in between insofar as they bear on the question of vision. Whether or not the spatial preoccupations of the book betokened an affinity for Apollonian structuralism—as Megill, following Derrida has claimed—or merely reflected Foucault's subject matter—as he himself later argued[85]—*The Order of Things* does not seem quite as obsessively fixed on *le regard* as his earlier work. Or rather, it seems so only in Foucault's account of the Classical Age. As in *Madness and Civilization*, he describes the onset of that period in terms of the breakdown of an assumed unity of word and image before the end of the sixteenth century. In a culture based on semantic resem-

83. Foucault, *The Order of Things: An Archaeology of the Human Sciences* (New York, 1970).

84. See, for example, John R. Searle, "*Las Meninas* and the Paradoxes of Pictorial Representation," *Critical Inquiry*, 6 (Spring, 1980), pp. 477–488; Joel Snyder and Ted Cohen, "Reflections on *Las Meninas*: Paradox Lost," *Critical Inquiry*, 7 (1981), pp. 429–447; Svetlana Alpers, "Interpretation Without Representation, or, the Viewing of *Las Meninas*," *Representations*, 1 (February, 1983), pp. 31–42; Claude Gandelman, "Foucault as Art Historian," *Hebrew University Studies in Literature and the Arts*, 13, 2 (Autumn, 1985), pp. 266–280; Hubert L. Dreyfus and Paul Rabinow, *Michel Foucault: Beyond Structuralism and Hermeneutics* (Chicago, 1982), pp. 21–26; Merquior, *Foucault*, pp. 46–50; and Guégen, "Foucault and Lacan on Velázquez: The Status of the Subject of Representation."

85. Foucault, "Space, Knowledge, Power" in *The Foucault Reader*, p. 254.

blances, images were understood to be decipherable hieroglyphs of meaning. The result was "a non-distinction between what is seen and what is read, between observation and relation, which results in the constitution of a single, unbroken surface in which observation and language intersect to infinity."[86]

For reasons that are not clear and which Foucault unfortunately never deemed worthy of explication, the Classical Age emerged when this unity is shattered and images no longer resembled readable texts. Both Bacon and Descartes, if with different motivations, denounced thinking through resemblances or similitudes (which, it will be recalled, Foucault used as synonyms in this book) and warned against the illusions to which it led. One implication of the breakdown of this unity, first evident in Miguel de Cervantes, was the growing awareness of the binary and representative nature of the sign, which freed it from the assumption that it bears an intrinsic figural or iconic resemblance to what it signifies. As an arbitrary human tool, language came to be understood as a neutral medium of communication. Inclined toward nominalism, language in the Classical Age also privileged the most neutral verb possible: the verb "to be."

Another implication of the breakdown was the compensatory unleashing of perception in general, and vision in particular, as the sole means of ascertaining reliable knowledge about the external world. According to Foucault, "The manifestation and sign of truth are to be found in evident and distinct perception. It is the task of words to translate the truth if they can; but they no longer have the right to be considered a mark of it. Language has withdrawn from the midst of beings themselves and has entered a period of transparency and neutrality."[87] The Classical Age is thus dominated by a new faith in the power of direct and technologically enhanced observation and by a concomitant taxonomic ordering of its

---

86. Foucault, *The Order of Things*, p. 39.

87. Ibid., p. 73. Foucault's analysis of the eclipse of language in the Classical Age has been implicitly disputed by John W. Yolton in *Perceptual Acquaintance from Descartes to Reid* (Oxford, 1984), where it is argued that a semantic dimension exists even in perception for Descartes and his followers.

findings in the visible space of the table. Although such tables are necessarily linguistic, the names they arrange in spatial relations are assumed to be utterly without density of their own. The triumph of natural history was thus the triumph of a new visual order.

> One has the impression that with Tournefort, with Linnaeus or Buffon, someone has at last taken on the task of stating something that had been visible from the beginning of time, but had remained mute before a sort of invincible distraction of men's eyes. In fact, it was not an age-old inattentiveness being suddenly dissipated, but a new field of visibility being constituted in all its density.[88]

Other senses such as touch and hearing were denigrated as scientific language struggled to turn itself as much as possible into a transparent record of the observing gaze.

Moreover, to the extent that visual knowledge was dominant in the Classical Age, an observing eye was assumed to exist, capable of seeing the visible tables, but from a position outside of them. Because it so vividly exemplified this assumption, *Las Meninas* was, according to Foucault, a brilliant representation of representation in the Classical Age.[89] For in it, the absent sovereigns, visible only in their reflections in the small mirror on the back wall of the painter's studio, are the ones who "see" the picture in front of us. But in this doubled space of representation, the seeing subject can only be inferred, not perceived directly. We are thus not yet in a fully humanist age characterized by the positive appearance of Man.

> In Classical thought, the personage for whom the representation exists, and who represents himself within it, recognizing himself therein as an image or reflection, he who ties together all the interlacing threads of the "representation in the form of a picture or a table"—he is never to be found in that table itself. Before the eighteenth century, *man* does not exist.[90]

88. Foucault, *The Order of Things*, p. 132.

If then, it is only with the end of the visual regime of the Classical Age that full-fledged humanism emerges, what is the connection for Foucault between ocularcentrism and the rise of Man? At first glance, there does not seem to be any, which would call into question the significance of the antivisual discourse in Foucault's work, at least at this stage of it. For when he came to describe the end of natural history and its replacement by biology at the time of Georges Cuvier, he explicitly stressed the new emphasis on invisible, anatomic and organic structures, which supplanted the empirical classifications of the Classical table. "The visible order, with its permanent grid of distinctions," he wrote, "is now only a superficial glitter above an abyss."[91] With the concomitant emergence of historical consciousness, functional analogy and succession—temporal rather than spatial values—replace the static order of the Classical Age. Life, labor, and language all break free from the domination of the taxonomic gaze. The putative transparency of language gives way to a growing opacity that culminates in the appearance of pure "literature" in Mallarmé.

And yet, in a subtle way, the post-Classical, humanist *episteme*, as Foucault described it, was still hostage to the primacy of sight, if mobilized in a new visual regime. This continuity across the seemingly abrupt rupture in discursive formations becomes evident in the light of Foucault's argument about Bichat, Pinel, and Freud in *Madness and Civilization* and his highly speculative claim about the link between the later sciences of man and the medical gaze in *The Birth of the Clinic*. In those works, he insisted that even as the surface of the body was penetrated to let the hitherto invisible become the object of scrutiny, even as language was introduced

89. Painted in 1656, *Las Meninas* is normally interpreted as an example of baroque rather than classical art, and Velázquez is understood as having subverted any confidence in the objectivity of the phenomenal world in favor of a subjective perspectivalism. See, for example, José Antonio Maravell, *Velázquez y el espíritu de la modernidad* (Madrid, 1960). Foucault, however, did not differentiate between the baroque and classical eras, which may have reflected his Gallocentrism. See Gandelman, "Foucault as Art Historian," p. 268, for reflections on this issue.

90. Foucault, *The Order of Things*, p. 308.

91. Ibid., p. 251.

to supplement the psychiatric gaze, vision did not falter as the dominant cognitive sense. It was for this reason that at the same time modern biology was positing "life" as its object, it paradoxically discovered "death" at its heart.[92]

But in an even more fundamental sense, the primacy of the visual was preserved in Foucault's account of the rise of the human sciences. For with the eclipse of the Classical Age,

> man appears in his ambiguous position as an object of knowledge and as subject that knows; enslaved sovereign, *observed spectator*, he appears in the place belonging to the king, which was assigned to him in advance by *Las Meninas*, but from which his real presence has for so long been excluded. As if, in that vacant space towards which Velázquez's whole painting was directed, but which it was nevertheless reflecting only in the chance presence of a mirror, and as though by stealth, all the figures whose alternation, reciprocal exclusion, interweaving, and fluttering one imagined (the model, the painter, the king, the spectator) suddenly stopped their imperceptible dance, immobilized into one substantial figure, and demanded that the entire space of the representation should at last be relaxed to one corporeal gaze.[93]

In this extremely important paragraph, Foucault revealed the extent to which humanism was based in his view on the replacement of the absent spectator, the king, by the "observed spectator," Man in a still visually constituted epistemological field. Thus, the arrival of this "strange empirico-transcendental doublet"[94] meant that Man functioned both as an allegedly neutral metasubject of knowledge and as its proper object, viewed from afar. Even phenomenology, Foucault once again insisted, fell prey to this way of perceiving the world, showing its "insidious kinship, its simultaneously promising and threatening proximity, to empirical analyses of man."[95]

Only with the later triumph of an opaque and self-referential concept of language did the visually determined humanist *episteme* begin to be effaced enough for Foucault to claim that "man has been a figure occurring between two modes of language."[96] With writers like Roussel and Bataille—as well as others Foucault mentions, such as Artaud and Blanchot—the crisis of ocularcentrism had reached a point at which an epistemic shift away from humanism was on the horizon. Now those hitherto forbidden elements that had been consigned to the realm of darkness ever since the onset of the Classical Age, such as madness, difference, and transgressive eroticism, could be rescued from the domination of light, transparency, and homogenizing "sameness." For with the weakening of the Classical and humanist paradigms went a concomitant questioning of the translucency of language which had accompanied it ever since the breakdown of the preclassical unity of word and image. But rather than a return to that prelapsarian state in which latent meaning was available to be deciphered, the post-humanist condition would be characterized more by the mutual opacity Foucault celebrated in his studies of Roussel and Magritte.

The Order of Things marked the last great instance of what has become known as Foucault's archaeological period, which was brought to a close by his methodological treatise, *The Archaeology of Knowledge*. Near the end of that work, he contended that a painting could be conceptualized as a "discursive practice . . . not a pure vision that must be transcribed into the materiality of space . . . it is shot through . . . with the positivity of a knowledge (*savoir*)."[97] And elsewhere, he regretted, as already mentioned, the term "medical gaze" in *The Birth of the Clinic*. Both of these remarks might be interpreted as a weakening of his visual concerns, the former because it seemed to reduce the order of the visual to that of the discur-

92. Ibid., p. 232.
93. Ibid., p. 312 (italics added).
94. Ibid., p. 318.
95. Ibid., p. 326.
96. Ibid., p. 386. In French, of course, *figure* also means face, which suggests the famous final metaphor of the book.
97. Foucault, *The Archaelogy of Knowledge*, p. 194.

sive, the latter because it undercut the stress on the metasubjective observer characteristic of the natural and human sciences as Foucault had described them. But in fact, all that they implied was a more heightened awareness of the anthropocentric fallacy involved in positing a synthetic, unified subject, or even a more phenomenologically grounded one, doing the looking. For it was precisely this transcendental subject that *The Order of Things* claimed was a function of a specific visual regime rather than a precondition of vision as such. Vision, Foucault now seemed to suggest, could help constitute an *episteme* without the implied presence of an absent sovereign or his humanist surrogate, whose gaze totalized the visual field. Here, he showed a continued filiation to Sartre whose paranoid ontology of the gaze in *Being and Nothingness* had not required an actual subject looking at an objectified other. And he demonstrated as well a similarity to Lacan with his distinction between the eye and the gaze.

The generalizable experience of being observed by an unknown and omnipresent "eye" was, in fact, precisely what Foucault analyzed in his powerful investigation of panopticism in his next major work, *Discipline and Punish* of 1975.[98] He had been sensitive to the relations between social and political constraint and the objectifying power of the gaze as early as *The Birth of the Clinic*, where he linked the rise of modern medicine directly to the reforms of the French Revolution:

> This medical field, restored to its pristine truth, pervaded wholly by the gaze, without obstacle and without alteration, is strangely similar, in its implicit geometry, to the social space dreamt of by the Revolution. . . . The ideological theme that guides all structural reforms from 1789 to Thermidor Year II is that of the sovereign liberty of truth: the majestic violence of light, which is in itself supreme, brings to an end the unbounded, dark kingdom of privileged knowledge and establishes the unimpeded power of the gaze.[99]

98. Foucault, *Discipline and Punish: The Birth of the Prison*, trans. Alan Sheridan (New York, 1979).

But it was only in *Discipline and Punish*, the first major fruit of his so-called genealogical method,[100] that Foucault analyzed the more subtle social mechanism that allowed domination to extend beyond the boundaries of an all-seeing sovereign or a despotic revolutionary state.

Foucault began with an evocation of the spectacle of sovereign power in the Classical Age. With characteristic visual éclat he described the torture and execution of the failed regicide Damiens in 1757 as a "theatrical representation of pain"[101] in which the power of the monarch was literally inscribed in the visible flesh of the condemned man. As in his earlier accounts of the constitution of madness, the medical gaze in the clinic, and the taxonomic system of natural history, the privileging of visual observation is evident. Not only does it appear in the "spectacle of the scaffold" of the ancien régime, but it continues as well through the "great theatrical ritual"[102] of the Revolutionary guillotine.

But as in his earlier analyses, Foucault noted the decay of the Classical mode in favor of a more complicated but still visually determined alternative in the nineteenth century. Although acknowledging its prototype in the military schools, military camps, and clinics of the eighteenth century—and he might have added the court society at the end of Louis

99. Foucault, *The Birth of the Clinic*, pp. 38–39.

100. Derived largely from Nietzsche, genealogy reversed the distancing, contemplative gaze of traditional historical analysis. Instead, it "shortens its vision to those things nearest to it—the body, the nervous system, nutrition, digestion and energies; it unearths the periods of decadence and if it chances upon lofty epochs, it is with suspicion—not vindictive but joyous—of finding a barbarous and shameful confusion. . . . Effective history studies what is closest, but in an abrupt dispossession, so as to seize it at a distance." Foucault, "Nietzsche, Genealogy, History," in *Language, Counter-memory, Practice*, pp. 155–156.

101. Foucault, *Discipline and Punish*, p. 14. As de Certeau noted, *Discipline and Punish* combined such representational tableaux with other optical features, "analytic tableaux (lists of ideological 'rules' or 'principles' relating to a single phenomenon) and figurative tableaux (seventeenth–nineteenth century engravings and photographs)." De Certeau, "Micro-techniques and Panoptic Discourse: A Quid Pro Quo," *Humanities in Review*, 5 (Summer and Fall, 1982), p. 264.

102. Ibid., p. 15.

XIV's reign[103]—he, like Jacques-Alain Miller, chose Bentham's model prison as the most explicit version of the new ocular technology of power.[104] For it was here that the disciplining and normalizing function of the gaze was at its most blatant. Reversing the principle of the dungeon, the Panopticon, with its hidden and invisible God, was an architectural embodiment of the most paranoid Sartrean fantasies about the "absolute look." The object of power is everywhere penetrated by the benevolently sadistic gaze of a diffuse and anonymous power whose actual existence soon becomes superfluous to the process of discipline. The Panopticon, Foucault wrote, is a "machinery that assures dissymmetry, disequilibrium, difference. Consequently, it does not matter who exercises power. Any individual, taken almost at random, can operate the machine."[105]

Complementing the role of the gaze—or rather, the sensation of always being its target—in the control and rehabilitation of criminals is the prophylactic power of surveillance (literally super-vision) which is designed to prevent potential transgressions of the law. Here the external look becomes an internalized and self-regulating mechanism that extends the old religious preoccupation with the smallest detail that was still immense "in the sight of God."[106] Although by no means restricted to its ocular dimension,[107] this new mechanism of control was first and foremost a part of the visual economy of the modern world.

103. For an analysis of the shift from spectacle to surveillance at the court of Louis XIV, which places it around 1674, see Jean-Marie Apostolidès, *Le roi-machine: Spectacle et politique au temps de Louis XIV* (Paris, 1981). He argues that by the end of his reign, the Sun King had absented himself from the spectacle and become an empty place in the power structure of the monarchy, which gave the impression of being able to see without being seen. The same pattern, it has also been claimed by Christine Buci-Glucksmann, marked the role of the sovereign in *Las Meninas*. See her "Une archéologie de l'ombre," p. 24. If these anticipations of the epistemic/practical shift from spectacle to surveillance are correct, then the precision of Foucault's periodization is called into question.

104. In a subsequent interview, Foucault claimed that he came upon the Panopticon while working on the clinic, well before Miller's 1973 essay. See "The Eye of Power," in *Power/Knowledge*, p. 146.

105. Foucault, *Discipline and Punish*, p. 202.

106. Ibid., p. 140.

The normalizing effects of the institutions and practices of surveillance were successful enough, according to Foucault, to dispense with the more heavy-handed displays of sovereign power needed earlier to render the population docile. Napoleon's reign, he contended, was the transitional moment, as the emperor "combined in a single symbolic, ultimate figure the whole of the long process by which the pomp of sovereignty, the necessarily spectacular manifestations of power, were extinguished one by one in the daily exercise of surveillance, in a panopticism in which the vigilance of intersecting gazes was soon to render useless both the eagle and the sun."[108] Thus, implicitly taking issue with the arguments of Guy Debord, to be discussed shortly, Foucault concluded that "our society is one not of spectacle, but of surveillance. . . . We are neither in the amphitheatre, nor on the stage, but in the panoptic machine."[109]

That our imprisonment in this machine owed much to the well-intentioned goals of the Enlightenment and the Revolution it helped spawn Foucault did not doubt. "The 'Enlightenment' which discovered the liberties," he argued, "also invented the disciplines."[110] Explicitly drawing on Starobinski's analysis, he linked the Panopticon to Rousseau's utopian vision of crystalline transparency.

> I would say Bentham was the complement to Rousseau. What in fact was the Rousseauist dream that motivated many of the revolutionaries? It was the dream of a transparent society, visible and legible in each of its parts, the dream of there no longer existing any zones of darkness. . . . Bentham is both that and the

107. In the "Eye of Power" interview, one of Foucault's interlocutors, Michelle Perrot, reminded him that Bentham also suggested that tin tubes be used to link the chief inspector with each prisoner through sound as well as sight (p. 154). In the age of electronic wiretapping and other such devices, surveillance is, of course, as much aural as visual. For a discussion, see David Lyon, "Bentham's Panopticon: From Moral Architecture to Electronic Surveillance," *Queen's Quarterly*, 98, 3 (Fall, 1991).

108. Foucault, *Discipline and Punish*, p. 217.

109. Ibid.

110. Ibid, p. 222.

opposite. He poses the problem of visibility, but thinks of a visibility organized entirely around a dominating, overseeing gaze. He effects the project of a universal visibility which exists to serve a rigorous, meticulous power. Thus Bentham's obsession, the technical idea of the exercise of an "all-seeing" power, is grafted on to the great Rousseauist theme which is in some sense the lyrical note of the Revolution.[111]

Although Foucault took pains to avoid the implication that all modern technologies of power derived from the Rousseauist-Benthamite principle of perfect visibility,[112] he nonetheless acknowledged its importance in constituting and then controlling the next phenomenon he investigated: that of sexuality. "With these themes of surveillance, and especially in the schools," he claimed, "it seems that control over sexuality becomes inscribed in architecture. In the Military Schools, the very walls speak the struggle against homosexuality and masturbation."[113] The sciences of man, intended to help in the macrological control of populations as well as in the micrological normalizing of individuals, drew on the mixture of the gaze and discourse that Foucault had identified with psychoanalysis as early as *The Birth of the Clinic*. Although he now stressed the power of discourse, such as that of the confession, in constituting the very notion of sexuality, he insisted on the importance of spatial, visual controls in policing it. Nowhere was this function as evident as in the ostracism of the sexual "pervert" whose very deviance was "written immodestly on his face and body because it was a secret that always gave itself away."[114] In so arguing, Foucault implicitly complemented Sartre's contention in *Saint*

111. Foucault, "The Eye of Power," p. 152. There is, to be sure, a certain slippage here from the emphasis in *Discipline and Punish* on the theatrical spectacle of the revolutionary guillotine—a residue of the Classical Age's spectacular visual style—to the antitheatrical surveillance of the nineteenth century anticipated by Rousseau.

112. See his disclaimer in "The Eye of Power," p. 148.

113. Ibid., p. 150.

114. Foucault, *The History of Sexuality*, vol. 1, *An Introduction*, trans. Robert Hurley (New York, 1982), p. 43.

Genet that Genet's sexual identity was produced by the gaze of the other, which "raped" him from behind.[115]

To mention Genet is to open the question of possible resistance to the process of visually induced objectification and normalization. For certain of his works—such as the film he made with Jean Cocteau, *Un chant d'amour*—have been interpreted as challenges to the voyeuristic sadism of modern culture.[116] Can Foucault himself be said to have offered a visual antidote, or indeed any antidote, to the disciplinary power of the gaze? How strong a weapon was his "art of seeing" in thwarting the visual policing of bodies and the spaces they inhabited? Or did he implicitly draw on other senses in his famous evocation of "bodies and pleasures" as a counterweight to the domination of sexuality in the constitution of the self?

At times, as we have noted, Foucault did explicitly call on the disruptive power of images, especially against the claims of language to represent a perfectly self-contained and self-sufficient system. In his introduction to Binswanger, it will be recalled, he criticized psychoanalysis in general and Lacan in particular for failing to acknowledge the irreducibly visual dimension of dreams. His analyses of Roussel and Magritte also emphasized the power of sight to subvert the homogenizing drive toward the "Same" implicit in naive linguistic versions of representation, as in turn they pitted language against visual immediacy. What in *The Order of Things* Foucault called "heterotopias"[117] were disturbingly inconsistent spatial configurations that undermined the alleged coherence of the dominant visual regime. Indeed, one might say that against both linguistic and visual *trompe l'oeil*, he preferred a kind of catachresis that preserved ambiguity, otherness, and chiasmic intersection. There is thus a moment of

---

115. Foucault rarely dealt directly with Genet, although he included him with Jean Cocteau and William Burroughs among "the great homosexual writers of our culture." Interview entitled "Sexual Choice, Sexual Act: Foucault and Homosexuality," in *Politics, Philosophy, Culture: Interviews and Other Writings, 1977–1984*, ed. Lawrence D. Kritzman, trans. Alan Sheridan et al. (New York, 1988), p. 297.

116. Laura Oswald, "The Perversion of I/Eye in *Un chant d'amour*," *Enclitic*, 7 (Fall, 1983).

117. Foucault, *The Order of Things*, p. xviii.

truth in Rajchman's contention that, for Foucault, seeing was "an art of trying to see what is unthought in our seeing, and to open as yet unseen ways of seeing."[118]

And yet, in all of his attempts to problematize the given visual order and expand the boundaries of what could be seen, Foucault never provided a genuinely positive alternative. Whether an archaeology, a genealogy or, to invoke one of his final formulations, an "analytic,"[119] Foucault's own method was resolutely antitheoretical precisely because of the time-honored complicity of theory and vision.[120] As demonstrated by his frequent criticisms of Merleau-Ponty, he also resisted an ontology of embodied vision in which a superior kind of perception might replace problematic "high altitude" philosophies of consciousness. When he invoked vision against the self-sufficiency of language, it was always to emphasize its revelation—or perhaps rather construction—of a world of shadows or opacity, never transparency or clarity. As Wilhelm Miklenitsch put it, "His concern has in effect been, at all times, to valorize the experience of the eye's *punctum caecum*—its blind spot, which is found on the retina where the optic nerve is born—in a thought that grasps finitude and Being."[121]

With characteristic ascetic rigor, Foucault thus resisted exploring vision's reciprocal, intersubjective, communicative potential, that of the mutual glance. *Le regard* never assumed for him its alternative meaning in English as well as French: to pay heed to or care for someone else. The

118. Rajchman, "Foucault's Art of Seeing," p. 96.

119. In his interview, "The Confession of the Flesh," in *Knowledge/Power*, Foucault calls for an "analytic of power," not a theory (p. 199).

120. For discussions of this issue, see David F. Gruber, "Foucault and Theory: Genealogical Critiques of the Subject"; Ladelle McWhorter, "Foucault's Move Beyond the Theoretical"; and Peg Birmingham, "Local Theory," all in *The Question of the Other: Essays in Contemporary Continental Philosophy*, eds. Arleen B. Dallery and Charles E. Scott (Albany, N.Y., 1989). For a counteropinion that despite Foucault's intentions, the totalizing gaze of theory did reappear in his work, see de Certeau, "The Black Sun of Language: Foucault," in *Heterologies*, p. 183.

121. Wilhelm Miklenitsch, "La pensée de l'épicentration," *Critique*, 471–472 (August–September, 1986), p. 824.

"care of the self" which he explored in his final work included a visual dimension only to the extent that it involved a "certain manner of acting visible to others."[122] But the ethical cum aesthetic self-fashioning he found so compelling did not go beyond a kind of dandiacal display, which left out more interactive affective ties, such as those in the family.[123] As de Certeau pointed out,[124] Foucault may have focused so insistently on the dangers of panopticism that he remained blind to the other micropractices of everyday life that subvert its power. For all his professed interest in resistance, Foucault may have too hastily absorbed all power relations into one hegemonic ocular apparatus.[125] Although he may have believed that the disciplinary society of the panopticon was itself being replaced by a new "society of control" based more on computerized than visual surveillance—at least so Deleuze has argued[126]—

122. Foucault, "The Ethic of the Care for the Self as a Practice of Freedom: An Interview," *Philosophy and Social Criticism*, 12, 2–3 (1987), p. 117. His final major work was *The Care of the Self*, trans. Robert Hurley (New York, 1986).

123. As Mark Poster has noted, Foucault treated the family largely in terms of the external discourses that acted on it from without, rather than its internal dynamics, which may include a dimension of mutual regard. See Poster, "Foucault and the Tyranny of Greece," in *Foucault: A Critical Reader*, ed. David Couzens Hoy (New York, 1986), p. 219.

124. De Certeau, "Micro-techniques and Panoptic Discourse: A Quid Pro Quo," pp. 259–260.

125. According to Jeffrey Minson, "as a compelling image of surveillance, the Panopticon tends to put all types of surveillance at par, conflating surveillance over the governed with surveillance over the governers, making centralized hierarchical authority within corporate structures, municipal or governmental departments politically indistinguishable from centralization of power and authority over such entities. The Panopticon also offers an inviting metaphor for all disciplinary power, modern *pouvoir-savoir* functioning as a mirror image of sovereign power and hence as a totalizing image of disciplinary society. Finally, in one grand bipolar sweep, by which power (society) can be identified with one of its forms, disciplinary surveillance can be offered as the key to understanding power-in-general." Minson, *Genealogies of Morals: Nietzsche, Foucault, Donzelot and the Eccentricity of Ethics* (London, 1985), p. 97.

126. Gilles Deleuze, "Postscript on the Societies of Control," *October*, 59 (Winter, 1992).

Foucault never explored in any depth the role visual experience might play in resisting it as well.

It is, moreover, unlikely that he held out any hope for another sense as the antidote to the hegemony of the eye, as was the case with certain French feminists. They may have chosen to turn to touch or smell as more consonant with female than male sexuality, but Foucault was always too skeptical of any search for essentializing immediacy—and also too unconcerned with women's sexual experience—to feel that this choice provided an answer. Indeed, as he emphasized in one of his last interviews, "I am not looking for an alternative. . . . What I want to do is not the history of solutions, and that's the reason why I don't accept the word *alternative*. I would like to do the genealogy of problems, of *problématiques*. My point is not that everything is bad, but that everything is dangerous."[127] There was therefore no real escape from the current "empire of the gaze" into a more benign heterotopic alternative. For wherever Foucault looked, all he could see were scopic regimes of "*malveillance*."[128]

⊙

If Foucault's critique of the dominant scopic regime focused on the disciplining and normalizing effect of being the object of the gaze, that of Guy Debord and his Situationist collaborators stressed the dangers of being its subject. That is, for them, seduction by the Spectacle of modern life was far more politically nefarious than Big Brother's omnipresent watchfulness. Moreover, unlike Foucault, they doggedly held out hope for a utopian reversal of the current order in which the participatory Festival would supplant the contemplative Spectacle, and a new and healthier subject would emerge. Accordingly, they sought to intervene in a more directly activist way than Foucault to bring about this end, hoping to turn the current scopic regime against itself.

127. Foucault, "On the Genealogy of Ethics: An Overview of Work in Progress" in *The Foucault Reader*, p. 343.
128. Foucault, "The Eye of Power," p. 158.

In the long run, their legacy seems to have been more critical than constructive, as their redemptive project, like so many others, faltered in the aftermath of May, 1968. Twenty years later, the Situationists, who so fervently sought to unite art and life and thus make the Revolution, were in danger of being turned into yet another canonized entry in the dreary succession of modernist movements seeking to outdo their predecessors in radicality.[129] Radical "situations" in the streets were replaced by "artworks" in museums. Even their central concept of the Spectacle had begun to lose some of its critical force, as postmodernists either unashamedly embraced it as a benign phenomenon or claimed that its descriptive power was no longer appropriate in the twentieth-century's *fin-de-siècle.*

Whatever the mixed results of the Situationist project to overthrow bourgeois society, there can be no doubt that it contributed significantly to the undermining of the dominant visual order. Its own roots were, in fact, in several earlier movements and discourses that had challenged the hegemony of the eye.[130] Although its ultimate affinity with older mil-

---

129. In 1989, their "works" were the subject of exhibitions at the Centre Pompidou in Paris, the ICA (Institute of Contemporary Arts) in London, and the ICA in Boston. Although aware of the irony of bestowing aesthetic credentials on a movement that sought to dismantle the institution of art, the organizers, Peter Wollen and Mark Francis, felt that no other way was possible to retrieve their ideas and rescue their projects. Accompanying the exhibitions was a splendid catalogue, *On the Passage of a Few People Through a Rather Brief Moment in Time: The Situationist International, 1957–1972,* ed. Elisabeth Sussman (Cambridge, Mass., 1989), several of whose essays wrestled with the dilemma of "spectacularizing" Situationism.

130. The best historical account of the movement is Peter Wollen, "Bitter Victory: The Art and Politics of the Situationist International," in *On the Passage of a Few People Through a Rather Brief Moment in Time.* Wollen emphasizes their debt to Western Marxism and Surrealism. See also Edward Ball, "The Great Sideshow of the Situationist International," *Yale French Studies,* 73 (1987), pp. 21–37; Mark Shipway, "Situationism," in *Non-Market Socialism in the Nineteenth and Twentieth Centuries,* ed. Maximilien Rubel and John Crump (London, 1987); and Greil Marcus, *Lipstick Traces: A Secret History of the Twentieth Century* (Cambridge, Mass., 1989), which places them in a tradition of antinomian protest stretching from medieval chiliasm to punk rock. Unlike Wollen, he stresses their linkage to Dadaism rather than Surrealism and generally ignores their roots in Western Marxism. For a less

lennial/anarchistic religious movements cannot be denied, in more immediate political terms Situationism was a child of Western Marxism, the tradition launched by Georg Lukács with *History and Class Consciousness* in 1923.[131] Not only did the Situationists share Lukács's stress on criticizing the totality of social relations, his redemptive hope for a unity of subject and object, and his celebration of workers' councils,[132] but also they adopted his critique of reification as the major obstacle to revolutionary change. To the extent that Lukács's concept of reification was indebted to Bergson's assault on the spatialization of time,[133] the Situationists absorbed some of the antivisual pathos of his argument.

Like Foucault, they also came to understand the value of examining space as a locus of domination as well as its resistance. Here the work of the French Marxist Henri Lefebvre was especially important, even if the Situationists came to quarrel with him over the priority of their shared

---

sympathetic assessment of their history, see the chapters on the "Specto-Situationists" in Stewart Home, *The Assault on Culture: Utopian Currents from Lettrism to Class War* (London, 1988). He writes from the perspective of the dissidents who broke with Debord in 1962 to form the Second Situationist International.

131. For my own attempt to trace its history, see *Marxism and Totality: The Adventures of a Concept from Lukács to Habermas* (Berkeley, 1984). Wollen correctly notes that like other accounts of the tradition by Perry Anderson, Mark Poster, and Russell Jacoby, it marginalizes the importance of Surrealism and the Situationists.

132. Lukács, to be sure, soon abandoned his faith in the councils in favor of the Leninist Party. The Situationists, like the *Socialisme ou Barbarie* group led by Cornelius Castoriadis and Claude Lefort, were more dogged believers in their importance, but they too sought some role for radical intellectuals as the organized mediators of theory and practice. See, for example, their famous 1966 pamphlet, "On the Poverty of Student Life," reprinted in *Situationist International Anthology*, ed. and trans. Ken Knabb (Berkeley, 1989), p. 334. One of the often cited contradictions in Situationist theory was its celebration of play and consumption, on the one hand, and its productivist reliance on workers' councils, on the other.

133. The most sustained attempt to make this link can be found in Lucio Colletti, "From Bergson to Lukács," in *Marxism and Hegel*, trans. Lawrence Garner (London, 1973). For a different assessment of Bergson's influence, see Andrew Feenberg, *Lukács, Marx and the Sources of Critical Theory* (Towata, N.J., 1981), p. 208. He rejects the link because of its irrationalist implications, but doesn't discuss the issue of the spatialization of time.

ideas.[134] Lefebvre, once on the fringes of Surrealism in the 1920s, had passed through orthodox Stalinist and Marxist Humanist phases, to emerge in the 1960s as a guiding light of the New Left. As one of the *Arguments* group, which included Edgar Morin, Kostas Axelos, Jean Duvigneaud, and Pierre Fougeyrollas, he helped to popularize and transform the Hegelian Marxism of Lukács. Of particular importance for the Situationists were his emphases on everyday life, mass consumption, and the urban spatial environment as loci of revolutionary struggle.[135] In what he called the "bureaucratic society of controlled consumption," alienation reached its crescendo, with sterile, functional new cities like Mourenx sapping all the spontaneity out of quotidien existence. But, for Lefebvre, and the Situationists as well, the urban festival, reestablishing the "right to the city,"[136] was still a viable possibility, once the commodity fetishism of the modern spectacle was undermined.

That visual experience would become a major battlefield in the service of revolution was inevitable, because of the strong link between any critique of fetishism, Marxist or otherwise, and that of idolatry.[137] Insofar as commodities were the visible appearances of social processes whose roots in human production were forgotten or repressed, they were like the idols worshiped in lieu of the invisible God. The fact, moreover, that in French *spectacle* also means a theatrical presentation suggests that in invoking it

134. See, for example, the vituperative denial of any influence in "The Beginning of an Era," from the *Internationale situationniste*, 12 (September, 1969), reprinted in Knabb, ed., *Situationist International Anthology*, p. 228. For an account of Lefebvre's career, see *Marxism and Totality*, chap. 9. His continued interest in the issue of visuality is shown in such later works as *The Production of Space*, trans. Donald Nicholson-Smith (Oxford, 1991), originally published in 1974. See, for example, his discussion of the sinister effects of the eye's totalizing hegemony over the other senses on page 286.

135. Henri Lefebvre, *Everyday Life in the Modern World*, trans. S. Rabinovitch (New York, 1971). In French, Lefebvre published several volumes under the title *Critique de la vie quotidienne*, the earliest in 1947.

136. Lefebvre, *Le droit à la ville* (Paris, 1968).

137. See, for example, David Simpson, *Fetishism and Imagination* (Baltimore, 1983), and W. J. T. Mitchell, "The Rhetoric of Iconoclasm: Marxism, Ideology and Fetishism," in *Iconology: Image, Text, Ideology* (Chicago, 1986).

as the antithesis to festival, Lefebvre and the Situationists were drawing on the long-standing suspicion of theatrical illusion evident in Rousseau and before.[138]

They were also clearly indebted to the iconoclastic impulse—in both senses of the word—in Surrealism, which manifested itself in several politically motivated modernist movements during the postwar era. One was the so-called Cobra group of artists led by the Dane Asger Jorn, the Belgian Christian Dotrement, and the Dutchman Constant Nieuwenhuys, who were active from 1948 to 1951 in several countries; another was the Imaginist Bauhaus, organized by Jorn and the Italian artist Giuseppe Pinot-Gallizio, which functioned from 1953 to 1957.[139] Many of the figures who would join with Debord to found the Situationist International, officially launched at Cosio d'Arroscia in 1957 and dissolved fifteen years later, were already active in these movements.

A third influence was Lettrism, an international group launched by Isidore Isou (born Jean-Isidore Golstein) in Rumania during the Second World War.[140] Indebted to the tradition of Dadaist scandal, the Lettrists first made their mark in France by interrupting a lecture by Michel Leiris in Paris in 1946, a lecture that was itself on Dadaism. The young Debord, born in 1931, was soon attracted to their orbit rather than that of the Surrealists, whose fascination with the Freudian unconscious he did not share. But with characteristic contentiousness, he quickly broke with Isou to help form a more politically radical splinter group called the Lettrist International in 1952.[141] Significantly, the journal they founded was entitled *Potlatch*,[142] thus evoking the same wasteful destruction of specular reciprocity and exchange that Bataille had found so seductive.

138. See Jonas Barish, *The Anti-Theatrical Prejudice* (Berkeley, 1981).

139. For Jorn's life and work, see Guy Atkins, ed., *Jorn in Scandinavia: 1930–1953* (London, 1968); *Asger Jorn: The Crucial years: 1954–1964* (London, 1977); and *Asger Jorn: The Final Years: 1965–1973* (London, 1980).

140. For accounts of its origins and development, see the essays edited by Stephen C. Foster, *Lettrisme: Into the Present*, a catalogue for a 1983 exhibition at the University of Iowa Museum of Art that was published in *Visible Language*, 17, 3 (1983). See also Marcus, *Lipstick Traces*, for an account of Isou, pp. 246ff.

But before the rupture, the first of many sectarian quarrels Debord would initiate or join, Lettrism left an important mark on his theory and practice. Besides providing a model for creating disruptive aesthetic situations with political implications—Isou himself had been a Communist in Rumania—the Lettrists also helped Debord and his colleagues focus on visual issues in a number of different media. Lettrist poetry was notable for its insistence on the material importance of the signifiers on the page, which involved introducing nonstandard alphabets such as Morse Code, braille, flag languages, and hieroglyphs into their work. As in the case of other visually oriented "concrete poetry," they hoped to undermine the semantic transparency of the word, replacing it with "hypergraphy" (*métagraphie*) or "super-writing."

Conversely, their painting, most notably that of Maurice Lemaître, sought to disrupt visual purity by introducing letters and words, often as cryptic rebuses or pictograms. According to Jean-Paul Curtay, although earlier artists such as Georges Braque, Picasso, or Klee had used writing and symbols for their figurative value, "only after the appearance of superwriting did critics begin to see signs on their canvases and to read them as 'visual texts.' Isou had thus shifted the paradigm of art. To paint had become to organize signs."[143] Their work was also opened to the incorporation of sign/images from popular culture, such as cartoons, often subversively recaptioned, which were to have a strong impact on the Situationists.

The Lettrists' visual practice included experimental or what they called "discrepant" cinema, which extended beyond the halting efforts of the

---

141. The immediate cause of the break seems to have been Isou's refusal to countenance the disruption of a press conference by Charlie Chaplin in October, 1952. See *Documents relatifs à la foundation de l'internationale situationniste*, ed. Gérard Berreby (Paris, 1985), pp. 147ff. Along with Debord, Michèle Bernstein, Serge Berna, Jean-Louis Brau, and Gil J. Wolman left Isou's group. The LI, as it was known, had a very fluid membership, twelve of whom were expelled in its first two years. See Home, *The Assault on Culture*, p. 17.

142. Its issues are collected as *Potlatch*, ed. Guy Debord (Paris, 1985).

143. Jean-Paul Curtay, "Super-Writing 1983—America 1963," in Foster, ed., *Lettrisme: Into the Present*, p. 23.

Surrealists in the 1920s and 1930s.[144] In 1951, Isou produced a film entitled *Treatise on Slobber and Eternity* (*Traité de bave et d'éternité*) and Lemaître another called *Is the Feature on Yet?* (*Le film est déjà commencé?*). Here they attempted to demonstrate what Isou called the transition from the constructive or "amplic" (*amplique*) to the "chiseling" (*ciselante*) phase of an art form. In his "Esthetics of the Cinema" of 1952 and elsewhere,[145] Isou explained that chiseling involved a direct attack on or even destruction of the medium in which the work was grounded, for example the scratching or tearing of the celluloid filmstrip. Along with disjunctive editing, in which the sound and the image were out of synch, and chiseling of the soundtrack, in which its integrity was also undermined, this assault on the seeming transparency of the image, as well as on its primacy,[146] was designed to break the illusion of representation it provided. So too was Lemaître's idea of "syncinema," a performance art that introduced actual actors from the film into the real space of the audience, thus closing the gap between passive spectator and the object of his or her gaze. In 1962, he would present a work called *An Evening at the Movies* (*Un soir au cinéma*), which projected images, often hypergraphs, onto the bodies of the spectators themselves.

Shortly before he broke with Isou, Debord completed the first of a se-

144. Frédérique Devaux, "Approaching Lettrist Cinema," in Foster, ed., *Lettrisme: Into the Present*. See also Dominique Noguez, "The Experimental Cinema in France," *Millennium Film Journal*, 1 (Spring–Summer, 1978). Although virtually forgotten for many years, Lettrist film was recognized as significant in the early 1950s. Jean Cocteau gave Isou's first effort the Avant-Garde award at the 1951 Cannes Film Festival.

145. For a list of his publications, see the bibliography appended to Devaux's essay. Not surprisingly, it includes a piece written after the break with Debord entitled *Contra le cinéma situationniste, néo-Nazi* (Paris, 1979).

146. As one of the voices in Isou's *Traité* put it, "Destroy the photograph for the sake of speech, do the inverse of what one has done in this domain, the contrary of what one *thought was the cinema*. Who ever said that the cinema, whose meaning is *movement*, must absolutely be *the movement of the photography* and not *the movement of the word?* . . . The photograph bothers me in the cinema." Isou, *Traité de bave et d'éternité*, in *Oeuvres de Spectacle* (Paris, 1964), p. 17.

ries of experimental "films," entitled *Screaming for Sade* (*Hurlements en faveur de Sade*).[147] Although its initial version presented chiseled images, the final one went even further in assaulting the visual expectations of the viewer. Its sound track included words from many disparate sources uttered by several expressionless voices. When they spoke, the screen was white. When they were silent, which was about four-fifths of the film's one hour and twenty minutes, the screen was black. Not surprisingly, the event produced the scandal that Debord expected—those *hurlements* elicited by sadistically subjecting the audience to so mind-numbing an experience[148]—when it was first shown to a non-Lettrist audience in London at the ICA (Institute for Contemporary Art) in 1952. In subsequent years he would remain unremittingly hostile not only to mainstream cinema but also to its apparent critics, such as Jean-Luc Godard.[149]

According to Thomas Levin, Debord's early films, more Dadaist than Lettrist in inspiration, followed a logic that could be called "the mimesis of incoherence"[150] in which the meaningless reality of the world is duplicated with uncompromising severity. Later, he would realize that the political function of cinema could be better served by refunctioning representational images rather than obliterating them entirely. Although the priority of sound over image evident in *Hurlements* was not reversed, Debord's subsequent films—*Sur le passage de quelques personnes à travers une assez courte unité de temps* (1959), *Critique de la séparation* (1959), *La société du spectacle* (1973), *Réfutation de tous les jugements, tant élogieux*

147. Guy Debord, *Oeuvres cinématographiques complètes: 1952–1978* (Paris, 1978). For an excellent account of his films, see Thomas Y. Levin, "Dismantling the Spectacle: The Cinema of Guy Debord," in *On the Passage of a Few People Through a Rather Brief Moment in Time*.

148. Debord was not the first to advocate screaming with de Sade. According to Denis Hollier, the first version of Bataille's essay "Le 'Jeu Lububre'" was to be called "Dali hurle avec Sade." See his *Against Architecture: The Writings of Georges Bataille*, trans. Betsy Wing (Cambridge, Mass., 1989), p. 122.

149. See, for example, his 1966 diatribe against Godard in Knabb, *Situationist International Anthology*, pp. 175ff.

150. Levin, *"Dismantling the Spectacle,"* p. 90.

qu'hostiles, qui ont été jusqu'ici portés sur le film 'Société du spectacle' (1975), and *In girum imus nocte et consumimur igni* (1978)[151]—contained appropriated visual material juxtaposed with and often ironically undercut by the sound commentary.

Here Debord drew on a favorite Situationist technique known as *détournement* that suggests diversion, deflection, or hijacking, often for illicit purposes. Anticipated by Lautréamont's creative plagiarism, Dada photomontages, Duchamp's readymades, and Brecht's principle of *Umfunktionerung*, it meant confronting the Spectacle with its own effluvia and reversing their normal ideological function. Asger Jorn had called for and practiced "detourned painting"[152] in which elements from previous works of art were parodically devalued and reinvested with fresh meaning through their integration in a new ensemble. He also overpainted kitsch paintings, which he called "modifications," in the hope of releasing their utopian potential. Debord and his major collaborators in the movement, Raoul Vaneigem, Michèle Bernstein (Debord's wife from 1954 to 1971),[153] René-Donatien Viénet, and Attila Kotányi, extended the technique to all aspects of visual culture, from comic books to wall posters, billboards to pornography, cinema to graffiti. "We can build," they contended, "only on the ruins of the spectacle."[154]

In accord with their injunction to realize the utopian promise of art in everyday life, they also sought to challenge the spectacle in kinesthetic terms. Following Ivan Chtcheglov's "formulary for a new urbanism,"[155] they tried to counteract the "banalization" of the city by randomly wan-

151. Their scripts and some stills are contained in his *Oeuvre cinématographiques complètes*. The films themselves were removed from distribution by Debord in response to the innuendoes against him in the wake of the unsolved murder of his friend and sponsor Gérard Lebovici in 1985. See Marcus, *Lipstick Traces*, p. 452.

152. Asger Jorn, *Peinture détournée* (Paris, 1959). See also "Detournement as Negation and Prelude" in *Internationale Situationniste*, 3 (December, 1959), reprinted in Knabb, ed., *Situationist International Anthology*, pp. 55–56.

153. The best account of her role in the movement can be found in Marcus, *Lipstick Traces*, pp. 374ff.

154. "Questionnaire" in *Internationale Situationniste*, 9 (August, 1964), reprinted in Knabb, ed., *Situationist International Anthology*, p. 139.

dering through it, either solo or in groups, following their "psychogeo-graphical" impulses. What they called the *"dérive"* (drifting) went beyond the voyeuristic strolling of the *flâneur* or even the Surrealists' aimless ram-bling in the countryside.[156] The hope, according to Chtcheglov, was com-plete, liberatory disorientation through a kind of openness to the hidden wonders of urban space. "This project," he wrote, "could be compared with Chinese and Japanese gardens of illusory perspectives [*en trompe l'oeil*]—with the difference that those gardens are not designed to be lived in all the time—or with the ridiculous labyrinth in the Jardin des Plantes, at the entry to which is written (height of absurdity, Ariadne unem-ployed): *Games are forbidden in the labyrinth.*"[157] For the Situationists, drawing on the same image Bataille and other French critics of ocularcen-trism would find so congenial, the city turned labyrinth was precisely where games—like the smashing of storefront windows or neon signs—were to be played. Only there could the repressive visual order of Hauss-mann's "boulevardized" Paris, brought to its logical conclusion in the nightmare sterility of Le Corbusier's purist urban fantasies, be thwarted. Only there could the practice of urban nomadism *détourne* the modern cityscape into a liberated zone in which authentic life would loosen the deathgrip of dessicated images.

Repeatedly evoked in the twelve issues of their journal, *Internationale Situationniste*, published from 1958 to 1969,[158] and in many of their oc-

155. This 1953 text is included in Knabb, ed., *International Situationist Anthology*, pp. 1–4. He was nineteen when it was written under the pseudonym Gilles Ivain. A few years later, he was denounced by the LI and soon after was committed to an asylum. Relations with the SI were resumed in the late 1950s, which allowed his seminal text to appear in its journal. See the brief discussion in Christopher Gray, ed. and trans., *The Incomplete Work of the Situationist International* (London, 1974), p. 4; and Home, *The Assault on Culture*, pp. 18ff.

156. Debord, "Theory of the Dérive," *Internationale Situationniste*, 2 (December, 1958), reprinted in Knabb, ed., *International Situationist Anthology*, pp. 50–54. Breton's *Nadja* anticipates the urban *dérive* to some extent.

157. Chtcheglov, "Formulary for a New Urbanism," p. 3.

158. They were reissued in one volume called *Internationale Situationniste 1958–1969* (Paris, 1975).

casional pamphlets, the concept of the Spectacle was most extensively elaborated in Debord's *Society of the Spectacle* of 1967. Appearing several years after certain of his rivals, most notably the Dane Jorgen Nash, were purged from the movement,[159] it helped solidify his role as its central spokesman, comparable to Breton in Surrealist circles.[160] It also introduced the movement's central concept to a more general audience than anything else in the history of Situationism. *Le Nouvel Observateur* went so far as to call it "the *Capital* of the new generation."[161] The May events of 1968 were by no means the outcome of Situationist agitation, but they were inflected theoretically by Debord and his collaborators' ideas.

Society of the Spectacle opened with a citation from Ludwig Feuerbach's *The Essence of Christianity* which expressed suspicion of the illusions of representation and condemned the worship of sacred images. What followed were 221 numbered paragraphs divided into nine chapters; although the two English translations interspersed the text with various pictures and other graphic material, the original French did not.[162] The initial section demonstrated the way in which Debord had grafted the antiocular discourse onto the Western Marxist totalizing critique of reification and fetishism. "In societies where modern conditions of production prevail," the opening paragraph stated, "all of life presents itself as an immense accumulation of *spectacles*. Everything that was directly lived has moved away into a representation."[163] This accumulation was composed of the discrete images detached from life, separated from their

159. The split with the "Nashists," as they became known, took place in 1962. For the orthodox SI version, see "The Countersituationist Campaign in Various Countries," in Knabb, ed., *Situationist International Anthology*. For an account defending the "legitimate status of the Second International," see Home, *The Assault on Culture*, chap. 7.

160. The comparison was made even earlier by Asger Jorn in his *Signes gravés sur les églises de l'Eure et du Calvados* (Copenhagen, 1964), p. 294.

161. *Le Nouvel Observateur,* November 8, 1971, cited in Knabb, ed., *Situationist International Anthology*, p. 387.

162. Debord, *La Société du Spectacle* (Paris, 1967; 1st trans. Detroit, 1970; 2d trans. Detroit, 1977). All quotations are from the improved translation.

163. Ibid., par. 1.

original context, and reunited as an autonomous world apart from lived experience. "As a part of society it is specifically the sector which concentrates all gazing and all consciousness."[164]

Debord was careful not to demonize vision as such, but rather the way in which it functioned in Western society.[165] "The spectacle," he warned, "is not a collection of images, but a social relation among people, mediated by images."[166] It is the material objectification of alienated socioeconomic relations, the "true reflection of the production of things, and the false objectification of the producers."[167] It operates by radically separating individuals, preventing dialogue, thwarting unitary class consciousness. Its very separation from the productive life of those who passively consume it reflects the division of labor and cleavage between State and Society generated by the dominant mode of production, which it duplicates in inverted form. It is thus the other side of money, "the money which *one only looks at*, because in the spectacle the totality of use is already exchanged for the totality of abstract representation."[168] The spectacle, in short, "is *capital* to such a degree of accumulation that it becomes an image."[169] It arrives in its mature form at the "moment when the commodity has attained the *total occupation* of social life."[170]

But if not reducible to the tyranny of images per se, the spectacle as Debord described it certainly drew on the traditional privileging of the

164. Ibid., par. 3.

165. Raoul Vaneigem likewise was careful to distinguish between malevolent and benign versions of sight. In his 1979 work, *The Book of Pleasures*, trans. John Fullerton (London, 1983), he claimed that *"the eye of power destroys what it gazes on,"* but "the disturbingly deep gaze of lovers . . . is indelibly marked with sensual delirium— how everything will one day be" (pp. 83–84).

166. Ibid., par. 4.

167. Ibid., par. 16.

168. Ibid., sect. 49.

169. Ibid., par. 34.

170. Ibid., par. 42. It should be noted that although most of Debord's analysis dealt with Western consumer societies, he also included totalitarian or "bureaucratic capitalist" societies. The former were "diffuse spectacles" and the latter "concentrated." See pars. 64 and 65.

eye in Western thought. It was, he claimed, "the heir of all the weaknesses of the Western philosophical project which was to understand activity, dominated by the categories of *seeing*; indeed, it is based on the incessant deployment of the precise technical rationality which grew out of this thought."[171] Typical of this deployment was the sinister spatialization of time and the destruction of memory against which Bergson had railed. The spectacle, Debord wrote, is the *"false consciousness of time."*[172] Equally characteristic was the triumph of contemplation over action, the society of the spectacle being precisely the place "where the commodity contemplates itself in a world which it has created."[173] Whatever pleasure such a world provides is only a simulacrum of the real thing, a "pseudo-joy which contains repression in it."[174] Debord's bleak diagnosis of the mystification of everyday life and domination of true by false needs, with its echoes of Herbert Marcuse's then widely remarked critique of "one-dimensional society," was not without its optimistic antithesis. Standard forms of working-class organization may have been bankrupt—Bolshevism, he wrote, was complicitous with "the domination of the modern spectacle: the *representation* of the working class has opposed itself radically to the working class"[175]—but there were hopes for a new nondominating vanguard that would help the masses to unmask the illusions that enslaved them. The goal was a nonstatist society of self-managing workers' councils in which the spatial separation and passive contemplation of the spectacle would be undone.

In cultural terms, the task was to end the very distinction between art and society in a grand sublation, indeed to overcome the independent realm of culture itself. Interestingly, in the light of the subsequent postmodernist rediscovery of the baroque, Debord praised it for being the

171. Ibid., par. 19.
172. Ibid., par. 158.
173. Ibid., par. 53.
174. Ibid., par. 59.
175. Ibid., par. 100.

first to mingle the historical and the aesthetic and thus anticipate the negation of art as a realm in itself. More recent avant-garde movements carried the project still further, but still with limitations: "Dadaism wanted *to suppress art without realizing it*; surrealism wanted *to realize art without suppressing it*. The critical position later elaborated by the *situationists* has shown that the suppression and the realization of art are inseparable aspects of the same *overcoming of art*."[176] This overcoming cannot be done merely in thought, but in the radical restructuring of social relations dominated by images. Only then, Debord concluded his book, will the dealienation of mankind occur and "dialogue arm itself to make its own conditions victorious."[177]

What was new in Debord's critique was its hyperbolic contention that society *as a whole* had been turned into a gigantic spectacle, in which the visible form of the commodity totally occupied everyday life, uniting production and consumption in one monstrous system. No one before him, as Jonathan Crary has noted, put the definite article before "spectacle" and demonized it so thoroughly.[178] It is, nonetheless, easy to discern in his analysis many familiar motifs of the antiocular discourse: the contrast between lived, temporally meaningful experience, the immediacy of speech, and collective participation, on the one hand, with "dead" spatialized images, the distancing effect of the gaze, and the passivity of individuated contemplation, on the other. For all their hopes for happiness in the festival of unalienated existence, there was something of the ascetic suspicion of "the lust of the eyes" in the Situationists' relentless hostility

176. Ibid., par. 191.

177. Ibid., par. 221. Dialogue, to be sure, is a future possibility, not one permitted to true revolutionaries in the present. In defense of their frequent practice of excluding internal dissidents, the Situationists would condemn the "ideology of dialogue." See Knabb, ed., *Situationist International Anthology*, p. 177.

178. Jonathan Crary, "Spectacle, Attention, Counter-Memory," *October*, 50 (Fall, 1989), p. 97. He does note the use of the term in a more positive sense by the painter Fernand Léger in his 1924 essay, "The Spectacle," in *Functions of Painting*, trans. Alexandra Anderson (New York, 1973).

to visual pleasure in the present. When Debord insisted that "revolution is not 'showing' people life, it is making them live,"[179] there was a touch of the stern Rousseauist injunction to force people to be free by compelling them to shut their eyes to illusion, whether they wanted to or not.

Situationism's radical critique, already influential in the student strike in Strasbourg in 1966, reached its most receptive audience amidst the festival that was May, 1968. The international in its title gained added meaning, as offshoots appeared in other countries and its works were translated into more than ten foreign languages. But with the defeat of the student movement, its historical moment was soon over. Its journal ceased publication in 1969; its last conference was held in Venice that same year. Following more internecine squabbling and the resignations of central figures like Bernstein and Vaneigem, the Situationist International dissolved itself in 1972.[180] In its fifteen-year history, only seventy individuals had actually been official members, and because of the frequency of splits and exclusions, never more than twenty belonged at one time.

Although Debord held fast to his intransigent critique of the spectacle,[181] he soon faded, as it were, from view, with only the occasional film to remind the public of his existence. Like Althusser, whose antiocular critique of ideology was also powerful in the same period,[182] his fortunes were tied to the French infatuation with Marxism. When it collapsed, he no longer seemed very relevant to current problems. Foucault's "specific intellectual," with his antiutopian acceptance of the ubiquity of power and the inescapability of surveillance, captured the mood of the 1970s

179. Debord, "For a Revolutionary Judgment of Art" (February, 1961), in Knabb, ed., *Situationist International Anthology*, p. 312.

180. For Debord's version of its final years, see his "Notes to Serve toward the History of the S.I. from 1969–1971," in *The Veritable Split in the International* (Paris, 1972).

181. See, for example, his *Préface à la quatrième edition italienne de "La Société du spectacle"* (Paris, 1979), and his *Commentaires sur la société du spectacle* (Paris, 1988).

182. Wollen calls them "mirror images of each other, complementary halves of the ruptured unity of Western Marxism . . . one, so to speak, abstractly romantic, the other abstractly classical" ("Bitter Victory," p. 56). What united them, however, was their shared distrust of the hegemony of the eye.

and 1980s much more accurately than did Debord's still "universal intellectual" with his unyielding pretention to speak for and about the totality. It became easy for more skeptical thinkers like Philippe Lacoue-Labarthe to tax the Situationists for being "caught up in a sort of Rousseauist reverie of *appropriation*—which was in the end merely set against all forms of *representation* (from the image to the delegation of power)."[183] Although the rage and destructive energy of the Situationist movement spilled over into popular cultural phenomena, such as punk rock,[184] its political analysis no longer attracted much interest.

Situationism was doomed to ultimate frustration from the beginning. Its stress on play and the festival was incoherently related to its celebration of workers' councils and intransigent faith in the proletariat as the subject of history. Its contempt for the elitism of traditional working class parties was undercut by its own sectarian intolerance of dissent. Its penchant for totalizing critique and redemptive politics made anything short of a utopian reversal of the status quo seem a defeat. Its critical appropriation of mass culture was often blind to gender issues, which allowed it to recycle sexist images of women with little discomfort. And finally, its hope to sublate art and life and reenchant the banal life world failed to do justice to the complex differentiations that characterized what Habermas has called the uncompleted process of modernity.[185]

And yet what survived the shipwreck of Situationism as a political movement was precisely its assault on the spectacle, which fit so well with the more wide-ranging denigration of the visual in recent French

183. Philippe Lacoue-Labarthe, *Heidegger, Art and Politics: The Fiction of the Political*, trans. Chris Turner (Cambridge, Mass., 1990), p. 65.

184. See Marcus, *Lipstick Traces*, for the linkages. He contends that not only the negative side of Situationism but also some of its millenarian hopes survived in groups like the Sex Pistols.

185. Habermas's critique of other attempts to unite art and life, most notably those of the Surrealists, appears in "Modernity versus Postmodernity," *New German Critique*, 22 (Winter, 1981); for a sample of the discussion it provoked, see Richard J. Bernstein, ed., *Habermas and Modernity* (Cambridge, Mass., 1985). Without acknowledging it, however, Habermas's own work echoes one of Debord's key concepts, that of the "colonization of everyday life," which in his lexicon becomes the "colonization of the lifeworld."

thought. Thus subsequent critics of everyday life, such as Michel de Certeau, could echo Debord in arguing that "from TV to newspapers, from advertising to all sorts of mercantile epiphanies, our society is characterized by a cancerous growth of vision, measuring everything by its ability to show or be shown and transmuting communication into a visual journey."[186] Also belittling a high-altitude "Icarian" perspective on the city, de Certeau praised instead the Daedalus-like walker who prowls its labyrinthine spaces.[187] Others like Maurice Blanchot could agree that "the everyday loses any power to reach us; it is no longer what is lived, but what can be seen or what shows itself, spectacle and description, without any active relation whatsoever. The whole world is offered to us, but by way of a look."[188] By the 1970s, scarcely any discussion in France or elsewhere of the manipulative power of mass culture could resist blaming its spectacular dimension.[189]

Although Debord claimed that the full-blown society of the spectacle had emerged only in the 1920s, historians like Jean-Marie Apostolidès could project the role of the spectacle in politics as far back as the reign of Louis XIV.[190] And others, like T. J. Clark, himself once a member of the English section of the Situationist International, could employ it to make

186. Michel de Certeau, *The Practice of Everyday Life*, trans. Steven F. Rendall (Berkeley, 1984), p. xxi.

187. Ibid., pp. 92–93. The Icarus/Daedalus contrast could, of course, have been derived from Bataille as well as Debord.

188. Maurice Blanchot, "Everyday Speech," *Yale French Studies*, 73 (1987), p. 14. Blanchot credits Lefebvre more than Debord for his interest in the theme of the everyday.

189. For an overview of its function in the work of American writers like Daniel Boorstin, Richard Sennett, Daniel Bell, Christopher Lasch, and Jerry Mander, see Patrick Brantlinger, *Bread and Circuses: Theories of Mass Culture and Social Decay* (Ithaca, 1983), chap. 8. They tend to focus more on the effects of television than did the Situationists, who were more involved with the cinema. For an interesting attempt to apply Debord's analysis to English culture in the nineteenth century, see Thomas Richards, *The Commodity Culture of Victorian England: Advertising and Spectacle, 1851–1914* (Stanford, 1990).

190. Apostolidès, *Le roi-machine*, pp. 148ff. On Debord's dating, see *Commentaires sur la société du spectacle*, p. 13.

sense of the Paris of the Impressionists.[191] The penchant for French fascists to deny the existence of the Holocaust could be blamed by Alice Yaeger Kaplan on the denigration of memory in the society of the spectacle.[192] Even theologians like Jacques Ellul could praise Debord's "rigorous and explanatory"[193] thought and employ it in the service of a religious defense of the word against the image.

The loose and unfocused reception of the Situationists' central concept has, in fact, led one observer to wonder "how far the anti-spectacle attitude is from the iconoclastic fear of idolatry found in the ascetic sectors of the three major Western religions, and that what is 'real' is what cannot be represented."[194] Whether or not this is the case, it is clear that the concept of the spectacle could be detached from its subversive political function and become a merely descriptive tool to describe current cultural conditions. In the 1980s, postmodernist writers like Jean Baudrillard stopped worrying and found a way to accept and even celebrate what Debord and his colleagues had found so troubling: the ubiquity of images without referents and the reification of experience. Baudrillard, who also exhorted his readers to "forget Foucault,"[195] giddily embraced rather than castigated the "hyperreal simulacrum" of reality.

191. T. J. Clark, *The Painting of Modern Life: Paris in the Art of Manet and His Followers* (Princeton, 1984), pp. 9ff. The document recounting his 1967 exclusion, along with two other British members, is included in Knabb, ed., *Situationist International Anthology*, pp. 293–294. Its vituperative and punishing tone captures the Situationists at their most sectarian.

192. Alice Yaeger Kaplan, *Reproductions of Banality: Fascism, Literature and French Intellectual Life* (Minneapolis, 1986), p. 168. A similar analysis has been applied to other fascists, for example, by Russell Berman, "Written Right Across Their Faces: Ernst Jünger's Fascist Modernism," in *Modernity and the Text: Revisions of German Modernism*, eds. Andreas Huyssen and David Bathrick (New York, 1989), and to more recent art, for example, by Hal Foster, "Contemporary Art and Spectacle," in *Recodings: Art, Spectacle, Cultural Politics* (Port Townsend, Wash., 1985).

193. Jacques Ellul, *The Humiliation of the Word*, trans. Joyce Main Hanks (Grand Rapids, Mich., 1985), p. 115.

194. Jon Erickson, review of Greil Marcus, *Lipstick Traces*, in *Discourse*, 12.1 (Fall–Winter, 1989–1990), p. 135.

195. Jean Baudrillard, *Oublier Foucault* (Paris, 1977).

Although some commentators reproached Baudrillard for having left the insights of Debord behind,[196] others contended that he was right to move beyond a critical concept of the spectacle, which was no longer adequate to the nonvisible, uncongealed world of data flows that loomed before us.[197] During the heyday of Situationism, Raoul Vaneigem had optimistically predicted that "the spectacle's degeneration is in the nature of things, and the dead weight which enforces passivity is bound to lighten. Roles are eroded by the resistance put up by lived experience, and spontaneity will eventually lance the abscess of inauthenticity and pseudo-activity."[198] Baudrillard cynically responded that what had really degenerated was spontaneous, lived experience and all that was left were the hyperreal effects of pure simulation, "whose operation is nuclear and genetic, and no longer specular and discursive."[199]

Whether or not Baudrillard's critique of Debord represented a more broadly shared postmodernist restitution of the power of images is a theme that will have to be addressed in our final chapter. For now, suffice it to say that both Foucault's critique of surveillance and Debord's of the spectacle provided a generation of critics with new ammunition in their struggle against the hegemony of the eye. Still more was offered by commentators on the greatest technological extensions of visual experience in the modern world: photography and the cinema. Roland Barthes and Christian Metz revealed no direct debt to Foucault or Debord, but their work shared nonetheless in the denigration of the gaze that so permeated French thought in the twentieth century.

196. See, for example, Douglas Kellner, *Jean Baudrillard: From Marxism to Postmodernism and Beyond* (Cambridge, 1989), p. 214.

197. Jonathan Crary, "Eclipse of the Spectacle," in *Art After Modernism: Rethinking Representation*, ed. Brian Wallis (New York, 1984), p. 287; and "Spectacle, Attention, Counter-Memory," p. 107. Crary, to be sure, is careful not to draw the same complacent conclusions from this change as Baudrillard.

198. Raoul Vaneigem, *The Revolution of Everyday Life*, trans. Donald Nicholson-Smith (London, 1983), p. 98. The original title was *Traité de savoir-vivre à l'usage des jeunes generations* (Paris, 1967).

199. Jean Baudrillard, "Simulacra and Simulations," in *Selected Writings*, ed. Mark Poster (Stanford, 1988), p. 167.

CHAPTER EIGHT

The Camera as Memento Mori: Barthes, Metz, and the Cahiers du Cinéma

I crave, I long for Abstinence from
Images, for every Image is bad.

ROLAND BARTHES[1]

It is in fact essential to know that
cinema in its entirety is, in a
sense, a vast *trucage*.

CHRISTIAN METZ[2]

The interrogation of vision, as we have had ample opportunity to note, was frequently widened to include the eye's technological extensions. Inventions such as the telescope, the microscope, and the camera obscura were instrumental—in a literal as well as a metaphorical sense—in fostering the Cartesian perspectivalist scopic regime so dominant during most of the modern era. Others, such as the photograph and the stereoscope, made no less of a contribution to its growing crisis in the nineteenth century. Indeed, the critique of ocularcentrism as a whole was powerfully abetted by the questions about visual experience posed by the puzzling implications of new technologies and the scientific discourses surrounding them.[3]

As a result, virtually all of the theorists already examined were compelled to ponder the meaning of these extensions in the human capacity

1. Roland Barthes, "The Image," *The Rustle of Language*, trans. Richard Howard (Berkeley, 1989), p. 356.

2. Christian Metz, "*Trucage* and the Film," *Critical Inquiry*, 3, 4 (Summer, 1977), p. 670.

3. The best general account is Jonathan Crary, *Techniques of the Observer: On Vision and Modernity in the Nineteenth Century* (Cambridge, Mass., 1990).

to see. As might be expected, they generally concentrated on the two most culturally potent inventions: photography and the cinema. Bergson set the tone for many who followed with his suspicious disdain for both the snapshot's violent interruption of the flow of temporal duration and the cinema's inept attempt to restore its vitality. Others, like the Surrealists and Sartre, were often personally enamored of films and photographs, but became gradually disabused of their early infatuation.[4] Lettrist and Situationist film practice revealed more of a rage against the medium than a belief in its emancipatory potential. Novelists like Claude Simon and Alain Robbe-Grillet struggled to incorporate the new visual media in their prose techniques, or even tried to master them themselves.[5] Neither the spectacle nor surveillance in its current form could be imagined, the critics of these phenomena often argued, without the aid of television, the cinema, and photojournalism, which took much of the blame for their ubiquity.

It was not, however, until the amalgamation of structuralist, psychoanalytic and Marxist theory in the late 1960s and early 1970s that the critics of ocularcentrism devoted their full attention to photography and film. Armed with Althusserian and Lacanian arguments against the humanist subject, sympathetic to the demolition of that same subject in the so-called *nouveau roman* of the previous decade, anxious to situate ideology in material apparatuses rather than mere "false consciousness," a number of prominent theorists probed as never before the problematic implications of the new visual technologies.

4. See Glenn Willmott, "Implications for a Sartrean Radical Medium: From Theatre to Cinema," *Discourse*, 12.2 (Spring–Summer, 1990); Robert Harvey, "Sartre/Cinema: Spectator/Art That Is Not One," *Cinema Journal*, 30, 3 (Spring, 1991); and Gertrud Koch, "Sartre's Screen Projection of Freud," *October*, 57 (October, 1991). Koch claims that Sartre's understanding of the link between film and the gaze anticipated Lacanian film theory (p. 16). Merleau-Ponty, on the other hand, did not lose his enthusiasm. See "The Film and the New Psychology," in *Sense and Non-sense*, trans. Hubert L. Dreyfus and Patricia A. Dreyfus (Evanston, Ill., 1964).

5. For analyses, see Bruce Morrissette, *Novel and Film: Essays in Two Genres* (Chicago, 1985); and David Carroll, *The Subject in Question: The Languages of Theory and the Strategies of Fiction* (Chicago, 1982).

Although it would be impossible to do justice to all of the figures involved or all of the nuances of their work, two in particular are worth singling out for special attention: Roland Barthes with reference to the camera and Christian Metz in regard to film. Some sixteen years apart in age, they were nonethless close friends and frequent collaborators whose work showed considerable mutual influence.[6] This chapter will begin by analyzing Barthes's lifelong fascination with photography, culminating in his final book, *Camera Lucida*. It will then conclude by exploring the stunningly antiocularcentric film theory developed in the wake of Lacan and Althusser by Metz and his colleagues at the *Cahiers du Cinéma*.

⊙

It is a convention of the massive literature on Roland Barthes to emphasize the labile and unpredictable nature of his career.[7] Barthes the sober structuralist decoder transformed himself into the hedonist "professor of desire," seeking ecstatic *jouissance* beyond the mere *plaisir* of binary oppositions. The militant Marxist with his "euphoric dream of scientificity"[8] became the self-conscious expert on the nuances of love. The celebrant of textuality turned into a champion of the body, which could both be read as a legible text and as the limit of legibility. He who had solemnly proclaimed the death of the author, drowned in a sea of intertextuality,

6. Barthes's importance for the younger Metz is evident throughout the latter's work, which contains many positive references. For Barthes's appreciation of Metz, see his 1975 essay, "To Learn and to Teach," *The Rustle of Language*.

7. See, for example, Philip Thody, *Roland Barthes: A Conservative Estimate* (Atlantic Highlands, N.J., 1977); Annette Lavers, *Roland Barthes: Structuralism and After* (London, 1982); Jonathan Culler, *Roland Barthes* (New York, 1983); Steven Ungar, *Roland Barthes: The Professor of Desire* (Lincoln, Nebr., 1983); Philippe Roger, *Roland Barthes, roman* (Paris, 1986); Ginette Michaud, *Lire le fragment: Transfert et théorie de la lecture chez Roland Barthes* (Ville LaSalle, Quebec, 1989); Steven Ungar and Betty R. McGraw, eds., *Signs in Culture: Roland Barthes Today* (Iowa City, 1989). For a bibliography of Barthes's own work and the secondary material up until 1982, see Sanford Freedman and Carole Anne Taylor, *Roland Barthes: A Biographical Reader's Guide* (New York, 1983).

8. Roland Barthes, "Réponses," *Tel Quel*, 47 (Autumn, 1971), p. 97.

nonetheless fashioned himself into an internationally renowned "writer" on the level of a Sartre or a Malraux. The shy observer from a distance, still metaphorically residing in the tuberculosis sanatoriums in which he had spent much of his youth, came to exhibit himself publicly as the central character in an autobiographical "novel."[9] In short, to cite a typical assessment, "from the very beginning, Barthes struggled to break the signs, to proliferate meanings, to exceed structure, classification, and stereotypes."[10]

Yet throughout all of the kaleidoscopic mutations and playful disruptions of his identity, Barthes retained an unremittingly intense interest in the theme that fascinated so many of his compatriots: the status of the visual in contemporary culture. He was also passionately interested in music and the ear—he learned to play the piano at an early age and also studied voice—and was fascinated as well by taste and even smell.[11] But Barthes was drawn even more frequently to what he called the "dioptric arts"[12]—theater, painting, cinema, and literature. He also tried his own hand as an artist, and shortly after his death in 1980 an exhibition of his paintings and sketches was mounted in Rome.[13] Even when it came to his fervent linguistic interest, Barthes admitted, "I have a disease: I *see* language. . . . Hearing deviates to scopia: I feel myself to be the visionary and voyeur of language."[14]

Although his attitude defies reduction to unequivocal hostility, many of the criticisms of visual phenomena already encountered reappeared in

9. The epigraph to *Roland Barthes*, trans. Richard Howard (New York, 1977), says "it must all be considered as if spoken by a character in a novel."

10. John O'Neill, "Breaking the Signs: Roland Barthes and the Literary Body," in *The Structural Allegory: Reconstructive Encounters with Recent French Thought*, ed. John Fekete (Minneapolis, 1984), p. 195.

11. Barthes wrote about Japanese food in *The Empire of Signs* and was very interested in Brillat-Savarin's *Physiologie du goût*. See *The Rustle of Language*.

12. Barthes, "Diderot, Brecht, Eisenstein," in *Image-Music-Text*, trans. and ed. Stephen Heath (New York, 1977), p. 70.

13. "Roland Barthes: Carte Segni," at the Casino dell'Aurora in Rome, February–March, 1981, cited in Ungar, *Roland Barthes*, p. 85.

14. Barthes, *Roland Barthes*, p. 161.

his work. Accepting the arguments of the *Annales* school historians and Georg Simmel, he contended that the modern age had reversed the medieval hierarchy of the senses, putting sight on top in place of hearing and touch.[15] One of the most insistent debunkers of the classical French fetish of clarity in language, Barthes was also an early champion of Alain Robbe-Grillet's visually self-conscious fiction, which he admiringly read to imply that sight, revealing a world of opaque objects, "cannot lead to reflection."[16] Barthes was, moreover, among the first to recognize the importance of Bataille's violent narrative of the enucleated eye.[17] Sensitive to the role of visual experience in the maintenance of modern "mythologies," he also produced telling critiques of such phenomena as *The Family of Man* photo exhibition and the *Paris-Match* cover of a black soldier in a French uniform, which anticipated Debord's "society of the spectacle" by a decade.[18]

15. Barthes, *Sade, Fourier, Loyola*, trans. Richard Miller (New York, 1976), p. 65; and "Taking Sides," in *Critical Essays*, trans. Richard Howard (Evanston, Ill., 1972), p. 164.

16. On the dangers of clarity, see Barthes, *Writing Degree Zero*, trans. Annette Lavers and Colin Smith (Boston, 1970) and "Roland Barthes on Roland Barthes" (April, 1979 interview in *Lire*) in *The Grain of the Voice: Interviews 1962–1980*, trans. Linda Coverdale (New York, 1985), p. 332. On Robbe-Grillet, see "Literal Literature," "There is No Robbe-Grillet School," and "The Last Word on Robbe-Grillet," in Barthes, *Critical Essays*, as well as his foreword to Bruce Morrissette, *The Novels of Robbe-Grillet* (Ithaca, 1975). The citation comes from "There Is no Robbe-Grillet School," p. 92. For a discussion of Barthes on Robbe-Grillet, which also emphasizes the novelist's divorce of sight from knowledge, see Claudio Guillén, *Literature as System: Essays Toward the Theory of Literary History* (Princeton, 1971), pp. 355ff. Most recently, Fredric Jameson has pointed out that Robbe-Grillet's work can "be read today less as an affirmation of the visual over the other senses than as a radical repudiation of phenomenological perception as such." *Postmodernism, or, the Cultural Logic of Late Capitalism* (Durham, N.C., 1991), p. 135.

17. Barthes, "The Metaphor of the Eye," *Critical Essays*. He also wrote admiringly of Bataille's overturning of the normal corporeal hierarchy through his appreciation of "The Big Toe." See Barthes, "Outcomes of the Text," in *The Rustle of Language*. For a critical analysis of his formalist reading of Bataille, see Brian T. Fitch, "A Critique of Roland Barthes' Essay on Bataille's *Histoire de l'oeil*," in *Interpretation of Narrative*, eds. Mario J. Valdés and Owen J. Miller (Toronto, 1978).

18. Barthes, *Mythologies*, trans. Annette Lavers (New York, 1972; original ed., 1957).

An avid exponent of the virtues of semiology, Barthes sought to apply it to the "'language' of the human image-repertoire"[19] in everything from film to fashion. His insistence that the body and its gestures could be treated as a visible text earned him a comparison with physiognomists like Lavater.[20] Many of the interrogations of the visual already encountered in this narrative, such as Sartre's discussion of the imagination and Lacan's of the mirror stage, provided him critical tools unavailable in the writings of his masters in linguistics: Saussure, A. J. Greimas, and Louis Hjelmslev.

Although at times Barthes seemed to be seeking the reduction of visual experience to a readable code, no less amenable to semiological analysis than any other, elsewhere he recognized the resistance of language's own materiality, including its visual dimension. Thus, for example, he was fascinated by the ambiguous implications of the fashion designer Erté's decorated alphabet with its "erotographic" and "semioclastic" transformation of letters into women's bodies.[21] He also savored the visual rhetoric of baroque artists like Giuseppe Arcimboldo.[22] And he wrote with evident relish about the opaque "empire of signs" he encountered in Japan in a work splendidly illustrated with color photos.[23] He had in fact devoted so much attention to these issues that after his death it was possible to compose an entire exhibition of his writings on visual themes with their accompanying artifacts, which was entitled "Roland Barthes: Le Texte et l'Image."[24]

19. Barthes, "Semiology and the Cinema," interview in *Image et Son* (1964); reprinted in *The Grain of the Voice*, p. 37.

20. Michael Shortland, "Skin Deep: Barthes, Lavater and the Legible Body," *Economy and Society*, 14, 3 (August, 1985).

21. Barthes, "Erté, or à la lettre," *The Responsibility of Forms: Critical Essays on Music, Art and Representation*, trans. Richard Howard (New York, 1985); for analyses, see Betty R. McGraw, "Semiotics, Erotographics, and Barthes' Visual Concerns," *Substance*, 26 (1980), pp. 68–75; and Ungar, *Roland Barthes*, pp. 91ff., and "From Writing to the Letter: Barthes and Alphabetese," in *Visual Language*, 11, 4 (Autumn, 1977). "Semioclasm" is Ungar's term.

22. Barthes, "Arcimboldo, or Magician and Rhétoriqueur," *The Responsibility of Forms*.

Perhaps nowhere was his concern for the visual as explicit as in his frequent musings on photography, which culminated in one of his most deeply felt and self-revelatory texts, *Camera Lucida*.[25] In a posthumously published essay of 1977 entitled "Right in the Eyes," which dealt inter alia with Richard Avedon's photographs, Barthes hinted at the reason for his concern. "Science," he wrote, "interprets the gaze in three (combinable) ways: in terms of information (the gaze informs), in terms of relation (gazes are exchanged), in terms of possession (by the gaze, I touch, I attain, I seize, I am seized): three functions: optical, linguistic, haptic. But the gaze *seeks*: something, someone. It is an *anxious* sign: singular dynamics for a sign: its power overflows it."[26] What, it must be asked, did Barthes mean by the anxiety of the seeking gaze, and how did it manifest itself in particular in the photograph, as he understood it?[27]

His earliest attempt to provide an answer came in a 1961 essay entitled "The Photographic Message," published in the inaugural issue of the journal *Communications*.[28] Written at the height of his semiology cum

23. Barthes, *The Empire of Signs*, trans. Richard Howard (New York, 1982).

24. The show was held at the Pavillon des Arts in Paris from May 7th to August 3, 1986; the catalogue was published under the same name that year.

25. Barthes, *Camera Lucida: Reflections on Photography*, trans. Richard Howard (New York, 1981). Although he wrote sporadically on the cinema, he was clearly more interested in the still photograph. For a comparison, see Steven Ungar, "Persistence of the Image: Barthes, Photography, and the Resistance to Film," in Ungar and McGraw, eds., *Signs in Culture*. Barthes, to be sure, was also deeply attracted to the theater, which he acknowledged was perhaps at "the crossroads of the entire *oeuvre*" (*Roland Barthes*, p. 177).

26. Barthes, "Right in the Eyes," *The Responsibility of Forms*, p. 238.

27. Why Barthes called the gaze a sign is also an intriguing question, especially because at the outset of this very essay, which was unpublished at his death and may not have been completed, he wrote that "a sign is what repeats itself . . . the gaze can say everything but cannot repeat itself, 'word for word.' Hence, the gaze is not a sign, yet it signifies . . . the gaze belongs to that realm of signification whose unit is not the sign (discontinuity) but *signifying* [*signifiance*], whose theory Benveniste has proposed" (p. 237). Whatever the proper terminology for the gaze, the crucial point is the anxiety surrounding it for Barthes.

28. Barthes, "The Photographic Message," in *Image-Music-Text*.

ideology critique period, but showing the residues of his earlier schooling in phenomenology, it argued that the autonomous structure of the photograph could be broken down into two elements that created "the photographic paradox." The first was its denotative capacity to imitate the world. "Certainly the image is not the reality," Barthes wrote in words cited earlier, "but at least it is its perfect *analogon* and it is exactly this analogical perfection which, to common sense, defines the photograph. Thus can be seen the special status of the photographic image: *it is a message without a code*."[29] But photographs also had a second-order capacity to signify, which Barthes identified with their connotative power: the cultural resonances activated by their reception.

Because of the power of the analogical dimension of the medium, which gives the impression that is pure denotation, photography often seems to escape the rhetorical power of its connotative overlay. For Barthes, this ability was the source of its mythological potential, its confusion of artifice with nature, its ability to contribute to what elsewhere he called "the reality effect."[30] Could the photograph escape myth and actually become a true simulacrum of the world, unmediated by cultural coding? Interestingly, Barthes acknowledged that although rare, such possibilities did exist when the picture taken—and here he was talking of the press photograph in particular—was of a traumatic event. For "the trauma is a suspension of language, the blockage of meaning. . . . One could imagine a kind of law: the more direct the trauma, the more difficult is connotation; or again, the 'mythological' effect of a photograph is inversely proportional to its traumatic effect."[31]

Barthes's discrimination between an analogical, denotative dimension of photography and its connotative, socially constituted overlay reappeared at various moments throughout his career.[32] It even survived the critique of more absolutist semiologists like Umberto Eco, who claimed

29. Ibid., p. 17.

30. Barthes, "The Reality Effect," *The Rustle of Language*. In this 1968 essay, he included photography in the milieu that gave rise to the realistic novel in the nineteenth century (p. 146).

31. Barthes, "The Photographic Message," p. 31.

nothing phenomenologically pure, no codeless message, was prior to the process of codification.[33] Whether or not their arguments successfully undermine the distinction cannot be decided now, although, as has been argued in chapter 2, Charles Sanders Peirce's triad of symbol, icon, and index might help restore it. What is more interesting for our purposes is Barthes's identification of photographic denotation with emotional trauma, which provides a clue to answer the question of why the seeking gaze produced anxiety.

His next effort to treat the subject, "Rhetoric of the Image," written in 1964,[34] supplies still other possible explanations. It dealt primarily with advertising images, which Barthes claimed could be understood as presenting three messages: linguistic, coded iconic, and noncoded iconic. Once again, he contrasted the denotative, analogous quality of the last of these with the connotative, rhetorical, semiologically legible quality of the first two. He also repeated his claim that "*it is precisely the syntagm of the denoted message which 'naturalizes' the system of the connoted message.*"[35] What was new in this essay was Barthes's description of what photographic denotation presented to the eye of the beholder. "It establishes," he wrote, "not a consciousness of the *being-there* of the thing (which any copy could provoke) but an awareness of its *having-been-there*. What we have is a new space-time category: spatial immediacy and temporal anteriority, the photograph being an illogical conjunction between the *here-now* and the *there-then*."[36] The implication of this argument was profound, for now Barthes had uncovered a further source of the anxiety

32. It reappeared again, for example, in the 1977 interview he gave "On Photography," reprinted in *The Grain of the Voice*, p. 353. In first counterposing connotation and denotation in *Mythologies*, Barthes drew on the glossematics of Louis Hjelmslev, but reversed its belief in the priority of the latter over the former. See his discussion in *S/Z*, trans. Richard Miller (New York, 1974), p. 7.

33. Umberto Eco, "Critique of the Image," in *Thinking Photography*, ed. Victor Burgin (London, 1982), pp. 33ff.

34. Barthes, "Rhetoric of the Image," *Image-Music-Text*.

35. Ibid., p. 51.

36. Ibid., p. 44.

surrounding the photographic image. That is, beyond the fact that the denotative power of photographs was most evident when they showed explicit traumas, the inevitable aura of a lost past attached to *all* photographs suggested an implicit trauma as well: the pain associated with mourning that loss.

Among the conclusions Barthes drew from this new insight was the radical disparity between photography and cinema: "Film can no longer be seen as animated photographs: the *having-been-there* gives way before a *being-there* of the thing."[37] In a subsequent essay of 1970 devoted to the stills taken from the Russian director Sergei Eisenstein's *Ivan the Terrible*, Barthes elaborated the implications of his argument.[38] In the still, he claimed, something was revealed that the continuous motion picture obscured. That something he dubbed "the third meaning" beyond the informational and symbolic level of the film. Borrowing a term from Julia Kristeva, he called it the level of *signifiance*, which was not equivalent to that of signification or communication. Whereas the latter two produced what Barthes called the "obvious" sign, a meaning which seeks out the viewer, *signifiance* provided only "obtuse meanings" instead. Defining obtuseness variously as blunted, rounded in form, and greater than the "right angle" of meaningful narrative, Barthes also linked it explicitly to Bataille's notion of expenditure and Mikhail Bahktin's idea of the carnivalesque. Resisting metalinguistic translation, outside of the circuit of semantic exchange, not a copy of anything in the real world, obtuse meaning was visual counternarrative: "disseminated, reversible, set to its own temporality . . . counterlogical and yet 'true'."[39] It remains a fragment of a whole, which can never be reunited through the setting in motion of the cinematic apparatus.[40]

From these three essays can be discerned some of the sources of the un-

37. Ibid., p. 45.

38. Barthes, "The Third Meaning: Research Notes on Some Eisenstein Stills," *Image-Music-Text*.

39. Ibid., p. 63.

canny doubleness of photographs for Barthes, their paradoxical, anxiety-inducing effect. Beyond their meaningful, communicative, connotative "obviousness," which gives them their ideological force and makes them vulnerable to semiological demystification, they also contain an "obtuse" meaning that defies description in linguistic terms. Although on one level, such obtuseness seemed to function for Barthes as a laudable disruption of the smooth workings of myth and ideology, on another, it suggested a deeper problem. For denotation, instead of being a straightforward analogical representation of nature, turns out to point to a traumatic reality that is no longer there, a fragment of a whole that can never be revealed.

What precisely that absent hurt was for Barthes became clearer in his remarkable autobiographical "novel," *Roland Barthes* of 1975, which significantly began with a portfolio of photographs from Barthes's youth. To understand their role, it is necessary to acknowledge Barthes's enthusiastic reception of one of the most influential texts in the French antiocular-centric discourse, Lacan's essay on the mirror stage. According to his own testimony, Barthes "needed" a psychology when he was working on *A Lover's Discourse*, which was published in 1977, and found Lacan's psychoanalysis especially useful.[41] But as one of his leading commentators, Steven Ungar, has noted, Lacanian themes can be found as early as *S/Z*, published in 1970, and perhaps even in some of his writings in 1968.[42]

Barthes also claimed that his own notion of the "image-repertoire" was not as negatively inflected as Lacan's "Imaginary."[43] In many ways, how-

40. For a thorough discussion of the pivotal role of the fragment in Barthes's entire *oeuvre*, see Michaud, *Lire le fragment*. For a complementary discussion of the detail, see Naomi Schor, *Reading in Detail: Aesthetics and the Feminine* (New York, 1987), chap. 5.

41. Barthes, "Of What Use Is an Intellectual?" (1977 interview), in *The Grain of the Voice*, p. 274.

42. Ungar, *The Professor of Desire*, p. 81. For confirmation, see the 1970 interview, "*L'Express* talks to Roland Barthes," in *The Grain of the Voice*, p. 93.

43. Barthes, "Of What Use Is an Intellectual?" p. 275.

ever, the term inevitably brought with it the implication of ideology, which others like Althusser eagerly exploited in the late 1960s.[44] Thus, for example, Barthes's celebrated invidious comparison between Text and Work was based on the claim that whereas the former was in the realm of the symbolic, the latter was only the "imaginary tail of the Text."[45] Similarly, Barthes echoed Lacan's attack on ego psychological notions of subjective wholeness, claiming that the "je" was a problematic construct able to experience only the limited "pleasure" that was undermined by the "bliss" of decentered, linguistic expenditure. "What Lacan means by *imaginaire*," he told an interviewer in 1975, "is closely related to analogy, analogy between images, since the image-repertoire is the register where the subject adheres to an image in a movement of identification that relies in particular on the signifier and the signified. Here we reencounter the theme of representation, figuration, the homogeneity of images and models."[46] Now, instead of invoking the analogical function of the photograph as an "obtuse" antidote to the "obvious" workings of narrativized ideology, Barthes linked it with Lacan's Imaginary, implying a certain distrust of the *méconnaissances* it engendered.

In *Roland Barthes*, a text whose main theme he later called "not the problem of bliss, but that of the image, the image-repertoire,"[47] the splitting of the centered "je" was enacted in a number of ways. The very title of the book—in French it was called *Roland Barthes par Roland Barthes*— and its injunction to be "considered as if spoken by a character in a novel"[48] problematized the status of both its author and its subject. Because of its Dionysian challenge to the serene image of an Apollonian self, the book has been called "a parody of *Ecce Homo*."[49]

44. Gregory L. Ulmer has argued that "Barthes's interest in the Imaginary may be seen as part of the 'politics of the Imaginary' that emerged after the May '68 events in France" ("The Discourse of the Imaginary," *Diacritics*, 10 [March, 1980], p. 66).

45. Barthes, "From Work to Text," *Image-Music-Text*, p. 157.

46. Barthes, "Twenty Key Words for Roland Barthes" (1975 interview), *The Grain of the Voice*, p. 209.

47. Ibid., p. 232.

48. Barthes, *Roland Barthes*, epigraph.

Within the text, there were four ways in which Barthes referred to "himself:" "I," "he," "R. B.," and "you." Only the first of these, he stressed, was the pronoun of the image-repertoire, but "an image-repertoire that tries to undo itself, unravel itself, to dismember itself, through mental structures that are no longer only those of the image-repertoire, without being, for all that, the structure of truth."[50] Barthes's playful use of the other "shifters," to use Roman Jakobson's famous term for pronouns with no determinant meaning, promoted still further the unraveling of his identity.

The book itself was comprised of loosely related fragments— "biographemes"[51] as Barthes called them in *Sade, Loyola, Fourier*—defying integration into a meaningful whole. Beginning with an uncaptioned photograph prior to the title page, it followed with thirty-five disparate images, accompanied by captions of varying length, of the young Barthes, family, friends, and places of his youth, as well as two images of writing and a hospital chart. They were, he informs the reader, "the author's treat to himself, for finishing the book . . . images which enthrall me, without my knowing why."[52] Then came some 225 short sections, occasionally interrupted by more visual material, including everything from photos and doodles to cartoons and an anatomy sketch from Diderot's *Encyclopedia*. The texts and images were explicitly irreducible to illustrations of each other, but commentators have often seen a certain pattern in their sequential arrangement that has seemed Lacanian in inspiration.

That is, the preponderance of images in the first part of the book and of text in the second suggests the transition, to be sure incomplete, from the Imaginary to the Symbolic stages. As if to make the association even

49. Gregory L. Ulmer, "Fetishism in Roland Barthes's Nietzschean Phase," *Papers in Language and Literature*, 14, 3 (Summer, 1978), p. 351. For another deconstructionist reading of *Roland Barthes* that compares its author with Nietzsche, see Paul Jay, *Being in the Text: Self-Representation from Wordsworth to Roland Barthes* (Ithaca, 1984), p. 175.

50. Barthes, "Twenty Key Words for Roland Barthes," *The Grain of the Voice*, p. 215.

51. Barthes, *Sade, Loyola, Fourier*, p. ix.

52. Barthes, *Roland Barthes*, unnumbered page after second photo.

more explicit, the initial, uncaptioned photo prior to the title page is of a youngish woman on a beach striding in very soft focus toward the camera; in the illustrations list at the end, she is identified as the "narrator's mother." In the album itself, there is an oval of the smiling mother, this time with the infant Roland in her arms. Underneath, Barthes has placed the caption "The mirror stage: 'That's you'." According to one commentator, this photograph "is perhaps the Flying Dutchman's 'ancient mark' that consecrates him in early childhood to the god Imaginary."[53] But significantly, as another has noted, this page is not placed at the actual point of origin of Barthes's book, but rather at the midpoint of the photo album.[54] Barthes may thus be both evoking and denying the search for the origin of identity in the founding moment of the mirror stage. The oval mother/son shot perhaps functions as the negative of the other photos or is anamorphically related to them, gesturing to a reality that is not on the same plane as the one they reflect.

Barthes, moreover, claimed that his personal transition from the period when he was dominated by the image-repertoire to the one in which writing replaced it occurred when he left the sanatorium for the last time in 1945.[55] As his age at the time, twenty, was a bit late for a strict psychoanalytic interpretation to make sense, it is clear that Barthes was not really holding to the Lacanian schema in any rigorous way. Or perhaps he was emphasizing the impossibility of ever really leaving the Imaginary behind. This interpretation is given more weight by the caption opposite two images of himself, one in 1942, the other in 1970, in which he wrote of the experience of not believing that is how one actually looks: "You are the only one who can never see yourself except as an image; you never see your eyes unless they are dulled by the gaze they rest upon the mirror or the lens . . . even and especially for your own body, you are condemned to the repertoire of its images."[56]

53. Lynn A. Higgins, "Barthes' Imaginary Voyages," *Studies in Twentieth Century Literature*, 5, 2 (Spring, 1981), p. 163.
54. Michaud, *Lire le fragment*, p. 111.
55. Barthes, *Roland Barthes*, p. 3.

But however much he remained captive to his image-repertoire, however fascinated he was by the images of his childhood, Barthes maintained that in his role as semiologist and cultural critic, he was compelled to resist their lure, or at least try. Noting that Saussure's bête noire was analogy, he claimed that "when I resist analogy, it is actually the imaginary I am resisting: which is to say: the coalescence of the sign, the similitude of signifier and signified, the homeomoporphism of images, the Mirror, the captivating bait."[57]

But how difficult it was to leave the Imaginary behind Barthes candidly acknowledged. At his most structuralist moments, he conceded, he had succumbed to the temptation to view objects panoramically, as if from the top of the Eiffel Tower. Even the poststructuralist recourse to an experimental writing of fragments, like that of *Roland Barthes* itself, was not fully successful. "I have the illusion to suppose," he admitted, "that by breaking up my discourse I cease to discourse in terms of the imaginary about myself, attenuating the risk of transcendence, but since the fragment . . . is *finally* a rhetorical genre and since rhetoric is that layer of language which best presents itself to interpretation, by supposing I disperse myself I merely return, quite docilely, to the bed of the imaginary."[58]

Appropriately, *Roland Barthes* ends with a fragment called "the monster of totality" in which Barthes ambivalently evokes both the threat and the promise of holistic stasis, based on an image of an almost Baudelairean *luxe, calme, et volupté*. Or rather the written text ends there, for after it come three final images, which ironically call into question the totalizing power of the image. The first is of an eighteenth-century anatomical drawing of the stems of the vena cava accompanied by the caption, "To write the body. Neither the skin, nor the muscles, nor the bones, nor the nerves, but the rest: an awkward, fibrous, shaggy raveled thing, a clown's coat."[59] The second is of two doodles, which he calls "the signifier with-

56. Ibid., p. 31.
57. Ibid., p. 44.
58. Ibid., p. 95.
59. Ibid., p. 180.

out the signified," and the third a sample of Barthes's handwriting, which ends with the defiant claim, "One writes with one's desire, and I am not through desiring."[60]

Significantly, however, these final images, which seem to question visual totalization and valorize symbolically generated, life-affirming desire, are not photographs. When Barthes returned to the theme of the photograph in *Camera Lucida*, his belief that it was anything but an affirmation of life was made more explicit than ever before. In the mountain of commentary generated by this text, there is universal recognition that Barthes's reflections betrayed the personal grief he felt at the recent death of his beloved mother.[61] The general importance of trauma in photographs, which he had stressed in his earliest meditations on the subject, now had a striking confirmation on the level of particular experience. His own accidental demise shortly after the book's publication—he was struck down by a laundry truck after leaving a lecture at the Collège de France in February, 1980, and died a month later of his injuries—only added to the poignancy of his argument for later readers. "Few texts," a typical commentator opined, "are so morbid as *La Chambre claire*."[62]

Few texts have also been subjected to as thorough an exegesis, as it obviously struck a respondent chord among those who had been immersed in the antiocularcentric discourse for a considerable time. Everything from its title (the original is in French, not Latin—that is, in Barthes's "mother tongue") to its dedication (an homage to Sartre's *L'Imaginaire*, which suggested the return of a phenomenological perspective) has been probed for meaning. No less energy has been spent analyzing the absence

60. Ibid., pp. 187–188.

61. In addition to the discussions in the books listed above, see Jean Delord, *Roland Barthes et la photographie* (Paris, 1981); Tom Conley, "A Message Without a Code?" *Studies in Twentieth Century Literature*, 5, 2 (Spring, 1981); Chantal Thomas, "La photo du Jardin d'Hiver," *Critique*, 38, 423–424 (August–September, 1982); Roland Sarkonak, "Roland Barthes and the Specter of Photography," *L'Esprit Créateur*, 32, 1 (Spring, 1982); Jacques Derrida, "The Deaths of Roland Barthes," *Philosophy and Non-Philosophy Since Merleau-Ponty*, ed. Hugh J. Silverman (New York, 1988).

62. Conley, "A Message Without a Code?" p. 153.

of a photo of Barthes himself, who was so prominently represented in *Roland Barthes*, and even more significantly, the absence of an image of his mother, whose haunting presence in a photograph is described, but not shown. Even the number of its sections, forty-eight, has been the object of interpretation, appearing to some as an inverted reference to the age of his mother at her death.

Although this is not the place for yet another minute dissection of this remarkable book, certain points warrant emphasis in connection with our larger theme. First, Barthes once again seemed concerned with what he had called the denotative rather than connotative quality of photographs, their analogical rather than semiotic function. The title itself, he explained in a later interview, was meant to evoke that implication: "I try to say that what is terrible about a photograph is that there is no depth in it, that it is *clear evidence* of what was there."[63] But now, unlike in his 1961 essay on "The Photographic Message," the analogical and denotative meant more than just an uncoded message; they implied instead the Imaginary with all of its problematic lures. To make this case necessitated more than a coolly detached analysis from afar. Barthes thus chose several photographs that moved him personally and then reflected on them in the hope of distilling the essence of the medium. "This," he acknowledged, "is a phenomenological method, an entirely subjective one."[64] It was, however, a "vague, casual, even cynical phenomenology"[65] concerned with two themes classical phenomenology occluded: desire and mourning.

The results were divided into two parts: the first twenty-four sections invited comparison with a "pleasure of the image" comparable to Barthes's earlier "pleasure of the text"; the second twenty-four stressed pain instead. Even in the first part, Barthes's morbid preoccupation with death was

63. Barthes, "From Taste to Ecstasy" (1980 interview), in *The Grain of the Voice*, p. 352. The title also expressed something else. For Barthes, the chemical process of fixing the image was ultimately more important than the perspectival system of camera obscura optics, because it allowed the referential residue that he saw as essential to the image's ability to "wound" the viewer in ways to be explained below.

64. Barthes, "On Photography" (1980 interview), in *The Grain of the Voice*, p. 357.

65. Barthes, *Camera Lucida*, p. 20.

apparent; describing the referent of the photograph as its "Spectrum," he remarked that "this word retains, through its root, a relation to 'spectacle' and adds to it that rather terrible thing which is there in every photograph: the return of the dead."[66] Echoing Sartre's description in *The Words* of his experience posing for his grandfather's camera, Barthes wrote that "once I feel myself observed by the lens, everything changes: I constitute myself in the process of 'posing,' I instantaneously make another body for myself, I transform myself in advance into an image. . . . I feel that the Photograph creates my body or mortifies it, according to its caprice. . . . The Photograph is the advent of myself as other, a cunning dissociation of consciousness from identity."[67] By thus being transformed from a subject to an object, by becoming a specter of himself, Barthes wrote, "I have become Total-Image, which is to say, Death in person. . . . Ultimately, what I am seeking in the photograph taken of me (the 'intention' according to which I look at it) is Death: Death is the *eidos* of that photograph."[68]

But it was not only the memento mori produced by his own reification in the camera's eye that made photography so necrophilic for Barthes. For at least certain images of others also "wounded" him in ways that awoke the specter of mortality. Once again operating with binary—or if Derrida is right, supplementary[69]—logic, Barthes distinguished between what he called the "studium" and the "punctum" of photographs. The former is the publically available meaning of the image, its connotatively charged subject matter determined by the cultural context in which it is received.

66. Ibid., p. 9.

67. Ibid., pp. 11–12. Barthes's complicated relation to Sartre has been treated in Lavers, *Roland Barthes*, pp. 66ff. One significant biographical similarity is the loss of their fathers, both naval officers, when they were very young—Sartre at fifteen months and Barthes when he was three. Interesting in light of Barthes's fascination with photos of his dead mother is that Sartre was said to have replied to questions about his father by dryly saying that "he was only a photo in my mother's bedroom" (cited in Annie Cohen-Solal, *Sartre: A Life*, ed. Norman Macafee, trans. Anna Cancogni [New York, 1987], p. 4).

68. Ibid., p. 15.

69. Derrida, "The Deaths of Roland Barthes," p. 285.

Like the "obvious sense" he had described in "The Third Meaning," it signified in rhetorical ways that were always coded, and thus could be decoded by semiotic analysis. A photograph's "studium" produced only the limited pleasure of recognition, comparable to that of the "readerly" text he had described in *S/Z*.

In contrast, the "punctum" was that unexpected prick, sting, or cut that disturbed the intelligibility of the culturally connoted meaning. Often a detail whose power was impossible to generalize for all viewers, it defied reduction to a code, serving as the analogon of something prior to codification. Like the "writerly" text with its experience of *jouissance* or a Japanese Haiku, the "punctum" could produce a higher order of emotional intensity. Evident in erotic photos, which Barthes distinguished from pornographic ones precisely because of their ability to take the viewer out of the frame into a "blind field" charged with desire of the unseen, it was also present in images of a very different kind: those that spoke of irretrievable loss. As he had argued in "The Rhetoric of the Image," it was the "having-been-there" of the photographic image that made it so poignant.

The precise object of his own mourning was not hard to discern. In the first part of *Camera Lucida*, Barthes spoke of the "punctum" of landscapes as evoking an uncanny, Baudelairean fantasy of utopian bliss, like that of the maternal body.[70] In the second part, he more explicitly developed the personal loss he experienced with his own mother's death. Searching for a photograph whose "punctum" would reactivate his connection with the lost object, he found one taken in 1898 of his then five-year-old mother and her seven-year-old brother in a conservatory, then called a Winter Garden. It serves, as Derrida notes, as the "*punctum* of the entire book."[71] In this image of his mother as a child, an image he refused to reproduce

70. According to Lynn A. Higgins, Barthes's travel writing on Japan and China displayed a similar mood. Such countries "were consistently experienced as maternal. Modestly claiming to describe only a 'fantasized Japan', a 'hallucinated' China, he situates his travel texts in the domain of the Imaginary" ("Barthes' Imaginary Voyages," p. 163).

71. Derrida, "The Deaths of Roland Barthes," p. 286.

for the disinterested "studium" of his readers, Barthes was able to discover what he called "the Ariadne thread" that led him through the labyrinth of all the world's photographs to find the essence of the Photograph.

Commenting on Jean-Joseph Goux's contention that whereas Judaism suppressed the image to avoid worshiping the Mother, Christianity elevated the image-repertoire above the paternal Law, Barthes acknowledged that his seduction by the Winter Garden photo might seen as confirming his debt to Catholicism. But then, he protested, his reaction was too specific to be made a mere instantiation of so general a phenomenon: "In the Mother, there was a radiant, irreducible core: my mother. . . . What I have is not a Figure (the Mother), but a being, and not a being, but a *quality* (a soul): not the indispensable, but the irreplaceable."[72] That is, the actual presence of the photo's concrete referent, its actually having once been there, is what moved him most. Almost like Balzac, with his bizarre fear that photographs dangerously remove the outer spectral layers of the subject's body,[73] he believed in an objective trace left behind. Barthes even went to far as to say he preferred black and white to color images, because the latter seem to add something extraneous to the physical residue of the original referent.

Strictly speaking, then, photographs are different from Proustian recollections of lost time; they are more than exercises in nostalgia abolishing the distance between past and present. Instead, Barthes argued, they ratify the existence of what was. Elaborating on his original insight, he explained that "the realists, of whom I am one and of whom I was already one when I asserted that the Photograph was an image without code—even if, obviously, certain codes do inflect our reading of it—the realists do not take the photograph for a 'copy' of reality, but for an emanation of *past reality*: a *magic*, not an art."[74]

72. Barthes, *Camera Lucida*, p. 75. Derrida argues that "he is right to protest against the confusion between that which was his mother and the Figure of the Mother, but the metonymic power (one part for the whole or no name for another, etc.) will always come to inscribe both in this relation without relation" ("The Deaths of Roland Barthes," p. 287).

73. This belief was reported by Nadar in "My Life as a Photographer," *October*, 5 (Summer, 1978), p. 9.

But if a form of magic, photography is not in the service of redemption or tragic catharsis. It provides no anamnestic totalization, no means of making history—personal or collective—intelligible. Rather than helping in the dialectical recuperation of death's negativity, it merely records it. "The photograph," Barthes insisted, "is undialectical: it is a denatured theater where death cannot be 'contemplated,' reflected and interiorized. . . . The Photograph is violent: not because it shows violent things, but because on each occasion *it fills the sight by force*, and because in it nothing can be refused or transformed."[75] And what precisely cannot be ignored is its message of what Barthes called "flat death," yielding up no meaning beyond mortality. "In front of the photograph of my mother as a child," Barthes confessed, "I tell myself: she is going to die: I shudder, like Winnicott's psychotic patient, *over a catastrophe which has already occurred*. Whether or not the subject is already dead, every photograph is this catastrophe."[76]

Not surprisingly, such an experience makes photography a bizarre medium filled with "mad images, chafed by reality."[77] Society deals with its threat by turning it into a mere art form, for example in cinema, or by disseminating it so widely that it forces all other images to the margins, becoming the banal and omnipresent "reality" of normal life. Barthes concluded *Camera Lucida* by claiming that photography can be either mad or tame: "tame if its realism remains relative, tempered by aesthetic or empirical habits . . .; mad if this realism is absolute and, so to speak, original, obliging the loving and terrified consciousness to return to the very letter of Time: a strictly revulsive movement which reverses the course of the thing, and which I shall call, in conclusion, the photographic *ecstasy*."[78]

74. Barthes, *Camera Lucida*, p. 88. For a suggestive reading of Barthes's stress on the meaningless unintentionality of the photograph, which compares it with the realist novel's impersonal "free indirect style," see Ann Banfield, "L'Imparfait de l'Objectif: The Imperfect of the Object Glass," *Camera Obscura*, 24 (1991).

75. Ibid., pp. 90–91.

76. Ibid., p. 96.

77. Ibid., p. 115.

78. Ibid., p. 119.

Ecstasy, the death of the centered self, thus follows when photography's madness punctures routinized, culturally coded perception and forces the viewer to confront the undialectical, unrecuperable, unintelligible annihilation awaiting us all. No wonder the seeking gaze is an *"anxious* sign" whose power overflows it. Looking through its image-repertoire for consoling experiences of mirror-stage wholeness, hoping to reunite with the maternal body of bliss, it finds instead "flat death," which violently resists revitalization of any kind. For all of Barthes's obvious attraction to the photographic image, for all his openness to the blissful wounds it inflicts, the result is a chilling lament, a thanatology of vision, which contributes a new and plaintive note to the chorus of those made anxious by the domination of the eye.[79]

⊙

In 1963 and 1964, Barthes gave two interviews to the film journals *Cahiers du Cinéma* and *Image et Son*, in which he spoke with cautious optimism about the prospects for a semiology of film.[80] Acknowledging that he went to the movies at least once a week, he claimed that despite the importance of the denotative, analogical power of the filmed image, its connotative implications, most explicitly foregrounded by the use of montage, permitted a decoding somewhat akin to that of literature. Such an approach would have to emphasize the metonymic structure of film narrative, which would require uncovering its syntagmatic rather than

79. It might, of course, be possible to situate Barthes in a tradition, best exemplified by Blanchot, of French writers who follow Heidegger in trying to face rather than escape from death. Thus Ulmer writes, "Barthes' confrontation with death in the deliberate use of the aphorism and the fragment must be seen as not a flight from death, but a therapeutic acceptance" (Ulmer, "Fetishism in Roland Barthes' Nietzschean Phase," p. 349). *Camera Lucida*, however, seems more like a surrender than a mere acceptance. In any case, what is important for our purposes is his morbid linkage of death and the photographic image.

80. Barthes, "On Film," *Cahiers du Cinéma*, 147 (September, 1963), and "Semiology and Cinema," *Image et Son* (July, 1964), both reprinted in *The Grain of the Voice*.

paradigmatic means of signification (a distinction to be explored shortly in Metz's work). But even though films drew on many different connotative systems, Barthes concluded, "there is perhaps beyond all this a great 'language' of the human image-repertoire. That is what is at stake."[81]

In 1975, however, Barthes published an essay with a radically altered tone and a very different conclusion. Significantly entitled "Leaving the Movie Theater," it served as his contribution to a special issue of the journal he helped edit, *Communications*, devoted to "Psychoanalysis and Cinema."[82] Confessing his relief at escaping from a movie, he compared watching a film to being under a hypnotic spell, for

> it sustains in me the misreading attached to Ego and to image-repertoire. In the movie theater, however far away I am sitting, I press my nose against the screen's mirror, against that "other" image-repertoire with which I narcissistically identify myself . . . the image captivates me, captures me: I am *glued* to the representation, and it is this glue which established the *naturalness* (the pseudo-nature) of the filmed scene. . . . Has not the image, statutorily, all the characteristics of the *ideological*?[83]

Only by replacing a "narcissistic body," gazing into the screen/mirror, with a "perverse body," focusing on everything in the movie-going experience *not* on the screen might the ideological hypnosis of the cinema be avoided.[84]

81. Barthes, "Semiology and Cinema," p. 37.

82. Barthes, "En sortant du cinéma," *Communications*, 23 (1975); in translation as "Leaving the Movie Theater," in *The Rustle of Language*.

83. Barthes, "Leaving the Movie Theater," p. 348.

84. Barthes's contrast between a narcissistic and perverse body recalls an earlier distinction made by the psychologist Henri Wallon between the spectator's "visual series" and his "proprioceptive series." Whereas the former involves watching the "unreal" diegetic action on the screen, the latter concerns the sense of the real body doing the watching. See Wallon, "L'acte perceptif et la cinéma," *Revue internationale de filmologie*, 13 (April–June, 1953).

Barthes's new "resistance to film," as one commentator has called it,[85] might be deemed idiosyncratic, if not for the remarkable commonality of opinion expressed in the issue of *Communications* where it first appeared. The invitation to speculate on the implications of psychoanalysis for the film seems to have unleashed in a wide variety of thinkers a hostility to the medium per se astonishing in its intensity. Not only evident in the texts by non–film critics like Félix Guattari and Julia Kristeva,[86] it could also be detected, with varying degrees of ferocity, in those by theorists who devoted their entire professional energies to writing about film, such as Christian Metz, Jean-Louis Baudry, Thierry Kuntzel, and Raymond Bellour. Barthes was not the only French thinker at this time who was anxious to "leave the movie theater."

To make sense of the change that occurred during the late 1960s and early 1970s in film studies, a change whose effects are clearly registered in the contrast between Barthes's interviews and his essay, requires a brief glance backward at the history of French film criticism and theory. Pioneers in the development of the medium, the French were also in the forefront of those who discussed its aesthetic, cultural, social, and even

85. Ungar, "Persistence of the Image: Barthes, Photography, and the Resistance to Film."

86. In "Le divan du pauvre," Guattari, continuing the denunciation of classical psychoanalysis he had begun with Gilles Deleuze in *Anti-Oedipus* in 1972, contended that "the cinema has become a gigantic machine to model the social libido, while psychoanalysis has never been more than a small artisanal enterprise reserved for selected elites" (p. 96). The "famialist, Oedipal and reactionary" cinema, he wrote, "conducts a mass psychoanalysis, seeking to adapt men not to the out-moded, archaicisms of Freudianism, but to those that are implicated in capitalist (or bureaucratic socialist) production" (p. 103). In "Ellipse sur la frayeur et la séduction spéculaire," Kristeva contended that specularity in general and the cinema in particular can both express and smooth over transgressive impulses—her term is "lektonic traces"—coming from what she calls the "semiotic," the presymbolic realm of signification associated with the mother. Citing St. Augustine, she claims that film realizes his project of experiencing monotheistic, symbolic transcendence. Only if disrupted by laughter can the cinema escape its complicity with authority and order: "If not for that demystification," she concluded, "the cinema would be nothing but another Church" (p. 78). An English translation of this essay appeared as "Ellipsis on Dread and the Specular Seduction," *Wide Angle*, 3, 3 (1979).

philosophical significance.[87] After the First World War, such writers as Louis Delluc, Émile Vuillermez, Léon Moussinac, Jean Epstein, and Henri Diamant-Berger turned journals like *Le Film* and *Le Journal du Ciné-club* into forums for what one commentator has called "possibly the most comprehensive and sophisticated theory of the medium available at the time."[88] They were joined by advocates of the avant-garde potential of the film, such as Blaise Cendrars and the Surrealists, whose enthusiasms (and disillusionment) have been encountered in an earlier chapter.

After 1945, French film theory was increasingly informed by phenomenology, following Merleau-Ponty's injunction that "the movies are peculiarly suited to make manifest the union of mind and body, mind and the world, and the expression of one in the other. . . . The philosopher and the movie maker share a certain way of being, a certain view of the world which belongs to a generation."[89] The most vigorous and influential exponent of what might be called phenomenological realism was André Bazin, who famously insisted that photography and the cinema "satisfy, once and for all and in its very essence, our obsession with realism."[90] For Bazin, the tyranny of Cartesian perspectivalism, which dominated Western painting, was lifted as the picture frame, separating subject and object, was replaced by the movie screen, helping to bring them once again together.

87. For a useful survey of French films beginning with the Lumière brothers and Georges Méliès, see Roy Armes, *French Cinema* (New York, 1985). On the early period, see Richard Abel, *French Cinema: The First Wave, 1915–1927* (Princeton, 1984). For a selection of classical critical texts, see Richard Abel, ed., *French Film Theory and Criticism: 1907–1939*, 2 vols. (Princeton, 1988). It should be noted that the making and interpreting of films were often carried out by the same figures, a practice continued with the involvement of directors like Jean-François Truffaut, Claude Chabrol, Jean-Luc Godard, and Eric Rohmer in the *Cahiers du Cinéma* in the 1950s.

88. Stuart Liebman, "French Film Theory, 1910–1921," *Quarterly Review of Film Studies*, 8/1 (Winter, 1983), p. 2.

89. Merleau-Ponty, "The Film and the New Psychology," pp. 58–59. On the importance of phenomenology, see Dudley Andrew, "The Neglected Tradition of Phenomenology in Film Theory," *Wide Angle*, 2, 2 (1978).

90. André Bazin, "The Ontology of the Photographic Image," in *What Is Cinema?*, trans. Hugh Gray (Berkeley, 1967), p. 12.

Learning from the even earlier example of Bergson, whose distrust of film he nonetheless rejected, Bazin stressed the cinema's capacity to portray a world of living flux, "objectivity in time."[91] He was thus suspicious of attempts to analyze the cinematic experience scientifically, and minimized the importance of the montage of juxtaposed images in its development. Although he called the dream of total cinema an idealist myth of perfect representation, Bazin nonetheless expressed evident wonder at the ontological power of the filmed image. Like the great German film critic and theorist Siegfried Kracauer, with whom he has often been compared, Bazin marveled at the film's "redemption of physical reality."[92] Whereas in the theater, he argued, we share a reciprocally self-conscious awareness with the performers on the stage, "the opposite is true of the cinema. Alone, hidden in a dark room, we watch through half-open blinds a spectacle that is unaware of our existence and which is part of the universe. There is nothing to prevent us from identifying ourselves in imagination with the moving world before us, which becomes *the* world."[93]

Phenomenological realism seemed the perfect theory to explain the importance of recent cinematic developments, most notably the films of

91. Ibid., p. 14. On Bazin's debt to Bergson, see Dudley Andrew, *André Bazin* (New York, 1978), pp. 20ff. It should be noted that earlier French film critics like Jean Epstein and Émile Vuillermez were at times able to find some inspiration in Bergson, as did Gilles Deleuze in the 1980s. For evidence of their interest, see Abel, ed. *French Film Theory and Criticism*, vol. 1, pp. 108, 148, and 205. Deleuze's more extensive rescue of Bergson comes in *Cinema I: The Movement Image*, trans. Hugh Tomlinson and Barbara Hammerjam (Minneapolis, 1986), pp. 8ff. Another anticipation of phenomenological realism can be found in Delluc's notion of *photogénie*. See Abel, ed., *French Film Theory and Criticism*, vol. 1, pp. 107ff.

92. Siegfried Kracauer, *Theory of Film: The Redemption of Physical Reality* (Oxford, 1960); for short comparisons, see Andrew Tudor, *Theories of Film* (London, 1964), chap. 4, and V. F. Perkins, *Film as Film: Understanding and Judging Movies* (London, 1972), chap. 2. More recent research on Kracauer has, however, stressed certain differences. See, for example, Miriam Hansen, "Decentric Perspectives: Kracauer's Early Work on Film and Mass Culture," *New German Critique*, 54, (Fall, 1991). For a critique of Bazin's position from a nonsemiological point of view, see Noël Carroll, *Philosophical Problems of Classical Film Theory* (Princeton, 1988), chap. 2.

93. Bazin, "Theater and Cinema, Part Two," in *What Is Cinema?*, vol. 1, p. 102.

Jean Renoir and the Italian Neorealist Roberto Rosselini, which Bazin and his followers like Amédée Ayfre hoped would help revivify postwar European culture.[94] Unlike the veristic documentary, which depended on the fiction of a detached observing eye, neorealism, with its penchant for deep-focus cinematography, could be defended in Merleau-Pontyan terms as a holistic enterprise reuniting viewer and viewed in the flesh of the world. As Edgar Morin, another commentator who adopted an attitude of phenomenological wonder toward the medium, concluded, "The cinema achieves a sort of resurrection of the archaic vision of the world in recovering the virtually exact superposition of practical perception and magical vision—their syncretic conjunction."[95]

Morin, an ex-member of the French Communist Party, was still a Marxist and had worked with Barthes on the leftist journal *Arguments* in the late 1950s. But Bazin wrote for Emmanuel Mounier's Catholic organ *Esprit*, among other journals, and Ayfre was a priest, so phenomenological realism was often surrounded by an aura of religiosity and Platonic idealism that would not easily survive the intensifying politicization of film criticism in the late 1960s.[96] Nor would the other main contribution of

94. Bazin, "An Aesthetic of Reality: Neo-Realism (Cinematic Realism and the Italian School of the Liberation)," in *What Is Cinema?*, vol. 2, trans. Hugh Gray (Berkeley, 1971); and Ayfre, "Neo-Realism and Phenomenology," in *Cahiers du Cinéma: The 1950's: Neo-Realism, Hollywood, New Wave*, ed. Jim Hillier (Cambridge, Mass., 1985).

95. Edgar Morin, *Le cinéma ou l'homme imaginaire: Essai d'anthropologie* (Paris, 1956), p. 160. Morin emphasized the roots of the cinema in what he called the "*cinématographe*," the expansion of perception through technological innovations in the nineteenth century. Only later, he argued, did these become the basis for the signifying language of film per se.

96. After Ayfre died in 1963, one of his followers, Henri Agel, attempted to continue the phenomenological tradition in *Poétique et Cinéma* (Paris, 1973), but with little success. Other phenomenological theorists included Roger Munier, *Contra l'image* (Paris, 1963) and Jean-Pierre Meunier, *Les structures de l'expérience* (Louvain, 1969). See the discussion in J. Dudley Andrew, *The Major Film Theorists: An Introduction* (Oxford, 1976), chap. 9. In the English-speaking world, perhaps the most important theorist influenced by phenomenological approaches, in his case Heidegger's, was Stanley Cavell. See *The World Viewed: Reflections on the Ontology of Film* (Cambridge, Mass., 1979).

Bazin's journal *Cahiers du Cinéma* in the 1950s: the celebration of the great creative filmmaker—more than a mere director—and his unique *mise en scène*.

The so-called *politique des auteurs* had been launched by such texts as Jacques Rivette's 1953 apotheosis of Howard Hawks and François Truffaut's diatribe the following year against traditional French directors.[97] Although Bazin himself was to remain relatively aloof,[98] the *Cahiers* would be filled with essays extolling the ability of Hollywood *auteurs* heroically able to transcend the commercial pressures placed on them by the giant studios. The journal even briefly opened its pages to the *auteurist* extremism of a group of cultic (and politically reactionary) theorists led by Michel Mourlet who were known as the MacMahonians because of their link with the MacMahon Theater in Paris.[99]

A decade later, such panegyrics seemed too indebted to the bourgeois humanist fetish of the individual genius, too beholden to suspect notions of romantic subjectivity, to satisfy critics anxious to apply the lessons of Marxist aesthetics—or more precisely, modernist Marxist aesthetics—to the cinema.[100] The introduction of Brecht's ideas, first by the more covertly political Joseph Losey and then in the more explicitly militant ver-

97. Rivette, "The Genius of Howard Hawks" (May, 1953), in *Cahiers du Cinéma: The 1950's: Neo-Realism, Hollywood, New Wave*, and Truffaut, "A Certain Tendency of the French Cinema" (January, 1954), in *Movies and Methods: An Anthology*, ed. Bill Nichols (Berkeley, 1976).

98. Bazin, "On the *politique des auteurs*" (1957), in *Cahiers du Cinéma: The 1950's*, ed. Jim Hillier.

99. Michel Mourlet, *Sur un art ignoré* (Paris, 1965); his article of the same name appeared in the *Cahiers* in 1959, with a somewhat distanced introduction by the editors.

100. For an account of the politicization, see D. N. Rodowick, *The Crisis of Political Modernism: Criticism and Ideology in Contemporary Film Theory* (Urbana, Ill., 1988). See also Dana B. Polan, *The Political Language of Film and the Avant-Garde* (Ann Arbor, Mich., 1985), which situates the changes in the larger project of politicized film beginning with Eisenstein. Many of the relevant texts are collected in Hillier, ed., *Cahiers du Cinéma: 1960–1968*. As John Caughie points out in *Theories of Authorship* (London, 1981), already by 1960, in the work of such critics as Fereydoun

sion championed by Barthes and Bernard Dort,[101] were decisive. So too was the example of Jean-Luc Godard's self-consciously political experiments in cinematic alienation, which held out the hope of realizing the dream of transferring Brechtian theatrical techniques to the screen. Here the "new wave" French cinema seemed to offer an antidote to the domination of the classical Hollywood movie, exemplified by the Welles, Hitchcocks, Premingers, Hawks, Fullers, and Rays so lionized by *auteur* theory.

In the early 1960s, French film theory was thus already debunking the idealization of the medium as a magical evocation of reality and questioning the priority of perception over signification. In addition, the "death of the author" championed by Barthes and Foucault in literary and philosophical terms had its counterpart in the death of the *auteur* in film studies; in both cases, the authority of authorial intention and creative point of view were denied.[102] Not surprisingly, self-effacing practitioners of the "new novel" like Robbe-Grillet were appreciated for their screenplays as

Hoveyda, the *auteur* as a living human being was being replaced by the *auteur* as a critical construct, the *mise en scène* becoming a relatively autonomous concept.

It should be noted that the more radical experiments of Lettrist and Situationist filmmakers, which were discussed in chap. 7, were ignored by the *Cahiers du Cinéma* critics. Debord and his colleagues responded by belittling the revolutionary pretensions of New Wave film, claiming that "in the final analysis the present function of Godardism is to forestall a situationist use of the cinema" ("The Role of Godard" [1966], in *Situationist International Anthology*, ed. Ken Knabb [Berkeley, 1981], p. 176).

101. Losey, "The Innocent Eye" (1960), in *The Encore Reader*, ed. Charles Marowitz, Tom Hale, and Owen Hale (London, 1965); Dort, "Towards a Brechtian Criticism of Cinema" (1960), in *Cahiers du Cinéma: 1960–1968: New Wave, New Cinema, Reevaluating Hollywood*, ed. Jim Hillier (Cambridge, Mass., 1986); Barthes, "Mother Courage Blind" (1954), "The Brechtian Revolution" (1955), and "The Tasks of Brechtian Criticism" (1956), all in *Critical Essays*; and "Diderot, Brecht, Einstein," in *Image-Music-Text*. For accounts of the reception of Brecht, see Hillier's introduction to *Cahiers du Cinéma: The 1960's*, pp. 10ff.; and George Lellis, *Bertolt Brecht, Cahiers du Cinéma and Contemporary Film Theory* (Ann Arbor, Mich., 1982).

102. For a later version of the critique, see Jean-Louis Baudry, "Author and Analyzable Subject," in *Apparatus: Cinematographic Apparatus: Selected Writings*, ed. Theresa Hak Kyung Cha (New York, 1980).

well.[103] The semiological attempt to expose the workings of cinema's reality effect, which Barthes cautiously defended in his interviews of 1963 and 1964, went hand in hand with the Brechtian project of exposing devices and providing audiences critical distance from the spectacle before them. Rather than visual experiences based on the analogical redemption of physical reality, films became texts to be decoded. They were thus better understood as conventional languages than ontological revelations.

In this endeavor, a new generation of critics came to dominate the *Cahiers du Cinéma*. Bazin had died in 1958 and was replaced by Eric Rohmer, and then for a short while by Jacques Rivette. But by the mid-1960s, the dominant editorial voices were those of Jean-Louis Comolli, Jean Narboni and Jean-André Fieschi. Their most theoretically sophisticated collaborator was Christian Metz, who also worked with Barthes on *Communications* and at the Centre d'Études de Communications de Masse at the École des Hautes Études en Sciences Sociale. Along with Pascal Bonitzer, Jean-Pierre Oudart, Jean-Louis Baudry, and Marcelin Pleynet, the latter two connected more with the journals *Cinéthique* and *Tel Quel* than the *Cahiers*,[104] they intensified the resistance to the cinephilic phenomenological and *auteur* theories of film. Moving beyond the semiotic decoding of filmic texts to a critique of the institutional, material, and psychological underpinnings of the cinema, they left behind the narrow focus on what Gilbert Cohen-Séat had once called the "filmic fact" for the "cinematic fact."[105] When the ideological implications of the

---

103. Jacques Doniol-Valcroze, "Istanbul nous appartient," *Cahiers du Cinéma*, 143 (May, 1963), pp. 55ff. Whether or not Robbe-Grillet was as self-abnegating as his work seemed to suggest was called into question by the remark in his autobiography, *Le miroir qui revient* (Paris, 1985), that "I have never spoken of anything else but myself" (p. 10). But certainly in the context of the 1950s and 1960s, he was taken to be undercutting narrative as the product of an authorial point of view.

104. For a discussion of the linkages among the *Cahiers du Cinéma*, *Cinéthique*, and *Tel Quel*, see Rodowick, *The Crisis of Political Modernism*, chap. 3.

105. Metz, *Language and Cinema*, trans. Donna Jean Umiker-Sebeok (Bloomington, Ind., 1974), discusses this distinction on page 9, where he says that semiology must concern itself primarily with only the filmic fact. After 1968, the cinematic fact would come to the fore once again.

"apparatus" as a whole became foregrounded, it resulted in the post-1968 paroxysm of politically charged hostility that culminated in the famous issue of *Communications* devoted to psychoanalysis and the cinema.

Before reaching this extreme conclusion, however, the semiological analysis of film, developed with greatest penetration in the essays Metz wrote from 1964 to 1968,[106] attempted with apparent dispassion to address a number of fundamental issues. How scientific can the study of cinema be? What are the similarities and differences between verbal linguistic systems and the visual language of the cinema? What are the roles of denotation and connotation in cinematic signification? What is the nature of cinematic narration and how can its codes be classified? Is the essence of film montage or the image? What is the most fundamental unit of cinematic analysis? Metz's answers to such questions, which often frustratingly shifted from essay to essay, invited many long and searching critiques.[107]

Only a few of their points have to be stressed before passing on to the post-1968 turn in French film theory. First, although semiotics seemed at times to substitute a purely structuralist or formalist for a phenomenological interpretation of film, Metz, like Barthes, retained certain phenomenological assumptions, which surfaced whenever he wrestled with the relationship between denotation and connotation, analogical and

106. These are available in Metz, *Film Language: A Semiotics of the Cinema*, trans. Michael Taylor (Oxford, 1974); *Language and Cinema*; and *Essais Sémiotiques* (Paris, 1977).

107. See, for example, Andrew, *The Major Film Theories*, chap. 8; and *Concepts in Film Theory* (Oxford, 1984), chap. 4; Richard Thompson, "Introduction: Metz Is Coming," *Cinema*, 7, 2 (Spring, 1972); Alfred Guizetti, "Christian Metz and the Semiology of the Cinema," *Journal of Modern Literature*, 3, 2 (April, 1973); Stephen Heath, "The Work of Christian Metz," *Screen*, 14, 3 (1973); Michel Cegarra, "Cinema and Semiology, *Screen*, 14, 1–2 (1973); Brian Henderson, "Metz: Essais I and Film Theory," *Film Quarterly*, 28, 3 (Spring, 1975); James Roy MacBean, *Film and Revolution* (Bloomington, Ind., 1975), chap. 16; Sol Worth, "The Development of a Semiotic of Film," *Semiotica*, 3 (1976); and Mary C. Baseheart, "Christian Metz's Theory of Connotation," *Film Criticism*, 4, 2 (1979). Finally, for a sovereign glance backward after the storm had calmed, see Jean Mitry, *La sémiologie en question: langage et cinéma* (Paris, 1987).

coded signification.[108] In particular, he stressed the incomplete reducibility of shots to words, resisted an overreliance on montage, and emphasized the importance of the "diegetic" underpinnings of narration. Diegesis, a concept introduced to cinema studies by Étienne Souriau, referred to the film's represented material, the "profilmic" events, characters, and landscapes that constituted the totality of its denotation, the signifieds to which the film's signifiers referred, the implied space of its narrated fiction.

According to Metz, the importance of diegesis suggested a fundamental difference between film and the still photograph. Following the early Barthes, he argued that whereas the latter earned its analogical, denotative power from the physical transfer of indexical traces, the former also gained its denotation from the cumulative effect of the articulated movement of images over time, the lifelike result of the persistence of vision in the eye.[109] Barthes had also been right, Metz claimed, to equate the photograph with the evocation of a past event, while films provided the sensation of living presence. The reason for this effect is that movement in real life is also conveyed to us by the eyes, and "because movement is *always* visual, to reproduce its appearance is to duplicate its reality."[110]

Although this argument is curiously unappreciative of the ways in which movement can be tactile, aural, and even kinesthetic as well as visual, it is important for our purposes because it demonstrates that from the very beginning Metz was struggling to explain the curious reality effect of the cinema. Unlike theater, in which the actual living figures in front of the spectator were paradoxically too real, too present in flesh and

108. Metz's struggle to find a successful way to deal with this issue continued into the 1970s. See his 1972 essay, "Connotation Reconsidered," *Discourse*, 2 (Summer, 1980). Although he paid lip service to Eco's critique of Barthes (*Film Language*, p. 113), he resisted the conclusion that denotation was at root only connotation not yet decoded.

109. Metz, *Film Language*, p. 98.

110. Ibid., p. 9. For a recent scientific discussion of the relation between movement in films and in normal perception that supports Metz's position, see Joseph Anderson and Barbara Anderson, "Motion Perception in Motion Pictures," in *The Cinematic Apparatus*, ed. Teresa de Lauretis and Stephen Heath (New York, 1980), p. 87.

blood, and thus undercut the realistic impact of the diegetic action they portrayed, the cinematic spectacle provided a powerful impression of reality. Following the psychological, Merleau-Pontyan argument of Jean Mitry in his just published *Esthetique et psychologie du cinéma*,[111] Metz claimed that

> attempts to explain the "filmic state" by hypnosis, mimicry, or other procedures wherein he is entirely passive, never account for the spectator's participation in the film, but only for the circumstances that render that participation not impossible. The spectator is indeed "disconnected" from the real world, but he must then connect to something else and accomplish a *"transference"* of *reality*, involving a whole affective, perceptual, and intellective *activity*, which can be sparked only by a spectacle resembling at least slightly the spectacle of reality.[112]

The issue then was precisely how that transference occurred, how the spectator projected a reality effect onto the screen. In this initial essay, Metz could only point to the importance of time and motion as part of the "secret" of motion pictures, but the ground was broken for his more elaborate psychologically informed explanations a few years later.

In the work that followed his earliest efforts, Metz seemed to bracket the phenomenological and psychological origins of the cinematic experience and concentrate instead on decoding its formal systems of signification.

111. Mitry, *Esthetique et psychologie du cinéma*, vol. 1 (Paris, 1963). The second volume appeared in 1965, shortly after Metz's essay. For accounts of Mitry's importance, see Andrew, *The Major Film Theorists*, chap. 7, and Brian Lewis, *Jean Mitry and the Aesthetics of the Cinema* (Ann Arbor, Mich., 1984). The attempt to apply psychology to film went back at least as far as Hugo Munsterberg's 1916 *The Film: A Psychological Study*. For a history of the interaction between cinema and psychiatry, see Krin Gabbard and Glen O. Gabbard, *Psychiatry and the Cinema* (Chicago, 1987).

112. Metz, *Film Language*, pp. 11–12. One of his colleagues, Raymond Bellour, maintained an interest in the parallels between hypnosis and film. See Janet Bergstrom, "Alternation, Segmentation, Hypnosis: Interview with Raymond Bellour," *Camera Obscura*, 3, 4 (1979).

But he retained his emphasis on the importance of lifelike and present-oriented movement as the essence of film. It appeared not only in his controversial insistence that narrative was the necessary basis of the cinema[113] but also in his belief—similar to that informing much narratological theory of the realist novel—that syntagmatic rather than paradigmatic signification was the primary source of its intelligibility. Whereas paradigmatic relationships involve potential substitutions of absent terms for present ones, either through similarity or opposition, syntagmatic ones combine already present terms, which are linked through linear transformations over time. Syntagmatic analysis focuses on the question of why one unit of narration is preceded or followed by another—for example, through relations of spatial synchronicity, temporal succession, or causality. Attempting to chart the "large syntagmas" controlling narrative cinema, Metz came up with a complicated system of eight fundamental varieties, whose details need not concern us now. What is important to note is that even throughout his most semiologically formalist phase, he never lost sight of the fact that the coded language of the film was dependent on the simulacrum of lived experience produced by its analogical, denotative foundation in movement over time. For all his apparent similarities to the synchronic structuralism so influential in the 1960s, most notably that of Lévi-Strauss, Metz retained a diachronic emphasis that he never abandoned.

For Barthes, it was precisely a stubborn belief in the analogical, denotative capacity of the photograph that allowed him, once he appropriated Lacan's notion of the Imaginary, to mount a powerful attack on the problematic implications of the medium itself. A similar chain of reasoning can be discerned in Metz with regard to film. There were important differences concerning the issue of the photograph's evocation of death for Barthes and the film's of life for Metz, but nonetheless in both cases a psychoanalytic reading of the implications of the respective media led to a radical critique of each that went well beyond the "scientific" neutrality of the semiotics they advocated in the early 1960s. A decade later, Metz, who

113. Metz's stress on narrative was attacked by Cegarra in "Cinema and Semiology."

had been chastised for ignoring the ideological implications of film a short while before,[114] could denounce the widespread attitude of "loving the cinema" as nothing more than "a mirror reduplication of the film's own ideological inspiration, already based on the mirror identification of the spectator with the camera (or secondarily with the characters, if any)."[115]

The change, although prepared by the earlier interest in Brecht, came only in the wake of the events of 1968 and the rapid absorption in film studies of Althusserian and Lacanian ideas, often filtered through the radical modernism of the *Tel Quel* circle around Philippe Sollers.[116] Derrida's notion of *écriture* as a dissemination of coherent intelligibility also gradually had an impact, especially on the critique of narrativity that soon dominated French cinema studies.[117] The *Cahiers*' new direction, which accompanied a positive reevaluation of Russian revolutionary film-

114. For example, by Cegarra, "Cinema and Semiology," and MacBean, *Film and Revolution*.

115. Metz, *The Imaginary Signifier: Psychoanalysis and the Cinema*, trans. Celia Britton, Annwyl Williams, Ben Brewster, and Alfred Guzzetti (Bloomington, Ind., 1977), p. 14. Metz resisted the claim that the two periods of his work were radically different. At times, he claimed that he was always deeply critical: "From the beginning on semiotics was an endeavor to de-mystify dominant cinema; and it was not so easy in 1963 or 1964 to say that narrative cinema was coded when the very principle of the ideological dominance of that narrative cinema is to pretend to be uncoded" ("Discussion," in *The Cinematic Apparatus*, ed. de Lauretis and Heath, p. 168). But at other times, he protested that he was always trying to be a neutral scientist; to an interviewer's question, "Am I correct in saying that your work is not oriented towards values, ethical or aesthetic, but toward description, exposition and a science?" he answered: "Oh, yes, a science, except that science is a big word. . . . Science remains the goal, but I would hesitate to use the word science except as a very far away target—a direction of mine" ("The Cinematic Apparatus as Social Institution—An Interview with Christian Metz," *Discourse*, 1 [1979], p. 30).

116. For accounts, see Lellis, *Bertolt Brecht, Cahiers du Cinéma and Contemporary Film Theory*, chap. 6; Rodowick, *The Crisis of Political Modernism*, chap. 3; William Guynn, "The Political Program of the *Cahiers du Cinéma*, 1969–1977," *Jump Cut*, 17 (1978); and Maureen Turim, "The Aesthetic Becomes Political: A History of Film Criticism in *Cahiers du Cinéma*," *The Velvet Light Trap*, 9 (Summer, 1973).

117. Perhaps the first major impact of Derrida's ideas on film theory came in Jean-Louis Baudry's essay, "Écriture/fiction/idéologie," *Tel Quel*, 31 (Autumn, 1967). For

makers like Eisenstein and Dziga Vertov and a turn away from Hollywood, was announced in a widely remarked, two-part editorial signed by
Comolli and Narboni in the October and November issues of 1969 called
"Cinema/Ideology/Criticism."[118] A major stimulus to the piece was the
founding of the new radical film journal *Cinéthique* a year earlier, which
stressed the economic underpinnings of cinema as an institution.[119] Here
critics like Pleynet, Baudry, and Jean-Paul Fargier were beginning to raise
the stakes of the debate over the nature of film, seeing it as the culmination of an ideological project that antedated even the origins of capitalism.[120] This project expressed the "ideology of the visible" whose links
with Western ocularcentrism were explicitly spelled out in a 1970 *Cahiers
du Cinéma* essay by Serge Daney. Here he suggested we "call into question
what both serves and precedes the camera: a truly blind confidence in the
visible, the hegemony, gradually acquired, of the eye over the other senses,
the taste and need a society has to put itself in spectacle, etc. . . . The
cinema is thus bound up with the Western metaphysical tradition of seeing and vision whose photological vocation it realizes."[121]

Although the *Cahiers* editors did not share all of *Cinéthique*'s judgments about specific films, together the two journals, and others following them like *Screen* in England,[122] developed a critique of the pernicious

---

a discussion of its importance, see Rodowick, *The Crisis of Political Modernism*,
pp. 23ff. For a general analysis of Derrida and film theory, see Peter Brunette and
David Wills, *Screen/Play: Derrida and Film Theory* (Princeton, 1989).

118. It is available in English in several venues, including *Screen*, 12, 1 (Spring, 1971)
and Bill Nichols, ed., *Methods and Movies* (Berkeley, 1976).

119. For an account, see Thomas Elsaesser, "French Film Culture and Critical
Theory: *Cinéthique*," *Monogram*, 2 (Summer, 1971). One of the seminal essays was
Marcelin Pleynet and Jean Thibaudeau, "Économique, idéologie, formel," *Ciné-
thique*, 3 (1969).

120. See, in particular, Baudry's essay of 1970, "Ideological Effects of the Basic Cinematographic Apparatus," *Film Quarterly*, 27, 2 (Winter, 1974–1975). Baudry's
work of this period is collected in *L'effet cinéma* (Paris, 1978).

121. Serge Daney, "Sur Salador," *Cahiers du Cinéma*, 222 (July, 1979), p. 39; cited in
Jean-Louis Comolli, "Machines of the Visible," in *The Cinematic Apparatus*, ed. de
Lauretis and Heath, p. 125. It was Comolli who coined the phrase "the ideology of
the visible."

implications of the medium that went beyond anything before in the history of film criticism. Neither specific films nor certain techniques nor idealist film theories like *auteurism* or phenomenologial realism were the problem, but rather the very cinematic "apparatus" (*appareil* or *dispositif*) itself.[123] Although including the technological development of the medium, the term "apparatus" went beyond a mere fascination with chemicals and machines. Indeed, the claim that film technology was neutral and based on advances in pure science was precisely what apparatus theory set out to dispute.[124]

Very much in the air in France in the post-1968 era, "apparatus" was

122. For an account of the reception of French film theory in England, see Colin MacCabe, *Tracking the Signifier: Theoretical Essays: Film, Linguistics, Literature* (Minneapolis, 1985). For a critique, see Andrew Britton, "The Ideology of Screen: Lacan, Althusser, Barthes," *Movie*, 26 (Winter, 1978/1979).

123. As Joan Copjec has noted, the two French terms have a slightly different meaning. *Appareil* connotes a machine or device, whereas *dispositif* suggests these meanings as well as an arrangement. The former, she writes, "is usually used in a mechanical or anatomical sense, attached to an organ of reproduction. *Dispositif* can be used to signal an adherence to a philosophical tradition which includes, among others, Bachelard, Canguilhem, Foucault, which sets itself against the empiricist position that facts exist outside the science that discovers them. According to this theory—of the apparatus, or phenomeno-techniques, or veridical discourses—truths are internal to the signifying practices that construct them" (Copjec, "The Anxiety of the Influencing Machine," *October*, 23 [Winter, 1982], p. 57). The two major essays by Baudry to be discussed below differ in that the first uses *appareil* in its title ("Cinéma: effets produits par l'appareil de base"), while the second is called "Le dispositif: Approches métapsychologiques de l'impression de réalité."

124. On the issue of technology, see Jean-Louis Comolli, "Technique et idéologie: Caméra, perspectif, profondeur de champ," *Cahiers du Cinéma*, 229 (May, 1971); 230 (July, 1971); 231 (August, 1971); 233 (November, 1971); 234–235 (December, 1971–January, February, 1972); and 241 (September, 1972), essays which are condensed in English as "Technique and Ideology: Camera, Perspective, Depth of Field," *Film Reader*, 2 (January, 1977); also, Stephen Heath, "The Cinematic Apparatus: Technology as Historical and Cultural Form," in de Lauretis and Heath, eds., *The Cinematic Apparatus*. There was a significant French theorist of this period who presented a more neutral version of technology, Jean-Patrick Lebel. His *Cinéma et ideologie* (Paris, 1971) contested Pleynet's claims about the medium as a whole. It was in turn attacked by Comolli in the articles cited above for distorting the role of science in the invention of the cinema.

employed by Bachelard to examine "phenomeno-technologies" rather than unmediated phenomenological perception, by Althusser to designate "ideological state apparatuses (*appareils*)," and by Foucault to talk of *dispositifs* of power and sexuality. But it was a renewed interest in Freud's usage that most inspired its adoption by film theorists. In a widely discussed passage from *The Interpretation of Dreams*, he had suggested that rather than conceptualizing the psyche as monolithic and undifferentiated, "we should picture the instrument which carries out our mental functions as resembling a compound microscope, or a photographic apparatus, or something of the kind. On that basis, psychical locality will correspond to a place inside the apparatus at which one of the preliminary stages of an image comes into being."[125]

Derrida had called attention to this passage in his 1966 essay, "Freud and the Scene of Writing," in which he praised Freud for moving beyond optical metaphors to those of *écriture*, such as the "mystic writing pad," instead.[126] But Baudry and his followers remained entranced by the idea that the psyche could be construed as a dynamic optical machine, for it implied that the cinema might be profitably understood as a kind of external version of the same apparatus. Indeed, the very distinction between inner and outer was problematized as the apparatus embraced the complex interaction of camera, screen, projector, and spectatorial consciousness. Lacan's argument about the mirror stage only reinforced this belief in the projective intertwining of inner and outer, in ways that will be examined shortly.

In addition, Freud's evocation of technologies of optical enhancement, such as the microscope, suggested another connection: that between

125. Freud, *Standard Edition*, vol. 5, trans. and ed. James Strachey (London, 1973), p. 536. The encounter between psychoanalysis and the cinema began in the 1920s, for example in G. W. Pabst's film *Secrets of a Soul*. For a discussion, see Anne Friedberg, "An *Unheimliche* Maneuver between Psychoanalysis and the Cinema: *Secrets of a Soul (1926)*," in *The Films of G. W. Pabst: An Extraterritorial Cinema*, ed. Eric Rentschler (New Brunswick, N.J., 1990).

126. Derrida, "Freud and the Scene of Writing," *Writing and Difference*, trans. Alan Bass (Chicago, 1978). For another deconstructionist critique of optical metaphors in Freud, see Sarah Kofman, *Camera obscura: de l'idéologie* (Paris, 1973), chap. 2.

the cinema and the Cartesian perspectivalist scopic regime, which had emerged along with these technical innovations. Against Bazin's claim that the screen was different from the frame of traditional painting, they contended that the perspectivalist mode of representation, with all its artificial privileging of the fixed, monologic eye, had in fact persisted in photography and the cinema. Extrapolating from the arguments of such predecessors as the art historian Pierre Francastel,[127] they claimed, as Pleynet put it, that "the film camera is an ideological instrument in its own right, expressing bourgeois ideology before expressing anything else. . . . It produces a directly inherited code of perspective, built on the model of the scientific perspective of the Quattrocento."[128] It is thus complicitous, they contended, with an ideology of the visible in which "the human eye is at the center of the system of representation, with that centrality at once excluding any other representative system, assuring the eye's domination over any other organ of the senses and putting the eye in a strictly divine place."[129]

The monocular vision of the camera, Baudry added in his seminal essay, "The Ideological Effects of the Basic Cinematographic Apparatus," "lays out the space of an ideal vision and in this way assures the necessity of a transcendence," which "seems to inspire all the idealist paeans to which the cinema has given rise [such as we find in Cohen-Séat or Bazin]."[130] This visual regime goes along with an idealist belief in the homogeneity of all Being and the transcendent subject who can view it from afar. The disincarnation of that subject's eye is furthermore abetted by the way in which it is no longer tied to a concrete body situated in a specific time and space, but can roam freely wherever the camera can go. Rather than sug-

127. Francastel, *La figure et la lieu* (Paris, 1967). According to Mitry, however, the film theorists confused Francastel's claim that perspective was a figurative space with their own argument that the real space of the cinema was perspectival. See his *La sémiologie en question*, p. 61.
128. Pleynet with Thibaudeau, "Économique, idéologique, formel," p. 10.
129. Ibid.
130. Baudry, "The Ideological Effects of the Basic Cinematographic Apparatus," p. 42.

gesting multiple and perhaps conflicting points of view, the moving camera negates differences and produces a singular subject effect. This subject seems continuous, linear, and coherent, but is really produced by what another contributor to the debate, Jean-Pierre Oudart, called an ideological "suture."[131] Borrowed from the Lacanian Jacques-Alain Miller, the term referred to a signifier that seemed to "sew up" the lacks and absences that language can never actually fill.[132] Such techniques as shot/reverse shot alternations foster visual sutures, Oudart claimed. They stitch together the dispersed and contradictory subjectivities of the actual spectator into a falsely harmonious whole by encouraging him or her to identify seriatim with the gazes of the characters in the film, gazes which seem to come from centered and unified subjects.

To explain the fundamental process of identification that underlay such techniques, Baudry, Pleynet, Oudart, and those who came after them turned increasingly to Lacanian psychoanalysis—or at least a simplified version of it. Moving away from a semiological reading of films as decodable texts, they sought instead what Bertrand Augst has called "a metapsychology of the spectator."[133] That pitiable creature, they argued, was "chained, captured, or captivated"[134] by the spectacle projected on the screen in front of him in the darkened room (the word "captivate" was especially apposite, Baudry noted, because its reference to the head sug-

131. Oudart, "Cinema and Suture," *Screen*, 18, 4 (Winter, 1977–1978) originally in *Cahiers du Cinéma*, 211 (April, 1969) and 212 (May, 1969).

132. Jacques-Alain Miller, "Suture (Elements of the Logic of the Signifier)," *Screen*, 18, (1977–1978); originally in *Cahiers pour l'analyse*, 1 (1966). For discussions, see Stephen Heath, "Notes on Suture," *Screen*, 18, 4 (1977–1978); reprinted in his *Questions of Cinema* (Bloomington, Ind., 1981); Daniel Dayan, "The Tutor-Code of Classical Cinema," and William Rothman, "Against the System of Suture," both in *Movies and Methods*, ed. Bill Nichols; Kaja Silverman, *The Subject of Semiotics* (New York, 1983), chap. 5; and Noël Carroll, *Mystifying Movies: Fads and Fallacies in Contemporary Film Theory* (New York, 1988), pp. 183ff.

133. Augst, "The Lure of Psychoanalysis in Film Theory," in Cha, ed., *Apparatus*, p. 421.

134. Baudry, "Ideological Effects of the Basic Cinematic Apparatus," p. 44.

gested precisely the hierarchy Bataille had sought to undo with his image of an acephalic, wounded and bleeding body). The result was a state of consciousness simulating a dream, an old comparison in the history of film theory, but now given a more sinister twist, as it implied regression. "The arrangement of the different elements—projector, darkened hall, screen—in addition from [*sic*] reproducing in a striking way the *mise-en-scène* of Plato's cave (prototypical set for all transcendence and the topological model of idealism) reconstructs the situation necessary to the release of the 'mirror stage' discovered by Lacan."[135]

That reconstruction takes place because, like the young child, the moviegoer suffers from limited corporeal mobility and becomes dependent on hypertrophied visual experience, which produces a superreal sense of reality that cannot be tested.[136] As a result, the reality effect of the film is ultimately based on the misrecognition of a reconstituted mirror stage, in which two types of identification take place. A secondary level based on the image of characters on the screen, similar to the type of identification that Brecht attacked in the theater, is grounded in a more primary level, unique to the cinema. Here the viewer identifies with the camera eye as transcendental, omniscient subject. "Thus the spectator identifies less with what is represented, the spectacle itself," Baudry wrote, "than with what stages the spectacle, makes it seen, obliging him to see what it sees; this is exactly the function taken over by the camera as a sort of relay."[137]

As a result of its restaging of the misrecognitions of specular identification, the cinema must be exposed as "an apparatus destined to obtain a precise ideological effect, necessary to the dominant ideology: creating a

135. Ibid., p. 45.

136. This contention makes sense if it is understood to mean that the viewer is inhibited from testing the diegetic reality depicted on the screen—whether or not what is seen is a "real" plane crash or only a model—and not the experience of viewing a film as opposed to "real life," which can always be tested by such devices as sticking one's hand in front of the projector.

137. Baudry, "Ideological Effects of the Basic Cinematic Apparatus," p. 44.

fantasmatization of the subject, it collaborates with a marked efficacy in the maintenance of idealism."[138] In short, it is the cinema's complicity with the Imaginary and all of its ideological functions rather than its ability to be "read" semiologically as a connotatively rich Symbolic language that produces its politically nefarious effect. What Bellour called "symbolic blockage" meant that film contained the disruptive implications of language and produced instead narratives restoring equilibrium and reconciliation.[139] It thus functions alongside of those other ideological apparatuses, schools, churches, newspapers, and so on, that Althusser saw as essential buttresses of the status quo.[140]

Or rather, the cinema in its dominant realist form served that function for Baudry and some of his followers in the early 1970s,[141] who held out a faint hope for an alternative, modernist cinema that would bare the device, wake the spectator from his or her regressive dream, and break the spell of illusion. If the ideological "work" of the cinema were explicitly challenged, they claimed, then what Althusser called a subversive "knowledge effect" might ensue. Some filmmakers, such as Robert Bresson, had in fact been able to unstitch the threads of the sutured subject.

This Brechtian-inspired hope ill-accorded, however, with Althusser's pessimism about the permanence of ideology no matter what the system and was easy prey for critics influenced by Derrida's deconstruction of the

138. Ibid., p. 46.

139. Raymond Bellour, "Le blocage symbolique," *Communications*, 23 (1975), pp. 348–349.

140. Althusser, "Ideology and Ideological State Apparatuses (Notes towards an Investigation)" in *Lenin and Philosophy and Other Essays*, trans. Ben Brewster (New York, 1971). Among them he had included "the cultural ISA (Literature, Arts, sports, etc.)" (p. 143), a category in which cinema would presumably belong. Althusser followed Gramsci in extending the idea of the state to embrace private as well as public apparatuses. The film critics who followed him did not, however, emphasize the state in their analyses of ideology.

141. Bellour, for example, argued that a close relationship existed between the nineteenth-century realist novel and the classical American cinema, both using the same reality-effects exposed by Barthes in *S/Z*. See Bergstrom, "Alternation, Segmentation, Hypnosis: Interview with Raymond Bellour," p. 89.

truth/illusion opposition.[142] In fact, Narboni and Comolli were far more skeptical about the possibility of releasing film's allegedly demystifying potential, and sought to distance themselves explicitly from Baudry's position on at least this one question.[143] The spectator may not be entirely passive, they claimed, but the work he or she did "is not only a work of decipherment, reading, elaboration of signs. It is first of all and just as much, if not more, to play the game, to fool him or herself out of pleasure, and in spite of those knowledges which reinforce his or her position of non-fool; it is to maintain—if the spectacle, its play make it possible—the mechanism of disavowal at its highest level of intensity."[144]

By his next major statement, an essay simply called "The Apparatus" that appeared in the 1975 special issue of *Communications* on "Psychoanalysis and the Cinema," Baudry himself was evincing little confidence in a nonideological cinema. As a result, "apparatus theory," as it became known, invited the frequent reproach that it posited the completely watertight mechanism of control, what one critic dismissed as a "delirium of clinical perfection."[145] In this second essay, Baudry explored in greater detail than in "Ideological Effects of the Basic Cinematographic Apparatus" the allegory of Plato's cave—where shackled prisoners stare at shad-

142. Rodowick, *The Crisis of Political Modernism*, pp. 96ff., develops such a critique. He concludes that "it is in fact the optical metaphor criticized by Baudry that finally turns Oriental perspective against a Western optical centering, difference against continuity, and a knowledge-effect against the illusory fantasy of an omniscient, transcendental subject. Even in the discourse of political modernism, the metaphor of visibility retains its power as the measure of the unity of subject in the field of perception, posting self-identical being as the locus of knowledge and the master of the world that is its object of thought" (p. 103).

143. Narboni and Comolli, "Cinema/Ideology/Criticism (2)," *Screen Reader I*, p. 41. Rodowick argues, however, that they too didn't go far enough in problematizing the distinction between illusion and truth, ideology and science.

144. Comolli, "Machines of the Visible," p. 140.

145. Joan Copjec, "The Delirium of Clinical Perfection," *The Oxford Literary Review*, 8, 1–2 (1986). See also Mary Ann Doane, "Remembering Women: Psychical and Historical Constructions in Film Theory," in *Psychoanalysis and Cinema*, ed. E. Ann Kaplan (New York, 1990), p. 52. They attack Baudry for precisely the opposite reason adduced by Rodowick, who focuses more on the earlier essay.

ows on the wall before them and mistake them for real objects—as an explanation of the cinema's remarkable power. The cave story, with its confusion of reality and simulacrum, could be understood—with considerable license[146]—to express a long-standing, unquenchable desire which also motivated, through a kind of demonic teleology, the invention of the cinema more than two millennia later.[147] That desire, Baudry claimed, was for regression to the earliest psychic state of oneness with the world, the overcoming of subject and object in a kind of primitive narcissism.

Here the cave's obvious resemblance to the womb was important, as was the linkage between vision and the oral stage which the analyst Bertram Lewin had posited.[148] Such a utopia of archaic satisfaction, Baudry speculated, was "anterior to the 'stade du miroir,' to the formation of the self, and therefore founded on a permeability, a fusion of the interior with the exterior."[149] As a consequence, "the usual forms of identification, already supported by the apparatus would be reinforced by a more archaic mode of identification, which has to do with the lack of differentiation between the subject and his environment, a dream-scene model which we find in the baby/breast relationship."[150] The cinema could thus be called an artificial hallucinatory psychosis in which perceptions and representations were confusingly intertwined. No liberating use of the cinema, he now tacitly admitted, could dismantle such an apparatus.

146. For a telling critique of Baudry's use of the Platonic myth, and much else in the apparatus argument, see Carroll, *Mystifying Movies*, p. 19.

147. Interestingly, Bazin had also written of "the myth of total cinema" as antedating the actual invention of film, and claimed that "the concept men had of it existed so to speak fully armed in their minds, as if in some platonic heaven." (*What Is Cinema?*, p. 17). Where he differed from Baudry was in his refusal to turn this observation into a reproach.

148. Bertram Lewin, "Sleep, the Mouth and the Dream Screen," *Psychoanalytic Quarterly*, 15 (1946), and "Inferences from the Dream Screen," *International Journal of Psychoanalysis*, 29 (1948). Lewin claimed that the visual "dream screen" was a hallucinatory representation of the mother's breast, and thus a surrogate for that perfect state of gratification following feeding.

149. Baudry, "The Apparatus," *Camera Obscura*, 1 (Fall, 1976), p. 117.

150. Ibid., p. 120.

"One cannot overestimate the impact of Baudry's work in this period,"[151] as D. N. Rodowick has aptly noted. It was clearly evident in the transformation of Metz from the coolly analytical cine-semiologist of *Film Language* and *Language and Cinema* to what can be called the militant cinephobe (or at least postcinephile) of his next important work, *The Imaginary Signifier*, published in 1977.[152] Two of the four sections of that book appeared alongside Baudry's essay on "The Apparatus" in the 1975 special issue of *Communications*; a third was explicitly written "with respect to his remarkable analyses."[153]

Much of Metz's argument, in fact, merely reiterated the main points of the psychoanalytic/Marxist critique made by Baudry, Comolli, Narboni, and others in *Cinéthique* and the *Cahiers du Cinéma*. Although he later protested that he had never been an orthodox Lacanian,[154] the work starts by asserting that "reduced to its most fundamental procedures, any psychoanalytic reflection on the cinema might be defined in Lacanian terms as an attempt to disengage the cinema-object from the imaginary and to win it for the symbolic, in the hope of extending the latter by a new province."[155] That cinema-object had become, in the terminology of Melanie Klein, a "good" rather than "bad" object which was adored too uncritically by most of its commentators. They should instead sublimate their visual love into a rigorous epistemophilia exposing the ideological workings of the cinematic apparatus. Straightforward visual pleasure, Metz implied with an asceticism that would have done the Iconoclasts proud, must be vigilantly resisted.

To interrogate what he called "the scopic regime of the cinema," Metz

151. Rodowick, *The Crisis of Political Modernism*, p. 89.

152. "To be a theoretician of the cinema," Metz wrote, "one should ideally no longer love the cinema and yet still love it: have loved it a lot and only have detached oneself from it by taking it up again from the other end, taking it as the target for the very same scopic drive which had made one love it" (*The Imaginary Signifier*, p. 15).

153. Ibid., p. 5.

154. Metz, "The Cinematic Apparatus as Social Institution—An Interview with Christian Metz," p. 8.

155. Metz, *The Imaginary Signifier*, p. 3.

repeated many of the claims made by his colleagues: the spectator's primary identification was with the omniscient camera eye, the screen was like (if not precisely equivalent to) a mirror reinforcing a specular identity, film realism compared with that of the theater was hyperrealistic, Quattrocento perspective still defined the spatial order of the dominant cinema, phenomenological realist theory was a form of idealism, the lowered mobility of the spectator's body led to a regressive dreamlike state, and so on. "The institution of the cinema," he could accordingly conclude,

> requires a silent, motionless spectator, a *vacant* spectator constantly in sub-motor and hyper-perceptive state, a spectator at once alienated and happy, acrobatically hooked up to himself by the invisible thread of sight, a spectator who only catches up with himself at the last minute, by a paradoxical identification with his own self, a self filtered out into pure vision. . . . All that remains is the brute fact of seeing: the seeing of an outlaw, of an *Id* unrelated to any *Ego*, a seeing which has no features or position, as vicarious as the narrator-God or the spectator God.[156]

Metz did add to, nuance, and even implicitly correct some of the arguments of his predecessors in significant ways. He complained that Baudry, while right to find parallels between the mirror stage and cinematic experience in "over-perception and under-motricity," had underestimated the important difference that movie-watching occurred without the spectator's own body image on the screen.[157] He also tacitly questioned the argument in "The Apparatus" about primary narcissism, the nostalgia for undifferentiated oneness, as the source of the precinematic desire to see.

156. Ibid., pp. 96–97.

157. Metz, "The Cinematic Apparatus as Social Institution—An Interview with Christian Metz," p. 20. One might, however, respond by recalling the importance of transitivism in the etiology of the mirror state for Lacan. That is, the identification with the body of the other is also part of the process of subject formation. See Jacqueline Rose, "The Imaginary," in *Sexuality and the Field of Vision* (London, 1986), p. 196, for a discussion of this issue.

Instead, he introduced the concept of scopophilia or voyeu
what Lacan had called the scopic drive, to explain the unt
tance between the subject of desire and its object, which
nonparticipatory cinematic experience.[158] The viewer is like ;
cause he is isolated in the audience—Metz, like Barthes,[159] clai.   ⌐vie
spectatorship was inherently antisocial—and sees a scene that cannot look
back at him: "In the spectator's voyeurism there is no need for him to be
seen (it is dark in the cinema, the visible is entirely confined to the screen),
no need for a knowing object, or rather an object that wants to know, an
object-subject to share in the activity of the component drive."[160]

Although this argument tacitly contradicted Baudry's claim in "The
Apparatus" that cinematic viewing was based on the regressive wish to
conflate subject and object in an undifferentiated whole, it nonetheless
shared with it the same negative evaluation of the medium's effect. So too
did Metz's related emphasis on the importance of two other pathological
aspects of cinematic viewing: disavowal and fetishism. The former, *Ver-
leugnung* in Freud's vocabulary and also sometimes translated as denegation, referred to the complex interaction of belief and nonbelief that
characterized psychological reactions to such phenomena as the "castration" of girls. That is, the little boy both thinks girls have lost their penises
and denies that very belief. In film terms, Metz claimed the same mechanism of mingling presence and absence worked to allow the viewer to

158. Linking the cinema to voyeurism, it should be noted, was a time-honored argument, extending at least as far back as Walter Serner's 1913 essay, "Kino und
Schaulust," reprinted in *Kino-Debatte: Texte zum Verhältnis von Literatur und Film
1909–1929*, ed. Anton Kaes (Tübingen, 1978).

159. As early as his 1963 interview, "On Cinema," Barthes had admitted, "I would
prefer of course to go the movies alone, because to me, the cinema is a completely
projective activity" (p. 11).

160. Ibid., p. 96. Cavell also acknowledges the voyeurism of cinematic viewing, but
turns it in a less malevolent direction: "How do movies reproduce the world magi-
cally? Not by literally presenting us with the world, but by permitting us to view it
unseen. This is not a wish for power over creation (as Pygmalion's was), but a wish
not to need power, not to have to bear its burdens. . . . In viewing films, the sense of
invisibility is an expression of modern privacy or anonymity" (*The World Viewed*,
p. 40).

believe in the reality of what was on the screen, while at the same time "knowing" that it was a simulacrum. More subtle than notions of cinematic hypnosis or hallucination, disavowal also allowed Metz to speak of the dreamlike state of film-watching more in terms of daydreams than their nocturnal counterparts. Whereas the latter entailed a total loss of control, the former allowed the dreamer to move in and out of his fantasy in a way closer to the film spectator's actual behavior in the theater.

Disavowal also worked for Metz to reinforce voyeurism by denying any reciprocity between viewer and viewed: "The film is not exhibitionist. I watch it, but it doesn't watch me watching it. Nevertheless, it knows that I am watching it. But it doesn't want to know. This fundamental disavowal is what has guided the whole of classical cinema into the paths of 'story' relentlessly erasing its discursive basis, and making it (at best) a beautiful closed object."[161] Here Metz introduced the linguist Émile Benveniste's famous distinction between "story" (or sometimes "history") and "discourse," the former being a narratorless narration, the latter foregrounding the narratorial voice. Film, at least in its classic form, disavowed its discursive underpinnings, presented itself as a "real" story on display for the voyeuristic spectator. But it is not the voyeurism of an interaction in which the object of the gaze is exhibitionistically making itself available, but rather that of an object that disavows its awareness that it is on view (a conceit abetted by the normal taboo against actors looking directly into the camera).

The import of this disavowal is that film masks its workings, a masking which suggests that *trucage*, a term used normally for trick photography alone, is close to the essence of film itself.[162] Although paradoxically granted a higher "reality quota" than the still photography because of its apparent ability to "reproduce life," film was in fact based more on deceit. As Comolli was to put it, "However refined, analogy in the cinema is a deception, a lie, a fiction that must be straddled—in disavowing, knowing but not wanting to know—by the *will to believe* of the spectator, the

161. Ibid., p. 94.
162. Metz spells out this argument in "*Trucage* and the Film."

spectator who expects to be fooled and wants to be fooled, thus becoming the first agent of his or her own fooling."[163]

Disavowal, according to psychoanalytic theory, is intimately linked to fetishism. Put schematically, the fetish is the subject's disavowal of the differences between the sexes as a defense against castration anxiety, which itself echoes the more primary "loss" of the mother's breast through weaning. Splitting in two, the ego both perceives sexual difference in the presence or absence of the penis and denies it by displacing the "lost female penis" onto something else, which it fetishistically idealizes. The missing phallus finds an imaginary surrogate, which both puts something in its place, either metaphorically or metonymically, and affirms the disavowed lack. Like suturing, it ideologically binds the wound, restoring the good object, while at the same time "knowing" that it (the absent penis) is still lacking.

In the case of film, Metz claimed,[164] the missing object is the referent, the profilmic diegetic action, which is absent and yet compensated for by what he calls love for the very technique of the cinema. Such an idealizing fixation on the apparatus of signification comes before the secondary fetishes of specific signifieds (for example, movie stars) that also serve as surrogates for the absent object. "The cinema fetishist," he writes, "is the person who is enchanted at what the machine is capable of, at the *theater of shadows* as such. . . . The fetish is the cinema in its *physical* state."[165] At its most extreme, it leads to that cinephilic love affair with the medium that must be disrupted if the ideological effects of the apparatus are to be overcome.

Even the most well-meaning avant-garde filmmakers, those who sought

---

163. Comolli, "Machines of the Visible," p. 139.

164. Later Metz would protest that he didn't equate film with fetishism in all respects, only two: disavowal and taking the apparatus as a substitute for the penis. See his disclaimer in "The Cinema Apparatus as Social Institution—An Interview with Christian Metz," p. 11. For two very different critiques of his use of fetishism, see Carroll, *Mystifying Movies*, pp. 42ff., and Kaja Silverman, *The Acoustic Mirror: The Female Voice in Psychoanalysis and Cinema* (Bloomington, 1988), pp. 2ff.

165. Ibid., p. 74.

to counteract the ideological implications of the apparatus, were in danger of fetishizing its technical capacities, however critical the use to which they hoped to put them.[166] As Metz remarked in a later essay, reflexive films seeking to bare the device are still the prisoner of the apparatus they seek to disrupt. "When one undertakes to raise the purpose of the film one degree higher, the imaginary raises itself (without being wished or invited) the same degree higher because you have to shoot the second degree thing, the second degree imaginary, and you can shoot it only from a third degree imaginary point of view."[167]

With arguments like these, it is not surprising that an American dissertation on his work, published in 1980, could conclude with bewildered exasperation that "despite his repeated professions of great love for the cinema, Metz may not have real respect and affection for the seventh and liveliest art."[168] Indeed, one might say of the entire psychoanalytic/Marxist, semiological approach that it self-consciously sought to suppress its cinephilic instincts and produce what Bellour called "a disentangling of the fascination, which can only be effected through the reconstruction of what founds it."[169] As such, it can justly be seen as a culminating moment in the French critique of ocularcentrism, a moment in which the "frenzy of the visible"[170] seemed to engender a counterphobic panic of its own.

⊙

The Imaginary Signifier was not, however, the last time Metz pondered the relation between film and fetishism. In an essay written in 1984 on

166. For a development of this point based on French film theory, see Constance Penley, *The Future of an Illusion: Film, Feminism and Psychoanalysis* (Minneapolis, 1989), chaps. 1 and 2.

167. Metz, "Third Degree Cinema," *Wide Angle*, 7, 1/2 (1985), p. 32.

168. George Agis Cozyris, *Christian Metz and the Reality of Film* (New York, 1980), pp. 167–168.

169. Bergstrom, "Alternation, Segmentation, Hypnosis: Interview with Raymond Bellour," p. 97.

170. Comolli, "Machines of the Visible," p. 122.

"Photography and Fetish,"[171] he returned to the theme, but now with special reference to Barthes's argument in *Camera Lucida* concerning the link between photographs and death.[172] "Film," he argued, "gives back to the dead a semblance of life, a fragile semblance, but one immediately strengthened by the wishful thinking of the viewer. Photography, on the contrary, by virtue of the objective suggestion of its signifier (stillness, again) maintains the memory of the dead *as being dead*."[173] From one perspective, this meant that photography was better suited than film to the mourning process, which Freud had identified with the healthy withdrawal of libido from the lost object. But from another, it could also mean that it was more likely than film to become fetishized.

This latter acknowledgment required Metz to depart tacitly from his earlier analysis. Now he claimed that the absent object whose loss produced the compensatory fetish was not profilmic reality per se, but whatever was positioned off-frame, like the emotionally charged trauma that produced Barthes's *punctum*. "The off-frame effect in photography," he wrote, "results from a singular and definitive cutting off which figures castration and is figured by the 'click' of the shutter. It marks a place of irreversible absence, a place from which the look has been averted forever."[174] Filmic off-space also existed, as when characters filtered in and out of the frame with their voices still audible to the audience.

But film, he now conceded, was "more difficult to characterize as a fetish. It is too big, it lasts too long, and it addresses too many sensorial channels at the same time to offer a credible unconscious equivalent of a lacking part-object."[175] Although it was able to activate fetishism end-

---

171. Metz, "Photography and Fetish," *October*, 34 (Fall, 1985); first delivered as a talk in 1984.

172. Metz also referred to the more recent work of Philippe Dubois, *L'acte photographique* (Paris, 1983), which also equates photography with "thanatography." For an analysis of Barthes's own complicated attitude toward fetishism, see Ulmer, "Fetishism in Roland Barthes's Nietzschean Phase."

173. Metz, "Photography and Fetishism," p. 84.

174. Ibid., p. 87.

175. Ibid.

lessly by evoking a variety of such objects, it could not become one in and of itself. Interestingly, it was because the photograph exceeded its visual function and could become a physical object that it was more likely to become a fetish: "Most of all a film cannot be *touched*, cannot be carried and handled: although the actual reels can, the projected film cannot. . . . Film is more capable of playing on fetishism, photography more capable of itself becoming a fetish."[176]

Metz's revised reflections on the issue of fetishism and film, in one of the few pieces he published during the virtual silence that followed *The Imaginary Signifier*, suggested a certain retreat from the Lacanian-Althusserian apparatus theory model that had dominated the post-1968 French discussion. Ironically, as it spread elsewhere with great success—in 1987, Metz's work could be said to verge on "orthodoxy in many [English and American] university cinema study programs"[177]—it began to flag in France. One obvious reason was the change in political climate, which made the type of militant Marxism of the early 1970s *Cahiers du Cinéma* seem obsolete to many. Cinephilia seemed no longer as unremittingly bourgeois as before, and some of the old loves of the journal returned to respectability.[178]

But more important, a number of problems in the model itself came increasingly to the fore. As already noted, apparatus theory at its most militant seemed hopelessly ahistorical, reducing the cinema, as it did, to little more than the realization of a teleological project at least as old as

176. Ibid., pp. 88–90.

177. Gabbard and Gabbard, *Psychiatry and the Cinema*, p. 179. See, for example, Dana B. Polan, "'Above All Else to Make You See': Cinema and the Ideology of Spectacle," *Boundary 2*, 11, 1 and 2 (Fall, Winter, 1982). There were, to be sure, exceptions, such as Stanley Cavell, Dudley Andrew, Noël Carroll, and William Rothman, who vigorously resisted French film theory. By the late 1980s, Metz's star was clearly on the wane in the English-speaking world. For many, the new paradigm was non-psychoanalytic cognitivism, developed by David Bordwell and others, which also began to have an audience in France. See the special issue of the French journal *Iris*, 9 (Spring, 1989) devoted to "Cinema and Cognitive Psychology."

178. Lellis, *Bertolt Brecht, Cahiers du Cinéma and Contemporary Film Theory*, p. 163.

Plato's cave and as fundamentally grounded as the yearning for reentry into the womb. Metz himself came to concede that long-term changes in family structure might alter the psychic structure underlying cinema.[179] Critics like Jean Louis Schefer contended that without acknowledging such historical variations, film theory could only produce an abstract, essentialized and overly homogeneous subject.[180]

No less problematic was apparatus theory's virtual indifference to the nonvisual dimensions of the film experience, most notably sound. *Cahiers du Cinéma* theorists like Pascal Bonitzer and Michel Chion increasingly turned their attention to the role of sound in the history of the cinema, even during its silent phase.[181] Bonitzer's stress on the off-screen voice was, in fact, one of the stimuli to Metz's tacit revision of his theory of fetishism. Although it was always possible to assimilate sound to the Lacanian Imaginary and see it functioning in tandem with the gaze to create a sutured subject,[182] doing so at least undercut apparatus theory's own version of the "ideology of the visible." And, as a result, it could also open up the possibility of seeing tensions between aspects of the film experience that might work against ideological closure.

Other difficulties in the theory further undermined its power. The essentially analogical slippages between philosophy, psychology, technology, and politics so easily made in the post-1968 era came to seem too loosely metaphorical and empirically underdefended to survive critical

179. Metz, "The Cinematic Apparatus as Social Institution—An Interview with Christian Metz," p. 8.

180. Jean Louis Schefer, *L'homme ordinaire du cinéma* (Paris, 1980).

181. Pascal Bonitzer, *Le regard et la voix* (Paris, 1976), and *Le champ aveugle: Essais sur le cinéma* (Paris, 1982); and Marcel Chion, *La voix au cinéma* (Paris, 1982). In the English-language literature, the most important considerations of this theme appeared in Silverman, *The Acoustic Mirror*, and the "Cinema/Sound" issue of *Yale French Studies*, 60 (1981). See also Roy Armes, "Entendre, C'est Comprendre: In Defense of Sound Reproduction," *Screen*, 29, 2 (Spring, 1988), which specifically addresses the issue of the French film theorist's obsession with the visual.

182. See, for example, Peter Wollen's comments in "Discussion," in *The Cinematic Apparatus*, ed. de Lauretis and Heath, p. 60.

scrutiny. Gilles Deleuze, claiming that the linguistic approach had been "catastrophic"[183] and the notion of the Imaginary a muddle, turned to a logic of moving images he claimed had been anticipated by Bergson. Metz himself was compelled to acknowledge that "you can't equate things—you can only find out that certain features of the cinematic situation have something to do with the Mirror Stage, the Imaginary, the Symbolic."[184] The political strategies implied by the theory—at times a Brechtian modernist baring of the device, at others a cry of impotent outrage at the cinematic apparatus *tout court*—were also perceived as contradictory and uncertain. So too was its attitude toward the avant-garde film's attempt to disrupt mainstream narrative, which was at times applauded, at others denounced. Even its assumption that film spectatorship was an inherently isolating experience, to be explained in psychological rather than sociological terms, was called into question.

Nor was it clear that the film theorists had really understood all of the implications of the psychoanalytic theory they so eagerly adopted. Lacan's own considerations on the visual had developed from his early mirror stage argument to the more complicated dialectic of the eye and the gaze in the *Four Fundamental Concepts of Psycho-analysis*. Whereas the former could be understood to support the idea of specular identity in a misrecognized image of wholeness, the latter suggested a more chiasmic intertwining of two visual fields without sublation, or even a crossing of the linguistic and the visual. In such intertwinings, multiple desires remain unfulfilled and the subject is split, not sutured.

In much of the film theory under discussion, for example, Baudry's first apparatus essay ("Ideological Effects of the Basic Cinematographic Apparatus") or Oudart's study of suture, only the first argument was really taken seriously: the screen is the mirror in which an ideological subject is constructed. When an alternative model was posited, such as in Baudry's second major essay ("The Apparatus") where regression to a state earlier than the mirror stage is understood as the cinema's goal, its implicit tension with the first was not thematically foregrounded.[185] Thus, typically, Metz could write of voyeurism as a one-way process, claiming that the screen does not look back at the spectator, whereas Lacan had claimed that the tin can floating on the water did in some sense "look back" at him, catching him in the scopic field of the "gaze."

In a trenchant discussion of this problem, Joan Copjec has claimed that French film theory was thus more unintentionally beholden to Foucault's totalizing notion of panopticism than to Lacanian theory properly understood.[186] Lacan's seminars, she points out, cannot be used to claim a direct lineage from Renaissance perspective to the cinema, contrary to Pleynet, Baudry, and Comolli's claims. For they introduce other visual modalities, such as anamorphosis and the Bataillean *informe*, to complicate the picture. "In film theory," she writes, "the subject identifies with the gaze as the signified of the image and comes into existence as the realization of a possibility. In Lacan, the subject identifies with the gaze as the signifier of the lack that causes the image to languish. The subject comes into existence, then, through a desire which is still considered to be the *effect* of the law, but not its *realization*. . . . The conflictual nature of Lacan's culpable subject sets it worlds apart from the stable subject of film theory."[187]

The most substantial challenge to apparatus theory's version of the ideological subject came from those critics who noted its blindness to a theme that increasingly came to the fore in the 1970s and 1980s: gen-

183. Gilles Deleuze, *Pourparlers* (Paris, 1990), p. 76; originally from a 1983 interview.

184. Metz, "The Cinematic Apparatus as Social Institution—An Interview with Christian Metz," p. 20.

185. On one level, to be sure, Baudry's second model was commensurate with the first. That is, both posited a narcissistic identity, whether in the mirror stage or in pre-Oedipal oneness with the mother's body, as the apparatus's goal. In contrast, Lacan's eye/gaze dialectic was more conflictual and was based on the irreducibility of otherness to sameness in visual (and psychic) experience.

186. Joan Copjec, "The Orthopsychic Subject: Film Theory and the Reception of Lacan," *October*, 49 (Summer, 1989); see also Rose, "The Imaginary," and Craig Saper, "A Nervous Theory: The Troubling Gaze of Psychoanalysis in Media Studies," *Diacritics*, 21, 4 (Winter, 1991).

187. Ibid., pp. 70–71. For another challenge to Metz that argues for a more conflicted notion of the Imaginary, see Thomas M. Kavanagh, "Film Theory and the Two Imaginaries," in *The Limits of Theory*, ed. Kavanagh (Stanford, Calif., 1989).

der.[188] Lacan's own problems with this issue were also being scrutinized with special vigor during these years. And some of the criticism spilled over onto the debate about film. Interestingly, it was in the English-speaking world that feminist film criticism most intensely developed, following the path-breaking critique of the "male gaze" by Laura Mulvey in her 1975 essay on "Visual Pleasure and Narrative Cinema."[189] It launched a remarkably rich, productive, and still lively debate, which involved, inter alia, Mary Ann Doane, Peter Wollen, Jacqueline Rose, Claire Johnston, Stephen Heath, E. Ann Kaplan, Elisabeth Lyon, Pam Cook, Maureen Turim, Annette Kuhn, Kaja Silverman, Teresa de Lauretis, Miriam Hansen, Constance Penley, Judith Mayne, Janet Bergstrom, Patricia Mellencamp, Tania Modleski, Patricia Petro, Linda Williams, Sandy Flitterman-Lewis, and D. N. Rodowick. Here many questions raised in the interrogation of the visual by French intellectuals for decades entered the Anglo-American arena with special urgency.

In France, the interaction of feminism and film theory was ironically far less intense, although it ultimately arrived on the rebound from the Anglo-American discussion.[190] The specific challenges to dominant cinema by women filmmakers like Germaine Dulac, Marie Epstein, or Agnès Varda were rarely, if ever, subjected to sustained analysis.[191] Metz

188. Soon after, a purely gendered analysis of the gaze was itself called into question by those who stressed race or sexual preference as no less significant. See, for example, Jane Gaines, "White Privilege and Looking Relations: Race and Gender in Feminist Film Theory," *Screen*, 29, 4 (Autumn, 1988).

189. Mulvey, "Visual Pleasure and Narrative Cinema," *Screen*, 16, 3 (Autumn, 1975).

190. See, for example, Bellour's response to Bergstrom in "Alternation, Segmentation, Hypnosis: An Interview with Raymond Bellour," pp. 87ff. In a contribution to a collective volume on *Le western* in 1966, Bellour had dealt with representations of women, but without the psychoanalytic approach he now agreed was fundamental to understanding the importance of male desire in structuring the camera's gaze. For feminist critiques of Bellour's claim that film could only be based on the male gaze, see Janet Bergstrom, "Enunciation and Sexual Difference," *Camera Obscura*, 3/4 (1979); Silverman, *The Acoustic Mirror*, pp. 204ff., and Sandy Flitterman-Lewis, *To Desire Differently: Feminism and the French Cinema* (Urbana, 1990), pp. 15ff.

191. For a feminist analysis of their work, see Flitterman-Lewis, *To Desire Differently.*

spoke for many of his colleagues when he defensively claimed in 1979, "I think that it's up to the women's movement. . . . I think it would be to some extent . . . how could I say . . . *unfair*, dishonest, when a man takes a very publicly and openly and overtly feminist position, because men have no right to speak for women, at their place."[192] For reasons that are not fully clear, the French women's movement did not actively take up this challenge, at least in comparison with their Anglo-American counterparts.[193]

Still, it was in France that one of the major tools for the debate over the gendering of the film subject was forged, that being the discourse of difference, which was most vigorously pursued in the body of thought that came to be known as deconstruction. Jacques Derrida's own ruminations on visual issues, characteristically impossible to reduce to a simple valorization or condemnation of the eye, stimulated an explicitly feminist theorizing about the implications of privileging sight. Here thinkers like Hélène Cixous, Julia Kristeva, Catherine Clément, Michèle Le Doeuff, and most notably Luce Irigaray added new and powerful arguments to the critique of ocularcentrism. Without wanting to reduce feminist theory to a variant of a predominantly male lament, the following chapter hopes to demonstrate that within the discourse of gender difference there were still new reasons for rejecting the putative nobility of sight.

192. Metz, "The Cinematic Apparatus as Social Institution—An Interview with Christian Metz," p. 10.

193. A glance at recent studies of French feminism—for example, Claire Duchen, *Feminism in France from May '68 to Mitterand* (London, 1986); Elaine Marks and Isabelle de Courtivron, eds., *New French Feminisms: An Anthology* (New York, 1981); Jeffner Allen and Iris Marion Young, eds., *The Thinking Muse: Feminism and Modern French Philosophy* (Bloomington, Ind., 1989); and Elisabeth Grosz, *Sexual Subversions: Three French Feminists* (Sydney, 1989)—reveal not a single reference to film theory. For two exceptions that prove the rule, see Kristeva, "Ellipse sur la frayeur et la séduction spéculaire" and Catherine Clément, "Les charlatans et les hystériques," both in *Communications*, 23 (1975).

CHAPTER NINE

"Phallogocularcentrism": Derrida and Irigaray

Borges is correct: "Perhaps universal history is but the history of several metaphors." Light is only one example of these "several" fundamental "metaphors," but what an example! Who will ever dominate it, who will ever pronounce its meaning without first being pronounced by it? What language will ever escape it?

JACQUES DERRIDA[1]

I always privilege the ear over the eye. I am always trying to write with my eyes closed.

HÉLÈNE CIXOUS[2]

Investment in the look is not as privileged in women as in men. More than any other sense, the eye objectifies and it masters. It sets at a distance, and maintains a distance. In our culture the predominance of the look over smell, taste, touch and hearing has brought about an impoverishment of bodily relations.

LUCE IRIGARAY[3]

Deconstruction, it is often suggested, provided a vital stimulus to feminist thought, sometimes negative, but most often positive.[4] That stimulus, this chapter hopes to demonstrate, was intimately connected to its exploration of the role of vision in Western patriarchal culture. To appreciate the full import of French feminist critiques of the mutual implication of ocularcentrism and phallocentrism, most notably that of Luce Irigaray, is to go beyond their complicated debt to Lacanian psychoanalysis and acknowledge the "seminal" role of Derrida's critique of logocentrism. Or to

1. Jacques Derrida, "Violence and Metaphysics," *Writing and Difference*, trans. Alan Bass (Chicago, 1978), p. 92.

2. Hélène Cixous, "Appendix: An Exchange with Hélène Cixous," in Verena Andermatt Conley, *Hélène Cixous: Writing the Feminine* (Lincoln, Nebr., 1984), p. 146.

3. Luce Irigaray, interview in *Les femmes, la pornographie et l'erotisme*, ed. Marie-Françoise Hans and Gilles Lapouge (Paris, 1978), p. 50.

4. See, for example, Alice A. Jardine, *Gynesis: Configurations of Woman and Modernity* (Ithaca, 1985), who claims, "Derrida, after Lacan, has had the deepest influence on both feminist and antifeminist thinking in France, with the scales tending to tip in

play a bit with a Derridean term, the "dissemination" of deconstructive ways of thinking must be accounted one of the main sources of the critique of visually engendered "sameness," a critique which was so much a part of the French feminist defense of "difference." That defense was aimed at thwarting the totalizing effects of what might be called, in the spirit of deconstructionist neologizing, "phallogocularcentrism."

Such an analysis, however, invites several obvious objections. The first follows from the evident impropriety of using metaphors of male semination (in- or dis-) to account for the genesis of what Alice Jardine has called "*gynesis*—the discourse of 'woman' as that *process* diagnosed in France as intrinsic to the condition of modernity."[5] Can one, after all, blithely turn Irigaray and her colleagues into Derridean disciples, dutiful daughters who merely "apply" his ideas to gender issues? He may have encouraged speaking or writing "like a woman," but was that the same as speaking or writing "as a woman"?[6] Isn't it, moreover, problematic to re-

---

the direction of the latter the more orthodox the Derridean: Hélène Cixous and Sarah Kofman, for example, are the most skeptical with regard to feminism, while a writer like Luce Irigaray remains as unorthodoxly one (feminist) as the other (Derridean)" (p. 181). See also, Elizabeth Grosz, *Sexual Subversions: Three French Feminists* (Sydney, 1989), pp. 26–38; Linda Kintz, "In-different Criticism: The Deconstructive 'Parole'," in *The Thinking Muse: Feminism and Modern French Philosophy,* ed. Jeffner Allen and Iris Marion Young (Bloomington, Ind., 1989); Gayatri Chakravorty Spivak, "French Feminism in an International Frame," in *In Other Worlds: Essays in Cultural Politics* (New York, 1988); "Displacement and the Discourse of Women," in *Displacement: Derrida and After,* ed. Mark Krupnick (Bloomington, Ind., 1983); and "Feminism and Deconstruction, Again: Negotiating with Unacknowledged Masculinism," in *Between Feminism and Psychoanalysis,* ed. Teresa Brennan (London, 1989); and Naomi Schor, "This Essentialism Which Is Not One: Coming to Grips with Irigaray," Diana Fuss, "Reading Like a Feminist," and Robert Scholes, "Éperon Strings," all in *Differences,* 1, 2 (Summer, 1989).

5. Jardine, *Gynesis,* p. 25.

6. This distinction, implicit in the French expression *parler-femme,* has become fundamental in recent feminist criticism. For a helpful discussion of its implications which tries to go beyond it, see Fuss, "Reading Like a Feminist." Whereas speaking or writing *like* a woman suggests a linguistic mode available to anyone, if "he" or "she" chooses to use it, speaking or writing *as* a woman depends on deep-seated social, historical, and arguably biological factors that have created gendered subject positions that are far less open to choice.

duce the feminist consideration of visual issues to little more than another variation on a theme developed time and again by a wide variety of male thinkers? How can we assume, in short, that women like Irigaray needed the theories of men like Derrida to alert them to the evils of the "male gaze"?[7]

It might further be objected that for all his hostility to "phallogocentrism," including that which he detected in Lacan, Derrida often self-consciously distanced himself from the mainstream feminist movement. Aligning himself with Nietzsche, he argued that "feminism, indeed, is the operation by which woman wants to come to resemble man, the philosophical dogmatist who insists on truth, science, objectivity—together with the whole virile illusion, the whole castration effect that goes along with it. Feminism wants castration, even that of woman. It wants to lose its style."[8] Even more explicitly hostile to feminism was Derrida's colleague Sarah Kofman, who denounced it as inherently phallocentric, no matter the gender of its defender.[9]

7. Such a question may come more easily to American than French critics. As Toril Moi has noted, "French feminists on the whole have been eager to appropriate dominant intellectual trends for feminist purposes, as for instance in the case of the theories of Jacques Derrida and Jacques Lacan. Although not entirely absent, intellectual separatism (the desire to do without 'male' thought; or the search for an all-female space within patriarchal culture) has had less impact on feminist thought in France than in some other countries" (Introduction to *French Feminist Thought: A Reader*, ed. Toril Moi [New York, 1987], p. 1). Irigaray's method, Margaret Whitford acknowledges, "implies a certain parasitism" in that she frequently reworks terms from writers like Lacan and Derrida (*Luce Irigaray: Philosophy in the Feminine* [London, 1991], p. 3).

8. Derrida, "The Question of Style," in *The New Nietzsche: Contemporary Styles of Interpretation*, ed. David B. Allison (New York, 1977), p. 182. A slightly different translation appears in *Spurs: Nietzsche's Style*, trans. Barbara Harlow (Chicago, 1979), p. 65. Elsewhere, he claimed with more caution, "I am not against feminism, but I am not simply for feminism" ("On Colleges and Philosophy: Jacques Derrida and Geoff Bennington," *ICA Documents*, 5 [London, 1986], p. 71). See also his "Women in the Beehive: A Seminar with Jacques Derrida," in *Men in Feminism*, ed. Alice Jardine and Paul Smith (New York, 1987).

9. Sarah Kofman, "Ça cloche," in *Les fins de l'homme*, ed. Philippe Lacoue-Labarthe and Jean-Luc Nancy (Paris, 1981).

There are also possible objections that might be raised concerning the nature of the deconstructionist examination of visuality. Although it has sometimes been claimed that in Derrida, "one finds an anti-ocular, antispatial stance so radical that all positions seem to be wiped away as soon as they become visible,"[10] it would be imprecise to call the suspicious approach Derrida does take to the primacy of vision in Western culture a straightforward "critique" of ocularcentrism. Although that word might well fit other French thinkers of this century, and it has been used accordingly in this study, it may well be inappropriate in Derrida's case. For he generally rejected the normal use of critique as a means to uncover the truth hidden by ideological mystifications and in so doing facilitate their overthrow.[11] Instead, he preferred the notion of "reading," in particular that of a double reading, which refused to resolve itself like a stereoscope into a single, three-dimensional image.[12] Examining both the "inside" and "outside" of texts, at once putting their content and rhetoric under erasure and reinscribing them in a new register, such a reading exemplified the cardinal deconstructionist virtue of undecidability. For submitting texts

10. Allan Megill, *Prophets of Extremity: Nietzsche, Heidegger, Foucault, Derrida* (Berkeley, 1985), p. 260. For an account that emphasizes instead the ambiguities in Derrida's attitude toward vision, see John McCumber, "Derrida and the Closure of Vision," in *Modernity and the Hegemony of Vision*, ed. David Michael Levin (Berkeley, 1993).

11. See, for example, the remarks in his July 10, 1983, "Letter to a Japanese Friend," in *Derrida and Différance*, ed. Robert Wood and Robert Bernasconi (Evanston, 1988), p. 3. Occasionally, however, he would forget his own injunction and adopt the language of critique, for example in the discussion with the Marxists Jean-Louis Houdebine and Guy Scarpetta in *Positions*, trans. Alan Bass (Chicago, 1981), where he protested, "Must I recall that from the first texts I have published, I have attempted to systematize a deconstructive critique precisely against the authority of meaning, as the *transcendental signified* or as *telos*, in other words history determined in the last analysis as the history of meaning" (p. 49). For an analysis that discusses the residues of and resistances to critique in Derrida, see Kevin Hart, *The Trespass of the Sign* (Cambridge, 1989).

12. As such texts as *Glas* and "Tympan" suggested, he also experimented with "double writing," in which the single voice of the author was bifurcated. For a discussion of double reading, see Naomi Schor, "Reading Double: Sand's Difference," in *The Poetics of Gender*, ed. Nancy K. Miller (New York, 1986).

to a process of "soliciting"[13] or shaking up did not mean for Derrida exposing their problematic assumptions as corrigible illusions, but rather treating them as knots to be untied again and again without end.

Moreover, insofar as everything that goes under the rubric of "vision" might be understood as a textual construct for Derrida rather than a perceptual experience—"I don't know what perception is and I don't believe that anything like perception exists," he once exclaimed[14]—the hypertrophy of something designated vision per se could not be subjected to a critique, even if deconstruction permitted such an approach. The blind spots—"punctum caecum" was a privileged deconstructionist term—revealed by double readings were metaphors for the unknowable that no amount of revelation could illuminate. However "apocalyptic" the tone of deconstruction might be, it was "an apocalypse without vision, without truth, without revelation."[15] No feminism interested in undoing the effects of patriarchal oppression, it might be thought, could be inspired by so Sisyphean a scenario. No theory so blatantly lacking in a redemptive, utopian impulse could fuel the feminist quest for radical change.[16]

And yet notwithstanding all these cogent objections, unless deconstruction's distinctive contribution to the ongoing crisis of ocularcentrism is acknowledged, the rise of a heterodox feminism in France, which struck yet another blow against the alleged nobility of the eye, cannot be understood.[17] Or to avoid the impression of a simple one-directional causal-

<hr />

13. According to Derrida, "sollus" in archaic Latin means the whole, while "citare" means "to put in motion" ("Force and Signification," in *Writing and Difference*, p. 6).

14. Derrida, "Discussion," in *The Structuralist Controversy: The Languages of Criticism and the Sciences of Man*, ed. Richard Macksey and Eugenio Donato (Baltimore, 1972), p. 272.

15. Derrida, "Of an Apocalyptic Tone Recently Adopted in Philosophy," *Semeia*, 23 (1982), p. 94.

16. Such a reproach is leveled against Derrida by Whitford in *Luce Irigaray*, pp. 123ff. For a more positive reading of the implications of deconstruction for feminism—she calls Derrida "the purveyor of hope," at least in comparison with Lacan—see Andrea Nye, *Feminist Theory and the Philosophies of Man* (London, 1988), pp. 186ff.

17. Another indication of Derrida's contribution to the crisis of ocularcentrism can be discerned in the way his work was absorbed into the debate about film discussed in

ity—for Derrida may well have learned a thing or two from his feminist colleagues—it might be said that a synergistic interaction between deconstruction and French feminism added still more fuel to the antiocularcentric fire. Insofar as some of Derrida's writings on this theme antedate Irigaray's, however, it makes sense to begin with a close examination of his complicated and ambiguous ruminations on visuality in its various guises, and then investigate the uses to which Irigaray put them, as well as her own unique contributions to the debate. We hope to show as a result that French feminism—or rather certain of it exponents, for the movement as a whole resists reduction to one common denominator—radicalized the antivisual components in deconstruction. Moving beyond Derrida's characteristic ambivalence, Irigaray in particular produced a less insistent double reading of the pernicious effects produced by the hypertrophy of the visual.

⊙

Deconstruction has been notoriously impatient with the traditional game of tracing intellectual influences, but it is difficult to ignore hearing in Derrida's work the echoes of many arguments already encountered in previous chapters. Bergson's protest against the spatialization of time, Nietzsche's critique of Apollonian art, Bataille's strictures against heliocentric notions of form, Starobinski's exposure of the dialectic of transparency and obstacle in Rousseau, Heidegger's attack on enframing in the age of the worldview, Merleau-Ponty's interest in the chiasm of the visible and invisible, and Barthes's rejection of the traditional French fetish of linguistic clarity all provided threads for the intertextual web that can be

---

the previous chapter. See, for example, Serge Daney's remarks cited by Jean-Louis Comolli, "Machines of the Visible," in *The Cinematic Apparatus*, ed. Teresa de Lauretis and Stephen Heath (New York, 1985), p. 126. The most explicit use of deconstruction in French film studies came in the work of Marie-Claire Ropars-Wuilleumier, *Le Texte divisé* (Paris, 1981). A similar impact might be traced in the work of Philippe Lacoue-Labarthe and Jean-Luc Nancy on literature. See, for example, their *The Literary Absolute: The Theory of Literature in German Romanticism*, trans. Phillip Barnard and Cheryl Lester (Albany, N.Y., 1988), where they deconstruct the specular "eidesthetics" of the Romantics.

called deconstruction. So too did Emmanuel Levinas's elevation of Hebraic iconoclastic notions of ethics over idolatrous Hellenic ontology and Edmond Jabès's stress on the word over the image, which will be discussed in the following chapter. Here the effects of Derrida's own Jewish background must be acknowledged.[18] And finally, the impact of the twentieth-century revolution in communications media, which was so important for thinkers from Heidegger to Baudrillard, may also be detected in Derrida's work.[19]

Derrida's sustained thematic engagement with visual themes began as early as his initial encounters with phenomenological and structuralist theory in the 1960s. As noted before, his first work on Husserl, the 1962 introduction to the latter's *Origin of Geometry* and *Speech and Phenomena* of 1967,[20] focused on the important link between vision and Husserl's impoverished concept of temporality. According to Derrida, phenomenology's reliance on the primacy of perception led it to posit the possibility of immediacy, which privileged presence over other temporal modes. Husserl's eidetic intuition with its debt to the visual notion of *eidos* assumed the "self-same identity of the actual now" revealed in his telling

18. Derrida has discussed the personal effects of his origins as an Algerian Jew in the interview he gave *Le Nouvel Observateur* in 1983, reprinted in Wood and Bernasconi, eds., *Derrida and Différance*. For an account of its intellectual importance which stresses the issue of sight, see Susan A. Handelman, *The Slayers of Moses: The Emergence of Rabbinic Interpretation in Modern Literary Theory* (Albany, N.Y., 1982), chap. 7; and Megill, *Prophets of Extremity*, chap. 8. For more extensive accounts of the complicated Derrida/Levinas relationship, see Robert Bernasconi, "The Trace of Levinas in Derrida," in *Derrida and Différance*, ed. Wood and Bernasconi; and "Levinas and Derrida: The Question of the Closure of Metaphysics," in *Face to Face with Levinas*, ed. Richard A. Cohen (Albany, N.Y., 1986); and many of the essays in Robert Bernasconi and Simon Critchley, eds., *Re-reading Levinas* (Bloomington, Ind., 1991).

19. For arguments to this effect, see Gregory L. Ulmer, *Applied Grammatology: Post(e)-Pedagogy from Jacques Derrida to Joseph Beuys* (Baltimore, 1985); and Mark Poster, *The Mode of Information: Poststructuralism and Social Context* (Chicago, 1990).

20. Derrida, *Edmund Husserl's Origin of Geometry: An Introduction*, trans. John P. Leavy (Stony Brook, N.Y., 1978) and *Speech and Phenomena and Other Essays on Husserl's Theory of Signs*, trans. David B. Allison (Evanston, Ill., 1973).

metaphor of "im selben Augenblick."[21] What this theory forgot, however, was the impurity of perception, its inevitable intertwining with language, which opened up a more complex temporal horizon.

> As soon as we admit this continuity of the now and the not-now, perception and nonperception, in the zone of primordiality common to primordial impression and primordial retention, we admit the other into the self-identity of the *Augenblick*; nonpresence and nonevidence are admitted into *the blink of the instant*. There is a duration to the blink, and it closes the eye.[22]

Using the same metaphor previously encountered in Bataille and other critics of ocularcentrism, Derrida concluded that language—in particular, the phoneme—"is the *phenomenon of the labyrinth*. . . . Rising toward the sun of presence, it is the way of Icarus. . . . Contrary to the assurance that Husserl gives us a little further on, 'the look' cannot 'abide'."[23] Believing that it could was not merely a fallacy of Husserlian phenomenology, Derrida suggested, but of Western philosophy as a whole with its "metaphysics of presence." Ever since the Platonic emphasis on form, he added in a later essay on Husserl, such a visually abetted temporal bias has ruled Western thought: "All the concepts by which *eidos* or *morphe* could be translated and determined refer back to the theme of *presence in general*. Form is presence itself. Formality is what is presented, visible, and conceivable of the thing in general. . . . The metaphysical domination of the concept of form cannot fail to effectuate a certain subjection to the look."[24] Such subjection, moreover, had a gender dimension that

21. Derrida, *Speech and Phenomena*, p. 62.

22. Ibid., p. 65.

23. Ibid., p. 104. Derrida's fascination with labyrinths, as well as other spaces hidden to view like crypts, invites comparison with that of Deleuze and Guattari with the figure of the rhizome or root-system. See, for example, *A Thousand Plateaus: Capitalism and Schizophrenia*, trans. Brian Massumi (Minneapolis, 1987). All of these metaphors are deep structures, but without the intelligible regularity assumed by structuralist theory.

permeated Western philosophy from virtually its beginnings: "The idea of form in Aristotle, for example, is regularly linked with the male."[25]

Even Heidegger, whose hostility to visual primacy was far more explicit than Husserl's, was not spared Derrida's criticism.[26] For despite his emphasis on time and critique of visually informed *theoria*,[27] Heidegger, because of his ontological quest for forgotten origins (*archia*), remained complicitous with a metaphysics of presence. The difference between Being and beings, which he had posited, was itself forgotten, as Heidegger privileged a notion of presence evident as early as Parmenides: "a present under the heading of that which endures and persists, near and available, exposed to vision or given by hand."[28]

Phenomenology's fatal implication in the metaphysical tradition was reinforced by another fallacy besides its reliance on visual presence: its equally problematic faith in the primacy of the voice over writing. Derrida's complicated defense of *écriture* suggested that however much he may have been unhappy with ocular immediacy, he was no less critical of similar effects produced by other senses. Insofar as presence was suggested by the speaker hearing his own voice, aurality could be as much of a source of deception as sight: "This self-presence of the animating act in the trans-

24. Derrida, "Form and Meaning," in *Speech and Phenomena*, p. 108.

25. Derrida, interview in Raoul Mortley, *French Philosophers in Conversation* (London, 1991), p. 104.

26. Derrida, "*Ousia* and *Gramme*: Note on a Note from *Being and Time*," in *Margins of Philosophy*, trans. Alan Bass (Chicago, 1982). For a comparison of their thought, see Herman Rapaport, *Heidegger and Derrida: Reflections on Time and Language* (Lincoln, Nebr., 1989); and "Time's Cinders," in *Modernity and the Hegemony of Vision*, ed. David Michael Levin (Berkeley, 1993).

27. The deconstructionist attitude toward visually based *theoria* was close to Heidegger's, despite the confusion caused by the appropriation in America of the term "theory" to apply to deconstruction itself (e.g., Paul de Man, *The Resistance to Theory* [Minneapolis, 1986]). Derrida, however, self-consciously put the term in quotation marks and wrote of "theoretical jetties" to indicate forces rather than forms in "Some Statements and Truisms about Neologisms, Newisms, Postisms, Parasitisms, and Other Small Seismisms," in *The States of "Theory:" History, Art and Critical Discourse*, ed. David Carroll (New York, 1990).

28. Derrida, "*Ousia* and *Gramme*," p. 32.

parent spirituality of what it animates, this inwardness of life with itself, which has always made us say that speech [*parole*] is alive, supposes, then that the speaking subject hears himself [*s'entend*] in the present."[29] There was, to be sure, another implication produced by listening to the voice of the other, an implication to be examined shortly, but insofar as any sense might produce the effect of presence, it was in need of deconstruction.

If such a procedure required greater awareness of the importance of language, in particular of writing, how did structuralism with its debt to Saussurean linguistics fare in Derrida's estimation? In a number of different essays and *Of Grammatology*, published in 1967, Derrida sought to demonstrate that for all their apparent oppositions, phenomenology and structuralism shared several problematic assumptions.[30] Not only did Saussure and those who followed him like Lévi-Strauss phonocentrically privilege the voice over writing, not only did they show a nostalgia for origins as fervent as that of a Heidegger, not only did they fall victim to the metaphysics of presence, but they also espoused a visually determined notion of form that could be seen by the cool gaze of the dispassionate scientist. The nineteenth-century "panoramagram," invented by Émile Littré to show objects on a flat surface in their true visual depth, was, Derrida insisted, "the very image of the structuralist instrument."[31]

To bring movement and play back into such Apollonian structures, Derrida claimed, required an appreciation of Nietzsche's Dionysian notion of force. Careful to warn against the simple replacement of form by force, which would repeat the binary logic of structuralism itself, he argued for an interminable interaction of the two. "Like pure force, Dionysus is worked by difference. He sees and lets himself be seen. And tears out (his) eyes. For all eternity, he has had a relationship to his exterior, to visible form, to structure, as he does to his death. This is how he appears (to himself)."[32] Dionysus's contradictory relation to blindness and vision

29. Derrida, *Speech and Phenomena*, p. 78.

30. Husserl's own structuralist side is highlighted in "'Genesis and Structure' and Phenomenology," in *Writing and Difference*.

31. Derrida, "Force and Signification," in *Writing and Difference*, p. 5.

is thus the eternal difference that pits force against form. Similarly, the spatial notion of a center, which is so important to structuralist notions of order, must be both preserved and erased.[33] Although at one point, Derrida asks "is not the center, the absence of play and difference, another name for death?"[34] at another, he calls it "an absolutely indispensable" function, which must be situated in a force field, but not undone.[35] Such an argument implies that "ocular-" as well as the other "centrisms" deconstruction sought to challenge cannot be entirely extirpated.[36]

But, Derrida insisted, they should be severely shaken, in order to produce the effect in writing that one commentator has compared to Op Art in its dizzying overload of the perceptual system.[37] How, it must be asked, does writing relate to visual experience? Aren't marks on the page just as evident to the eye as pictures, photographs, or the visible manifold of "real objects"? Although Derrida's position may be, as Geoffrey Hartman has put it, that of a "Hebrew rather than a Hellene: aniconic yet intensely graphic,"[38] isn't the grapheme itself inevitably visible?

Here too Derrida's answer was a double reading. Insofar as traditional philosophy and linguistics tended to suppress the materiality of the sign and see it as a transparent window on the world of purely mental, symbolic discourse, it must be chastened for having forgotten the sensual na-

---

32. Ibid., p. 29.

33. Derrida, "Structure, Sign and Play in the Discourse of the Human Sciences," in *Writing and Difference*. This essay also appeared in *The Structuralist Controversy* with a transcript of the discussion afterward.

34. Derrida, "Ellipsis," in *Writing and Difference*, p. 297.

35. Derrida, "Discussion" after "Structure, Sign and Play in the Discourse of the Human Sciences," in *The Structuralist Controversy*, p. 271.

36. A similar conclusion follows from Derrida's "Violence and Metaphysics: An Essay on the Thought of Emmanuel Levinas," in *Writing and Difference*. For all his appreciation of Levinas's critique of Hellenic ontologizing in the name of Hebraic ethics, he nonetheless refuses to make the opposition absolute, citing instead James Joyce's chiasmic "JewGreek is greekjew. Extremes meet" (p. 53).

37. Gregory Ulmer, "Op Writing: Derrida's Solicitation of *Theoria*," in *Displacement*.

38. Geoffrey H. Hartman, *Saving the Text: Literature, Derrida, Philosophy* (Baltimore, 1981), p. 17.

ture of every medium of discourse. Poets like Mallarmé, who resurrected visible poetry, and Pound, influenced as he was by Ernest Fenollosa's work on Chinese ideograms, had understood the need to register the irreducible materiality of visible signifiers. So too had Freud when he compared the dream work to hieroglyphic rather than purely phonetic writing. In contrast, linguists like Saussure, who had rejected the pictographic origins of language in favor of a notion of the pure arbitrariness of signs, had failed to realize the nonphonetic visible dimension of writing.[39]

It was precisely to support this claim that Derrida introduced the neologism "différance" in his influential essay of that title written in 1968.[40] This term, "literally neither a word nor a concept,"[41] acquires at least one of its multiple acceptations through visual rather than aural means: the "a" that cannot be heard, but is there to be seen in its idiosyncratic spelling. As such, "différance" performatively enacts Derrida's "grammatological" resistance to the putative primacy of speech over the written word.

To put it another way, as the Derridean Rodolphe Gasché has emphasized, specular or reflective discourses of identity, in which words allegedly mirror thoughts without remainder, have metaphorically forgotten the silver backing, the tain, behind every mirror image.[42] When the tain becomes, as it were, visible, the mirror loses its capacity to reflect; when the materiality of language is foregrounded, signifiers cannot be taken as simple doubles of what they signify: mere transparent vehicles of signification.

But insofar as language must itself be understood as dependent on what Derrida called "arche-écriture," its infrastructural workings can never become fully apparent to the eye or even available to the penetrating structuralist gaze claiming to reveal the diacritical *langue* beneath the surface of *parole*. Although the figurative, ideographic dimension of writing should

39. Derrida, *Of Grammatology*, pp. 32ff. In his discussion of anagrams, Saussure came close to the insight that graphemes are prior to phonemes, but, Derrida claims, he hesitated to draw this full conclusion (p. 245).

40. Derrida, "Différance," in *Margins of Philosophy*.

41. Ibid., p. 3.

42. Rodolphe Gasché, *The Tain of the Mirror: Derrida and the Philosophy of Reflection* (Cambridge, Mass., 1986).

not be forgotten, Derrida argued, neither should it be made its essence. "I have often insisted on the fact," he told interviewers in 1971, "that 'writing' or the 'text' are not reducible *either* to the sensible or visible presence of the graphic or the 'literal'."[43] Their hidden workings should themselves be understood in terms of a kind of invisible materiality.

Even on the level of purely visual representation, Derrida suggested, perfect specularity is problematic. For the reflective interplay of apparently identical images is based on an inevitable disunity that already defines the first image, "for what is reflected is split *in itself* and not only as an addition to itself of its image. The reflection, the image, the double, splits what it doubles. The origin of the speculation becomes a difference. What can look at itself is one; and the law of the addition of the origin to its representation, of the thing to its image, is that one plus one makes at least three."[44] Although the two images may be apparently identical, there is always a surplus, an invisible otherness, that necessarily disrupts their specular unity. Mimicry, visual or linguistic, is never perfect because there is no self-contained, entirely unified original referent prior to the speculative process which could be seamlessly reproduced.[45] Mimesis should not become what Derrida calls "mimetologism," a visual version of logocentrism, which was evident in the close relationship of theatricality to theory.[46] Even Lacan's concept of the mirror stage, Derrida suggested, if applied without awareness of the cracks that disrupt its smooth opera-

43. Derrida, *Positions*, p. 65.

44. Derrida, *Of Grammatology*, p. 36. Derrida returned to the metaphorics of reflection in "The Laws of Reflection: Nelson Mandela, in Admiration," in *For Nelson Mandela*, ed. Jacques Derrida and Mutapha Tlili (New York, 1987). Here specular paradoxes are connected in positive ways to Mandela's relation to the law and the admiration that he evokes in Derrida.

45. See his analysis of Mallarmé's *"Mimique"* in "The Double Session," in *Dissemination*, trans. Barbara Johnson (Chicago, 1982).

46. Deconstruction's general suspicion of the traditional theater of imitation was evident in particular in the work of Philippe Lacoue-Labarthe. See, for example, his "La césure du spéculatif," *L'imitation des modernes* (Paris, 1976). Here he links the Greek tragedy with speculative idealism and contrasts it with the German *Trauerspiel*, as implicitly recovered by Hölderlin.

tion—as was the case with certain French film theorists—suppresses the otherness that can never be entirely mastered by specular identity.[47]

Another way to express the difference that splits seemingly identical reflections, linguistic or visual, is through what Derrida called the problematic of "the trace." Acknowledging his debt to Levinas's critique of ontology, with its suspicion of visual presence, he attributed the trace to the memory of an ever-receding origin that always remains elusively outside of what it produces in the present. The temporal spacing of the trace never leads to spatial simultaneity and full visibility, but rather to interminable delay (*différance* as deferral). "*The (pure) trace is différance,*" Derrida contended. "It does not depend on any sensible plenitude, audible or visible, phonic or graphic. It is, on the contrary, the condition of such a plenitude. Although it *does not exist*, although it is never a *being-present* outside of all plenitude, its possibility is by rights anterior to all that one calls sign (signified/signifier, content/expression, etc.), concept or operation, motor or sensory. This differance is therefore not more sensible than intelligible."[48]

Derrida's vigilant refusal to valorize one side of a binary opposition, such as sensible, over another, such as intelligible, meant he was just as critical of theorists who believed in the possibility of doing away with the illusions of sight as he was of those who believed visual experience could provide illuminations of the truth. Thus, *Of Grammatology* roundly criticizes utopian desires to replace theatricality and "spectacle" entirely by

47. Derrida's celebrated critique of Lacan's seminar on Poe's "The Purloined Letter," in his "The Purveyor of Truth," *Yale French Studies*, 52 (1975), argues in effect that Lacan's entire theory replicates the mirror stage in its claim that the story can be understood as an allegory of the truth of psychoanalysis. Derrida in contrast stresses the ways in which "The Purloined Letter" exceeds this specular interpretation. For further discussion, which argues that Derrida himself makes tacit truth claims open to the same objection, see Barbara Johnson, "The Frame of Reference: Poe, Lacan, Derrida," in *The Critical Difference: Essays in the Contemporary Rhetoric of Reading* (Baltimore, 1980). For a Derridean critique of Lacanian film criticism, see Peter Brunette and David Wills, *Screen/Play: Derrida and Film Theory* (Princeton, 1989).

48. Derrida, *Of Grammatology*, p. 62.

"festival," the distanced gaze of subjects looking voyeuristically at objects from afar by a participatory "community of speech where all the members are within earshot."[49] Here Rousseau and Lévi-Strauss were the targets, although elsewhere he directed a similar argument against Antonin Artaud.[50]

With Starobinski's analysis as his guide, Derrida claimed that Rousseau's yearning for crystalline transparency blinded him to the chain of representational supplementarity that rendered his project futile. "The concept of the supplement is a sort of blind spot in Rousseau's text, the not-seen that opens and limits visibility."[51] Failing to acknowledge the inevitability of supplementarity meant a comparable blindness to representation. "What Rousseau criticizes in the last analysis is not the content of the spectacle, the sense *represented* by it, although that *too* he criticizes: it is re-presentation itself."[52] For Derrida, the yearning to do away entirely with representation—politically, theatrically, or imagistically—turns out to be another form of the metaphysics of presence.

Even Heidegger, whose analysis of the age of the world picture included a powerful critique of representational ways of thinking, could not entirely escape representation. "It will be difficult to avoid the question," Derrida wrote in a later piece entitled "Sending: On Representation," "whether the relationship of the epoch of representation to the great Greek epoch is not still interpreted by Heidegger in a representative mode, as if the couple *Anwesenheit/repraesentatio* still dictated the law of its own interpretation, which does no more than to redouble and recognize itself in the historical text it claims to decipher."[53] Representations,

49. Ibid., p. 136.

50. Derrida, "The Theater of Cruelty and the Closure of Representation," *Writing and Difference*, p. 244. Another obvious target of the same reproach would be Debord, whose work, however, Derrida ignored.

51. Derrida, *Of Grammatology*, p. 163.

52. Ibid., p. 304.

53. Derrida, "Sending: On Representation," *Social Research*, 49, 2 (Summer, 1982), p. 322.

Derrida argued, were "sendings" (*envois*), which never reach their final destination or reunite with the object or idea they represent.[54] Because of their inevitable "destinerrance," their interminable wanderings (like that of the Jews), representations can never be replaced by the pure presence of what they re-present. But neither can their difference from the "things" they represent be completely effaced in the name of a realm of pure simulacra entirely without a trace of reference (as theorists like Baudrillard were to argue).[55]

A similar double reading informed one of his most influential essays, "White Mythology: Metaphor in the Text of Philosophy" of 1971. Here he argued against the impossible dream of ridding philosophy of its metaphorical, rhetorical medium of expression; even the ideal of clarity was, after all, based on a photological metaphor invoking visual experience.[56] No metalanguage of literal concepts could purify thought of its metaphoric pollution, no supersensible realm could free itself of its entanglement in the sensual. But metaphors based on sense experience were open to a deconstructive reading, which could unsettle them, even if they could not be dissolved entirely.

54. See also the comparable analysis in *The Post Card: From Socrates to Freud and Beyond*, trans. Alan Bass (Chicago, 1987). It should be noted that insofar as postcards generally have pictures on one side, they are instantiations of the imbrication of the visual and the graphic, rather than pure examples of *écriture*.

55. There are, to be sure, places in his work where Derrida does seem to approach Baudrillard's position, for example, in his discussion of Mallarmé in *Dissemination*, where he writes: "We are faced then with mimicry imitating nothing; faced, so to speak with a double that doubles no simple. . . . This speculum reflects no reality; it produces mere 'reality-effects.' . . . In this speculum with no reality, in this mirror of a mirror, a difference or dyad does exist, since there are mimes and phantoms. But it is a difference without reference, or rather a reference without a referent" (p. 206).

56. In "Force and Signification," he had already written that light and dark was "the founding metaphor of Western philosophy as metaphysics. The founding metaphor not only because it is a photological one—and in this respect the entire history of our philosophy is a photology, the name given to a history of, or treatise on, light—but because it is a metaphor. Metaphor in general, the passage from one existent to another, authorized by the initial *submission* of Being to the existent, the *analogical* displacement of Being, is the essential weight which anchors discourse in metaphysics" (p. 27).

No metaphor was in as much need of such an unsettling as the founding trope of Western metaphysics, the privileging of whiteness over blackness, light over darkness: "The white mythology which resembles the culture of the West: the white man takes his own mythology, Indo-European mythology, his own *logos*, that is the *mythos* of his idiom, for the universal form of that he must still wish to call Reason."[57] Not only does such a metaphor express the domination of one race over another, but it also derives from the time-honored privileging of the sun as the dominant locus of signification: "Value, gold, the eye, the sun, etc. are carried along, as has been long known, by the same tropic movement. Their exchange dominates the field of rhetoric *and* of philosophy."[58]

In its dominant form, which has ruled metaphysics from Plato to Descartes and beyond, the sun was the giver of natural light (*lumen naturale*), the source of "the very opposition of appearing and disappearing, the entire lexicon of the *phainesthai*, of *aletheia*, etc., of day and night, of the visible and the invisible, of the present and the absent—all this was possible only under the sun. Insofar as it structures the metaphorical space of philosophy, the sun represents what is natural in philosophical language."[59] Such a sun, seeming to return each day after a trip around the earth, was also the symbol of specular sameness and circular unity for Western man, who identified with its daily progress across the sky: "The sensory sun, which rises in the East, becomes interiorized, in the evening of its journey, in the eye and the heart of the Westerner. He summarizes, assumes and achieves the essence of man, 'illuminated by the true light.'"[60] Insofar as the operation of metaphoric exchange itself was understood in terms of analogical equivalence (difference reduced to sameness) or interiorizing anamnesis (the ingathering through memory of alienated otherness) rather than disseminating supplementarity, it too betrayed a

57. Derrida, "The White Mythology: Metaphor in the Text of Philosophy," *Margins of Philosophy*, p. 213.
58. Ibid., p. 218.
59. Ibid., p. 251.
60. Ibid., p. 268.

logic of detemporalizing sameness rather than the infinite deferral of *différance*. "The tenor of the dominant metaphor will return always to this major signified of ontotheology: the circle of the heliotrope."[61] In contrast, as Geoffrey Hartman was to put it, "the blackness of ink or print suggests that *écriture* is a hymn to the Spirit of the Night."[62]

As a result, a philosophy acknowledging the importance of *écriture* would inevitably seem to be challenging the naive project of a completed "enlightenment."[63] Although Derrida—like Foucault before him—sought to fend off the charge that he was simply anti-Enlightenment in a totalizing way,[64] the cumulative effect of his interrogation of sight, at least for many of his critics, was to strengthen the hold of what Peter Sloterdijk has called cynical over critical reason in poststructuralist thought.

Derrida's double reading of the solar metaphor, in fact, showed that its links to the Enlightenment were not total. For there were other dimensions of that metaphor without specular or illuminating implications. The sun is also a star, after all, like all the other stars that appear only at night and are invisible during the day. As such it suggests a source of truth or properness that was not available to the eye, at least at certain times. Even more powerfully destructive of sight was the sun as an object of the gaze, for its light was capable of blinding and dazzling as well as illuminat-

---

61. Ibid., p. 266.

62. Hartman, *Saving the Text*, p. xix.

63. Deconstruction has accordingly often been called "counter-Enlightenment" in implication, for example, by Jürgen Habermas in *The Philosophical Discourse of Modernity: Twelve Lectures*, trans. Frederick Lawrence (Cambridge, Mass., 1987).

64. In "On Colleges and Philosophy" (p. 69), Derrida protested, "Of course in some situations I am totally on the side of the Enlightenment. It depends on the analysis of the situation—the forces against which we have to fight in terms of Enlightenment as rationality, criticism, absolute suspicion against obscurantism, etc. But, on the other hand, we know that the philosophy of the Enlightenment, reduced to its common features, implies many things that I think we have to suspect and deconstruct. . . . I think we should be on the side of Enlightenment without being too naive, and on some occasions be able to question its philosophy." For Foucault's similar protest, see "What Is Enlightenment?" in *The Foucault Reader*, ed. Paul Rabinow (New York, 1984), p. 45.

ing. The burning sun, which Bataille in particular had celebrated for its thwarting of the Icarian yearning for transcendence,[65] presented a potent alternative to the Platonic sun of cool reason. Heliotropic metaphors are thus always imperfect, implying both turning toward and turning away from the sun, the source of illumination as well as blindness.

But insofar as language cannot escape its metaphoricity, a plural metaphoricity that resists reduction to a univocal master trope, there is no way to purge language (and by extension, philosophy) of its sensory, especially visual, entanglements. In this sense, Derrida's refusal to be cast as a simple anti-Enlightenment thinker has some plausibility. For paradoxically, by insisting on the rhetoricity of language (which might be construed as a counter-Enlightenment claim), he also acknowledged that our metaphorically informed bias for illumination and transparency cannot be completely undone.

Derrida's resistance to radical rejections of ocularcentrism, his unwillingness to countenance antivisual purism, did not, however, mean he lessened his hostility to the traditional privileging of the eye. Instead, like Nietzsche, he fought against any hierarchizing of the senses, seeking instead to explore their interdependence.[66] His special fascination with the complicating role of other senses has been widely remarked. Even smell and (not always good) taste, the "chemical senses" that reverse the distancing function of sight, did not escape his attention ("How," he once irreverently asked, "could ontology get hold of a fart?").[67]

But it was touch and hearing that seemed most compelling. Derrida's

---

65. The penultimate footnote of "The White Mythology" cites all of the relevant texts of Bataille on visual themes. Derrida's major consideration of Bataille, "From Restricted to General Economy: A Hegelianism Without Reserve," in *Writing and Difference*, ends by contrasting visual images in Hegel and Bataille. For a consideration of the intertextual traces of Bataille's *Story of the Eye* in Derrida's *Glas*, see John P. Leavy, Jr., *GLASary* (Lincoln, Nebr., 1986), pp. 76ff.

66. For a typical deconstructionist appropriation of Nietzsche, see Sarah Kofman, *Nietzsche et la métaphore* (Paris, 1972), p. 154, where she compares Nietzsche and Bataille as critics of the nobility of the eye.

67. Derrida, *Glas*, trans. John P. Leavy (Lincoln, 1986) p. 69. For a discussion of Derrida on taste and smell, see Ulmer, *Applied Grammatology*, pp. 53ff.

stress on texts as tactile textures with hinges, breaks, and crevices, his attention to the importance of the hand even in the aurally inclined Heidegger,[68] led one commentator to go so far as to claim that "especially haptic qualities are demanded of the deconstructionist performer, spectator, and reader; not to follow optically the 'line of ideas' in a text or in a picture and see only the representation proper, the surface, but to probe with the eyes the pictorial texture and even to enter the texture and probe below the texture."[69] Such "touching" with the eye did not lead to a secure tactile experience of being firmly planted on the ground, for all grounds, all foundations, were suspect, however they may be construed. We are, as Nietzsche knew, swimming in an endless sea, rather than standing on dry land. To "touch" a trace, groping blindly in the dark, is no more the guarantee of certainty than to see its residues.

Derrida's attitude toward hearing was similarly ambivalent. Although Sarah Kofman suggested that deconstruction might require a "third ear" to catch what normal philosophy couldn't hear, not all listening experiences were equally valuable.[70] As already noted, Derrida criticized the effect of hearing one's own voice as the justification for speech's alleged preeminence over writing. It was on the basis of this experience that Hegel could claim that hearing was even more ideal, more dialectically effective than sight. For whereas the latter always acknowledged the existence of the object prior to and after the event of seeing, the former identified the sound entirely with its being heard. It could thus serve as the model of perfect sublation, preserving both objectivity and interiority.[71]

68. Derrida, "*Geschlecht* II: Heidegger's Hand," in *Deconstruction and Philosophy*, ed. John Sallis (Chicago, 1987).

69. Claude Gandelman, *Reading Pictures, Viewing Texts* (Bloomington, Ind., 1991), p. 140. Such surface/depth metaphors are, however, generally alien to deconstruction. See also Gregory L. Ulmer, "The Object of Post-Criticism," in *The Anti-Aesthetic: Essays on Postmodern Culture*, ed. Hal Foster (Port Townsend, Wash., 1983), p. 93.

70. Sarah Kofman, *Lectures de Derrida* (Paris, 1984), p. 30.

71. Derrida, "The Pit and the Pyramid: Introduction to Hegel's Semiology," in *Margins of Philosophy*, p. 92.

But if this version of hearing was obviously problematic for Derrida, another was less so. In several places, he invoked the Levinasian "ear of the other"[72] as an ethical antidote to the metaphysics of presence. In so doing, however, he carefully distanced himself from a competing theoretical tradition that also privileges the ear as a communicative organ: hermeneutics.[73] Even Heidegger's reliance on aural metaphors, he charged, remained hostage to logocentrism. Although Gadamer protested that Heidegger's version of hearing was more complicated than Derrida had allowed, the latter remained unconvinced.[74] For him, the ear was less a means of coming to a common agreement through patient listening, less the locus of the reception of the Word, than an impediment to common understanding. Insofar as the ear was defined as "the distinct, differentiated, articulated organ that produces the effect of proximity, of absolute properness, the idealizing erasure of organizing difference,"[75] Derrida resisted its claims. But understood as the other's ear, it functions to disrupt

72. Derrida, *The Ear of the Other: Otobiography, Transference, Translation*, ed. Christie McDonald, trans. Peggy Kamuf and Avital Ronell (Lincoln, Nebr., 1982). For an analysis of the ethical implications of his position, see Diane Michelfelder, "Derrida and the Ethics of the Ear," in *The Question of the Other: Essays in Contemporary Continental Philosophy*, ed. Arleen B. Dallery and Charles E. Scott (Albany, N.Y., 1989).

73. According to Hans-Georg Gadamer, "The primacy of hearing is the basis of the hermeneutical phenomenon, as Aristotle saw" (*Truth and Method* [New York, 1975], p. 420). David Couzens Hoy finds common ground between Derrida and Gadamer on the basis of their attitude toward hearing: "Derrida overcomes the objections raised against the idea of a dialogue with a written text. Hearing and reading are no longer so disanalogous, for hearing is also a kind of reading—an *interpretation* of the universality of the proposition in terms of the concreteness of the situation" (*The Critical Circle: Literature and History in Contemporary Hermeneutics* [Berkeley, 1978], p. 82). What Hoy underestimates is Derrida's hostility to "interpretation" and his resistance to listening as an activity of mutual understanding.

74. Gadamer, "Letter to Dallmayr," in *Dialogue and Deconstruction: The Gadamer-Derrida Encounter*, ed. Diane P. Michelfelder and Richard E. Palmer (Albany, N.Y., 1989), p. 95. This collection shows deconstruction's hostility to hermeneutics in performative as well as constative ways; throughout Derrida and his supporters steadfastly resist entering into a constructive dialogue with Gadamer and his defenders.

75. Derrida, "Tympan," *Margins of Philosophy*, p. xvii. The phrase "absolute properness," a favorite deconstructionist target, drew on the multiple meanings of the French word "propre": cleanliness, possession, property, even propriety.

presence and undercut the authority of the speaker or author, with his authenticating signature, for "it is the ear of the other that signs."[76]

The physical configuration of the ear was also significant for Derrida. In the familiar terms of Nietzsche and Bataille, the ear could be understood as a labyrinth (the spiraling canals of the inner ear) and a vibrating membrane (the tympanum or middle ear),[77] which produced delay and distancing. Like other organs opening to the world—most notably the anus and vagina[78]—it problematized the distinction between inner and outer, producing a sensation of uncanniness. Even the different sizes of ears, Derrida suggested, could imply resistance to sameness or what one commentator has called "earsplitting."[79] Thus, hearing the "glas" or knell of the bell was no less important than looking into the "glace" of the mirror.[80]

In all of his considerations of the senses, Derrida sought to uncover their multiple implications, discerning in each a tendency toward sameness and a countertendency toward difference. Thus, for example, in his 1983 essay on "The Principle of Reason: The University in the Eyes of Its Pupils," an essay that plays with the metaphorics of light and vision in the Western tradition of rational education, Derrida insisted that

> it is not a matter of distinguishing here between sight and non-sight, but rather between two ways of thinking of sight and light, as well as between two conceptions of listening and voice. But it is true that a caricature of representational man, in the Heideggerian sense, would readily endow him with hard eyes permanently open to a nature that he is to dominate, to rape if necessary, by fixing it in front of him, or in swooping down on it like a bird of prey.[81]

Such a caricature—drawing on Aristotle's distinction between animals with "hard, dry eyes" and those that have eyelids—is not, however, the only version of visual experience that might serve as the basis for a university of the future.

76. Derrida, *The Ear of the Other*, p. 51.

77. Another membrane with a similar function is the hymen. Even the eye, he claimed, should be understood as a membrane. See *Dissemination*, pp. 284–285.

> The chance for this event [a nontechnologically dominated
> university] is the chance of an instance, an *Augenblick*, a "wink"
> or a "blink," it takes place "in the twinkling of an eye," I would
> say, rather, "in the twilight of an eye," for it is in the most crepus-
> cular, the most westerly situations of the Western university that
> the chances of this "twinkling" of thought are multiplied.[82]

The eye that knows when to blink or shut is thus preferable to one that stares without eyelids in the full glare of the light of reason; but such an eye still at times knows when to look. The same refusal to choose between one sense over another, commensurate with the deconstructionist preference for undecidability over closure, can also be detected in Derrida's attitude toward the crucial question of the relation between perception and language. At times, he seemed to imply that insofar as there was no pure perception, no unmediated "natural" interface between mind and world, it was necessary to understand the latter as a text to be "read," or more precisely, read doubly. In the case of the visual, such an injunction has led to the widespread impression that deconstruction simply privileged language over perception, following the oft-cited words from *Of Grammatology*, "il n'y a pas de hors-texte."[83] Thus, one commentator claims that "Derrida's answer to the question, 'What is an image?' would undoubtedly be 'Nothing but another kind of writing, a kind of graphic sign that

78. Derrida's frequent introduction of invagination as a positive term, for example, in "Living On: Border Lines," in *Deconstruction and Criticism*, ed. Harold Bloom (New York, 1979), has been useful in the feminist appropriation of his work.

79. Herman Rapaport, "All Ears: Derrida's Response to Gadamer," in Michelfelder and Palmer, eds., *Dialogue and Deconstruction*, p. 200. Rapaport notes that Derrida refuses to listen to Gadamer with the same size ears.

80. These are only two of the multiple meanings evoked in his *Glas*.

81. Derrida, "The Principle of Reason: The University in the Eyes of Its Pupils," *Diacritics*, 13, 3 (Fall, 1983), p. 10.

82. Ibid., p. 20.

83. Derrida, *Of Grammatology*, p. 158. Spivak renders this phrase both as "there is nothing outside of the text" and "there is no outside-text."

dissembles itself as a direct transcript of that which it represents, or of the way things look, or of what they essentially are.'"[84]

But if one takes seriously Derrida's refusal to purify language of its sensuous dimension, as well as his repeated denunciation of the reduction of "textuality" to the commonplace idea of written discourse,[85] if one remembers, that is, what Ulmer has called his pictorialization of the word as well as his grammatization of the image, then a more complicated understanding of his position may result. Only in this way can we make sense of his frequent introduction of visual material into his own texts, material that is, *pace* Geoffrey Hartman, at least still weakly iconic as well as intensely graphic.

The Truth in Painting, first published in 1978, is best known for Derrida's deconstruction of traditional ideas of the aesthetic, most notably that of Kant's Third Critique.[86] Arguing against the integrity of the work of art (the *ergon*), he showed that it is always polluted by its framing contexts (the *parergon*), so that any purely aesthetic discourse cannot itself avoid intermingling with those it tries to exclude—ethical, cognitive, or whatever. Nor can works of art themselves purport to represent the truth in an unproblematic way, say through mimesis of a real or ideal realm. For they are always penetrated intertextually by other impulses that deprive them of their putative disinterested, autonomous status. Cézanne's pledge "I owe you the truth in painting and I will tell it to you"[87] is thus, Derrida claimed, doomed to be betrayed. For what is inside and outside a picture is undecidable and no amount of ingenuity can make the frame impermeable. The dispute between Heidegger and the art historian Meyer Schapiro over the referent in Van Gogh's "Old Shoes with Laces," which

84. W. J. T. Mitchell, *Iconology: Image, Text, Ideology* (Chicago, 1986), p. 30.

85. See, for example, Derrida, "Some Statements and Truisms about Neologisms, Newisms, Postisms, Parasitisms, and Other Small Seismisms," where he claims that "deconstruction is all the less confined to the prisonhouse of language because it *starts* by tackling logocentrism" (p. 91).

86. Derrida, *The Truth in Painting*, trans. Geoff Bennington and Ian McLeod (Chicago, 1987).

87. Cited in ibid., p. 2.

Derrida discussed at some length, is impossible to resolve; there is no un-equivocal truth to be revealed, no matter how learned the disquisition.

Understood in one way, this argument appears fully congruent with the critique of ocularcentrism. Although Merleau-Ponty is unmentioned, Derrida's gloss on Cézanne can be seen as an implicit rejection of the argument in "Cézanne's Doubt" that the painter was in touch with a primordial reality prior to the split between subject and object. And his deconstruction of aesthetic discourses of framing, including the window-like frame around the traditional Western easel painting,[88] may well be indebted to Heidegger's attack on the *Gestell* (the enframing) responsible for turning the world into a picture to be viewed from afar. So too his extended analysis of the works of the painter Valerio Adami, in a chapter originally published in a series called "Behind the Mirror,"[89] can be understood as stressing the inevitability of writing—for example, Adami's own signature and fragments of texts, such as Derrida's *Glas* itself—even in the optical space of the canvas.

Elsewhere in *The Truth in Painting*, Derrida invoked the idea of the sublime as a concept that also defeats the rigorous framing function of the parergon, which tries to surround beautiful images. Noting, as Lyotard also did, that both Kant and Hegel associated the sublime with the Jewish taboo on representation,[90] he cited the familiar claim that "the sublime cannot inhabit any sensible form."[91] But as if to undercut the absoluteness of the interdiction, he included several pictures by Goya of a colossus, whose immensity is such that it supposedly cannot be taken in by the eye.

88. For an analysis of the replacement of the *cadre* (frame) by the *écart* (split) in Derrida, see Tom Conley, "A Trace of Style," in Krupnick, ed., *Displacement and After*. For a discussion of Derrida's fascination with ornaments and margins, see Ulmer, "Op Writing: Derrida's Solicitation of Theory," in idem.

89. The chapter is called "+R (Into the Bargain)," and first appeared in *Derrière le Miroir*, 214 (May, 1975). "+R" can also be read as "tr." for the trace of Adami's signature (the graphic) in the pictorial. *Truth in Painting* also contains an essay on the cartouches of Gérard Titus-Carmel, another artist whose work comes closer to post-modernist than modernist notions of visuality (as Allan Megill notes in *Prophets of Extremity*, p. 282).

90. Ibid., p. 134.

91. Ibid., p. 131.

Frequently throughout the book, in fact, Derrida introduced visual material of one kind or another, suggesting that the Jewish taboo was not absolute. Included are several of Magritte's works, which deal ambivalently with feet and shoes in ways that mock the attempts by Heidegger and Schapiro to identify the referent in Van Gogh's painting. But like all of the Surrealist painters' visual puns, they both invoke and cancel normal sight. So too, Derrida's deconstruction of painting's claim to truth leaves a faint residue of the visual, even as it relentlessly debunks its claim to univocal meaning. The frame may no longer enclose a window on the world, but it remains a dynamic site of chiasmic intertwining between inner and outer, iconic and graphic, that prevents total blindness. Like Duchamp's "pictorial nominalism," with which it has been suggestively compared,[92] deconstruction refuses to break entirely with the seen for the written.

A comparable implication can be drawn from Derrida's 1985 textual accompaniment to a portfolio of photographs by Marie-Françoise Plissart entitled "Right of Inspection."[93] A series of apparently interconnected images, some erotic, others violent, the portfolio invites narrative interpretation, as if it were a photo-novel. Derrida, however, deliberately resisted the role of authoritative commentator, refusing to provide a metadiscursive accompaniment that turns a disordered montage into a "story" recorded by the photographs.[94] Instead, he split his rambling commentary between two voices who argue about everything from the legal status of images and the referential dimension of photographs to the sexual dynamics of the gaze and the power of surveillance. His parergonal comments seem to penetrate and intermingle with the pictures rather than provide a firm border between what is in them and what is outside.

Photo*graphy*, he emphasized, must be understood as writing, which has

92. Carol P. James, "Reading Art Through Duchamp's *Glass* and Derrida's *Glas*," *Substance*, 31 (1981).

93. Marie-Françoise Plissart and Jacques Derrida, "Right of Inspection," trans. David Wills, *Art and Text*, 32, (Autumn, 1989). The original title, *Droit de regard*, suggests "the right to look," "the law(s) of looking," and the "right to oversee."

94. For an analysis of montage and collage as general principles of Derrida's work, see Ulmer, "The Object of Post-Criticism."

to be read as well as viewed. These photographs, one of his voices mused, may even somehow be "in French." Moreover, the inclusion of other, earlier photos in Plissart's images produces a *mise-en-abyme*, which thwarts the innocent eye. "Precisely, this abyssal inclusion of photographs within photographs takes something away from looking, it calls for discourse, demands a reading. These tableaux, scenes or stills provoke a deciphering beyond any simple perception. Instead of a spectacle they institute a reader, of either gender, and instead of voyeurism, exegesis."[95] Insofar as the photographic gaze suggests atemporal instantaneity, it must be disrupted by the haptic interference that "retouches" the image, suggested within Plissart's photos by erotic images of touching.

Derrida challenged any univocal reading of the images, which takes the "right to inspect" as license to hold the "thread of the labyrinth"[96] too tightly. So too he sought to unsettle the initial power of the photographer to fix meaning. "The appropriation of a point of view, for all its reliance on the contrivance of a photography, still unleashes violence. Possession—by that I mean leading to ecstasy—is negotiated through the right of inspection, and that right reverts to whoever possesses the camera, it reverts to the apparatus of capture held in one or the other's hands."[97] The counterpart to such violence, however, cannot be another totalizing point of view, which would be like a panopticon, but rather fragments, which deny any view of the whole: "no single panorama, but simply parts of bodies, torn-up or framed pieces, abyssal synecdoches, floating microscopic details, X-rays, sometimes focused, sometimes out of focus, hence blurred."[98] Indeed, even the word "fragment," Derrida warned, is prob-

95. Plissart and Derrida, "Right of Inspection," p. 27. The general importance of the figure of *mise-en-abyme* for Derrida is shown in his work on the poet Francis Ponge, *Signsponge*, trans. Richard Rand (New York, 1984). Significantly, one of Ponge's poems was entitled "Le soleil placé en abîme." For an analysis of the visual dimensions of this work, see Allan Stoekl, "Ponge's Photographic Rhetoric," in *Politics, Writing, Mutilation: The Cases of Bataille, Blanchot, Roussel, Leiris and Ponge* (Minneapolis, 1985).

96. Plissart and Derrida, "Right of Inspection," p. 35.

97. Ibid., p. 51.

98. Ibid., p. 74.

lematic because it suggests a lost totality or one yet to come, whereas "with regard to the photographic gaze and its apparatus, there is no such thing, it doesn't apply at all."[99]

Among Plissart's images there is one that shows a girl smashing a framed photograph, which Derrida turned into an allegory for iconoclasm:

> For a moment she resembles Moses holding the Table of the Law, the laws of the gaze [*le droit de regard*], which she shows held above her head before dashing it to the ground. The glass shatters like the stone Tablets, like the Decalogue. But what the photograph shows is more or less indescribable within the normal operations of objective representation (as if one had transgressed the Judaic prohibition against icons).[100]

His noting the paradox of the image showing what should be indescribable, however, suggests that Derrida's own attitude was not quite as iconoclastic as the Mosaic tradition,[101] despite his obvious debts to it. As in the case of *The Truth in Painting*, there is a residual trace of the visual here as well, which is manifest in subtle ways in his text. At one point, he referred obliquely to his earlier quarrel with Lacan over Poe's "Purloined Letter," suggesting that although looking has nothing to do with naive perception, "this is not to say that, by being bound to laws and to rights, it only belongs to the 'symbolic.' What happens here is at once entirely imaginary and symbolic."[102] Thus, although pictures have to be "read," their "language" includes the images of the Imaginary, as well as the words of the Symbolic.

Here Derrida drew on certain of Barthes's arguments about the referential moment in photography, about which he had written admiringly in an earlier piece.[103] "Of all the arts," he contended, "photography seems to

99. Ibid.

100. Ibid., p. 85.

101. Even that tradition, the next chapter will argue, was not unequivocally anti-visual.

102. Ibid., p. 53.

me the only one that does not suspend its explicit dependence on a visible referent. In the final analysis, however perverse or ingenious the montage might be, it is unable to produce or domesticate its referent. It must presume it to be given, a captive of what is captured by the apparatus."[104] Photography thus always contains a trace of a thing that was once there; as a result, "it's all about the return of the departed. . . . The spectral is the essence of photography."[105]

Only when photography becomes caught in the parergonal discourse of the aesthetic does it gain a certain distance from its referential function: "Where the referent is itself framed within the photographic frames, the index of the completely other, however marked it may be, nonetheless makes reference endlessly refer. The notion of the chimera is then admissible. If there is an art in photography . . . it is here. Not that it suspends reference, but that it indefinitely defers a certain type of reality, that of the *perceptible* referent."[106] So even when they are redescribed as art, an irreducible trace of the visible residue of what was once there remains in photographs, however much they require reading rather than mere perceptual "seeing."

Derrida's complicated musings on the intertwining of vision and blindness, the shown and the said, the iconic and the graphic, were given an even greater opportunity for expression when he was invited in 1989 by the Louvre to curate an exhibition of its drawings.[107] In one of those uncanny coincidences that seem almost implausibly contrived, Derrida reported in his catalogue essay that he was unable to meet with the museum staff for their first scheduled meeting because he suddenly suffered a facial

103. Derrida, "The Deaths of Roland Barthes," in Hugh J. Silverman, *Philosophy and Non-Philosophy Since Merleau-Ponty* (New York, 1988).

104. Ibid., p. 90.

105. Ibid., p. 34.

106. Ibid., p. 91.

107. Derrida, "*Mémoires d'aveugle: L'autoportrait et autres ruines*," catalogue of exhibition at the Louvre's Napoleon Hall, October, 26, 1990–January 21, 1991 (Paris, 1991); for a discussion, see Meyer Raphael Rubinstein, "Sight Unseen," *Art in America* (April, 1991).

paralysis that left his left eye unable to blink. After he recovered two weeks later, the meeting took place and on the way home, the theme of the exhibition came to him. Playing with the name of the museum, he jotted down the phrase "l'ouvre où on ne pas voir" (the opening where one can't see). Shortly thereafter, he woke in the night with a dream in which he fought with a blind man, which he related to memories he had of competing with his brother as a child in drawing. Less skilled than his brother, he turned to writing in compensation. Not only did the dream reawaken strong feelings of the competition between the word and the image, but the very act of writing the dream down in the dark, when he was unable to see what he was doing, also struck Derrida as significant.

The result was a show of works around the themes of blindness, self-portraiture, and the idea of the ruin, which he entitled "Mémoires d'aveugle" (Memories of the Blind). Composed of some forty-three drawings, mostly self-portraits, some images of blindness and one of ruins (which acted as a metonym of the show as a whole), the exhibition sought to present a network of relationships between drawing and blindness. For Derrida, the act of drawing itself necessitates a moment of non-seeing in which the artist depicts the ruins of a previous vision. Or rather, there is no initial vision that is not already a ruin (a visual analogy to his familiar argument that there is no original word or thing prior to its representation). The delay and temporalization produced by the memory of the earlier trace also means that there is no specular identity, especially when the artist paints him- or herself. Instead a chiasmic exchange occurs, which is complicated still further by the substitution of the beholder in the place of the painter in front of the canvas.

Self-portraits are, moreover, of special interest because they inevitably entail the intervention of writing, for the visual image alone cannot convey the information that the portrait is by the artist himself. To generalize the lesson that images and writing are always intertwined, Derrida's catalogue invokes many of the texts already encountered in this narrative: E. T. A. Hoffmann's "The Sandman," Baudelaire's poem "Les Aveugles," Merleau-Ponty's *Visible and the Invisible*, and Bataille's *Story of the Eye*, as well as others such as Paul de Man's essay on Derrida's account of Rousseau, "The Rhetoric of Blindness." As in the case of his textual accompaniment to "Right of Inspection," his own contribution is less a master commentary then an intertextual crossroad that facilitates the interaction of linguistic and iconic musings on the theme of blindness and insight.

Significantly, it concluded with a reflection on drawings of the blindings of Samson and St. Paul, which raise questions of gender and violence. Following Freud's insight into the link between castration and blindness, Derrida noted that in the Western tradition, the most heroic blind figures are virtually all male. Women's blindness is most frequently depicted in terms of crying, an activity also identified with figures like Augustine and Nietzsche. Tears, Derrida argued, are the most exalted kind of blindness: "If the eyes of all animals are destined for sight, and perhaps from there to the scopic knowledge of the *animale rationale*, only man knows how to go beyond seeing and knowing because only he knows how to cry. . . . Only he knows that tears are the essence of the eye—and not sight. . . . Revelatory blindness, apocalyptic blindness, that which reveals the very truth of the eyes, this would be the gaze veiled by tears."[108]

But such an apocalypse, it will be recalled, is for Derrida one in which the veil can never be ripped away to reveal a fully illuminated truth. Eyes that cry implore rather than see; they invite the question from the other: whence the pain? Only a feminism that knows the value of the veil of tears, Derrida seemed to be suggesting, can preserve the insights provided by such blindness. Only women who resist mimicking the dominant male scopic regime can avoid merely inverting the hierarchy that it supports.

⊙

It is precisely because traditional feminism failed to avoid this mimicry that Derrida, like Nietzsche before him, was unsympathetic toward it. What is sometimes called "liberal feminism" sought the extension of all the rights and privileges normally enjoyed by males to females as well.[109]

108. Derrida, *Mémoires d'aveugle*, p. 128.
109. For a critical discussion of the liberal feminist tradition, see Zillah R. Eisenstein, *The Radical Future of Liberal Feminism* (New York, 1981).

As a result, its ideal was to turn women into rational individuals on the Enlightenment model of bourgeois men, a model whose virtues it did not question. For Olympe de Gouges, the bold author of the "Declaration of the Rights of Women and the Citizen" during the French Revolution, the goal was equality, not difference.

In terms of the metaphorics of vision, this meant accepting the dominant ocularcentric tradition and hoping that women would now be allowed to find their way out of the shadows into its light. Thus, for example, Mary Wollstonecraft's *A Vindication of the Rights of Women* could praise women like Catherine Macauley for a writing style in which "no sex appears, for it is like the sense it conveys, strong and clear," and adopt for herself a God's-eye view: "Let me now as from an eminence survey the world stripped of all its false delusive charms. The clear atmosphere enables me to see each object in its true point of view, while my heart is still."[110] For all her hostility to Rousseau, Wollstonecraft shared his disdain for the glittering superficiality of aristocratic women in the salon culture of the *ancien régime* and hoped to make women pure and transparent instead.[111]

When modern feminist theory emerged in 1949 in France with the publication of Simone de Beauvoir's *The Second Sex*,[112] the model to be emulated had altered considerably—Sartre's existential cum socialist hero rather than the *animale rationale* of the bourgeois Enlightenment—but two assumptions remained fundamentally the same: to be free meant

110. Mary Wollstonecraft, *A Vindication of the Rights of Women*, ed. Carol H. Poston (New York, 1975), pp. 105, and 110.

111. For a discussion of this dimension of her thought, see Joan B. Landes, *Women and the Public Sphere in the Age of the French Revolution* (Ithaca, 1988), p. 129. She argues that Wollstonecraft shared Rousseau's bias for the bourgeois public sphere, which is verbal rather than iconic and male rather than female. My only emendation of this claim would be to stress the still visual dimension of the public sphere, where language is to be transparent and lucid.

112. Simone de Beauvoir, *The Second Sex*, trans. H. M. Parshley (Harmondsworth, 1972). For recent considerations of its importance, see Mary Evans, *Simone de Beauvoir: A Feminist Mandarin* (London, 1985), and Judith Okely, *Simone de Beauvoir* (London, 1986).

women should become like men, and freedom meant being the active, transcending gazer, not the passive object of the gaze.[113] Determined to reject biologism, de Beauvoir spurned any positive consideration of the woman's body, such as its maternal function. Instead, she accepted the Sartrean notion that only transcendence of the body, of materiality itself, might provide an escape from reification. Only leaving the darkness of immanence to emerge "into the light of transcendence"[114] was the way to liberate women.

Nor did de Beauvoir question her own evident interiorization of male notions of physical beauty.[115] Although her analysis of specifically women's oppression drew her inevitably away from the individualist premises of *Being and Nothingness* and tacitly closer to Merleau-Ponty,[116] de Beauvoir never explicitly challenged Sartre's premise that the state of otherness produced by the gaze was always a condition of inferiority.

Only in the wake of the events of 1968 and the intellectual turmoil surrounding them did French feminism radically reject most of these assumptions.[117] Sharing many of the psychoanalytic and Marxist premises so powerful in other discourses of the era, influenced by the structuralist and poststructuralist stress on language, open to anthropological analyses of exchange and patriarchy, and uninhibited about probing the specificity of the female body and its capacity for sexual *jouissance*, a wide variety of women generated a new (at times anti-"feminist") feminism that in many

---

113. De Beauvoir also introduced Sartre's dialectic of the keyhole in her 1943 novel, *She Came to Stay* (Cleveland, 1954), pp. 306ff.

114. De Beauvoir, *The Second Sex*, p. 675.

115. Okely points out that they continued to dominate her self-perception in later years too, as shown by passages in her autobiographical writings (p. 123).

116. For an analysis that stresses the subtle subversion of those premises in *The Second Sex*, see Sonia Kruks, "Simone de Beauvoir and the Limits to Freedom," *Social Text*, 17 (Fall, 1987).

117. For a history, see Claire Duchen, *Feminism in France: From May '68 to Mitterand* (London, 1986). For a bibliography of relevant works, see Elissa D. Gelfand and Virginia Thorndike Hules, eds., *French Feminist Criticism: Women, Language and Literature: An Annotated Bibliography* (New York, 1985).

ways avoided the limitations that led Nietzsche and Derrida to spurn its more traditional predecessor. And in so doing, they infused the interrogation of vision with a sensitivity to gender it had hitherto lacked.

Virtually all the major contributors to the post-1968 French feminist debate, most notably Julia Kristeva, Hélène Cixous, Monique Wittig, Michèle Montrelay, Catherine Clément, Margaret Duras, and Michèle Le Doeuff, had something striking to say about the link between ocularcentrism and phallocentrism, which soon became a familiar theme in the international discussion as well.[118] But none gave it the thematic weight that Luce Irigaray did. And although many aspects of Irigaray's work were heatedly challenged by other French feminists who questioned her reading of Freud or bemoaned her indifference to Marx,[119] her stress on the role of vision in patriarchal domination remained, to my knowledge, virtually uncontested. Indeed, it rapidly became a staple of feminist criticism outside of France as well.[120]

An important thread in Irigaray's analysis of the links between phallocentrism and ocularcentrism involved her appropriation of the Nietzschean critique of liberal feminism in the name of *femina vita* further developed by Derrida (and others like Eric Blondel).[121] Rather than aspir-

118. As mentioned earlier, in the Anglo-American world, it was particularly potent in feminist film theory. But it appeared as well in all considerations of the visual arts, high and low. See, for example, Rosemary Betterton, ed., *Looking On: Images of Femininity in the Visual Arts and Media* (London, 1987); and Griselda Pollock, *Vision and Difference: Femininity, Feminism and the Histories of Art* (London, 1988).

119. Among the most prominent critiques were Monique Plaza, "'Phallomorphic Power' and the Psychology of 'Woman'," in *Ideology and Consciousness*, 4 (Autumn, 1978) and Sarah Kofman, *The Enigma of Woman*, trans. Catherine Porter (Ithaca, 1985).

120. For a recent synoptic discussion, see Nancy S. Love, "Politics and Voice(s): An Empowerment/Knowledge Regime," *Differences*, 3, 1 (1991).

121. In his 1971 essay, "Nietzsche: Life as Metaphor," Blondel wrote that according to Nietzsche, "when confronted by the *theoretical* man—i.e. the voyeur (*theoria* means vision or sight)—who appeals to visual if not voyeuristic theories of contemplation, clarity, 'divine insight,' intuition, and so forth, the *vita femina* learns to close her eyes to herself, to take refuge in the superficiality of her dress, her appearance" (in Allison, ed., *The New Nietzsche*, p. 159).

ing to the condition of men, seeking to emulate their search for theoretical, speculative or evidential truth and eidetic essences, women,[122] she argued, should positively embrace their identification with precisely what defeats such a quest: the dissimulating veil that "hides" the truth. Whereas the dominant philosophical tradition at least since Plato had devalued women because they were outside the truth, closer to undetermined matter than to ideal form, Nietzsche and Derrida had appreciated what they saw as women's lack of essence and resistance to a unified style, their stubbornly enigmatic inaccessibility, which saved them from full incorporation into the specular economy of phallogocentric culture. Instead of seeking a firm ground, a philosophy built on visible foundations, women swam in the moving sea, the fluid medium that both frightened and attracted Nietzsche.[123]

In *Spurs*, Derrida had pitted *écriture* against style, suggesting that "if style were a man (much as the penis, according to Freud, is the 'normal

122. To write "women" rather than "woman" departs in a significant way from Derrida's reading of Nietzsche, in which "woman" becomes a "name for the nontruth of truth," as Gayatri Chakravorty Spivak has called it ("Feminism and Deconstruction, Again: Negotiating with Unacknowledged Masculinism," in Brennan, ed., *Between Psychoanalysis and Feminism*, p. 212). In the plural, the term implies actual actors in the world, rather than a placeholder for *différance*. As such, I think it better corresponds to Irigaray's use of Derrida's argument. See, for example, her protestation in a 1982 interview, "I don't particularly care for the term *feminism*. It is the word by which the social system designates the struggle of women. . . . I prefer to say the struggles of women, which reveals a plural and polymorphous character." (Interview with Lucienne Serrano and Elaine Hoffman Baruch, in *Women Writers Talking*, ed. Janet Todd [New York, 1983], p. 233).

123. In *Amante Marine* (Paris, 1981), Irigaray wrote that she "chose to examine Nietzsche in terms of water because it is the place of the strongest interpellation, it is the element of which he is the most afraid. In *Zarathustra*, we hear his fear of the deluge. Water is what disturbs rigidity of both frozen forms and mirrors. It is a place which I wouldn't call opposite but different, in relation to the sun" (p. 43). Yet, compare Nietzsche's tremulous exultation in *The Gay Science*: "At last the horizon appears free again to us, even granted that it is not bright; at last our ships may venture out again, venture out to face any danger; all the daring of the lover of knowledge is permitted again; the sea, *our* sea, lies open again; perhaps there has never yet been such an 'open sea'" (*The Portable Nietzsche*, ed. Walter Kaufmann [New York, 1971], p. 448).

prototype of fetishes'), then writing would be a woman."[124] For Irigaray, as well as other French theorists such as Kristeva and Cixous, the issue of the relationship between woman and writing (or language in general) was central.[125] *Parler n'est jamais neutre*, as the title of one of Irigaray's books insisted.[126]

This is not the place to address the plausibility of their complicated arguments for a unique woman's language, an *écriture féminine* or *parler-femme* somehow connected to the *voix maternelle*.[127] Nor is it necessary to join the heated controversy stirred by Kristeva's argument that certain men—specifically avant-garde writers—as well as women can express a "semiotic" maternal tongue of drives prior to the "symbolic" language of rational significations. It suffices for our purposes to note that these various claims for a special women's relationship to language were frequently couched in antiocular terms, often pitting the temporal rhythms of the body against the mortifying spatialization of the eye. For as Alice Jardine has remarked, in France, "woman" or "the feminine" has not only been a metaphor for a certain kind of reading and writing, but also "a tool for declaring war on the Image within the more general twentieth-century iconoclastic imagination."[128]

Many of the leading French feminists, in fact, appropriated the critique of Apollonian clarity, precise definitions, transparent representations and good form developed by Barthes and Derrida.[129] Their principled rejec-

124. Derrida, *Spurs*, p. 57.

125. For useful overviews, see Toril Moi, *Sexual/Textual Politics: Feminist Literary Theory* (London, 1985) and Nye, *Feminist Theory and the Philosophies of Man*, chap. 6.

126. Irigaray, *Parler n'est jamais neutre* (Paris, 1985). For a helpful account of her general approach to linguistic issues, beginning with her dissertation on *Le langage des déments* (Paris, 1973), see Whitford, *Luce Irigaray: Philosophy in the Feminine*, chap. 2.

127. Not all French feminists, it should be noted, accepted the idea of a woman's language. See, for example, the disclaimer in "Variations on Common Themes," from *Questions féministes*, 1 (November, 1977); reprinted in Elaine Marks and Isabelle de Courtivron, eds., *New French Feminisms* (New York, 1981), p. 219.

128. Jardine, *Gynesis*, p. 34.

tion of a philosophical metalanguage—"there is simply no way I can give you an account of 'speaking (as) woman'"; Irigaray contended, "it is spoken, but not in metalanguage"—[130] was likewise consonant with the disdain for high altitude thinking and a God's-eye view so ubiquitous in the antiocularcentric discourse. So too was their insistence on a language of proximity rather than distance, a language closer to the senses of touch and taste than sight. In Irigaray's terms, "this 'style' or 'writing' of women tends to put the torch to fetish words, proper terms, well-constructed forms. This 'style' does not privilege sight; instead it takes each figure back to its source, which is among other things *tactile*."[131]

For French feminism, the issue of language was intricately intertwined with that of the psyche; the grammatical and the psychological subjects, its proponents understood, were impossible to disentangle. For Irigaray, trained as an analyst by Lacan and the author of a dissertation on the language of senile dementia, the role of the visual in the constitution of the linguistic/psychological subject—or rather its different role in the constitution of male and female subjects—was of particular importance. As early as 1966, she wrote that "distortions of language can . . . be related to a distortion of the specular experience."[132]

In her efforts to explore the gendered dimension of that experience, Irigaray was compelled to confront the implications of Lacan's influential argument about the mirror stage. She proved a most undutiful daugh-

129. Cixous's prose, for example, has been praised for promoting "the release of semiotic energies which the male simply squanders in specular or oedipal constraints, known as the product of the 'mirror stage'. . . . Cixous's texts always resemble novels written outside the Occidental tradition. The tempo of their writing—indeed their lack of style—is in cadence with lacunary moments of grammatical inconsistencies, sentence fragments, image signs, portmanteau words, litanic inscriptions, and jets of letters of infinite regress. The novels in this manner appear often nightmarish" (Conley, *Hélène Cixous: Writing the Feminine*, p. 86).

130. Irigaray, *This Sex Which Is Not One*, trans. Catherine Porter and Carolyn Burke (Ithaca, N.Y., 1985), p. 144.

131. Irigaray, "The Power of Discourse," in *This Sex Which Is Not One*, p. 79.

132. Irigaray, "Communications linquistique et spéculaire," *Cahiers pour l'analyse*, 3 (May–June, 1966), p. 55.

ter.[133] In 1974, she published her most important book, *Speculum of the Other Woman*, which was directed explicitly against Freud and implicitly against Lacan's reading of him.[134] Her impertinence earned Irigaray's dismissal from the Department of Psychoanalysis at the University of Paris VIII (Vincennes) and banishment from Lacan's seminar.

Irigaray's critique of Lacan's complicated and problematic attitude toward women and the construction of the feminine subject unleashed a flood of polemics on both sides of the question.[135] With reference to the issue of vision, controversy swirled around everything from the implications of his choice of Bernini's statue of an ecstatic St. Theresa on the cover of *Encore, Séminaire XX* (and his claim to know female *jouissance* just by looking at it) to his personal ownership of Courbet's infamous painting of a vagina, "The Origin of the World."[136] Although his subtle appreciation of the chiasmic intertwining of the eye and the gaze allowed

133. Jane Gallop, *The Daughter's Seduction: Feminism and Psychoanalysis* (Ithaca, 1982) argues that in one respect Irigaray remains beholden to the Law of the Father, in her resistance to incestuous love with him (pp. 78ff). For an argument that Kristeva rather than Irigaray is more dutiful, see Elizabeth Grosz, *Jacques Lacan: A Feminist Introduction* (London, 1990), p. 150.

134. Irigaray, *Speculum of the Other Woman*, trans. Gillian G. Gill (Ithaca, 1985). Significantly, Irigaray refused to name the father, Lacan, in the text, although he appears in the notes. In the volume of essays originally published in 1977, *This Sex Which Is Not One*, Irigaray more explicitly criticized Lacan's texts on women, most notably *Encore, Séminaire XX*.

135. His writings on the subject are available in *Feminine Sexuality: Jacques Lacan and the école freudienne*, ed. Juliet Mitchell and Jacqueline Rose, trans. Jacqueline Rose (New York, 1982). For defenses of his position, see the editors' introductions; Eugènie Lemoine-Luccioni's review of *Speculum* in *Esprit*, 43, 3 (1975); and Ellen Ragland-Sullivan, *Jacques Lacan and the Philosophy of Psychoanalysis* (Urbana, Ill., 1987). For typical critiques, see Catherine Clément, *The Lives and Legends of Jacques Lacan*, trans. Arthur Goldhammer (New York, 1983); and David Macey, *Lacan in Contexts* (London, 1988). For somewhat more balanced accounts, see Gallop, *The Daughter's Seduction*; and Grosz, *Jacques Lacan*.

136. Rainer Mack, "Reading the Archaeology of the Female Body," *Qui Parle*, 4, 1 (Fall, 1990), p. 79, where he notes that Lacan had put a sliding wooden panel with a hidden trigger over the painting, thus enabling him to control the gaze directed at the woman's sex.

Lacan to challenge the traditional Cartesian perspectivalist visual order, he had not escaped, his critics charged, the no less traditional privileging of the "male gaze" in Western culture.

Speculum of the Other Woman focused in particular on Lacan's mirror stage argument, which it situated in the twin contexts of Freud's theory of child development and Plato's theory of ideas.[137] In certain respects, Irigaray implicitly drew on Derrida's defense of *différance* against the tyranny of sameness, as well as his identification of "woman" with what escapes that tyranny. Both Freud and Lacan, she claimed, remained unaware of "the blind spot of an old dream of symmetry"[138] between the sexes. This blind spot was evident not only in Lacan's privileging of the phallic signifier in the Symbolic stage, but also in his description of the visual constitution of the ego in the Mirror Stage. Like Kristeva, she challenged the notion that the Imaginary must be based on visual experience alone.[139] Like Cixous and Clément, she argued that Freud's was a "voyeur's theory."[140]

Noting the general dependence of psychoanalysis on photological metaphors ("the dark continent of femininity") and its complicity with the Idealist tradition of equating truth with *eidos*, Irigaray claimed that

137. As Toril Moi has pointed out, *Speculum* is itself organized like a speculum with the first section on Freud mirrored in the last on Plato. In the middle are more fragmented and heterogeneous chapters grouped under the title "Speculum," which are like the vaginal hole reflected in the curved glass. See Moi, *Sexual/Textual Politics*, pp. 130ff.

138. This is the title of the first section of *Speculum*, which deals with Freud.

139. As Kristeva told an interviewer in 1984, she wanted to "make more detailed the archaic stages preceding the mirror stage because I think that the grasping of the image by the child is the result of a whole process. And this process can be called *imaginary*, but not in the specular sense of the word, because it passes through voice, taste, skin and so on, all the senses yet doesn't necessarily mobilize sight." ("Julia Kristeva in Conversation with Rosalind Coward," in *Desire, ICA Documents* [London, 1984], p. 22). Kristeva, however, was interested in children of both sexes, and stressed the availability of this imaginary, which she identified with the semiotic, for male avant-garde artists. Irigaray believed in an already gendered pre-Oedipal situation.

140. Hélène Cixous and Catherine Clément, *The Newly Born Woman*, trans. Betsy Wing (Minneapolis, 1986), p. 82.

Freud was still trapped in an economy of "presence" in which woman could be figured only as a lack, an absence, a default. The critical expression of this bias came in the psychoanalytic descriptions of castration anxiety and penis envy, which were grounded in accounts of visual experience. According to Freud, the alarming sight to the boy of the little girl's or mother's "absent" genitals, her unrepresentable "hole," was the mechanism that unleashed these emotions.

> The little girl, the woman, supposedly has *nothing* you can see. She exposes, exhibits the possibility of a *nothing to see*. Or at any rate she shows nothing that is penis-shaped or could substitute for a penis. This is the odd, the uncanny thing, as far as the eye can see, this nothing around which lingers in horror, now and forever, an overcathexis of the eye, of the appropriation by the gaze, and of the *phallomorphic* sexual metaphors, its reassuring accomplices.[141]

The "overcathexis of the eye" is evident as well in the psychoanalytic claim—and here Lacan more than Freud was the target—that the ego is formed by a reflection in a mirror. "If this ego is to be valuable," Irigaray notes, "some 'mirror' is needed to reassure it and re-insure it of its value. Woman will be the foundation for this specular duplication, giving back man 'his' image and repeating it as the 'same.'"[142] This mirror is, how-

141. Irigaray, *Speculum of the Other Woman*, p. 47.
142. Ibid., p. 54. For a general account of women and mirrors in literature which is indebted to Irigaray, see Jenijoy La Belle, *Herself Beheld: The Literature of the Looking Glass* (Ithaca, 1988). For a defense of Lacan against Irigaray, see Ragland-Sullivan, p. 275, where she writes, "Her understanding of the mirror stage seems limited to its literal, visual aspect, which she reduces to the genetic or biological. The mirror stage is, of course, a metaphor for a mimetic process that occurs in intersocial relations— with or without a mirror . . . a metaphor for the alienation that first forms the ego from the outside world through identification with others." If so, one must ask why Lacan was so interested in the work of Wallon and others about actual behavior in front of mirrors, which Ragland-Sullivan herself adduces to show that his ideas have an empirical ground (p. 17). And even if the results are called a "mere" metaphor, Irigaray is surely right to question its implications. Perhaps more telling is Ragland-

ever, flat and thus replicates the image as if it were merely a precise duplicate of the self. To the extent that women identify with the narcissistic subject created by such flat mirrors, they are imprisoned in a male specular economy in which they are always devalued as inferior versions of the male subject, as mere objects of exchange, dead commodities, in a "hom(m)osexual" circuit of sameness (in which the *homme* was the only standard of value). Here a more drastic *méconnaissance* is added to that Lacan attributed to the mirror stage in general, especially when what is suppressed is the mother-daughter relationship, "the *dark continent* of the *dark continent*."[143]

One solution would be to shatter the mirror, to go "through the looking glass," like Alice in Wonderland, with whom (a Luce) Irigaray could easily identify.[144] For on the other side of the mirror, behind the screen of male representations, is an underground world hidden from the surveyor's categorizing gaze, a world where women might whirl and dance out of the glare of the sun. Here is "what resists infinite reflection: the mystery (hysteria?) that will always remain modestly *behind every mirror*, and that will spark the desire to see and know more about it."[145] Here what she calls "la mystérique," combining mystery, hysteria, mysticism (the "dark night of the soul"), and the feminine, finds its natural home.

Another alternative is a different, more benign kind of mirror. For "if an *other* image, an *other* mirror were to intervene, this inevitably would

---

Sullivan's further charge that "Irigaray has confused the fixing of a species-specific *Gestalt* during the mirror stage with the phallic fixing of sexual identity that occurs *after* the mirror stage" (p. 277). She does, however, acknowledge that Lacan never took back his symbolic depiction of the female genitalia as an absence, a hole.

143. Irigaray, *Le corps-à-corps avec la mère* (Paris, 1981), p. 61. For a critical analysis of the discussion of the mother in Irigaray and other French feminists, see Domna C. Stanton, "Difference on Trial: A Critique of the Maternal Metaphor in Cixous, Irigaray, and Kristeva," in *The Thinking Muse*. For a more sympathetic response, see Madelon Sprengnether, *Spectral Mother: Freud, Feminism, and Psychoanalysis* (Ithaca, 1990).

144. Irigaray, "The Looking Glass, from the Other Side," in *This Sex Which Is Not One*.

145. Irigaray, *Speculum of the Other Woman*, p. 103.

entail the risk of mortal crisis,"[146] or at least it would for the universality of the male subject. That other mirror is the concave speculum, used by gynecologists to investigate the female genitalia. Its invention in the mid-nineteenth century by the French doctor Joseph Récamier could be interpreted darkly as a technological advance in the male exploration and conquest of the woman's body,[147] and Irigaray did acknowledge its ability to act as an instrument to spread the vaginal lips and allow the male eye to penetrate, "to see, notably with speculative intent."[148] But she preferred to stress two more positive implications of the speculum which made it more than a tool of male "hysteroscopic" desire: its revelation that the female genitalia are more than just a hole, an absence, and the disruption of specular mimesis, formal integrity, and autorepresentation produced by its curved surface. "(The/a) woman is always already in a state of anamorphosis in which the figure becomes fuzzy."[149] Like the Lacan of the *Four Fundamental Concepts of Psychoanalysis,* a work she unfortunately neglected to discuss, Irigaray thus implied the possibility of visual experience that was more chiasmic than specular, at least when the mirror was curved or, as she once put it, *"folded back on itself."*[150]

But even such a speculum remains too dependent on the visual to do justice to the woman's body, in particular to her sexuality. Although the eye can get inside the vagina—a feat Irigaray notes was literally depicted in Bataille's *Story of the Eye*—"it will be unable to take in the whole of the female sexual equipment with *one* look, as some of it will have remained 'outside.'"[151] In a certain sense, the woman's body is like the tain of the mirror, outside of any specular representation, although on some level the material support of that representation. Women's sexuality is thus best

---

146. Ibid.

147. See, for example, Elaine Showalter, *Sexual Anarchy: Gender and Culture at the Fin de Siècle* (New York, 1990), p. 124.

148. Irigaray, *Speculum of the Other Woman,* p. 144.

149. Ibid., p. 230.

150. Irigaray, "Questions," in *This Sex Which Is Not One,* p. 155.

151. Ibid., p. 89.

understood in nonvisual terms. As she put it in an essay entitled "This Sex Which is Not One,"

> Within this logic [that of Western thought], the predominance of the visual, of the discrimination of form and individualization of form, is particularly foreign to female eroticism. Woman takes pleasure more from touching than from looking, and her entry into a dominant scopic economy signifies, again, her consignment to passivity: she is to be the beautiful object of contemplation. While her body finds itself thus eroticized, and called to a double movement of exhibition and of chaste retreat in order to stimulate the drives of the "subject," her sexual organ represents the *horror of nothing to see*.[152]

Within a scopic economy, the female genitalia may seem like an absence, but within a haptic one, they are far richer than their male equivalent. Whereas the penis is a singular organ needing something outside itself to provide gratification, the vaginal lips, clitoris, labia, vulva, and so on, are multiple—"this sex which is not one"—and thus capable of self-touching. Autoaffection, Irigaray contends, not autorepresentation is the mark of female sexuality. Hidden female lips, she speculated elsewhere,[153] may even have the same etymological source as the word "labyrinth," which is so powerful an image in the antiocularcentric discourse.

Not only are the female genitalia plural and female sexuality based more on touch than sight, but the woman's body is also less firmly divided into inner and outer than the man's. Its form is less unified and solid, closer to the fluidity that is expressed by menstrual blood, milk, and tears.[154] Echoing Bataille's defense of *informe* and the waste products

---

152. Irigaray, *This Sex Which Is Not One*, p. 26.

153. Irigaray, "The Gesture in Psychoanalysis," in Brennan, ed., *Between Feminism and Psychoanalysis*, p. 135.

154. Irigaray did not ignore sperm or the common ability to generate saliva and sweat, but she claimed that man "cathects these only in a desire to turn them into the self (as same). Every body of water becomes a mirror, every sea, ice" (ibid., p. 237).

of the body, Irigaray argued that only a "mechanics" of fluids rather than solids can avoid the reduction of female difference into male sameness.[155] "We would thus escape from a dominant *scopic* economy," she contended, "we would be to a greater extent in an economy of *flow*."[156]

Not only would such an alternative call into question the psychological underpinnings of that scopic economy, but it would also challenge its philosophical correlate (and, she added in a later essay, Western science as well).[157] Like Derrida, Irigaray sought to link the hegemonic tradition of Western thought ever since Plato, the tradition of "specula(riza)tion," with the privileging of the eye. Like Bataille, she foregrounded the repressed materiality, irreducible to images of visible matter, that such a tradition rejected as heterogeneous waste. Like Heidegger, she bemoaned the reduction of the world to a standing reserve for the manipulative subject. Like Baudry, she located the fatal starting point of the ocularcentric project in the dream of perfect representation evident in Plato's myth of the cave. But more than all of them, she identified that "other" of heliocentric, idealist rationality with women, who are "never anything but the still undifferentiated opaqueness of sensible matter, the store (of) substance for the sublation of self, or being as what is, or what he is (or was), here and now."[158]

In her striking reinterpretation of Plato in *Speculum of the Other Woman*, Irigaray sought to read his myth of the cave as a metaphor for escaping the womb or *hystera*, where "the properties of the eye, of mir-

---

Why, she wondered, did Lacan always conceptualize the *petit objet a* as a solid rather than a fluid object?

155. Irigaray, "The 'Mechanics' of Fluids," in *This Sex Which Is Not One*. Cixous also contended that water is the quintessential feminine element. See, for example, "The Laugh of the Medusa," in *New French Feminism*, p. 260.

156. Irigaray, "Questions," in *This Sex Which Is Not One*, p. 148.

157. Irigaray, "Is the Subject of Science Sexed?" *Cultural Critique*, 1 (Fall, 1985).

158. Irigaray, *Speculum of the Other Woman*, p. 224. For a helpful reading of her discussion of Plato's cave, see Andrea Nye, "Assisting at the Birth and Death of Vision," in *Modernity and the Hegemony of Vision*, ed. David Michael Levin (Berkeley, 1993).

rors—and indeed of spacing, of space, time, of time—are dislocated, disarticulated, disjointed, and only later brought back to the perspective-free contemplation of the truth of the Idea."[159] Plato's alternative to the cave/womb is a realm of unchanging Forms, beyond the fluid world of becoming, whose highest manifestation, the Idea of the Good, he equated with the sun itself.[160]

The cave myth can thus be read as a kind of phantasmic primal scene in which the role of the mother in engendering culture is elided in favor of the father, the solar origin of Ideas, the specular fount of sameness. The painful birth process is forgotten, repressed, in the service of a male myth of autogenesis: *"Sun, ex-stasy of the copula. Cause of all that is. Focus of a jouissance which now is reduced to merely dazzling the eye. Luminescent receptacle. Matrix for reproducing images."*[161] Those images more and more become part of the intelligible rather than sensible world, for the latter still conjures up too much of the materiality identified with women.

Eidetic intuition—and here Irigaray applied Derrida's critique of Husserl to Plato—"does away with the interposition, the intervention, the mediation of any kind of path or trail, the need for the opening of any *diaphragm*, disavows any division by a *paraphragm*."[162] Such a visually grounded philosophy forgets the materiality of the eye socket (the cave or womb) and privileges instead the pupil, the hole through which sight takes place, an allegedly pristine sight whose ultimate manifestation is divine vision, perfect incorporeality. Such a standard produces a kind of blindness itself, "for the optics of Truth in its credibility without doubt (*créance sans doute*), its unconditional certainty, its passion for Reason, has veiled or else destroyed the gaze that remained mortal. With the re-

159. Ibid., p. 253.

160. The gendered heliotropism of the Western tradition was also the target of Cixous in *Portrait du Soleil* (Paris, 1973). For a general account of her work that details her frequent critique of ocularcentrism, see Conley, *Hélène Cixous*.

161. Irigaray, *Speculum of the Other Woman*, p. 303.

162. Ibid., p. 320. I take "paraphragm" to mean something that divides into side-by-side sections.

sult that it can no longer see anything of what had been before its conversion to the Father's law."[163]

The only kind of sight, Irigaray later conceded, that might escape this fatal phallogocentric economy, was "the Buddha's gaze at the flower," which is "not a distracted or predatory gaze, it is not the lapse of the speculative into the flesh, it is at once material and spiritual contemplation that provides an already sublimated energy to thought."[164] But absent such a selfless, nurturant relation to the world, the gaze fosters an interpersonal interaction whose sinister implications recall those Sartre had so pessimistically described in *Being and Nothingness*.

Indeed, much of Irigaray's work implied that visual experience was inevitably caught in a dialectic of domination in which women were always the victims. As a result, she frequently invited the reproach of essentialism, of remaining within a discourse that reified gender differences into permanent, even biologically given, aspects of the human condition. Her subtle technique of mimicking traditional male assumptions about women, parodically parroting the master's discourse, produced, so some critics charged, mere anodyne displacements rather than effective subversions. Her emphasis on the specific qualities of the female genitalia, although reversing the traditional male horror of their alleged "absence," reinforced the assumption of a difference in kind between men and women. Her privileging of the pre-Oedipal mother could lead, other critics worried, to a narcissistic politics of the Imaginary. Even Irigaray's claim that fluids should be given equal status with solids was vulnerable to the charge that she was generating a positive term in a way which simply imitated the valorization of positivity characteristic of the dominant discourse.

Although it would be unfair to reduce these and other criticisms of Irigaray to a single common denominator, in many cases the larger issue they raise concerns the relation between difference in general and sexual

163. Ibid., p. 362 (translation emended).

164. Irigaray, "Love Between Us," in *Who Comes After the Subject?*, ed. Eduardo Cadava, Peter Conner, and Jean-Luc Nancy (New York, 1991), p. 171.

difference. Derrida resisted turning differences into opposing terms in a binary structure that is visible, as it were, to the eye. "Woman" was thus a placeholder for *différance*, not a positive concept, and male/female a dichotomy to be deconstructed.[165] In Irigaray's appropriation of Derrida, however, it sometimes seemed as if she reconstructed the dichotomy, albeit with a different evaluation of the terms. Whereas he was content to undermine subject positions of whatever gender, Irigaray often felt compelled to argue for a new feminine subjectivity empowering those who were the victims of patriarchal domination.[166] Because of her frequent insistence on the unalterable distinctions between male and female bodies, even her most stalwart defenders were obliged to admit that those victims were not discursively constituted for her in solely cultural or social terms.[167]

The debate over Irigaray's alleged essentialism, indeed over the vexed role of "ontological" essentialism for feminism in general, has reached levels of polemical intricacy that need not detain us now.[168] More impor-

---

165. Derrida, however, has not always been completely consistent on this point. In a recent commentary on Levinas, he complained that "E.L.'s work seems to me to have always rendered secondary, derivative, and subordinate alterity as sexual difference, the trait of sexual difference, to the alterity of a sexually non-marked wholly other. It is not woman or the feminine that he has rendered secondary, derivative, or subordinate, but sexual difference. Once sexual difference is subordinated, it is always the case that the wholly other, who is *not yet marked* is *already* found to be marked by masculinity." "At this very moment in this work here I am," in *Re-reading Levinas*, ed. Robert Bernasconi and Simon Critchley (Bloomington, Ind., 1991), p. 40. The implication is that sexual difference should not be turned into a version of difference *tout court*.

166. For example, when she asks the question in a review of Elizabeth Schüssler Fiorenza's *In Memory of Her: A Feminist Theological Reconstruction of Christian Origins*, "can a claim to equality be acceptable without a fundamental respect for the subjective rights of both sexes, including the right to a divine identity?" (Irigaray, "Equal to Whom?" *Differences*, 1, 2 [Summer, 1989], p. 73).

167. For a recent consideration of the cultural and historical constitution of sexuality that tacitly challenges Irigaray, see Thomas Laqueur, *Making Sex: Body and Gender from the Greeks to Freud* (Cambridge, Mass., 1990).

168. See, for example, Plaza, "'Phallomorphic Power' and the Psychology of "Woman"; Rosi Braidotti, "The Politics of Ontological Difference," in Brennan, ed.,

tant to note are the ways her work powerfully informed the feminist contribution to the critique of ocularcentrism. Although her recent remarks about the Buddhist gaze suggest that Irigaray on occasion loosened the tie between gender and vision, the overwhelming majority of her references to it suggested a fundamental—even "essential"—connection. Derrida's "double reading" of sight became a far more univocal single reading in her work and that of many French feminists. When that analysis was combined with the no less intransigent denigration of the gaze in other quarters, such as the film theory we previously examined, its impact was reinforced still further.[169]

Inevitably, a certain backlash occurred, as feminists outside of France sought to nuance the critique of the gaze. Some commentators wondered if the imputation of voyeurism to all Western philosophy and science had elevated de-eroticized visual experience to vision per se, and thus missed the communal, nonobjectifying potential in a vision informed by desire.[170] Such a vision was closer to the proximate sensuality that Irigaray attributed solely to touch and smell. Others contended that visual plea-

---

Between Feminism and Psychoanalysis; Whitford, *Luce Irigaray*, chap. 6; Schor, "This Essentialism Which Is Not One: Coming to Grips with Irigaray"; Fuss, "Reading Like a Feminist"; Scholes, "Éperon Strings"; Kate Mehuron, "An Ironic Mimesis," in *The Question of the Other: Essays in Contemporary Continental Philosophy*, ed. Arleen B. Dallery and Charles E. Scott (Albany, N.Y., 1989); Judith P. Butler, *Gender Trouble: Feminism and the Subversion of Identity* (New York, 1990); Tania Modleski, *Feminism Without Women: Culture and Criticism in a "Postfeminist" Age* (New York, 1991); and Nancy Fraser and Sandra Lee Bartky, eds., *Revaluing French Feminism: Critical Essays on Difference, Agency, and Culture* (Bloomington, Ind., 1992). It has even become possible to attack radical antibiologism as "cultural essentialism." See Toril Moi, "Patriarchal Thought and the Drive for Knowledge," in Brennan, ed., *Between Feminism and Psychoanalysis*, p. 193.

169. According to Brunette and Wills, *Screen/Play*, "Irigaray is perhaps the most striking example of a feminist use or adaptation of Derridean practice. . . . Given the interest shown in Derrida's work by French feminist theorists, it is surprising that his name has not been more frequently invoked by feminist film theory" (p. 20). Perhaps the explanation is that only when feminists like Irigaray had reduced his double reading of the visual to a single one could it be used by the kind of Manichean feminist film theory that demonized the "male gaze" by combining apparatus theory and gender.

sure, rather than being a virtual synonym for sexual harassment, could be legitimately experienced by women as well as men, and indeed even women's bodies could be the benign objects of visual appropriation by the lesbian gaze.[171] The public experience of female spectatorship in the cinema, moreover, could be seen as helping to liberate women from the private sphere.[172] Still others argued that without paying attention to differences in visual experience produced by class, racial, and other nongender determinations, Irigaray had fallen prey to the same homogenizing logic she so disliked in the dominant phallogocentric economy.[173]

However telling these criticisms were, they did little to counteract the antiocularcentric effect produced by the feminist appropriation of Derridean and other arguments against the hegemony of the eye. By the 1980s, a deep suspicion of the visual representation of women in the spectacle of modern life had become a given of much cultural criticism. Nowhere was this assumption as prevalent as in the discourse of postmodernism, whose genesis cannot be fully understood without appreciating the feminist critique of the eye.[174] That discourse will be the con-

170. Evelyn Fox Keller and Christine R. Grontkowski, "The Mind's Eye," in *Discovering Reality: Feminist Perspectives on Epistemology, Metaphysics, Methodology, and Philosophy of Science*, ed. Sandra Harding and Merrill B. Hintikka (Dordrecht, Holland, 1983), p. 220.

171. See, for example, Teresa de Lauretis, *Alice Doesn't: Feminism, Semiotics, Cinema* (Bloomington, Ind., 1984).

172. See Giuliana Bruno, "Streetwalking Around Plato's Cave," *October*, 60 (Spring, 1992).

173. This critique is a staple of all more Marxist-inflected feminisms, e.g., Spivak, "French Feminism in an International Frame"; Patrice Petro, "Modernity and Mass Culture in Weimar: Contours of a Discourse on Sexuality in Early Theories of Perception and Representation," *New German Critique*, 40 (Winter, 1987); and Carole-Anne Tyler, "The Feminine Look," in *Theory Between the Disciplines: Authority, Vision, Politics*, ed. Martin Kreiswirth and Mark A. Cheetham (Ann Arbor, Mich., 1990).

174. For a discussion of the connections, see Craig Owens, "The Discourse of Others: Feminism and Postmodernism," in *The Anti-Aesthetic*. Lyotard, the main French celebrant of postmodernism, was clearly aware of Irigaray's work, even if he drew on it infrequently. In *Discours, Figure* (Paris, 1971), he refers to an early essay on

cluding target of this Icarian overview, the final chapter in this unabashedly synoptic metanarrative, of the interrogation of vision in twentieth-
century French thought.

---

linguistic themes, which he finds too phenomenological (p. 348). In his 1976 essay
"One of the Things at Stake in Women's Struggles," he cites *Speculum* in the context
of a discussion of the feminist critique of metalanguages. He defends Irigaray against
the accusation, presumably made by Lacanians, that she confuses the phallus as a
symbolic phenomenon with the penis as an empirical one (one, that is, which can
actually be seen). For Lyotard, the belief that the symbolic is a metalanguage that
can be neatly distinguished from its referential double is precisely what feminism
helpfully undermines (*The Lyotard Reader*, ed. Andrew Benjamin [Oxford, 1989],
p. 119).

CHAPTER TEN

The Ethics of Blindness and the Postmodern Sublime: Levinas and Lyotard

Why *blindness?* Because it is
impossible to deduce a prescription
from a description.

JEAN-FRANÇOIS LYOTARD[1]

Even when he does not regard
me, he regards me.

EMMANUEL LEVINAS[2]

Vision, it bears repeating, is normally understood as the master sense of
the modern era, variously described as the heyday of Cartesian perspectivalism, the age of the world picture, and the society of the spectacle or
surveillance. It will come therefore as no surprise that the critique of modernity would find congenial many of the same arguments against the
hegemony of the eye that we have been tracing in this study. In France,
and not there alone, that critique has spawned a wide-ranging discussion
of the alleged advent of a postmodern era, whose characteristics and implications are still being vigorously contested.

From one perspective, postmodernism has seemed the apotheosis of the
visual, the triumph of the simulacrum over what it purports to represent,
a veritable surrender to the phantasmagoric spectacle rather than its sub-

1. Jean-François Lyotard, *The Differend: Phrases in Dispute*, trans. Georges Van Den
Abbeele (Minneapolis, 1988), p. 108.

2. Emmanuel Levinas, "Ethics and Politics," *The Levinas Reader*, ed. Seán Hand (Oxford, 1989), p. 290.

version. Images, it is claimed, are now set completely adrift from their referents, whose putative reality has ceased to provide a standard of truth or illusion. What Jean Baudrillard has dubbed the "hyperreal" world of simulations means we have become seduced by images that are signs of nothing but themselves.[3] Because such images now precede their referents—Baudrillard calls it "the precession of simulacra"[4]—they can no longer be understood in terms of the panopticon or the spectacle, concepts that imply a prior intentionality using visual means for other ends, such as the maintenance of power or the perpetuation of capitalism. We are no longer even in front of a mirror, but rather stare with fascination at a screen reflecting nothing outside it.

Postmodernism, one recent commentator tells us, must therefore be understood as "the transformation of reality into images," while another adds that it is best understood as "a figural, as distinct from discursive regime of signification."[5] We live, a third tells us, in an obscene world of "hypervisibility: the terror of the all-too-visible, the voracity, the total promiscuity, the pure concupiscence of the gaze."[6] As such, it resurrects

3. According to his widely discussed chronology, the successive phases of the image are as follows: "It is the reflection of basic reality—it masks and perverts a basic reality—it masks the *absence* of a basic reality—it bears no relation to any reality whatever: it is its own pure simulacrum" ("The Precession of Simulacra," in *Art After Modernism: Rethinking Representation*, ed. Brian Wallis [New York, 1984], p. 256). For a sample of Baudrillard's writings on these themes, see Mark Poster, ed., *Selected Writings* (Stanford, 1988). For evaluations of his work, see André Frankovits, ed., *Seduced and Abandoned: The Baudrillard Scene* (New York, 1984); for a critique, see Douglas Kellner, *Jean Baudrillard: From Marxism to Postmodernism and Beyond* (Oxford, 1989).

4. Baudrillard, "The Precession of Simulacra." The term "simulacrum," it should be noted, was already used by Bataille and Klossowski to indicate the noncommunicable dimension of signs. See Pierre Klossowski, "À propos du simulacre dans la communication de Georges Bataille," *Critique*, 195–196 (1963).

5. Fredric Jameson, "Postmodernism and Consumer Society," in *The Anti-Aesthetic: Essays on Postmodern Culture*, ed. Hal Foster (Port Townsend, Wash., 1983), p. 125; Scott Lash, *Sociology of Postmodernism* (London, 1990), p. 194. For a dissenting voice that claims that postmodernism questions "the dominant *photological imagination* of modernism" (p. 145) and gives primacy instead to the labyrinthine aurality of the ear, see Thomas Docherty, *After Theory: Postmodernism/Postmarxism* (London, 1990).

what Christine Buci-Glucksmann has celebrated as the flamboyant, anamorphic "madness of vision" most vividly expressed in the baroque.[7]

From the same perspective, the main proponent of the postmodern hysteria of the visual, if one looks past the faddish figure of Baudrillard, is Jean-François Lyotard.[8] For wasn't it Lyotard who called his *Discours, figure* a "defense of the eye" and an attack on the "sufficiency of discourse"?[9] Wasn't it Lyotard who chastised Lacan for reducing the unconscious to a language, and privileging the Symbolic over the Imaginary, rather than acknowledging the force of visual "thing-images" in the dream-work?[10] Wasn't it Lyotard who criticized Derrida's notion of the "trace" and "archewriting" for failing to take into account the positive presence of the "other" of discourse?[11] And wasn't it Lyotard who insisted that painting should be understood as a libidinal machine in which the primary process becomes visible?[12]

If postmodernism teaches anything, however, it is to be suspicious of single perspectives, which, like grand narratives, provide totalizing accounts of a world too complex to be reduced to a unified point of view. In

6. Meaghen Morris, "Room 101 or A Few Worst Things in the World," in Frankovits, ed., *Seduced and Abandoned*, p. 97.

7. Christine Buci-Glucksmann, *La folie du voir: De l'esthétique baroque* (Paris, 1986). See also her *La raison baroque: De Baudelaire à Benjamin* (Paris, 1984), and *Tragique de l'ombre: Shakespeare et le maniérisme* (Paris, 1990). Buci-Glucksmann, to be sure, identifies the baroque scopic regime as part of modernity, evident in the Paris explored by Walter Benjamin, but her analysis of its characteristics make it even more suitable for postmodernity.

8. For a comparison of the two, see Julian Pefanis, *Heterology and the Postmodern: Bataille, Baudrillard and Lyotard* (Durham, 1991). He contrasts Baudrillard's radical antiproductivism with Lyotard's "nonpositive affirmation of the productive system" (p. 86).

9. Jean-François Lyotard, *Discours, figure* (Paris, 1985), p. 11.

10. Ibid., p. 260.

11. Lyotard, "Sur la théorie," in *Dérive à partir de Marx et Freud* (Paris, 1970), pp. 228–229.

12. Lyotard, "La peinture comme dispositif libidinal," *Des dispositifs pulsionnels* (Paris, 1980).

the case of postmodernism and vision, and *a fortiori* of Lyotard's role in its formulation, no monocular, transcendental gaze will do. In fact, from a different perspective, the one that has been adopted in this study, post-modernism may be understood as the culminating chapter in a story of the (enucleated) eye. Or rather, it may paradoxically be at once the hyper-trophy of the visual, at least in one of its modes, *and* its denigration.[13]

This case can be made, to compound the paradox, only if the rise of postmodern thought is tied to the revival of interest in France in one of the most premodern of cultural phenomena. For an essential, if unex-pected, element in this story is the intense fascination with Judaism that gripped many French intellectuals in the 1970s and 1980s. Focusing on the work of the central figure responsible for that development, Emman-uel Levinas will help reveal the unexpected links between the traditional iconoclastic Jewish attitude toward visual representation and a powerfully antiocular impulse in postmodernism. For Lyotard was not speaking for himself alone when he admitted in 1986 that Levinas's books have been "my companions for twenty years."[14]

⊙

The impact of anti-Semitism on French intellectual life from the time of Voltaire through that of Vichy and beyond has often been remarked.[15]

13. This is not the place to probe the complex visual practices of postmodernist artists on the international scene, but it is clear that many of them have been deeply affected by the antiocularcentric discourse—e.g., the photographers Cindy Sherman, Victor Burgin, and Mary Kelly, the architect Peter Eisenman, and the video/performance artist Dan Graham. See Stephan W. Melville, "Critiques of Vision and the Shape of Postmodernity" (unpublished paper). For a discussion of the Conceptual Art of the 1960s and 1970s which shows its mobilization of many of the same impulses, see John C. Welchman, *Word, Image and Modernism: An Analysis of the Orders of Relations between Visuality and Textuality in the Modern Period*, Ph.D. diss., Courtauld Insti-tute of Art (London, 1991), chap. 4.

14. Jean-François Lyotard, *Peregrinations: Law, Form, Event* (New York, 1988), p. 38. The text is from the 1986 Wellek Library Lectures at the University of California, Irvine.

The importance of philo-Semitism, in contrast, has been less frequently noted.[16] In the disappointing aftermath of the 1968 events, however, one of the most arresting developments in France was in fact a new appreciation for the legacy of Judaism.[17] The contribution of North African Jews in France, such as the poet Edmond Jabès and the psychoanalyst André Green, both of whom came from Egypt, was increasingly acknowledged. The importance of Derrida's Algerian Jewish roots also became evident when the texts he devoted to Jabès and Levinas in 1964 became more widely known; he criticized Hegel's attitude toward the Jews in *Glas*, and played with his own identity as "Reb Derissa."[18] Among disillusioned former leftists in the 1970s and 1980s, the flight from "Mao to Moses," as the newspaper *Liberation* jocularly put it,[19] was a frequent enough trajectory to warrant public attention. The erstwhile *enragé* and secretary to the elderly Sartre, Pierre Victor, reassumed with considerable fanfare his original name Benny Lévy and entered a Talmudic academy. Others like Alain Finkielkraut became public spokesmen on Jewish issues. And as already

15. See, for example, Arthur Hertzberg, *The French Enlightenment and the Jews: The Origins of Modern Anti-Semitism* (New York, 1968) and Jeffrey Mehlman, *Legacies of Anti-Semitism in France* (Minneapolis, 1983).

16. Philo-Semitism, to be sure, may have its own dangers, expressing as it sometimes does an exaggerated love for the Jews, which totalizes and homogenizes them as much as its putative opposite. In the case of the French appropriation of the Jewish disdain for idolatry, such dangers are perhaps best shown in the Lyotard essay, "Figure Foreclosed," to be discussed below.

17. Many French Jewish intellectuals rediscovered the virtues of their heritage. See Judith Friedlander, *Vilna on the Seine: Jewish Intellectuals in France Since 1968* (New Haven, 1990).

18. Jacques Derrida, "Edmond Jabès and the Question of the Book," and "Violence and Metaphysics: An Essay on the Thought of Emmanuel Levinas," in *Writing and Difference*, trans. Alan Bass (Chicago, 1978). The last essay in this collection, "Ellipsis," ends with a quotation from "Reb Derissa." His critique of Hegel's attitude toward the Jews appears in *Glas* (Paris, 1974), p. 64. For an analysis of Derrida's debts to a heretical Jewish tradition of rabbinical hermeneutics, see Susan A. Handelman, *The Slayers of Moses: The Emergence of Rabbinic Interpretation in Modern Literary Theory* (Albany, N.Y., 1982), chap. 7.

19. "Un Génération de Mao à Moïse," *Libération* (Paris, December 21, 1984), p. 36.

noted, such previously tabooed subjects as the Jewish origins of psycho-analysis became a source of interest and even pride.

An explicitly acknowledged reason for this new fascination with Jewish themes was the importance of the biblical interdiction of graven images. Interestingly, one of the justifications for their hostility advanced by earlier anti-Semitic French intellectuals like Maurice Bardèche and Robert Brasillach was precisely the atomizing effect of the taboo, which they claimed undermined the beneficent power of images in films to create a popular community.[20] Now the reverse implication was drawn, as a multitude of scholars, Jews and Gentiles alike, pondered its wisdom.[21] Literary critics like Jean-Joseph Goux explored the implications of iconoclasm for everything from modern abstract art and the fall of the gold standard to the Nazi persecution of the Jews and the Marxist theory of commodity fetishism.[22] Theologians like the Protestant Jacques Ellul claimed that Christianity properly understood was no less hostile to the primacy of sight than Judaism, and vehemently denounced the current "humiliation of the word"[23] in the society of the spectacle. More secular cultural critics like Louis Marin and Claude Gandelman conducted intense dialogues

20. For a discussion of their preference for silent films over talkies, see Alice Yaeger Kaplan, *Reproductions of Banality: Fascism, Literature, and French Intellectual Life* (Minneapolis, 1986), p. 182.

21. See, for example, Adèlie and Jean-Jacques Rassial, eds., *L'interdit de la représentation* (Paris, 1984).

22. Jean-Joseph Goux, *Les iconoclastes* (Paris, 1978).

23. Jacques Ellul, *The Humiliation of the Word*, trans. Joyce Main Hanks (Grand Rapids, Mich., 1985). Ellul, it might be noted, was partly Jewish in background, which may help to account for his deep attraction to the iconoclastic tradition in Protestantism, especially Kierkegaard and Barth. He followed Nelly Vialleneix, the author of *Kierkegaard et la parole de Dieu* (Paris, 1977), in claiming that Kierkegaard was the first philosopher to attack the primacy of sight. See the discussion in *The Humiliation of the Word*, p. 37. For an analysis of his hostility to images, see my "The Rise of Hermeneutics and the Crisis of Ocularcentrism," in *The Rhetoric of Interpretation and the Interpretation of Rhetoric*, ed. Paul Hernadi (Durham, N.C., 1989). For an earlier French consideration of the religious significance of images and the modern world, written from a Catholic perspective, see Amédée Ayfre, *Conversions aux images?: Les images et dieu; Les images et l'homme* (Paris, 1964).

over the comparative role of images in Jewish and Christian thought.[24] Others like Jean-Jacques Rassial pondered the Nazi obsession with identifying Jews by sight, which deliberately transgressed the ethical implications of the taboo.[25] Even the topos of the "wandering Jew" could be assimilated to that profoundly antiocular image of the labyrinth, in which infinite temporal deferral replaced timeless spatiality and unmediated presence.[26]

With increased scrutiny, the Jewish tradition became more complicated than it seemed at first glance. Roland Goetschel pointed to the role of visible cherubim in Jewish theology, Pierre Prigent noted the importance of funereal paintings and synagogue decorations between the second and sixth centuries, and Claude Gandelman stressed the importance of iconic representation in the textuality of the late Kabbalah.[27] Warnings against

24. Claude Gandelman and Louis Marin, "Dialogue," *Peinture: Cahiers théoriques*, 14/15 (May, 1979).

25. Jean-Jacques Rassial, "Comme le nez au milieu de la figure," *L'interdit de la représentation*.

26. Derrida implies the connection in his essay on Jabès, p. 69. Another deconstructionist, Paul de Man would return to the theme of the wandering Jew in "Conclusions: Walter Benjamin's 'The Task of the Translator'," in *The Resistance to Theory* (Minneapolis, 1986), p. 92. For an analysis of the relation between the labyrinth image and temporal deferral in writing, see Werner Senn, "The Labyrinth Image in Verbal Art: Sign, Symbol, Icon?" *Word and Image*, 2, 3 (1986).

27. Roland Goetschel, "Les métamorphoses du Chérubin dans la pensée juive," in *L'interdit de la représentation*; Pierre Prigent, *Le Judaïsme et l'image* (Tübingen, 1990); Claude Gandelman, "Judaism as Conflict between Iconic and Anti-iconic Tendencies: The Scripture as Body," in *Die Handbuch der Semiotik*, ed. Posner and Sebeok (Berlin, 1990). Outside of France, other scholars have also nuanced the general assessment of the Jewish prohibition. See, for example, Irving Massey, *Find You the Virtue: Ethics, Image, and Desire in Literature* (Fairfax, Va., 1987), and Daniel Boyarin, "The Eye in the Torah: Ocular Desire in Midrashic Hermeneutic," *Critical Inquiry*, 16, 3 (Spring, 1990). Boyarin argues that one must distinguish between the theosophical doctrine that God is invisible, the normative command not to look at Him if He can be seen, and the prohibition on picturing Him. He argues that a biblical and Rabbinic tradition of a visible God was forgotten during the Middle Ages when the threat of Hellenic influences produced anxieties that led to a more rigorous antiocular version of Judaism. There was, however, a tradition of Midrashic hermeneutics

graven images, it was realized, need not mean hostility to all images as such. But by and large, the French reception of the Jewish taboo was in accord with the attitude expressed by Jabès when he confessed in the "egoist museum" page of *Le Nouvel Observateur* in 1985, "I have little taste for images."[28]

The full import of the taboo was apparent in the remarkable work of Emmanuel Levinas, who came to France in 1923 from Lithuania, where he was born in 1906. He was first influential in his adopted country as an early interpreter of German phenomenology; his *Théorie de l'intuition dans la phénomenologie de Husserl* of 1930, according to Paul Ricoeur, "quite simply founded Husserlian studies in France."[29] Levinas was an enthusiastic reader of Heidegger's *Being and Time* and present at the famous debate between its author and the neo-Kantian Ernst Cassirer in Davos, Switzerland in 1929.[30] Before discovering phenomenology, however, he had also been strongly influenced by Bergson, whose seminal contribution to the critique of ocularcentrism has already been detailed.[31] Bergson's stress on temporality helped him to move beyond the visually inflected bias for presence in Husserl's eidetic intuitionism.

But it was Levinas's religious training that gave his work its special pre-

---

in which the recovery of God's visibility was ardently sought. For a discussion of a similar search among Jewish mystics, see Gershom Scholem, "*Shi ur Komah*: The Mystical Shape of the Godhead," in *On the Mystical Shape of the Godhead: Basic Concepts in the Kabbalah*, trans. Joachim Neugroschel (New York, 1991).

28. Edmond Jabès, "J'ai peu de goût pour les images," *Le Nouvel Observateur* (February 22, 1985), p. 78.

29. Paul Ricoeur, "L'originaire et la question-en-retour dans le *Krisis* de Husserl," in *Textes pour Emmanuel Lévinas*, ed. François Laruelle (Paris, 1980), p. 167. See also Richard A. Cohen, "Absolute Positivity and Ultrapositivity: Husserl and Levinas," in *The Question of the Other: Essays in Contemporary Continental Philosophy*, ed. Arleen B. Dallery and Charles E. Scott (Albany, N.Y., 1989).

30. Even after the issue of Heidegger's Nazism became so vigorously discussed in France in the late 1980s, Levinas could still call *Being and Time* "one of the most beautiful books in the history of philosophy" ("Admiration and Disappointment: A Conversation with Philippe Nemo," in *Martin Heidegger and National Socialism*, ed. Gunter Neske and Emil Kettering, trans. Lisa Harries (New York, 1990), p. 149.

occupation with visual issues.[32] The Lithuanian Judaism of his youth, he later recalled, was markedly sober in tone, resistant to "a certain drunkenness of spirit at the popular level."[33] Its emphasis was on the Talmud, on, it might be said, observing the law rather than observing the world. Levinas also became interested in the dialogical theology of Martin Buber and Franz Rosenzweig then being developed in Frankfurt, although he resisted their celebration of Hasidism and the Kabbalah. Buber's stress on verbally mediated, intersubjective "I-Thou" rather than visually constituted, subject-object "I-It" relations left its imprint on Levinas, despite his rejection of the symmetrical reciprocity at its root.[34] Rosenzweig's critique of the Hegelian idea of totality in *The Star of Redemption* also strongly inspired Levinas's preference for infinity, which eluded a God's-eye view of the whole.[35]

Levinas was also an eager reader of contemporary French literature, in particular Valéry and Proust. He was introduced to them in the 1920s by a fellow student in Strasbourg, Maurice Blanchot, who became his life-

31. Levinas frequently acknowledged his debt to Bergson, for example, in the "Dialogue with Emmanuel Levinas" conducted by Richard Kearny in *Face to Face with Levinas*, ed. Richard A. Cohen (Albany, N.Y., 1986), p. 13.

32. Levinas has insisted that his "point of departure is absolutely non-theological" ("Transcendence et Hauteur," *Bulletin de la Société Française de la Philosophie*, 56 [1962], p. 110). But it is impossible not to detect religious concerns in even his most rigorously philosophical work. For a helpful discussion of the complicated relation of religion and philosophy in Levinas, see Susan A. Handelman, *Fragments of Redemption: Jewish Thought and Literary Theory in Benjamin, Scholem and Levinas* (Bloomington, Ind., 1991).

33. Levinas, "Entretien avec Emmanuel Lévinas," in Salomon Malka, *Lire Lévinas* (Paris, 1984), p. 103.

34. Levinas's proximity and distance from Buber can be seen in his 1958 essay, "Martin Buber and the Theory of Knowledge," in *The Levinas Reader*. "It is impossible," he agrees with Buber, "to remain a spectator of the Thou, for the very existence of the Thou depends on the 'word' it addresses to me" (p. 66).

35. Emmanuel Levinas, *Totality and Infinity*, trans. Alphonso Lingis (The Hague, 1969). He acknowledges his debt to Rosenzweig in "Entretien avec Emmanuel Lévinas," p. 105. For other similarities between their positions, see Handelman, *Fragments of Redemption*.

long friend.[36] Although at that time politically conservative and even a contributor to anti-Semitic journals like *Combat*, Blanchot later acknowledged Levinas as his "clandestine companion."[37] His own remarkable work was preoccupied with visual themes, so much so that it is hard to know how much Blanchot influenced Levinas or vice versa on this issue.[38] Not surprisingly, Blanchot was also a significant presence in the theorizing of other figures encountered in this study, such as Bataille, Foucault, and Derrida. As such, he may have been instrumental in preparing the ground for the later reception of Levinas's ideas.

As early as 1932, Blanchot had denounced the alleged French passion for clarity in prose as a foreign imposition, contrasting it with a "vivid flame" that dazzles and even blinds the eye.[39] Blanchot's 1941 novel (or what he preferred to call a *récit*) *Thomas the Obscure*[40] explored the paradoxical relations between night and day, blindness and insight, the eye and the field of vision. In many other places in his work, Blanchot probed the complex tension between language, especially literary language, and

36. On their relations, see Joseph Libertson, *Proximity, Levinas, Blanchot, Bataille and Communication* (The Hague, 1982).

37. Maurice Blanchot, "Our Clandestine Companion," in *Face to Face with Levinas*. During the war, Blanchot's politics changed, and he helped Levinas's wife escape from the Nazis. For examinations of the anti-Semitic dimension of his career, see Mehlman, *Legacies of Anti-Semitism in France*, and Allan Stoekl, *Politics, Writing, Mutilation: The Cases of Bataille, Blanchot, Roussel, Leiris, and Ponge* (Minneapolis, 1985).

38. See, for example, Levinas's glowing review of Blanchot's *L'espace littéraire*, "Maurice Blanchot et le regard du poète," in *Monde Nouveau*, 98 (March, 1956), in which their shared position is very evident. Blanchot's nuanced reception of Heidegger may also have influenced Levinas's later work, such as *Totality and Infinity*. For a short discussion, see Herman Rappaport, *Heidegger and Derrida: Reflections on Time and Language* (Lincoln, Nebr., 1989), p. 121.

39. Blanchot, "La culture français vue par un Allemand," *La Revue Française* (March 27, 1932).

40. Blanchot, *Thomas the Obscure*, new version, trans. Robert Lamberton (New York, 1973). Levinas discusses it in his 1946 essay, "There Is: Existence without Existents," in *The Levinas Reader*. For a discussion of the difference between a novel and a *récit*, see Blanchot, "The Song of the Sirens: Encountering the Imaginary," in *The Gaze of Orpheus*, ed. P. Adams Sitney, trans. Lydia Davis (Barrytown, N.Y., 1981).

vision.[41] For example, in "Parler, ce n'est pas voir," Blanchot wrote, "To speak is not to see. Speech frees thought from this optical requirement which has dominated our approach to things for thousands of years in the Western tradition, and invited us to think under the guarantee of light or under the threat of the absence of light."[42] Implicitly acknowledging the importance of the Jewish taboo, he noted that "whoever sees God dies."[43]

Orpheus's gaze was for Blanchot the founding act of writing because it crosses the threshold of death and seeks in vain to return to an immediacy of visual presence that cannot be restored.[44] Eurydice's disappearance represents the futility of sight and the compensatory function of a literary surrogate (Orpheus's song), which functions more in the realm of what Lacan would have called the Symbolic than the Imaginary (or perhaps in that of the unsymbolizable Real).[45] Literature is thus, to borrow the title of Foucault's essay on Blanchot, "the thought from outside,"[46] based on

41. For general accounts of Blanchot's visual concerns, see P. Adams Sitney's Afterword to *The Gaze of Orpheus*, and Steven Shaviro, *Passion and Excess: Blanchot, Bataille, and Literary Theory* (Tallahassee, Fla., 1990), pp. 5ff. As Paul de Man was to note, his writings refused to shed light on the dark recesses of language: "The light they cast on texts is of a very different nature. Nothing, in fact, could be more obscure than the nature of this light." "Impersonality in Blanchot," in *Blindness and Insight* (Minneapolis, 1983), pp. 62–63.

42. Maurice Blanchot, "Parler, ce n'est pas voir," *L'entretien infini* (Paris, 1969), p. 38.

43. Maurice Blanchot, "Literature and the Right to Death," in *The Gaze of Orpheus*, p. 46. See Boyarin, "The Eye in the Torah," for a critique of this assumption about Jewish fears of looking at God.

44. Blanchot, "The Gaze of Orpheus," in *The Gaze of Orpheus and Other Literary Essays*. For an interesting analysis of this piece which stresses its problematic gender dimensions, see Karen Jacob, "Two Mirrors Facing: Freud, Blanchot, and the Logic of Invisibility," *Qui Parle*, 4, 1 (Fall, 1990). She points out the extent to which Eurydice is always the object of Orpheus's gaze and lacks any reciprocity. Blanchot, she claims, repeats the dynamic of visual reification of female subjectivity posited by Sartre in *Being and Nothingness*.

45. For a discussion of the Real as opposed to the Symbolic in Blanchot, see Shaviro, *Passion and Excess*, p. 27.

46. Michel Foucault, *Maurice Blanchot: The Thought from Outside*, trans. Brian Massumi, with Maurice Blanchot, *Michel Foucault as I Imagine Him*, trans. Jeffrey Mehlman (New York, 1987), where he writes that, for Blanchot, "fiction consists not

language which perpetually thwarts the desire for authorial presence and plenitudinous meaning. Indeed, for Blanchot, being itself—the mystery of the *il y'a*—can never fully reveal itself to the human gaze. As Ann Smock has noted, there is thus an affinity between Levinas and Blanchot in their "concern for being's effacement itself: concern, precisely, *lest* it show, lest being be robbed of that indefiniteness, that seclusion, that *foreignness* from which it is inseparable. Together Blanchot and Levinas reverse the terms in which *Being and Time* poses the question of authenticity."[47] They abandon the traditional philosophical preoccupation with ontology based on "the eternally present order of vision."[48] It was for this reason that Blanchot suggested in such works as *Faux pas* and *La folie du jour* that noontime, the hour of greatest visibility, was also the hour of greatest danger, the time when looking at the sun brought blindness.[49] Nor was the night any more conducive to lucid vision. What Blanchot called "the writing of the disaster" meant relinquishing any fixed star in the visible firmament—thus literally "dis-aster"—as the ground of meaning. In so doing he reversed that contemplative appreciation of the starry heavens that Hans Blumenberg has shown was a fundamental premise of Western metaphysics.[50]

On the level of interpersonal relations, Blanchot called for a community that can never be built on visual interaction. Writing of "the community of lovers" in Marguerite Duras's novel *The Malady of Death*, he contended that the heroine is an "anti-Beatrice, Beatrice having her being

---

in showing the invisible, but in showing the extent to which the invisibility of the visible is invisible . . . language about the outside of all language, speech about the invisible side of words" (pp. 24–25).

47. Ann Smock, Translator's Introduction to Blanchot, *The Space of Literature* (Lincoln, Nebr., 1982), p. 8.

48. Levinas, "The Servant and Her Master," *The Levinas Reader*, p. 157.

49. Blanchot, *Faux pas* (Paris, 1943); *La folie du jour* (Paris, 1973). For Levinas's appreciation of the latter, see his "Exercises sur *La folie du jour,*" in his *Sur Maurice Blanchot* (Montpellier, 1975).

50. Maurice Blanchot, *The Writing of the Disaster*, trans. Ann Smock (Lincoln, Nebr., 1986); Hans Blumenberg, *The Genesis of the Copernican World*, trans. Robert M. Wallace (Cambridge, Mass., 1987).

wholly in the vision one has of her, a vision that presupposes the full scale of the seeable, from the physical sight that strikes one like lightning to the absolute visibility where she is no longer distinguishable from the Absolute itself: God, and the *theos*, theory, the ultimate of what can be seen."[51] Against the Dantean privileging of visual presence and the specular fusion of souls, he posited an ethical alternative that denied the importance of mutual recognition. "An ethics is possible only when—with ontology (which always reduces the Other to the Same) taking the backseat—an anterior relation can affirm itself, a relation such that the self is not content with recognizing the Other, with recognizing itself in it, but feels that the Other always puts it into question to the point of being able to respond to it only through a responsibility that cannot limit itself and that exceeds itself without exhausting itself."[52]

These words, written by Blanchot in 1983, were an explicit paraphrase of his friend Levinas's position, which had been developed long before. Levinas's entire project may, in fact, be characterized, *grosso modo*, as the vindication of the "meontological" (from *meon*, nonbeing), ethical impulse that had been buried under the ontological preoccupation of the dominant Western tradition. "The Good," he contended, "is before being."[53] He explicitly tied ethics to the Hebraic taboo on visual representation and contrasted it again and again to the Hellenic fetish of sight, intelligible form, and luminosity. "The proscription of images," he insisted, "is truly the supreme command of monotheism."[54] Even if the biblical words describing Moses's meeting with God on Sinai suggest a visible "face-to-face" encounter, what they really meant was a divine verbal command, for all God showed, according to the famous passage in Exodus 33, was His back.[55]

51. Maurice Blanchot, *The Unavowable Community*, trans. Pierre Joris (Barrytown, N.Y., 1988), p. 52.

52. Ibid., p. 43.

53. Levinas, "Substitution," *The Levinas Reader*, p. 112.

54. Levinas, "Reality and Its Shadow," *The Levinas Reader*, p. 141.

55. Levinas, "Revelation in the Jewish Tradition," *The Levinas Reader*, p. 204.

The word made flesh in the Christian tradition was thus a falling away from the Jewish stress on the voice and the ear. "In sound, and in the consciousness termed hearing, there is in fact a break with the self-complete world of vision and art. In its entirety, sound is a ringing, clanging scandal. Whereas, in vision, form is wedded to content in such a way as to appease it, in sound the perceptible quality overflows so that form can no longer contain its content. A real rent is produced in the world, through which the world that is *here* prolongs a dimension that cannot be converted into vision."[56] Such a conversion was typical of an aesthetic rather than ethical stance toward the world, that of Aaron rather than Moses, because it privileged formal presence rather than the substantive commands from an absent interlocutor.

For Levinas, the two meanings of "regard" should therefore be rigorously separated, for to care for the Other meant refusing to turn him or her into an object of visual knowledge or aesthetic contemplation. Going beyond Debord's historical analysis of the society of the spectacle, he insisted that vision itself was the root of the problem: "The 'turning' of the constituted into a condition is accomplished as soon as I open my eyes: I but open my eyes and already enjoy the spectacle."[57] Regard in the sense of caring thus meant keeping the eyes shut, thwarting the violent "avidity of the gaze" in the service of generosity.[58] It also meant resisting the temptation of formal reciprocity to which even Buber's I-Thou principle had succumbed, for such a principle risked specular reduction of difference into sameness. Although Levinas often talked about "face-to-face" encounters, it was the summons to hear the Other's call rather than seeing his or her visage that mattered.[59] "The face," he insisted, "is not in front

56. Levinas, "The Transcendence of Words," *The Levinas Reader*, p. 147.

57. Levinas, *Totality and Infinity*, p. 130.

58. Ibid., p. 50.

59. Levinas, "Ethics as First Philosophy," *The Levinas Reader*, p. 83. According to Handelman, "Despite the connotations of the word, he maintains that 'face' is *not* originally founded on any visual perception" (*Fragments of Redemption*, p. 209). See also the discussion of this issue in Jill Robbins, "*Visage, Figure*: Reading Levinas's *Totality and Infinity*," *Yale French Studies*, 79 (1991).

of me (*en face de moi*), but above me; it is the other before death, looking through and exposing death. Secondly, the face is the other who asks me not to let him die alone, as if to do so were to become an accomplice in his death."[60] According to Levinas's notion of "substitution," the ethical self was the hostage of the other, who is always in asymmetrical and hierarchial relation to the self. Rather than the shame induced by a Sartrean reifying look,[61] real ethical responsibility came from an eminently non-visual source.

In addition to commands to the ear, ethical interaction manifests itself in touch, which is also basically temporal in nature.[62] Whereas visual relations with others foster instrumental manipulation—Levinas approvingly cited Heidegger's distinction between *Vorhandenheit* (presentness-at-hand) and *Zuhandenheit* (readiness-at-hand), as well as Bergson's dictum, "to recognize an object is to know how to use it"[63]—touch allows a more benign interaction. Instead of the distance between subject and object congenial to sight, touch restores the proximity of self and other, who then is understood as neighbor. It also entails a more intimate relation to the world. "As Merleau-Ponty in particular has shown," Levinas wrote, "the I that constitutes the world comes up against a sphere in which it is by its very flesh implicated; it is implicated in what it otherwise would have constituted and so is implicated in the world."[64]

Touch, moreover, is connected to the primacy of doing over contemplation, in particular a kind of doing that reveals the vulnerability of the self to the world. For Levinas, Edith Wyschograd has suggested, "touch is

---

60. Levinas and Richard Kearny, "Dialogue with Emmanuel Levinas," pp. 23–24.

61. Levinas also disputed Sartre's reduction of alterity to nothingness and his belief in the totalizing project of the self. Levinas's version of intersubjectivity was accordingly far more hopeful than that of the Sartre of *Being and Nothingness*.

62. For a helpful explication of this theme, see Edith Wyschograd, "Doing Before Hearing: On the Primacy of Touch," in *Textes pour Emmanuel Lévinas*, and her *Emmanuel Levinas: The Problem of Ethical Metaphysics* (The Hague, 1974), pp. 137ff.

63. Levinas, "Interdit de la représentation et 'droits de l'homme,'" in Rassial, ed., *L'interdit de la représentation*, pp. 112–113.

64. Levinas, "Ethics as First Philosophy," *The Levinas Reader*, p. 79.

not a sense at all; it is in fact a metaphor for the impingement of the world as a whole upon subjectivity. . . . to touch is to comport oneself not in opposition to the given but in proximity with it."[65] Touch, Levinas contended, can thus be understood as the phenomenological ground of religious ritual, which has no instrumental telos, no usefulness in the practical world. This kind of doing may even be more primordial than the hearing of ethical commands; it certainly is more fundamental than the theoretical contemplation of a world of objects through the eyes.

The most benign mode of touching, which may even go beyond touching normally understood is the caress. It is the opposite of the grasp, which takes possession of what it holds.[66] Nor does it lead to a fusion, which overwhelms the otherness of the Other. "The caress," Levinas writes,

> is a mode of the subject's being, where the subject who is in contact with another goes beyond this contact. Contact as sensation is part of the world of light. But what is caressed is not touched, properly speaking. It is not the softness or warmth of the hand given in contact that the other seeks. The seeking of the caress constitutes its essence by the fact that the caress does not know what it seeks. This "not knowing," this fundamental disorder, is the essential.[67]

65. Wyschogrod, "Doing Before Hearing: On the Primacy of Touch," p. 199.

66. Levinas, "Beyond Intentionality," in *Philosophy in France Today*, ed. Alan Montefiore (Cambridge, 1983), p. 103, where he discusses Husserl's epistemology in terms of grasping. In his 1967 essay, "Language and Proximity," in *Collected Philosophical Papers* (Dordrecht, Holland, 1987), Levinas claimed that "the visible caresses the eye. One sees and hears like one touches" (p. 118). Here he conflated the senses in a way reminiscent of Merleau-Ponty's effort to evoke an equiprimordiality prior to their differentiation, but in general, he preferred to respect their differences. For a reading of this essay, which takes it to mean that Levinas never completely broke with ocularcentrism, see Paul Davies, "The Face and the Caress: Levinas's Ethical Alterations of Sensibility," in David Michael Levin, ed., *Modernity and the Hegemony of Vision* (Berkeley, 1993).

67. Levinas, "Time and the Other," *The Levinas Reader*, p. 51.

What was taken as the problematic gender implication of Levinas's description of the caress initially aroused the ire of feminists like Simone de Beauvoir, who accused him of reducing women to passive objects of male sensual pleasure.[68] But by the 1980s, and a more nuanced appreciation of Levinas' reversal of the normal hierarchy of self and other, the logic of his argument began to attract feminist supporters, such as Catherine Chalier and Luce Irigaray.[69] For them, one of the most attractive dimensions of his work was its usefulness for a feminist ethics. Not only did Levinas suggest the condition of maternity as the ideal model of selfless submission to the needs of the other, but he also explicitly privileged the feminine as that which was outside the specular economy of the male gaze. For Levinas, the feminine was "a mode of being that consists in slipping away from the light. The feminine in existence is an event different from that of spatial transcendence or of expression that goes toward light. It is a flight before light. Hiding is the way of existing of the feminine, and this fact of hiding is precisely modesty. So this feminine alterity does not consist in the object's simple exteriority."[70]

In the Bible, the role of women as unobserved observers was essential, Levinas claimed. For the world that it depicts "would not have been structured as it was—and as it still is and always will be—but for the secret presence, to the verge of invisibility, of these mothers, these wives and daughters, but for their silent footsteps in the depth and opaqueness of reality, depicting the dimensions of interiority itself and making the

68. Simone de Beauvoir, *The Second Sex*, trans. H. M. Parshley (New York, 1970), p. xvi, n. 3.

69. Catherine Chalier, *Figures du féminin. Lecture d'Emmanuel Lévinas* (Paris, 1982); Luce Irigaray, "The Fecundity of the Caress: A Reading of Levinas's *Totality and Infinity*, Section IV, B, 'The Phenomenology of Eros'," in Richard A. Cohen, ed., *Face to Face with Levinas*. For a discussion of Irigaray's debt to Levinas, see Elisabeth Grosz, *Sexual Subversions: Three French Feminists* (Sydney, 1989), p. 141. In a later essay, "Questions to Emmanuel Levinas: On the Divinity of Love," in *Re-Reading Levinas*, ed. Robert Bernasconi and Simon Critchley (Bloomington, Ind., 1991), Irigaray is more critical of the sexist presuppositions of his work and also argues for a greater openness to mysticism than Levinas's.

70. Levinas, "Time and the Other," *The Levinas Reader*, p. 49.

world habitable."[71] Heidegger's *Heimat* only becomes truly a home with a woman's invisible nurturance, which opens up the dimension of intimacy lacking in men with their lofty yearnings for fame in the glare of the public realm.

⊙

Female modesty and domesticity, ethical commands from an absent God, religious ritual as the model of practical action—Levinas's worldview was anything but that of a "progressive" thinker who would become a likely hero to his most advanced French contemporaries. Indeed, his political statements, based on a religious variant of Zionism, could betray a troubling insensitivity to universalist values.[72] And yet, as mentioned earlier, no less an arbiter of the radically new than Jean-François Lyotard found in him a powerful inspiration.

An explanation is not difficult to provide. For if, as is often argued, postmodernism's critique of the modernist project was in large measure also a rejection of the Enlightenment, it should be no surprise that the unabashedly counter-Enlightenment philosophy of Levinas would find a congenial reading. And a fortiori it is no mystery that his powerful critique of the ocularcentric premises of the *siècle des lumières* would also find an appreciative audience. By 1984, the French popular press could thus justly claim that Levinas was "à la mode,"[73] with Lyotard as one of the main celebrants.

Lyotard's own roots were in the more "pagan" philosophies of Marxism and phenomenology, and it would have been hard to predict his fascination for Levinas at the beginning of his career. He became politically active during the Algerian struggle for independence and, in 1954, at the

71. Levinas, "Judaism and the Feminine Element," *Judaism*, 18, 1 (Winter, 1969), p. 32.
72. See, for example, his denial of the status of "other" to the Palestinians in his 1982 interview "Ethics and Politics," in *The Levinas Reader*, p. 289.
73. "La mode Lévinas," *Le Monde* (November 23, 1984), p. 21.

age of thirty, joined the ultraleftist group *Socialisme ou Barbarie*, led by
Cornelius Castoriadis and Claude Lefort.[74] His first major philosophical
publication appeared in the same year, a short introduction to phenomenology, which perfunctorily cited Levinas's works on the subject but was
more obviously indebted to Merleau-Ponty.[75] Although Lyotard abandoned his affiliation with *Socialisme ou Barbarie* in 1964 and its offshoot
Pouvoir Ouvrier two years later, and although he would increasingly come
to criticize Merleau-Ponty in ways that will be examined shortly, he continued to dispense "lessons in paganism"[76] well into the 1970s. Like many
other French intellectuals of the period, he became increasingly interested
in Nietzsche.[77] Polytheism, not the one true God of the Jewish tradition,
was Lyotard's avowed credo, which was underlined by his celebrated dismissal of a single master historical narrative in *The Postmodern Condition*.[78] Lacking Levinas's irenic instincts, he privileged dissensus over consensus, agonistic struggle over the pacific adjudication of differences.

Moreover, unlike Levinas, Lyotard often wrote with relish on visual
themes, trenchantly analyzing such artists as Cézanne, Duchamp, Barnett
Newman, Ruth Francken, and Daniel Buren, as well as experimental cinema and photography. Nor did he share the Jewish thinker's general disdain for the category of the aesthetic, which in fact he sought to rescue
from its inferior status among contemporary philosophers.[79] He was thus

74. For his later account of this episode, see Lyotard, "A Memorial for Marxism: For
Pierre Souyri," in *Peregrinations: Law, Form, Event*. Lyotard's first professional position was teacher of philosophy in a *lycée* in the Algerian city of Constantine, which he
began in 1950.

75. Lyotard, *La phénoménologie* (Paris, 1954).

76. Lyotard, "Lessons in Paganism," in *The Lyotard Reader*, ed. Andrew Benjamin
(London, 1989). The original was published in 1977.

77. See, for example, his essay "Notes on the Return and Capital," in *Semiotext(e)*, 3,
1 (1978).

78. Lyotard, *The Postmodern Condition: A Report on Knowledge*, trans. Geoff Bennington and Brian Massumi (Minneapolis, 1984).

79. For an account of Lyotard's complex attitude toward aesthetics, see David Carroll,
Paraesthetics: Foucault, Lyotard, Derrida (New York, 1987), chap. 2.

drawn to Adorno's *Aesthetic Theory*, whose "diabolical" critique of theoretical totalizations and negative dialectics he admired.[80]

And yet, for all their differences, it is clear that Levinas provided Lyotard with valuable inspiration in his transformation from a leftist phenomenologist to the major French defender of postmodernism. To make sense of his debt, however, it will be necessary first to clarify Lyotard's complicated attitude toward the visual during the earlier phases of his career. For even before he absorbed the full measure of Levinas's critique of the eye, Lyotard already harbored some of the same reservations about the alleged nobility of sight so pervasive in twentieth-century French thought.

At the same time he was drifting away from the heterodox Marxism he had shared with other members of *Socialisme ou Barbarie*, Lyotard was also coming to terms with psychoanalysis.[81] In the mid-1960s, he attended Lacan's seminars in Paris, and was intrigued by his attempt to rescue Freud from ego psychology through the use of structural linguistics, as well as by his critique of Merleau-Ponty's phenomenological search for a primordial ontology of vision prior to the split between subject and object. But one aspect of Lacan's position failed to persuade him. As he later put it,

> I myself felt a bit resistant to Lacan's teaching. It has taken me over twenty years to understand this resistance. It has nothing to do with the concept "A," the big A in Lacan's schema. On the contrary, this

80. Lyotard, "Adorno as the Devil," *Telos*, 19 (Spring, 1974). He nonetheless chastised Adorno for not going far enough in relinquishing his nostalgia for an impossible totality. See also his ruminations on Adorno's micrological challenge to speculative philosophy in "Presentations," *Philosophy in France Today*, ed. Alan Montefiore (Cambridge, 1983), and "Discussions, or Phrasing 'after Auschwitz'," in *The Lyotard Reader*. Although this is not the place to explore them, there are some important parallels between Adorno and Levinas. For a discussion, see Hent De Vries, *Theologie im Pianissimo & Zwischen Rationalität und Dekonstruktion: Die Aktualität der Denkfiguren Adornos und Levinas'* (Kampen, 1989).

81. The verb drift (*dérive*) is Lyotard's own, for he chose—perhaps with deliberate irony—the same term we have seen introduced by the Situationists to describe his disenchantment in *Dérive à partir de Marx et Freud*.

concept seems to me to supply a foundation for the split between desire and demand, that is to say, between what Lacan calls the Real, which is relevant to the order of desire or the "Id," and the Imaginary, which belongs to the economy of the Ego demands. The anger I felt against Lacan's reading of Freud was related to the third term, the Symbolic, to which the entire field of language and knowledge belongs.[82]

Lyotard's rejection of Lacan's notion of the Symbolic, and much else as well, was manifest in the book he fashioned from his *doctorat d'état* in 1971, *Discours, figure*.[83] A sprawling, ambitious, and thematically diffuse work, it touched on many of the themes and figures already encountered in this narrative, from Quattrocento perspective to its anamorphic distortion, from Descartes's *Dioptrique* to Merleau-Ponty's *Visible and Invisible*, from the visual poetry of Mallarmé's "Un coup de dés" to Freud's notion of foreclosure, from Breton's defense of hallucination to Derrida's critique of the *Augenblick* in Husserl. The results defy easy paraphrase or reduction to a theoretical system, as indeed does much of Lyotard's deliberately elusive work.[84] But what can be said with some confidence is that the disparate analyses in the book are all loosely tied together by the contrast, at

82. Lyotard, *Peregrinations*, p. 10.

83. Lyotard, *Discours, figure* (Paris, 1971); the following quotations are taken from the 4th edition (1985). Among the most insightful interpretations of the book in English are Bill Readings, *Introducing Lyotard: Art and Politics* (London, 1991), sect. 1; David Carroll, *Paraesthetics*, chap. 2; Geoff Bennington, "Lyotard: From Discourse and Figure to Experimentation and Event," *Paragraph*, 6 (October, 1985); Maureen Turim, "Desire in Art and Politics: The Theories of Jean-François Lyotard," *Camera Obscura*, 12 (Summer, 1984); and Peter Dews, "The Letter and the Line: Discourse and Its Other in Lyotard," *Diacritics*, 14, 3 (Fall, 1984).

84. Commentators hesitant to "betray" Lyotard's resistance to paraphrase have struggled to find a mode of presentation commensurate with his own performative ideals. See, for example, Geoff Bennington, *Lyotard: Writing the Event* (Manchester, 1988); and Readings, *Introducing Lyotard*. For reasons I have detailed elsewhere ("Two Cheers for Paraphrase: The Confessions of a Synoptic Intellectual Historian," in *Fin-de-siècle Socialism and Other Essays* [New York, 1988]), I am less anxious about the costs of paraphrase and so will not attempt a Lyotardian reading of Lyotard.

once maintained and deconstructed, between the two terms in Lyotard's title: discourse and figure.

The cluster of meanings surrounding the first of these signifiers is somewhat easier to specify than those around the second. For Lyotard, discourse implies the domination of textuality over perception, conceptual representation over prereflexive presentation, rational coherence over the "other" of reason. It is the realm of logic, concepts, form, speculative reciprocity, and the symbolic. Discourse thus serves as the locus of what normally passes for communication and signification in which the materiality of signifiers is forgotten. Whether in the guise of dialectical sublation or diacritical synchronicity, discourse entails a belief in transparency and lucidity.

Figurality, in contrast, is what injects opacity into the discursive realm. It works against the self-sufficiency of linguistic meaning, introducing an unassimilable heterogeneity into putatively homogeneous discourse. Very much like Bataille's notion of excess, it transgresses the limits of the knowable and the communicable, preventing the recuperation of the incommensurable into one systematic order.[85] The figural is not so much the simple opposite of the discursive, an alternative order of meaning, as it is the principle of disruption that prevents any order from crystallizing into full coherence. As Lyotard later put it, "I did not try in *Discours, figure* to oppose language and image. I was suggesting that a (discursive) principle of readability and a (figural) principle of unreadability shared one in the other."[86]

For Lyotard, the figural embraces a welter of different meanings. It includes the rhetorical tropes that defy literal signification, those "figures of speech" that traditional philosophy tries in vain to banish. It also implies notions of configuration, shape and image, although without the bias for clarity and lucidity that traditionally accompanies those terms. It suggests as well the inescapability of designation and reference to something out-

85. For a discussion of Lyotard's implicit debt to Bataille, see Pefanis, *Heterology and the Postmodern*, p. 86.
86. Lyotard, "Interview," *Diacritics*, 14, 3 (Fall, 1984), p. 17.

side a closed, self-referential discursive system. Figurality is tied as well to the unique temporality of what Lyotard calls "the event," unexpected happenings that undermine the stasis of a synchronic system—such as the diacritical oppositions of structuralist linguistics—as well as the emplotted coherence of a grand narrative.

More precisely, Lyotard distinguishes among "figure-images," which violate the perceptual recognition of objects' outlines (e.g., as in Cubist art), "figure-forms," which problematize the space of visibility itself in which outlines might appear (e.g., the abstract expressionism of a Jackson Pollock), and finally, "figure-matrices," which are simply invisible, although they somehow surge up into the realm of visibility as a principle of pure difference. Their relation to the unconscious will be examined shortly.

Insofar as *Discours, figure* begins with a section called "le parti pris du figural" in which Lyotard explicitly claims "this book is a defense of the eye,"[87] it might seem as though he has not yet fully accepted the wholesale critique of ocularcentrism. And indeed, his complicated argument cannot be reduced to so simple a formula. For Lyotard expressly distances himself from a religious tradition that trusts only in the Word given directly to the ear, as well as a philosophical tradition that dismisses sense experience as the enemy of the truth. Instead, he invokes Breton's dictum that "the eye exists in a savage state" and Merleau-Ponty's attempt to explore the chiasmic intertwining of the visible and the invisible.[88]

What, however, becomes readily apparent is that Lyotard's avowed defense of the visual is not comparable to those made by believers in speculative mirroring, empirical observation, visionary illumination, or eidetic intuition. For Lyotard, the eye must be understood as a source of disruptive energy: "l'oeil, c'est la force."[89] And it is a force that resists recupera-

87. Lyotard, *Discours, figure*, p. 11.

88. Ibid., p. 11. For a discussion of his debt to and differences from Merleau-Ponty, see Jean-Loup Thébaud, "La chair et l'infini: J. F. Lyotard et Merleau-Ponty," *Esprit*, 6 (June, 1982).

89. Ibid., p. 14.

tion into a harmonious intertwining in the flesh of the world. There is no Hegelian sublation of the discursive and the figural in a higher third. Whereas discourse follows the graphic logic of what Lyotard calls "the letter," in which conventional meaning reigns, the figure is beholden to the visual space of "the line," where opacity, intensity, and the nonrecognizable dominate.[90] There is no way to make the two entirely commensurate.

Thus for all his obvious debts to phenomenology's critique of Cartesian perspectivalism, Lyotard rejects Merleau-Ponty's attempt to turn Cézanne's painting into an emblem of a successful restoration of a primordial state before the split between subject and object. Like Lacan, he eschews nostalgia for any *voyure* anterior to the chiasm. Instead of reconciliation, he calls for "deconciliation," in which the figural is "not attached to the visible, nor to the I-You of language, nor to the One of perception, but to the Id of desire. And not to the immediate figures of desire, but to its operations."[91]

In the latter part of the book, the desiring Id begins in fact to crowd aside the unsublatable dialectic of discourse and figurality. The phenomenological understanding of perception and the body, especially that of Merleau-Ponty, is now explicitly faulted for dissimulating libidinal desire. The change occurs after his discussion of Mallarmé's radical subversion of traditional poetry through the introduction of antisignifying visual material. Here, as David Carroll has noted,

> an impasse of sorts is reached in *Discours, figure*. For when the alternative between the discursive and the figural—defined in predominantly visual terms—is overcome in Mallarmé's poetry, not only the alternative, but the notion of art supporting such a definition of the figure, can now be seen as deficient. It is as if the figural had become too stable, too visible, too easily located in a particular poetic practice—no matter how radical it is claimed to be—to continue to serve a critical function.[92]

90. Ibid., pp. 211ff. In *Économie libidinale*, the same function would be fulfilled by what he called "the tensor." See the essay of the same title in *The Lyotard Reader*.

What Lyotard puts in its place is libidinal desire, understood as a force or energy, which follows the imperatives of discharge and intensity rather than signification. Most interesting for our purposes is that the "figure-matrix," which is his term for the ground of desire, is invisible. At most it appears as an inverse trace of primary process in secondary processes. "Not only is it not seen," he writes, "but it is no more visible than readable. It belongs neither to plastic nor to textual space: it is difference itself, and as such, it does not suffer being put in the form of an *opposition*, which is what its spoken expression would demand, or in the form of an image or a form, which its plastic expression would suppose. Discourse, image, and form all miss it equally because it resides in all three spaces together."[93]

It is here that Lyotard's quarrel with Lacan's notion of the Symbolic becomes manifest. In a section entitled "The Dream-work Does Not Think,"[94] he challenges Lacan's contention that the unconscious is structured like a language (a complaint already made in Foucault's earlier work on Binswanger which Lyotard, however, ignored).[95] For if it were, there would be no significant difference between consciousness and the unconscious. Rejecting the identification of condensation with the linguistic operation of metaphor and displacement with metonymy, Lyotard argues that "it is futile to attempt to bring everything back to articulated language as the model for all semiology, when it is patently clear that language, at least in its poetic usage, is possessed, haunted by the figure."[96] Dreams also make use of rebuslike figures that defy reduction to language alone; they are like Magritte's paintings, "many of which are not plays

91. Ibid., p. 23.

92. Carroll, *Paraesthetics*, p. 37.

93. Lyotard, *Discours, figure*, p. 278.

94. It is translated in *The Lyotard Reader*, from which the following quotations are taken.

95. Foucault, Introduction to Ludwig Binswanger, *Le rêve et l'existence*, trans. Jacqueline Verdeaux (Paris, 1954), p. 27.

96. Lyotard, "The Dream-Work Does Not Think," p. 30.

on words but games played by the figure on the words which form its legend."[97]

According to Lyotard, Lacan fails to acknowledge that the plastic embodiment of signifiers affects their meaning. He refuses to "concede to figurability its two functions: the one operative *inside* the writing system, creating figures with letters, heading not only in the direction of the hieroglyph, but in the direction of the rebus; the other, however, about which Lacan says not a word, trading on the designatory power of language, and simply replacing . . . the signified by one of its designates, the concept by one of its objects."[98] That is, Lacan fails to understand the figural as an internal principle of disruption, which pits the materiality of signifiers against what they try to signify. And he also ignores the importance of the referential function of language, the figure's ability to designate visible objects in the world that cannot be recuperated into purely linguistic concepts. The desire expressed in figurality must therefore be understood not as the decipherable source of latent intelligibility lurking beneath the manifest content of the dream. It is rather a primal phantasm that disrupts the intelligible, breaking the laws of language, "at once discourse and figure, a tongue lost in a hallucinatory scenography, the first violence."[99]

Unfortunately, Lyotard confined his analysis solely to texts in Lacan's *Écrits*. He neglected, however, to examine the more complicated analysis of the eye and the gaze in the seminars included in *Four Fundamental Concepts of Psychoanalysis*, perhaps because they were not available in print until almost a decade after they were delivered in 1964. Lacan's appreciation of the nonsublatable imbrication of the visual and linguistic was more in evidence in this later work. The apparently rigid separation of the Imaginary and the Symbolic, against which Lyotard railed in *Discours, figure*, was thus not so watertight for Lacan after all.

Nonetheless, Lyotard's defense of the phantasmic "figure-matrix" which disrupts the intelligibility of the signifying system won him plaudits from

97. Ibid., p. 28.
98. Ibid., p. 39.
99. Ibid., p. 51.

those like Gilles Deleuze and Félix Guattari, who also rejected structuralism and its apparent residue in Lacan.[100] In their *Anti-Oedipus* of 1972, they praised his restitution of "the theory of pure designation"[101] for resisting the imperialism of the textual. "The extreme importance of J.-F. Lyotard's recent book," they argued, "is due to its position as the first generalized critique of the signifier. . . . He shows that the signifier is overtaken towards the outside by figurative images, just as it is overtaken towards the inside by the pure figures that compose it—or more decisively, by 'the figural' that comes to short-circuit the signifier's coded gaps."[102]

Even more important, they claimed, is Lyotard's challenge to the traditional psychoanalytic emphasis on the Oedipus complex, which was still shared by Lacan. For the analysis of the figure-matrix in *Discours, figure* undermines any notion of the unconscious as the site of a theatricalized representation, such as that operative in the Oedipal triangle. It thus prepares the way for what they call schizoanalysis, which interprets the unconscious hydraulically as a desiring machine, producing unrepresentable, uncodable, unterritorializable flows of libidinal energy. "To overturn the theater of representation into the order of desire-production," they contended, "this is the whole task of schizoanalysis."[103] Although faulting

100. Guattari was analyzed by Lacan. For a defense of the latter's position, see Ellie Ragland-Sullivan, *Jacques Lacan and the Philosophy of Psychoanalysis* (Urbana, Ill., 1987), pp. 87ff. Interestingly, Lyotard's argument was less favorably received by deconstructionists, who rejected his attempt to make something positive and liberating about figural desire. See, for example, Bennington, "Lyotard: From Discourse and Figure to Experimentation and Event," where he wonders, "Why should we assume an essentially *psychic* root to the problem of the figure? Is there not something still too ontological and even corporeal here, which will give rise quite soon in Lyotard's work to the 'libidinal band' of *Économie libidinale*? And concomitantly, is not the emphasis on *transgression* too simple and optimistic, apparently falling short of the recognition that transgression also confirms the law that it breaks? . . . And does this not in fact, against the general deconstructive drift of the book . . . re-construe the difference between difference and opposition as an opposition rather than a difference, and thus allow the earlier notion of discourse its revenge after all?" (p. 23).

101. Gilles Deleuze and Félix Guattari, *Anti-Oedipus: Capitalism and Schizophrenia*, trans. Robert Hurley, Mark Seem, and Helen R. Lewis (Minneapolis, 1983), p. 204.

102. Ibid., p. 242.

103. Ibid., p. 271.

Lyotard for reintroducing a certain notion of lack in his concept of desire, which they insisted should instead be understood entirely in affirmative terms, Deleuze and Guattari nonetheless acknowledged in him a kindred spirit.

The affinity between their positions was no less explicitly registered by Lyotard, who wrote a long appreciation of *Anti-Oedipus* in 1972 entitled "Capitalisme énergumène" stressing the anti-Marxist implications of their argument.[104] In the work that followed *Discours, figure* in the early 1970s, most notably the collections *Des dispositifs pulsionnels* and *Économie libidinale*,[105] Lyotard spelled out an alternative libidinal politics, which showed how far he had come since his days with Lefort and Castoriadis. Capitalism, for all its despotic attempts to regulate economic exchange, he argued, also unleashes libidinal intensities that thwart containment. There is no utopian order, he contended, in which these could or should be reigned in. It is also fruitless to oppose a general economy of expenditure to a restricted one of exchange, as the former always already inhabits the latter. In a sense, capitalism is thus more radical than socialism, for it cynically liquidates all structures and mystifications and refuses to put new ones in their place.

However one judges Lyotard's libidinal politics—and he himself came to doubt its plausibility[106]—it is more important to note the presence of

104. Lyotard, "Capitalisme énergumène," *Des dispositifs pulsionnels* (Paris, 1979). "Energumen" means one possessed by an evil spirit, a fanatical enthusiast.

105. Lyotard, *Des dispositifs pulsionnels* (Paris, 1973) and *Économie libidinale* (Paris, 1974). Of the latter, Julian Pefanis writes, "It is, if you like, a Deleuzian text in the sense of being schizophrenic and nonnegotiable in a poetic way: the reader is left little room to move except in the direction of the flow. What it lacks in the clarity of its outcome is replaced by the intensity of its expression, its irrepressible antagonism and agonism" (*Heterology and the Postmodern*, p. 91).

106. See, for example, his remarks in his conversation with Jean-Loup Thébaud, *Just Gaming*, trans. Wlad Godzich (Minneapolis, 1985), p. 90: "It is not true that one can do an aesthetic politics. It is not true that the search for intensities or things of that type can ground politics, because there is the problem of justice." *Économie libidinale* he came to call "my evil book" in which he had self-indulgently tried in his prose to "destroy or deconstruct the presentation of any theatrical representation

similar arguments about visual phenomena in his work of the same era. That is, he frequently celebrated precisely those disruptive, unrepresentable, invisible impulses that shattered traditional notions of visual experience. In 1971 and 1972, he published essays on "Freud According to Cézanne" and "Psychoanalysis and Painting," in which he attacked Freud's aesthetic theory for privileging the symbolic content of a work of art over its plastic means. These always resisted reduction to intelligible significance.[107] He then analyzed works by artists like Cézanne, Delauney, and Klee in "Painting as Libidinal Apparatus" in 1972, and hyperrealist art the following year.[108] In all these works, Lyotard subordinated the clarity of the dispassionate gaze to the workings of figural desire, which ruptures the smooth surface of the canvas to penetrate deep into the viewer's unconscious.

Not surprisingly, he would find Marcel Duchamp's explicitly "anti-retinal" art congenial. In his 1977 *Les transformateurs Duchamp*, Lyotard approvingly contended that Duchamp's

> dissolution of visual ensembles doesn't have as its goal the rediscovery of a body or ego prior to the Cartesian body, a "flesh," as Merleau-Ponty says, opening to a world without established referents. . . . No ambition to *heal* the deformities which float in the confines of the visual field nor restore the curvilinear space where the supposed chiasmic extension rules them. It is necessary to blind the eye that believes in something; it is necessary to make

---

whatsoever, with the goal of inscribing the passage of intensities directly in the prose itself without any mediation" (*Peregrinations*, p. 13). See also his negative evaluation of the "desperation" behind this book in his interview with Willem van Reijen and Dick Veerman in *Theory, Culture and Society*, 5 (1988), p. 300.

107. Lyotard, "Freud selon Cézanne," in *Des dispositifs pulsionnels*, and "Psychoanalyse et peinture," *Encyclopaedia Universalis*, 13 (Paris, 1972).

108. Lyotard, "La peinture comme dispositif libidinal," and "Esquisse d'une économie de l'hyperréalisme," in *Des dispositifs pulsionnels*. He would return to the question of hyperrealism in a later text on Jacques Monory, *L'assassinat de l'expérience par la peinture* (Paris, 1984).

a painting of blindness, which plunges the self-sufficiency of the eye into disarray.[109]

What Duchamp called the "Miroirique" produced an anamorphic distortion of specularity in which the incommensurabilities—the "paradoxical hinges"—within visual experience and between discourse and figurality remained unreconciled.[110]

In an essay of 1973 entitled "Acinema," Lyotard extended his analysis of libidinal economy to the cinema, which repeated many of the same complaints against traditional films elaborated by other commentators from Bergson to Debord and Metz.[111] Arguing for the priority of flow and movement over stasis, he denounced the cinema for seeking ways to stabilize visual experience and provide formal closure. "All so-called good form," he charged, "implies the return of sameness, the folding back of diversity upon an identical unity."[112] Through conventional plot resolutions, mechanisms of identification, and the reality effect produced by editing and synchronization of sound and image, films provide an ideological simulacrum of meaningful unity. They thus act "as the orthopedic mirror analyzed by Lacan in 1949 as constitutive of the imaginary subject of *object a*."[113]

"Acinema," in contrast, will destroy the illusion of unity and coherence. It will be a *détournement*—Lyotard introduced the Situationist term but attributed it solely to Pierre Klossowski—that will be like Bataille's potlatch of signs: "It is essential that the entire erotic force invested in the

109. Lyotard, *Les transformateurs Duchamp* (Paris, 1977), p. 68.

110. Lyotard would introduce the same notion of antispecular mirroring in his discussion of Ruth Francken, in which he also invokes the familiar image of the labyrinth. See his "The Story of Ruth," *The Lyotard Reader*, p. 264.

111. Metz, in fact, cautiously drew on *Discours, figure* in *The Imaginary Signifier: Psychoanalysis and Cinema*, trans. Celia Britton, Annwyl Williams, Ben Brewster, and Alfred Guzzetti (Bloomington, Ind., 1982), e.g., pp. 229–230, 287. Lyotard's critique of Lacan's belief in the unconscious as a language seems to have moved Metz away from the more rigorously structuralist beliefs of his earlier work.

112. Lyotard, "Acinema," *The Lyotard Reader*, p. 172.

113. Ibid., p. 176.

simulacrum be promoted, raised, displayed and burned in vain. It is thus that Adorno said the only truly great art is the making of fireworks: pyrotechnics would simulate perfectly the sterile consumption of energies in *jouissance*."[114] Acinema achieves this end either by extreme immobilization, producing films that are like tableaux vivants, or by extreme mobilization, which creates "lyric abstractions."[115] In both cases, the "orthopedic" subject of traditional narrative cinema is dismantled. Vision once again is paradoxically allowed to reveal those invisible figure-matrices pulsing through the unconscious.[116]

⊙

The post-1968 Lyotard, with his libidinal preoccupations and celebration of unconstrained desire, may seem a long way from an appreciative reader of Levinas's austere defense of ethical rigor, feminine modesty, and ritual observance. And in fact, *Discours, figure* and the collection immediately following contain only passing and not always unreservedly positive references to Levinas's work.[117] And yet in two other essays written in 1969 and 1970, Lyotard showed how important Levinas's ruminations on the

114. Ibid., p. 171.

115. Ibid., p. 177.

116. Lyotard's extreme hostility to the representational function of film has earned him the reproach of Maureen Turim, who notes, "The danger of a purely Lyotardian analysis is that, in its concentration on the description of the apparatus of libidinal engagement, it tends to ignore the representation that remains in the art object. Once this release of the imaginary is accompanied by representational elements, it becomes important to consider how concepts such as architecture, landscape, bodies, violence, curiosity and memory are being presented." "The Place of Visual Illusions," in *The Cinematic Apparatus*, ed. Teresa de Lauretis and Stephen Heath (New York, 1985), pp. 146–147. For further critical reflections that treat the unexamined gender assumptions of his argument, see Jacqueline Rose, "The Cinematic Apparatus: Problems in Current Theory," in de Lauretis and Heath, pp. 179ff.

117. In *Discourse, figure*, for example, he contrasts Levinas's argument that ethical prescriptions involve listening alone with his own defense of the eye (p. 12). He also criticizes Derrida's attempt to read Levinas in somewhat Hegelian terms as reconciling eye and ear (p. 48).

Jewish taboo on graven images had become in his thinking. The second of these, the intricately argued "Jewish Oedipus," has already been mentioned in the context of the French philo-Semitic reception of Freud. Here Lyotard sets up an opposition between Greek tragedy, exemplified by Sophocles's *Oedipus*, and Jewish ethics, which he claims is manifest in Shakespeare's *Hamlet*. The difference between them begins with the hero's ability in the former to realize his incestuous desires, whose consequences are then representable on the theatrical stage. In the latter, however, the hero fails to accomplish his forbidden goal and remains always beholden to the prohibiting word of the Other (the Father's no). "Oedipus fulfills his fate of desire" Lyotard writes; "the fate of Hamlet is the non-fulfillment of desire; this chiasma is the one that extends between what is Greek and what is Jewish, between the tragic and the ethical."[118]

Also prohibited in the Jewish scenario is a speculative dialectic of reconciliation, either between the son and mother or the son and father.[119] Nor is there any reconciliation within the self, which remains permanently "dispossessed" by the imperatives of the Other. There can be therefore no anamnestic totalization, such as that posited by Platonic philosophy. Not surprisingly, the taboo on graven images is at the root of this impossibility: "In Hebraic ethics representation is forbidden, the eye closes, the ear opens in order to hear the father's word. The image figure is rejected because of its fulfillment of desire and delusion; its function of truth is denied. . . . Thus one does not *speculate*, one does not ontologize, as Emmanuel Levinas would say."[120]

Another casualty of the Jewish taboo is the Greek search for knowledge, which is based on the notion of truth as representable in language. Instead, Jewish truth "works" rather than speaks; in psychoanalytic terms, it is like the dream-work or acting out rather than representation. "The

---

118. Lyotard, "Jewish Oedipus," *Driftworks*, ed. Roger McKeon (New York, 1984), p. 42.

119. The role of the daughter is never really discussed in these analyses. Her potential reconciliation with the mother, so important for feminists like Irigaray, is never explored.

120. Lyotard, "Jewish Oedipus," p. 42.

ethical rejection," Lyotard claims, "affects not only ontological fulfillment, that of Christ, but also that of cognition, the Odyssey of knowledge."[121] Through a complex reading of the triangulated relationships in *Hamlet*, Lyotard tries to show that Hamlet's murder of Polonius is an acting out that does not know—cannot represent to its perpetrator—its true motives. He then extrapolates this analysis to make sense of Freud's controversial account of Moses in *Moses and Monotheism*.

> Just as Hamlet by killing Polonius on the other stage will fail to recognize his parricidal desire and remain seized by the task intimated by the voice, in the same way the Hebrew people—by killing Moses in an *acting-out*—forgoes recognizing itself as the father's murderer and cuts off the path of reconciliation, the one traced by the desire to see: the Christian path that announces at its end the vision of the father.[122]

Psychoanalysis itself, he concludes, partakes of the Jewish taboos against specularity, anamnestic totalization, theatricality, and visual presence. There is, however, one salient difference between it and its religious avatar which is enabled by Freud's atheism: the renounced desire to see could be transformed into a desire to know, which explains the scientific pretensions of the theory. But alongside the language of knowledge in Freud, Lyotard insisted, there is always the truth work of desire that disrupts the project of full cognition, undermining the Greek dream of beautiful form and visual presence, even in its modern scientific guise.

Where does the prohibited image go then in Judaism? Lyotard's remarkable—even outrageous—answer can be found in the essay he composed late in 1968, but which was not published until sixteen years later, entitled "Figure Foreclosed."[123] Composed originally for a conference on

121. Ibid., p. 44.

122. Ibid., p. 52.

123. The essay first appeared in *L'Écrit du Temps*, 5 (Winter, 1984), preceded by Lyotard's explanation for the delay and followed by no fewer than seven responses. In English, it appears in *The Lyotard Reader*, from which the following quotations come.

Freud and the question of the figure, it was by its author's own admission a "brutal" and "wicked text,"[124] whose delay may well have been due to Lyotard's own hesitations about its potentially misunderstood content. And indeed, one of the seven respondents provided by the journal in which it finally did appear pointed to certain uncomfortable echoes of language found in anti-Semites like Edouard Drumont.[125]

Lyotard's provocative premise was that Judaism must be understood as a form of psychopathology. And yet, "Figure Foreclosed" should not be read as a convoluted exercise in anti-Semitism. For in the context of Lyotard's distrust of conventional notions of psychological "health," an attitude evident in the mutual admiration between him and Deleuze and Guattari, the attribution of pathology must be understood with some irony. Judaism is also described in the essay as patriarchal, a charge that is linked with its hostility to images. But here too there was room for misunderstanding. For Lyotard's position cannot be simply reduced to a conventional feminist critique of inequality, especially if his debt to Levinas, whose work he was reading at the time, is recalled.[126]

"Figure Foreclosed" begins with two epigraphs from Freud concerning the likely existence of mother-goddesses prior to father-gods. Lyotard then speculates that Freud himself shared the Jewish loss of memory of such goddesses, a loss that must be understood as evidence of a kind of psychic illness. "The science he founded has not fully recovered from the religious malady," Lyotard writes, "and . . . inherits from it that overestimation of the father which Freud sees as its major symptom."[127] Along with the repression of the mother goes a certain hostility to images, evident both in Judaism and psychoanalysis.[128] For, according to Lyotard, "the mother is visible; the father is not. . . . The father is a voice, not a figure. He is not initially situated in the visible world."[129]

124. Lyotard, "Contre-temps," L'Écrit du Temps, 5, (Winter, 1984), p. 64.

125. Léon Poliakov, "Une Lettre," L'Écrit du Temps, 5 (Winter, 1984), p. 117.

126. Lyotard notes his concurrent reading of Levinas in "Contre-temps," p. 63. For a similar analysis of the relation between the Jewish taboo and the rejection of the mother, written in 1978, see Goux, "Moïse, Freud: La prescription iconoclaste," in Les iconoclastes.

What then is the nature of the psychopathology that produces the loss of the visible mother and the domination of the invisible father's voice? Freud himself had considered religion, Judaism included, as a kind of collective obsessional neurosis,[130] but Lyotard introduced a more radical explanation. Borrowing, with some license,[131] Lacan's notion of foreclosure or *foreclusion* (Freud's *Verwerfung*) as opposed to repression (*Verdrängung*), he argued that the Jewish hostility to images expressed a kind of psychosis. Whereas repression still permitted what was problematic to remain in the unconscious, allowing it to be displaced, condensed, and so forth in neurotic symptoms amenable to transferential projection and ultimate working through, foreclosure did not. Repression, that is, included "thing-presentations" in the psyche, like the visual representations in the dream-work, not just "word-representations." Foreclosure, in contrast, meant the intolerance of such problematic material, which was cast

127. Lyotard, "Figure Foreclosed," p. 70.

128. He notes, however, that in *Moses and Monotheism* a certain revenge of the figural can be discerned, despite all of Freud's efforts to banish it. This argument is similar to the one cited above concerning the ambiguities in psychoanalysis toward knowledge.

129. Lyotard, "Figure Foreclosed," p. 85. One might ask for whom the mother is visible. For surely, the neonate can have no visible memory of the body from which he or she came. The link must be made by those who witness the birth and who then tell the child who his or her mother is. It is also arguable that the mother's voice plays as crucial a role as her visible presence. For a discussion of this issue, see Kaja Silverman, *The Acoustic Mirror: The Female Voice in Psychoanalysis and Cinema* (Bloomington, Ind., 1988).

130. Freud, "Obsessive Actions and Religious Practices," *Standard Edition*, ed. James Strachey, vol. 9 (London, 1959). This 1907 paper provided the kernel of Freud's later ruminations on religion. For an overview, see Paul W. Pruyser, "Sigmund Freud and His Legacy: Psychoanalytic Psychology of Religion," in *Beyond the Classics? Essays in the Scientific Study of Religion*, ed. Charles Y. Glock and Phillip E. Hammond (New York, 1973).

131. One of his respondents, Isi Beller, in fact complained that Lyotard displayed an inadequate understanding of Lacan's meaning. See his "Le Juif pervers," *L'Écrit du Temps*, 5 (Winter, 1984), pp. 138ff. If, however, it is recalled that Lacan's notion of foreclosure was built on his earlier concept of scotomization, then Lyotard's emphasis on its visual dimension will not seem so strained.

out of the psyche instead. (*Verwerfung*, it will be recalled, literally means "thrown out.")

The result of this process was hallucinatory psychosis rather than dreams or transference neuroses, approaching a kind of schizophrenia.[132] The motivation for so violent a rejection was extreme castration anxiety. Once fusion with the visible mother was prohibited by the incest taboo and the threat of castration, all nostalgia for goddess-mothers had to be abandoned on the collective level. All that was left is the attenuated yearning for surrogate gratifications through what Lacan called "objects a." "This is the sense reality," Lyotard writes, "with its immanent transcendence, the maternal reality which Merleau-Ponty wanted to uncover beneath the perceptions articulated in language, and which Levinas rejects as false transcendence."[133] That is, whereas phenomenology continues the futile Greek and Christian search for visual plenitude, for reconciliation with the mother via sublimation, the Jewish taboo on graven images remains entirely on the side of the invisible father, the sayer of the word.

Psychoanalysis is only an imperfect manifestation of the psychosis that produced Judaism, because on one level Freud actually tried to *be* the father (of his new science) rather than listen to the father's word. It is nonetheless the mark of psychoanalysis's greatness that it generally prefers to observe the law (in the sense of obeying the word) rather than observe the world (in the sense of seeing it). That more than one religious tradition or one psychological theory is at stake, Lyotard implied, is shown by the importance of the Jewish "psychosis" for launching nothing less than the West's historicity, which he identified not with intelligible metanarratives of dialectical reconciliation, but rather with the succession of eternally nonrecurring events. "When castration is foreclosed," he wrote, "culpability evades all reconciliation, all mediation with or by reality which is posited as a co-creature, as a witness to the ordeal. This is the price that has to

132. Ibid., p. 82. One of his respondents, Eugène Enriquez, claimed that paranoia rather than schizophrenia best characterizes the Jewish collective pathology, for what is really foreclosed is the murder of the father. See "Un peuple immortel?" *L'Écrit du Temps*, 5 (Winter, 1984), pp. 131ff.

133. Ibid., p. 86.

be paid if history is to begin. . . . Historicity presupposes foreclosure, and the renunciation of compromise, myth and figure, the exclusion of female or filial mediation, a face to face encounter with a faceless other."[134]

Efforts to "cure" this psychosis by reabsorbing the foreclosed image into the collective psyche of mankind, turning history into a story of redemption, Lyotard explicitly rejected as dialectical mystification: "The dialectic is the expanded form of the neurotic symptom known as compromise formation. In so far as they are dialectical forms of thought and practices, Christianity, Hegelianism and 'marxism' must be numbered amongst the many attempts that have been made to reach a compromise, those (futile) attempts to restore the West from psychosis to neurosis."[135] Thus, although it may appear as if characterizing Judaism as a psychotic repudiation of the mother would betoken disdain for its legacy, Lyotard in fact implied the very opposite: the "malady" is more liberating than the "cure," insofar as it frees us from the vain hope of reconciliation and fusion. The wandering Jew is an emblem of the radical heterogeneity that makes history possible.[136]

The writings that followed Lyotard's libidinal economy phase, for all their abiding protestations of pagan polytheism,[137] gave evidence of the

---

134. Ibid., pp. 95–96. Significantly, he cites Levinas's *Quatre lectures talmudiques* (Paris, 1976) in support of this claim.

135. Ibid.

136. For Lyotard's general views on history, see his "The Sign of History," in *Post-Structuralism and the Question of History*, ed. Derek Attridge, Geoff Bennington, and Robert Young (Cambridge, 1987).

137. Such protestations were not, to be sure, meaningless. They did reflect his refusal to embrace the fundamental religious premise of Levinas's position. In his conversation with Jean-Loup Thébaud, Lyotard explained that his paganism "consists in the fact that each [language] game is played as such, which implies that it does not give itself as the game of all the other games or as the true one. This is why the other day I was saying that I was betraying Levinas because it is obvious that the very way in which I take over his doctrine or his theory, or his description of the prescriptive, is alien to his own. In his view, it is the transcendental character of the other in the prescriptive relation, in the pragmatics of prescription, that is, in the (barely) lived experience of obligation, that is truth itself. This 'truth' is not ontological truth, it is ethical. But it is a truth in Levinas's own terms. Whereas for me, it cannot be the truth"(*Just Gaming*, trans. Wlad Godzich [Minneapolis, 1985], p. 60).

presence of Levinas's privileging of Jewish over Greek attitudes even more explicitly than before. For now he no longer needed to find the ground of unintelligibility in transgressive desire; he could find them instead in the incommensurability of language games. Most notably he could argue that the ethical language game, that of prescriptives based on the command from the other, could never be reconciled with the language game of description based on the visible presence of ontological reality. No longer calling on the figure-matrix in the unconscious as an antidote to linguistic imperialism, he thus tacitly dropped the complicated "defense of the eye" motivating his antistructuralist writings of the 1960s and early 1970s.[138]

Just Gaming, Lyotard's dialogue on justice with Jean-Loup Thébaud of 1979, liberally drew on Levinas's categorical distinction between ontology and ethics, the language games of understanding and obligation.[139] In *The Differend* of 1983, in which "regimes of phrases" replaced the apparently still too humanist notion of language games, a long excursus on Levinas formed the backbone of the chapter on obligation. Here the I's blindness, the abandonment of its narcissistic image, is praised for preventing prescriptive phrase regimes from being derived from descriptive ones.[140] Even Lyotard's newfound admiration for Kant was tempered by his realization that Levinas provided a more rigorous repudiation of metalinguistic "images" of prescriptive commands.[141] And when he was compelled to enter

138. In *Peregrinations*, Lyotard would wonder if *Discourse, figure* "remains too close to a conception of the unconscious coming directly from Freud," and he reproached himself for forgetting "that the polymorphic paganism of exploring and exploiting the whole range of intensive forms could easily by swept away into lawful permissiveness, including violence and terror" (pp. 11, 15).

139. Lyotard and Thébaud, *Just Gaming*; see especially pp. 22, 25, 35, 37, 41, 45, 60, 64, 69, and 71. Philippe Lacoue-Labarthe was correct to say to Lyotard, "You go so far as to take up for yourself the motif of 'the otherwise of being' and of the Jewish refusal of ontology, as well as that of the 'passivity' (of the absolute privilege of the receiver previous to the distinction between activity and passivity, autonomy and heteronomy)" ("Talks," *Diacritics*, 14, 3 [Fall, 1984], p. 30).

140. Lyotard, *The Differend*, pp. 166ff.

141. See especially Lyotard, "Levinas' Logic," in Cohen, *Face to Face with Levinas*, pp. 130ff.

the heated French debate over Heidegger's politics in the late 1980s, he explicitly drew on Levinas's analysis to criticize Heidegger's mistaken belief that freedom was a function of Being rather than obedience to the ethical Law.[142]

It was, however, in Lyotard's influential discussion of postmodernism that his Levinas-inflected critique of ocularcentrism fully came into its own. This is not the place to attempt yet another sorting out of the various meanings that have accrued to the term in the past two decades,[143] and even less to launch another rocket in the (increasingly tiresome) battle over its implications. Suffice it to say that Lyotard's 1979 report to the Conseil des Universités of the Government of Quebec, *The Postmodern Condition: A Report on Knowledge,* along with his 1982 essay "Answering the Question: What Is Postmodernism?" provided an international rallying point for the dispute, especially when they were counterposed to Habermas's celebrated statement of 1980, "Modernity—An Incomplete Project."[144]

Although much of the attention was focused on Lyotard's identification of postmodernism with incredulity toward emancipatory metanarratives and the rejection of rational metadiscourses of legitimation, his argument

142. Lyotard, *Heidegger and "the jews,"* trans. Andreas Michel and Mark S. Roberts (Minneapolis, 1990), pp. 81, 84, and 89. Lyotard explains the entire anti-Semitic tradition in terms of Western culture's inability to accept a people—he calls them "the jews" with a lower case to suggest more than an empirical category—who represent an ethical "otherness" beyond Being. He also draws on his earlier analysis of the antidialectical, anticonciliatory nature of Jewish wandering, which he interprets partly in psychoanalytic terms.

143. For a helpful survey, see Allan Megill, "What Does the Term 'Postmodernism' Mean?" *Annals of Scholarship,* 6 (1989), pp. 129–151.

144. Both of Lyotard's works are available in English as *The Postmodern Condition: A Report on Knowledge,* trans. Geoff Bennington and Brian Massumi (Minneapolis, 1984). Habermas's essay can be found in Foster, ed., *The Anti-Aesthetic.* For an important example of the many attempts to comment on the debate, see Richard Rorty, "Habermas and Lyotard on Postmodernity," in *Habermas and Modernism,* ed. Richard J. Bernstein (Cambridge, Mass., 1985). For my own thoughts on the issues in the debate, see "Habermas and Modernism" and "Habermas and Postmodernism," in *Fin-de-siècle Socialism and Other Essays* (New York, 1988).

also made important claims concerning the visual issues so prominent elsewhere in his work. Indirectly, they appeared in his attack on the alleged goal of communicative transparency in Habermas, which rehearsed the arguments Foucault and others make against Rousseau. Similarly, his critique of a single narrative of history was reminiscent of that rejection of "Icarian, high-altitude thinking" already noted in Bataille, Merleau-Ponty, de Certeau, and other critics of the totalizing gaze from afar. "The idea," he warned, "that thinking is able to build a system of total knowledge about clouds of thought by passing from one site to another and accumulating the views it produces at each site—such an idea constitutes *par excellence* the sin, the arrogance of the mind."[145]

More directly, Lyotard's debt to the antiocularcentric discourse was evident in the most fundamental criterion he provided for distinguishing between modernism and postmodernism: their respective attitudes toward the aesthetics of the sublime first developed by Longinus in third-century A.D. Greece and then resurrected by Boileau in the seventeenth century and Burke and Kant in the eighteenth. The sublime, Lyotard was careful to point out, should not be confused, as Habermas failed to realize,[146] with the Freudian notion of sublimation. The latter, as already noted, he identified with reconciliation and the search for plenitudinous visual presence. The sublime, in contrast, was the experience that "alludes to something which can't be shown or presented (as Kant said, *dargestellt*)."[147] It occurs only "when the imagination fails to present an object which might, if only in principle, come to match a concept."[148] In a certain sense, it was the opposite of Greek tragedy with its theatrical representation of reconciliation. As Burke noted, "the sublime was no longer a matter of elevation (the category by which Aristotle defined tragedy), but a matter of intensification."[149]

145. Lyotard, *Peregrinations*, pp. 6–7.
146. Lyotard, *The Postmodern Condition*, p. 79.
147. Lyotard, "The Sublime and the Avant-Garde," *The Lyotard Reader*, p. 197.
148. Lyotard, *The Postmodern Condition*, p. 78.
149. Lyotard, "The Sublime and the Avant-Garde," p. 205.

Modern and postmodern art both instantiate an aesthetics of the sublime, but with an important difference. For modernism still remains nostalgic for something lost.

> It allows the unpresentable to be put forward only as the missing contents; but the form, because of its recognizable consistency, continues to offer to the reader or viewer matter for solace and pleasure. Yet these sentiments do not constitute the real sublime sentiment, which is an intrinsic combination of pleasure and pain: the pleasure that reason should exceed all presentation, the pain that imagination or sensibility should not be equal to the concept.[150]

Those misguided interpretations of modern art, such as Kojève's of Wassily Kandinsky, which seek in abstraction a version of total optical purity, are thus covertly Hegelian in their lament for a lost totality.[151] Postmodernism, in contrast, is willing to live with the pain of unrepresentability. It eagerly embraces, Lyotard implied, the psychopathology of the Jewish taboo on images and rejects any nostalgia for reunification with the mother.

That Lyotard's valorization of the postmodern sublime was closely tied to his Levinasian reading of the taboo is abundantly clear in his frequent references to Kant's evocation of the key passage in *Exodus* prohibiting images as the very model of the sublime. Not only does such a citation appear at a crucial point in *The Postmodern Condition*, but it surfaces as well in at least three other places in his work.[152] Invidiously contrasting,

150. Lyotard, *The Postmodern Condition*, p. 81.

151. Lyotard, "Philosophy and Painting in the Age of Their Experimentation: Contribution to an Idea of Postmodernity," *The Lyotard Reader*, p. 187.

152. Lyotard, *The Postmodern Condition*, p. 78; "Newman: The Instant," *The Lyotard Reader*, p. 246; "The Sublime and the Avant-Garde," p. 204; "The Sign of History," p. 172. Once again, the same argument appears in Goux's "Moïse, Freud: La prescription iconoclaste," where Freud's admiration for Michelangelo's statue of Moses as sublime rather than beautiful is tied explicitly to the notion of unrepresentability (p. 18). Interestingly, neither Lyotard or Goux discusses Hegel's equally insistent identification of Judaism as a "religion of sublimity."

as did Levinas, totality and infinity, Lyotard also embraced Kant's claim that "optical pleasure when reduced to near nothingness promotes an infinite contemplation of infinity."[153] And he endorsed as well Kant's belief, which anticipated both Bataille's celebration of *informe* and Levinas's critique of Hellenism, that "formlessness, the absence of form" is "a possible index to the unpresentable."[154]

When Lyotard helped curate a postmodern "manifestation" or "nonexhibition" at the Centre Georges Pompidou in the spring of 1985, entitled "Les Immatériaux," he attempted to demonstrate the links between his ideas and new technologies, such as videos, holographs, satellites, and computers.[155] Seeking to evoke the disappearance of a material world visible to the scientific gaze, the show led its visitors, or rather allowed them to wander mapless, through a maze of some sixty-one different "zones," which culminated in a space filled with word-processing and data-storing devices. It was not surprisingly called "the labyrinth of language." As John Rajchman has noted, "In the world of 'Les Immatériaux,' everything starts in the body and ends in language. . . . [It] was a phenomenologist's nightmare; everywhere one was shown the replacement of the material activities of the 'lived body' with artificial ones, or with formal or immaterial languages. One entered a world of simulation of the body."[156]

As they meandered, the visitors listened to earphones, which pumped a

153. Lyotard, "The Sublime and the Avant-garde," p. 204.

154. Lyotard, *The Postmodern Condition*, p. 78. Lyotard would continue to rely on the notion of the Jews as the inassimilable other of Western theoretical discourse in later works, such as *Heidegger and "the jews."*

155. There was no ordinary catalogue accompanying "Les Immatériaux," but instead several texts produced by the interaction of different authors on computers and notes showing facsimiles of sketches and work documents for the show. In addition, two ancillary books were published: Élie Théofilakis, *Modernes et après? "Les Immatériaux"* (Paris, 1985) and *"1984" et les présents de l'univers informationnel* (Paris, 1985). For an attempt to relate Lyotard's work to computers, see Mark Poster, *The Mode of Information: Poststructuralism and Social Context* (Chicago, 1990), chap. 5. For an excellent account of the exhibition's importance, see John Rajchman, "The Postmodern Museum," *Art in America*, 73, 10 (October, 1985).

156. Rajchman, "The Postmodern Museum," pp. 114 and 116.

melange of texts into their ears depending on the change in their location. No coherent narrative made the journey through the maze meaningful, but a sense, often manic, of temporality was fostered nonetheless. "One of the preponderant dimensions of postmodernity," Lyotard and his colleagues explained, "is time; its conquest is one of the latest challenges. The manifestation introduces for the first time this parameter in privileging sonoral communication (tied to the flow of time) in relation to visual communication."[157]

Visual stimulation remained, even if it didn't lead to much communication. In fact, "Les Immatériaux" provided many examples of simulated images in which "reality" was metamorphosed and hybridized into simulacra of hyperreality.[158] Appropriately, one of the voices in the earphones was that of Baudrillard, prophesizing the arrival of the era of the simulacrum. As a result, the exhibition suggested an implicit answer to a crucial question Lyotard himself never squarely addressed: What happens to the foreclosed visual material thrown out of the psyche? If psychoanalysis could talk of the return of the repressed, what of the return of the foreclosed? The answer may be precisely that phantasmagoric realm of images without referents, "the precession of simulacra" that Baudrillard identifies with the present cultural order. The postmodern suspicion of the visual, paradoxically fueled by Lyotard's pagan appropriation of Levinas's arguments against the Greeks, is thus best understood as the reverse side of its celebration of the hyperreal simulacrum, rather than the simple negation of that celebration. Whereas in the case of Lyotard (and the Jewish tradition as Levinas presented it), the figure was foreclosed, in the case of Baudrillard's "hypervisuality," it might be said that reality was foreclosed instead. In both cases, what was lost was any hope for clarity of meaning and transparency of understanding. In both, the modernist faith that visuality and rationality can be reconciled was decisively rejected. What is

157. "Les Immatériaux," Centre National d'Art et de Culture Georges-Pompidou, brochure, p. 2.

158. *Modernes et après* contains several texts dealing with their implications, e.g., Edmond Couchet, "Hybridations," and Jean-Louis Weissberg, "Simuler—interagir —s'hybrider = Le Sujet rentrer sur scène."

perceived by the senses and what makes sense are split asunder. Not surprisingly, the dominant emotion evoked by this outcome was, as Lyotard frankly admitted in discussing "Les Immatériaux," mourning and melancholy for the lost illusions of modernism.[159] All that was left, he defiantly concluded, was "to reflect according to opacity."[160] All we postmoderns can do is wander aimlessly, as through the rooms of the Centre Pompidou, amidst the shifting clouds that are our disparate thoughts. "One cloud casts its shadow on another, the shape of clouds varies with the angle from which they are approached."[161] But the sun can never shine through them to illuminate our way.

159. Lyotard, "A Conversation with Jean-François Lyotard," *Flash Art* (March, 1985), p. 33.
160. Lyotard, "Philosophy and Painting in the Age of Their Experimentation," p. 193.
161. Lyotard, *Peregrinations*, p. 5.

Conclusion

It is now time to land our high-flying balloon and consider what has been gained by its bumpy voyage over the landscape of recent French thought on vision and visuality. The trip began by acknowledging how thoroughly infused our language is by visual metaphors, how ineluctable, to borrow Joyce's celebrated phrase, is the modality of the visible, not merely as perceptual experience, but also as cultural trope. It thus seemed fruitful to follow the unfolding of a loose discourse about visuality, rather than try to document actual transformations in sensual practices.

Inevitably, the interaction of such practices—whether based on technical enhancements of the ability to see or on social/political mobilizations of the results—with the discourse itself has had to be acknowledged. And the no less significant exchange between developments in the visual arts and the theoretical discussion surrounding them has had to be considered as well. For there is no privileged vantage point outside the hermeneutic circle of sight as perceptual experience, social practice, and discursive construct.

And yet, by focusing more of our attention on the French discourse about the visual than on visual practices per se, certain benefits, I hope, have accrued. First, a welter of overlapping attitudes, arguments, and assumptions shared by a large number of otherwise disparate thinkers has become apparent as never before. Virtually all the twentieth-century French intellectuals encountered on this voyage were extraordinarily sensitive to the importance of the visual and no less suspicious of its implications. Although definitions of visuality vary from thinker to thinker, it is clear that ocularcentrism aroused (and continues in many quarters to arouse) a widely shared distrust. Bergson's critique of the spatialization of time, Bataille's celebration of the blinding sun and the acephalic body, Breton's ultimate disenchantment with the savage eye, Sartre's depiction of the sadomasochism of the "look," Merleau-Ponty's diminished faith in a new ontology of vision, Lacan's disparagement of the ego produced by the mirror stage, Althusser's appropriation of Lacan for a Marxist theory of ideology, Foucault's strictures against the medical gaze and panoptic surveillance, Debord's critique of the society of the spectacle, Barthes's linkage of photography and death, Metz's excoriation of the scopic regime of the cinema, Derrida's double reading of the specular tradition of philosophy and the white mythology, Irigaray's outrage at the privileging of the visual in patriarchy, Levinas's claim that ethics is thwarted by a visually based ontology, and Lyotard's identification of postmodernism with the sublime foreclosure of the visual—all these evince, to put it mildly, a palpable loss of confidence in the hitherto "noblest of the senses."

Antiocularcentrism in several cases turned, in fact, into hostility to sight in virtually any of its forms. Critiques of specific historical manifestations of visuality worked cumulatively to discredit vision per se, and the effects were evident not only in France. For in the Anglo-American reception of French thought beginning in the 1970s, many of the same complaints were quickly echoed. Pragmatist philosophers like Richard Rorty, reprising John Dewey's earlier critique of the "spectator theory of knowledge," anthropologists like Stephen Tyler and David Howe, building on the media critiques of Marshall McLuhan and Walter Ong, film critics like Laura Mulvey and Mary Ann Doane, yoking together apparatus theory and the feminist suspicion of the male gaze, art historians like

Rosalind Krauss and Hal Foster, rebelling against the fetish of opticality in traditional modernist theory, students of photography like John Tagg and Abigail Solomon-Godeau, rejecting the formalist defense of photography's claim to aesthetic value, were all inspired to one degree or another by the French antiocularcentric discourse. By 1990, Fredric Jameson could effortlessly invoke its full authority in the opening words of his *Signatures of the Visible*: "The visible is *essentially* pornographic, which is to say that it has its end in rapt, mindless fascination; thinking about its attributes becomes an adjunct to that, if it is unwilling to betray its object."[1] Such a salutary "betrayal," it should now be apparent, had become almost second nature to many French theorists and those they inspired elsewhere.

Second, the extent to which the critique of ocularcentrism has helped fuel the concomitant weakening of faith among French intellectuals—and not them alone—in what can be broadly called the modern project of enlightenment has also become manifest. The sole scopic regime of modernity cannot be identified *tout court* with Cartesian perspectivalism; and yet, time and again precisely such a premise underlay many of the critiques of modernity so powerful among the thinkers examined in this study. Although it would be a mistake to turn the interrogation of the eye into nothing but a mere metaphor for a counter-Enlightenment debunking of rational lucidity—metaphors of this power are anything but "mere"—there is evident truth in the claim that they have often been intertwined. For when the visual is cast out of the rational psyche, it can return in the form of hallucinatory simulacra that mock the link between sense (as meaning) and the sense of sight.

But third, it cannot be denied that for all its hyperbolic rhetoric, for all its inclination to demonize, the antiocularcentric discourse has successfully posed substantial and troubling questions about the status of visuality in the dominant cultural traditions of the West. It has weakened any residual belief in the claim that thought can be disentangled entirely from the sensual mediations through which it passes, or that language can be

1. Fredric Jameson, *Signatures of the Visible* (London, 1990), p. 1.

shorn entirely of its sensual metaphoricality. It has shown the costs of assuming the eye, however it is understood, is a privileged medium of knowledge or an innocent instrument in human interaction. It has also highlighted the ways in which the concomitant denigration of other senses brings with it certain cultural losses that warrant redress. And finally, it has posed the vital question, how open is our sensual interaction with the world to radical change? Although an equally ruthless critique of the costs of privileging other senses might result in conclusions no less troubling, there can be no doubt that the French obsession with vision and visuality has proven extraordinarily productive.

A certain caution about the uncritical acceptance of all the discourse's implications may, to be sure, seem warranted. The figures who have contributed to its elaboration might, for example, be dismissed as mandarin intellectuals distrustful of the visual pleasures provided by modern mass culture. As such, they may appear open to the charge of playing the time-honored role of the privileged literate class disdainful of unlettered, mere pleasure-seeking hoi polloi. Only those who possess the power of the word, it might be argued, dread what Jacques Ellul calls its humiliation; only those who think themselves above the lust of the eyes, it might be claimed, resist the delights of the spectacle. For isn't there a covert asceticism in the denial of the pleasures of the gaze, even accounting for its often gendered bias?

But such reproaches, it can be argued in return, fail to do justice to the complexities of the antiocularcentric discourse, whose fascination with visual experience often betrays a keen attraction to its pleasurable side. Breton, Bataille, Merleau-Ponty, Foucault, Barthes, and Lyotard are all thinkers, after all, who show a keen personal appreciation of the lust of the eyes; even Metz has to resist a constant temptation to be seduced by the cinema. And when many of them do criticize the eye, it is for its supposed disincarnated coldness, which they contrast to the more proximate pleasures provided by other sense organs. As for the alleged elitism in their critique, there is no necessary connection between privileging language over perception—assuming this is what they in fact do—and the maintenance of cultural hierarchy. Indeed, those who control the production and dissemination of images may be as much of an elite as those who protest the power of those images over the masses. In short, the antiocularcentric discourse cannot be dismissed by turning it into little more than a weapon in the struggle over cultural capital.

Nor can it be undone by positing a normative notion of visuality which it fails to appreciate. If anything, this study shows the impossibility of assuming such a *point d'appui* exists. Although the introduction resisted a completely constructionist concept of the visual by citing recent scientific literature about the functions and limitations of the eye, it would be problematic to assume that the scientific debate over vision has itself reached a definitive conclusion. As the recent work of Jonathan Crary has so persuasively shown,[2] it was not so long ago that scientific certainties about visual experience were overturned in favor of others, which may also one day have their successors. Although there is much to be learned from experiments in the mechanics and physiognomics of sight, that complex mix of natural and cultural phenomena called visuality defies reduction to any normative model based on scientific data alone.

Indeed, it is precisely the proliferation of models of visuality that the antiocularcentric discourse, for all its fury against the ones it distrusts, tacitly encourages. Ocular-*ec*centricity rather than blindness, it might be argued, is the antidote to privileging any one visual order or scopic regime. What might be called "the dialectics of seeing"[3] precludes the reification of scopic regimes. Rather than calling for the exorbitation or enucleation of "the eye," it is better to encourage the multiplication of a thousand eyes, which, like Nietzsche's thousand suns, suggests the openness of human possibilities. Even the putatively voyeuristic "male gaze," a number of feminist film critics have come to acknowledge, can be understood as far more dispersed and plural than might seem at first glance.

2. Jonathan Crary, *Techniques of the Observer: On Vision and Modernity in the Nineteenth Century* (Cambridge, Mass., 1990).

3. Susan Buck-Morss uses this phrase as the title of her arresting account of Benjamin's search for "dialectical images" amidst the debris of bourgeois culture. *The Dialectics of Seeing: Walter Benjamin and the Arcades Project* (Cambridge, Mass., 1989).

A "women's cinema," they have argued, must do more than demonize visuality and the "apparatus" of film as necessarily complicitous with partriarchy; a more specifically female spectatorship should be nurtured as well.[4] When "the" story of the eye is understood as a polyphonic—or rather, polyscopic—narrative, we are in less danger of being trapped in an evil empire of the gaze, fixated in a single mirror stage of development, or frozen by the medusan, ontologizing look of the other. Permanently "downcast eyes" are no solution to these and other dangers in visual experience.

Among those visually infused practices that deserve a second look is that of enlightenment itself. Disillusionment with the project of illumination is now so widespread that it has become the new conventional wisdom. As Peter Sloterdijk observes in his magisterial account of the triumph of cynical over critical reason, "There is, to be concise, not only a crisis of enlightenment, not only a crisis of the enlighteners, but even a crisis in the praxis of enlightenment, in *commitment* to enlightenment."[5] Even as loyal a defender of the enlightenment project as Jürgen Habermas feels compelled, however reluctantly, to call the present era that of "Die neue Unübersichtlichkeit," "the new unsurveyability."[6] This multilevel crisis has many sources, and certainly the denigration of ocularcentrism is among them. Although by no means all of the protagonists in the history

4. See, for example, Teresa de Lauretis, who writes, "The project of women's cinema, therefore, is no longer that of destroying or disrupting man-centered vision by representing its blind spots, its gaps or its repressed. The effort and challenge now are to effect another vision: to construct other objects and subjects of vision, and to formulate the conditions of representability of another social subject" ("Aesthetic and Feminist Theory: Rethinking Women's Cinema," *New German Critique*, 34 [Winter, 1985], p. 163).

5. Peter Sloterdijk, *Critique of Cynical Reason*, trans. Michael Eldred (Minneapolis, 1987), p. 88.

6. Jürgen Habermas, *Die neue Unübersichtlichkeit* (Frankfurt, 1985). The English translation of this essay in *The New Conservatism: Cultural Criticism and the Historians' Debate*, trans. Shierry Weber Nicholsen (Cambridge, Mass., 1989) translates it as "the new obscurity," but "unsurveyability" better captures the sense of a lost God's-eye view.

reconstructed in this study lost faith in the efficacy of emancipatory cri- tique, many did weaken its premises by focusing so insistently on the neg- ative side of the dialectic of enLIGHTenment.

If, however, the still faintly visible positive side is not forgotten, it may be possible to salvage something from the debris. It is to that end that this study has risked an Icarian flight above the terrain of a discourse that knows all too well the dangers of approaching the sun. Fully aware that his perspective is not that of the figures on the ground (if, indeed, the meta- phor of ground is itself still viable in an age when philosophical founda- tions are routinely undermined), its author nonetheless hopes that he has provided some useful understanding of a discursive network that remains largely invisible at sea level.

Perhaps, to be sure, postmodern culture has gone beyond the point where a naive belief in the enlightening power of such endeavors can still be maintained. Perhaps we no longer need to worry about the benign ef- fects of the eye, or even its evil ones. In a parable about the current state of the human sciences, Michel Serres claims that contemporary modes of communication, based on codes and computers, have put an end to the reign of "panoptic theory." "The informational world takes the place of the observed world," he writes, "things known because they are seen cede their place to an exchange of codes. Everything changes, everything flows from harmony's victory over surveillance. . . . Pan kills Panoptes: the age of the message kills the age of theory."[7] The eyes of the all-seeing god, he concludes, have been transferred to the plumage of a peacock where "sight looks blankly upon a world from which information has already fled. A disappearing species, only ornamental, the peacock asks us to ad- mire, in the public parks and gardens where the gawkers gather, the old theory of representation."[8]

But judging from the alarm expressed by his compatriots at the omni- present power of the visual, Serres's confidence in so epochal a shift seems

7. Michel Serres, "Panoptic Theory," in Thomas M. Kavanagh, ed., *The Limits of Theory* (Stanford, Calif., 1989), pp. 45–46.
8. Ibid., p. 47.

premature. Representation and theory in their traditional guises may be under assault, surveillance and the spectacle may be widely decried, but the power of visuality has certainly survived the attack. Panoptes has managed to fend off his total transfiguration into the unseeing "eyes" of a peacock's tail (just as the postmodernist foreclosure of the visual into the realm of meaningless simulacra has been less than complete). The invisible, hermeneutic harmony of Pan (the son of Hermes) that Serres claims now reigns in "the age of the message" is still a long way off. And happily so, I would add, for vision and visuality in all their rich and contradictory variety can still provide us mere mortals with insights and perspectives, speculations and observations, enlightenments and illuminations, that even a god might envy.

Index

Abel, Elisabeth, 153n
Abel, Richard, 254n, 459n
Abbot Suger, 41
Abrams, M. H., 91n, 108
Abstraction, 26, 200, 246, 583
 in Renaissance art, 61
 in the French Revolution, 95
Action, 283–284
Adami, Valerio, 517
Adam-Salomon, Antoine Samuel, 138n
Adhémar, Jean, 113n
Adler, Laure, 111n
Adorno, Theodor W., 21n, 115n, 176–177n, 265, 562, 573
Aesthetics, 107, 160, 462, 516, 561, 571
 of framing, 421–423, 517–518
 of the sublime, 583
Agatharcus, 52n
Agulhon, Maurice, 97n
Aimée, 341, 345, 345n, 349
Alberti, Leon Battista, 52, 54, 55, 57, 58, 59, 60n, 61, 63, 133
 grid of, 54, 63
 idea of space, 67–68n

perspectivalism, 97, 189, 195, 315
Alderman, Harold, 271n
Alford, C. Fred, 333n
Alhazen, 38
Al-Kindi, 38
Allen, David W., 11n, 332n
Alloula, Malek, 140n
Alpers, Svetlana, 56n, 60–63, 60n, 61n, 64n, 72, 132–133, 315, 402n
Althusser, Louis, 14, 15, 329n, 331, 370, 372–380, 383, 430, 436, 437, 446, 472
 and ideology, 331, 370–376, 476, 588
 and Lacan, 372–377
American jazz, 238n
American pragmatism, 14n
Anaglyph, 162
Anamorphosis, 48, 48n, 74n, 164, 360, 362–364, 363n, 489, 534, 570
Anaxagoras, 24, 52n
Anderson, Barbara, 466n
Anderson, Joseph, 466n

Bergson, Henri, 14, 25, 135, 147, 149n, 151, 186, 191–208, 228, 239, 263, 266, 270, 283, 302, 310, 347, 418, 428, 498, 550, 557, 588
  and the body, 191–195
  critique of cinema, 164n, 198–201, 254, 311, 436, 460, 488, 572
  durée, 186, 197, 203, 205–207, 208n, 241, 268
  memory, 193, 428
  spatialization of time in, 418, 428, 498, 588
  and time, 81–82, 195–197
  use of images, 202–204
  vitalist bias, 198
Bergsonism, 192
Bergstrom, Janet, 467n, 476n, 490, 490n
Berlin, Isaiah, 106n
Berman, Marshall, 124n
Berman, Russell, 433n
Bernard, Claude, 173
Bernard (Saint), 13, 42
Bernasconi, Robert, 499n
Bernet, Rudolph, 267n
Bernstein, Michèle, 424, 430
Bersani, Leo, 346n
Bertillon, Alphonse, 143
Beufils, Marcel, 265n
Bichat, Marie-Françoise-Xavier, 394n, 405
Binswanger, Ludwig, 386, 387, 388, 413, 567
Birmingham, Peg, 414n
Bischoff, Rita, 216n, 217n
Bishop Berkeley, 73n, 78, 99
Blake, William, 109, 109n, 224–225
Blanc, Charles, 150
Blanchot, Maurice, 230, 388, 395n, 407, 432, 432n, 551–555

Blindness, 43, 99–101, 99n, 110, 260, 363, 390–391, 502, 510–511, 521–522, 580, 591
  in Bataille, 217, 218, 227, 259
  in psychoanalysis, 332
  in religion, 12, 12n
  of seers in Greek culture, 25
Blind spot, 8, 320, 355, 361, 414, 497, 507
Blondel, Eric, 526, 526n
Blumenberg, Hans, 21–22, 24n, 30n, 63, 64, 65n, 123n, 271n
Boccioni, Umberto, 205n
Body, 55, 56–57n, 104, 151, 152, 158, 161, 162, 166, 191–194, 252, 253n, 268, 289–290, 304, 310–311, 316, 405, 413
  against the eye, 161, 192, 379n, 528
  baser functions of, 221–222, 227, 310
  of king, 88
  as instrument of action, 193
  intellectualization of, 86
  as source of visual experience, 152, 155
Boethius, 177
Böhme, Hartmut, 28n, 30n
Bohr, Niels, 200n
Boiffard, Jean-André, 249, 250, 252
Boileau, 582
Bolla, Peter de, 45n
Bolyai, Farkas, 158n
Boman, Thorlieff, 23n
Bonitzer, Pascal, 464, 487
Bonald, Louis de, 106
Bonjour, Michel, 264n
Boorstin, Daniel, 432n
Borch-Jacobsen, Mikkel, 343n
Borcoman, James, 129n
Bordo, Susan R., 81n
Borel, Adrien, 222, 225
Börne, Ludwig, 239n

Chtcheglov, Ivan, 424
Cicero, 31n, 40
Cinema, 132, 135, 164n, 172, 183,
    198–201, 212, 238n, 253–259,
    311, 311n, 421–424, 434,
    436–437, 561, 592. *See also* Film
    apparatus, 444, 471–479, 484,
        486–490
    as deception, 482–483
    and dream, 254, 475
    as moving camera, 473–474
    and politics, 461, 462n, 465,
        469–470, 475–477, 487
    and time, 198–199
Cixous, Hélène, 333n, 491, 493n,
    526, 528, 531
Clair, Jean, 132n, 164n, 165
Clair, René, 254
Clarity, 47–48, 85, 90, 116, 118,
    214, 414, 439, 508, 528
Clark, Kenneth, 13n
Clark, Priscilla Parkhurst, 84n
Clark, T. J., 119, 155, 159, 432
Clarke, Samuel, 99n
Claudel, Paul, 244n, 315
Clay, Reginald S., 65n
Clement of Alexandria, 36
Clément, Catherine, 349n, 370n,
    491, 491n, 526, 531, 532n
Clérambault, Gaëtan Gatian de,
    339–340, 339n, 348n, 350
Clercq, Louis de, 140
Clifford, James, 16, 141n
Cocteau, Jean, 360n, 413, 413n
Cohen, Richard A., 387n, 551n,
    580n
Cohen, Ted, 402n
Cohen-Séat, Gilbert, 464
Cohn, Robert Greer, 178n
Colbert, Jean Baptiste, 88
Coleridge, Samuel Taylor, 108n
Colletti, Lucio, 196n, 418n
Color, 6, 9, 29, 32, 62, 77, 100,

107, 131, 151, 151–152n, 153,
    310
    in Dutch painting, 60
    Impressionists' use of, 154, 158
    in literature, 171–172, 174–177
    Sartre's hostility toward, 281
    theory of, 156
Columbus, Christopher, 63n
Commodity, 58–59, 427, 429, 548
    fetishism, 419
Communism, 237, 312, 372, 373
Comolli, Jean-Louis, 148–149, 154,
    187, 369, 464, 470, 471n, 477,
    477n, 479, 489
Comte, Auguste, 154
Concupiscentia ocularum (ocular
    desire), 13, 57n, 63, 89, 120, 124,
    166, 167, 169, 241, 366, 590
    critics of, 37, 63, 241
    in psychoanalysis, 332, 366, 575
Condillac, Étienne Bonnet de, 85,
    95, 99, 101, 191
Conley, Tom, 450n, 517n, 529n,
    537n
Conrad, Joseph, 153
Consciousness, 86, 192, 266–267,
    284, 290, 318, 345
    versus opacity, 282–283
Constable, John, 139
Constantine, 37
Constructivists, 214n
Cook, Albert, 51, 51n
Cook, Mark, 4, 4n, 7n, 9n, 10–11n
Cook, Pam, 490
Cooper, Barry, 298n
Copernican Revolution, 79
Copjec, Joan, 339n, 369, 471n,
    477n, 489
Corbin, Alain, 34n, 115n, 120n
Corneille, Pierre, 89
Cornford, F. M., 30n
Corot, Jean-Baptiste-Camille, 137,
    204

Deleuze, Gilles, 199, 200–201, 208n, 370n, 384, 387, 393n, 398, 400n, 487–488, 568–570, 576. *See also* Félix Guattari
    Anti-Oedipus, 569–570
    schizoanalysis, 567
Delhomme, Jeanne, 207n
Delluc, Louis, 183n, 459
Delord, Jean, 450n
De Man, Paul, 176, 501, 522, 549n
Demeny, Paul, 110
Democritus, 27, 52n
Department store, 120
Derrida, Jacques, 14, 33n, 87n, 93, 208n, 223n, 229n, 251n, 251, 267, 333n, 335, 335n, 364, 371n, 402, 450n, 453, 454n, 472, 476, 491, 493n, 493–523, 526, 527, 536, 537, 547, 549n, 563, 588
    critique of logocentrism, 493
    différance, 504, 510, 531, 539
    double reading, 496
    drawing and blindness, 521–523
    écriture, 251, 335, 469, 472, 501, 510, 527
    and feminism, 495, 497–498, 523, 526–527
    Glas, 170, 236, 517, 547
    and language, 501–506, 511, 515, 528–529
    Of Grammatology, 502, 506, 515
    and photography, 518–521
    textual construct verus perceptual experience, 497
    trace, 506, 512, 519, 522, 545
    The Truth in Painting, 516–517, 520
Desargues of Lyon, Gerard, 34, 79n
Descartes, René, 9n, 14, 21n, 39, 63, 67, 69–82, 84–85, 92, 101, 133, 151, 187, 189, 226, 263n, 266, 271, 288, 304–305, 316, 335, 403, 509

attitude toward the senses, 72–73
cogito, 268, 288, 304, 310, 313, 320, 322, 347, 359
demonstration versus narration, 79–80
Discourse on Method, 70, 71, 72–73, 79, 81
emphasis on vision, 69–82, 183
induction versus deduction in, 72, 72n, 74, 80
La Dioptrique, 70, 71–79, 261, 304, 315, 563
and perspectivalism, 69
philosophy of, 73, 97, 226, 263, 360, 363, 391, 401
theory of light, 71, 73–75, 90, 133n
Descombes, Vincent, 264n, 325n
Desire, 166, 167, 168, 169, 170, 207, 241, 292, 345, 351, 366, 368, 450, 451, 478, 540, 570
    in baroque, 48
    and gender, 168
    as possession, 292–293
    to know (*Wisstrieb*), 332, 574, 575
Desnos, Robert, 232, 252, 254
Destutt de Tracy, Antoine Louis Claude, 191
Devaux, Frederique, 422n
DeVries, Hent, 562n
De Waelhens, Alphons, 349n
Dewey, John, 588
Dews, Peter, 368n, 563n
Diamant-Berger, Henri, 459
Diamond, Hugh Welch, 144
Diderot, Denis, 85, 97–103, 146, 248, 248n, 363, 447
    attitude toward vision, 97–102
Didi-Huberman, Georges, 37n, 331
Diegesis, 466–467
Diksterhuis, E. J., 51n

Gravelle, Karen, 5n, 6n, 8, 77n
Great Schism, 41–42
Greaves, Roger, 145n
Greeks, ancient:
  affinity for sight/vision, 21–26,
    28–33, 555
  attitude toward language, 33,
    189
  compared to the Hebrews,
    23–24, 33–36, 499, 503,
    574–580
  contradictory attitudes toward
    vision, 27–28, 32–33
  and other senses, 22, 22n, 79n
  and vision, 21–34
  vision in art of, 22n, 23
  vision in metaphysics of, 55, 67
  vision in myths of, 28, 28n
  vision in philosophy of, 23,
    24–28
  vision in religion of, 23
  vision in science of, 23, 25
  worship of clarity and light, 227
Green, André, 336, 547
Green, Christopher, 205n
Greenberg, Clement, 159–161, 165
Gregory the Great, 41
Greimas, A. J., 440
Greuze, Jean Baptiste, 97
Grew, Raymond, 122n
Grid, 57, 60–61n, 156, 188, 189
  in the city, 115
Gris, Juan, 214
Grontkowski, Christine R., 541n
Grosseteste, Robert, 37, 81
Grosz, Elisabeth, 491n, 494n,
  530n, 559n
Gruber, David F., 414n
Guattari, Félix, 370n, 458, 458n,
  569–570, 576. See also Gilles
  Deleuze
Guégen, Pierre-Gilles, 383n, 402n
Guilbaut, Serge, 161n

Guillaume, Eugène, 156, 204
Guillaume, Paul, 320–321
Guizetti, Alfred, 465n
Guillén, Claudio, 40n, 53n, 188n,
  439n
Gurwitsch, Aron, 299
Gutenberg, Johann, 66, 68
Guynn, William, 469n
Guys, Gérard Constantin, 121

Habermas, Jürgen, 15, 233, 368n,
  431, 431n, 510n, 581–582, 581n,
  592
Hacking, Ian, 2, 2n, 35n, 70, 84,
  84n
Hall, Edward T., 5–6n, 7n
Hamann, Johann Georg, 106
Hamon, Philippe, 124n
Hampfstängl, 129
Handelman, Susan A., 23n, 33n,
  337n, 499n, 547n, 556n
Hansen, Miriam, 460n, 490
Hapsburg Empire, 47
Harries, Karsten, 53n, 81, 81n,
  189n
Harris, Neil, 143n
Harris, Zelig S., 15
Harriss, Joseph, 124n
Hart, Kevin, 496n
Hartman, Geoffrey, 108, 503, 510,
  516
Hartmann, Heinz, 348n
Harvey, Robert, 278n, 435n
Hausmann, Raoul, 180
Haussmann, Georges-Eugène,
  117–120, 425
Havelock, Eric, 26, 26n
Havet, Jacques, 264n
Hawkes, Howard, 462
Hawthorn, Geoffrey, 52n
Hay, Eloise Knapp, 182n
Hearing, 34–35, 41, 106, 196, 404,
  512–514. See also Ear

Hearing *(continued)*
  in hermeneutics, 106, 186
  as privileged by the Hebraic
    tradition, 35
Heath, Stephen, 465n, 471n, 474n,
  490
Hebrews:
  compared to the Greeks, 23–24,
    33–36
  emphasis on verbal, 23, 269, 556
  ethics of unrepresentability, 336,
    499, 503, 555
Hegel, Georg Wilhelm Friedrich,
  109–110, 188, 223, 235–236,
  263, 287, 290, 292, 306, 345,
  346, 368, 373, 375, 386, 512,
  518, 547, 579
Heidegger, Martin, 81, 265,
  269–275, 276, 284, 287, 291,
  297, 299, 301, 306, 316, 324,
  347, 351, 386, 387, 498, 499,
  501–502, 507, 513, 516, 518,
  536, 550, 560, 581
  attitude toward the Greeks,
    269–272
  dual concept of vision, 274–275
  world picture in, 51, 272, 507,
    517, 543
Heisenberg, Werner, 75n, 200n
Held, René, 238n, 277
Hell, John, 4n
Helmholtz, Hermann, 151–152
Hemingway, Ernest, 214n
Henderson, Brian, 465n
Henderson, Linda Dalrymple, 158n
Henry, Charles, 155
Henry VIII, 43
Hepworth, Barbara, 206n
Heraclitus, 270
Herder, Johann Gottfried von, 106,
  106n
Herding, Klaus, 95n
Hertz, Neil, 332n

Heterotopia, 386n, 413, 416
Heterogeneity, 227, 230, 579
Higgins, Lynn A., 448n, 453n
Himmelfarb, Gertrude, 383n
Hjelmslev, Louis, 440, 443n
Hobbes, Thomas, 64n
Hocke, Gustav René, 229n
Hockney, David, 251n
Hoffmann, E. T. A., 116, 332, 522
Holbein, Hans, 48, 362–364, 366
Hölderlin, Friedrich, 272, 273n
Hollander, Anne, 132n
Hollander, John, 171n, 177n, 178n
Hollier, Denis, 218, 229, 230n,
  343n, 353n, 365n, 387n, 401,
  423n
Hollywood, 462, 463, 470
Home, Stewart, 418n, 421n, 426n
Homosexuality, 340
Honour, Hugh, 109n, 110n
Hooke, Robert, 65
Horace, 170, 170n
Houlgate, Stephen, 109–110n
Howe, David, 588
Hoy, David Couzens, 513n
Huéscar, Antonio Rodriguez, 188n
Huet, Marie-Hélène, 94n
Hugo, Victor, 110, 225
Hulme, T. E., 202
Humanism, 16, 170, 316, 403,
  404, 406
Hume, David, 85, 283
Hunt, Lynn, 96n
Husserl, Edmund, 265–268,
  273, 282, 283, 287, 289, 299,
  301, 302, 303, 308, 318, 323,
  499–501, 537, 563
  Wesenschau (eidetic intuition),
    266–267, 268, 499, 537, 550
Hutcheon, Linda, 172n
Huygens, Constantin, 62, 65
Huysmans, Joris-Karl, 113n, 155,
  173

Lyotard, Jean-François *(continued)*
  Discours, Figure, 545, 563–570
  ethical language game, 580
  figurality in, 564–566, 568–569,
    572, 585
  figure-matrix, 565, 567, 568,
    569, 573, 580
  and Freud, 575–578
  interpretation of the eye, 565
  Just Gaming, 580
  and Lacan, 562–563, 567–570,
    577
  and Levinas, 561–562, 573–574,
    576, 579–581, 583–584
  La Phénomenologie, 266
  libidinal desire, 566–570, 573,
    579
  The Postmodern Condition, 561,
    581, 583

Macauley, Catherine, 524
MacBean, James Roy, 465n, 469n
MacCabe, Colin, 471n
MacCannell, Juliet Flower, 360n,
  366n, 369n
Macey, David, 246n, 334n, 338n,
  343n, 347, 347n, 351n, 362n,
  373n, 530n
Machery, Pierre, 377n
Madaule-Barthélémy, Madeleine,
  199n
Madison, Gary Brent, 307n, 318n,
  320, 322
Madness, 390–392, 407, 409. *See
  also* Insanity
  as spectacle, 390, 392
Magritte, René, 166, 165n,
  245–246, 245n, 246–247, 259,
  326, 351, 370n, 385, 399–400,
  407, 413, 518, 567
Maine de Biran, François-Pierre,
  151, 190, 191n
Mallin, Samuel B., 307n

Maloney, Clarence, 3n
Malebranche, Nicolas de, 77,
  80–81, 92
Malevich, Kasimir, 214n
Mallarmé, Stéphane, 172, 176–180,
  237, 239, 405, 504, 563, 566
Malraux, André, 139, 438
Mander, Jerry, 432n
Mandrou, Robert, 34–35, 34n,
  35n, 41, 43
Manet, Edouard, 137, 154, 155n,
  165, 170, 230, 385
Mannerism, 46
Mannheim, Karl, 201
Man Ray, 165n, 239n, 249,
  250–251, 252, 254, 259
Map, 118, 146
  in Dutch art, 60–61, 60–61n
  in vision, 63
Maravall, José Antonio, 35n, 46,
  47n, 49, 405n
Marcel, Gabriel, 264
Marcus, Greil, 417n, 420n, 424n,
  431n
Marcuse, Herbert, 428
Marey, Étienne-Jules, 133, 133n,
  137, 144–145, 145n, 163, 198,
  311
Maria Theresa, 47
Marin, Louis, 55n, 88, 88n, 548
Marinetti, F. T., 180
Maritain, Jacques, 206
Marot, Daniel, 35
Martin, John Rupert, 46n, 47n,
  60n
Marx, Karl, 189, 190, 234, 237,
  374, 375, 378, 377n, 525
Marxism, 195–196, 290, 372–379,
  418, 430, 436, 462, 479, 486,
  560, 562, 579
  Western, 17, 290, 373, 418, 426
Mary Magdalene, visuality of the
  cult of, 42n

Mourlet, Michel, 462
Mourning, 451, 485
Moussinac, Léon, 459
Müller, Johannes, 151–152
Muller, John P., 354n
Mulvey, Laura, 490, 588
Mumler, W. H., 130
Mundy, 244n, 247n
Munsterberg, Hugo, 467n
Muratori, Ludovico Antonio, 47
Murdoch, Iris, 27n
Music, 27, 92, 244, 265, 281, 314, 438
    in literature, 176–178, 201, 238
Muybridge, Eadweard, 133, 135n, 137, 144–145, 162, 198–199
Myers, F. W. H., 241

Nadar, (Gaspard-Félix Tournachon), 111–112n, 129n, 138n, 145–146, 145n, 213, 454n
Nadeau, Maurice, 231, 243
Nadja, 242
Nancy, Jean-Luc, 109, 109n, 498n
Narboni, Jean, 464, 470, 477, 477n, 479
Narcissism, 277, 333, 344, 344n, 368
Narcissus, 28, 350
Nash, Jorgen, 426
Nasio, Juan-David, 370n
Naturalism, 112–113, 138–139, 141, 146–147, 172–175, 179, 190–191
Nature, 138
Naville, Pierre, 242, 249n
Néagu, Philippe, 145n
Neale, Steve, 135n, 142–143n
Neo-Impressionism, 155
Neo-Kantianism, 263, 264, 301
Neo-platonism, 37, 54, 106, 108
    in Augustine, 37n
Nerval, Gérard de, 110

Newman, Barnett, 561
Newton, Isaac, 75, 75n, 84, 90, 99, 109, 109n, 150, 364
Niceron, Jean-François, 48, 74n
Nicholas of Cusa, 40, 40n, 189n
Niépce, Isadore, 125, 125n
Niépce, Joseph-Nicéphore, 125, 125n
Nietzsche, Friedrich, 31–32n, 40, 185, 187, 189–192, 200, 215, 229n, 235, 265, 271, 303, 495, 498, 502, 511, 512, 514, 523, 526, 561, 591
    critique of feminism, 495, 523, 526–527
Nieuwenhuys, Constant, 420
Nizan, Paul, 264
Nominalism, 74n, 403
Nougé, Paul, 238
Noguez, Dominique, 422n
Novalis, 108, 237
Nude, 154, 165, 166, 168–169
Nye, Andrea, 528n, 536n

Object, 52
    experience of being objectified, 276, 286, 288
Objectivity, 25, 393
Observation, 9, 29, 30, 81, 110–111n, 113, 186, 236, 271, 307, 398, 401, 403, 404
    as knowledge, 67
    as mode of scientific investigation, 70–71
    and speculation, 85, 186
Ocularcentrism, 3, 3n, 36, 80
    critics of, 8, 25, 33–36, 42, 101, 149–150, 163, 185–187, 191–192, 206, 209
    in Christianity, 36–38, 39–42
    in Greek thought, 21–34
    roots of, 29–30

Ocular regime:
  baroque, 45, 47
  denarrativization of, 50, 51
  multiplicity of, 62
  scientific/rational, 45, 47, 48, 49
  unified, 215
O'Dea, William T., 123n
Oedipus complex, 332, 350, 351,
  352, 353, 368, 569
Okley, Judith, 525n
Olscamp, Paul, 72n
Ong, Walter J., 2n, 22–23n, 41n,
  64, 66–69, 67n, 84n, 588
Ontology, 81–82, 271–275, 414
  of sight, 198, 388
Opacity, 91, 110, 288, 406, 414,
  564
  versus consciousness, 282–283
Op Art, 503
Optics, 7–8, 23, 25, 29, 38, 53,
  71–78, 125, 150, 153–154, 252,
  364
  instruments of, 65–66
  spiritual, 109
Orgel, Stephen, 46n
Origen, 36
Orpheus, 28
Ortega y Gasset, José, 161n, 187
O'Sullivan, Timothy, 139n
Other, 103, 287–290
  desire for, 368
Oudart, Jean-Pierre, 464, 474, 488
Owens, Craig, 131–132, 541n
Ozenfant, Amédée, 214
Ozouf, Mona, 95n

Painting, 51, 139, 152–169,
  314–316
  absorptive versus theatrical
    modes of, 98, 98n
  abstract, 51
  Dutch, 60–63
  history of, 29

narrative function of, 52, 52n
perspective in, 54–59, 76, 81,
  102, 154, 459
and Plato, 27, 27n
post-abstract, 52n
rationalization of, 62
Pan, 28, 594
Panofsky, Erwin, 41n, 51–52n,
  112n
Panopticon, 129n, 381–383, 407,
  410–411, 415, 415n, 489, 519,
  544
Papin sisters, 338–339, 341, 345,
  349
Paris Commune, 143
Parmenides, 24, 501
Paul (Saint), 13, 523
Paulsen, William R., 12n, 99n
Pawlowski, Gaston de, 158n
Paz, Octavio, 166, 167, 169
Peacham, John, 38, 39n
Pêcheux, Michel, 15, 17
Pefanis, Julian, 545n, 564n, 570n
Peirce, Charles Sanders, 129, 443
Pelerin, Jean (Viator), 59, 68
Penis envy, 532
Penley, Constance, 484n, 490
Perception, 5, 30, 35, 65–66, 101,
  105n, 151, 198, 248, 287, 299,
  302, 305, 414
  body as ground of, 191, 566
  of depth, 54–55
  as distinct from images, 283
  enhanced, 65
  from afar, 89
  and language, 199, 323, 371
  as source of ideas/knowledge,
    84, 299
  and truth, 300, 403
  unmediated, 157, 472
  visual, 67
Péret, Benjamin, 231, 237, 243,
  249n, 256
Perkins, V. F., 460n

Perniola, Mario, 24n
Perrot, Michelle, 117n, 411n
Perspective, 44, 51, 51n, 54–60,
  68, 79n, 137, 139, 188, 362
  aerial, 213–214
  atmospheric, 54
  and capitalism, 58–59
  critics of, 64
  as dominant/naturalized visual
    culture, 52, 53, 61, 62, 152,
    188
  geometrical rules and procedures,
    51, 204–206
  in history, 188–189
  illusion of, 51–52
  linear, 54, 206
  and literary point of view, 170,
    188
  lived versus geometric/
    photographic, 158
  multiple vantage points in, 54,
    200, 303–304
  perspectivalism, 186–187
  and science, 62
  in urban planning, 117–119
  vanishing point in, 58, 188
Petro, Patricia, 490, 541n
Phallocentrism, 493, 495, 538
  and ocularcentrism, 493, 526
Phantasmagoria, 115, 115n, 119,
  176–177n, 543
Phenomenology, 198, 206,
  212, 261–262, 265–275, 290,
  297–299, 325, 326, 347,
  370–371, 386–388, 395, 406,
  451, 459, 499–502, 550, 560
  of sight, 277
Philipon, Charles, 121
Phillips, Heather, 36n
Phillips, John, 36n, 43n, 45
Philo of Alexandria, 36
Philosophes, 84, 85, 89, 99, 102,
  103

Philosophy:
  Cartesian, 29, 69, 97, 226, 263,
    391, 400–401
  of the concrete, 264
  representation in, 268
  of science, 388
  visual bias in, 24, 39, 508
Photography:, 111, 111–112n,
  113n, 124–146, 148, 171,
  182–183, 243n, 249–253, 434,
  435, 436–437, 561, 589
  in Barthes, 441–445, 451–456
  as art, 125–126, 129, 136–141
  and cinema, 444, 455, 459, 466,
    473, 485–486
  as description, 112–113
  and Dutch art, 62, 149
  indexical quality of, 248
  and readymades, 161–162
  representation in, 68n, 151
  truth versus illusion in, 125–130
  uses of, 141–146
  as writing, 518–519
Physics:
  in Descartes, 73, 74–75
  in Newton, 75, 75n
Physiogomy, 97, 143, 440
Picabia, Francis, 238n, 254
Picasso, Pablo, 214, 224, 231, 281,
  421
Pichon, Eduard, 354, 354n, 372n
Picture, and window, 61n, 244, 518
Piel, Jean, 385n
Pilkington, Anthony, 206n
Pineal gland, 76–77, 77n, 80, 226,
  304
Pinel, Philippe, 391–392, 405
Pinker, Steven, 5n
Pinkney, David H., 117n
Pinot-Gallizio, Giuseppe, 420
Pirenne, M. H., 5n, 53n
Plateau, Joseph, 152, 166

in behavior control, 50, 391
binocular versus monocular,
105, 152, 184, 310
as biological function, 4, 5–7,
6n, 8, 151
as cultural construction, 3–5, 9,
149, 389
in cultural and social practices,
2–3, 587
dangers of, 44, 56–57n
deanthropomorphization of, 62,
72
dimensions of, 77
dual concept of, 29–30, 80–81,
303
as epistemology, 274–275
in etymology, 2, 2n
in history, 3–4
in languages, 2
malevolent power of, 28
as metaphor, 1, 1n, 2, 16, 27,
187, 190, 198, 272, 587
in myth, 28
as ontology, 274–275
perspectival, 53–60
psychological function of, 7
relation to language, 8–9, 33
in religion, 11–13
in religious practices, 39–41
and repression, 222
role of God in, 77
scientific knowledge of, 5–10, 62
separated from textual, 44–45,
57
status of, 24–29, 159–160
in technology, 3, 3n
Visionary tradition, 39–40, 309
Visual aids, 40, 42, 45
Visual cultures. *See also* Ocular
regime
multiplicity of, 62
Visual experience, 4, 113–115, 122

directed, 10–11, 63, 64–65
as natural, 132
passive, 62–63, 72, 75
received, 11
as related to culture, 4–5, 15,
150
Visual field, 4, 55, 57, 76, 81,
159n, 365–366, 401. *See also*
James J. Gibson
as commodity, 58–59
Visual phenomena, 71
Visual poetry, 179–180
Visual process as participatory, 30.
See also Subject/object dualism
Visual seduction, 46–47
Visual world, 4, 54–55, 76, 159n.
See also James J. Gibson
Vitrac, Roger, 232
Vitruvius, 52n, 65n
Vitz, Paul C., 136n, 151–152n,
164n
Voice, 93, 94
Voltaire, 83–84, 99, 101n
and Descartes, 84
Vorhandenheit, 271, 284, 285n,
286, 557
Vorticism, 159
Voyeurism, 91, 111, 169–170, 332,
412, 481–482, 488, 531, 540, 591
in Proust, 181, 182n, 183
in Sartre, 276, 289, 295
Vuillermez, Émile, 459

Waelhens, Alphonse de, 326
Wagner, Richard, 176, 176–177n
Wahl, Jean, 264
Wallon, Henri, 320, 343–344, 345,
346, 346n, 457n
Wartofsky, Marx W., 4–5
Watney, Simon, 208n, 243n, 250
Watson, Stephen, 327n
Watteau, Jean Antoine, 181

Designer: Patrick Dooley Design
Compositor: Modern Design
Text: 11/15 Garamond
Display: Garamond